THE PURSUIT OF LIBERTY

THE PURSUIT OF LIBERTY
A History of the American People

VOLUME ONE   TO 1877

THIRD EDITION

R. Jackson Wilson
Smith College

James Gilbert
University of Maryland

Karen Ordahl Kupperman
New York University

Stephen Nissenbaum
University of Massachusetts

Donald M. Scott
The New School for Social Research

HarperCollins*College* Publishers

Executive Editor: Bruce Borland
Developmental Editor: Judith M. Anderson
Project Coordination and Text Design: Ruttle, Shaw & Wetherill, Inc.
Cover Designer: Kay Petronio
Cover Illustration: Painting by Helen Lundeberg: "Pioneers of the West," 1934.
  National Museum of American Art, Smithsonian Institution. Transfer from
  General Services Administration.
Art Studio: Mapping Specialists Ltd.
Photo Researcher: Corrine Johns
Electronic Production Manager: Angel Gonzalez Jr.
Manufacturing Manager: Willie Lane
Electronic Page Makeup: Americomp
Printer and Binder: R.R. Donnelly & Sons Company
Cover Printer: The Lehigh Press, Inc.

For permission to use copyrighted material, grateful acknowledgment is made to the copyright holders on pp. C-1 through C-3, which are hereby made part of this copyright page.

The Pursuit of Liberty: A History of the American People,
Volume One   To 1877, Third Edition

Copyright © 1996 by HarperCollins College Publishers

HarperCollins® and ® are registered trademarks of HarperCollins Publishers Inc.

All rights reserved. Printed in the United States of America. No part of this book may be used or reproduced in any manner whatsoever without written permission, except in the case of brief quotations embodied in critical articles and reviews. For information address HarperCollins College Publishers, 10 East 53rd Street, New York, NY 10022. For information about any HarperCollins title, product, or resource, please visit our World Wide Web site at **http://www.harpercollins.com/college**.

Library of Congress Cataloging-in-Publication Data
The pursuit of liberty : a history of the American people / R. Jackson
    Wilson . . . [et al.]. — 3rd ed.
        p.   cm.
    Includes bibliographical references (p.) and index.
    ISBN 0-673-46921-2 (pbk. : v. 1). — ISBN 0-673-46922-0 (pbk. : v. 2)
    1. United States—History. I. Wilson, Raymond Jackson.
E178.1.P985 1996   95-35092
973—dc20   CIP

95 96 97 98   9 8 7 6 5 4 3 2 1

Brief Contents

Detailed Contents ... vii
Maps, Tables, and Figures ... xiii
Preface ... xv
Supplements ... xix
Acknowledgments ... xxiii
About the Authors ... xxv

1 FIRST ENCOUNTERS 1

Episode: Sir Walter Raleigh and the Beginnings of the British Empire 3
Europe's New World 24

2 THE COLONIES ESTABLISHED 47

Episode: 1622—Clash of Cultures in Virginia 49
Patterns of Settlement to Mid-Seventeenth Century 68

3 GROWTH AND DIVERSIFICATION 89

Episode: Witchcraft at Salem Village 91
New Peoples and New Patterns in the Later Seventeenth Century 109

4 THE EIGHTEENTH CENTURY 133

Episode: Runaway Slaves and Spanish Florida 135
Expansion and Consolidation 149

5 THE AMERICAN REVOLUTION 175

Episode: The Boston Massacre 177
The Coming of Independence 194

6 THE TRANSITION TO NATIONHOOD 215

Episode: George Washington, from General to President 217
The Making of the American Constitution 232

7 THE REPUBLIC ON TRIAL 251

Episode: Aaron Burr, Conspirator 253
Dissent and Conflict in the New Nation

270

8 BEYOND THE APPALACHIAN BARRIER — 293

Episode: The Trail of Tears—The Tragedy of the Cherokee Nation — 295
Expansion and the Market Economy — 316

9 THE AGE OF PARTY — 333

Episode: 1840—The Log Cabin Campaign — 335
Democracy and a New Politics — 351

10 A NEW NORTH — 379

Episode: The Garrisons—An Antebellum Family — 381
The Self-Made Society — 397

11 A NEW SOUTH — 423

Episode: Nat Turner's Rebellion — 425
Slavery and Southern Society — 440

12 EXPANSION AND THE CRISIS OF THE UNION — 463

Episode: Uncle Tom's Cabin — 465
Slavery, the West, and the Fate of the Republic — 483

13 HIS TERRIBLE, SWIFT SWORD — 511

Episode: Abraham Lincoln—From Politics to Martyrdom — 513
The Mighty Scourge of War — 528

14 RECONSTRUCTION — 553

Episode: Edisto Island—Land and Freedom — 555
Reunion and Reconstruction — 571

THE DECLARATION OF INDEPENDENCE — A–3
THE CONSTITUTION OF THE UNITED STATES OF AMERICA — A–6
AMENDMENTS TO THE CONSTITUTION — A–15
CREDITS — C–1
INDEX — I–1

Detailed Contents

Maps, Tables, and Figures	xiii
Preface	xv
Supplements	xix
Acknowledgments	xxiii
About the Authors	xxv

1 FIRST ENCOUNTERS 1

Episode: Sir Walter Raleigh and the Beginnings of the British Empire 3
Europe's New World 24
   Native American Cultures 24
   First Contacts 28
      Columbus 28
      John Cabot 29
      The Spanish 29
      The French 31
   The Impact of European Diseases 33
   First Colonies 34
      The Southwest 34
      Spanish and French Settlements in the East 35
   The English Approach to Colonization 38
   Jamestown 40
      Captain John Smith 41
   Indian Relations 42
      Colonies Established 44
CHRONOLOGY 45
SUGGESTIONS FOR FURTHER READING 46

2 THE COLONIES ESTABLISHED 47

Episode: 1622—Clash of Cultures in Virginia 49
Patterns of Settlement to Mid-Seventeenth Century 68
   The Southwest 69
   The Chesapeake 70
      Virginia 70
      Maryland 74
   New England 74
      Puritanism 75
      Plymouth 75
      Massachusetts Bay 77
   Middle Colonies 82
      New Netherland 82
      New Sweden 84
   Patterns 85
CHRONOLOGY 86
SUGGESTIONS FOR FURTHER READING 86

3 GROWTH AND DIVERSIFICATION 89

Episode: Witchcraft at Salem Village 91
New Peoples and New Patterns in the Later Seventeenth Century 109
   New Colonies 110
      The Carolinas 110
      Pennsylvania 112

Trade	114
The Atlantic	114
Mercantilism	115
Trade and Settlement in the Interior	116
New England to Florida: The Settled Colonies	**117**
New England	117
New York	119
The Chesapeake	120
Florida	121
Colonial Wars	**122**
The Pueblo Revolt	123
Bacon's Rebellion	123
King Philip's War	125
Glorious Revolutions	127
Patterns	**129**
CHRONOLOGY	130
SUGGESTIONS FOR FURTHER READING	131

4 THE EIGHTEENTH CENTURY 133

Episode: Runaway Slaves and Spanish Florida	135
Expansion and Consolidation	149
New Areas of Settlement	149
Immigration	149
Settlement of the Frontier in the East	151
American Indians and the Clash of Empires	154
The West	156
The Settled East	160
Religion and Colonial Elites	160
Economic Growth	164
Slavery in the Eighteenth Century	165
Social Order	166
The French and Indian War	168
Effects of the War	169
CHRONOLOGY	172
SUGGESTIONS FOR FURTHER READING	172

5 THE AMERICAN REVOLUTION 175

Episode: The Boston Massacre	177
The Coming of Independence	194
Novel Taxation	194
The Sugar Act	194
The Stamp Act	195
Constitutional Challenges	195
The Stamp Act Congress	196
The Townshend Acts, 1767	197
The Boston Tea Party and the Coercive Acts	199
The Quebec Act	201
The Continental Congress, 1774	201
First Shots	202
Washington Takes Command	204
Tom Paine's *Common Sense*	204
The Declaration of Independence	205
War	206
Indian Involvement	208
Turning Point	209
France Enters the War	209
The Home Front	210
Victory	210
CHRONOLOGY	213
SUGGESTIONS FOR FURTHER READING	213

6 THE TRANSITION TO NATIONHOOD 215

Episode: George Washington, from General to President	217
The Making of the American Constitution	232
The Confederation Period	233
Government Under the Articles	234
Achievements Under the Articles	235
Five Major Problems of the Confederation	237

The Philadelphia Convention	239
The Virginia and New Jersey Plans	240
The New Constitution	241
Powers of the Federal Government	241
Checks and Balances	242
Attitudes Toward Democracy	243
The Struggle for Ratification	244
Things Left Unsaid and Undone	245
Political Parties	246
Slavery	247
The Bill of Rights	248
CHRONOLOGY	249
SUGGESTIONS FOR FURTHER READING	249

7 THE REPUBLIC ON TRIAL 251

Episode: Aaron Burr, Conspirator	253
Dissent and Conflict in the New Nation	270
Partisan Politics	271
Defining the Executive Branch	271
Hamilton's Financial Program	272
The Whiskey Rebellion	274
Republicans Versus Federalists	274
The Election of 1800	276
Jefferson's Republicanism	277
Marshall and the Judiciary	279
Foreign Affairs	280
A Shaky Neutrality	281
Negotiations with France	282
Territorial Expansion	283
The Louisiana Purchase	284
Trouble with Britain	284
The War of 1812	287
The Hartford Convention	289
CHRONOLOGY	291
SUGGESTIONS FOR FURTHER READING	292

8 BEYOND THE APPALACHIAN BARRIER 293

Episode: The Trail of Tears—The Tragedy of the Cherokee Nation	295
Expansion and the Market Economy	316
Osceola and the Seminole Wars	316
The Expansion of Southern Agriculture	319
War	319
Land Hunger: The Rise of "King Cotton"	320
The Expansion of Northern Agriculture	323
Tecumseh, William Henry Harrison, and the Defeat of the Northwestern Indians	323
Land Hunger: The Rise of Wheat	327
Getting to Market: The Erie Canal	328
The Expansion of Market Agriculture	330
CHRONOLOGY	331
SUGGESTIONS FOR FURTHER READING	332

9 THE AGE OF PARTY 333

Episode: 1840—The Log Cabin Campaign	335
Democracy and a New Politics	351
Political Parties	351
Politics and the Panic of 1819	352
The Republican Consensus and Diplomacy	354
The End of the Dynasty	355
John Quincy Adams	357
The Election of 1828	358
The New Politicians	359
Politics and the Law	361

A New Theory of Party	362
The Two-Party Idea	362
Parties and the Government	363
Parties and "The People"	364
The Politics of Sectionalism	367
The Missouri Compromise	367
The Nullification Crisis	368
The Bank "War"	369
Jackson and His Party	370
And Tyler Too	372
The Travail of Martin Van Buren	373
The Whig Split	375
Government "By the People"	375
CHRONOLOGY	376
SUGGESTIONS FOR FURTHER READING	377

10 A NEW NORTH 379

Episode: The Garrisons—An Antebellum Family	***381***
The Self-Made Society	*397*
Economic Growth and Transformation	397
The Rise of Corporations	398
The Advent of the Railroad	399
Population	399
Urbanization	400
Technology, Growth, and Their Effects	402
The "Self-Made Man"	404
Middle-Class Evangelism	405
Charles Grandison Finney	406
Tracts and Missionaries	406
A New Model of Family Life	407
Changes in the Role of Women	409
A Feminist Alternative	410
An Age of Reformers	411
Utopian Communities	413
The Mormons	413
Workers' Movements	414
New Artists, New Ideas	415
CHRONOLOGY	420
SUGGESTIONS FOR FURTHER READING	420

11 A NEW SOUTH 423

Episode: Nat Turner's Rebellion	***425***
Slavery and Southern Society	*440*
Slavery and Market Capitalism	442
Slavery and Cotton	443
Slavery as a Social System	446
Varieties of Slave Experience	447
The Master's Power	448
Slaves' Responses to Servitude	449
Resistance	449
The Slave Family	449
Slave Culture	452
Slave Religion	453
The Social Structure of the South	453
Planter Rule	454
The Proslavery Argument	455
The Ideal of Southern Womanhood	458
CHRONOLOGY	460
SUGGESTIONS FOR FURTHER READING	461

12 EXPANSION AND THE CRISIS OF THE UNION 463

Episode: Uncle Tom's Cabin	***465***
Slavery, the West, and the Fate of the Republic	*483*
"Manifest Destiny"	485
The Mexican War	486
Mexican Independence	486
Texan Independence	487
The Texas Question	488
War	490
Slavery and Expansion	494
Slavery and Politics: The Election of 1848	495
The Crisis and Compromise of 1850	495

The Resumption of Expansion	498
The Kansas-Nebraska Act	498
"Bleeding Kansas"	500
The Rise of the Republican Party	501
Republican Ideology	502
The Rush to Disunion	503
The Dred Scott Case	503
John Brown's Raid	504
The Election of 1860	505
Southern Response to Lincoln's Election	506
CHRONOLOGY	508
SUGGESTIONS FOR FURTHER READING	509

13 HIS TERRIBLE, SWIFT SWORD   511

Episode: Abraham Lincoln—From Politics to Martyrdom	513
The Mighty Scourge of War	528
Building and Equipping Armies	528
Strategy—Theory and Practice	530
The Struggle Begins	532
Leadership and Opposition in Wartime	536
War and Slavery	538
The Struggle Climaxes	542
The Election of 1864	544
The Struggle Ends	546
The Toll of Total War	547
CHRONOLOGY	550
SUGGESTIONS FOR FURTHER READING	550

14 RECONSTRUCTION   553

Episode: Edisto Island—Land and Freedom	555
Reunion and Reconstruction	571
Lincoln's Plan for Reconstruction	573
Presidential Reconstruction Under Johnson	575
Black Codes	578
Congressional Reconstruction	579
Radical Reconstruction	581
The Republican Coalition in the South	584
Redeeming the States	588
The End of Reconstruction	593
CHRONOLOGY	594
SUGGESTIONS FOR FURTHER READING	595

THE DECLARATION OF INDEPENDENCE	A–3
THE CONSTITUTION OF THE UNITED STATES OF AMERICA	A–6
AMENDMENTS TO THE CONSTITUTION	A–15
CREDITS	C–1
INDEX	I–1

Maps, Tables, and Figures

MAPS

The Atlantic Rim: First Contacts	9
Spanish and French Explorations of North America	32
Indian Towns and European Settlements	39
Settlements at Mid-Century	85
Salem in 1692	101
Atlantic Trade Routes	115
Settlements at the End of the 17th Century	129
The Colonies in the 18th Century	161
European Claims to North America in 1754 and 1763	171
The Three Phases of the American Revolution	207
North America in 1783	236
Westward to the Mississippi, 1807	257
The Trans-Mississippi West, 1807	285
The Three U.S. Thrusts of 1812	288
The Campaigns of 1813	288
The British Advance, 1814	289
The War in the South, 1814–1815	289
The Cherokee Nation, About 1825	298
The Election of 1828	359
The Missouri Compromise, 1820–1821 and Admission of States, 1791–1821	368
The Election of 1832	370
The Election of 1840	374
Slavery in the United States, 1821 (After the Missouri Compromise)	443
The War for Texas Independence, 1836	487
The Election of 1844	489
The Oregon Boundary Dispute	491
The Mexican War, 1846–1848	493
Acquiring a Western Empire	499
The Compromise of 1850 and the Kansas-Nebraska Act	500
The Election of 1860	506
Alignment of States in 1861	529
The First Battle of Bull Run, July 21, 1861	532
The War for the Mississippi, 1862–1863	533
The Peninsular Campaign and the Second Battle of Bull Run, 1862	534
The Battle of Antietam, 1862	535
Gettysburg, July 1–3, 1863	543
The Chattanooga Campaign, 1863	546
Sherman's March Through the Confederacy, 1864–1865	547

The Final Virginia Campaign, 1864–1865	548
Edisto and Sea Islands	556
Reconstruction	592

TABLES AND FIGURES

Slave States, 1860—Proportion of White and Black Population	455

PREFACE

Some forty years ago, when the oldest of the authors of *The Pursuit of Liberty* was in the eighth grade, he had to take his first course on the history of the United States. His teacher was a legend in the school, a tough, slightly forbidding woman, who was determined that her students were going to learn something about the history of their country.

She gave her roomful of fourteen-year-olds a demanding task. They had to memorize 200 "facts" about American history, including their dates. When the final examination came, they had to write down their list of facts in the correct chronological order. You could choose any facts, as long as there were 200 of them and they were in chronological order. You might start with "1492—Columbus discovers America." Or you could begin with "1607—First English colony in America at Jamestown, Virginia." (In both cases, you would be a bit wrong. But that didn't matter. These "facts" were in the textbook, and the important thing was that you had learned them.)

Nowadays, of course, everything about learning history has changed. The authors' own children have come home from history classes in schools and colleges with their heads full of "concepts" instead of "facts." They don't think "1607—Jamestown" (or even "1587—Roanoke," which is closer to the truth). Instead, they are taught to talk about large and abstract matters like "The Confrontation of European and Native-American Cultures." They study grand processes such as "Industrialization, Immigration, and Urbanization." They seem to learn history in a more sophisticated and better way than memorizing some arbitrary list of 200 facts.

But there is a problem. Students who study American history today seem to know something in general, but nothing much in particular. They discuss abstractions and generalizations, but these are not connected with any firm grasp of relevant factual information. Have our best and most innovative teachers and professors simply replaced 200 facts with 20 vague concepts? The old problem was that history was a grab bag of names and dates and places. Students learned something in particular and nothing much in general. But the new problem, knowing the general but not the particular, is just as serious. Either way, studying history runs the risk of being a plain waste of time.

This dilemma is partly the result of the nature of history itself. There are large and general tendencies and there are particular facts. The difficult thing is to see how the two fit together. We tend to look at history the way we look at a painting. We focus on the foreground—the facts. Or we think about the background, about the general way the picture is structured and the kinds of claims it makes on our imagination. But when we study history, it is difficult to put the foreground and the background, the facts and the general concepts, together. We seem to choose between foreground and background, unable to see how each makes sense in terms of the other.

When most history textbooks try to bring specific facts and general concepts together, they do so by simply telling readers that this or that fact is an example of this or that general tendency. First comes a heading, something like "The Contact of European and Native American Cultures" or "Industrialization." Then comes a sentence or two of generalization. A little further on come the facts, such as "In 1607, an English colony was established at Jamestown, in Virginia," or "The first transcontinental railroad was completed in 1869."

Some important things are lost in this way of writing history. We are not asked to see or understand the relationship between fact and general concept at all. Did something called industrialization *cause* the first transcontinental railroad or did a host of facts, such as the building of that railroad, *cause* industrial development? Concrete facts and general concepts merely coexist in most textbooks, each of them inert and incapable of giving any sort of life to the other.

Perhaps worse, when students study history in textbooks of this sort, they get no sense of the human experience involved in either the specific events they find listed there or the generalizations they read and underline to study for next week's test. Most history textbooks contain no narrative, no stories, no accounts of the dramatic, sometimes triumphant, often shameful efforts and struggles of human beings. Human action is squeezed out of history and we are left with dead events and equally lifeless generalizations.

We have written *The Pursuit of Liberty* in the belief that we have found ways to solve these kinds of problems. We started with two convictions. First, we had to make it possible for students to see and understand the ways that specific sequences of human action were related to the general setting in which they took place. Second, historians ought not to keep a secret of the remarkably exciting and dramatic ways people actually acted in the past.

These two convictions have shaped our book and explain its unusual structure. Each chapter has two different parts. In the first, we tell the *story* of a very specific and concrete episode: a witchcraft hysteria in Salem Village, Massachusetts, in 1692, for example; or the massacre of a band of Native American Sioux people at Wounded Knee Creek in the Dakotas in 1890; or the rending struggle for custody of the infant known as Baby M in the 1980s. Episodes like these are the human material out of which history is made.

But history is more than stories. It involves coming to understand how the stories could have happened. To do this, we have to know something about the general context within which a specific episode took place. So the second part of each chapter is a discussion of the historical setting of the chapter's episode. The narrative of Salem witchcraft is followed by a discussion of new people and new patterns in the later seventeenth century; the Wounded Knee massacre by an examination of the westward expansion of European-American society into the territories of the Native Americans; the story of Baby M by a discussion of the tangled relationships between private morality and public politics that characterized American life in the 1980s.

And so we go through *The Pursuit of Liberty*, alternating between the specific and the general, between narrative and explanation. In the end we think our readers will have a much better grasp of the way history works, of the way that all the specific actions of people are shaped by the historical setting in which they take place. And we have faith, too, that some of our readers will learn the most important thing that history has to teach all of us: We all live in history, profoundly shaped by the society around us, by what it has been as well as by what it is now.

If this lesson is learned, then our readers will have learned what we already know, that learning history is a way of discovering our kinship with all those real people who have come before us, who have acted out their struggles, terrors, and occasional exaltations with the same anxiety and effort that go so deeply into all our lives. The past is inescapable, for everyone, whether one knows it or not. It is better to know it.

We have been gratified by the way teachers and students have responded to the first two editions of *The Pursuit of Liberty*. But along with many kind words have come criticisms and suggestions for change. In this third edition, we have done our best to respond to those criticisms we found valid, and to act on the suggestions we found useful. So this edition is more than a collaboration among the five of us. It is a larger collaboration with our readers and critics. Out of this larger collaboration have come a multitude of small but worthwhile changes and a number of large ones. All of the chapters have been carefully revised. But we have worked hardest throughout the book to continue to try to rescue American history from its traditional focus on the actions of politically important men of European descent, and to tell as well the legitimate history of women and all those "minorities" who have long been the true American majority. Our two chapters on the Jacksonian period, for example, have been completely reorganized and rewritten in ways that have allowed us to do even more justice to the story of the Native Americans' encounter with the relentless westward advance of European-American society.

Our coverage of the colonial period has been expanded from three chapters to four. But more than expanded coverage is involved. The episode for Chapter 2 has been entirely replaced with a story that focuses much more sharply on the complicated relationships in Virginia between Europeans and Native Americans. A new chapter has been added on the eighteenth century. Its episode tells the story of an English effort to dislodge the Spanish from their settlement at St. Augustine, Florida. But this is more than the story of a military encounter between European forces. It is a story in which African-American slaves, "runaway" slaves, and Native Americans take their important place in the action alongside the English and Spanish. The second half of this chapter is an exploration of the ways all these groups—and with them women and people from other European countries as well—were interacting to create distinctive and diverse societies, not just in the English colonies of the Atlantic coast, but all over North America.

We have added a new chapter on the period of Reconstruction that followed the Civil War. This chapter, whose episode is on the wrenching experience of African Americans on Edisto Island, South Carolina, has given us a chance to explore in much greater detail the long, difficult and often disappointing efforts of freed slaves to gain a decent measure of control over their own lives and destinies.

A new final chapter has been added to bring our history down to the present. Its episode is on the police beating of Rodney King, the criminal trials of the white policemen involved, and the riots in Los Angeles that followed during the spring of 1992. The second half of the chapter is our attempt to grasp the significance and meaning of the startling diversity that characterizes the United States as it prepares to enter the twenty-first century.

R. Jackson Wilson

James Gilbert

Karen Ordahl Kupperman

Stephen Nissenbaum

Donald M. Scott

SUPPLEMENTS

FOR INSTRUCTORS

- **Instructor's Resource Manual.** Prepared by the authors of *The Pursuit of Liberty*, this manual includes lecture suggestions, audiovisual materials, and suggestions for enhancing student involvement.

- **Test Bank.** This test bank, prepared by Dona Brown of the University of Vermont contains over 2000 objective, conceptual, and essay questions with an emphasis on critical thinking and making connections. All questions are keyed to specific pages in *The Pursuit of Liberty*.

- **America Through the Eyes of Its People: A Collection of Primary Sources.** Prepared by Carol Brown of Oakland Community College, this one-volume collection of primary documents portrays the rich and varied tapestry of American life; contains documents concerning women, Native Americans, African Americans, Hispanics, and others who helped to shape the course of U.S. history. Designed to be duplicated by instructors for student use, the documents have accompanying student exercises.

- **Primary Sources in Gender in American History.** Prepared by Ellen Skinner of Pace University, this collection includes both classic and unique documents from diverse perspectives covering the history of women and gender in American history. The book includes critical thinking questions, bibliography, and contextual headnotes and is available shrinkwrapped with *The Pursuit of Liberty* at a low cost.

- **Primary Sources in African American History.** Prepared by Roy Finkenbine of Hampton University, this compelling collection includes both social and political documents and covers the history of African Americans in America. The book includes critical-thinking questions, bibliography, and contextual headnotes and is available shrinkwrapped with *The Pursuit of Liberty* at a low cost.

- **American Impressions: A CD-ROM for U.S. History, Volume I.** This unique and ground-breaking CD-ROM for the U.S. History course is organized in a topical and thematic framework that allows in-depth coverage with a media-centered focus. Hundreds of photos, maps, works of art, graphics, and historical film clips are organized into narrated vignettes and interactive activities to create a tool for both professors and students. The first volume includes: "The Encounter Period," "Revolution to Republic," "A Century of Labor and Reform," and "The Struggle for Equality." A Guide for Instructors provides teaching tips and suggestions for using advanced media in the classroom. The CD-ROM is available in both Macintosh and Windows formats.

- **Visual Archives of American History, 2/e.** This two-sided video laserdisc explores history from the meeting of three cultures to the present. It is an encyclopedic chronology of U.S. history offering hundreds of photographs and illustrations, a variety of source and reference maps—several of which are animated—plus 50 minutes of video. For ease in planning lectures, a manual listing barcodes for scanning and frame numbers for all the material is available.

- **HarperCollins Comprehensive American History Transparency Set.** This vast collection of American history map transparencies will soon become a necessary teaching aid. This set includes over 200 map transparencies ranging from the first Native Americans to the end of the Cold War, covering wars, social trends, elections, immigration, and demographics. Included are a reproducible set of student map exercises, teaching tips, and correlation charts. This fresh and extensive map package provides complete geographic coverage of American history.

- **Discovering American History Through Maps and Views.** Created by Gerald Danzer of the University of Illinois at Chicago, the recipient of the AHAs 1990 James Harvey Robinson Prize for his work in the development of map transparencies—this set of 140 four-color acetates is a unique instructional tool. It contains an introduction on teaching history through maps and a detailed commentary on each transparency. The collection includes cartographic and pictorial maps, views and photos, urban plans, building diagrams, and works of art.

- **A Guide to Teaching American History Through Film.** Written by Randy Roberts of Purdue University, this guide provides instructors with a creative and practical tool for stimulating classroom discussion. The sections include "American Films: A Historian's Perspective," a list of films, practical suggestions, and bibliography. The film listing is presented in narrative form, developing connections between each film and the topics being discussed.

- **Video Lecture Launchers.** Prepared by Mark Newman, University of Illinois at Chicago, these video lecture launchers (each 2 to 5 minutes in duration) cover key issues in American history from 1877 to the present. The launchers are accompanied by an Instructor's Manual.

- **"This Is America" Immigration Video.** Produced by the American Museum of Immigration, these two 20-minute videos tell the story of American immigrants, relating their personal stories and accomplishments. By showing how the richness of our culture is due to the contributions of millions of immigrant Americans, the videos make the point that America's strength lies in the ethnically and culturally diverse backgrounds of its citizens.

- **TestMaster Computerized Testing System.** This flexible, easy-to-master computer test bank includes all the test items in the printed test bank. The TestMaster software allows you to edit existing questions and add your own items. Tests can be printed in several different formats and can include figures such as graphs and tables. Available for IBM and Macintosh computers.

- **QuizMaster.** This new program enables you to design TestMaster generated tests that your students can take on a computer rather than in printed form. QuizMaster is available separately from TestMaster and can be obtained free through your sales representative.

- **Grades.** A grade-keeping and classroom management software program that maintains data for up to 200 students.

FOR STUDENTS

- **Study Guide and Practice Tests.** This two-volume study guide, created by Dona Brown of the University of Vermont, includes chapter outlines, significant themes and highlights, a glossary, learning enrichment ideas, sample test questions, exercises for identification and interpretation, and geography exercises based on maps in *The Pursuit of Liberty*.

- **Learning to Think Critically: Films and Myths About American History.** Randy Roberts and Robert May of Purdue University use well-known films such as *Gone with the Wind* and *Casablanca* to explore some common myths about America and its past. Many widely held assumptions about our country's past come from or are perpetuated by popular films. Which are true? Which are patently not true? And how does a student of history approach documents, sources, and textbooks with a critical and discerning eye? This short handbook subjects some popular beliefs to historical scrutiny in order to help students develop a method of inquiry for approaching the subject of history in general.

- **Mapping American History: Student Activities.** Written by Gerald Danzer of the University of Illinois at Chicago, this free map workbook for students features exercises designed to teach students to interpret and analyze cartographic materials as historical documents. The instructor is entitled to a free copy of the workbook for each copy of the text purchased from HarperCollins.

- **TimeLink Computer Atlas of American History.** This atlas, compiled by William Hamblin of Brigham Young University, is an introductory software tutorial and textbook companion. This Macintosh program presents the historical geography of the continental United States from colonial times to the settling of the West and the admission of the last continental state in 1912. The program covers territories in different time periods, provides quizzes, and includes a special Civil War module.

Acknowledgments

We believe that everything that is said in *The Pursuit of Liberty* is true. Well, almost everything. But the book contains two unavoidable half-truths, both of them on the title page. Both are formulas that are imposed by the powerful conventions that govern the publication of books in our society. The first is the suggestion that an abstract corporate entity named HarperCollins College Publishers brought the book into existence. The second is that five individuals known as authors are responsible for all the words and ideas in the book. We would like to set the record straight on both these points.

The truth of the matter is that HarperCollins is not a corporate abstraction but a set of very specific people who have generously invested efforts, care, and talent in this book. Two of them, in particular, have been extremely helpful. Bruce Borland had the imagination and courage to set this third edition of *The Pursuit of Liberty* in motion. Judith Anderson brought to her editorial work seemingly inexhaustible reserves of intelligence, patience, and generosity of spirit. The book owes much to them.

The truth is, as well, that the writing of history is a collective enterprise. We owe an incalculable debt to generations of men and women who have labored to make the history of the American people comprehensible. We also owe a great deal to the people—many of them now mature men and women—who have been our students. We cannot repay them for all the history lessons they have given to us; we can only hope that some of their children may learn as much from our book as we have from them.

Newell G. Bringhurst
College of the Sequoias

John H. DeBerry
Somerset Community College

Ronald P. Formisano
University of Florida

Gerald J. Goodwin
University of Houston

James A. Hijiya
University of Massachusetts, Dartmouth

David Hudson
California State University, Fresno

Donald M. Jacobs
Northeastern University

Stephen J. Kneeshaw
College of Ozarks

Timothy Koerner
Oakland Community College

Jesus Luna
California State University, Fresno

Gerald W. McFarland
University of Massachusetts

Peter C. Mancall
University of Kansas

David Nasaw
City University of New York

Sheila Skemp
University of Mississippi

Ephraim Smith
California State University, Fresno

John Snetsinger
California Polytechnic University

Gary E. Thompson
Tulsa Junior College

Robert E. Weir
Bay Path College

In addition, we are most grateful to our consultants and critiquers whose thoughtful and constructive work contributed greatly to this edition. Their many helpful suggestions led to significant improvements in the final product.

The Pursuit of Liberty is also the product of some fine advice from other intelligent and dedicated people. Sometimes their suggestions have posed formidable tasks for us. Nonetheless, we are grateful to all our colleagues, particularly to: Katherine Abbott, Paul Francis Bourke, Dona Brown, Lawrence Foster, Ron Formisano, Paula Franklin, William Graebner, James Henretta, Marvin L. Jaegers, Stephen Kneeshaw, Gary Nissenbaum, Gregory Nobles, Thomas C. Parramore, Stephen Weisner, and Nancy Woloch.

About the Authors

R. JACKSON WILSON is a Professor of History at Smith College. He is a graduate of the University of Missouri and received his Ph.D. from the University of Wisconsin. He has taught at an unusually wide range of institutions, including the University of Arizona, the University of Wisconsin, Columbia University, the University of Massachusetts, Hartford College for Women, Yale University, the University of Pennsylvania, and the Flinders University of South Australia. He has been a fellow of the Woodrow Wilson Foundation, the National Endowment for the Humanities, the Charles Warren Center, Harvard University, and the National Humanities Center. He is the author of *In Quest of Community: Social Philosophy in the United States* and *Figures of Speech: American Writers and the Literary Marketplace, from Benjamin Franklin to Emily Dickinson* (1989).

JAMES GILBERT is Professor of History at the University of Maryland. He is a graduate of Carleton College and received his Ph.D. from the University of Wisconsin. He has taught at Teachers College, Columbia University; Warwick University in Coventry, England, and the University of Paris. He has held Fulbright Professorships in Sydney, Australia, and Amsterdam, the Netherlands. His books include *Writers and Partisans* (1968), *Designing The Industrial State* (1972), *Work Without Salvation* (1978), *Another Chance: Postwar America* (1981), *A Cycle of Outrage: America's Reaction to the Juvenile Delinquent in the 1950s* (1986), and *Perfect Cities: Chicago's Utopias of 1893* (1991). He is currently finishing a book on American religion.

KAREN ORDAHL KUPPERMAN is Professor of History at New York University. She is a graduate of the University of Missouri and holds an M.A. from Harvard University and a Ph.D. from Cambridge University. She is the author of *Providence Island, 1630–1641: The Other Puritan Colony* (1993), *Roanoke, The Abandoned Colony* (1984), and *Settling With the Indians: The Meeting of English and Indian Cultures in America, 1580–1640* (1980). Her edited books include *America in European Consciousness* (1995), *Major Problems in American Colonial History* (1993), and *Captain John Smith: A Select Edition of His Writings* (1988).

In 1980, her essay "Apathy and Death in Early Jamestown" won the distinguished Binkley-Stevenson award of the Organization of American Historians. Her book, *Providence Island*, won the Albert J. Beveridge Award, given by the American Historical Association, for the best book in American History including Canada and Latin America. She has been a Mellon Faculty Fellow at Harvard, a fellow of the National Humanities Center, and a National Endowment for the Humanities Fellow at the John

Carter Brown Library. In 1995–1996 she is the Times-Mirror Foundation Visiting Research Professor at the Huntington Library, and is Chair of the Council of the Institute of Early American History and Culture.

STEPHEN NISSENBAUM is Professor of History at the University of Massachusetts, Amherst, where he teaches cultural history. He is a graduate of Harvard College, holds an M.A. from Columbia University, and a Ph.D. from the University of Wisconsin. He has held fellowships from the National Endowment for the Humanities, the American Council of Learned Societies, and the American Antiquarian Society, and has been a fellow of the Charles Warren Center at Harvard. He has been the James Pinckney Harrison Professor of History at The College of William and Mary. He has served as president of his state humanities council, the Massachusetts Foundation for the Humanities. He is the author of *Sex, Diet, and Debility in Jacksonian America* (1988) and (with Paul Boyer) *Salem Possessed: The Social Origins of Witchcraft* (1974), which won the John H. Dunning prize awarded by the American Historical Association. He is currently writing a book about the history of Christmas in America.

DONALD M. SCOTT is a Professor of History at the Eugene Lang College of The New School for Social Research. He is a graduate of Harvard College and received his Ph.D. from the University of Wisconsin. He is the author of *From Office to Profession: The New England Ministry, 1750–1850*, and is co-author of *America's Families: A Documentary History* (1982). He has been a fellow at the Davis Center for Historical Studies, Princeton University, and a National Endowment for the Humanities Fellow at the American Antiquarian Society. He is currently working on a book on democracy and knowledge in nineteenth-century America.

THE PURSUIT OF LIBERTY

Chapter 1

First Encounters

Episode: Sir Walter Raleigh and the Beginnings of the British Empire

EUROPE'S NEW WORLD

Native American Cultures

First Contacts

The Impact of European Diseases

First Colonies

The English Approach to Colonization

Jamestown

Indian Relations

THE EPISODE: Twentieth-century people take the colonization of America for granted. Once Europeans knew of those vast lands, we assume, they would be eager to found settlements, looking forward to the growth of mighty empires and strong cultures. But the possibilities of America emerged slowly: Only decades after 1492 did Europeans develop a clear sense of the American continents. Colonization was not an obvious choice, nor did it promise much in the way of returns. Many possible investments were more promising than colonization.

Only a few people, such as Sir Walter Raleigh in the 1580s, were prepared to devote efforts to this new kind of endeavor. He had to convince his associates that colonization would pay off. Planting settlements in America soaked up money, and many investors saw nothing in return. Great empires did grow, but they rarely enriched those who founded them. Other, later, people reaped the benefits of the early efforts of the founders.

THE HISTORICAL SETTING: Colonization in America north of the Rio Grande did not appear to be a very attractive proposition to Europeans in the sixteenth century. The real question is why European men and women put their money into exploration and colonization instead of more promising enterprises. Even more difficult is explaining why thousands of men and women gave up their homes in Europe and braved the hazards of a grueling Atlantic voyage and of life in a strange, even hostile, environment. What did they expect? Why did they think it might be worth all the risks? Was life in Europe so difficult that they approached the gamble in a fatalistic spirit, or did they really believe they would make their fortunes in America?

What did the Indians make of the newcomers? The Native Americans' role was much more dynamic than modern readers realize. Popular culture has taught us to assume that once the Europeans arrived with their sophisticated technology—their guns, ships, and horses—the Indians were essentially forced to retreat in dismay. The story is actually much more complex. Although in some cases their predictions were not borne out by events, the natives made shrewd judgments on the evidence available to them and aided some plantations in order to get access to the European products they valued.

All the participants entered the new set of relationships with specific goals in mind. Often the situation turned out far different from their expectations. Many times events carried the participants into situations they never anticipated. Some results, such as the impact of European diseases on Native Americans, were completely unanticipated. Explorers, natives, and settlers were always reacting to unexpected circumstances. In many ways colonization was a constant series of improvisations, and America a giant laboratory for a great experiment in human relations.

Although North America was the last settled—and least promising—area in the newly revealed lands, Europeans had created settlements around its coasts by the first decade of the seventeenth century. France had the colony of Quebec, England had settled Jamestown, and Spain had St. Augustine in Florida and Santa Fe in New Mexico. All but St. Augustine were created within a few years of each other, and all signaled the beginning of permanent European occupation.

Sir Walter Raleigh and the Beginnings of the British Empire

On October 29, 1618, Sir Walter Raleigh was publicly executed in London, a city he had loved. Raleigh had once been among the richest and most powerful men in the kingdom. At the height of his influence, he had originated English colonization of America. Even the prosecutor who called for his execution said of him, "He hath been a star at which the world hath gazed."

Raleigh, like many great men and women of his time, viewed the world as a theater and saw himself as acting out predetermined roles. Thus, he stage-managed his own execution so that it would be remembered by all who saw or read about it. Onlookers marveled at his self-possession. As he was taken past the scaffold on which he was to die to the room where he was to spend his last night, he met a friend and asked him to come and witness the execution. He warned that there would be crowds: "I know not what shift you will make, but I am sure to have a place." When he was admonished for joking about such a serious matter, he answered, "Give me leave to be merry, for this is the last merriment that ever I shall have in the world: but when I come to the sad part, thou shalt see, I will look on it like a man."

He believed that he could go to his death calmly because he was innocent of the false charge of treason on which he had been convicted. No one had worked harder or devoted more of his life to serving England than he had; therefore, he could die with an easy conscience. On the morning of his execution he was "very cheerful." He ate heartily and smoked his pipe (his own settlers from the Roanoke colony had made smoking popular in England), "and made no more of his death, than it had been to take a journey; and left a great impression in the minds of those that beheld him."

It was customary for the condemned man to make a final speech on the scaffold. Raleigh first told the audience that the malaria he had caught on his American adventures might make him shake, but he would not shake with fear. When he saw some noblemen looking down from a window, he shouted so that they could hear him; instead, they came down and sat with him on the scaffold. Next he went through the list of charges against him, maintaining his innocence of all of them.

So effective was his speech and manner, according to one eyewitness, that many of his enemies who had come to gloat at his death found their feelings completely changed, "and turned their joy to sorrow, [and] it filled all men else with emotion and admiration." At the end he asked the spectators to join him in prayer. Then he distributed some small presents to those around him, saying, "I have a long journey to go, and therefore will take my leave."

Chapter 1 First Encounters

The spectators then left the scaffold and the executioner approached. Raleigh asked to see the ax. The executioner was upset and held back. Raleigh said to him, "I pray thee let me see it. Dost thou think that I am afraid of it?" As he tested the ax's edge with his finger, he remarked, "This is a sharp medicine, but it is a physician for all diseases." He then knelt down and put his head on the block. One of his friends said he should face east, toward Jerusalem, but he answered, "What matter how the head lie, so the heart be right." He refused a blindfold and controlled the event right up to the end. He said he would lift his hand when he was ready. The executioner, perhaps overcome with emotion, stood still despite the signal. Raleigh admonished him, "What dost thou fear? Strike, man!" Then the ax fell and Raleigh's life was over. The manner of his death would not be forgotten, even hundreds of years later.

Raleigh's fall was great because he had risen so high. No one could have guessed when he first made London his home, almost forty years before his death, that his life would follow a roller-coaster curve from obscurity to the heights of power and wealth, then down again to prison and a criminal's death. His life and death illustrate the grandeur and possibilities of the period of Queen Elizabeth I, England's great monarch. One of these possibilities was the creation of an English empire in America, which Raleigh worked tirelessly to bring about. Raleigh's career also illustrates the risks and dangers of the time: the schemes that helped build England's greatness and his own power also brought him to disgrace.

London was a powerfully exciting city at the end of the sixteenth century. Everyone felt it. The city was a magnet drawing the young in search of opportunities from all over England. Talented people came to find like-minded friends, and literary circles burgeoned. William Shakespeare and Ben Jonson created plays that drew high and low to the theater—a different play every day, sometimes two a day. Criers would travel through the city calling out the names of the plays, and fans would flock to the Globe Theatre and its rivals, where rich and poor jostled together.

On the Thames, ships set out for ports around the world, returning with unheard-of luxuries and exotic items—tobacco, chocolate, and sugar from America, silks and spices from the Orient. The whole world was opening up, and England was determined to be at the center. First Portugal and then Spain had been leaders in world exploration, but the English were determined to change this. No longer would England be an insignificant little country on the fringes of Europe!

The English were not just seeking glory for themselves, they were fighting for God and "true religion," by which they meant Protestantism. All Europe was involved in a great struggle over religion. As the sixteenth century opened, Europe was almost completely Roman Catholic, all countries paying homage to the pope in Rome. Beginning with Martin Luther's defiance in Germany in 1517, this unity was shattered. Luther argued not only that the Roman Catholic Church was corrupt, but that it had misread the Bible. He asserted that faith, not good works and sacraments, was the way to salvation. The movement he began spread over much of northern Europe. England became Protestant, as did the Netherlands and the Scandinavian nations. Germany, which was made up at that time of more than 300 small states and principalities, was split, as was France, between Catholics and Protestants.

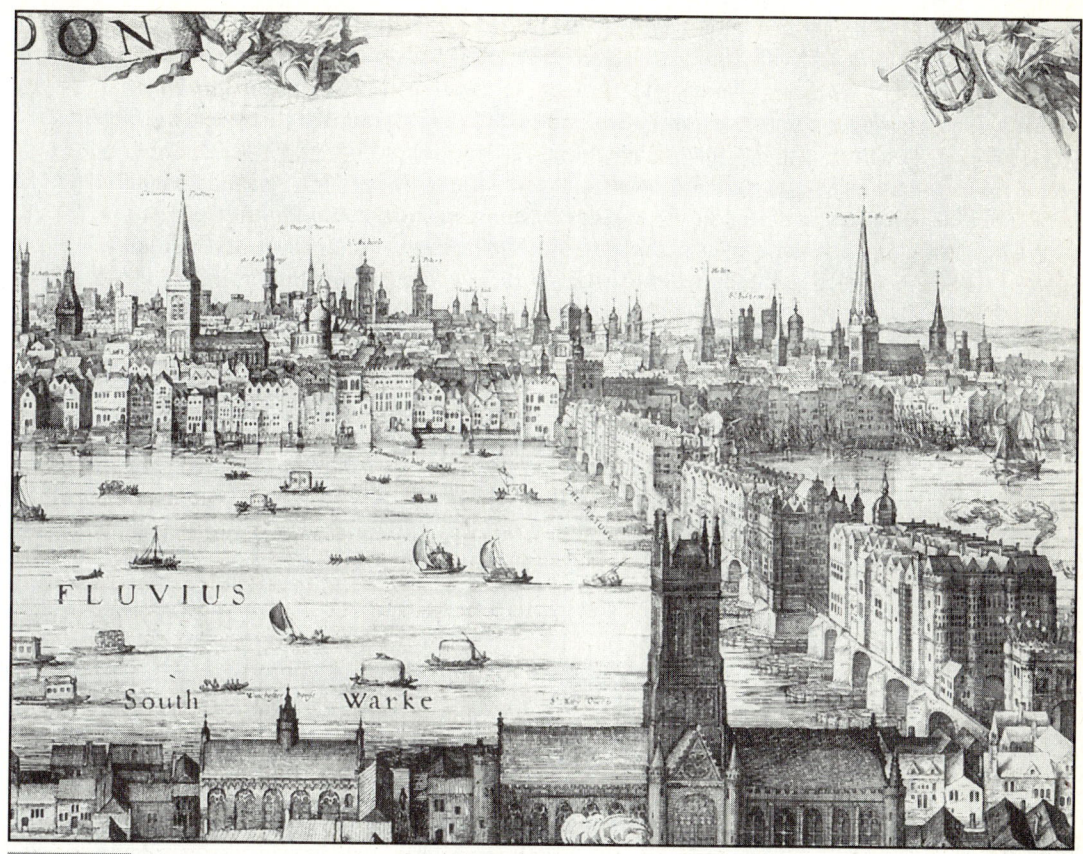

LONDON BRIDGE. John Visscher's 1616 engraving shows the city teeming with life and projects, with the ship-filled Thames River as its central artery.

Spain, the leader of the Roman Catholic nations, led the fight to try to force the newly Protestant countries back into allegiance to the pope. England, a much weaker nation, saw itself as leader of the Protestants. The English believed that God had specially selected them to carry the truth around the world. Their sense of national pride and their belief that they were fighting for truth against Spain, "the sword of that Antichrist of Rome," gave impetus to their attempts to build a great empire.

The nation looked to Queen Elizabeth, who symbolized England for her subjects. She could make them believe that God really had called the English to greatness. When the pope branded her a heretic, it only made them prouder of her. She was smart, even crafty, in dealing with foreigners and managed to build her country's prestige while spending as little money as possible. She brought the most glittering people to her court to adorn it, and she was loved by her people.

Her Roman Catholic predecessor, her half-sister Mary, had been a cold, reserved woman. Elizabeth, in her formal procession through the city on the day before her coronation in 1558, told the crowds, "I will be as good unto you as ever queen was to her people. . . . And persuade yourselves, that for the safety and quietness of you all, I will not spare, if need be, to spend my blood." Raleigh compared her court to a "great theater," and all acknowledged that she played the role allotted to her well.

This scintillating London was the place Sir Walter Raleigh loved best. He was a man of many talents, and the city gave him the chance to show them off. The literary world prized him for his poetry, and he could hold his own with the best of them in raucous evenings in the inns and taverns. He found a new world of interest in overseas ventures, and conferred with ship captains and mapmakers, who brought news of uncharted lands. He wanted a part in the great campaign to make the world acknowledge England's greatness. And, most important, the queen loved him. It was her love that made possible his great power and actions.

Elizabeth liked to have young, witty men at her court, and Raleigh, famous for his puns and clever verses, became her favorite soon after he came to live permanently in the city in 1582. The queen, who had now ruled for twenty-four years, was in her late forties; Raleigh was twenty years younger, but he courted her in his poems, writing that her eyes "set my fancy on fire" and her red hair held "my heart in chains."

The old story that he first caught her attention by putting his brand-new cloak on a puddle before her feet may very well be true. He wore beautiful and expensive clothes to please the queen and cultivated his dark, exotic good looks. He sported one huge pearl earring, which became his trademark.

Though he could play the lighthearted young suitor to the middle-aged Queen Elizabeth, Raleigh had already lived through a world of experiences before he came to London. He was certainly not born to that elegant world. His family was an old and distinguished one, but his father was not a rich man; Raleigh grew up on the family's farm in Devonshire in the west of England. This part of England looked out to the sea, and young Walter grew up hearing stories of great maritime exploits.

His mother had been married before, and Walter had older half brothers, John, Humphrey, and Adrian Gilbert. Humphrey was in his teens when Walter was born in 1554, and Raleigh looked up to him all his life. It was through Humphrey that Raleigh received introductions to many roles he would play as an adult. Humphrey was a pioneer in arguing for an empire that would make England great.

English men and women typically left home for good when they were about fourteen, and Raleigh was no exception. Young people of humble origins usually started their careers as servants, working in someone's home, farm, or workshop, but Raleigh prepared himself for the life of a gentleman by going off to war in 1568 with a company of gentlemen from Devonshire to fight on the side of the French Protestants, called Huguenots, against the Roman Catholic French. The vicious fighting was a brutal introduction to life for a young teenager. Young Raleigh returned home after four years a cynical eighteen-year-old.

When he returned to England in 1572, Raleigh registered at Oxford University, but apparently did not spend much time there. In 1575 he registered at the Inns of Court in London, which served as England's law school. Here, at the age of twenty-one, he became part of his older half brother Humphrey Gilbert's circle and was introduced to the plans being made for English exploration abroad. Gilbert was convinced that there must be a passage through the continent of North America that would allow the

English to reach the riches of the Orient, and he was trying to find backers for a scheme to look for it. Raleigh was entranced to be a part of such big plans. He began to evolve his personal style. He published his first book of poetry in 1576, and he became known for his rowdy style of life. His drunken exploits were legendary.

This exciting time was not to last, however, for there was more war in Raleigh's future. In 1580, when he was twenty-six, he went to England's most difficult war, that in Ireland. Earlier, in France, he could believe he was helping honest Protestants to free themselves of Roman Catholic tyranny, but the Irish war offered no such justification. England had ancient claims on paper to Ireland, but actually bringing Ireland under control was quite another matter. The religious conflict of Protestants versus Roman Catholics all over Europe made it imperative for England to control Ireland. The Irish had remained Roman Catholic when the English became Protestant, and the Irish hated the English. Therefore, the English feared that if Spain or some other Catholic power wanted to invade England, Ireland would offer them a good base. The English believed they had to conquer Ireland once and for all.

The fighting here was more vicious than in France, partly because the Irish, whom the English despised, used guerrilla tactics. English commanders, perhaps because their cause was so suspect, called the Irish "barbarians," even "cannibals," then used these names to justify English actions. One commander wrote from Ireland that the Irish "live like beasts, void of law and all good order." He said they were "more uncivil, more uncleanly, more barbarous and more brutish in their customs and demeanors, than in any other part of the world that is known." Therefore, according to the English, the most severe tactics were acceptable.

Sir Humphrey Gilbert had been commander in the Irish province of Munster in 1570, ten years before Raleigh went, and he had become famous as the most ferocious and brutal of all the English. When Raleigh went to Ireland, he must have had his beloved brother's actions in his mind. Gilbert had instituted a system of total war, in which women and children were executed along with soldiers. It was said that when his troops moved through the country not a living creature was left behind. He lined the path to his tent with the severed heads of those he had slaughtered, in order to "bring great terror to the people when they saw the heads of their dead fathers, brothers, children, kinsfolk and friends, lie on the ground before their faces, as they came to speak with the said colonel."

Raleigh was plunged immediately into the slaughter that was still going on ten years later when he arrived. He participated in the conquest of the Irish fortress at Smerwick, which was garrisoned by 400 Spanish and Italian volunteers who had come to help their fellow Roman Catholics as the English had helped the French Protestants. In addition, the fort held about 200 Irish women and children. The English commander, Lord Grey of Wilton, decreed that all the captives be killed, despite the fact that he had apparently promised them their safety if they surrendered.

Lord Grey ordered Raleigh and another captain to oversee the slaughter. The 200 men they commanded carried out the executions of the 600 captives that day. It must have been a horrifying experience. As a commander, Raleigh would have had to deal with the hundreds of condemned men, women, and children, who pleaded in agony as they waited their turn during that long day. The English forces, in order to kill so many in one day, would have had to take great care that their swords did not become dull. If they killed the victims with a thrust in the stomach, that would preserve the sword's sharpness but result in a slower and more painful death. Highly skilled soldiers could strike a clean blow through the neck without hitting any edge-dulling bone. Lord Grey's report to Queen Elizabeth described the slaughtered garrison: "as gallant and good personages as ever beheld."

That Raleigh never spoke of his Irish service in his later life indicates he found the memory painful. He knew he would have been treated the same way had he been captured in France. He sent his own analysis of the Irish problem to the court—a daring thing for a junior officer to do. He argued that the war was all wrong, that the Irish should be wooed rather than battered into submission. Having seen two vicious wars in which religion was an issue, he hoped for better solutions to England's problems.

<hr>

Finally, in 1582 Walter Raleigh came to London and found his natural home: the court of Queen Elizabeth. Raleigh's rise to preeminence among the queen's favorites meant fabulous wealth and power. Those she favored she showered with estates and monopolies over the production or import of key commodities. Raleigh, in addition to estates in England and Ireland, won monopolies on the importation of sweet wines, the export of woolen cloth—England's most important product—and tin production in Cornwall. This meant his agents could rake off a percentage of profits, and Raleigh's men saw that he always got his cut. He soon became the equivalent of a modern millionaire.

These monopolies, which could easily degenerate into mere corruption, were Elizabeth's way of concentrating national resources in the hands of men such as Raleigh who could then use them in great ventures that would benefit the entire country. Raleigh, probably more than anyone in England, was ready to make use of the opportunities such wealth offered. He reinvested his wealth in projects to raise England to great-nation status. He had learned well the lessons gained while listening to the great plans of Humphrey Gilbert and his advisers. Now that he was the queen's favorite, he suddenly had the wealth and power to try to make those dreams come true.

Walter Raleigh, like many of his countrymen, was unhappy with England's lowly position. The great superpower of the age was Spain, the leader of the Roman Catholic nations. English analysts argued that the source of Spain's preeminence was its great American empire and the fabulous riches of the Aztecs and Incas. While England had myopically focused on subduing the Irish threat, Spain had conquered half the New World and achieved unparalleled wealth and power.

The Spanish empire was a remarkable structure for the sixteenth century, because it was highly organized from top to bottom. All expeditions were sent out directly by the king, and the royal government required elaborate reports from everyone in the field, which were funneled through the Council of the Indies. These reports were actually read, often by the king himself, and new directions sent back. The empire functioned almost like a modern bureaucracy. All trade was licensed through the *Casa de Contratación* in Seville, which also kept accounts of all revenues. The empire was divided into two viceroyalties, New Spain and Peru, and each was divided into *audiencias,* which were again subdivided into *presidencias,* and so on. Everything went through the chain of command. No other American empire built by a European nation attempted anything quite like this.

When Raleigh looked at Spain, he saw clear lessons for England. Spain had become powerful through the riches the conquest produced. England was weak and backward because it had lagged behind. Nearly a century had passed since word of the newly discovered continents had spread over Europe. England had established claims to North America by the voyages of John and Sebastian Cabot, sent out within the first decade after 1492; yet the nation had done next to nothing to develop these claims. Raleigh and his associates, ashamed of English slackness, were determined to rectify that neglect.

With an American empire, England would also become a world-class power, and by doing so, it could both help itself and strike a blow at Spain. For the time being, nothing could be done about the Spanish possessions, but at least Spain could be prevented from taking over North America as well. And England could show the world how colonization ought to be done. Raleigh and his friends were disgusted by the Spanish example, which they interpreted as a ruthless search for gold to the exclusion of all else. When the Indians died out, the Spanish imported Africans in huge numbers to take their places as slaves on the plantations and in the silver mines.

A Spanish priest, Bartolomé de las Casas, wrote a book vividly depicting the suffering of the Indians, *A Brief Relation of the Destruction of the Indies,* published in 1552. It was translated into English as *The Tears of the Indians* in 1583, just at the time Raleigh was becoming interested in founding a colony, and it horrified the English public. Raleigh and other English promoters believed they could show the world an empire that would not inflict such injustice, either on Indians or on Africans.

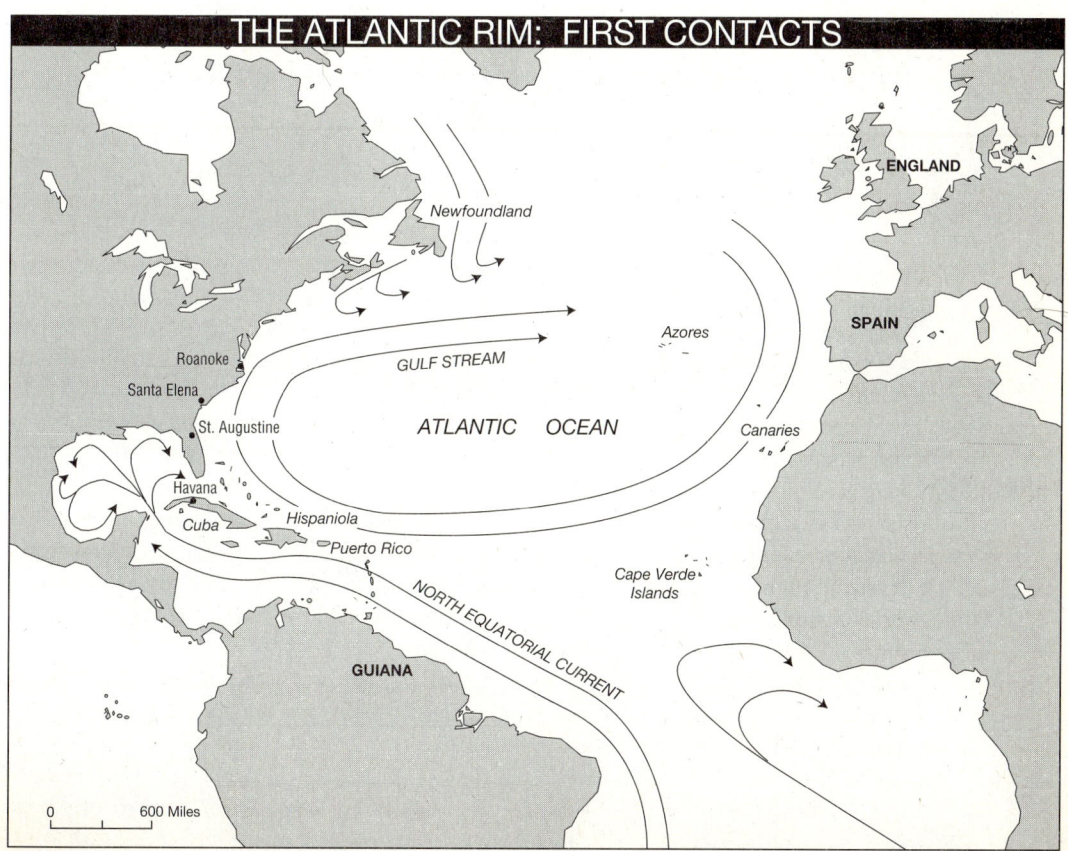

In 1584, when Raleigh began to plan for his first settlement at Roanoke, his associate Richard Hakluyt, a geographer, wrote a long treatise for Queen Elizabeth explaining why England needed colonies, and why she should help Raleigh. In this *Discourse of Western Planting* he quoted Las Casas to demonstrate that Spain's was an evil empire. Hakluyt and Raleigh strongly believed that the Indians and Africans who had been enslaved by the Spanish would rise up and greet the English as liberators, "to shake off from their shoulders the most intolerable and insupportable yoke of Spain." Hakluyt quoted numerous instances of torture and claimed 12 million Americans had died in the first forty years of Spanish rule, because of the Spaniards' "most outrageous and more than Turkish cruelties in all the West Indies, whereby they are everywhere there become most odious unto them."

This was mostly just big talk in the early 1580s. England had a long way to go before it could mount a successful challenge. The country was backward in every way. Though English ships went every summer to fish off the Grand Banks near Newfoundland, English mariners lacked the skill to navigate the much more difficult journey to the islands of the Caribbean and the coast north of Florida. When English ships sailed into those regions, they were forced to rely on Portuguese pilots to guide them, a humiliating experience.

Nor were the English competitive with the Spanish and Portuguese in the theoretical knowledge needed to make the maps and charts essential to colonization. Whereas Oxford and Cambridge, the ancient universities of England, disdained applied mathematics and geography as mere "practical" subjects unworthy of their notice, Spain and Portugal had long since established academies where sea captains learned the basic trigonometry required for navigation by stars and sun out of sight of land, and surveyors learned how to make accurate maps.

Raleigh, whose new wealth and position at court made action possible, was determined to change all this. Durham House, a London mansion given him by the queen, became a center of experts planning a new role for England, a kind of "think tank" where they could pool their knowledge. Raleigh amassed his own fleet and hired a young scholar from Oxford, Thomas Harriot, to create a textbook on navigation and teach it to his captains. Geographer Richard Hakluyt was also part of this group. He went on to devote his life to gathering all the information available about America, and he published it in massive collections, the most famous of which was *Principal Navigations, Voyages, Traffics, and Discoveries of the English Nation,* which appeared between 1589 and 1600. All this was part of the campaign to focus the nation's attention on America.

The Durham House group generated an atmosphere of tremendous excitement. England was poised for takeoff as a colonial power. The key problem was finding the money to finance ventures. Establishing a colony cost enormous amounts of money— comparable to building a large and continuously occupied station on the moon today—and, given the fact that it would take years before settlers could even establish themselves and become self-sufficient, it was unclear what they could produce that would repay such outlays of money. Spanish adventurers had discovered great riches in Mexico and Peru, but North America had no comparable riches to offer.

The English monarchy lacked the funds to help finance such projects. Colonization had to be underwritten by private investors, as a business proposition. Elizabeth gave Raleigh the exclusive right to colonize in North America so that he could then attract investors and colonists and set up his colonies as he wished. As with all monopolies, Raleigh would expect to make money off his colonies. He saw nothing wrong with mixing public service and private gain.

Raleigh knew just how his ventures would make money. He would set up a colony as an American base for his fleet, which could then dart out and attack Spanish ships as they carried the wealth of the Aztecs and Incas home to Spain. He knew that all the treasure produced in the Spanish colonies was carried every year to Havana and from there loaded onto huge ships known as carracks. Once a year a great convoy of these carracks, which were slow and clumsy, made its way from Havana to Seville. If English sailors could detach and capture even one ship, riches beyond belief would flow to the investors. This kind of piracy, known as privateering, was considered legal, even patriotic, because it was carried out against England's enemy.

An American colony, then, would allow Raleigh to do everything he wanted: strengthen England, enrich himself, and harm Spain. In 1584 he sent out a reconnaissance voyage to find a good location for his base. After a few weeks, his ships returned with the news that the Carolina Outer Banks offered the perfect site. The Outer Banks are long sandbars along the coast, and sheltered within them was little Roanoke Island—hidden away and yet close to the Spanish islands. Arthur Barlowe, one of the captains, described Roanoke as almost a paradise: "We found the people most gentle, loving, and faithful, void of all guile, and treason, and such as lived after the manner of the golden age. The earth bringeth forth all things in abundance, as in the first creation, without toil or labor."

Barlowe told Raleigh what he wanted to hear, and immediate plans were drawn up to send a colony. Only later would Raleigh realize that such lavish praise could not be true and only set up the colonists for greater failure later. It turned out that Roanoke was a very poor site. The sandbars that made up the island and the Outer Banks lacked the fertility to sustain a large English population, and the surrounding waters were so shallow that the great ships had to anchor miles out to sea, exposed to furious Atlantic storms and visible to the enemy. Roanoke, the first English colony, was useless for the purpose for which it was designed, but only long and painful experience would make that clear.

In the spring of 1585 Raleigh dispatched the first contingent of English colonists to America. After choosing the location, the next problem was to select the people who would go. Raleigh made the most obvious choice: the settlement would be made up of young men, preferably with military experience. They could then defend themselves against both the Indians and the Spanish, and they ought to be able to spend the rest of their time exploring. Raleigh thought of setting up a colony as similar to sending an expedition to France or to Ireland.

Anyone would probably have made the same choice, but we now know this was the worst possible model for a colony. The young men tended to fall apart in the isolation and frustration, and they were difficult to control. Ralph Lane, who was the governor of this first Roanoke colony, said that while the American "savages" posed great challenges to the settlement, many of his worst problems stemmed from "the wild men of my own nation." Also, these men, many of whom were veterans of the religious wars

AN INDIAN VILLAGE. John White painted the Carolina Algonquian village of Secoton after his return from Roanoke. White was eager to demonstrate to European audiences that the Indians encountered by the Roanoke colonists were not nomadic savages, but lived a settled village life. He showed corn at three different stages of growth, and included scenes of Indian religious and family life.

in Europe or English campaigns in Ireland, always thought of force as a solution to all situations. They visualized Indian relations as basically a question of which side would dominate, and they wanted to make sure the English would always be on top. Their attitudes and methods destroyed any possibility of peaceful and friendly relations with the Indians.

The little fleet carrying England's first American colonists set out in early spring of 1585. When they arrived at Roanoke on June 29, they immediately found out that the Outer Banks were a poor place for a colony. The *Tiger*, the ship carrying almost all the provisions that were to feed the colonists over the winter, ran aground on the treacherous sandbars. Everything was ruined. It was too late to plant food crops. And all winter long the stormy Atlantic was too dangerous to cross. This meant that the colonists would have to get all their food from the Indians—and of course the Indians had had no advance warning that they would be expected to keep over a hundred extra people fed for almost a year. It was a situation set up for disaster.

Nonetheless, the colonists set to work building their settlement under the direction of Ralph Lane. Meanwhile, Sir Richard Grenville, commander of the fleet, took some of the smaller boats and explored the sounds between the Outer Banks and the mainland. Grenville graphically taught the Indians what the coming of the Europeans would mean to them. One of his men kept a terse record of their stops:

> *The 12.* we came to the Town of Pomeiocke.
>
> *The 13.* we passed by water to Aquascococke.
>
> *The 15.* we came to Secotan and were well entertained there of the Savages.
>
> *The 16.* we returned thence, and one of our boats with the Admiral was sent to Aquascococke to demand a silver cup which one of the Savages had stolen from us, and not receiving it according to his promise, we burnt, and spoiled their corn, and Town, all the people being fled.

This is hard to believe. Grenville knew that the hundred-plus men he was leaving in Roanoke would be utterly dependent on the Indians for food. Yet here he was not only committing an incredibly hostile act, but destroying some of that food which would soon be in such short supply. Why would he do such a thing?

These colonizers saw all life as a struggle for domination. Grenville believed that either the colonists would dominate the Indians or vice versa. Despite what theorists like Hakluyt wrote in England, Grenville's thinking was much closer to the Spanish model. He and most of the leaders like him believed that if the colonists ever showed the slightest sign of weakness, the Indians would realize they had the upper hand and the English would be at their mercy. He honestly thought he was protecting the colonists in the most effective way.

Ralph Lane, fresh from service in Ireland, carried on in the same tradition after he and his colonists were left alone. When he wanted to ensure the cooperation of an Indian leader, he kidnapped his "best beloved son" and held him hostage. Because of such behavior, but even more because the colonists' incessant demands for food pressed the Indians so hard, relations deteriorated. Lane had expected fresh supplies from England in April, but they did not arrive. Meanwhile, the Roanoke chief, Wingina, had become rich and powerful because he had acquired so much English copper and so many European goods in return for corn. Lane became convinced Wingina was forming a large coalition to wipe out the settlement, so he and his men planned a pre-emptive strike. In a surprise attack on June 1, 1586, the colonists began their "slaughter, and surprise of the Savages" with the watchword of the day: "Christ our victory." Wingina was killed and his severed head displayed on a post. All possibility of good relations with the Roanoke Indians was over.

Now the situation was truly desperate. Food supplies were almost completely gone. A week later, June 8, the lookout sighted ships, "but whether they were friends or foes, he could not yet discern, but advised me to stand upon as good guard as I could." They turned out to be English, but not the anticipated supply fleet. These were the ships of Sir Francis Drake, who had been privateering in the Spanish colonies for almost a year and had arrived at Roanoke hoping to inaugurate its role as a rest and repair center. Instead, he found the colonists desperate and in disarray, unable to feed even themselves, much less all of Drake's men.

After some discussion, Drake agreed to take them all home. They sailed June 19, after Drake's impatient sailors threw overboard almost everything the settlers had collected in their year in America: "the most of all we had, with all our Cards maps, Books and writings, were by the Sailors cast overboard, the greater number of the Fleet being much aggrieved with their long and dangerous abode in that miserable road." Among the articles lost was a "fair chain" of native pearls Lane had hoped to present to Queen Elizabeth. This was the end of the first Roanoke colony. Raleigh's supply ships were already at sea, but they arrived to find the island deserted.

Lane's colony was not just a failure, however, nor had it ever been just a military outpost. Raleigh had sent along two men, his scientific adviser Thomas Harriot, and an artist named John White, to investigate the country and make a record of Indian life

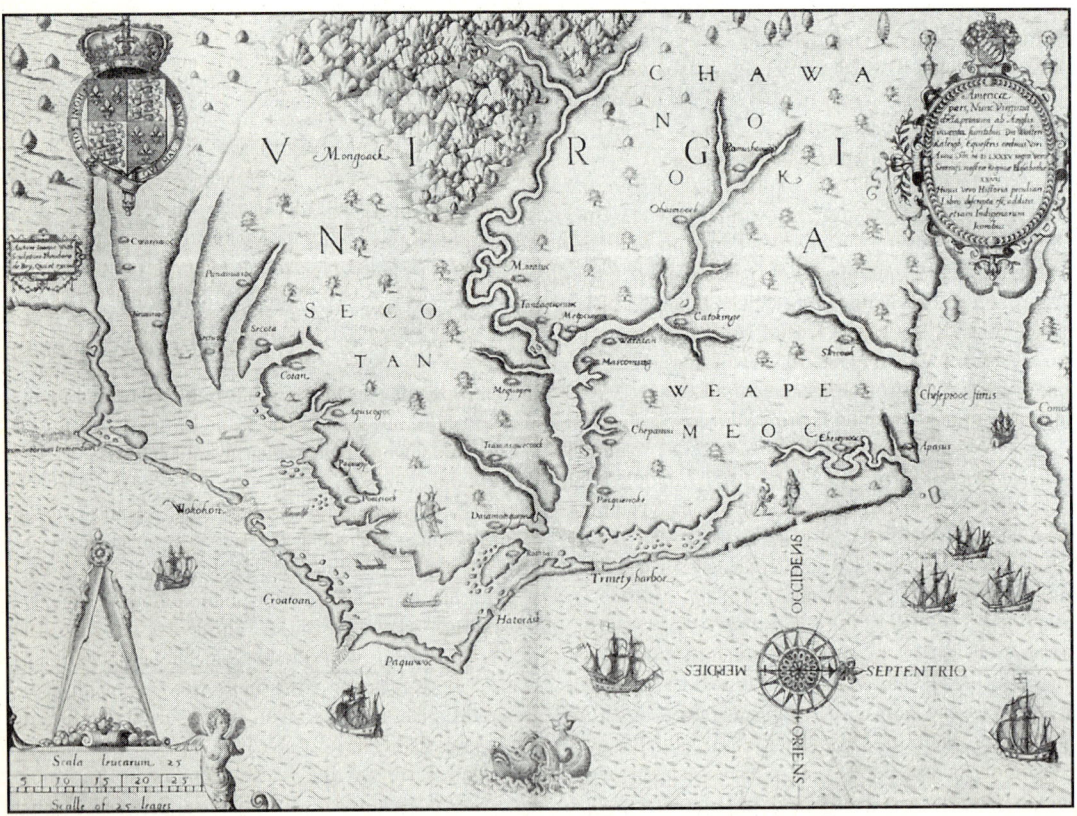

ROANOKE AND CHESAPEAKE BAY. Theodore DeBry engraved this map, based on an original by John White, for his edition of Harriot's *Briefe and True Report* (1590). The map demonstrates the sophistication of Harriot and White's survey of the immediate Roanoke area, and showed prospective investors that even though Roanoke was a poor site, Chesapeake Bay was nearby and was a good prospect for a permanent colony.

and culture and of the flora, fauna, and resources of the region. Harriot had prepared for the task by learning the Algonquians' language from two Indians, Manteo and Wanchese, who had been brought to England by the reconnoitering voyage in 1584. Harriot and White's report was the finest discussion of America's natural history and Indian life produced in the entire colonial period. They also created the most accurate map of any part of America done to that time. Moreover, an exploring party from Roanoke had discovered a much better site for a colony to the north, along one of the rivers that emptied into Chesapeake Bay. This site had what Roanoke lacked: It could shelter a settlement from enemy eyes, yet was approachable by oceangoing ships; the James River was navigable for many miles. So deep was the river that the largest oceangoing ship could be tied up to a tree branch.

Raleigh determined to try again, and in his plans for the new colony, his real genius shone through. Instead of tinkering with this or that aspect of the old plans, he realized that a completely new approach was called for. He decided to put his colony on Chesapeake Bay, and to scrap the idea of sending soldiers. This new venture was to have families for its settlers. Men, women, and children would go to America and work to become self-supporting. Only then could they live in peace and harmony with the Indians. And only families working on their own land would have the incentive to put in the effort to make a colony successful. Raleigh was among the first to acknowledge that women's skills were as important as men's contributions in setting up new societies in America.

The backing for the new colony was also arranged differently. Raleigh now realized that a single individual, no matter how wealthy and powerful, did not have the resources to sustain a large colonial venture. He created a joint-stock company, a kind of corporation, to sponsor the colony. Joint-stock companies, just emerging in England during the sixteenth century, were used to sponsor all kinds of activities, from Shakespeare's Globe Theatre to privateering voyages. They made it possible to pool funds and spread risks involved in big ventures.

John White, the painter, was one of the few members of Lane's colony whose enthusiasm was undiminished, and Raleigh chose him to be governor of the "City of Raleigh in Virginia." White, in turn, recruited many of the new settlers, including his pregnant daughter, Eleanor Dare, and her husband, Ananias. Eleanor was one of two women who were pregnant on board the ships. The trip across was always bad for passengers; it must have been almost intolerable for these women, and for children. Sixteenth-century ships lacked bunks or cabins. Passengers rolled up in blankets and slept on deck or, in bad weather, belowdecks. During storms, passengers were forced to remain below, where the stench quickly became intolerable. There were no toilet facilities, and seasick passengers contributed to the stench. Rats and cockroaches, stirred up by the ship's motion in a storm, and fleeing the water that inevitably leaked in, made sleeping difficult. America must have indeed looked like a paradise to this set of passengers when they finally arrived.

The settlers set out in the spring of 1587 with great enthusiasm; each family was to have 500 acres, a huge estate by English standards. The new formula, substantial families who would work hard because they worked for themselves, would produce a nearly self-sufficient plantation. This was the formula that led to success in later plantations. John White's colony should have been a glorious success, yet it became the famous Lost Colony.

How could this have happened? The answer lies in the perennial search for money. Investors had to be repaid, and sources of quick income had to be found. Raleigh had solved this problem by having his ships go privateering, but it now became clear that colonization and privateering did not mix. The fleet carrying the settlers was, as usual, under the direction of a Portuguese mariner, Simão Fernandes. Fernandes and John White hated each other, and White was horrified that Fernandes started privateering on the way to America despite the risk to the women and children. Then, when the ships made a brief stop at Roanoke on their way to Chesapeake Bay, one of Fernandes's men "called to the sailors in the pinnace, charging them not to bring any of the planters back again, but leave them in the Island saying that the Summer was far spent, wherefore he would land all the planters in no other place."

QUEEN ELIZABETH I. This portrait, painted to commemorate England's victory in 1588 over the Spanish Armada, shows the country's inflated claims to mastery as the Spanish ships go down to destruction in a God-sent storm in the right corner, and Elizabeth's hand rests on a globe of the world under a representation of the serene English fleet. Pearls such as those adorning her dress and hair were one goal of overseas colonies.

White and his colonists were stunned. Fernandes, putting privateering before the colony, was jeopardizing their lives and the entire enterprise. The colonists begged White to return and describe their situation to Raleigh. He at first refused, fearing he would be accused of desertion, but was "at the last, through their extreme entreating, constrained to return into England." He embarked August 27, 1587, shortly after the birth of his granddaughter, Virginia Dare, the first English child born in America. As he said good-bye, he could not know that no European would ever see any of the 114 colonists again.

The planters expected to be resupplied in the spring. Meanwhile, they told White they would attempt to move the settlement overland to Chesapeake Bay. As soon as he was back in England, White flew to Raleigh and infected him with his own sense of urgency. As White had expected, Raleigh received his news with great concern and authorized a large fleet and new supplies, which were gathered over the winter. Just as the fleet was ready to depart in the spring of 1588, word came from the Privy Council that no ships were to be allowed to leave English ports. Spain, fed up with English interference with its ships, had decided to invade England and bring that country to its knees once and for all. Because Queen Elizabeth "doth receive daily advertisements of the preparations of the King of Spain," the "intended voyage" to the aid of the Roanoke colonists was forbidden.

Raleigh's supply fleet was diverted to the national defense. Every ship was needed, because the "advertisements" reaching the queen's ears were correct. King Philip II of Spain had amassed the greatest armada the world had ever seen, to finish off England's resistance to his power. In one of the most dramatic moments in English history, the Spanish Goliath was met by the English David. Queen Elizabeth, at Tilbury to review the troops massed to resist the threatened invasion, gave one of her most famous speeches, in which she said, "I know I have the body of a weak and feeble woman, but I have the heart and stomach of a king, and of a king of England too, and think foul scorn that Parma or Spain, or any prince of Europe should dare to invade the borders of my realm." Never had she been more popular with her people. Storms (some said the hand of God) scattered the Spanish fleet, and many of the sailors were lost. Philip II's dream of finishing off England was not fulfilled.

But the armada did help kill Raleigh's Roanoke colony. Just as privateering was the reason the colony had first come into existence, now it was privateering, or at least the outcome of privateering, that ended it. No supplies were sent to the settlers in 1588, nor in 1589. Raleigh's attention was increasingly diverted to other projects. Elizabeth granted him large estates in Ireland, and he was collecting colonists and supplies to be sent there while his Roanoke colonists were being neglected. Only John White continued to put the Roanoke settlement first in his concerns, working constantly to attract attention to their plight. Twice White managed to get passage on small ships that he hoped would look for the planters, but each time the mariners just went privateering instead.

Finally, in 1590, White returned to Roanoke Island. The landfall was made at evening, and "we saw a great smoke rise in the Isle Roanoke near the place where I left our Colony in the year 1587, which smoke put us in good hope that some of the Colony were there expecting my return out of England." As they anchored near the spot, White and the sailors "sounded with a trumpet a Call, & afterwards many familiar English tunes of Songs, and called to them friendly; but we had no answer." Next morning they found the village deserted. The smoke came from brushfires kindled by lightning.

White was disappointed, but not desolate. He and his party found the word CROATOAN carved on a post. A Maltese cross would have indicated that the colonists had left in distress, but just the one word had been carved. And the settlers had carefully buried everything they could not take with them. They clearly had not been wiped out, nor had they left in a hurry. Croatoan, the home of Manteo, who had spent time in England, and the sole village that had remained friendly to the Lane colony, would be a natural place for them to go. White was actually encouraged.

But as the ships prepared to make the short journey south to Croatoan Island, a great storm blew up. The *Hopewell,* White's ship, lost two of its three anchors in attempts to avoid being hurled against the Outer Banks. With only one anchor standing between the ship and certain disaster, the master insisted on leaving that dangerous area. The second, smaller ship had already deserted the cause. White and the *Hopewell*'s master agreed to seek aid in the West Indies before resuming the search for the colonists, but the vagaries of wind and weather pushed them toward home.

Inexplicably, that was the last attempt to find the families of the Roanoke Lost Colony until 1603, when one ship made a slender effort. When Jamestown was founded in 1607, twenty years after the Lost Colony's abandonment, the settlers heard vague rumors of people like them who had lived on Chesapeake Bay until they had been wiped out by Powhatan, the dominant Indian leader of the region, but nothing of theirs was ever found.

Why was nothing done? The answer to that question lies in the basic conception of the English empire. Two things would have to change before colonies would be successful. One was the practice of associating colonization with privateering. The 1590s, the period when the colonists might still have been found if anyone had looked for them, was the great age of privateering; English ships swarmed over the Atlantic and West Indies, and they found they could be highly successful without a base such as Roanoke. As long as privateering was the goal, colonies were unnecessary. Privateering could bring in vast wealth with a single lucky strike; a settlement would be nothing but a drain for a long time and might never have anything to offer but basic agricultural commodities.

The idea that a single great man could control colonization also had to be abandoned. Even at the height of his wealth and power, Raleigh never had sufficient resources to people and supply Roanoke for as long as would be necessary. More important, his position was never secure. In the early 1590s he began to be edged out of the favorite's role at Elizabeth's court. The tall, young, glamorous earl of Essex had appeared at court and caught the queen's eye. Moreover, Raleigh was maturing and longed for a family of his own. The queen could not tolerate disloyalty among her courtiers. When Raleigh's secret marriage to Bess Throckmorton, one of the queen's ladies-in-waiting, was revealed by her pregnancy, Elizabeth threw both of them into prison in the Tower of London. She soon freed the couple, but sent them into exile in their country home at Christmas 1592. Bess Raleigh was never again allowed to come to court.

Raleigh worked from his country retreat to be allowed once again to see his queen and take up his court position as captain of her guard. He also worked to develop his plans for a British empire. He had been so proud and arrogant when in power that many rejoiced in his disgrace, but he knew he had not yet finished his part in history. What he needed was a big strike, something that would restore his fortunes with the queen and continue his campaign for English greatness in one grand gesture. In the West Country, his mind returned again and again to a story told him by a Spanish grandee, Sarmiento de Gamboa, who had been captured by his privateers in 1586. According to this account, the wealth of the Aztecs and Incas was excelled by a third great center, the fabulously rich city of El Dorado, which lay in the region of Guiana on the South American mainland.

Raleigh determined to put together a great fleet and find that golden city and its mines. He knew that however much he had offended Elizabeth, she would not ignore him if he brought such riches to England. In 1595 the fleet of five ships set off.

Amazed at the strangeness and beauty of the country, Raleigh wrote one of the great classics of exploration literature about Guiana on his return, but the practical results of the voyage were small. Raleigh's men, like many before and after them, found the web of marshes and tributaries marking the mouth of the Orinoco River extremely confusing. Raleigh interviewed many Indians and even some captured Spaniards who were also searching for the fabled gold, and he was thoroughly convinced that a rich mine existed, but though he wrote that "every stone that we stopped to take up promised either gold or silver by his complexion," none of the samples he brought back proved worthwhile.

He claimed this voyage had never been intended as anything more than a reconnaissance, and vowed to return. His quest was for the gold, but he was also attracted to the alien land and its strange people and beasts; Raleigh was convinced that the Amazons of ancient legend lived beyond the gold in the interior. He had gleaned this knowledge from his long and cordial talks with Indian leaders, who had also convinced him that the English would be welcome along the Orinoco. Raleigh, like Richard Hakluyt, believed the natives lived in terror of the cruel Spanish and that they would rise up to aid English liberators and would gladly share their wealth.

The Guiana voyage did not accomplish what Raleigh had intended; too many false hopes had been generated by other voyages. London had gone wild over tons of ore brought back by other voyages to other parts of America, and had turned against such ventures when it all proved worthless. Promises and rumors were not enough; provable ore or tangible gems were required to entice skeptical backers. Though Raleigh continued to nourish hopes of a gold mine in Guiana, he found no enthusiasm among those who would have to lay out money for another voyage.

The next year Raleigh turned his attention to the threat of Spain nearer home. In 1596 in association with his rival, the earl of Essex, and the lord admiral, Charles

Howard, Raleigh became involved in a massive plan to attack the great Spanish port of Cádiz, humiliating Spain and cutting off supplies to Spanish America. Nothing shows England's scale of values more clearly than this venture. At a time when Raleigh and the businessmen who had backed the City of Raleigh corporation could not spare one or two ships to seek the Lost Colonists, a great fleet of ninety-six English and more than twenty Dutch ships carrying 10,000 soldiers was amassed to take and loot Cádiz.

The Cádiz expedition was not a great success. The city was taken, but the forces spent their energies in a frenzy of sacking and pillaging. Nothing of permanent importance was gained; after about ten days the fleet left for home despite Essex's contention that Cádiz should be held for England. Raleigh, wounded in the initial attack, limped painfully for the rest of his life.

All had been worthwhile from Raleigh's point of view, however, because he had regained the queen's favor. He would never be singled out as before, but he was welcome at court and once again the recipient of favors. But the old queen's reign was drawing to a close. With her death in 1603, the first phase of England's interest in America, and especially the virulent anti-Spanish emphasis, would end. Elizabeth's successor, James I, who was also king of Scotland and the first of the long Stuart line of monarchs, wanted to avoid war at all costs. He sought to conciliate England's enemies rather than defy them. At times he even seemed to be pro-Spanish.

Raleigh was out of tune with the new regime. Most courtiers, seeing that Elizabeth was dying, had secretly approached James in Scotland to secure a place of favor in the new regime. Raleigh was one of the few who remained steadfastly loyal to Elizabeth right to the end. In flattering and fawning over the man who was soon to be king, other men hoped not only to enhance their own status in the new reign but also to harm those who might be rivals. Raleigh's refusal to play this game cost him heavily. His rivals poisoned the new king's mind against him, convincing James that Raleigh was plotting against him. When they met, James, indulging in one of the puns he loved so much, said: "On my soul, man, I have heard rawly of thee." Raleigh was soon hit by a series of blows; one by one he lost the sources of income and many of the estates that had been Elizabeth's gifts.

Soon the greatest blow of all fell: Raleigh was committed to the Tower of London on a charge of high treason. The charge was ludicrous; he was said to have conspired with Spain against England. It was almost as if the government had looked for the most far-fetched accusation they could have made. Even Raleigh's enemies considered it impossible that he, the leader of those who hated Spain, would have done anything to help that country.

But Raleigh did have many enemies; his arrogance in his days of power had alienated many. One courtier had said of him when he was at his most powerful that he was "the best hated man of the world, in Court, city, and country." Now in 1603 his humiliation created deep satisfaction at court, and crowds gathered to jeer him on his way to trial. Though his dignity and courage were to win over the crowd, he was convicted as everyone knew he would be and sentenced to a traitor's death.

King James was too smart to create a martyr, though, and offered Raleigh his life, to be spent in imprisonment in the Tower of London. The original sentence remained in effect; James could have him executed at any time.

Raleigh remained in prison for twelve years. He had an apartment and could receive guests; the Raleighs had a son during the Tower years. In some ways these were the most productive years of his life, for he devoted them to writing and to scientific experiments. Much of his reputation as a Renaissance man stems from this period. The governor of the Tower allowed him to cultivate a garden for his medicinal experiments, and he and his fellow prisoner, the earl of Northumberland, set up a laboratory. Thomas Harriot brought them books and worked with them.

Among Raleigh's frequent visitors was Henry, Prince of Wales, son and heir of King James. Henry was only fourteen when he began to visit Raleigh, but he already showed signs of the intelligence and independence that gave observers hope the kingdom would be run very differently when he came to the throne. Raleigh began to teach the boy about statecraft and policy; for Henry's benefit he began his great prose work, *The History of the World*. Prince Henry respected Raleigh, and remarked that "no king but my father would keep such a bird in a cage." But Henry died in 1612 at the age of eighteen of typhoid fever he caught from swimming in the foul Thames River. Raleigh, completely discouraged, quit writing his *History* after completing just one volume. Though its immediate object had been lost, the book went through many editions within a few years and is considered one of the great classics of English literature.

During his imprisonment, Raleigh's thoughts turned again and again to Guiana. King James was chronically short of money, so even he could not be indifferent to the gold Raleigh was sure existed there. If only he could return to the Orinoco, he was certain he could locate the mine. Raleigh began a campaign to present his case to the king.

While Raleigh spun his dreams of a great gold strike, other patriotic Englishmen had founded Jamestown in 1607, the first successful English colony in America. The colonial scene had changed greatly under the new regime. James I had shut down the thriving privateering war as soon as he acceded to the throne in 1603. National leaders were angry that England was completely out of America, except for the annual fishing voyages to Newfoundland, while Spain was now allowed a free hand in extracting treasure. Since James would allow no hostile acts against Spain, patriots had decided to do what they could. This peaceful colony would prevent Spanish expansion into North America, but would be far enough away from Spain's colonies to avoid conflict. On the other hand, if war were to break out, the new colony's location would prove useful as a base.

But the new colony's first decade was a dismal one. When Jamestown did begin to emerge from its poverty, the tobacco that was Virginia's gold seemed to many a poor commodity. King James hated to see England's American empire founded on smoke, and he hated the way the habit was spreading in England:

> It makes a kitchen of the inward parts of men, soiling and infecting them with an unctuous and oily kind of soot. Is it not a great vanity, that a man cannot heartily welcome his friend now, but straight they must be in hand with tobacco? that the sweetness of man's breath, being a good gift of God, should be wilfully corrupted by this stinking smoke?

So James was prepared to listen to Raleigh's rich dreams, and decided the possibility of a great gold strike that would bring immediate returns was worth a try. The king agreed to let Raleigh conduct another expedition to Guiana with one proviso: there must be no hostile actions against Spanish subjects. In accepting this restriction,

SIR WALTER RALEIGH AND HIS SON WAT, 1602.
Nine-year-old Wat clearly inherited his father's determination and recklessness. Once as a young man he told an unsavory story about his father at a dinner party. Raleigh slapped the young man across the face. Wat, who did not dare to strike his own father, immediately turned and hit the man sitting next to him, saying "Box about. 'Twill come to my father anon."

Raleigh was walking into a trap. Guiana was in the heart of the Spanish empire. It would be virtually impossible to go there without some clashes. He did not know how bad a trap James had set for him, however. James gave the Spanish ambassador an exact description of each of Raleigh's ships and their armaments as well as his itinerary. The Spanish knew exactly where he would be and how well he could defend himself as his little fleet set sail in June 1617.

Raleigh was now in his early sixties and not in good health. His Cádiz wound and a series of strokes suffered in the Tower had left him unsteady and in constant pain. This kind of buccaneering venture was a young man's game. Once it was under way, the expedition was plagued by problems. Devastating sickness broke out, killing many. Raleigh was too sick to travel into Guiana himself. He was forced to stay with the ships in the Caribbean while the exploring party, led by his associate Lawrence Keymis and Raleigh's son Walter, nicknamed Wat, set out up the river.

Raleigh was pleased to find that the Indians of the region remembered him; the news confirmed his belief that they would support the English against their Spanish "oppressors." He wrote to his wife, "To tell you that I might be here king of the Indians were a vanity, but my name hath still lived among them." But none of his other expectations held up. The tangled web of streams at the mouth of the Orinoco confused Keymis, who never even approached the area where the mine was thought to be, and soon the inevitable clash with Spanish soldiers occurred. Hotheaded young Wat Raleigh rashly led an attack in which he was killed, and his father's doom was sealed. Keymis returned empty-handed to tell Raleigh that his son was dead and the expedition compromised, then committed suicide in his cabin. Everything was over. Raleigh wrote to his wife, "I was loath to write, because I knew not how to comfort you: and, God knows, I never knew what sorrow meant till now."

Raleigh considered escape to France or some other friendly country, but ultimately returned to face execution on his original death warrant. King James offered to allow the king of Spain to execute Raleigh in Madrid, but Philip III wisely decided to allow James alone to bear the blame. Because he was a knight, Raleigh was allowed to die by the executioner's ax rather than suffer the horrible traitor's death.

With Raleigh's death in 1618, the Elizabethan plan for empire was ended for good, but he lived on through his writings and as a symbol. When Charles I, James's son and successor, was challenged by the new Puritan opposition, Raleigh was remembered as the man who had fought for the country's true destiny under England's great Queen Elizabeth and who had been brought down by the pettiness of a Stuart king. This opposition movement would ultimately bring Charles I to the same end as Raleigh on the executioner's block at the close of the English Civil War in 1649.

Puritan leaders also revived Raleigh's dream of a great English empire in America, but here they parted company with much of his legacy. The search for gold, already anachronistic when Raleigh set out on his last Guiana voyage, was abandoned. Instead, the enduring legacy was the one outlined by Thomas Harriot and John White at Roanoke. The real foundation of the English empire would be true colonies, settlements of English men and women who would re-create their native culture in a new environment. These colonies would enrich England by trade in commodities produced by Old World transplants.

Even in 1618 when Raleigh was executed, though many in England were doubtful about it, Virginia was building a sound economy on tobacco culture, and the colony's promoters had begun to encourage families there with the promise of free land. And Plymouth colony, composed of families each on their own farm, would soon be founded in New England. The British empire of which Raleigh had dreamed was already established.

Europe's New World

Raleigh's attempt to found the Roanoke colony was part of a long process of transplantation to the American continents. The Spanish had been involved in colonization for almost a century when Raleigh began his efforts in 1584. Moreover, the Indians were also the descendants of immigrants transplanted to the Americas thousands of years before.

When Europeans "discovered" America, they stumbled on continents that had been occupied for thousands of years by people who had developed a rich variety of cultures. The earliest explorers and colonists wondered who the Native Americans were and how they had come to America. Some Europeans thought they were the descendants of the Ten Lost Tribes of Israel. Modern archaeology has demonstrated that the American Indians share a common set of ancestors with modern Asian people.

During the last Ice Age (which began about 50,000 years ago and ended about 10,000 years ago), sea levels were lower. The Bering Strait between Siberia and Alaska was sometimes dry land. The ancestors of the modern Indians must have crossed this "land bridge" as they followed the big game animals of the period, such as mastodons. They were not conscious "immigrants." Probably only small groups found themselves on the American side, and they would have been unaware that they had crossed from one continent to another. Since the interior of the continent was under a huge glacier, their track would have taken them down the coast.

As these hunters moved over the land bridge and along the margin of the cold land, the weak and diseased would have fallen by the way. Hardship acted as a "disease filter," and many of the pathogens that constantly threatened the rest of the world were not imported into the Americas. The big game was plentiful and unwise to the ways of hunters, so, despite the cold conditions, food must have been relatively plentiful for these nomads. Scholars believe this initial small population expanded rapidly.

Major changes occurred about 10,000 years ago as the world began to warm up, and the great animals became extinct. The ancestors of the modern Indians gradually became more sedentary; that is, they remained in the same region all the time, although they may have moved according to the seasons within that region. They came to rely more and more on hunting small animals and gathering plants for food. This naturally led to cultivation of chosen plants, which reinforced a settled life.

NATIVE AMERICAN CULTURES

On the basis of the artifacts and other physical evidence these early Indians left behind, archaeologists describe a succession of increasingly

THE GREAT SERPENT MOUND FROM ADENA NEAR CINCINNATI, OHIO. Early explorers were only dimly aware of these massive structures and the complex cultures needed to build and maintain them. This thousand-year-old mound measures seventy-five feet across the serpent's open jaws, and its total length from head to triple-coiled tail is one quarter mile.

sophisticated cultures that grew up in the center of what would become the United States. At the same time that Christianity was beginning to win converts in the Old World, these people began to build large mounds for ceremonial and burial purposes in the New. We do not know what ceremonies were conducted around the mounds, some of which are shaped like animals. Nor do we know much about these cultures, centered in modern Ohio, which scientists have named the Adena and Hopewell cultures. The reasons for their disappearance are equally mysterious.

These early cultures were succeeded by one scholars call Mississippian, which is better understood. Although its great period had passed when Europeans became aware of America, Mississippian sites were still in use. The Spanish explorer Hernando de Soto met the heirs of Mississippian culture and saw their great structures as he traveled through the Southeast in 1539–1540.

This culture originated, as the name indicates, along the Mississippi River. Its most highly developed center was Cahokia, near modern St. Louis at the conjunction of the Mississippi and Missouri rivers. This city of 40,000 was the largest in North America not only then but for a long time to come. Boston held only 15,000 people when the American Revolution's first shots were fired. Cahokia was the center of a vast trade and cultural network. Things made there have been found across a wide territory, and many objects from all over the continent have been unearthed in Mississippian sites along the river.

The Mississippians centered their cities on enormous mounds built like flat-topped pyramids. In many cases the large central mound would be surrounded by many smaller mounds. Some sites were so extensive that they could not really be appreciated until airplanes flew over them in this century.

The size of their cities, and the fact that they were fortified, suggests that the Mississippians may have been developing political systems in which several villages became allied or even subservient to a stronger community. Spanish and French explorers who traveled through the Southeast described highly developed political systems along the Mississippi, such as among the Natchez Indians.

The English colonies were along the Atlantic coast, far from the great Mississippian centers. But English writers at Roanoke and Jamestown also described political groupings with strong Indian chiefs at their heads. Powhatan, the father of Pocahontas, was said to be building an empire when Jamestown was colonized in 1607. He had inherited the overlordship of six tribes from his father, and he was described as the "emperor" of thirty. Similarly in New England some tribes such as the Pequots and Narragansetts were emerging at the head of confederations partly as a result of their position in the new European trades. The Iroquois tribes to the west of New England had developed a very complex political league encompassing the Mohawks, Oneidas, Onondagas, Cayugas, and Senecas, and this league took an active part in the fur trade.

In the Southwest, very different patterns had developed. The Pueblo Indians lived in permanent towns built of adobe and were reliant, in that harsh environment, on highly sophisticated irrigation works. Though each pueblo was self-governing, they cooperated in technology. Recent migrants into the Southwest were Athapaskans, Navajos, and Apaches, who lived a more nomadic style of life based in part on raiding. European horses, runaways from settlements in Mexico, were already transforming their lives long before sustained contact with Europeans.

Names such as Algonquian, Iroquois, Athapaskan, and Sioux refer to Indian language families; they point to similar sources of these languages, just as French, Italian, Spanish, and Portuguese are grouped as Romance languages. The groupings do not imply that Algonquians, for example, would always be allies, or that they would even recognize any common elements with Algonquians from far away. There were many, often mutually unintelligible, languages within each group.

The newcomers wrote about "nations" and "empires," but, although the impact of European trade and settlement was pushing many natives in the direction of more-layered political organizations, much of that hierarchy was in the writers' own imaginations. Great variety of practices and cultures existed among American Indians, but they shared some characteristics. Indians were often organized at the village level, with some means for cooperation between villages when that was necessary. Chiefs usually worked by consensus, by getting the agreement of the people, rather than through coercion. Even warfare was usually a matter of men getting together to conduct a raid rather than a political decision by either a chief or an entire tribe. European observers, who were greatly impressed by the order and self-discipline in Indian communities, simply could not believe that they functioned without the kind of concentrated authority and ruthless law enforcement necessary in the Old World.

Work roles were evenly distributed within the villages. Men were responsible for hunting, war, and ceremonial practices. Women were the agriculturalists, and their role was seen as so important economically that, among many Indians, women actually owned the land, and children reckoned their descent through their mothers

WALPI PUEBLO IN ARIZONA. Spanish explorers were impressed by these cities. When the evidence of sedentary agricultural cultures was put together with legends of gold, Europeans easily convinced themselves that further exploration would lead to a big strike.

and grandmothers rather than their fathers and grandfathers. In the fields the women worked together; throughout the villages the emphasis was on sharing. This was the thing Europeans found most difficult to understand about Indian life: many possessions were held in common and a person attained status by giving away goods rather than accumulating them.

Justice and war operated on the principle of equilibrium. Peace reigned when relationships were evenly balanced. If something upset the peace, balance had to be restored. If a person was injured, it was up to the victim or the victim's village or clan to inflict an equal injury on the clan or village of the one who had done the harm. Intent did not matter. An accidental wrong was avenged just as an intentional one was. Nor was the retribution necessarily visited on the one who had originally caused the trouble. The goal was not to punish the guilty party or make him suffer, but to restore the balance.

This principle of repayment extended to diplomacy, where gift giving was essential. When the first party of explorers at Roanoke encountered a single Indian courageous enough to board their ships, they "gave him a shirt, a hat, and some other things, and made him taste of our wine, and our meat, which he liked very well." Instead of hurrying home with his prize, the explorers were surprised to see,

> He fell to fishing, and in less than half an hour, he had laden his boat as deep as it could swim, with which he came again to the point of the land, and there he divided his fish into two parts, pointing one part to the ship, and the other to the pinnace: which after he had (as much as he might) requited the former benefits received, he departed out of our sight.

The explorers had had their first lesson in Native American diplomacy. Reciprocity, maintaining the balance, was the important thing.

FIRST CONTACTS

For thousands of years after the glaciers melted, the two American continents were isolated from the rest of the world. There was one brief break in this isolation when Norse voyagers led by Leif Eriksson and Thorfinn Karlsefni established short-lived settlements in Labrador and Newfoundland about A.D. 1000. Accounts of these ventures written more than 200 years later, "The Greenlanders' Saga" and "Eirik the Red's Saga" told of their stay in America, and repeated voyages, which explored the coast from Baffin Island down into Maine. Remains of a settlement, an extension of settlements in Greenland, have been discovered by modern archaeologists in northern Newfoundland. But occupation was not sustained, and the Americas remained isolated.

America was "discovered," made known to Europeans, only after 1492. Spain and Portugal led the way in exploring and exploiting the new find. During the Middle Ages, these nations had come into close contact with advanced North African people—called "Moors" by the Europeans—who had developed mathematical and geographical knowledge far superior to that of the Europeans. The Portuguese, led by Prince Henry the Navigator, recognized the importance of their knowledge and brought North African scholars to their court. Through such technological and scientific breakthroughs, Europeans were able to consider the possibility of sailing west, over enormous stretches of uncharted ocean, in search of new routes to the riches of the East.

COLUMBUS

Many of the original explorers were Italian-born, but they looked for Atlantic nations to sponsor them. Columbus sought support in France and England as well as in Spain. In 1492, Spain was prepared to back his voyage—intended to find a

INDIAN WOMAN AND CHILD. Painted by John White in Roanoke, 1586. White painted the Carolina Algonquians as figures of great dignity. Here he shows the beginnings of cross-cultural exchange, because the girl has an Elizabethan doll one of the colonists has given her.

new route to the trade of the Orient—but other countries were skeptical of his plan.

Columbus returned with news that he had found land across the western ocean. Though we know his landfall was in the Caribbean, he believed (and maintained through all four of his voyages and to his dying day) that he had reached the Far East. Columbus's error symbolizes the problem confronting all of Europe in thinking about the discoveries. It would be a long time before many would realize that two huge, entirely new continents had been discovered.

The earliest landfalls were on islands. The Atlantic was dotted with islands and island groups, such as the Azores (discovered between 1427 and 1452), the Canaries, and Iceland and Greenland. Scholars naturally first thought that the newly discovered islands would be parts of such groups.

JOHN CABOT

That the islands were in fact on the margins of vast continents slowly became apparent. Giovanni Caboto, an Italian from Genoa like Columbus but known to us by the name he adopted in England, John Cabot, had been seeking backing for a voyage to Asia at the same time as Columbus. Shortly after Columbus returned from his first expedition in 1493, Cabot had made the English city of Bristol, whose fishing ships had ventured far out into the Atlantic, his headquarters. In 1497 he sailed west from Ireland and made a landfall on the North American coast somewhere in the latitude of 42 to 54 degrees (northern New England or southern Canada) and established grounds for an English claim in America. Though he did not find the rich spices and silks of the Orient, Cabot did report seas filled with fish; his voyage started an annual stampede of ships from all over western Europe to the Newfoundland Banks for the rich fishing.

THE SPANISH

The Spanish gradually mapped the coastline of South America, a process begun by Amerigo Vespucci's discovery of Guiana in 1501. In some ways it is appropriate that the New World should be named after Vespucci; he was the first to put forward the theory that new continents lay between Europe and Asia. South America's outline was fully known once Ferdinand Magellan's expedition had rounded the tip of the southern continent and crossed the Pacific to circle the globe, between 1519 and 1522.

As Spaniards began to investigate the newly found lands, they stumbled across the greatest Indian empires in America, those of the Aztecs in Mexico and the Incas in Peru. These Indians lived in highly organized state systems that even the ethnocentric Europeans recognized as genuine. Millions of people lived under Aztec control, which had been established around 1325, about 200 years before the Spanish arrived. The warlike Aztecs had succeeded earlier, more advanced people, the Mayas, whose culture was fading by the time the Europeans saw them. The Aztecs had inherited a form of written language, of numbers and calculation, and a calendar more accurate than any the Europeans had. The Incas, like the Aztecs, had advanced agricultural systems with irrigation networks. The Inca empire had built a remarkable web of paved roads superior to those in Europe. These Indian empires had large cities with huge public buildings, many constructed in the form of great stone pyramids. These Indians also possessed fabulous stores of wealth, rooms filled with gold tablets, and it was the gold that spurred on the conquest.

Conquest was not an occupation for the faint of heart. Most of the Spanish conquistadors were rough men ready to bear and inflict hardship in order to reach their goals. Millions of Native Americans were to die, most of new diseases to which they lacked immunity, before the conquest was completed. The first settlers were left by Columbus on islands in the Caribbean, where little wealth was found. Central America was the next target. In 1513 Vasco Núñez de Balboa found that only the narrow Isthmus of Panama separated the Pacific Ocean and the Caribbean at that point.

Rumors of the riches of the Aztecs lured an army of about 600 under the command of Hernando Cortés to attempt the conquest of Mexico in 1519. Their first entry into Tenochtitlán, the Aztec capital on the site of present-day Mexico City, was repulsed by Aztec forces organized by the emperor, Montezuma. The Spaniards had brought something far more deadly than bullets, however: a smallpox epidemic broke out in the city. One of Cortés's companions recalled the events much later: "When the Christians were exhausted from war, God saw fit to send the Indians smallpox, and there was a great pestilence in the city...." Because they had no prior exposure to it, the Indians lacked resistance to this European disease, and their ability to fight crumbled. When the Spanish entered the city they found "the streets, squares, houses, and courts were filled with bodies, so that it was almost impossible to pass. Even Cortés was sick from the stench in his nostrils."

The vast wealth discovered in Tenochtitlán spurred on further conquest. The Incas of Peru succumbed to a Spanish force under Francisco Pizarro in 1531–1533. The Inca ruler was tricked into surrendering. His people paid a stupendous ransom—more than 40,000 pounds of pure gold and silver—but the emperor was executed nonetheless. The discovery of such amazing wealth led to new conquests, always in the expectation of yet greater hoards. Expeditions invaded Ecuador, Chile, Argentina, and Bolivia. When no gold was found, leaders were tortured because the soldiers assumed they had hidden it away.

The conquistadors, who were largely ignorant of their own culture, had little appreciation for the sophisticated cultures they conquered, destroying artifacts, records, documents, and buildings in the search for riches. Gold was all that mattered. Some few priests and scholars worked frantically to save some artifacts, but little remained; these once-great cultures are mostly lost to us. By 1540 the conquest of Mexico, Central America, and Peru was largely accomplished.

The Spanish were interested in North America as well. In 1536 a Spanish gentleman named Cabeza de Vaca, survivor of an exploring expedition to Florida destroyed by shipwreck, turned up in Mexico City. He had been cast up on the Texas coast. With three other Spaniards, he had lived among the Indians there for six years. These four men had learned many of the Indians' skills, particularly in healing and the preparation of foods native to the region. They

NAVAHO WALL painting of the arrival of the Spaniards in the Southwest, Canyon del Muerto, Arizona. The expedition is accompanied by a priest dressed in black. The animals—horses, cows, pigs, and sheep—brought by the Europeans changed Indian life dramatically.

made their way on foot across the Southwest and down to Mexico; their stories of great cities, "populous towns and very large houses," seen on the way increased Spanish interest in exploration. Other early reports generated stories of seven golden cities of Cibola beyond the Rio Grande.

A huge expedition ventured out from Mexico in 1540 under Francisco Vásquez de Coronado, and these men quickly discovered a different reality. The environment was inhospitable; the Indians of the Southwest were superbly adapted to it, but it imposed real hardship on a large, roving expedition such as Coronado's. The great cities discovered by Coronado were the pueblos of the Zunis and Hopis. These pueblos were amazing feats, based on irrigation engineering that allowed the Indians to live a sedentary life year-round in that water-poor area, but they were not the gold-studded marvels for which the Spaniards yearned. Cibola (actually the Zuni pueblo Hawikuh) was, one of Coronado's men reported, "a small rocky pueblo, all crumpled up, there being many farm settlements in New Spain that look better from afar."

Coronado met resistance as he marched, which he put down promptly with great cruelty; a picture of the Europeans was firmly fixed in the Indians' minds by this first encounter. His expedition traveled, gathering information all the way, through the Southwest as far as central Kansas, a journey of 1,500 miles. Had he been interested in geography as much as gold, Coronado might have realized that the Arkansas River, on which he camped, was part of a major river system. He could have followed it to discover the Mississippi River, the central artery of the continent. Instead, he returned to Mexico after two years, to report a land barren of riches.

Simultaneously, Juan Rodríguez Cabrillo ventured all along the coast of California as far north as Oregon in 1542–1543. Cabrillo died on the voyage, and his crew returned in terrible condition to report no evidence of gold to the north, nor any sign of the western outlet of a passage through the continent. Concluding that the land north of Mexico not only offered no easy wealth, but exacted a heavy toll from those who attempted to travel in it, the Spanish largely ignored the Southwest for the next half-century. California was not to be colonized until the eighteenth century.

Spanish explorers were also curious about eastern North America. In the 1530s and 1540s, a Spanish party led by Hernando de Soto traveled through the Southeast. Their excitement grew as the expedition discovered the great mounds. Surely these Indians would possess riches like those of the Aztecs and Incas. No gold was found, but the search led the Spaniards all through the Southeast. De Soto's men crossed the Mississippi River, which he named Rio de Espíritu Santo, and were actually camped there while Coronado was nearby on the Arkansas. Since each had taken a circuitous route and the two never met, the combined reports of the two expeditions did not make the extent of the continent clear. Wishful thinking prevailed, and geographers decided that North America was at most 1,500 miles across (about half its actual extent).

THE FRENCH

France was also involved in exploration that revealed the shape of North America. Giovanni Verrazzano, an Italian from Florence who lived in France, sailed along the coast from south of Cape Fear, North Carolina, north past the mouth of the Hudson River. After a prolonged stop in what is now Newport Harbor, Rhode Island, "which we called 'Refugio' on account of its beauty," he continued to Newfoundland in 1524. So within a few decades of the first voyage of discovery by Columbus, the basic outline of the Americas was known.

Once Europeans understood that their New World consisted of two continents joined by a narrow isthmus, problems of conceptualization remained. Most thought of the great land masses, particularly the relatively unpromising northern one, as barriers to the trade routes they had hoped to chart, rather than as new opportu-

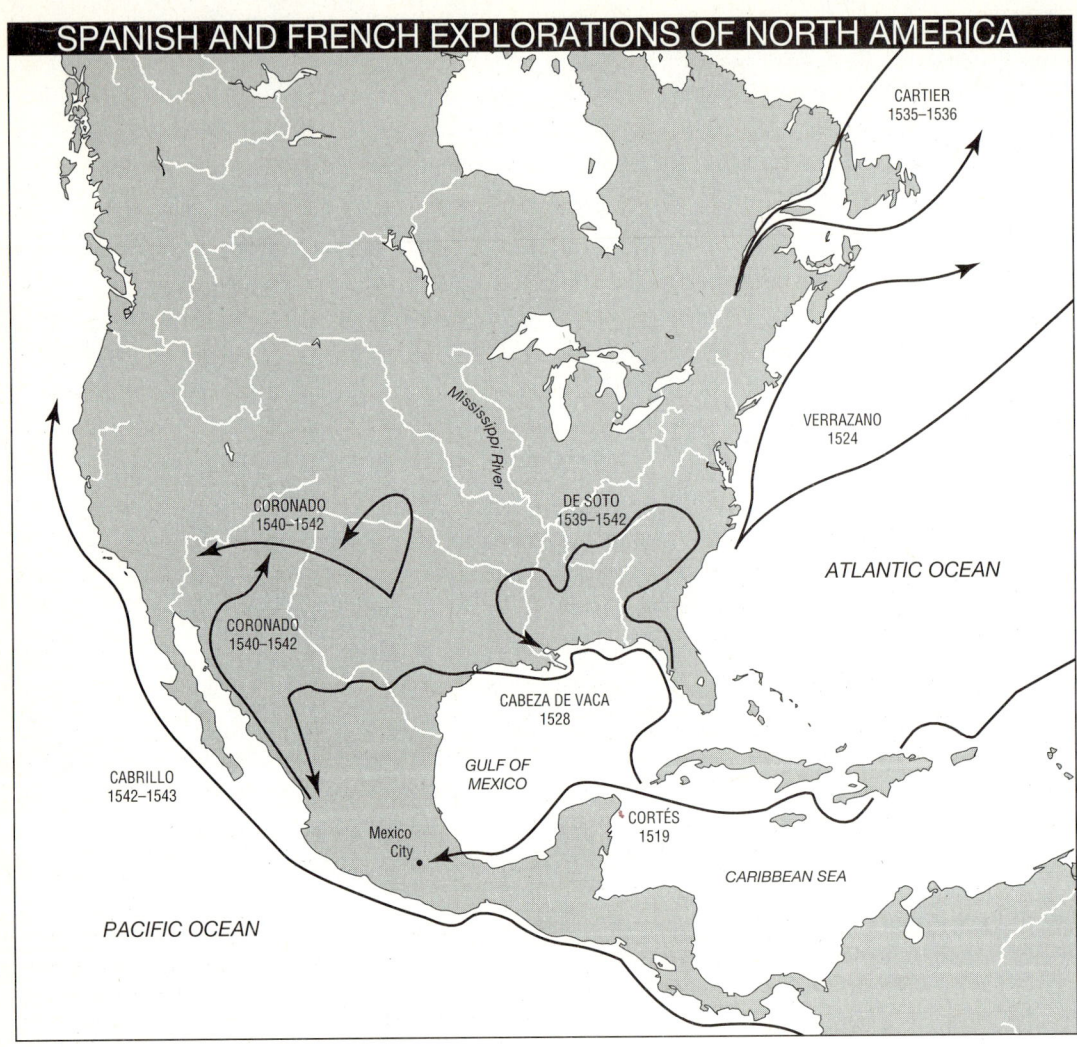

nities to be developed. Adventurers now began to explore the coasts, looking for likely entryways to passages that might cut right through to the East.

One waterway that looked promising was the St. Lawrence River. Jacques Cartier had explored it for France in two voyages in the 1530s. Convinced that the land "was the finest and most excellent one could find anywhere," he returned at the head of a colony that was planted near the modern city of Quebec in 1541. French backers hoped the settlement could support exploring voyages into the interior. The colony failed, partly because the planters were not prepared for the extreme cold of the Canadian winter, but the hope remained that the St. Lawrence might be the entrance to a system of rivers that would allow ships to travel right through the continent, especially when later explorers discovered the river's connection to the Great Lakes system. It would be centuries before the idea of a northwest passage was finally given up.

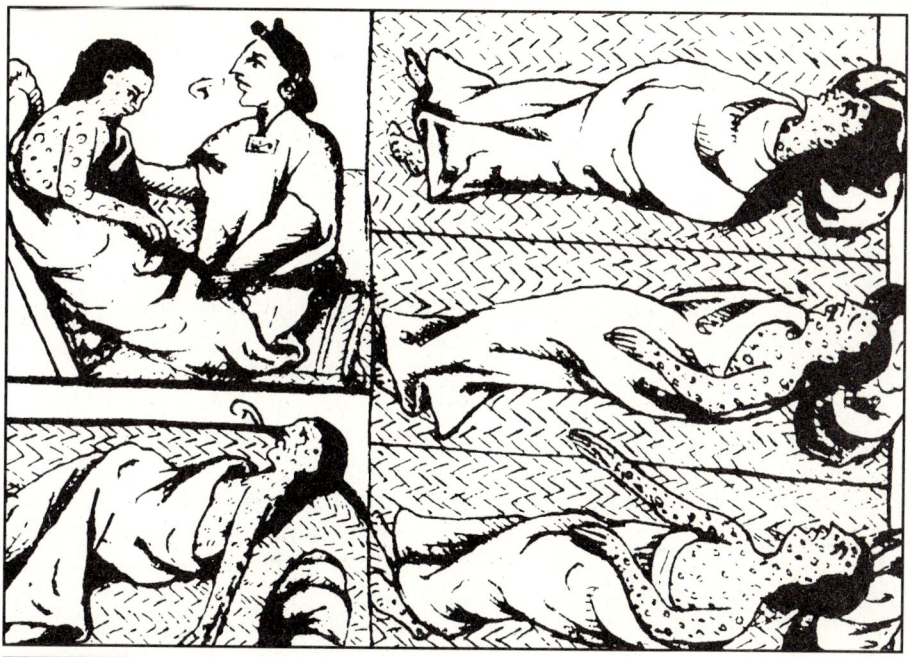

EUROPEAN DISEASES struck the Indians with unparalleled ferocity. Fray Bernardino de Sahagún, who accompanied Cortés, included this illustration of the impact of smallpox in his *General History of the Things of New Spain*.

THE IMPACT OF EUROPEAN DISEASES

So by the 1540s, the nature of the New World was becoming clear. What was less clear at the time was that exploration and the beginnings of colonization had produced a human event of massive proportions. The mixing of populations isolated from each other for 10,000 years brought consequences unprecedented in the history of the world, effects that can never be repeated as long as human beings remain on this planet.

The "disease filter" of cold through which the first immigrants to America had passed during the last Ice Age had been so efficient that most of the diseases present in the rest of the world did not exist in the Western Hemisphere. People acquire a degree of immunity to the bacteria and viruses that cause disease in their environment. Newborn babies inherit some resistance from their mothers. As that immunity wears off, they manufacture their own response to those pathogens that are always present. Even if they fall sick, they may have a milder case because they have some resistance. The Indians lacked acquired immunity to the pathogens the Europeans brought with them, and they were killed off by European diseases wherever the ships and their crews went. Plague, smallpox, and typhus, the great killers in Europe, felled many Indians. But others died of infections that were usually mild in Europe: influenza, colds, and measles. So devastating were these epidemics that scholars estimate 90 percent of the Indian population was destroyed in many places. One New England colonist wrote that "the twentieth person is scarce left alive."

The figures are horrifying. But the impact, physical and psychological, is incalculable. The process, initiated innocently by sixteenth-century explorers, was already well under way when the first colonists arrived, and may account for the ease with which Europeans were able to dominate. Powhatan told John Smith, "I have seen the deaths of all my people thrice." Three epidemics had swept through the Chesapeake *before* the Jamestown settlers even arrived. Alliances and political structures would have been in disarray. Religious systems, based on priestly power, including the power to heal, may have been assailed by doubt.

The diseases, because they affected the Indians but usually not the colonists, actually enhanced the reputations of the Europeans. One of the earliest Spanish accounts tells of how the Indians they encountered

> did not dare eat, drink, or do anything else of this life, without first asking permission from the Christians. They did this because they thought that these Christians had the power to kill them, or to give them life. For this reason, they believed that they were dying because the Christians had been made angry.

The Indians and the Europeans were both highly religious; both believed that events are controlled by God. Some Indians came to believe, as some colonists did, that the epidemics were, as one English colonist put it, "the hand of God" by which "the place is made so much the more fit, for the English Nation to inhabit in, and erect in it Temples to the Glory of God." No one understood how diseases are transmitted. In many cases the sickness would be carried by infected Indians to areas where the Europeans had never been. When the affliction broke out beyond the frontier, the Indians concluded that the colonists had the power to make sickness appear by remote control.

FIRST COLONIES

THE SOUTHWEST

In the Southwest, priests and soldiers, led by Juan de Oñate in 1598, began establishing a Spanish presence among the Indians in a huge territory the Spanish authorities called New Mexico. The southwestern Indians had adapted to their environment in different ways. Some, who later became known as Apaches and Navajos, had developed a roving culture that made use of the inhospitable land's changing offerings; these bands consisted of 50 to 300 people. Those whom we know as Pueblo Indians, including the Hopis and Zunis, had developed a sedentary life that harnessed the region's limited water supply. Their complexes of large, apartment-style houses were recognized by the Spaniards as true cities (*pueblo* is a Spanish word meaning either "town" or "people").

Though the pueblo-dwelling Indians cooperated with other cities for the immense irrigation projects that made their agriculture possible, neither they nor the Navajos and Apaches had a tribal identity. The names and the identity were imposed by the Spanish, who saw and labeled cultural similarities. Each village or band was completely independent; each was led by a person who was recognized as the moral leader of the community. The leader had no power of compulsion; persuasion was the only avenue to influence. The war leader, who organized defense and relations with outsiders, was much less important.

Oñate traveled among the pueblos, receiving expressions of fealty from their leaders, who knew from prior experience that resistance would be put down harshly. We do not know what they made of the ceremonies of submission, but it is clear that they did not sign over control of their lives to the Spanish. Throughout the region the Indians offered polite audiences, often adopting outward forms of Spanish life and religion while privately keeping their own culture intact. If pressure became too great, Indians would often simply move away from contact.

Pedro de Peralta, Oñate's successor, established the capital of Santa Fe by 1610 and sent out missionaries and soldiers to carry Spanish influence throughout the region. In those areas where the priests came first, the Indians recognized Spanish society as organized along proper lines, with the moral leader in charge. Because the pueblos were preexisting permanent structures, the priests were forced to set up their missions on the outskirts and to try to win the Indians over by making Christianity attractive to them. In many cases the priests were welcomed because they brought new agricultural technology that the Indians valued. Where military men set up forts and tried to compel Indian labor on their plantations, the Europeans looked alien and distasteful.

Spanish settlements north of Mexico were never more than peripheral to the main colonies, and Spain was never able to control the lands beyond the Rio Grande fully. Therefore, European influence was necessarily weaker, and these regions saw the development of a unique mixture of Indian and Spanish ways. Emissaries of Spanish culture found they had to adapt the religious, political, and social practices they offered to make them acceptable to Indian life; they were rarely in a position to impose their own ways. Often the Indians grafted outward forms and Spanish labels onto native government and religious structures. The resulting rich cultural mix is unique in the Americas.

SPANISH AND FRENCH SETTLEMENTS IN THE EAST

In the East, Spanish attention settled on Florida, because of the ever-present fear of privateering by French and English ships. All the great convoys leaving the Caribbean passed close to the tip of Florida, so control of that peninsula was seen as

FRENCH LANDING ON THE COAST OF FLORIDA. The exotic nature of the environment is vividly conveyed by the natives and alligators that come to greet the newcomers.

absolutely necessary to Spanish strategists. They acted quickly to forestall any other country's attempts to found colonies there.

In 1562 a group of French Huguenots (Protestants) erected a colony called Charlesfort on Port Royal Sound in South Carolina. Like many of the later English colonists, these men and women were fleeing religious persecution at home, and saw America as a place in which they could live and worship together. Though unsuccessful, this little settlement was the first to act on the idea that America offered the opportunity to create alternative societies, in which European minorities could live unmolested. Two years later, in 1564, the Huguenots tried again, this time in Florida. Their colony on the St. John's River was called La Caroline.

La Caroline faced the same problems that all colonies faced. They had to have a source of income, because no settlement could become self-sufficient quickly. Moreover, although the core of the settlers was the religious group, they also had to bring soldiers and others who were motivated more by greed and the search for adventure. Some of these young men embarked on a privateering venture, and the Spanish authorities, who had feared just such activities if any other European country had a colony in Florida, quickly cut short the life of the little colony in 1565.

Now Spain determined to create settlements of its own to prevent further problems. St. Augustine (San Agustin) was founded in 1565 under the governorship of a seasoned veteran, Pedro Menéndez de Avilés, near the site of La Caroline. Menéndez had great plans for the development of the Spanish presence along the East Coast. He sent missions to scout locations on the

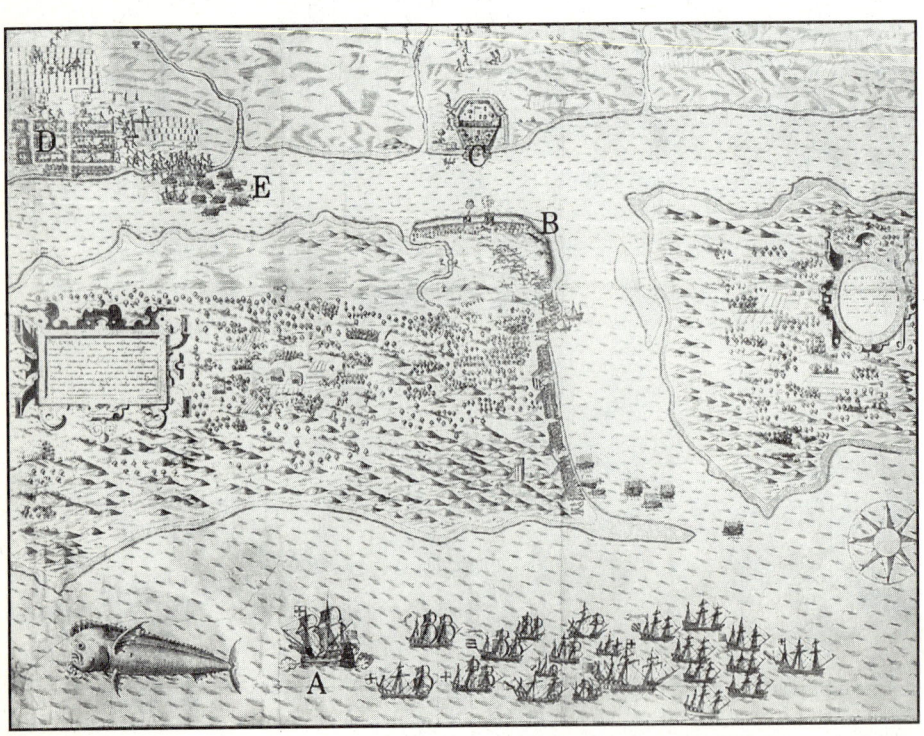

ST. AUGUSTINE, 1589, showing a remarkably settled town. The fish at the lower left corner is a dolphin.

coast of South Carolina, where the settlement of Santa Elena existed for a while (1572–1575). And Chesapeake Bay was the site of a short-lived Jesuit mission established in the early 1570s. The bay, like the St. Lawrence River, looked as though it might connect with inland rivers to provide a passage through the continent, and Spain was the first European country to explore it. Part of the Spanish leaders' concern was to protect Mexico as well as the ships leaving the Caribbean. Since no one knew the true extent of the continent from east to west, Europeans believed that men from colonies in the East might be able to attack the rich Mexican settlements by the overland route. Although the attempts to settle farther north were not sustained, St. Augustine remained and, after San Juan in Puerto Rico, is the first colony and the oldest European city in the United States.

The French, meanwhile, had more success in the far north. A series of voyages led by Samuel de Champlain, begun in 1602, followed up Cartier's discoveries. Champlain explored the coast of New England and the area around the St. Lawrence. Quebec, permanently settled in 1608, gave the French a key site for inland trade with powerful Indian confederations, particularly the Hurons.

France concentrated its colonial efforts on the fur trade. Quebec continued to be largely a trading post with a small population. In 1627 all of Canada held only 107 Frenchmen. The French presence was unique among European empires because they were able to construct a

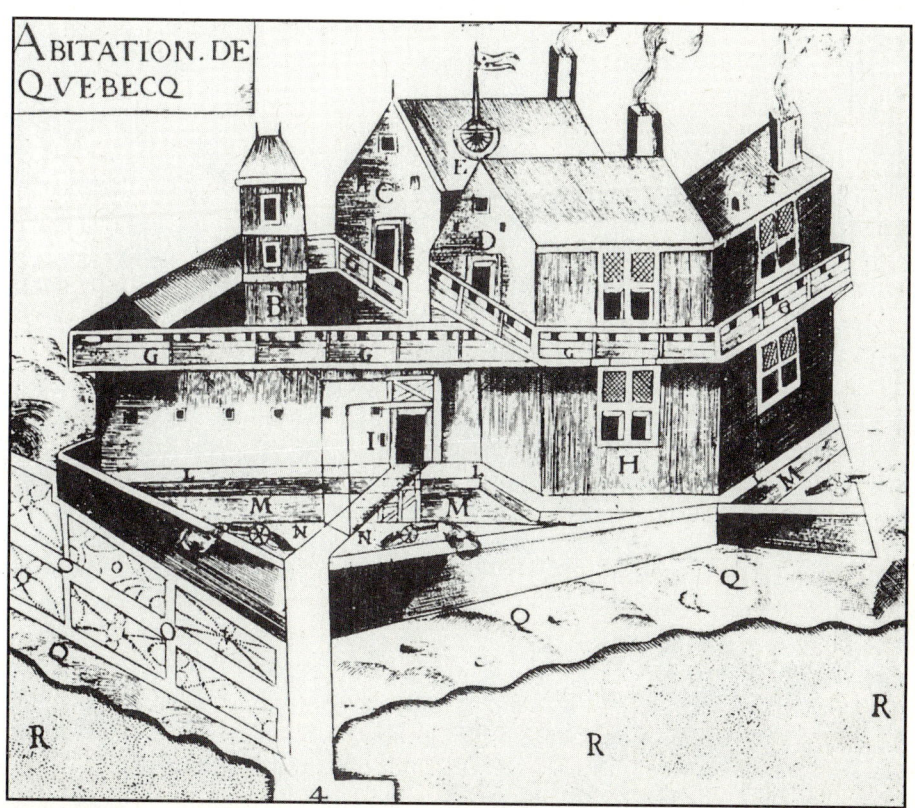

FRENCH HABITATION AT QUEBEC. Samuel de Champlain left a lively visual record of his expeditions. His drawing shows the colonists' adaptation to the cold winters. One could move about the settlement keeping exposure to the outside to a minimum.

mutually beneficial relationship with the Indians with whom they traded. Champlain understood the ceremonial importance of the exchange of goods, and did not treat the Indians merely as trading partners. He gave them military assistance against their enemies, and, because the colony included few farmers, the French did not compete for land and resources. By following the traditions laid down by Champlain, the French influence was carried far into the interior in the course of the seventeenth century. French traders, often accompanied or preceded by missionaries, developed warm relationships with many of the Indians with whom they dealt. Their activities carried them all through the heart of the North American continent.

THE ENGLISH APPROACH TO COLONIZATION

So, by 1607, England was the only Atlantic power without an established presence in America. There had been many English voyages of exploration, and English ships went to the Newfoundland Banks to fish every year, but no colonies existed. Individual exploits such as Sir Francis Drake's great voyage of 1577–1580, attacking and plundering Spanish colonies on both coasts of South America and venturing up the west coast of California, did little to change the picture. Drake claimed California, as "New Albion," for England, but he and his men found it cold and unpromising, the coast shrouded in "most vile, thick, and stinking fogs. Besides, how unhandsome and deformed appeared the face of the earth itself! showing trees without greenness in those months of June and July." England, with its attention tied up in Ireland, seemed unable to make the effort to establish a continuing presence anywhere in America. Indeed, it was Drake himself who carried home the hapless first colony at Roanoke in 1586, as he returned from a second privateering voyage.

The problems England faced were of two sorts. First, the Roanoke colony had demonstrated that such ventures were very expensive, requiring support over a very long period of time during which they could not be expected to repay investors. The English Crown was not prepared to put government money into colonization; therefore, a source of investment funds had to be found.

As Raleigh had realized in his final Roanoke venture, the joint-stock company was the solution to the problem of finance. By attracting many investors, the risk of investing could be spread and continuity of funding could be assured. The company would continue to exist even if one or more investors died. Joint-stock companies were founded to sponsor all kinds of ventures in sixteenth- and seventeenth-century England. Trade with the whole world boomed then and companies were set up to exploit it. The largest and most successful of these were the Muscovy Company, founded in the 1550s to trade along the northern sea route for Russian furs and wood products; the Levant Company, organized in the late 1570s to trade with the eastern Mediterranean nations for the spices and silks of the East; and the East India Company, chartered in 1599 to trade directly by sea with the Orient.

American colonies were naturally set up on the same lines, organized and paid for by joint-stock companies chartered by the government. But here the second problem arose. It centered on the expected rewards of colonization. Potential investors were hardheaded businessmen. The Muscovy, Levant, and East India companies were sure investments, with proven returns. What could America provide that would repay a massive outlay of capital? It was unlikely that the unpromising terrain of North America would ever furnish the silver and gold the Spanish had found in the south. Fish, as John Smith later pointed out, were a form of gold, but they could be obtained without the expense of colonies. France seemed to have the fur trade in the St. Lawrence area tied up. Even privateering did not require colonies; the English had demonstrated they could prey on Spanish shipping without permanent bases. There had to be a reason to assume the huge expense and problems of a colony.

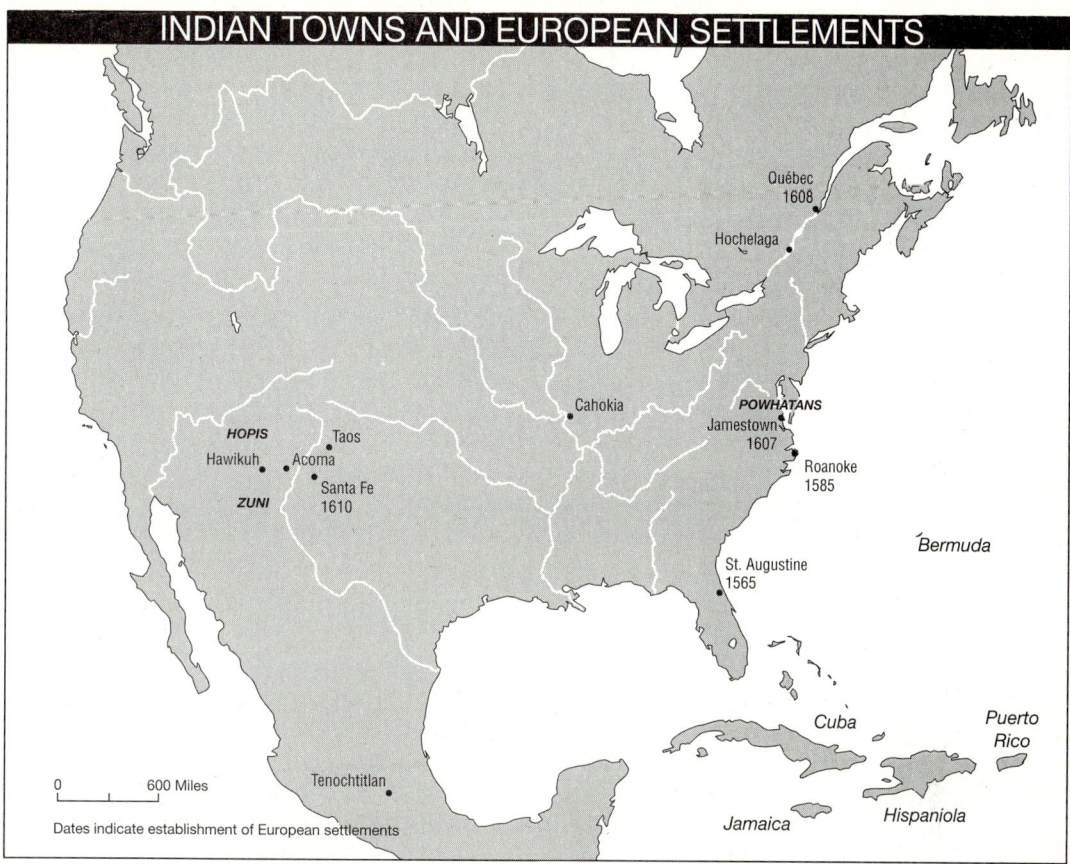

Why did England finally become sufficiently interested in American plantations to support them all the way to success? There were many reasons, some old, some new. The old ones—the dream of gold and of finding a passage through the continent—continued to inspire explorers. Jamestown, the first successful colony, was placed in 1607 on the deepwater port discovered by the Roanoke colonists on Chesapeake Bay partly because it was hoped that the mighty James River or one of the other rivers flowing into the bay would link up with inland rivers to form the northwest passage. No one yet realized how extensive the continent was from east to west.

To these old dreams was added a growing sense, already seen in Sir Walter Raleigh, that England was being left behind while Spain and other European countries were building worldwide trade networks. Knowledge gained in the twenty-year privateering war, from the middle of the 1580s to Elizabeth's death in 1603, made English mariners more confident. They no longer needed Portuguese pilots to navigate their ships.

Religious reasons also grew in importance. The English boast that they were the leaders of the Protestant religion seemed hollow when they allowed Roman Catholic nations to colonize and convert the American Indians and the English did nothing.

Domestic reasons added their weight. Many English people feared that their society was entering a state of decay as Queen Elizabeth I was replaced by James I. The organization of English society seemed to be breaking down, especially the local networks that supported people in hard times, and the mechanisms by which men and women entered adult life, formed families, and settled on an occupation.

Most English people earned their bread by farming, but some were involved in trades. Textile manufacture, the most important industry in England, was in trouble as improved techniques in Europe outclassed English cloth. The industry needed access to new dyes and fibers from America and other parts of the world. Colonies could help put English industry back on a firm footing. Although there might not be gold in Virginia, other products—such as medicines, timber, foods, and metals—might be developed by the hard work of colonists. These would not only enrich colonial investors and the country, they would free England of reliance on other European countries for products it needed. Captain John Smith pointed out that even "that contemptible trade of fish" could be lucrative, and fish would never run out: "Let not the meanness of the word fish distaste you, for it will afford as good gold as the Mines of Guiana or Potosi, with less hazard and charge, and more certainty and facility." There were, it seemed, many good reasons to develop American colonies.

JAMESTOWN

Heading off renewed French or Spanish attempts to settle in North America was a compelling reason for English colonization. The Spanish knew as well as the English that Chesapeake Bay was a good site. The English decided to plunge ahead in 1607 to keep Spain from renewing its attempt to plant a colony on the bay. And they planned to create a presence in the north that would forestall French attempts from the St. Lawrence. They hoped to create two new American settlements to mark out northern and southern claims. The name Virginia was applied to the entire coast of North America, so two Virginia Companies were set up to send out expeditions in 1607. One, based in London, was to found a colony on Chesapeake Bay. The other, headquartered in Plymouth, was to colonize on the Kennebec River in Maine. The Maine venture, called Sagadahoc, lasted less than a year, partly because of poor organization, but also due to the extremely cold winter "fit to freeze the heart of a plantation." The other Virginia colony lived on to become the first permanent English settlement in the New World—Jamestown.

Jamestown's planners had learned something from Roanoke's failure. A large joint-stock company was formed to ensure support over a long period of time. A massive propaganda campaign in favor of the colony was launched, with sermons, broadsides, and ballads carrying its message all over the country. English audiences were urged to "remember it is God's cause you have taken in hand." England's excess population would find a home in America, "our land abounding with swarms of idle persons, which having no means of labor to relieve their misery, do likewise swarm in lewd and naughty practices." The government authorized lotteries to help with finances. The country's attention focused on Virginia as it never had on Roanoke. Jamestown would not disappear from people's consciousness as the earlier attempt had.

Surprisingly, though, many of the same mistakes were repeated. Ignoring what Raleigh had learned from the Lane colony's failure, the Virginia Company sent an initial colony of young men of about the same size: a little over a hundred men. This group acted in many ways as Lane's had: they refused or were unable to grow food, so they tried to bully or cajole the Indians into selling them supplies. Their reliance on food from the Indians made them extremely vulnerable, so they often acted in a belligerent manner to prevent the Indians from taking advantage of that vulnerability. Their lack of self-discipline also meant the exploration they had been ordered to do—especially the searching for gold and for a passage through the continent—was done poorly if at all.

Captain John Smith vividly described the colonists' disillusionment and disorder:

> Being for the most part of such tender educations and small experience in martial accidents, because they found not English cities, nor such

fair houses, nor at their own wishes any of their accustomed dainties, with feather beds and down pillows, Taverns and alehouses in every breathing place, neither such plenty of gold and silver and dissolute liberty as they expected, they had little or no care of any thing, but to pamper their bellies, to fly away with our Pinnaces, or procure their means to return to England. For the Country was to them a miserie, a ruin, a death, a hell and their reports were, and their own actions there according.

Away from Jamestown, the colonists found the Indian aid sometimes vanished and they were left hungry and alone in an alien environment.

Many of the colonists found life in Jamestown more frustrating than they could bear. Throughout the first winter, more and more colonists fell sick and many died. Of the 108 colonists left in America in 1607, only 38 were alive the following spring. And this pattern was soon repeated. After its initial disappointments, the Virginia Company was reorganized in 1609 to try again on an even larger scale, demonstrating the power of a large joint-stock company. The newly reorganized company sent a huge fleet of nine ships with 500 new colonists to shore up the settlement. Part of the fleet—including most of the new government leaders–was shipwrecked on Bermuda, and did not arrive for an entire year (an event that inspired Shakespeare's play *The Tempest*). But most of the new colonists got through. These new settlers met disaster on an even larger scale than the first arrivals. Of the several hundred colonists left in Virginia in the fall of 1609, only 60 were alive the following spring.

CAPTAIN JOHN SMITH

Something was clearly very wrong; if promoters could not find the reasons for such massive failure, any hope for a permanent English presence in America seemed lost. One man claimed to know the answer and seemed to have the evidence to back him up: Captain John Smith. He had been in charge of the colony in between the two starving times, and during his tenure very few had died. He wrote volumes pointing out his success and making his case. Despite the quality of his evidence, though, few in London would listen to him.

Smith was an unusual man, one of the few colonial leaders who was not born to high rank. Apprenticed to a merchant, he had run away at the age of sixteen to find fame and fortune. Like Raleigh, he learned much at the "university of war" in France and then in eastern Europe. When he finally returned to England in his middle twenties, he had traveled all through Europe and into North Africa and Russia. He had experienced the extremes the world had to offer: he had been knighted on the field of battle in Hungary and

CAPTAIN JOHN SMITH. Smith deliberately presented himself as a gruff, hardened, plain soldier in contrast to lavishly costumed courtier-explorers like Raleigh.

had been a slave in Turkey. The Virginia Company, impressed by his survival skills, selected him to be one of their governing council in Virginia with the first colony in 1607.

None of the other councilors liked Smith; he never ceased to remind them that he was the only member of the government who knew anything about dealing with alien situations. Smith became president of the council in Virginia, but he gained the position, in September 1608, literally over the others councilors' dead bodies. Only when the others were either dead or too sick to rule did they let Smith take control.

John Smith felt that Virginia's problems lay in the design of the colony, and the kinds of men chosen. There were too many gentlemen—six times as many proportionally as in England. Not only did the gentlemen expect to do no work, they expected to be attended by servants who would work only for them and not for the colony as a whole. Many of the other colonists were either soldiers or what the Virginia Company called "the scum of the earth," not a promising bunch with which to build a new society or convert the Indians. Smith told the Virginia Company that "a plain soldier that can use a pick-axe and spade is better than five Knights." Quoting the Bible, he commanded that "he who does not work shall not eat." Even the gentlemen went to work felling trees; their soft hands became so blistered, and the work so painful to them, that Smith had to discipline them for the oaths they uttered as their axes hit the trees.

Through his policy of enforced labor, President Smith solved many of Jamestown's problems. Just getting the colonists up and moving brightened their outlook, and the work gave them a sense of purpose and hope for the future. Through their work they made conditions in the settlement better. Deep wells were dug so that the colonists would no longer sicken themselves by drinking groundwater, and secure houses were built. Food was planted, and Smith sent out expeditions to trade with the Indians for more supplies.

The proof of Smith's plan lies in his results: during his presidency the death rate fell almost to zero, and the few deaths were almost all from accidents. The upstart governor was replaced and forced out of the colony when the great new fleet came in 1609. The second wave of deaths, the reduction of the 500 colonists to 60, came after he left. He devoted the rest of his life to promoting colonization and analyzing what had gone wrong in Virginia.

The situation worsened in Virginia after 1609 under a series of governors. Finally, in 1611 Sir Thomas Dale arrived as governor and instituted a set of harsh new policies under a code called the Lawes Divine, Morall and Martiall. The colony's promoters may have thought the new system, carried on by Sir Thomas Gates after Dale left the colony, was similar to what Smith had instituted. In reality it was a code of the harshest severity, under which the colony languished. Virginia did manage to hold on, despite a prolonged war with the Indians, but just barely.

INDIAN RELATIONS

The Indians' role, particularly that of the great confederacy headed by Powhatan, was crucial in the early history of Virginia. Powhatan, who controlled much of what happened around Chesapeake Bay, was perfectly aware that he could have eliminated the colony at any time during its first years. Not only were the colonists weak and ill-adapted to the environment, Powhatan's people had wiped out a Spanish Jesuit mission near the same place in the 1570s. The question, then, is why did he allow the English to remain?

The answer seems to be that Powhatan, an extremely skillful strategist, wanted the trade goods the English brought with them, particularly metal tools and other equipment. Despite what the English believed, the Indians did not want to give up their own way of life in favor of a superior European way. But they did want tools that would make their *own* methods more efficient. Powhatan assumed that the English colony would remain a small trading post, and that he could always control the settlers by regulating their food supply. As the conduit for European trade goods, his power with his Indian clients would be enhanced. Powhatan told Smith that warlike acts would harm the colonists more than the Indians:

> What will it avail you, to take that perforce, you may quietly have with love, or to destroy them that provide you food? What can you get by war, when we can hide our provision and fly to the woods, whereby you must famish by wrong-

POWHATAN SPEAKING TO HIS PEOPLE. This is one of several inserts that adorned a map of Virginia published by John Smith. The figure of Powhatan was adapted from John White's portrait of a carved wooden idol he saw among the Carolina Algonquians. Artists and writers often borrowed from each other's accounts to enrich their own books about America.

ing us your friends. Think you I am so simple not to know, it is better to eat good meat, lie well, and sleep quietly with my women and children, laugh and be merry with you, have copper, hatchets, or what I want, being your friend?

Powhatan miscalculated on the future of Jamestown, but his reasoning on the information available to him was shrewd. After Captain Smith left the colony, relations deteriorated into a brutal intermittent war.

Powhatan's emissary in the early years was his dearest daughter, Pocahontas, who was about eleven years old when John Smith led the colony. She often carried messages back and forth between the Indians and the English. As an adult, she married English colonist John Rolfe. Pocahontas's marriage was followed by a cessation of the continuing hostilities between the English and the Powhatan confederacy, which had been draining to both sides. The truce gave the colonists the opportunity to move outside their fortifications and plan for the future.

COLONIES ESTABLISHED

By 1610, lasting colonies had been established by each of the colonizing powers. Spain had Santa Fe in the Southwest and St. Augustine in Florida. France had founded the colony of Quebec on the St. Lawrence and had sent parties far into the interior of the continent. England's colony in Virginia was precarious but alive. Santa Fe, Quebec, and Jamestown had all been founded within the same short span of time, marking a new kind of commitment to maintaining a presence in the northern regions of America. Each of the three colonies was small, little more than a holding party, and largely composed of young men. True settlement would come later, but it would be built on these foundations.

CHRONOLOGY

c. 1000	Norse settlements in Newfoundland	1582	Raleigh's appearance at Court
c. 1325	Establishment of Aztec empire	1584	Raleigh sends first reconnaissance voyage to Roanoke; Hakluyt writes *Discourse of Western Planting;* Manteo and Wanchese come to England
1492	Christopher Columbus, first voyage to America		
1497–1498	John Cabot's voyages establish English claim to North America		
c. 1500	Waning of Mississippian culture	1585	Roanoke colony set up as privateering base
1513	Balboa discovers Pacific Ocean across Isthmus of Panama	1585–1603	Privateering war between England and Spain
1517	Martin Luther's break with Roman Catholic Church	1586	Death of Wingina; first Roanoke colony returns home with Sir Francis Drake
1518	Conquest of Mexico by Spanish under Cortés	1587	Second Roanoke colony, composed of families under governorship of John White; this group is the Lost Colony
1519–1522	Magellan expedition rounds tip of South America and circles globe	1588	England defeats great Spanish Armada
1524	Verrazzano explores North America's east coast	1588–1590	Publication of Thomas Harriot's *Briefe and True Report of the New Found Land of Virginia* with paintings by John White
1531–1533	Conquest of Incas in Peru by Spanish under Pizarro	1590	John White's expedition to Roanoke finds site deserted
1533	Henry VIII breaks with Roman Catholic Church	1592	Raleigh expelled from court because of his secret marriage.
1534–1541	Jacques Cartier explores St. Lawrence River, attempts French colony near Quebec	1595	Raleigh's first voyage to Guiana
		1596	Raleigh participates in raid on Cádiz
1536	Cabeza de Vaca completes trek across southwestern North America	1598	Juan de Oñate establishes permanent Spanish presence north of Rio Grande
1539–1540	De Soto explores southeastern North America	1602–1608	Champlain explores New England and St. Lawrence area
1540–1542	Coronado expedition through North American Southwest	1603	Death of Queen Elizabeth; accession of James I; Sir Walter Raleigh arrested and sentenced to death
1542–1543	Cabrillo expedition along Pacific coast of North America		
1552	Publication of Las Casas's *Destruction of the Indies* (translated into English, 1583)	1607	Jamestown founded on Chesapeake Bay; Sagadahoc founded in Maine
		1608	Permanent settlement of Quebec by French colonists
1554	Birth of Sir Walter Raleigh	1608–1609	Captain John Smith president of Virginia
1558	Accession of Queen Elizabeth	1609	Virginia Company reorganized; second starving winter
1562–1565	French colony at Port Royal on South Carolina coast		
1565	San Agustin founded by Spanish in Florida	1610	Santa Fe established in new Mexico territory
		1611	Shakespeare's *The Tempest* performed at Court
1571–1572	Spanish mission on Chesapeake Bay destroyed by Indians	1612	Death of Prince Henry
1572–1575	Spanish settlement at Santa Elena on South Carolina coast	1617	Raleigh's second voyage to Guiana
		1618	Execution of Sir Walter Raleigh

SUGGESTIONS FOR FURTHER READING

SIR WALTER RALEIGH

Raleigh has been the subject of many biographies. Among the best recent ones are Robert Lacey, *Sir Walter Ralegh* (1973), and Stephen J. Greenblatt, *Sir Walter Ralegh: The Renaissance Man and His Roles* (1973). David B. Quinn has written a highly detailed history of the Roanoke colony, capping his lifetime of work on the subject: *Set Fair for Roanoke: Voyages and Colonies, 1584–1606* (1985). Karen Ordahl Kupperman, *Roanoke: The Abandoned Colony* (1984), offers a briefer history incorporating new work on English social history. The Roanoke documents are available in David B. Quinn and Alison Quinn, eds., *The First Colonists: Documents on the Planting of the First English Settlements in North America, 1584–1590* (1982). Thomas Harriot's *Briefe and True Report of the New Found Land of Virginia* (1588) has been republished in facsimile with the DeBry woodcuts of John White's paintings by Dover Books (1972). John White's paintings are available in *America 1585: The Complete Drawings of John White* (1984). On the connection between English activities in Ireland and American colonization, see Nicholas P. Canny, "The Ideology of English Colonization: From Ireland to America," *William and Mary Quarterly*, 3d ser., 30 (1973), 575–598.

EUROPE'S NEW WORLD

On Indian life before massive contact with outsiders, see the articles in Alvin M. Josephy, Jr., ed., *America in 1492: The World of the Indian Peoples Before the Arrival of Columbus* (1992). For an overview of evidence on prehistoric cultures, see Lynda Norene Shaffer, *Native Americans Before 1492: The Moundbuildng Centers of the Eastern Woodlands* (1992), and George E. Stuart, "Who Were the Mound Builders?" *National Geographic*, 142 (1972): 783–801. Bruce Trigger, ed., *The Northeast: Handbook of the Indians of North America*, vol. 15, gen. ed. William C. Sturtevant (1978), contains very readable articles by specialists on individual Indian tribes as well as general topics. It covers Indians all over the Northeast, including as far south as the Carolinas. James Axtell, *The Invasion Within: The Contest of Cultures in Colonial North America* (1985) offers a comprehensive analysis of English, French, and Indian relationships.

Charles Hudson, *The Southeastern Indians* (1976), offers a very full discussion of the culture of the Southeast, along with some materials on the impact of European colonization. Edward H. Spicer, *Cycles of Conquest: The Impact of Spain, Mexico, and the United States on the Indians of the Southwest, 1533–1960* (1962), discusses the cultures in the Southwest and the major changes wrought by the coming of Europeans. For New England Indians before and during contact, see Neal Salisbury, *Manitou and Providence: Indians, Europeans and the Making of New England, 1500–1643* (1982). On Indian life farther north see Bruce G. Trigger, *Natives and Newcomers: Canada's "Heroic Age" Reconsidered* (1985), and Olive Patricia Dickason, *The Myth of the Savage and the Beginnings of French Colonization in the Americas* (1982).

On the diseases that struck the Indians and other biological effects of the voyages to America, see Alfred W. Crosby, Jr., *The Columbian Exchange: Biological and Cultural Consequences of 1492* (1972), John W. Vetrano and Douglas Ubelaker, *Disease and Demography in the Americas* (1992), and Herman J. Viola and Carolyn Margolis, eds., *Seeds of Change: Five Hundred Years Since Columbus* (1991).

On the context of European expansion see K. G. Davies, *The North Atlantic World in the Seventeenth Century* (1974), and Carlo M. Cipolla, *Guns and Sails in the Early Period of European Expansion, 1400–1700* (1963). The most thorough and informed overview of all European exploration and the beginnings of colonization is David B. Quinn, *North America from Earliest Discovery to First Settlements: The Norse Voyages to 1612* (1977). See also his *England and the Discovery of America, 1481–1620* (1974). On Columbus and recent discussion surrounding his role, see William D. Phillips, Jr., and Carla Rahn Phillips, *The Worlds of Christopher Columbus* (1992), John Noble Wilford, *The Mysterious History of Columbus: An Exploration of the Man, the Myth, and the Legacy* (1991), and Kirkpatrick Sale, *The Conquest of Paradise: Christopher Columbus and the Columbian Legacy* (1990).

On early attempts to establish colonies in the Southeast, see Paul E. Hoffman, *A New Andalucia and a Way to the Orient: The American Southeast During the Sixteenth Century* (1990), and J. Leitch Wright, Jr., *Anglo-Spanish Rivalry in North America* (1971). On New France see Marcel Trudel, *The Beginnings of New France, 1524–1663*, trans. Patricia Claxton (1973). On the beginnings of Jamestown see Alden Vaughan, *American Genesis: Captain John Smith and the Founding of Virginia* (1975), and Karen Ordahl Kupperman, ed., *John Smith: A Select Edition of his Writings* (1988). Kenneth R. Andrews, *Trade, Plunder, and Settlement: Maritime Enterprise and the Genesis of the British Empire, 1480–1630* (1984), describes the manifold overseas interests of English investors and places America within that context.

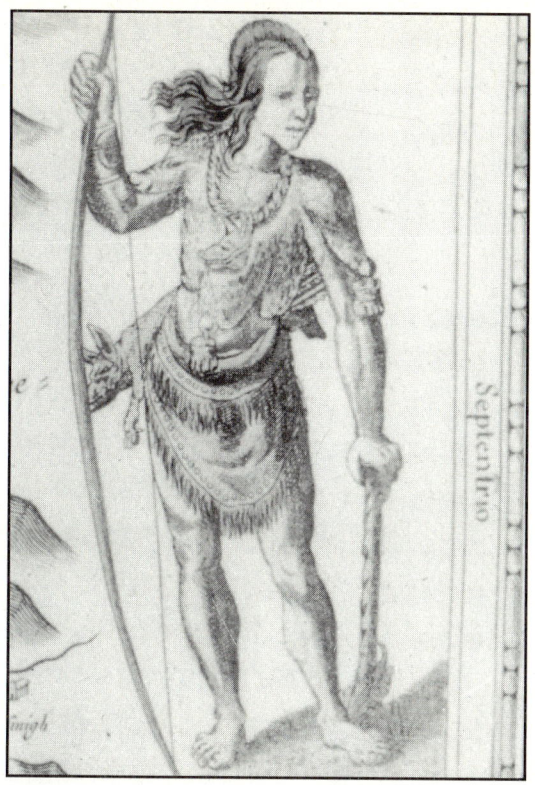

CHAPTER 2

The Colonies Established

Episode: 1622—Clash of Cultures in Virginia

PATTERNS OF SETTLEMENT TO MID-SEVENTEENTH CENTURY

    The Southwest

    The Chesapeake

    New England

    Middle Colonies

    Patterns

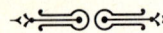

THE EPISODE: *Colonization was undertaken in a spirit of wishful thinking. Eager for England to become a world leader, promoters argued that the Indians would welcome colonists. Indian patterns of land use convinced early observers that plenty of unused land remained—enough to absorb all the settlers without disturbing Indian life. In fact, they argued, the Indians would only benefit from colonization. Christianity would save their souls and make their lives truly meaningful, and they would be offered the chance to become "civilized," both gifts of immense value. Had not the natives already welcomed trade and shown signs of wanting the Europeans to dwell among them?*

The Indians also viewed the early years through their own hopes and wishes. The early settlements looked so weak and straggling, and the men so pathetically unable to cope, that leaders such as Powhatan thought they would have no difficulty controlling the relationship. These English could not even grow their own food, so how could they ever threaten Indian life? The Indians, Powhatan thought, would have supplies of the metal tools and other goods the English brought, and could always call the tune.

Neither side saw clearly what the future held as Jamestown was founded. Certainly, no one anticipated the massive growth of the colony after 1618, and the sudden hunger for Indian land for Virginia's gold—tobacco. Seemingly overnight the Indians saw their way of life becoming impossible, and the colonists saw the natives as an obstruction to their own desires to live as independent men and women. The great attack of 1622, on the surface, was about conflict and the shedding of blood, but underneath it signalled recognition of the Indians' grim new reality.

THE HISTORICAL SETTING: *France, Spain, and England all had permanent settlements in existence by 1610. But in many ways the true beginning of colonization dates from about 1620, when Europeans finally realized they would not get the products they wanted from North America unless Europeans crossed the ocean and created them. In the 1620s colonial promoters began to reorganize their ventures in order to give ordinary men and women the incentives they needed to make the decision to emigrate, and they created the financial arrangements that made it possible to pay the colonists' way, as well as to reimburse those who advanced the money.*

Partly because these new arrangements coincided with bad conditions at home, Europeans began to flow into the colonies in the 1620s, and even more in the 1630s. Most early immigrants came from Britain, but Spain, France, the Netherlands, and Sweden also sent colonists. America became attractive when the sponsoring companies promised everyone who came land of their own. This incentive lured Europeans for whom such security was impossible at home, and the newcomers founded families with the goal of passing on estates to their sons.

But as colonists gained security, the Indians lost it. As the incoming Europeans steadily pushed back the frontier, the Indians were harassed by the free-ranging imported animals and found their lives rendered ever more difficult.

This chapter will look at the similarities and differences in the first wave of colonization, and the mechanisms by which colonies were established.

1622—CLASH OF CULTURES IN VIRGINIA

By 1622 the plantations in Virginia seemed to be truly settled and thriving. Tobacco, the great cash crop, was well established and the offer of land to all comers had allowed the little colony to spread along the James River for seventy miles on both sides. Moreover, peace had been achieved with the Indians after a long and troubling period of warfare. Opechancanough, chief of the region's tribes, had told the English that the peace between them was "so firm, as the Sky should sooner fall than it dissolve." The English had become so secure that they often went about without weapons, and they welcomed Indians into their houses freely.

MARCH 22, 1622: THE ATTACK

Friday, March 22, 1622, began like an ordinary day. At several of the plantations Indian neighbors came to call in the morning, bringing "Deer, Turkeys, Fish, Furs, and other provisions" to trade. They were invited to sit down to breakfast with their English hosts. Suddenly, these Indians, whom the English had come to think of as friends, snatched up the weapons lying about the houses and "basely and barbarously murdered" the English "not sparing either age or sex, man woman or child; so sudden in their cruel execution, that few or none discerned the weapon or blow that brought them to destruction."

 The attackers then spread over the fields and workshops and killed the English they found there. They knew where to find people because they had been welcomed into the plantations so often. "And by this means that fatal Friday morning, there fell under the bloody and barbarous hand of that perfidious and inhumane people, contrary to all laws of God and men, of Nature and Nations, three hundred forty-seven men, women, and children." Even more shocking, the Indian attackers mutilated the bodies of the dead, "defacing, dragging, and mangling the dead carcasses into many pieces, and carrying some parts away in derision, with base and brutish triumph."

 Edward Waterhouse, the secretary of the Virginia Company in London, put together the reports of the attack and published a book describing it. His readers were shocked by reports that the Indians treated most savagely the very people who had been most friendly to them. He pointed out that even wild animals will recognize their benefactors and save them from harm. Most prominent among these unjustly slaughtered English was George Thorpe, a leading gentleman, who had made the Indians'

THE GREAT POWHATAN ATTACK IN VIRGINIA, 1622, as illustrated by Theodore DeBry.

welfare his primary concern. He had actually been warned of the impending attack, but had believed that the Indians who were his friends would never harm him. Not only was he killed by "this Viperous brood," but they "cruelly . . . out of devilish malice, did so many barbarous despites and foul scorns after to his dead corpse, as are unbefitting to be heard by any civil ear." Waterhouse thought that Thorpe had become a martyr, and that the Indians had forfeited any claims to consideration.

Ten years of vicious warfare followed the uprising of 1622, and the English became truly established during this time, as the Indians lost ground. But both sides found the warfare draining and harsh.

INDIAN LIFE BEFORE COLONIZATION

Before it was named Virginia, the land around Chesapeake Bay was called Tsenacommacoh. In it, the "Great Emperor Powhatan," as Captain John Smith called him, ruled over some thirty tribes. These tribes gave a large part of their annual harvest to Powhatan, and he, in return, promised them protection and support in times of need. These people lived in abundance on the rich lands along the rivers branching out from the bay. Powhatan's title, werowance, the coastal Algonquian equivalent of "emperor," meant "he who is rich," and his wealth consisted of the accumulated food the werowance gathered in tribute.

The werowance was supported by captains called cockarouses, whose office involved giving advice, as well as governing villages subject to the werowance. They led the people in war. Equally important were the religious leaders, the priests and shamans. The priests functioned in the temples, conducting the religious ceremonies that kept the people in the proper relationship to the gods. The annual Green Corn ceremony in late summer was the greatest religious festival, but other observances throughout the year emphasized the people's dependence on the gods for the sun and the rain that made life possible.

The shamans, called "conjurers" by the English, were more individualistic. A person could consult a shaman for a particular problem or to seek greater success in hunting or war. The shamans were also healers. Both shamans and priests could rally the people in times of crisis.

One leader who combined many of these traits was Nemattanew, who was first seen by the English when they attempted to extend their control up the James River. Sir Thomas Dale led a force of 200 veteran soldiers up the James in 1611 into an ambush set up by Nemattanew. Though a settlement was created at the falls near modern Richmond, which was the farthest point to which an English boat could travel on the river, Nemattanew saw to it that the English paid a high price. Smith wrote that, because of his "courage and policy," Nemattanew was "accounted amongst the Savages their chief Captain."

Nemattanew was remembered, not only because of his military prowess, but because he made such a flamboyant appearance. The English called him "Jack of the Feathers" because, as George Percy wrote, "he used to come into the field all covered over with feathers and Swan's wings fastened unto his shoulders as though he meant to fly." Nemattanew assumed an almost magical role, and he began to use the people's belief in him to mount a defense of traditional Powhatan culture in the face of the English invasion. He told his followers that he could not be killed by English bullets, and they believed him because he had "so long escaped so many dangers without any hurt." He preached that strict adherence to the ways and beliefs of their ancestors could make them immune as well through "an Ointment that could secure them from our Shot." As Robert Beverley wrote at the end of the seventeenth century, Nemattanew, a "very cunning fellow, . . . took great Pride in preserving and increasing" their "Superstition concerning him, affecting everything that was odd and prodigious to work upon their Admiration."

YOUNG GO-BETWEENS

Not all relationships between settlers and natives were military or even hostile. Some individuals on both sides were able to cross cultural lines and meet as human beings. In the early years such relationships were forged by three children—Pocahontas, Henry Spelman, and Thomas Savage. Pocahontas was the beloved daughter of Powhatan. She was ten or eleven when Jamestown was founded in 1607, and she formed a human link between Jamestown and the Powhatans, carrying messages and presents and soothing anger on both sides. One official recalled fondly how she would playfully "get the boys forth with her into the market place and make them wheel, falling on their hands turning their heels upwards, whom she would follow, and wheel so her self." The colonists in Jamestown loved her presence as a relief from the grim reality in the fort. When she reached the age of puberty, Powhatan, who was an extremely loving father, sent her away from the English to live with Indian allies. But she was discovered by an expedition out looking for corn, which kidnapped her and took her back to Jamestown as a prisoner.

THE FLYER. John White painted this shaman, identified as a "conjurer" by Thomas Harriot. The bird on his head indicated his powers. Harriot wrote that "the inhabitants give great credit unto their speech."

Pocahontas became a convert to Christianity, was baptized with the name Rebecca, and married John Rolfe in 1614. She went to England with her husband and young son, Thomas, in 1616, where she was received at the court of King James and reunited with John Smith. Next year, as her ship back to Virginia was leaving, "it pleased God to take this Young lady to his mercy." Pocahontas was buried at Gravesend in England; she was only twenty-one years old.

The English boys played similar roles in early Virginia. Most ships and colonial forces carried a small number of boys, who could be called on to perform a variety of tasks. When Captain Christopher Newport came to Jamestown in January 1608, thirteen-year-old Thomas Savage was in his crew. Newport took Savage along when, only a month after their arrival, he and John Smith prepared to make a state visit to Powhatan. In order to cement the new English-Powhatan friendship, Newport "gave" Thomas Savage to Powhatan, telling him the boy was his son. The chief delighted in young Savage.

Pocahontas in London shortly before her death. Dressed as an English gentlewoman, she became the toast of London.

Once after Powhatan, in a fit of rage at the English, sent him back to Jamestown, Pocahontas came to the fort and begged Savage to return, because both she and her father loved him "exceedingly."

Another boy, Henry Spelman, a member of a distinguished English family, was sent to Jamestown at the age of fourteen, apparently because his family could not control him. He arrived in 1609 and almost immediately was given to one of Powhatan's adult sons, Parahunt, as a token of peace. Spelman later wrote one of the most revealing descriptions of Virginia Algonquian culture. Just as the Jamestown colonists had liked to have young Pocahontas come to the fort, Parahunt treated Spelman as a special pet. He noted that Parahunt "made very much of me, giving me such things as he had to win me to live with him."

Spelman later lived for a time among the Patawomekes, whose chief Japazaws also treated him as an honored guest. Spelman was particularly good with the chief's fretful baby and he wrote proudly, "None could quiet him so well as myself." When Japazaws found young Henry reading a Bible, he asked about a picture of the creation in it. Spelman explained the picture, "which the king seemed to like well of," and then Japazaws told him the creation story of his own people, which the boy judged "a pretty fabulous tale indeed."

These young emissaries were more than just pawns or hostages to see that the peace was kept. Genuine ties of affection were created. Just as Pocahontas called John Smith "Father" when they met in London, the English boys were thought of as sons by the chiefs to whom they were given. Powhatan greeted Thomas Savage in 1614 after the colonists and the Indians had endured four years of warfare with these words: "My child, you are welcome. You have been a stranger to me these four years." But still, the aging chief went on, "you are my child, by the gift of Captain Newport."

In living among the Indians, Spelman and Savage learned various native languages, just as Pocahontas learned English. The two English boys became key interpreters and aided in the spread of English settlements over the land. But their success in crossing cultural boundaries also created great suspicion. Many leaders on both sides feared that they had become too identified with the interests of the other side, or had become tainted and compromised by their long acquaintance with the alien culture. Spelman and Savage were never fully trusted in Jamestown. The colonists were in an impossible position: they were completely dependent on their interpreters, who alone knew the language and cultural ways of the natives; and yet they were never completely sure that Spelman and Savage would always keep the colonists' interests uppermost in their minds. One colonist wrote "We have sent boys amongst them to learn their Language, but they return worse than they went."

Suspicion broke out into open hostility in 1619 when Henry Spelman was put on trial in Jamestown, accused of having "unreverently and maliciously" disparaged Jamestown's governor, Sir George Yeardley, and telling Opechancanough "within a year there would come a governor greater than this." In fact Jamestown was anticipating the arrival of a more prestigious governor, Sir Francis Wyatt, but many wanted Spelman executed for having brought the colony's present government into disrepute. Some officials, fearing that he had crossed over the cultural line in his loyalties, alleged that Spelman "had in him more of the Savage than of the Christian." He was not executed, but rather was sentenced to serve as the governor's interpreter for seven years. Thus this man whom the leaders did not trust was placed in a position where trust was essential. They would have to depend on what he told them about the intentions of the Indians, even though they feared he might double-cross them. They were trapped by their dependence on Spelman's skills.

Thomas Savage was also treated with distrust. In October 1621 he began to hear rumors of the planning for a great attack on all the colonists. He collected stories of Opechancanough's attempts to get a quantity of a rare poison, and of an intended assembly of Indians from all over the Chesapeake region, called to create plans for attack on "every Plantation in the Colony." When Savage tried to convince the governor and his associates of the danger in which the colony stood, they ignored him, citing their "very great amity and confidence with the natives."

THE VIRGINIA COMPANY'S NEW POLICY

Life changed dramatically for both Indians and English in 1618 and the years that followed, as the forces that would change Tsenacommacah into Virginia became ever stronger. Powhatan died in 1618 and was shortly succeeded by a kinsman, possibly his brother, named Opechancanough. Opechancanough listened to Nemattanew, Jack of the Feathers, and was concerned about protecting Powhatan lifeways and culture. Those lifeways were under greater threat than ever before, because it was in 1618 that settlers began to pour into the colony in large numbers, seeking land on which to plant the new golden crop, tobacco. The colony began to expand by leaps and bounds, and little settlements along the river burgeoned into thriving plantations. The Indians found themselves pushed away from the waterway that had provided both their best land and their communication routes. While the planters took the land, their animals ruined the Indians' crops and wild food supply. Almost overnight, it seemed, the native way of life was rendered almost impossible.

No wonder Opechancanough listened with great interest to Nemattanew and his arguments that coexistence was not possible. Anyone with eyes could see that one side or the other was going to come out on top. The English for their part feared Nemattanew and always blamed him for every incident that occurred. Colonial officials told themselves that he was stirring up the Indians, and that if he could be captured, resentment and resistance would die down.

In fact the sources of native resentment and resistance were far deeper and more fundamental. The Virginia Company's new aggressive plan of colonization created much of the climate to which the Indians reacted. Company officials were convinced that the colony was too small to thrive, and that Virginia needed a large influx of settlers, so they made the colony attractive. People contemplating going over to Virginia were promised land of their own, fifty acres for each, and the same reward was also promised to each person who paid for the passage of another. With tobacco established

ADVERTISEMENT FOR TOBACCO. Smoking quickly became a fashionable habit in England and tobacco a profitable crop for the colonies. This advertisement shows the popular identification of pipe-smoking with Raleigh.

as a cash crop, and a representative assembly created to ensure that English law and custom would prevail, English planters began to pour into the colony at the rate of more than a thousand a year. Hard times and scarce land at home meant that these colonists would never have been able to own land in England. Virginia offered poor English men and women the chance of a lifetime. Soon the James River was lined with new settlements as far as the plantation at the falls, which was given the name Henrico.

Not only the poor were drawn to Virginia. It was also a land where gentlemen down on their luck could hope to rebuild their fortunes while using their leadership skills to help build the colony. One such was Sir John Berkeley, who had been forced to sell his ancestral home, Beverstone Castle in Gloucestershire. Said to be "estranged from his friends and reduced to poverty," he came to America in 1620 to take over direction of a Virginia Company project to construct an ironworks. Buying metal tools imported from England was extremely expensive and the supply was intermittent, so the colony placed a high priority on becoming self-sufficient in metalworking. No good ore had yet been located, but the falls near Henrico seemed to be a very good location for an ironworks.

WOMEN COLONISTS

The company was determined to make life in Virginia as normal as possible, which meant that the settlers must have the chance to live in families. In order to achieve this, company officers began to recruit and send over women of good character to make suitable wives for the colonists. The report of the first meeting of the Virginia Assembly in 1619 had stressed the need for women, saying, "In a new plantation, it is not known whether man or woman be more necessary." The Virginia Company acknowledged that the way to "tie and root the Planters' minds to Virginia" was through "the bonds of wives and children": "by long experience we have found that the Minds of our people in Virginia are much dejected, and their hearts enflamed with a desire to return for England only through the wants of the comforts without which God saw that Man could not live contentedly, no not in Paradise." The company resolved to send "young, handsome, and honestly educated Maids to Virginia."

One such was Anne Jackson, age twenty "or thereabouts," who sailed on the *Marmaduke* in 1621 with her brother, John. John Jackson had already lived in Virginia for some time, and had become a man of substance. He was one of two men chosen to represent the plantation of Martin's Hundred in the first meeting of the Virginia General Assembly in 1619. He had gone home and now he was taking his sister back with him. Anne Jackson represented just the kind of woman from a good family that company officials were looking for. The records noted that she was brought to the ship by her father, William Jackson, "a man of known honesty . . . by whose consent she comes." William Jackson was a gardener in the city of Westminster, now part of London, and the family had moved to London from Salisbury, where Anne was born. Anne and John both went to Martin's Hundred, seven miles up the river from Jamestown. Mary Ellyott, age nineteen, came to Martin's Hundred with her stepfather, Maximilian Russell, at the same time.

Some of the women went to a new plantation founded in the area south of the James River by Edward Bennett. They felt safer venturing across the ocean because they were going to a Puritan settlement. Like the Puritans who went to create Plymouth colony in New England at the same time, Edward Bennett felt so strongly about his religious convictions that he had left England and lived in Holland, which offered religious toleration, for a number of years. A wealthy and influential man, he had been an elder of the "ancient church" in Amsterdam. Bennett and his associates seized the opportunity presented by the opening of Virginia to create a godly settlement there.

The young women who went to Mr. Bennett's plantation were recommended by family members, who must have been reassured by the Puritan sponsorship of the settlement. Marie Daucks, a widow twenty-five years old, was recommended by her uncle who lived in London: "Mr. Slocum in Maiden Lane is her near kinsman by whom and other good testimonies her honesty and good Carriage is testified." Alice Jones, twenty-one, and Parnell Tenton, about twenty, traveled with Marie Daucks and Mary Ellyott in the *Warwick*. Parnell Tenton, who could reportedly "work all kinds of ordinary work" (sewing), was recommended for "her honest carriage" by Mr. Hobson, an officer of the Draper's Company. But it was her mother who brought her to the company docks for her embarkation for the unknown lands across the seas; Parnell's father was dead.

The company provided for the women's needs as they entered their new lives. Each was allotted a petticoat, a waistcoat, two pair of stockings, a pair of garters, two smocks, one pair of gloves, one hat and band, one round band, an apron, two pair of shoes, one towel, two coifs (hair dressings), a neckcloth, and yarn to knit stockings. The Virginia Company also provided two psalm books and twelve catechisms for the women to use on the voyage and in Virginia. The presence of these young women and all the others like them in the early 1620s marked the beginning of something like normal life in Virginia.

VIRGINIA LOTTERY. King James I authorized the Virginia Company to launch a nationwide lottery to help finance the Jamestown colony. The lottery proved to be a successful device both in bringing in money and in publicizing the venture.

INDIAN CONVERSION

Another sign of the renewed commitment to Virginia was the plan to create a school at Henrico, an "Indian college," in which young natives could be trained in European culture and Christianity. Collections were taken up in England and pious men and women contributed to what they saw as a noble cause. Ten thousand acres were set aside in Virginia, and the income from that land was to support the college. George Thorpe, who came to head the project, was idealistically dedicated to the campaign to bring the Indians "to Civility and to the embracing of our Christian religion." He planned that gentle persuasion, education, and preaching would replace force and warfare. Thorpe hoped for as close a relationship with his Indian friends as Thomas Savage and Henry Spelman had. But there would be no doubt about who was being changed. The Indians were all expected to become English. No one would cross the line the other way, as some feared Spelman and Savage had.

George Thorpe had already had experience of attempting to educate a Virginia native. When Pocahontas went to England in 1616 with her husband, John Rolfe, and her infant son Thomas, she had been accompanied by several young men and women, some of whom remained in England. One of these young men came to live with George Thorpe, who referred to him in correspondence as his "Virginia Boy." This young American took his host's name and was baptized Georgius Thorpe on September 19, 1619, but unfortunately the church register that mentions baptism of the *Homo Virginae* also records his burial on September 27. His impending death had presumably led to the hurried baptism.

George Thorpe left a comfortable life and his wife and children in England to take up the challenge of converting the Indians when he sailed for America in March 1620. Thorpe was a prominent gentleman in Gloucestershire and had been a member of parliament and a gentleman of the king's privy chamber. He had invested large sums in the Virginia Company and in the creation of Berkeley Hundred in the colony, but gossip said that it was in order to escape his creditors that he "did secretlie flie out of England to Virginia." He was a neighbor of ironworks manager Sir John Berkeley in England, and they apparently hoped to solve their financial problems by the expedient of emigrating. Thorpe was committed to the idea that if the Indians were only treated gently and lovingly, and exposed in a positive way to English technology and religion, they would voluntarily leave their "savagery" and become converts to the Christian way of life. Thorpe took two Bibles, two copies of the Book of Common Prayer, and three copies each of two classic devotional works. He chose two of the most popular books of their sort, Arthur Dent's *The Plaine Man's Pathway to Heaven* and Lewis Bayly's *The Practice of Piety*. The *Plaine Man's Pathway* was first published in 1601, and had gone through twenty-five editions by 1640. Similarly, *The Practice of Piety*, originally published about 1610, appeared in sixty editions by the end of the seventeenth century. These books were reprinted so often because they provided the kind of guidance that ordinary men and women needed in trying to find the way to a satisfying relationship to God. What they could do for English people, they might also accomplish for America's natives.

George Thorpe wrote home to his associates on the Virginia Company Council not long after his arrival, saying that Virginia exceeded even his expectations. Backers in England had been disturbed by reports that many English colonists died during the first months in Virginia, but Thorpe wrote that he "had never had my health better in my life than I have had since my coming into this Country." He said that he thought that "more do die here of the disease of their mind than of their body." Others had written that settlers died of broken hearts. The "disease of their mind" was a deep depression produced by the profoundly disorienting environment. Almost all the colonists were from towns and cities, and unused to rural occupations, much less life cut off from all familiar surroundings and friends and family. Strange foods added to the disorientation, and Thorpe thought the problem was "having this country victuals overpraised" before they came "and by not knowing they shall drink water here." Large numbers of new arrivals apparently gave up and died when the struggle to keep going seemed too great.

Those already in Virginia were overjoyed when Thorpe, a leading English gentleman, chose to emigrate. They believed that only the presence of true leaders, men of high birth, could motivate the colonists and get them working. John Pory, the colony's secretary, wrote that Thorpe's appearance was "as of an Angel from heaven, neither did I ever see any man's face out of my native country, that did more joy me. He will help to bear our burden." The colony's governor, Sir George Yeardley, had hoped that the company would choose Thorpe to succeed him when his term was up. (He was actually succeeded by Sir Francis Wyatt.)

Thorpe set out to win the Indians' love and loyalty by good treatment. He criticized the colonists, saying that "there is scarce a man amongst us that doth so much as afford them a good thought in his heart." Everyone who worked under Thorpe was required to treat the natives well, and any harshness was punished severely. He tried to grant the Indians' every wish. One example that was told and retold was the story of the English mastiffs. The Indians complained to him about these huge fierce dogs, who were very hostile to them, and Thorpe had the dogs killed in the Indians' presence. He warned the Virginia Company against listening to men who wrote home complaining of his actions, and said those complaints would come from men he had punished for drunkenness and other faults.

Thorpe believed that the way to win the Indians for Christianity was to lure them with manufactured goods. His strategy was to approach them through "the book of the world as being nearest to their sense." He wrote home that "they begin more and more to affect English fashions, and will be much allured to affect us by gifts if the Company would be pleased to send something in matter of apparel and household stuff to be bestowed upon them, I mean the kings."

Thorpe made a special effort to form a close friendship with Opechancanough. He offered to build the chief an English-style house to replace what Edward Waterhouse in London referred to as his own "den or hog-sty, made with a few poles and sticks, and covered with mats after their wild manner." Opechancanough particularly loved the lock and key, "as locking and unlocking his door a hundred times a day, he thought no device in all the world was comparable to it." Thorpe's plan called for the Indians to allow some of their children to come and live among the English and be educated as Christians. He even offered to "pay" for such children with trade goods. The Virginia General Assembly decreed that each plantation should make an effort "by just means" to acquire some Indian boys, "Of which children the most towardly boys in wit and graces of nature" were to be taught "the first Elements of literature, so as to be fitted for the College intended for them." Thorpe even hoped some English families would go and live among the Indians.

Thorpe and Opechancanough often discussed religion, and the chief had come to see, Thorpe reported, that "our God was a good God, and better much than theirs." Thorpe promised Opechancanough that "if he would serve our god, he should be partaker of all those good things we had, and of far greater than sense of reason ever could imagine." Opechancanough and his people seemed to love Thorpe more than all the other English colonists, and with good reason. But Opechancanough demanded that mutual trust must be shown. If the Indians were to hand over their precious children for training as English men and women, then the English could not prohibit the Indians from having guns and other English weapons. Trust must be reciprocated. While Thomas Savage was warning of Opechancanough's assembling of all his allies for the attack, Thorpe's belief in the trust between the chief and him ruled perceptions in Jamestown.

Some more-experienced colonists thought Thorpe's plan to win over the Indians through kindness was ridiculous. After the uprising, William Capps, an "ancient

A Werowance of Virginia engraved by Theodore DeBry from a painting by John White. The square of copper around his neck is a badge of office, and his folded arms were a "sign of wisdom."

planter," wrote that "Thorpe he hath brought such a misery upon us by letting the Indians have their head and none must control them. The Governor stood at that time for a Cypher whilst they stood ripping open our guts." Captain John Smith wrote that the Company had always been unrealistic, saying that they had criticized him earlier for "discovering the Countries about us, building of forts, and such unnecessary fooleries, where an Egg-shell (as they wrote) had been sufficient against such enemies."

NATIVE REACTIONS

Just as dissension existed in the English camp over Thorpe's campaign and its backing by Governor Wyatt, so the Indians also split over the wisdom of accepting the new policy. Nemattanew, Jack of the Feathers, countered the appeal of Christianity and preached his vision of a revitalized native religion and culture. He assured his followers that they could not be killed by English weapons, and restored pride and purpose to them. Some writers, both at the time and ever since, have argued that Opechancanough's apparent acceptance of Thorpe and his message was faked, and that he and Nemattanew were biding their time until they had enough weapons stockpiled to attack the English. Whatever the truth about their intentions, events soon forced them to act.

Early in March 1622 Nemattanew came to the house of "one Morgan," a man who was famous for having desirable trading goods. Our information about what happened next is sketchy and only comes from hostile English sources written after the great attack. They say that Nemattanew convinced Morgan to go to Pamunkey to trade, but "the Savage murdered him by the way." Two or three days later, Nemattanew showed up at Morgan's house wearing his cap. When his two young servants asked where Morgan was, Nemattanew reportedly replied that he was dead. They then tried to capture him to take him to George Thorpe for interrogation but, "Jack so moved their patience, they shot him." They then put Nemattanew into a boat to take him to the governor, seven or eight miles away, but the prophet soon realized he was dying. "Jack, finding the pangs of death upon him, desired of the Boys two things; the one was, that they would not make it known he was slain with a bullet; the other, to bury him amongst the English." He could not bear to have his followers know that he had been brought down by an English bullet.

Opechancanough "much grieved and repined" at "the loss of this Savage." He threatened revenge but the English threatened even greater counter-revenge. Therefore, he "cunningly dissembled his intent, with the greatest signs he could of love and peace, yet within fourteen days after he acted."

Christopher Brooke, a member of the Virginia Company in London who had served with George Thorpe in parliament, published a long *Poem on the Late Massacre in Virginia,* which praised "Brave" Thorpe

> Who did'st attempt to make those Indians know
> Th'Eternal GOD; their sinewy necks to bow
> To his obedience; and on that ground
> To make them apt to what thou did'st propound
> For our Commerce with them; their good, our peace
> And both to help with mutual increase.

Brooke went on to excuse Thorpe for being "credulous" of "their seeming shew" and said that if the English were as numerous as the sands they still could not "loose the hold the Devil hath, Or bring them to the knowledge of our Faith." The uprising had convinced observers in England that it was hopeless to try to convert the Virginia natives.

However, even the most indignant could not deny that the Indians had grievances. Even Virginia Company propagandist Edward Waterhouse admitted the Indians' "daily fear" that the English "in time by our growing continually upon them, would dispossess them of this Country." As the colonists poured in to take up land and turn it into tobacco fields, the natives were acutely aware of what the future held.

And not only was their land threatened, but their culture was at stake. Christopher Brooke's poem gives the most important clue as to why the natives struck as they did early in 1622, and why they focused their anger on men such as George Thorpe. Thorpe, through his dedication and commitment to drawing the Indians with good treatment, represented the greatest threat of all. He wanted to entice them to leave their own religion and culture, and to bow "their sinewy necks" to the Christian God. A military challenge might kill natives, but Thorpe sought to destroy their very way of life. Indian leaders were particularly dismayed because some of their young men and women had been lured by the trade goods the English offered them, and by the novel

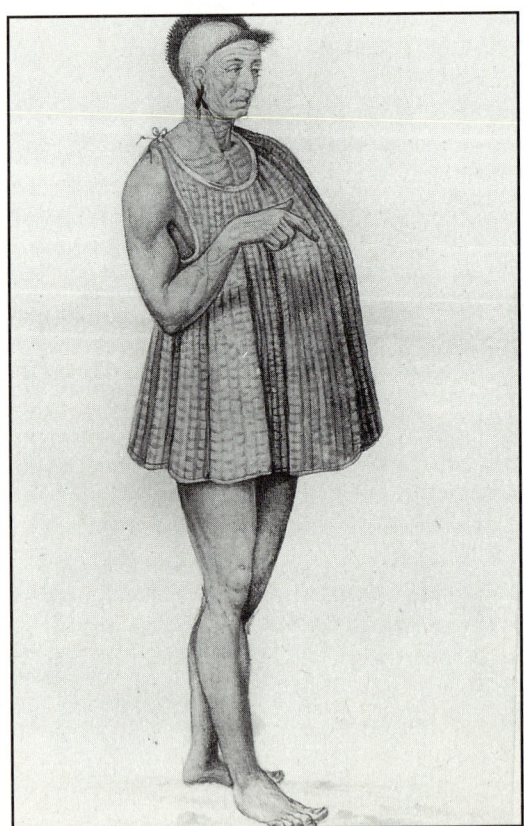

PRIEST OF SECOTAN engraved by Theodore DeBry from a painting by John White. Harriot wrote that these religious leaders were "well stricken in years and as it seemeth, of more experience than the common sort."

style of life at the plantations. They feared the loss of their own culture if the younger generation was seduced by the new.

These fears were well-founded, as reports of the fighting showed. Some natives, "whose souls they had formerly saved," warned English friends of the planned attack. Through this means Jamestown was ready and was spared. One story was told at length by the survivors. An Indian (the storyteller did not think it worthwhile to give his name) who was described as "belonging to one Perry," but who lived with another man named Pace, was approached by his brother and told to kill Pace at the appointed time. The brother intended to kill Perry, and then more natives would come to kill all the others. Instead the first man told Pace, who had treated him "as a Son." Pace rowed three miles across the James to Jamestown, so by this means Jamestown, and the lives of many English, were saved. The English gave the credit to God, who had moved the heart of this one convert. He must have represented just the kind of identity conflict that Opechancanough and the other Indian leaders feared most.

THE FIGHTING

The story of how Jamestown was spared illustrates just how highly coordinated the attack was. The reports all agree that the attack came at precisely the same time at all the plantations all along both sides of the river. The scope and precision of the event challenged English views of the nature of the "savage" and made those who reflected on it realize what they were up against. Though the survivors wrote of their "grief and shame" at being "thus butchered by so naked and cowardly a people," they also warned company officials in London that confronting the Powhatans would not be easy.

Martin's Hundred, where Anne and John Jackson had settled, suffered terribly in the attack. Everything but two houses and "a piece of the church" was destroyed. John Jackson's child was killed, one of at least six, including "a sucking child." Almost eighty colonists from Martin's Hundred appeared in the official Virginia Company list of the dead, including women, boys, and men. Some were named and some not. Maximilian Russell, Mary Ellyott's stepfather, was among the dead, and Mary herself may have been one of the unnamed women. The sixty-two surviving colonists fled to Jamestown, and only about thirty went back to try to keep the little settlement alive.

Edward Bennett's plantation was also hard hit, with fifty dead. The list there included Alice Jones, "Mary Dawks," and "Parnel, a maid." The three women who had traveled so hopefully to that godly settlement across the seas had found a different reality.

Casualties were high at "Captaine Berkeley's Plantation seated at the Falling Creek, some 66 miles from James-City in Virginia." Heading the list of the twenty-seven dead was "John Berkeley, Esquire." With him died most of the workers intended to operate the ironworks. Robert Williams and Giles Bradshaw were killed along with their wives and children, and John Howlet and his son were both among the dead. For all these, the dream of beginning life anew in America was over. Others held on in the face of such danger. Some "stragglers" gathered and fortified themselves at "Beggars-bush" and "Mistress Proctor, a proper, civil, modest Gentlewoman" also fortified and held her plantation, even though her husband, John, was away. Alice Proctor was one of the women who came in 1621. Finally the English authorities forced her to retreat to Jamestown, threatening to burn her house themselves if she did not agree to leave.

News of the great attack arrived in England in late June, and spread over the land in countless letters. A young law student, Simonds D'Ewes, recorded in his diary the "exceeding bad news" of the actions of the "inhuman wretches we had given peace to thus long." A play on the *Tragedy of the Plantation in America* was rushed onto the stage, but no copies have survived. The general opinion in England was that the uprising now freed the English to wage open war and that they had been restrained before only by good Christian impulses. Still underestimating the foe they faced, the royal government agreed to send some old arms from the Tower of London that were "altogether unfit, and of no use for modern service." The Virginia Company, completely abandoning the earlier emphasis on winning over the Indians through good treatment, argued that now the colonists could use all kinds of tactics:

> *by force, by surprise, by famine in burning their Corn, by destroying and burning their Boats, Canoes, and Houses, by breaking their fishing Weirs, by assailing them in their huntings, whereby they get the greatest part of their sustenance in Winter, by pursuing and chasing them with our horses, and bloodhounds to draw after them, and mastiffs to tear them, which take this naked, tanned, deformed Savages, for no other than wild beasts. . . .*

Those who were captured could be enslaved, condemned to "servitude and drudgery," freeing English colonists for "Arts and Occupations, which are more generous."

Virginia Company propaganda may have talked boldly of how the March uprising had freed the hands of the planters to give up their policy of peaceful coexistence and replace it with determined vengeance, but those actually in the colony knew better. A very large confederation of Indians opposed the English, and they were well armed and skillful. One source reported that the Indians were "very bold" and that they used muskets "as well or better than an Englishman." English commanders were reduced to stratagems such as calling a truce meeting and then offering the Indian leaders poisoned wine to seal the bargain. Captain John Smith, stuck in London for almost a decade, offered to go to Virginia and set things right. If he were given a force of 100 soldiers and 30 sailors, he claimed he could "enforce the Savages to leave their Country, or bring them in that fear and subjection that every man should follow their business securely." The company never even considered his offer seriously.

THE AFTERMATH

Leaders in England might talk boldly of how the colonists would strike at the Indians, but in reality life in Virginia was very hard, and reports telling the truth leaked back to England. George Sandys wrote to a company officer in London about the colony's plight and of "how the heavy hand of God hath suppressed us, the living being hardly able to bury the dead . . . I am afraid we have not lost less than 500 by sickness." John Rolfe was one of the dead from disease. Many more died in the fighting that followed

INDIAN WARRIOR. Captain John Smith wrote of this Susquehannock that "such great and well proportioned men, are seldom seen, for they seemed like Giants to the English." The Susquehannocks were situated near Delaware Bay and controlled the early fur trade throughout the region.

the uprising, Henry Spelman among them. Colonist Peter Arondelle wrote home that "Spelman's death is a just revenge," because "we ourselves have taught them how to be treacherous by our false dealing." Spelman was twenty-eight when he died and had been "one of the best Interpreters in the Land" half his life. As Arondelle wrote, "It is a great loss to us for that Captain was the best linguist of the Indian Tongue of this Country."

Young Richard Frethorne came to Martin's Hundred about Christmastime, 1622; he may have traveled on the *James*, which set sail on July 31, only a short while after news of the attack arrived in London. In March 1623 (one year after the attack), he wrote to his minister back in England and to his mother and father begging them to get him out of Virginia and to bring him back home. Martin's Hundred, he wrote, was "in great danger, for our Plantation is very weak." A full year after the surprise attack, he said they had only thirty-two fighting men, for when the "Rogues overcame this place last, they slew 80 Persons." They had not been able to plant crops the previous summer and food was so short, Frethorne wrote his parents, that "you have given more than my day's allowance to a beggar at the door."

Frethorne's only help and comfort came from another John Jackson, who was a gunsmith in Jamestown. Jackson befriended Frethorne when he accompanied the Martin's Hundred barge to Jamestown and gave him a place to stay out of the rain. Young Richard said that Jackson, who was like a second father to him, "much marveled that you would send me a servant to the Company. He said I had been better knocked on the head, and Indeed so I find it now to my great grief and misery, and [he] saith, that if you love me you will redeem me suddenly." Frethorne wrote that they were all awaiting the arrival of a supply ship, the *Seaflower*, and that his master had told all the servants they would be eating "the bark of trees, or mold of the Ground" if it did not come soon, and he concluded "I thought no head had been able to hold so much water as hath and doth daily flow from my eyes."

CAPTIVES

But Frethorne also reported some stunning news—not all those mourned as casualties of the 1622 attack were actually dead. He wrote that two Indians had been captured recently and the English had decided to "make slaves of them." These captives told them that some of the English who disappeared in 1622 had been taken as captives, "and now these two Indians that they have taken do tell us that the Indians have 15 alive with them." One of these was Jane Dickinson, who was ransomed from the Indians by Dr. Ralph Pott early in 1623. Jane's husband had been killed in the attack and she was taken prisoner. Ten months after her capture, and after "enduring much misery" among the "Cruel savages," "it pleased God so to dispose the hearts of the Indians" that they freed her and "divers others" for "a small ransom." Now, however, the unscrupulous Dr. Pott, who paid two pounds of beads for her release, was trying to force her to work for him indefinitely, saying that she had to work off both the remainder of her dead husband's term of servitude and the price of the ransom. Saying that her service with Dr. Pott "much differeth not from her slavery with the Indians," she petitioned the governor and council to release her from this obligation, "of the first by her widowhood, of the second by the law of nations, considering she hath already served ten months, too much for two pounds of beads."

Another captive was Anne Jackson, who had settled with her brother John at Martin's Hundred. We do not know what happened to her or how the links were set up, but in April of 1626 John Jackson and another man went "with certain Indians unto Pamunkey." In 1628 Anne turned up in Jamestown again. How she arrived back in English company is unknown, but the record hints that she may have become a "white Indian" and have been converted to the native way of life.

George Thorpe's original vision, of Indians and English coming together in a new Virginia society, was no longer thought desirable. Indians brought into the English plantations were now only made into slaves. But Anne Jackson's experience hinted at the possibility of another kind of coexistence, one in which *Indian* communities welcomed individual English men and women who made the commitment to live as Indians on terms of equality. On an individual level the Indians were able to accomplish what the English were not. Some of these men and women would later play the same interpreter's role as Henry Spelman and Thomas Savage.

There would be many such converts, most of them women, throughout the colonial period. The original plans had never seen this as a possibility—all the conversion was to be one way, from native to "civilized." And if there was one thing the English authorities thought they knew for sure, it was that women's lives were truly dreadful among the Indians. Therefore, the presence of Anne Jackson and the prospect of the sympathetic stories she might tell about Indian life were unsettling indeed. The Virginia General Court ordered "that Anne Jackson which Came from the Indians shall be sent for England with the first opportunity of Shipping and that her brother John Jackson shall give security for her passage and keep her safe till she be shipped aboard." The last part of the order is the tip-off. The court feared that if Anne Jackson were not kept "safe" in her brother's custody, she would make her way back to the Indians among whom she had lived for so long.

Anne Jackson's arrival back in London went unremarked, so we will never know how her stories of life among the Virginia Indians were received among her English friends and neighbors. The published and widely circulated Virginia Company denunciations of the Indians must have made a graphic impression. Anne Jackson's experience could have balanced that impression if she had been given a voice.

Richard Frethorne's fate is uncertain. He was gone from Martin's Hundred by early 1625, when a census of all the plantations was taken, but whether his parents redeemed him or he simply died we cannot know. The same census revealed healing in the Jackson family even before Anne's return. John Jackson and his wife, also named Ann, lived on at Martin's Hundred, and, while mourning the child killed in 1622, they now had a new baby, "a Child aged 20 weeks." Survivors like John Jackson and his wife Ann, who continued securely within the English plantations and who married and had children, were the people of the future in Virginia.

Patterns of Settlement to Mid-Seventeenth Century

True colonization began about 1620. Early attempts to settle had been tentative because planners had no clear idea what colonies were supposed to accomplish. Jamestown in Virginia, like Santa Fe in New Mexico, was fueled by dreams of gold. Such unrealistic aims led to a poor choice of colonists. The early colonies were all composed of single young men who had little interest in creating new societies—or even in remaining in America more than a few years. When no easily obtainable wealth was discovered, these same young men became unruly, and settlements crumbled.

By 1620 planners had come to realize several important truths about America. The only source of riches was the abundant furs, and these were soon depleted in most regions. Only the far north, the area of French settlement, continued to provide a great return of furs. The other product that was easily brought from America was fish, also from the far north. But neither of these products required colonies, and the fur trade flourished best when Indian life was not disturbed by farmers competing for their resources. The other goods backers had hoped to import from America—principally timber products, dyes, and drugs—either were not found or were more expensive to carry across the sea than they were worth.

Thus by 1620, all the old dreams were dead, and there seemed no reason to invest the huge sums of money necessary to found colonies.

But policy makers in Europe were beginning to think of America in new terms, and to see the lands across the ocean as a place to export excess population from Europe. These exported people could then *develop* valuable commodities to enrich themselves and their backers at home.

This new conception of colonization meant that men and women would leave Europe permanently, not expecting to be rotated home in a few years. They would come expecting to have families here, and their children would be Americans, wholly committed to the new land. After some experimentation and considerable disappointment, policy makers discovered that one thing was needed to lure such committed immigrants—land. Men and women would take the enormous step of leaving behind everything they had known and embarking for a new life in an uncertain world if they were promised land of their own which they could pass on to their children. Once backers had hit on this solution, the tiny trickle of colonists became a mighty stream. Land was the magnet that drew ordinary men and women to America.

This new way of thinking was possible about 1620 (slightly earlier or later in different locations) not only because experience of North America had been so disappointing, but also because the situation in Europe had become progressively worse. Since the early sixteenth century the population had been growing dramatically, and inflation of the money supply caused prices to rise. Incomes lagged far behind prices. More people were poor, and the poorest were poorer than before. The available land seemed insufficient for all who sought work. Now "wandering poor," people with no place to go, threatened the social order. Cold weather and poor harvests—produced by conditions so hostile that historians have dubbed the sixteenth and seventeenth centuries the Little Ice Age—created suffering, even occasional periods of famine. The situation was particularly bad in England, so many men and women were prepared to consider emigration to America now in hope of a better life and land of their own. Wealthy men were prepared to pay their passage as an investment in hope of enriching themselves and restoring order at home.

Another reason for emigration also became important at about this time—religious persecution or the fear of persecution in the future. This theme had already appeared in the attempt by French Protestants to settle in South Carolina and Florida in the middle of the sixteenth century. Now, in the seventeenth century, many Europeans feared that they would suffer for religious reasons, and America was attractive as a place where they could create communities of like-minded people and worship unmolested by the authorities. Because of the assumption that the people of any nation would follow the religion of the monarch, religion became a matter of political concern. Europe was exploding in wars over religion—the Thirty Years' War in Germany began in 1618 over the religious allegiance of the German states, France had been torn by religious strife between Roman Catholics and Protestants, and the Protestant Netherlands sought to free itself of control by Roman Catholic Spain. Often it was Protestants who fled persecution, but Maryland was founded by English Catholics fearing persecution by Protestants.

All these reasons—the offer of land and the independence that went with land ownership, and the hope of being free to follow their own consciences in a community of like-minded men and women—combined in the 1620s and 1630s to initiate a great rush of colonists to America's East Coast. Despite superficial differences, the colonies created at this time shared great similarities. The flow to all colonies involved a mixed group of all ages and both sexes. Some areas, such as Virginia, attracted a higher proportion of young, single men, but all regions put a premium on settlement by families.

All the colonial regions also went through a roughly similar pattern of relationship to the land and the Indians. All began with a period of experimentation and discouragement, with sickness at the beginning. All also built relatively good relations with neighboring Indians. But, as the colonies began to grow and spread over the land, each experienced a devastating period of warfare with displaced Indians that forced the colonies to confront the reality of colonization.

THE SOUTHWEST

These general patterns fit all the colonies on the East Coast more or less well. New Mexico in the West forms something of an exception, because it remained a small and distant outpost of New Spain in this period. Nonetheless, the twin themes of land and religion operated in New Mexico. The little fort at Santa Fe was renewed at the end of the 1620s and in the 1630s by the migration of a small but steadfast group of married soldiers and their families who settled on the land. In 1629 Santa Fe also received an expedition of thirty Spanish Franciscan priests led by Fray Estevan de Perea and dedicated, with the help of the twenty or so priests already in New Mexico, to creating a successful mission to the Indians that would replace the native religion with Christianity. They also sought to sustain the little settlement that Juan de Oñate had founded at Santa Fe two decades earlier. Indian resistance had been met with harsh reprisals by Oñate, culminating in the destruction of the pueblo of Acoma and the enslavement of all its people in 1599; every man had been sentenced to haveone foot cut off to prevent any future rebellions. Thus the Indians had learned the price of resistance, but they had also been cured of any interest in supporting colonization. Oñate was punished for his deeds when he returned to the Spanish authorities, but the damage was done in New Mexico.

In the 1630s, the priests, committed by their vows to a life of poverty and service, hoped to make the Indians see another side of Spanish culture, one that would win their love as well as their fear. Fifty mission churches already existed in New Mexico. The Indians, knowing the price of resistance, allowed the friars into their pueblos. Soon reports of 86,000 baptisms and many miracles were brought to Europe by Fray Alonso de Benavides, who had led the missions in New Mexico since 1626. At about the same time Franciscans were also moving beyond St. Augustine to establish missions among the Florida Indians.

Christian missionaries, whether Protestant English or Roman Catholic Spanish, all believed fervently that one could not be a Christian without living in a "civilized" manner, that is, in the European style. The missionaries always worked to convince the Indians to adopt their cultural patterns in dress, marriage, and government. Like George Thorpe in Virginia the Spanish Franciscans introduced the Indians to European goods, hoping to bring them to Christianity by making them desire what the Christians had. A Franciscan in Florida echoed Thorpe's emphasis on the "Book of the World" when he said "this world is the route to the other ... gifts can break rocks." Also like Thorpe, the Franciscans' greatest hopes lay in educating Indian children.

Initial enthusiasm and hopes gave way to the realization that in many cases the Indians had simply added the Christian religion to their own pantheon and had added European practices rather than relinquishing traditional ways. As priests increasingly attempted to force Indian converts to give up all native practices, resistance became overt. Conflict also developed between the priests and Spanish governmental officials in New Mexico. Each side accused the other of mistreating the Indians under their control. So extreme was this friction that the Franciscans actually excommunicated three of the New Mexico governors and denounced others to the Inquisition in Mexico. Such infighting made the Indians more skeptical of the values the Spanish brought with them. For many reasons, Santa Fe remained small, but Spain was committed to keeping the settlement alive.

THE CHESAPEAKE

VIRGINIA

Virginia entered a period of enormous growth after 1618. The colony had suffered through a long period of conflict and disaffection among the colonists. Now it was entering a new phase, initiating the trial-and-error process by which promoters began to understand what it would take to create a successful and thriving colony.

When Pocahontas married John Rolfe, peace settled over Virginia for a time, giving the struggling settlers badly needed breathing room. Economic security came through Rolfe's experiments with tobacco. The colony would not be attractive to immigrants and backers without some product of value that could be sold in Europe. Tobacco was to be that product. The native Virginia tobacco was considered too harsh, so Rolfe experimented with more acceptable West Indian strains until he found one that could flourish in Chesapeake conditions. When this tobacco began to sell in England, the Virginia economy entered a period of growth that was soon to produce a boom, based, as the skeptics said, "on smoke."

Now that the economic future looked brighter, Virginia Company promoters in London began to consider how the settlement could be made secure. The backers knew that a critical mass of colonists must be created by adding more immigrants to the 350 there in 1616. Tobacco culture was labor-intensive, so if it were to succeed on the scale necessary, many hands would be needed. Moreover, if the colony were ever to be more than just an outpost, it would have to be filled with people who intended to stay, not temporary employees expecting to be rotated home after a tour of duty. So the Virginia Company began to think in terms of true transplantation of English society.

The transformation of Virginia into a successful agricultural colony involved more than just sending people. They would have to be the right kind of people, committed to a future of hard work. The promoters also realized (as Raleigh had thirty years before) that a settlement composed primarily of men would always fail. Only colonies that contained a fair proportion of women ever succeeded. This was true partly because women's skills in food preservation and clothing manufacture were essential to survival. But more importantly, unless settlers had families to work for, they had no real commitment to the land. Families were encouraged to emigrate and women were recruited to go to the colony as servants and prospective brides.

Thousands of colonists went over in the years after 1618, attracted by a new set of offers the Virginia Company made, which introduced the principle of private property to the plantations. Most colonists went as indentured servants, which meant they agreed to work a specified number of years in return for their passage over. Servitude was a normal part of life in England. Traditionally, English men and women left their parents' home at about the age of fourteen. The lucky few with relatively wealthy parents became apprentices. The master to whom a boy was apprenticed promised to teach him his trade and to place him on the track that would allow him eventually to become a member of a guild. Guilds controlled the skilled professions, which were open only to those who entered through prescribed channels.

Most young adults in England became servants. Each fall, hiring fairs were held around the country, where servants and masters negotiated contracts that bound them together for one full year. A servant found away from the master's farm or shop at any time during the year would be whipped and returned. Similarly, the master, even if disaster befell him, was required to keep the servant and provide food, housing, and clothing for the entire year. This system gave servants a degree of control over their lives. If a master had a bad reputation, servants avoided him. This tradition of servitude was adapted to become the indentured servitude that brought servants to the American colonies.

The system of servitude through annual contracts allowed men and women to prepare for adult life and learn a craft. Servitude was a stage of life rather than a social condition. Even families that could afford to have servants might put their own children out as servants. After about a decade spent in such contracts, servants accumulated enough money to marry and set up a separate household. Young men and women, because they were on their own and often some distance from home by the time they married in their mid-twenties, chose their own marriage partners. The couple then built a new network of friends and neighbors when they settled down.

When the system was working well, most families had some land and a place to live. The landlord, often the local lord of the manor, would oversee the life of the area, dispensing justice and regulating relationships. Village life centered on the church, which offered social activities such as festivals and church ales as well as religious functions. Most English people identified with their local area. When they referred to their "country," they usually meant their county.

Now, with the population explosion and economic hard times, much of this traditional order seemed to be breaking up, and many were forced to face the fact that they would never have a place of their own in England. It was for this reason that the plan of emigration to America began to make sense to young English men and women.

The Virginia Company realized that colonists would work hard to make the venture succeed only if they were promised land of their own. Why should they labor to enrich investors in London? Now each servant, man or woman, was guaranteed fifty acres when the indenture was up. Also, those who paid the way of another or bought a share of stock in the Virginia Company were guaranteed fifty acres for each transaction as well. This "headright" system seemed to offer genuine opportunity, and many ordinary men and women took up the offer.

The plan would work only if some wealthy men put up money in advance to get the prospective colonists to Virginia, and this would only happen if profits were offered in return. Huge resources were needed to finance the colony's development, so the Virginia Company offered groups of Englishmen the chance to claim huge tracts of land in Virginia if they would take responsibility for sending over their own colonists and providing them with equipment and supplies. These "particular plantations," including Martin's Hundred, were like a series of small corporations—franchises—within the main Virginia Company, and many who invested in them reaped handsome rewards.

With new incentives in place both for going over as a colonist and for investing in sending settlers, the population grew by leaps and bounds, and the plantations quickly spread along the James River. The company allowed the colonists to form a general assembly (later to become the House of Burgesses), the first representative body in English America, to discuss common problems. This momentous step was a practical solution to the colonial government's inability to impose laws on all the settlements; it was far better that the planters agree on what should be done. John Rolfe wrote a letter home giving news of the assembly's first meeting in June 1619. He also noted the arrival of twenty Africans sold to the settlers as servants.

As the plantations spread along the river, seizing the best land in Virginia, the pressure on the Indians became intolerable. Powhatan died in 1618, just as the tobacco boom began. He never learned how badly his strategy had failed. His brother, Opechancanough, took over leadership of the confederacy and, by 1622, determined to stop the English once and for all through the

SETTLED LIFE IN VIRGINIA. This engraving by Theodore DeBry argues visually that colonists could live a normal life in America.

great attack of March 22, 1622. Almost 350 English colonists fell that day.

News of the attack hit the Virginia Company hard but the subsequent investigation yielded far more stunning information: the 350 killed by Indians were just a fraction of total deaths. Of the thousands sent to Virginia under the new plan, most had died. The colony had been ill-prepared to receive them. Food and housing were inadequate. Moreover, the environment was unhealthy for newcomers throughout the Chesapeake. Malaria, introduced in a mild form by the English and later in a more deadly form from Africa, killed many throughout the seventeenth century. Most immigrants were sickly during their first two years, as their bodies became acclimatized to the malaria parasite. During this period, known as the "seasoning," large numbers, sometimes up to half, of newcomers succumbed. If colonists survived two years, their chances of living a normal span were good, but most in the region were sickly all their lives, and even the normal life span there was short by the standards of English colonies to the north.

Only a portion of this picture could be seen in the 1620s. When the royal investigators looked at Virginia after 1622, they realized that, of 3,000 people sent to Virginia since 1618, less than one-third were alive when the Indians attacked. Negligence and bad planning had killed many more English subjects than the Indians had. Gossips in England now said that the whole enterprise was nothing more than "a more regulated kind of killing of men." The king could not allow his subjects to be condemned to death through the bad management of a private company. He took the charter away from the Virginia Company in 1624, making Virginia the first royal colony, with a governor appointed by the king. The phase of privately sponsored colonization was over in Virginia, though joint-stock companies would be allowed to found later settlements.

From the colony's standpoint, however, development went on as before. As long as economic conditions remained dismal in England, people would continue to take a chance on America. Terrible death rates were not enough to stem the flow of hopeful servants and planters, and tobacco production expanded at an incredible rate. In the 1630s thousands of English immigrants poured into the Chesapeake region and spread over the land. In 1615, colonists had exported 2,000 pounds of tobacco; in 1620, it was 40,000 pounds; and by 1629, 1,500,000 pounds. Virginia was growing according to a pattern that would typify the South: concentration on a single crop, sometimes to the exclusion even of growing their own food.

Growth was even greater in the 1630s, the decade of huge migration to all the colonies. Almost 9,000 men and women came to the Chesapeake during that ten-year period, and the tobacco colonies were firmly established.

Opechancanough had not stopped the process, and he saw his people suffer through ten years of murderous warfare after 1622 while the plantations expanded at an even greater rate. In 1644 he tried again with another great attack. This time he was so old that he had to be carried out to watch the fighting on a stretcher. Again, casualties were high, but the colony was now too strong and the English population too large.

The Indians carried out this 1644 attack in a fatalistic spirit, preferring death to the life of a conquered people. Those who survived the colony's punitive warfare were forced to acknowledge the Virginians' dominion over them. Now no barrier remained to the rapid expansion of the English population throughout the region in the search for new land for tobacco.

Tobacco was the gold of Virginia. Though concentration on one crop brought problems, it provided a firm foundation for an English presence in America. The pattern was set, and the lessons learned. All future English colonies would be made up of families. All colonists would come expecting to mix their labor with the American soil to produce commodities to sustain them. And settlers would come to create new societies, expecting to live out their lives in their new homes.

MARYLAND

The other Chesapeake colony was Maryland, founded in 1634 at the height of the great influx of new colonists into America. Maryland was created as a religious refuge for Roman Catholics who feared future persecution in England even though King Charles I was sympathetic to their plight, and authorized the colony. Only Maryland of all the colonies founded in this period was a proprietary colony belonging to one man, Cecilius Calvert, Lord Baltimore. All other colonies founded in the 1620s and 1630s were settled by companies created for the purpose.

Even though the entire colony belonged to him, Lord Baltimore faced the problem the Virginia Company had confronted earlier—the land was worthless without labor to develop it. The colony had to be populated in order to make it successful, and the only way to populate it was through the headright system—the offer of land to all comers—combined with indentured servitude. Thus although it looked very different on paper, Maryland's economy and society followed Virginia's model.

Contemporaries called Maryland "a good poor man's country," meaning that immigrants, if they survived the dangerous seasoning, could become landowners and substantial citizens, even officeholders. Most colonists in Maryland, as elsewhere on America's East Coast, lived on farms of a few hundred acres in the seventeenth century, and families worked on their farms alongside servants. One persistent problem, however, was the unfavorable sex ratio of approximately three men for every woman. Wives' roles in the household were crucial, and their commitment to the family's success often led them to go out and work in the fields with the men in the early years, work that women in England did not do. Moreover the logic of the colonial situation demanded that men and women marry and have children. The enormous gamble involved in emigrating and the drive required to survive the period of servitude and build a farm all made sense only if colonists had families to inherit the stake they had created. Passing land on to one's children was the ultimate goal.

In order to achieve the goal of security for themselves and their families, Maryland's Catholics, like the Puritans in New England, settled together around their churches and supported each other. Since life expectancy, even for those who survived seasoning, was relatively short, neighbors often took on the task of raising orphaned children and even of overseeing their inheritance. Neighbors thus assumed the roles that kin would have played in England.

Maryland had already been settled by a large number of Virginia Protestants when it was founded as a separate colony in 1634, and Protestants continued to come into the colony from Virginia. Thus, although there were Catholic districts, Maryland could not be an exclusive Catholic preserve and had to create a system that would allow all colonists to live together in peace. In 1649 the English parliament, led by the Puritans who had won the Civil War, executed Charles I. The Puritans, under the leadership of Oliver Cromwell, took control of the government, and their regime lasted until 1660. Maryland's Catholics feared that they would lose their privileges, especially if Protestant colonists complained of persecution. Therefore in 1649, under Governor William Stone, a Protestant, the assembly passed the "Act Concerning Religion," which guaranteed freedom of worship to all "professing to believe in Jesus Christ," and forbidding colonists to call each other "heretic, Schismatic, Idolater, Puritan, Independent, Presbyterian, popish priest, Jesuit, Jesuited papist, Lutheran, Calvinist, Anabaptist, Brownist, Antinomian, Barrowist, Roundhead, Separatist." Although there were to be many clashes between Protestants and Catholics, the principle of toleration was firmly established.

NEW ENGLAND

In 1620 while Virginia's tobacco economy was becoming established, a colony of Puritan separatists and others were settling Plymouth in New England. A decade later the colony of Massachusetts Bay was founded at Boston, and the flow of immigrants, both to New England and to the Chesapeake, became a torrent.

PURITANISM

New England was settled largely by Puritans, men and women who wished to push the Church of England to become more Protestant. The Church of England, although it rejected the authority of the pope, had retained many of the ceremonies and the hierarchical structure of the Roman Catholic Church. Puritans, like many other Protestants, argued for decentralization and allowing each congregation to govern itself. They adhered to the doctrine of the priesthood of all believers, arguing that all who were true believers had the same access directly to God and the same duty to interpret God's word in the Bible. Ordained priests and their superiors, the bishops, thus had no right to tell other Christians what to believe.

Puritans believed in predestination, the idea that no one could become a true believer without the aid of God's grace. They believed that human beings are naturally so sinful that they cannot approach God in a truly pure-hearted way. God, because he is all-loving, selects some for salvation and gives them grace, the power to believe. All other humans are condemned because of their sins. To human beings this choice must seem arbitrary, because humans cannot see as God sees, but the choices are all made according to God's master plan that has existed from the beginning of the world. Those who were saved were called the Elect, the chosen.

Although they knew that they could do nothing to cause God to choose them, Puritans did believe that they could create some of the preconditions for the godly life. They argued that the Church of England should be stripped of all ceremonies and practices that were not mentioned in the biblical description of the life of Christ or in the early churches set up by the apostles. And they stressed preaching that stirred the heart, spontaneous prayer, and Bible study to open the hearts of the congregation instead of set ceremonies. Puritans stressed literacy, arguing that the priesthood of all believers required each Christian to read and interpret the word of God.

Most Puritans were content to work within their own congregations to try to bring the Church of England closer to their way of thinking. In the early years of the seventeenth century, many of the bishops in England actually favored the Puritan point of view and allowed experimentation. Some Puritans, however, thought that such gradual change would not work, and argued for separation from the Church of England and withdrawal into self-governing congregations. These were often called Brownists after an early separatist thinker. Few people, even other Puritans, approved of the separatists, because they were prepared to abandon all those still within the Church of England and to see them damned.

PLYMOUTH

Although Puritanism within the Church of England was widely tolerated in the early seventeenth century, separatism was not. Therefore separatists left England and settled in Holland, the only country in Europe that offered religious toleration. One group went there in 1607, the year that Jamestown was founded. The separatists thrived in Holland, but they longed for a chance to live in an English land again, and accepted the opportunity offered by the new concept of colonization in America to try to create a community that would be both English and congenial to their religious beliefs. In 1620 the Pilgrims who had gone to Holland in 1607 crossed the ocean to found the little colony of Plymouth in Massachusetts. New England had a bad reputation in England as a cold and forbidding place with little to offer, a land, as Captain John Smith wrote "more to affright than to delight one." Smith, who believed that New England offered rich possibilities for settlers of the right sort, nonetheless acknowledged that the country had been "esteemed as a cold, barren, mountainous, rocky Desert." Those reports suited the Pilgrims perfectly, because they hoped to be left alone in their refuge.

William Bradford, Plymouth's long-serving governor, kept a journal in which he recorded the development of the little colony. *Of Plymouth Plantation* was rediscovered and published only a little over a century ago. He portrayed the arriving Pilgrims as falling on their knees to thank God, "who had brought them over the vast and furious ocean" and "set their feet on the firm and stable earth."

Plymouth colony was funded by a joint-stock company, merchants who invested in the hopes of making a profit. The backers were not particularly interested in the project's religious mission, except that it would give the immigrants a stronger sense of purpose. The company's sponsorship created a continuing problem, as the colonists, like those in Virginia earlier, were under intense pressure to begin reimbursing their backers. So burdensome was this pressure and interference that after a few years the colonists agreed to pool their resources and assumed the burden of the entire debt just to end their relationship with the merchants.

The Pilgrims had left England with a patent authorizing them to set up a particular plantation in Virginia. Other separatists from Holland did go to Virginia at the same time. But the Plymouth colonists went to New England instead. They chose this location because it would keep others away from them, but they did not have any legal authorization to settle or govern themselves in New England. The backers had forced them to take a large number of skilled men who were not Puritans to help build and protect the settlement, but now that the patent was no longer valid, these "strangers" were not bound to obey the Pilgrim leaders. In order to solve this problem the leaders brought together all the free (that is, not servants) adult men while they were still on their ship, the *Mayflower*. These men worked out a simple statement outlining the principles by which they would agree to be governed, and formally setting the colony up as a "Civil Body Politic." Forty-one men then signed the Mayflower Compact, signifying that they would abide by the decisions made by the government created under it "for the general good." Like the assembly in Virginia, the Mayflower Compact reflected leaders' understanding that in the colonial context government must have the consent of the governed.

The Pilgrims set up a democratic form of government. Each adult male head of a household of good character was eligible to be a freeman, to vote and hold office. At first all voters came together to make decisions, but after 1638 Plymouth moved to a representative system in which each town elected delegates to the assembly, called the General Court. The governor and his council were also elected. The General Court was responsible for handing out land grants, and, despite the misgivings of some leaders who wanted the colonists to live compactly together, the colony spread rapidly with generous grants.

Partly because it remained relatively small in numbers, Plymouth had relatively peaceful relationships with its Indian neighbors, chiefly the Wampanoags. The Pilgrims' leadership worked hard to regulate these relationships, especially the acquisition of Indian land. But the Indians also had shrewd leadership in the person of the Wampanoag chief Massasoit, who realized that he could make use of the new group of people in his midst. In the autumn of 1621 when the Pilgrims had brought in their first harvest, Massasoit visited them with "some ninety men." Pilgrim hunters had shot some "fowl," and Massasoit's men "went out and killed five Deer." Together the English and Wampanoags feasted for three days. Edward Winslow, who wrote this account of the first Thanksgiving, concluded his letter home by saying "And although it be not always so plentiful, as it was at this time with us, yet by the goodness of God, we are so far from want, that we often wish you partakers of our plenty."

In order to keep an eye on the Pilgrims and to make sure that Massasoit's interpretation of events prevailed, his ally, named Squanto, went to live with them. Squanto is one of the most remarkable men in early American history. He had been kidnapped by an unscrupulous English ship captain along with nineteen others, and sold into

MASSACHUSETTS BAY COMPANY SEAL. The legend issuing from the Indian's mouth is a quotation from the Acts of the Apostles in the Bible, in which St. Paul tells about his dream in which "a man of Macedonia" appeared to him and said "Come over into Macedonia and help us."

slavery in Spain in 1614. Somehow he escaped and made his way across Europe to England, where he made contact with men interested in the development of New England. His new friends arranged for his return to Cape Cod, and he arrived back just before the Pilgrims came there. Squanto found that his entire tribe, the Patuxets, had died in a massive epidemic that had spread over the land in 1616. In fact, the Pilgrims took over the Patuxets' cleared fields and house sites for their original settlement. Squanto was thus coming home when he came to live at Plymouth.

Squanto served as an interpreter and go-between for the Pilgrims, but he was not just their tool. He clearly shaped their relationships with neighboring Indian tribes in ways that he chose, and he was widely respected, even feared, by other natives. Squanto, like many others on both the Indian and the European sides, found that his life was completely changed by colonization. Faced with such conditions, he invented a new role that allowed him to live a useful and satisfying life.

The colony was overshadowed by the foundation of the megacolony of Massachusetts Bay in 1630, but Plymouth kept its independent existence as the "Old Colony" until it was absorbed by Massachusetts in 1691.

MASSACHUSETTS BAY

At the end of its first decade, in 1630, little Plymouth colony was swamped by the creation of a huge settlement centered on Massachusetts Bay. This colony was settled by more mainstream Puritans, those who were prepared to work within the Church of England to bring change. They hoped that by emigrating to America and creating proper models of churches and religious communities they could create a model for those back in England. The colony's leader, John Winthrop, spoke to the first contingent of settlers on board ship as they ventured to America, and he told them that "the eyes of all people are upon us." In a famous simile that has often been repeated, he said "we must Consider that we shall be as a City upon a Hill." Winthrop warned that if the colonists failed to live up to their goals, God would withdraw his support, and "we shall be made a story and a by-word through the world."

Massachusetts Bay's founders had studied the early difficulties in other colonies, and they aimed to correct errors that others had made. First, all earlier colonies had begun small—Roanoke, Jamestown, and Plymouth all began with just over 100 people. Massachusetts Bay began with several thousand brought in a great fleet of ships. The settlers provided a huge pool of aid and comfort to each other as they quickly set up several towns. Settlers continued to pour into New England during the 1630s, and the people in the colony supported themselves by selling supplies to the newcomers.

Secondly, all other colonies had suffered from interference from backers in London, who had hounded the colonists about repaying them for their huge investment and had tried to control events in the colony from afar. The Massachusetts Bay settlers made sure that they would not suffer in this way. The colony's leaders refused to go unless the sponsors allowed them to take their charter with them. With the charter safely in Boston, the leaders in America could control the settlement's development. The company charter was converted into the colony's government, with the board of directors serving as the council.

Thirdly, other colonies had not had much control over selection of prospective settlers. Massachusetts Bay was the first colony that exercised careful control over the choice of colonists and ensured that almost everyone who came believed in the same goals. Moreover, Massachusetts Bay had the most balanced population from the beginning, with a relatively normal distribution of men and women and all ages. Families were an important part of the immigrant stream.

Finally, all other colonies had been plagued by money problems from the beginning. Investors had put in huge sums and expected to be repaid quickly. The prominent Puritans who helped finance Massachusetts Bay did not make such demands. Moreover, many of the families who chose emigration had some funds of their own, having actually sold property in England to pay for the voyage. Thus they did not begin their American life burdened by debt as indentured servants did. Instead, they brought money with them and were able to buy their supplies from settlers who had arrived before them.

All these new approaches were necessitated by dramatic change in England. Not only was the English economy in terrible shape at the end of the 1620s, but the government and Church of England together seemed to be committed to forcing Puritans to conform. England seemed headed on a collision course to disaster. In 1629 King Charles I dissolved the parliament and vowed to rule without it. While the king began to violate the constitution in his search for ways to tax his subjects without parliament's consent during the 1630s, church authorities began to prosecute leading Puritan ministers, who were forced to flee the country or go into hiding. Puritans believed in Providence, the idea that Christians could read God's will by looking at events. The terrible economic conditions, combined with bad harvests and harsh winters, and new outbreaks of the bubonic plague, convinced Puritans that God was trying to tell England that the country must reform. Puritan preachers pictured God as standing on the threshold preparing to leave England if the country did not reform. Because the king and the head of the church seemed determined to keep on the wrong course, they argued that they must save themselves by creating a new England across the ocean. Because the stakes were so high, wealthy Puritans were willing to give money, and substantial men and women were prepared to give up everything and start life anew.

Because the colony began with such large numbers, it very quickly spread over the land. An early party had created a settlement at Salem, and the main group in 1630 centered on Boston. Within the first year the Boston settlement had spun off several more communities, and, with more than a thousand people coming in each year, the process of new town formation continued. The Massachusetts Bay leaders modified the headright system of the earlier colonies. Instead of granting land to individuals, a large grant for an entire town would be given to a group of settlers, often people who had emigrated together

In America, where the system could be designed from scratch, major rifts appeared. One area of conflict concerned theology, and particularly the idea that humans could not save themselves, but must be chosen by God to be saved. Ministers, in order to help their congregations face the awesome question of whether they were among the Elect, began to preach about the steps to conversion, breaking the process down into many small stages. Some members of the congregations were offended by this, arguing that such preaching implied that men and women could actually control the process, and they accused the ministers of deviating from the true Puritan message.

JOHN WINTHROP. Winthrop, a lawyer and member of the minor county gentry in England, became the great leader of Massachusetts Bay.

from the same part of England. This founding group would form both a town government and a church congregation. These would then grant newcomers land within the town and a part in the town government. When the elders judged the town to be full, more recent arrivals would be directed to another newly opening community. Families sometimes moved once or several times before settling permanently in a community. This system ensured orderly settlement, and the perpetuation of the Puritan system wherever farms were opened up.

Massachusetts Bay was spared the problems that other colonies had, but it generated its own problems, many of which had to do with the settlers' Puritanism. In England, where they had been forced to work within the existing system, Puritans could agree on what needed to be done.

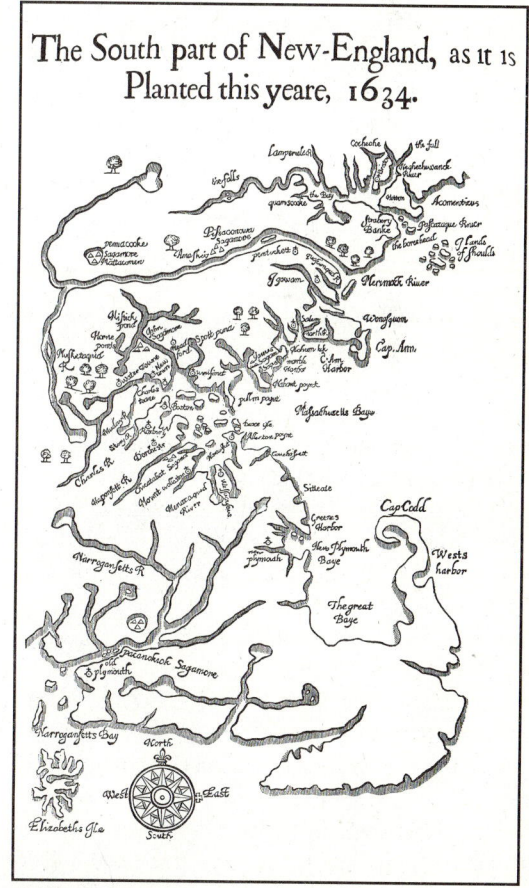

MAP OF NEW ENGLAND from William Wood's *New England's Prospect* (1634), showing the dramatic spread of new towns in the first few years of Massachusetts Bay.

By the middle of the 1630s this conflict had reached crisis proportions. One parishioner in particular, Anne Hutchinson, began to accuse the ministers in public. The doctrine of the priesthood of all believers implied that women as well as men could be priests. But when Anne Hutchinson's discussion groups of neighborhood women began to grow larger and to attract men as well as women, the authorities decided to act. Hutchinson's movement had grown so large and so militant that it seemed to threaten to tear the colony apart. The ministers tried Hutchinson for "erroneous opinions," and, although her knowledge of the Bible was equal to that of the university-trained ministers, they found her guilty of claiming that she had had direct revelations from God and expelled her and many of her followers from the colony.

Roger Williams, originally an honored man among the ministers in Massachusetts Bay, also began to take up radical ideas that the colony's leaders found dangerous. He argued that the colonists were hypocrites if they did not become separatists and denounce the practices of the Church of England. He also criticized the legal basis on which English settlers took over Indian lands. Williams was also expelled.

Roger Williams moved south of Massachusetts Bay and founded the colony of Rhode Island, where Anne Hutchinson and others critical of developments to the north found refuge. Rhode Island, like Maryland in the Chesapeake, offered religious toleration to the variety of people who fled there. Williams became a convert to the Baptist religion, and the first Baptist church in America was founded in Rhode Island in the year 1639.

Another area of conflict that developed in Massachusetts Bay by the middle of the 1630s concerned the connection between religion and government. No one who was not a member of a congregation was allowed to vote or hold office. In the early days, anyone who professed Puritanism could become a church member. But by the middle of the 1630s the churches had taken to examining those who applied for membership to see if they were truly among the Elect. Each candidate had to describe his or her conversion experience and the congregation then judged whether it was acceptable. Critics argued that only God could judge people's hearts, and that such a practice could only encourage hypocrisy. The most dramatic story would be the most compelling, whereas the true convert might be much more quiet about the experience.

Some leaders were particularly troubled about restricting voting and office-holding to those the congregations thought were "Visible Saints," and saw this as a perversion of the English system of government. Thomas Hooker, one of New England's most honored ministers, felt so strongly about this that he led a party of people to found Hartford on the Connecticut River. In Connecticut civil and religious life were strictly separated.

The Hooker party's trek was one of several that went to settle along the Connecticut River, a major trade route, in the middle of the 1630s. These settlements were related to another great conflict in the New England colonies, the Pequot War of 1636–1637. The Pequot Indians had become powerful because of their prime location on the shore of Long Island Sound. They and their rivals, the Narragansetts of Rhode Island, played pivotal roles in the early trade with the Dutch and English, even before settlement, and the Pequots had established overlord relationships with smaller and less powerful tribes living along the Connecticut River. Dutch traders had moved up the river and built a trading post near Hartford in 1633. Plymouth colony had also established a trading post on the river. These European traders began to deal directly with the river tribes. When Massachusetts Bay colonists also began to move onto the river in large numbers a year or two later, the Pequots sought to keep control over their tribes and to control the trade.

Several incidents occurred, and Massachusetts Bay, in consultation with other New England colonists, decided that they must make war on the Pequots before the Pequots made war on them. They interpreted the Pequots as tyrants and saw the war as a way of freeing the smaller tribes. Some tribes, notably the Mohegans, de-

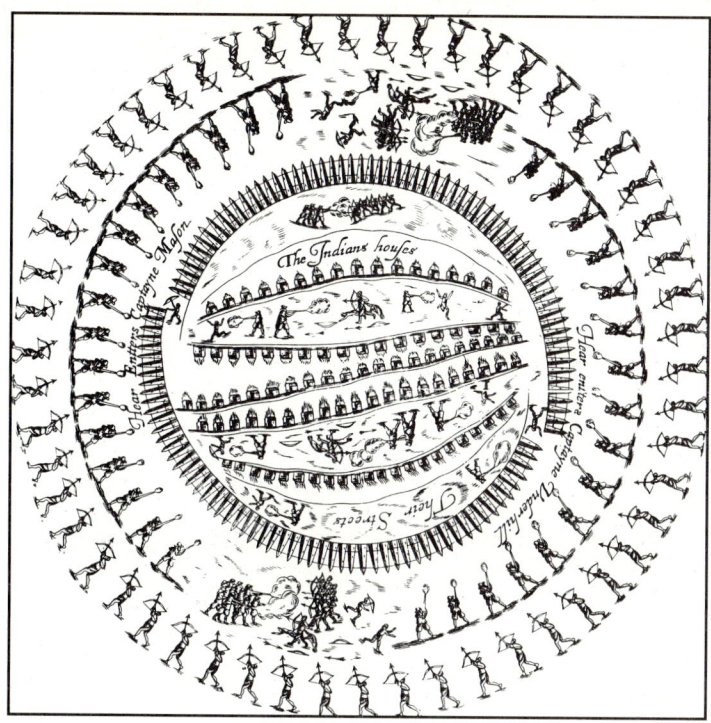

PEQUOT FORT AT MYSTIC, from John Underhill's *Newes from America*. Underhill was a military leader in the Pequot War, and this stylized picture shows the Pequots desperately trying to escape their burning fort as the English marksmen pick them off.

cided to fight on the English side, and the Narragansetts remained neutral, which helped the English.

The war culminated when the English forces surrounded the major Pequot fort near Mystic, Connecticut. The English set the fort on fire and shot the Indians as they fled. Somewhere between 300 and 500 Indians—old men, women, and children as well as fighting men—were killed. The Indians were astonished at the ferocity of this kind of warfare, which was alien to them. Their war was mostly fought to obtain captives or goods and, as one Englishman wrote, "they might fight seven years and not kill seven men." Captain John Underhill, who led the forces at Mystic, reported the reaction of the Narragansett allies: "Our Indians came to us, and much rejoiced at our victories, and greatly admired the manner of English men's fight: but cried *mach it, mach it*; that is, it is naught, it is naught, because it is too furious, and slays too many men." The defeated Pequots were disbanded, and the male leaders sold into slavery in the West Indies. But all Indians in southern New England now realized the price of resistance. It would be many years before Indians tried again to block the flow of settlement.

Meanwhile life in Massachusetts Bay was settling into permanent patterns, and leaders were concerned about creating secure economic foundations. All colonies had to find a product that could be sent back to Europe to pay for manufactured goods they desperately needed. In Virginia that product was tobacco. In New England this problem was delayed because the colony's economy was sustained for the first ten years by the steady influx of new settlers, all of whom brought goods with them as well as money to buy supplies when they landed and began to build houses.

But after 1640 the great flow of new colonists slowed back to a trickle. War broke out in England between the king's supporters and the parliament, led by the Puritans. It no longer seemed necessary to emigrate in order to protect the Puritan religion. Now the New England colonies were plunged into a deep recession, and they anxiously sought a secure economic footing. Most New Englanders produced basic foodstuffs on their farms. They could feed themselves, but not produce an income. Self-sufficiency was the preferred solution, but experimentation convinced colonial leaders that they could not produce the cloth and metal goods they would need for such a large population. The answer lay in trade. New Englanders began to ship fish to Europe and to trade their agricultural surplus to other colonial regions, particularly the Chesapeake and the islands of the West Indies. This began the process of tying the colonial regions together.

MIDDLE COLONIES

NEW NETHERLAND

In the Middle Colonies, as in the Chesapeake and New England, settlement began on a small scale in the 1620s and accelerated in the 1630s. In 1624, a tiny group of thirty families came to found New Netherland. Rather than being concentrated, these families were spread out in order to establish the Dutch claims. Some were deposited on Governor's Island, others along the Connecticut shore, on the Delaware River, and at Albany (Fort Orange). This plan was unworkable, and when Governor Peter Minuit took control in 1626, he concentrated the settlers on Manhattan Island. Minuit energetically took control and set the settlers to work providing houses for the colonists, and a mill to grind their grain as well as a fort. The little colony was expensive to maintain, and it remained small; many colonists even returned to Europe in the early years. The Netherlands, as the only country in Europe offering toleration, attracted a wide variety of people. New Netherland mirrored its parent, and was composed of peoples from all over Europe speaking many different languages. It was extremely difficult to achieve any sense of unity among this disparate population.

New Netherland faced the same problem as the English colonies—how to attract settlers to develop the land, and how to pay for their passage. Holland did not have the same kind of economic crisis that England faced in the early seventeenth century, so the problem was even more difficult to solve. In 1628 the company instituted the patroonship system, which in some ways was similar to the particular plantation system in Virginia. The aim in both cases was to grant land only to investors who brought over people to work on the land, thereby transferring the cost of colonization to wealthy individuals. New Netherland's system differed from the Virginia plan in that patroons had more powers; for example, they had jurisdiction over criminal cases within their plantations. Patroons, who were required to pay the Indians for their land, were given huge grants on condition that they settle fifty families on the land at their own expense within four years.

Most successful among the early patroonships was that around Albany settled by Kiliaen van Rensselaer. By choosing a site high up on the river, Van Rensselaer hoped to control the flow of furs down the Hudson River. The river had become a major colonial trade artery from the time of its discovery twenty years earlier and had been carefully sounded and charted. The new patroonship's location also linked it to the Mohawk River valley and its trade.

The fur trade was crucial to the development of New Netherland, as symbolized by the colony's seal—a beaver surrounded by wampum. The Dutch pioneered the use of wampum, made from Long Island Sound quahog shells, in the fur trade. Although wampum had always been important to American Indians for its spiritual and ceremonial value, it now became a kind of money, and prices were given in lengths (called

NEW AMSTERDAM, 1651.

fathoms) of wampum strings. Europeans even sometimes used wampum as money in trading with each other. But the fur trade also retarded the growth of New Netherland because the major investors in Europe tried to keep a monopoly of the trade for themselves. Most patroonships failed because this company monopoly made them unprofitable, and the population of New Netherland remained small throughout the 1630s.

In 1637 Willem Kieft became governor, and he set out to bring order and a sense of purpose to the colony through strict rule. At the same time, the company back in Holland decided to confront the problem of populating the colony. The investors finally gave up their monopoly of the fur trade and offered land free to families that would come over to farm. This new scheme was codified in the Charter of Freedoms and Exemptions issued in 1640, which promised

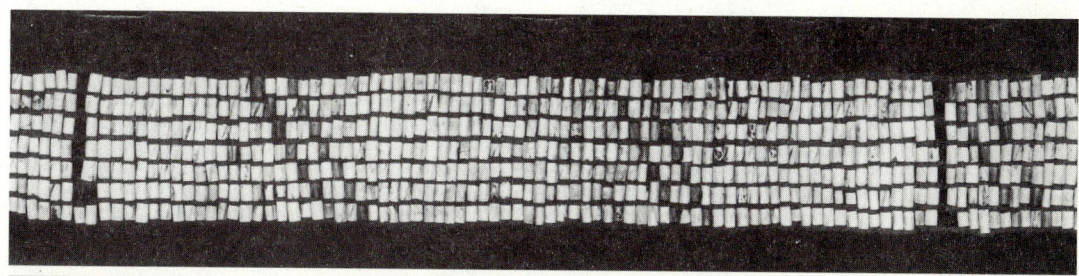

WAMPUM BELT. These belts, which had spiritual significance, were used to carry messages, and record treaties. Badges of office made of wampum were worn by Indian leaders.

200 acres free to anyone who brought a family of five, including servants. Patroons could still achieve large land grants if they paid for more settlers' transportation. Under this new system more colonists were attracted to New Netherland.

The colony's growth provoked a devastating Indian war between 1641 and 1645, that threatened to wipe out the settlements along the Hudson River. As in other colonies on the East Coast, the war was caused by large new demands for land as the colony grew, as well as the devastating effects of imported animals, cows and pigs especially, that were allowed to run free. The Indian population was reduced by 1,000 during that warfare.

After 1645 Peter Stuyvesant became governor. The war and the colony's slow growth had taught the company in Holland that colonists needed more say in government decisions, and Stuyvesant instituted this new policy. Now the colony began to thrive, with larger numbers and lively trade, and a higher proportion of the newcomers came in family groups. Stuyvesant governed until Dutch rule ended with the English conquest in 1664, and he presided over the time of greatest growth.

NEW SWEDEN

Although he had been removed from New York, Peter Minuit was not finished in America. He soon reappeared on the Delaware River as leader of New Sweden in 1638. The area was claimed by New Netherland, and the Dutch saw the new colony as trespassing, although many Dutch people were involved in it. The English colonies of Maryland and New Haven also claimed land in Delaware Bay. The colony, composed of Swedes and Finns, was always small, and it was attacked and absorbed by New Netherland in 1655.

Despite its short independent life, the little colony of New Sweden is interesting because it created a relationship with the neighboring Indians that was unique on America's East Coast. The sponsoring company back in Sweden was very lax about supplying the settlers or keeping in touch with them. Long periods of time, as much as six years, elapsed between the arrivals of company ships. Therefore, in order to survive the colonists had to invent a new way of life in partnership with the powerful Susquehannock Indians.

Ships from many colonies came to Delaware Bay and the Swedes traded with them. They obtained food and wampum from traders from New England, principally Connecticut. The food was for themselves, but they traded the wampum to Susquehannocks, who carried it far inland and traded the wampum for furs. The Swedish colonists then traded the furs to the New Englanders for the wampum and food. The colonists of New Sweden thus functioned as middlemen in the carrying of an item of native manufacture, wampum, and the fueling of the English fur trade. The whole trade was overseen and directed by the Susquehannocks. Wampum, which formerly had been very rare in the interior, was

PETER STUYVESANT. Stuyvesant was a tough military veteran when he took over the governorship of New Netherland. He returned to New York after the English conquest and lived the rest of his life on his farm, the Bouwerie.

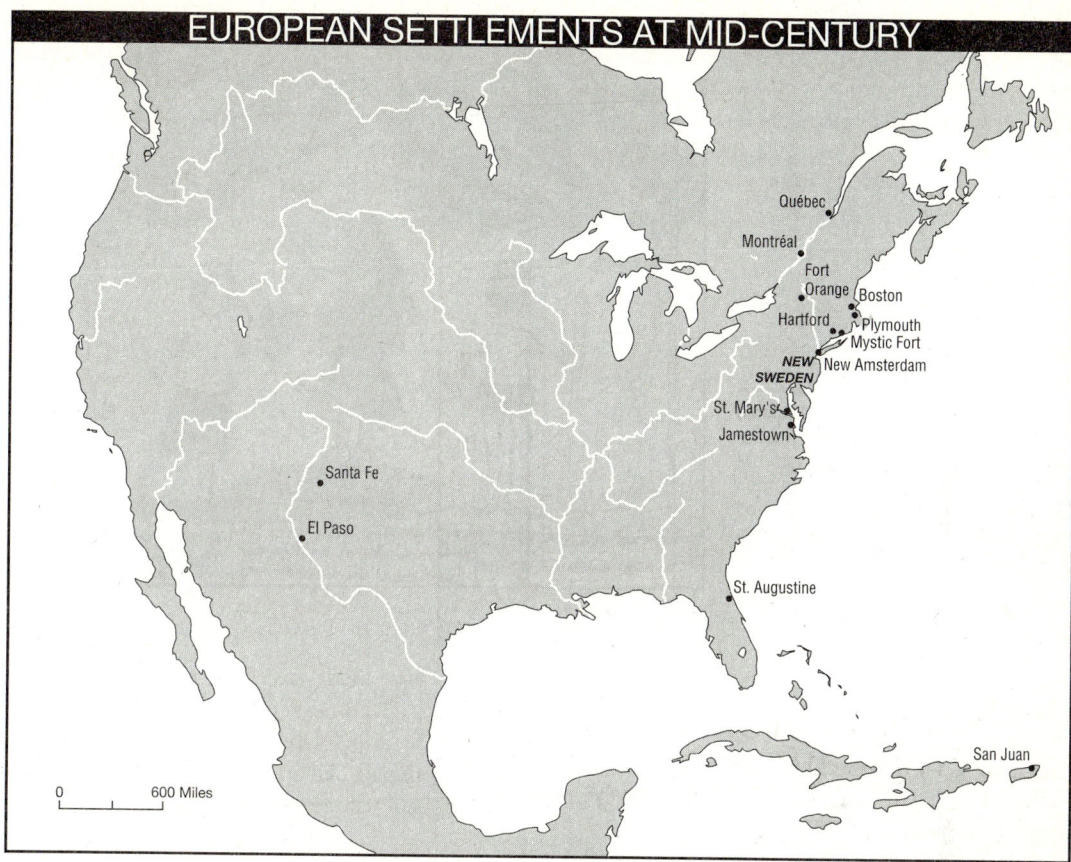

prized by the Indians because of its spiritual and ceremonial value. After 1655 New Sweden was part of New Netherland until the latter's capture in 1664.

PATTERNS

By the middle of the seventeenth century, patterns were firmly set that had not been foreseen in the early years of the century. The American colonies were well established, with large numbers of people settled in them. Moreover, these people had immigrated for good. Drawn by the offer of land of their own, they came expecting to remain, and to establish families that would inherit their land.

European practices had been redesigned and adapted to make all this possible. Joint-stock companies sponsored colonization, and offered their investors the chance to spin off smaller ventures of their own under the particular plantation and patroonship system. The European custom of servitude for young people became the indentured servitude that made immigration possible for many young colonists and made development possible for landowners. The granting of land to servants whose time was up, the freedmen, perpetuated the system and enlarged the areas of settlement.

Indians who had initially worked with Europeans in trade and in allowing early settlement had seen their populations plummet and their lands contract. Most had been weakened even before the takeoff of large-scale colonization by the diseases brought by earlier traders and explorers. They had not anticipated the massive influx of settlers that would transform trading stations and outposts into settlements. After an attempt at resistance in almost every colony, Indians found themselves pushed into enclaves, often forced away from the coast into the territory of other tribes. Their former lands were taken up and made into farms for settlers. As the European disadvantaged found opportunity to become independent landowners in America, the Indians in the original regions of settlement lost their independent life and the base that had supported it.

CHRONOLOGY

1616–1618	Introduction of headright system in Virginia;	1630	Massachusetts Bay settled
		1634	Founding of Maryland
	Women sent in large influx of new colonists after 1618	1633–1636	Founding of first Connecticut River towns
1617	Death of Pocahontas	1636	Roger Williams founds Rhode Island after expulsion from Massachusetts
1618	Death of Powhatan		
1619	First meeting of Virginia Assembly;	1636–1637	Pequot War
	Introduction of Africans into Virginia	1638	Anne Hutchinson expelled from Massachusetts;
1620	Plymouth colony founded by Pilgrims in New England;		New Sweden founded;
	Mayflower Compact		Absorbed by New Netherland in 1655
1621	First Thanksgiving in Plymouth	1639	First Baptist church founded in Rhode Island
1620s	Renewal of Spanish commitment in New Mexico	1640	New Netherland Charter of Freedoms and Exemptions
1622	Concerted Indian attack on Virginia plantations led by Opechancanough	1644	Second great Indian attack on Virginia plantations
1624	Virginia Company charter revoked; New Netherland founded	1649	Maryland Act Concerning Religion

SUGGESTIONS FOR FURTHER READING

1622: CLASH OF CULTURES

Three articles by J. Frederick Fausz are essential to understanding the background of events in Virginia: "George Thorpe, Nemattanew, and the Powhatan Uprising of 1622," *Virginia Cavalcade* (Winter 1979), 111–117; "Opechancanough: Indian Resistance Leader," in David G. Sweet and Gary B. Nash, eds., *Struggle and Survival in Colonial America*, 21–35; and "Middlemen in Peace and War: Virginia's Earliest Indian Interpreters, 1608–1632," *Virginia Magazine of History and Biography*, 95 (1987), 41–64. Our knowledge of the Powhatans and Indian culture in the Chesapeake has been illuminated by three recent books by Helen Rountree, *The Powhatan Indians of Virginia: Their Traditional Culture* (1989), *Pocahontas's People: The Powhatan Indians of Virginia Through Four Centuries* (1990), and Rountree, ed., *Powhatan Foreign Relations, 1500–1722* (1993). Indian relations in early Virginia are the subject of Nancy Lurie's pathbreaking article, "Indian Cultural Adjustment to European Civilization," in James Morton Smith, ed., *Seventeenth-Century America: Essays in Colonial History* (1959), 33–60, and Gary B. Nash, *Red, White, and Black: The Peoples of Early America* (1974, 1982, 1992).

Virginia Company letters and meeting minutes are found in Susan Myra Kingsbury, ed *The Records of the*

Virginia Company of London, 4 vols. (1906–1935); Richard Frethorne's letters to his minister, Mr. Bateman, and to his mother and father are in volume IV. On George Thorpe see Eric Gethyn-Jones, *George Thorpe and the Berkeley Company: A Gloucestershire Enterprise in Virginia* (Gloucester, 1982). For an exciting description of modern excavation of the Martin's Hundred site see Ivor Noël Hume, *Martin's Hundred* (New York, 1982).

PATTERNS OF SETTLEMENT TO MID-SEVENTEENTH CENTURY

Spanish Colonization

On Spanish colonization see David J. Weber, *The Spanish Frontier in North America* (1992). For studies that illuminate the tensions produced by Spanish-Indian confrontations in the Southwest see Ramón Gutiérrez, *When Jesus Came, the Corn Mothers Went Away: Marriage, Sexuality, and Power in New Mexico, 1500–1846* (1991), Elizabeth A. H. John, *Storms Brewed in Other Men's Worlds: The Confrontation of Indians, Spanish, and French in the Southwest, 1540–1795* (1975), and Marc Simmons, *The Last Conquistador: Juan de Oñate and the Settling of the Far Southwest* (1991).

The Chesapeake

Edmund S. Morgan, *American Slavery, American Freedom: The Ordeal of Colonial Virginia* (1975), offers a challenging interpretation of the early colonial experience and the growth of slavery. The essays in Thad W. Tate and David L. Ammerman, eds., *The Chesapeake in the Seventeenth Century: Essays on Anglo-American Society* (1979), take up important aspects of the problems of Virginia's founding. The classic book on the controversial end of the Virginia Company and the transition to royal government is Wesley Frank Craven, *The Dissolution of the Virginia Company: The Failure of a Colonial Experiment* (1932). On the life of ordinary colonists see James R. Perry, *The Formation of a Society on Virginia's Eastern Shore, 1615–1655* (1990), and James Horn, *Adapting to a New World: English Society in the Seventeenth-Century Chesapeake* (1994).

New England

On Puritanism and its impact on life in New England see Charles E. Hambrick-Stowe, *The Practice of Piety: Puritan Devotional Discipline in Seventeenth-Century New England* (1982), Harry S. Stout, *The New England Soul: Preaching and Religious Culture in Colonial New England* (1986), and Charles L. Cohen, *God's Caress: The Psychology of Puritan Religious Experience* (1986). On challenges to establishment Puritanism see Philip F. Gura, *A Glimpse of Sion's Glory: Puritan Radicalism in New England, 1620–1660* (1984), and Carla Gardina Pestana, *Quakers and Baptists in Colonial Massachusetts* (1991).

For Plymouth Colony see George F. Willison, *Saints and Strangers: the Story of the "Mayflower" and the Plymouth Colony,* rev. ed. (1966), George D. Langdon, *Pilgrim Colony: A History of New Plymouth, 1620–1691* (1966), and John Demos, *A Little Commonwealth: Family Life in Plymouth Colony* (1970).

On the founding of towns in Massachusetts Bay see Virginia DeJohn Anderson, *New England's Generation: The Great Migration and the Formation of Society and Culture in the Seventeenth Century* (1991), and John Frederick Martin, *Profits in the Wilderness: Entrepreneurship and the Founding of New England Towns in Seventeenth-Century New England* (1991). David Cressy deals with the continuing relationship between the colonists and their homes in *Coming Over: Migration and Communication between England and New England in the Seventeenth Century* (1987).

On expansion into Connecticut and Rhode Island see two books by Bruce C. Daniels, *The Connecticut Town: Growth and Development, 1635–1790* (1979), and *Dissent and Conformity on Narragansett Bay: The Colonial Rhode Island Town* (1983).

The Middle Colonies

New Netherland is the subject of Oliver A. Rink, *Holland on the Hudson: An Economic and Social History of Dutch New York* (1986). On the colony both before and after the English takeover see Michael Kammen, *Colonial New York: A History* (1975). On the relations between colonists and the Iroquois see Daniel Richter, *The Ordeal of the Longhouse,* and Matthew Dennis, *Cultivating a Landscape of Peace: Iroquois-European Encounters in Seventeenth-Century America* (1990).

On New Sweden see Stellan Dahlgren and Hans Norman, *The Rise and Fall of New Sweden: Governor Johan Risingh's Journal, 1654–1655, in its Historical Context* (1988).

CHAPTER 3

Growth and Diversification

Episode: Witchcraft at Salem Village

NEW PEOPLES AND NEW PATTERNS IN THE LATER SEVENTEENTH CENTURY

- New Colonies
- Trade
- New England to Florida: The Settled Colonies
- Colonial Wars
- Patterns

THE EPISODE: In 1692, one of the most remarkable events in American history took place. It began in a small village just outside the town of Salem in the British colony of Massachusetts. A group of young people, most of them female, began to have what their elders called "fits." Then they started to accuse adults of being witches, who were in league with the Devil. The little community was terrified. Almost everyone believed the Devil was real and that he could visit the earth and take possession of people's souls if they agreed to make a covenant with him. So the people of Salem Village set out to combat what they believed was a conspiracy, set afoot by the Devil himself. Within a few weeks, hundreds of women and men had been accused of being witches. Soon the highest authorities in the colony intervened, not to restore calm but to stamp out the "Satanic" conspiracy. Dozens of people were put on trial, and several confessed. By the time the hysteria and the trials ended, nineteen supposed witches had been hanged.

THE HISTORICAL SETTING: The Salem witchcraft accusations took place in a world that was changing dramatically. The first phase of English colonization was over, and all the colonies, old and new, followed different lines of development in the last decades of the century. Fewer immigrants were English. Now they came from other parts of Britain—Scotland and Ireland—and from all over Europe. The colonies on America's East Coast became more cosmopolitan and the American tradition of ethnic diversity became established.

The regions began to look quite different from each other as the patterns that would typify them in the next century became set. New England, after astonishing population growth, had reached the limits of its development as a self-contained farming region and was forced to accept links with the rest of the Atlantic world through trade. Such opening to the world created apprehension and Salem Village's crisis was one result of such fears. The Middle Colonies also experienced change. New Netherland became New York when it was seized by the English in the 1660s, and Pennsylvania was founded as a Quaker refuge in the 1680s. The region of fine harbors and fertile land became the new magnet for migrants from Britain and Europe. The Chesapeake established slavery as its labor system in these years, and the native-born were predominant in the population. These "creoles" started life with enormous advantages and formed the nucleus of the gentry families that would dominate the Chesapeake in the eighteenth century and beyond. The Carolinas were founded in the 1660s, and followed yet another variant of the pattern. They attracted immigrants from Europe as the Middle Colonies did, but South Carolina especially attracted planters from Barbados, who brought a full-blown slave system with them.

Each of the older regions experienced a major Indian war at the time these patterns were becoming set, as the natives tried to stop the expansion and protect what was left of their lands. The Pueblos of New Mexico also rose up and expelled the Spanish settlers and Catholic priests for a time. But in every region the war marked the end of armed Indian resistance, and thus these conflicts contributed to the establishment of the new secure patterns of settlement.

Witchcraft at Salem Village

The two girls were strangely sick. Betty Parris, who was nine years old, and her cousin, eleven-year-old Abigail Williams, often stared dully into space. Sometimes they went down on their hands and knees and made hoarse, choking sounds. At other times they simply fell to the floor and screamed. The girls lived in the house of Betty Parris's father Samuel, a minister, in a small settlement called Salem Village, in the English colony of Massachusetts. It was January 1692.

At first, Samuel Parris kept quiet about the girls' behavior. But as the minister of the town, he was more carefully watched by his neighbors than any other man. His house stood at the center of the village, just down a dirt road from the tavern and not far from the only meetinghouse, or church. Something had to be done, so Parris sent for the village doctor. Since the minister's family was considered the most important family in the village, the doctor proceeded seriously and carefully. He examined the girls, consulted his medical books, and tried various medicines. Nothing worked, and his books gave him no clue. Finally, he gave up. The girls, he told the Reverend Parris, were not physically sick at all but had been touched by "the evil hand."

No one in Massachusetts in 1692 needed to be reminded that the doctor was talking about witchcraft. Four years earlier, in Boston, an Irish woman called Witch Glover had been hanged for bewitching four children. One of Boston's most famous ministers, Cotton Mather, had taken one of the bewitched children into his own house to try to cure her. Mather had then published a book on witchcraft, a book read in every town of the Massachusetts Bay Colony. Samuel Parris had a copy.

Practically everyone in the colony believed that the Devil actually did visit the earth, persuading men and women to join him, and giving them a witch's power to torment innocent people. All over Europe at this time, witches were being accused, convicted, and hanged or burned at the stake. The people of Salem Village were just as superstitious as Europeans and other Americans. Cotton Mather was one of the best-educated men in the colony. Samuel Parris had attended Harvard College. The doctor who first examined Betty Parris and Abigail Williams was an educated scientist. All of these men believed in witchcraft. If such sophisticated community leaders accepted the idea that "the evil hand" was at work, what could be expected of the plain farmers of Salem Village?

As soon as gossip leaked out about Betty Parris and Abigail Williams, their young friends began to have similar fits. Between January and September of 1692 a group of about a dozen girls steadily acted bewitched. At nine, Betty Parris was the youngest of the afflicted children; the oldest of the group were two young women of twenty. Today they would probably all be called teenagers. This group of teenage girls was joined

Cotton Mather accepted the witchcraft trials of 1692 as an appropriate way to deal with people who had been possessed by the devil. Years later, though, he had second thoughts. He still believed in witches but had decided that fasting and prayer might "cure" a witch—a better solution than hanging.

from time to time by other afflicted persons, some of them adults, but most of them young people. A few adults argued that the girls were only pretending and that a good spanking would cure them. But most of the people of Salem Village, of nearby Salem Town, and of the whole Massachusetts Bay Colony took the girls' fits seriously.

At first the girls did not name anyone as their tormentors. All over Salem Village, parents and other relatives prayed and fasted. Samuel Parris called in the ministers of several neighboring towns, and they too prayed and fasted. The questions in their minds were: Who was bewitching the girls? Whom had the Devil persuaded to join him in witchcraft? Finally, on February 25, some of the girls called out three names. Whether the afflicted children had a plan or not, they were very shrewd—in the way that even truly disturbed or insane people can be shrewd. They named three women who were, for different reasons, very marginal and vulnerable.

The first was Tituba, a slave in the house of Samuel Parris. Tituba was from one of the islands of the West Indies, where Parris had worked as a merchant before coming to Salem to preach in 1689. She probably was part African American and part Native American. Tituba was married to another slave, John Indian, who also belonged to Parris. During dark winter afternoons in the Parris kitchen, Tituba had no doubt told weird stories of the islands to Betty and Abigail. She had also shown magic tricks to the village girls who were now afflicted.

The second person identified by the afflicted girls was Sarah Good. In her own way she was even more vulnerable than Tituba. Her husband was a laborer who had never held a job for long. Sarah herself was something of a hag. She smoked a pipe, muttered to herself, and often went begging from door to door in the village.

The third supposed witch was a prosperous old woman named Sarah Osburne. After her husband died, she had offended the town by living with an overseer on her farm. Although she eventually married the man, she had stopped going to church. She had a bad reputation.

In 1692 there were no regular judges in Massachusetts. Court hearings were presided over by members of the colonial legislature, known as assistants. So the parents and relatives of some of the afflicted children went to the two assistants of Salem Town and asked for the arrest of Tituba, Sarah Good, and Sarah Osburne on a charge of witchcraft.

March 1 was an exciting day for the village. The constables and uniformed military guard went out with drums to meet the two assistants coming from Salem Town. With this military escort the assistants marched into the meetinghouse, which had been converted into a courtroom. The assistants took their seats on a platform at the front of the church, with the afflicted girls facing them in the front pew. Almost everyone else in the village crowded in. Sarah Good was then brought forward for preliminary questioning.

One of the assistants, John Hathorne, was a stern, dark man who took his work very seriously. He leaned forward toward cranky Sarah Good and began to question her:

HATHORNE: Sarah Good, what evil spirit have you familiarity with?

SARAH GOOD: None.

HATHORNE: Have you made no contract with the devil?

SARAH GOOD: No.

HATHORNE: Why do you hurt these children?

SARAH GOOD: I do not hurt them. I scorn it.

HATHORNE: Who do you employ, then, to do it?

SARAH GOOD: I employ nobody.

HATHORNE: What *creature* do you employ, then?

SARAH GOOD: No creature. But I am falsely accused.

HATHORNE: Have you made no contract with the devil?

SARAH GOOD: No.

Up to this point, Hathorne had not shaken this stubborn woman. She simply denied everything, saying in a tough old voice, "I scorn it!"

But Hathorne and the other assistant, Jonathan Corwin, had made a decision before opening the court. They would accept the testimony of the afflicted children about who it was that tormented them. Hathorne and Corwin believed that even if Sarah Good were standing innocently before the judges, her "shape," or spirit, might attack the girls. If the afflicted girls said that Sarah Good's shape was pinching or hurting them, then she would be put in jail for a full-scale witch trial and possible hanging.

According to the legal procedures of the day, Sarah Good was not told of this decision in advance. Nor was she represented by a lawyer. Hathorne's next move was very important. It established the pattern for all the hearings that would follow. The clerk's record of the testimony continued:

> Hathorne desired the children all of them to look upon her and see if this were the person that had hurt them. And so they all did look upon her, and said this was one of the persons that did torment them. Presently they were all tormented.

Here was the key to Hathorne's prosecution of the witches: "Presently they were all tormented." Here, for the first time, the afflicted girls learned that their moaning and screaming could not only attract favorable attention, but could defeat the most stubborn adult testimony. After a short time the girls quieted down. They still said they were being tormented by the shape of Sarah Good, the cranky woman who at that moment was standing so still in the meetinghouse. Hathorne returned to the attack. Sarah Good held her ground for a moment, but then she began to break down:

> HATHORNE: Sarah Good, do you not see now what you have done? Why do you not tell us the truth? Why do you thus torment these poor children?
> SARAH GOOD: I do not torment them.
> HATHORNE: Who was it, then, that tormented the children?
> SARAH GOOD: It was Osburne.

In her panic, Sarah Good tried to save herself by pointing an accusing finger at Sarah Osburne. But in doing so she sealed her own fate. Hathorne and Corwin reasoned this way: Sarah Good was not afflicted. Therefore, unless she were a witch, how could she know that Sarah Osburne attacked the children? Hathorne could see that Sarah Good was going to pieces, and he hurried the process:

> HATHORNE: What is it you say when you go muttering away from persons' houses?
> SARAH GOOD: If I must tell, I will tell.
> HATHORNE: Do tell us then.
> SARAH GOOD: If I must tell, I will tell. It is the commandments.

Hathorne sensed that she was lying. Sarah Good might still have saved herself if she could have repeated even some of the Bible's Ten Commandments. But when Hathorne asked her to name one, she hedged:

> HATHORNE: What commandment is it?
> SARAH GOOD: If I must tell, I will tell. It is a psalm.
> HATHORNE: What psalm? After a long time [the clerk recorded], she muttered over some part of a psalm. . . . Her answers were given in a very wicked, spiteful manner, with base and abusive words and many lies.

Sarah Good was taken away, and her husband was questioned briefly. The clerk recorded his curious testimony:

> It was here said that her husband had said that he was afraid that she either was a witch or would be one very quickly. The worthy Mr. Hathorne asked him his reason why he said so

THE WITCH HOUSE. This elegantly gabled building, constructed in 1675, is a fine example of seventeenth-century domestic architecture in New England. Its fame, however, is not architectural: It was the home of Jonathan Corwin and became known as the Witch House.

of her. He answered that it was her bad carriage [attitude] to him, and indeed, said he, I may say with tears that she is an enemy to all good.

Once finished with questioning Sarah Good, Hathorne and Corwin then called Sarah Osburne, who quickly panicked. She tried to claim that she herself had been bewitched. To save herself, she tried to throw suspicion on Tituba's husband, John Indian, by claiming that she had been attacked by "a thing like an Indian, all black." But the afflicted girls would not let her join their circle. They accused her just as they had Sarah Good, and she was taken away. The assistants then sent for Tituba, who was to be the star of the day.

Tituba's situation was frightening. From the time little Betty Parris first accused Tituba, Parris had regularly beaten her (as a slaveowner, he had that authority over her body). But he had sometimes prayed for her (as a minister, he claimed that authority over her spirit). By March 1 she had worked out a shrewd plan. She would confess. But she would also save herself by throwing greater suspicion on others and by claiming that she was no longer working with the devil. Parris and the others might take this to mean that his prayers had worked, and she had been redeemed from the devil's grasp.

Once more Hathorne took the lead in the questioning. At first, Tituba's answers sounded like Sarah Good's, and the afflicted girls behaved the same way:

HATHORNE: Tituba, what evil spirit have you familiarity with?

TITUBA: None.

HATHORNE: Why do you hurt these children?

TITUBA: I do not hurt them.

HATHORNE: Who is it then?

TITUBA: The devil for aught I know.

But then Tituba began to execute her plan. As soon as she began to confess, the afflicted girls calmed down. It was as though Tituba's confession released them from their spells for the time being.

HATHORNE: Did you ever see the devil?

TITUBA: The devil came to me and bid me serve him.

HATHORNE: Who have you seen?

TITUBA: Four women sometimes hurt the children.

HATHORNE: Who were they?

At this point Tituba had to be careful. For the moment, at least, the children were quiet. But she had to name names that the assistants and the village farmers would accept. She also had to try to protect her husband, John Indian. Sarah Osburne had testified that she was bewitched by "a thing like an Indian, all black." Now Tituba invented a "tall man from Boston," dressed in black, to throw suspicion off John Indian. She also accused her two codefendants, Sarah Osburne and Sarah Good, of being witches.

Then Tituba began to weave a tale of witches, devils, and strange animals. The citizens of the village listened in fascinated horror.

TITUBA: There is four women and one man. They hurt the children. And they lay all upon me and they tell me if I will not hurt the children, they will hurt me.

HATHORNE: What also have you seen?

TITUBA: Two rats, a red rat and a black rat.

HATHORNE: What did they say to you?

TITUBA: They said serve me.

HATHORNE: Why did you not tell your master?

TITUBA: I was afraid they would cut off my head if I told.

HATHORNE: What attendants hath Sarah Good?

TITUBA: A yellow bird. And she would have given me one.

HATHORNE: What meat did she give it?

TITUBA: It did suck her between her fingers.

HATHORNE: What hath Sarah Osburne?

TITUBA: A yellow dog. She had a thing with a head like a woman, with two legs and wings.

HATHORNE: What else have you seen with Osburne?

TITUBA: Another thing. Hairy. It goes upright like a man. It hath only two legs.

HATHORNE: What clothes doth the man [the "tall man from Boston"] go in?
TITUBA: He goes in black clothes. A tall man with white hair, I think.

At the mention of these creatures, the afflicted girls began to behave strangely again. The timing was perfect. Hathorne had to ask Tituba who was bewitching the girls. His question gave Tituba a chance to end her testimony in a helpful way. She could again throw suspicion on someone else. Doing so would prove that she wanted to help hunt down the witches. But then she could claim that she could no longer "see." This would prove that she had been liberated from the devil's power, and had been "saved." (It would also spare her the risk of having to choose any other villagers to identify as witches.)

HATHORNE: Do you see who it is that torments these children now?
TITUBA: Yes, it is Goody [short for "Goodwife," a common way of addressing married women] Good. She hurts them in her own shape.
HATHORNE: And who is it that hurts them now?
TITUBA: I am blind. I cannot see.

Tituba, Sarah Good, and Sarah Osburne were questioned several more times during the next few days. On March 7 they were sent to jail in Boston to await a full trial. Sarah Osburne fell ill and died on May 10 without a trial. Sarah Good had a baby in jail, which died—confirming everyone's suspicion that she was an evil woman. With the three "witches" in jail, Salem Village might have calmed down. But Tituba had said that four women, plus the tall man from Boston, were tormenting the afflicted girls. And they continued to be afflicted. This meant more witches were on the loose.

Shortly after Tituba, Sarah Good, and Sarah Osburne had been taken away, Salem Village had a day of fasting and prayer. Once more the ministers of the neighboring towns came to meet with Parris. Once more the girls were watched, prayed over, and questioned. Finally, they called out a name, a name that shocked everyone and started the trials off in a new direction. The girls named Martha Cory, who was not a slave like Tituba, not a hag like Goody Good, and not a sinner like Goody Osburne. Martha Cory was an upstanding member of the village congregation. For the first time the girls had accused an adult with a solid reputation. If Martha Cory could be suspected, then no woman in Salem Village would be safe.

The warrant for Martha Cory's arrest was dated March 19, but because that day was a Saturday, she was not to be arrested until the following Monday. On the Sunday between she showed up at the meetinghouse, where a visiting minister, Deodat Lawson, was going to preach. Lawson had once been the minister of Salem Village and was now living in Boston. He came to Salem to witness the witchcraft proceedings, and he had spent the night in Parris's house, where he watched Abigail Williams go through a violent fit of possession.

This was to be no ordinary Sunday service. Goodwife Cory herself came bravely into the meetinghouse and took her place. But during prayers and the sermon, the afflicted girls fell into their fits of possession. Ordinarily, it would have been a serious offense even to whisper, doze off, or look out the window during church services. In the meetinghouses, men were assigned the job of patrolling the aisles during the sermon—which might last several hours—to prod or even hit people who misbehaved or did not pay attention. But the afflicted girls were able to break all the usual rules. Abigail Williams yelled out at the minister, and several of the other girls joined in. Finally, Abigail pointed to an exposed beam above the head of Martha Cory and called out, "Look where Goody Cory sits on the beam, suckling her yellow bird betwixt her fingers."

The girls had learned Tituba's lessons well. From the time of her "confession" to the end of the trials, they often mentioned strange animals, especially the yellow bird. Martha Cory, of course, was simply sitting in her place. But when the girls cried out, all eyes looked overhead to the beam where her "shape" was supposed to be sitting with its sinister yellow bird. When Cory came before the assistants the next day, most of the villagers had already made up their minds that she was guilty.

The visiting minister, Deodat Lawson, wrote an account of Martha Cory's subsequent examination by Hathorne and Corwin:

> On Monday the 21st of March, the magistrates of Salem were appointed to come to the examination of Goodwife Cory. And about twelve of the clock, they went into the meeting house, which was thronged with spectators. Mr. Noyes [a minister who had come over from Salem Town] began with a very pathetic [sad] prayer. Goodwife Cory, being called to answer what was alleged against her, desired to go to prayer. This was much wondered at, in the presence of so many people.

Martha Cory was a very proud and rugged woman. When two officers of the town had first come to her farm to ask her about the charges of witchcraft, she had laughed at them. Now, in her examination, she was trying to beat the village at its own game. If they could pray, then she would pray herself. But Hathorne refused:

> The magistrates told her they would not admit it. They came not there to hear her pray, but to examine her in what was alleged against her. The worshipful Mr. Hathorne asked her why she afflicted these children. She said she did not afflict them. He asked her who did, then? She said, "I do not know. How should I know?"

Hathorne began with the same questions he had put to Sarah Good and Sarah Osburne. Once more, the suspected witch denied everything. Once more, the afflicted girls had fits. Every time Martha Cory moved an arm or bit her lip, the girls acted afflicted in the same parts of their bodies:

> The number of afflicted persons were about that time ten. Those were most of them at Goodwife Cory's examination, and did vehemently accuse her in the assembly of afflicting them, by biting, pinching, strangling, etc. And that they did in their fit see her likeness coming to them, and bringing a book to them. She said she had no book. They affirmed that she had a yellow bird that used to suck betwixt her fingers. Being asked about it, she said she had no familiarity with any such thing. She was a Gospel woman, which title she called herself by. And the afflicted persons told her, Ah! She was a Gospel witch.
>
> It was observed several times that if she did but bite her under lip in time of examination, the persons afflicted were bitten on their arms and wrists and produced the marks before the magistrates, ministers, and others. If she did but pinch her finger, or grasp one hand hard in the other, they were pinched and produced the marks before the magistrates and spectators.

Then the afflicted girls threw terror into the entire audience by saying that there was a gathering of witches that very moment in front of the meetinghouse!

> The afflicted persons asked her [Martha Cory] why she did not go to the company of witches which were before the meeting house, mustering? Did she not hear the drumbeat? They accused her of familiarity with the devil, in the shape of a black man whispering in her ear. They affirmed that her yellow bird sucked betwixt her fingers in the assembly.
>
> She denied all that was charged upon her, and said they could not prove a witch. She was that afternoon committed to Salem prison.

Once the afflicted girls and their supporters had succeeded in their attack on Martha Cory, they were able to accuse anyone in the village. During the last week of March and the first days of April, several more women with sound reputations were arrested and brought before the assistants. The village was in a deepening panic. Neighbors began to suspect each other, and people quickly forgot the difference between evidence and common gossip.

The panic spread from Salem Village to Salem Town, and then to the rest of the Massachusetts Bay Colony. By April 11, the examinations had to be moved from the village to the larger meetinghouse in Salem Town. The deputy governor and several other leading citizens of the colony came up from Boston to observe the proceedings. The afflicted girls were no longer a local phenomenon. Now they were watched and wondered at by people from all parts of Massachusetts.

In the middle of April, with spring well on its way, the first break showed in the ranks of the afflicted girls. One of the women identified as a witch in early April was Elizabeth Proctor, whose husband owned a large farm in the southern part of the village. The Proctors' maidservant, Mary Warren, was one of the afflicted girls. But the Proctors did not believe in witchcraft at all, and they had the courage to say so in public. At Elizabeth Proctor's examination some of the girls had screamed out that her husband, John, was also a witch—or a wizard, as male witches were called. This accusation alarmed Mary Warren. She did not like Mrs. Proctor at all, but she seems to have had a twenty-year-old's crush on John Proctor, who was a middle-aged man. Outside the meetinghouse, she began to say that the afflictions were all a "sport," that John Proctor was not a wizard at all.

When the other afflicted girls found out about Mary Warren's betrayal, they accused *her* of being a witch. On April 18 she was arrested and brought before the assistants. Suddenly, she had moved from the favored pew of the afflicted girls into the seat of fear where she had watched grown men and women collapse in panic. This was a crucial point in the trials. If Mary Warren could hold her ground against the screams of the afflicted girls, the stares of the audience, and the sternness of Hathorne, then the trials might come to a halt.

Samuel Parris himself kept the official record of the scene:

> As soon as she was coming toward the bar, the afflicted fell into fits.
>
> HATHORNE: Mary Warren, you stand here charged with sundry acts of witchcraft. What do you say for yourself? Are you guilty or not?
>
> MARY WARREN: I am innocent.

> HATHORNE: Hath she hurt you (speaking to the sufferers)? Some were dumb. Betty Hubbard [one of the afflicted girls] testified against her, and then said Hubbard fell into a violent fit.
>
> HATHORNE: You were a little while ago an afflicted person. Now you are an afflictor. How comes this to pass?
>
> MARY WARREN: I look up to God and take it to be a great mercy of God.
>
> HATHORNE: What? Do you take it to be a great mercy to afflict others?

This trick question of Hathorne's took Mary Warren by surprise. At the same time, all the afflicted girls began to howl. It was too much for the young woman to bear. She broke down and became incoherent. She struggled from time to time to regain control of herself, but it was no use. By now the fits may have become real hysteria, which Mary Warren and some of the other girls could no longer start or stop at will.

> Now Mary Warren fell into a fit, and some of the afflicted cried out that Goody Cory and Proctor and his wife came in their apparition [their "shapes"] and struck her down.
>
> Mary Warren continued a good space in a fit, and she did neither see, nor hear, nor speak.
>
> Afterwards, she started up, and said, "I will speak," and cried out, "Oh I am sorry for it. I am sorry for it," and wringed her hands, and fell a little while into a fit again. And then she came to speak, but immediately her teeth were set, and then she fell into a violent fit, and cried out, "Oh, Lord, help me! Oh, Good Lord, save me!"
>
> And then afterward she cried again, "I will tell! I will tell!" And then she fell into a dead fit again.

Mary Warren was taken to Salem to jail, where she was questioned again and again by the assistants and ministers. Finally, on May 12, she admitted that both the Proctors were witches. By then, she had probably lost her weak hold on reality. She confessed that she herself had signed "the Devil's book," and she wildly accused several other people of witchcraft.

What was happening in Massachusetts in 1692 was really quite simple—though the reasons it happened were subtle and complex. A group of teenage girls caused a brief revolution. In January they were ordinary girls, taking orders from adults, working very hard in their homes or as servants, listening to long sermons in church on Sundays and other days. By the spring of 1692 they held an enormous amount of power—even the power of life and death—over a large number of the adult citizens of Massachusetts. They had begun by accusing poor old women and slaves. But within a few weeks they were charging ministers, merchants, and other solid citizens. They were able to terrify tough old pioneer farmers. And behind them stood the power of the Massachusetts government to send innocent men and women to the gallows.

As panic gripped Salem and the rest of the colony during the summer of 1692, displays of both courage and cowardice could be seen, sometimes in the same family or individual. One such mixture of responses occurred in the case of George Jacobs, a toothless village elder who shuffled about with the aid of two canes. Jacobs's household included his son and daughter-in-law—a woman "crazy in her senses, who had been so several years," according to local gossips. There were four grandchildren, the eldest a teenager named Margaret. Jacobs's servant, Sarah Churchill, was one of the afflicted girls.

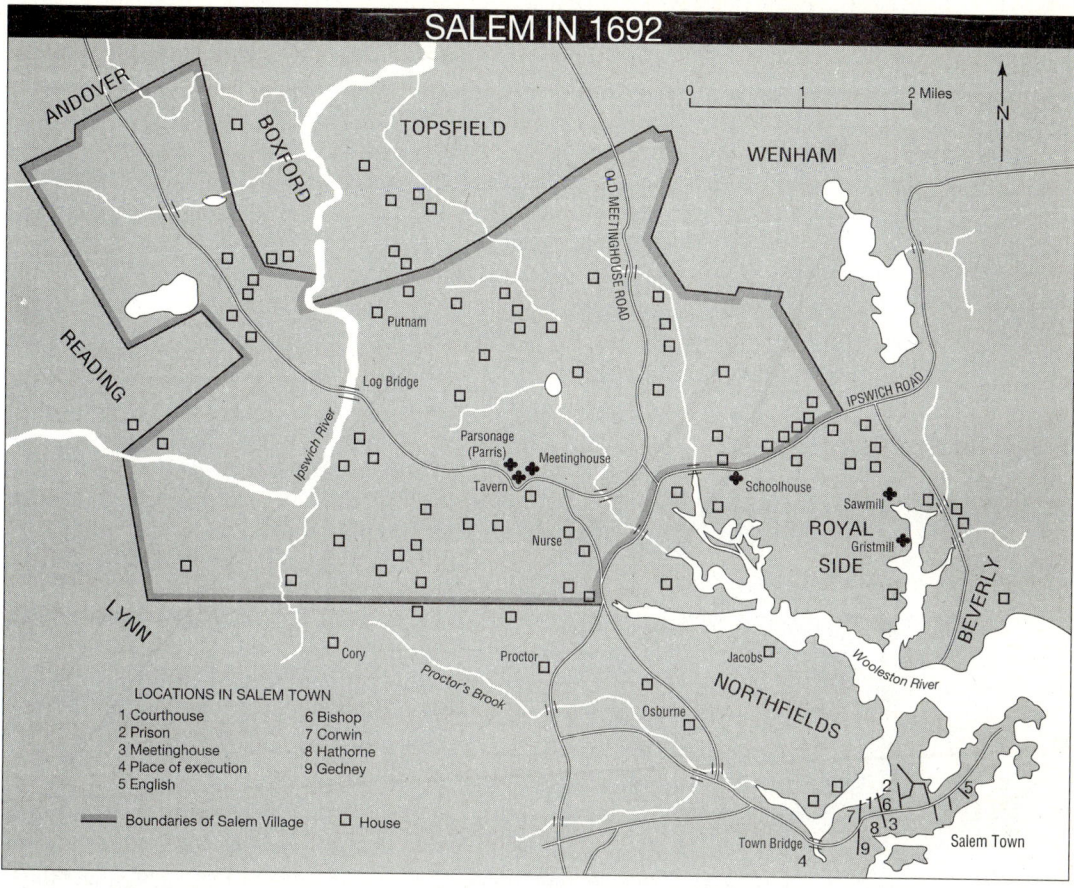

Old Jacobs, like John Proctor, had scoffed openly at the girls' claims that they were possessed by witches. He even went so far as to mock his own servant Sarah as a "witch bitch." Unfortunately for Jacobs, no one in Salem in 1692 could make such remarks and escape reprisal. On May 10 Jacobs was summoned to answer to charges of being a wizard. Jacobs, like John Proctor and Martha Cory, was crisp and caustic in his examination, because he considered the accusation completely ridiculous:

> HATHORNE: Here are them that accuse you of acts of witchcraft.
>
> JACOBS: Well, let us hear who they are and what they are.
>
> HATHORNE: Abigail Williams.
>
> JACOBS: [Laughing] I am falsely accused. Your worships, all of you, do you think this is true?
>
> HATHORNE: Nay, what do you think?
>
> JACOBS: I never did it.
>
> HATHORNE: Who did it?
>
> JACOBS: Don't ask me. I am as innocent as the child born tonight. You tax me for a wizard. You may as well tax me for a buzzard.

But it was no use. Old Jacobs was sent away to the Boston jail. His son and namesake, George Jr., did not wait to undergo a similar examination. Instead, he fled the colony, leaving not only his crazed wife but also their four children to face the consequences of having a close relative declared a wizard. The consequences were not long in coming. The town officers soon dragged Mrs. Jacobs before the afflicted ones. At first the girls did not recognize her. Then one—probably her servant, Sarah Churchill—cried out: "Don't you know the old witch? And then they cried out at her, and fell down in their fits." Mrs. Jacobs spent the next ten months in prison as a suspected witch, with her three youngest children left to the care of sympathetic neighbors.

Margaret, the eldest Jacobs child, had even worse luck. She was brought in to give testimony against her grandfather. Afraid that she would be denounced herself as a witch, Margaret "confessed" in order to save her life, accusing both her grandfather and the Reverend George Burroughs, a former village minister, of being wizards. Only after her grandfather and Burroughs had been put in prison did Margaret finally summon the courage to recant her confession. She wrote from prison, denying her previous accusations, but the court ignored this statement and Margaret remained in jail for another year, where she wrote or dictated this confession:

> The humble declaration of Margaret Jacobs unto the Honored Court now sitting at Salem:
>
> I was cried out upon by some of the possessed persons. The Lord above knows I knew nothing. They told me if I would not confess, I should be put down into the dungeon and would be hanged. But if I would confess, I should have my life. This did so afright me, with my own vile, wicked heart, to save my life made me make the confession I did, which confession is altogether false and untrue. What I said was altogether false, against my grandfather, and Mr. Burroughs, which I did to save my life and to have my liberty. But the Lord, charging it to my conscience, made me in so much horror that I could not contain myself before I had denied my confession, which I did, though I saw nothing but death before me, choosing death with a quiet conscience than to live in such horror.
>
> *Margaret Jacobs.*

The girl managed to visit the Reverend Burroughs before his execution in August, however, and received his forgiveness. Old Jacobs was also told of her recantation before his own execution and, although his property had already been confiscated, he showed his pleasure at Margaret's brave act of conscience by including her in his will. After her grandfather's death, Margaret wrote from prison to her vanished father describing her experiences. She ended her letter by stating simply: "My Mother poor Woman is very Crazy, and remembers her kind love to you." Margaret's letter probably never reached her father.

By this time, almost two dozen more people had been arrested, and many more were being accused every day. By the last week of May, nearly fifty people had been sent to the dark, crowded Boston jail, waiting for their final trials. The accused were no longer outcasts or simple local farmers. One of those arrested in May, for example, was Philip English, the foremost shipowner of Salem Town. (He later escaped from jail and fled to New York.)

At last, on May 28, the afflicted girls named the Master Wizard. They had been questioned for weeks by the assistants and ministers about "the tall man from Boston" that Tituba had first mentioned on March 1. Everyone presumed he was the guiding hand behind the entire witches' plot. The magistrates summoned him to court, and on May 31 a tall man from Boston walked into the Salem meetinghouse. His name was John Alden. He was the descendant of the Plymouth Colony's famous lovers, John and Priscilla Alden. This John Alden was more famous as a soldier than a lover, for he was a sea captain who had fought bravely in recent battles with the Indians.

Alden would never have come to Salem by his own choice, since he thought that the accusation of witchcraft was insanely foolish. But the deputy governor of the colony, William Stoughton, ordered him to appear for questioning. So Alden marched into court to face his accusers. Later, writing in the third person, he gave an angry description of what took place.

> John Alden was sent for by the Magistrates of Salem upon the accusation of a company of poor, distracted, or possessed creatures or witches. And being sent by Mr. Stoughton, arrived there the 31st day of May, and appeared at Salem Village before Mr. Gedney a third assistant, Mr. Hathorne, and Mr. Corwin.
>
> Those wenches being present, who played their juggling tricks, falling down, crying out, and staring in people's faces, the Magistrates demanded of them several times who it was of all the people in the room that hurt them?

Could the girls pick from the crowd a man they had never seen before—except perhaps for his "shape"? For a moment the girls were helpless.

> One of these accusers pointed several times at one Captain Hill, there present, but spoke nothing. The same accuser had a man standing at her back to hold her up. He stooped down to her ear. Then she cried out Alden, Alden, afflicted her. One of the Magistrates asked her if she ever had seen Alden. She answered, No. He asked her how she knew it was Alden. She said the man had told her so.

The assistants had to be careful, for Alden was an important man and a war hero. They ordered a ring of men to stand in the street; then they took the girls outside to see whether they could pick Alden out of the ring. Somehow, the girls immediately selected him, and the assistants ordered him arrested. His sword was taken from him, and he was brought back inside. But Alden was no poor slave or hag of Salem Village. He stood his ground to the end:

> Mr. Gedney bid Alden confess, and give glory to God. Alden said he hoped he would give glory to God, but appealed to all that ever knew him, and challenged any one that could bring in anything that might give suspicion of his being such a one [a wizard.] They bid Alden look upon the accusers, which he did, and then they fell down. Alden asked Mr. Gedney, what reason could be given why Alden looking upon him did not strike him down as well? But no reason was given that I heard.
>
> Alden told Mr. Gedney that there was a lying spirit in them [the afflicted girls], for I can assure you that there is not a word of truth in all these say of me. But Alden was again committed to the marshal.

Alden spent the next fifteen weeks awaiting trial, not in prison but under guard at his Boston home. This special treatment was due to his friendship with the colony's leading ministers—men like Cotton Mather of Boston—and with important officials, including the colony's governor. A number of ministers met with Alden from time to time in order to pray and fast for his "deliverance," but whether they meant deliverance from the charge itself or from being a wizard was uncertain.

Although Alden was a strong and self-assured man, he began to doubt his chances of escaping trial. Finally, in September 1692, after several witches had been hanged, he fled to friends in neighboring Duxbury and pounded on their door at midnight, shouting: "The devil is after me!" His friends smuggled Alden to safety in New York. There he joined other well-to-do or prominent individuals who had left Massachusetts rather than face the Salem court. There was no democracy among witches in the Bay Colony. With wealth or influence one had a far better chance of reaching safety in colonies like New York than did the ordinary citizen accused of witchcraft. The following year, Alden was declared innocent by special proclamation, and the "tall man from Boston" returned to Massachusetts, his person and property untouched.

Meanwhile, during the storm of arrests and imprisonments, a ship from England was bringing the man who would eventually control the outcome of events, Sir William Phips. He had recently been appointed the first royal governor of the Massachusetts Bay Colony.

Phips was born in New England, the son of a poor farmer in Maine. He had made a fortune in Boston and had added to it in the Caribbean islands, not far from where

Judge William Stoughton of the Court of Oyer and Terminer was a stubborn and overbearing man whose insistence that Rebecca Nurse be hanged was one of the low points of the vengeful trials. He was also a generous contributor to Harvard University.

Samuel Parris had worked as a merchant and had bought Tituba and John Indian. Phips found a sunken Spanish ship near Haiti and raised a treasure in gold worth well over a million dollars. England's king at the time, James II, had knighted Phips as a reward. Sir William was also the hero of several battles against the Indians and the French in America. After a trip to England he was returning home as a wealthy hero and the governor of Massachusetts.

When Sir William's ship sailed into Boston harbor in May 1692, he knew nothing of the witchcraft trials because he had been at sea for weeks. He was horrified at the news. Like almost everyone else at the time, Phips believed in witchcraft, but he was determined to get to the bottom of things. Dozens of suspected witches were in Boston jail awaiting trial. At the end of May, Phips appointed a special court to try the prisoners. He named seven judges, with his deputy governor, William Stoughton, as the chief justice. The court was called a Court of Oyer and Terminer. (This old English term was derived from French words meaning "to hear" and "to put an end to.") Verdicts of innocent or guilty were to be handed down by a jury picked from the men of Salem Town, where the trials were to take place.

The prisoners had to put their faith in the court. The judges were men of high standing in the colony. The accused could at least hope that the court would be careful about hanging respectable men and women who had been accused by a group of hysterical young girls. What the prisoners did not know, at first, was that most of the judges were just as severe as Hathorne.

Before they opened the Court of Oyer and Terminer, the judges made three decisions that hurt the chances of the accused witches. First, they decided to accept as evidence the records of the examinations Hathorne and Corwin had conducted in the village. These records—some of which were taken down by Samuel Parris himself—contained more than straightforward question-and-answer testimony. They also included biased vivid descriptions of the behavior of the afflicted girls. So the court was ready to take their fits and screams as "evidence." The second decision the members of the court made was to accept testimony about the "shapes" that could be seen only by afflicted persons. Third, and perhaps most important, the judges decided that anyone who *confessed* to being a witch would not be punished. They were reasoning that a confession was a sign that the accused person had broken the hold of the devil, and could be redeemed. But this meant that confession was rewarded, and it encouraged some, like Tituba, to accuse other innocent people in their confessions.

On June 2 the judges began their work by trying a woman named Bridget Bishop. Stoughton probably chose her because the case against her was strong, and because she was vulnerable. She was the wife of a tavern keeper in Salem Town and she had a suspect reputation. Also, several confessing witches had said she was one of their leaders. The jury quickly found her guilty, and the judges sentenced her to death. She was given a few extra days of life by an embarrassing discovery: there was no Massachusetts law providing the death penalty for witches. The colonial legislature, known as the General Court, quickly passed such a law. On June 10 the sheriff took Bridget in a cart to the top of Gallows Hill, where she was hanged. The first "witch" was gone.

But many more accused men and women were waiting, and Hathorne and Corwin were still conducting examinations in the village, turning up more and more suspects. Sometimes as many as fifty new witches were accused in a single day, no longer just in Salem Village but all over eastern Massachusetts. One week, then two weeks passed after the hanging of Bridget Bishop. But still the judges did not meet again. They were quarreling among themselves about the meaning of the afflicted girls' testimony concerning "shapes." This kind of evidence, which was called spectral evidence (from *specter,* or ghost), was considered all-important. Without it there would not be a case against a single suspected witch. The quarreling judges turned to the ministers of Boston and nearby towns to decide the question. The ministers finally decided that spectral evidence should be used, as long as the judges and jury were "careful" with it.

On June 28 the court met again, to try Rebecca Nurse. Goodwife Nurse was from a large and prosperous farm family of Salem Village. She was an old woman and nearly deaf. But she was a member of the church, and before the witchcraft panic she had been a respected old grandmother. The jury took the ministers' advice about being careful in admitting spectral evidence. This time, they ignored the shrieking, afflicted girls and brought back a verdict of not guilty. Chief Justice Stoughton quickly bullied the jury into reversing its verdict, however. Then Rebecca Nurse's relatives went to Governor Phips and persuaded him to stop the hanging. But it was no use. When Stoughton and others heard about Phips's action, they insisted that he change his mind.

Neither the jury nor the governor could save Rebecca Nurse, and on Tuesday, July 19, she was hanged. Four other women were hanged the same day. One was the hag of Salem Village, Sarah Good. When she was about to die, one of the ministers tried to persuade her to confess and save herself. Goody Good might well have done so. She had spent months in prison. One child had died there with her. A second child had been arrested as a witch, though she was only five years old. But these things had only toughened the old woman's will. "You are a liar," she spat back at the preacher. "I am no more a witch than you are a wizard. If you take my life away, God will give you blood to drink." With that, she went up the ladder to the waiting rope.

At the September meeting of the Court of Oyer and Terminer, one man refused to plead either innocent or guilty. He was Giles Cory, the husband of Martha Cory, who had already been condemned. Under an old English law, Cory was taken into a vacant field beside the prison in Salem Town and tortured. Heavy stones were piled on his chest, but he would not surrender and say either innocent or guilty. Instead—according to legend, at least—he said only "More weight!" By afternoon he had been crushed to death. Three days later, on September 22, the sheriff hauled eight more convicted witches to the top of Gallows Hill to die, bringing the total executed to twenty—not counting the several who had already died in prison.

After the hangings of September 22, as suddenly as it had begun, the panic was over. The afflicted girls had gone too far. In the early fall of 1692 they began to accuse almost everyone, including the pious wives of well-known ministers. One girl even claimed that Cotton Mather, the colony's leading minister, was a wizard. Several of the girls began to see the shape of Lady Mary Phips, the governor's wife! These charges simply could not be accepted.

The trials that began in Salem Village were stopped by some of the leading citizens of the colony. They had finally become convinced that the entire affair had been a terrible mistake. On October 26, before the Court of Oyer and Terminer opened again, the General Court ordered a new meeting of ministers to consider the problem. Three

THE HANGING OF WITCHES. This 1655 drawing shows women convicted of witchcraft being hanged in England. Four are dead already—at least the hangman is checking them to make sure they are dead. Three more are waiting below the gallows, and others are watching from the prison behind the barred window.

days later, the General Court dismissed the trial court, and Governor Phips began releasing prisoners on bond. In November, following the advice of the ministers, the governor established a new court, with new rules. In the new trials spectral evidence would not be accepted. And, just as important, confessing witches *would* be hanged. One by one, the prisoners were tried and found innocent. Five still insisted on confessing, and they were sentenced to hang, though Phips overruled the court and allowed even these five to live. It was too late for Sarah Good, Martha Cory, John Proctor, old Jacobs, and the rest who had died. But the Salem witch trials were over at last.

Salem Village and the rest of the colony then started the impossible task of settling accounts. The released prisoners were required to pay for food and rent during their time in prison. Some remained in jail for several months until these bills were paid. Samuel Parris's congregation voted to dismiss him, and he left Salem Village in disgrace. No one knows what happened to little Betty Parris, but her younger brother went insane and died while still a young man.

In January 1697, five years after Betty Parris and Abigail Williams had first been afflicted, the General Court voted a fund worth about $30,000, to be distributed among the relatives of the dead and the surviving witches. The money proved small compensation for the terrible anguish people had endured. When it was divided up, the lives of Martha and Giles Cory, for example, turned out to have been worth about $50.

After any tragedy, people's minds eventually turn to other matters. In Salem Village the families of the dead gradually and painfully made peace with the families of the afflicted girls. By 1706 the little town was calm. But on August 25 of that year, the meetinghouse was once more filled to overflowing. A young woman named Anne Putnam had come to ask for admission to membership in the church. According to New England church custom, she had to make a public confession, after which the members of the church would vote on whether to accept her.

As a young girl of twelve, Anne Putnam had been one of the most active of the afflicted girls. Now, at the age of twenty-six, she was asking for full admission into the adult community. The congregation was seated while the new minister read her confession aloud to them:

> I desire to be humbled before God for that sad providence in the year about '92. I, then being in my childhood, was made an instrument for the accusing of several persons of a grievous crime, whereby their lives were taken away from them. I now have good reason to believe they were innocent persons. What was said or done by me against any person, I can truly say I did not out of any anger, malice, or ill-will. What I did was done ignorantly, being deluded by Satan. I desire to lie in the dust, and to be humbled for it, and earnestly beg forgiveness of God, and from all those unto whom I have given just cause of sorrow and offence.

The minister finished reading, and then asked the congregation to vote. Sitting in the meetinghouse were many relatives of the innocent men and women whom Anne Putnam had helped imprison and hang. They must have scowled and clenched their hard farmers' fists. But they voted along with the rest of the congregation, unanimously, to accept Anne Putnam's plea for forgiveness. Shakily, she sat down. The travail of Salem Village had finally ended.

New Peoples and New Patterns in the Later Seventeenth Century

The years between 1640 and 1660 were a time of upheaval in English life that saw civil war, the execution of Charles I, and an experiment with Puritan rule. No new colonies were founded during this period. But with the restoration of the Stuart line and the return of Charles II to the English throne, a new phase of colonization began. New colonies were founded, and these attracted broad streams of immigration. And many of the older colonies continued to draw settlers in large numbers. So, interest in colonization continued on two levels: investors saw the plantations as a good place to put their money; and ordinary men and women saw America as a place offering opportunities they lacked at home.

The colonies were dramatically different in the later seventeenth century from the pattern earlier in the century. First, and foremost, they drew complex populations. The voluntary immigrant stream after mid-century was composed of people from all over Britain and Europe, not just from England. New Netherland had seen such a migrant pool from the beginning. Now mixed populations became the rule in the colonies, although the New England colonies received relatively fewer new immigrants and therefore retained a more homogeneously English population than other regions.

Secondly, a large percentage of newcomers were involuntary immigrants from Africa. During the later seventeenth century slavery became established as the labor system of the southern colonies, and slaves were present in all colonies. Even the minister in Salem Village, Samuel Parris, owned a slave, Tituba. This added yet another kind of complexity to colonial populations. Slavery also meant that the difference between the style of life of those who owned numbers of slaves and those who had few or none became increasingly greater. Colonists who started well-off, especially sons and daughters born in America, became wealthier. A man or woman who received an estate from parents got a start in life that newcomers could not match. Even in the middle and northern colonies, such "social distance" between rich and poor grew, although the extremes were less far apart than in the south.

The new colonies founded in the later seventeenth century shared design characteristics that set them apart from the earlier settlements. All these colonies were the property of one or a small number of proprietors, replacing the joint-stock company form that sponsored most of the successful early colonies. Several founders of later colonies took their rights as proprietors seriously and seized the opportunity to experiment with novel forms of government. Like earlier colonies, they offered land to colonists. They also offered a degree of religious toleration, and thereby attracted many who, fearing persecution in Europe, welcomed the chance to create a new life for themselves and their families in an atmosphere of freedom.

NEW COLONIES

THE CAROLINAS

The Carolina coast had always been considered an attractive site for settlement. The French Protestant Huguenots, the Spanish, and the English had all tried to create settlements there during the sixteenth century. But all had failed, and Carolina remained unsettled until after the middle of the seventeenth century. When the time came, the Carolinas were created in a unique way.

Rights to colonize were granted to a group of men by Charles II as a reward for their loyalty in supporting King Charles I during the Civil War. Eight aristocratic proprietors were given the grant of Carolina, which originally included both North Carolina and South Carolina, in 1663. Although the constitution they drew up for Carolina included provision for creation of an aristocratic, almost feudal, structure in the colony, the proprietors followed the lead of other successful English colonies in offering self-government through an elected assembly, religious toleration, and a generous headright system—originally 150 acres for every immigrant.

The immigrants from Europe to Carolina, as in all the colonies in the later seventeenth century, were largely from areas other than England. Some English religious dissenters came, who were excluded from civic life at home because of their religious beliefs. Other immigrants were from Scotland, still a separate country, Scots-Irish from Northern Ireland, and Huguenots from France.

But many of the earliest Carolina planters, especially in the southern part, did not come directly from Europe but rather from the English colony of Barbados in the Caribbean. That colony had become extremely rich as a sugar-producing island, and wealthy planters were prepared to set up their sons as planters in South Carolina. Drawing settlers from Barbados carried momentous consequences, because slavery was already well-established in the sugar islands. In the older mainland plantations in the Chesapeake, the transition from indentured servitude of Europeans to permanent slavery of Africans was in its early stages and the proportion of slaves in the population remained fairly small in the 1660s. In South Carolina, by contrast, slavery was the principal labor system from the beginning on the plantations, and slaves made up a large percentage of the population.

The Barbadian immigrants received enormous land grants and, using their slaves, set up large-scale plantations. The city of Charleston was created in 1670 as a planned city, with streets and squares laid out in advance, and many of the planters chose to live in the city, spending much of their time away from their plantations. South Carolina was set apart from other colonies by the scale of its commitment to slavery. It also differed in its wealth. South Carolina was to be the most lucrative of all the mainland colonies, and therefore was accorded most importance in the eyes of English officials. Charleston society maintained an opulence of style not seen in the other colonies. Travelers remarked that the Charleston people lived like the nobility in England: "State, magnificence, and ostentation, the natural attendants of riches, are conspicuous, among this people." They also kept up with the latest fashions from England, in dress, the theater, books, and music. Huge landholdings meant that parents of this elite class could endow all their children, women as well as men, with estates. Women thus became important in the maintenance of family position, and intermarriage within this elite cemented relationships.

FORCED LABOR. This English handkerchief shows slaves, male and female, working in the fields. Working alongside them is a European criminal, who has been "transported" and temporarily reduced to the condition of a slave.

The sources of this wealth changed over time. The plantations were first set to work growing provisions to be sold to the Caribbean colonies. But much more lucrative was the trade in deerskins with neighboring Indians. More than 50,000 skins were exported annually. Unfortunately the trade also led to the enslavement of many Indians, who were encouraged to acquire European goods in the expectation of paying for them later with deerskins. The European traders set the prices for their trade goods so high that Indians were never able to pay off their debts and, for many, slavery was the result. The deerskins, like the furs farther north, were slowly depleted, and as the trade brought increasing conflict on the frontier, it receded in importance.

Other kinds of enterprises took the place of the trade in deerskins in the economy. Ultimately rice culture became the most important. Slaves' knowledge of African modes of cultivation was extremely important in the trial-and-error period when Carolinians learned how to produce rice, but the European masters reaped the profits. Indigo, the extremely valuable dye crop, was also important. It had been introduced through the efforts of young Eliza Lucas, who had carried out extensive experiments until she perfected her knowledge of its culture and processing.

In 1691 Carolina was informally separated into two colonies with the appointment of separate governors. The government had always been the scene of stormy debates and active plotting as various groups vied for control of the colony. North Carolina, originally Albemarle County within Carolina, had seen its interests ignored as the proprietors focused on the richer land to the south, and the colony had seen several conflicts with dictatorial governors. One problem was the pirates, including the infamous Blackbeard, who infested the Outer Banks and terrorized coastal settlers.

North Carolina's settlers, like those away from the tidewater region in South Carolina, were religious dissenters from England, or from other parts of Britain, as well as from France. The colony also welcomed Swiss and German immigrants, and specialized recruiters began to operate in these countries.

As North Carolina began to grow, it paid the price for the activities of the deerskin traders on the frontier. The Tuscarora Indians attacked frontier settlements in 1711. Count Christophe von Graffenried, the Swiss and German immigrants' leader, transmitted the natives' complaints: the settlers "cheated the Indians in trading, and would not allow them to hunt near their plantations, and under that pretense took away from them their

BLACKBEARD THE PIRATE. Edward Teach, known as Blackbeard, previously based in Jamaica, operated within the Outer Banks of North Carolina, where he was tolerated by members of the colonial government. He was killed by a royal navy ship in 1718. The portrait shows him with smouldering matches under his hat, pieces of lighted wick necessary for shooting matchlock muskets.

game, arms, and ammunition. . . . These poor Indians, insulted in many ways by a few rough Carolinians more barbarous and unkind than the savages themselves, could not stand such treatment much longer, and began to think of their safety and vengeance, what they did very secretly." But the final cause of the outbreak of war was the foundation of the Swiss settlement of New Bern in 1710, which seemed to forecast a whole new wave of Europeans on the land. The Tuscaroras ultimately left the region and joined the Iroquois League in New York. South Carolina men had joined the northern colony in fighting the Tuscaroras, and in 1715 the South Carolina frontier was inflamed when the Yamasee Indians rose up against the activities of the traders, many of whom had contrived to enslave Indians. But the result of the Indian wars, as in the other colonies, was to cripple Indian resistance and to clear the frontier for continued settlement.

North Carolina's economy more closely resembled that of Virginia, its neighbor to the north, and the settlers marketed their produce through Virginia. North Carolina was a colony of modest farms, many engaged in subsistence agriculture, with some production for export. Wedged in between opulent South Carolina and Virginia, its planters were often ridiculed as lazy and unambitious. William Byrd of Virginia wrote of them, "The Men, for their Part, Just like the Indians, impose all the Work upon the poor Women. They make their Wives rise out of their Beds early in the Morning, at the same they lie and Snore, till the Sun has run one third of his course, and disperst all the unwholesome Damps. . . . To speak the Truth, tis a thorough Aversion to Labor that makes People file off to N. Carolina, where Plenty and a Warm Sun confirm them in their Disposition to Laziness for their whole Lives." Byrd's comment, like many similar ones, was a class-based judgment. Byrd owned hundreds of slaves and lived as a gentleman; he certainly did no physical labor. His remarks on the North Carolinians involved the disdain of the gentleman for those he considered beneath him.

PENNSYLVANIA

Pennsylvania, like the New England colonies and Maryland before it, was created as a religious experiment. The founder, William Penn, was a Quaker, a dissenting sect that emphasized the experience of God within each believer rather than more formal types of worship. Where the Puritans emphasized study of the written word, for Quakers the Bible was valuable because it confirmed what they knew from their own insight. The Quakers carried many of the tenets of Protestantism to their most extreme conclusions. Taking literally the Protestant idea of the "priesthood of all believers," they had no ordained ministers. They refused to bear arms, or to take oaths, and they insisted that all are equal in the eyes of God. Women preached as often as men in Quaker meetings. In fact, the Quakers represented exactly the outcome that many had feared from Puritanism's earlier challenge to authority. They were persecuted in England, and thus many were eager to emigrate after Penn founded Pennsylvania in 1681.

Pennsylvania's early years resembled those of Massachusetts Bay in some ways. The colony was set up on utopian lines. Penn expected colonists to give their loyalty and hard work in exchange for his provision of freedom of conscience and liberal political rights. He envisioned his colony as consisting of farming families living in close-knit communities, and he planned the city of Philadelphia to be a model of design. The immigrants came largely in family groups, with, as in Massachusetts, about a third of the number coming as servants. Almost 8,000 people came in the first five years.

Pennsylvania differed from Massachusetts Bay in important ways. Where the earlier colony had been founded by a company that had allowed the colonists to take control of their own affairs from the beginning, Pennsylvania was a proprietary colony, the property of William Penn. Penn wanted to keep close supervision of developments in the colony so that he could keep it in line with his paternalistic ideas. He had to spend much of his time in England looking after the colony's affairs. Inevitably, friction developed between the absent proprietor and the settlers actually experiencing the problems of colonization.

Pennsylvania also differed from the early Puritan colonies in that, like all regions in the

WILLIAM PENN'S NEGOTIATION WITH THE DELAWARES. This idealized rendition of the founding of Pennsylvania, implying peace and mutual benefit, was painted by Benjamin West many years later.

later seventeenth-century, it attracted immigrants from all over Britain and Europe. Although almost all these people held religious ideas similiar to those of the Quakers and came fleeing persecution, Pennsylvania never had the kind of cultural unity that New England enjoyed with its almost exclusively English population. Where Penn had anticipated a kind of melting pot in which all these people would come together, in reality they preferred to settle in enclaves with people from their home territories. Names such as Germantown demonstrate the cocoons in which newcomers sought the company of those who shared their culture. Although the Quakers retained political control of the colony for its first half-century, culturally it was divided, and suspicions often developed between the various groups in place of the cooperation that Penn had looked for.

TRADE

THE ATLANTIC

Pennsylvania's economic future lay in trade throughout the Atlantic world. Pennsylvania, and the Middle Colonies generally, shared this type of economic development with New England. Both regions were suited to family farming, which produced food for families, with some surplus to sell. These regions, growing moderate amounts of many crops, differed from the southern colonies, which produced large quantities of a small number of commodities, all of which were for sale. The southern colonies had no problem in paying for the manufactured goods all settlers had to buy from England; sale of their tobacco, rice, and indigo paid for them. The middle and northern colonies, lacking a product to sell in England, did have a problem.

New Englanders began to solve their financial problem early through the fishing trade. They became involved in large-scale fishing and began to sell fish in Europe as well as in America. As New England and then the Middle Colonies began to grow food surpluses, traders sold these to planters in the southern colonies and in the Caribbean who did not want to divert their slaves' energies away from profitable crops into growing food. They also sold timber products such as barrel staves made from the apparently limitless woods.

These activities involved the merchants in international commerce because trade was not specialized in this period. When their ships landed in a port, merchants exchanged their cargoes for whatever product was available. The next port of call would be the place where the captain reckoned he could sell that new cargo. For example, a load of fish might take a ship to Spain, where the captain could pick up a cargo of sweet wine—sherry or madeira. The wine might be sold in the West Indies, where a cargo of sugar could be loaded, and this sugar might be brought to New England to be made into rum. Thus merchants from New England and the Middle Colonies were drawn into a trading pattern that covered the entire Atlantic region. No one knew as a ship left home port when it would return; often many months, even years, would elapse while it was at sea. Ultimately most merchants also became involved in the slave trade. Slaves were treated as just another cargo. These mercantile activities caused profound unease among many New England Puritans because trade threatened to open the colony to the "profane" world that their parents had fled. Seaports such as Salem became divided over the eagerness with which some people took advantage of new opportunities for economic gain, and the witchcraft crisis was an extreme index of their uneasiness.

Samuel Parris, Salem Village's minister, understood the ways that trade, with its individualistic, profit-seeking values, might undermine New England's traditional "godliness." He himself had been a merchant in Barbados before he had failed and turned to the ministry. And just two years before his own daughter became "afflicted," he had bitterly contrasted the desire of merchants for "filthy lucre" with the demanding spiritual purposes of those who preached the gospel. "The

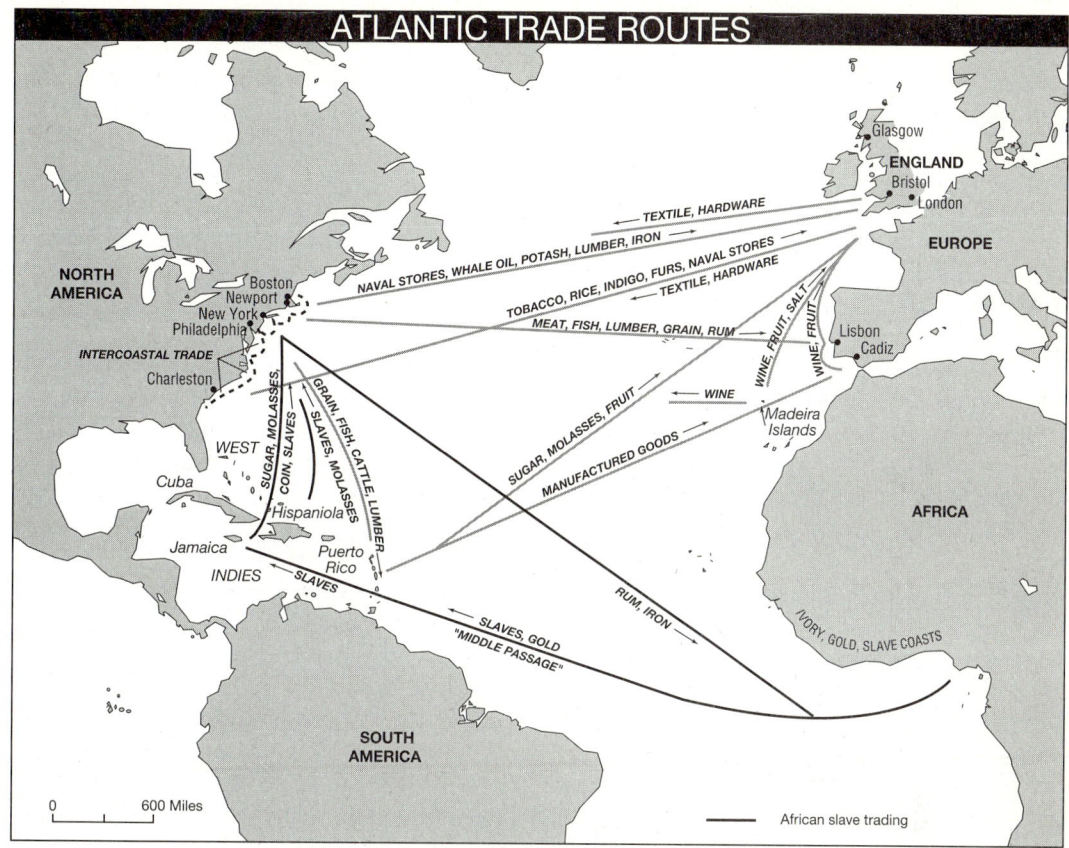

work of the Lord," he said, is done "deceitfully" if it is done "merely as a trade—to pick a living out of it." "Ministerial employment is the Lord's work. Aye, but when a man aims chiefly at himself in it, then he does it deceitfully, for he converts . . . God's service to his own private profit. . . . The ministry is a most noble calling; aye, but it is a bad trade—a pernicious trade indeed."

Parris seems to have understood his congregation of farmers very well. In 1692, a startling pattern of witchcraft accusations had emerged. The accusers were from the families of farmers in an outlying agricultural settlement. But the accused were mostly people who had close connections with nearby Salem Town, and with its prosperous elite of shipowners and merchants. The afflicted girls of Salem Village had no knowledge of sociology or economic theory, but they did seem to have an instinctive sense that they could tap an agrarian village's resentment of the larger, more progressive, and wealthier port town. Even Tituba, Samuel Parris's slave, may have grasped this subtle fact. When she was asked who led the conspiracy of witches, she did not single out anyone in the village, but claimed that it was a "tall man from Boston"—an even larger and wealthier port than Salem Town.

MERCANTILISM

Commerce in the seventeenth century depended very much on personal relationships. American merchants often benefited from being within the English trading system, with its representatives stationed in many ports of call. English merchants tried to make sure that Americans worked in cooperation with their trade rather than as competitors. Economic doctrine of the time was based on Mercantilism, the theory that in order to be secure a country should keep its trade within a closed system. Colonies, in this theory, were supposed to supply raw materials the parent country lacked, and then to buy all of the processed goods they needed from the home country. Thus the country that founded colonies would never be dependent on outsiders for raw materials, and the colonies' purchasing power would keep the parent economy healthy.

Mercantilism was supported by the English Navigation Acts, which were designed to regulate trade and keep it within the English system and to force colonial merchants to pay the same customs duties that English merchants paid. The first Navigation Act was passed in 1651, and many more followed throughout the colonial period. In the eighteenth century American merchants sometimes came to resent the restrictions the acts placed on their trade and successfully evaded them.

Successful American merchants built up their own set of relationships, often placing agents, called factors, in various places where their trade took them. The factor, often a member of the merchant's family, could assemble a cargo so that when a merchant's ship arrived it would be able to reload quickly and lose no time in getting to the next opportunity. The Pennsylvania Quakers were particularly successful in the Atlantic trade because they treated all other Quakers as family members. The Quakers became famous for keeping their word and living up to their responsibilities. Their huge network gave them great advantages.

For many reasons the Middle Colonies pulled ahead of New England in trade and as a magnet for new immigrants. Their central location and superb trading facilities were important; New York's harbor is one of the best natural harbors in the world. Moreover, the land in the Middle Colonies was far more fertile than New England's. The New Englanders had been very successful, and their population had grown dramatically in the seventeenth century, but such success also had its price. The land could not sustain such a large population, and by the end of the century New England was importing food. The Middle Colonies' population also grew through natural increase, and they were able to continue to absorb huge numbers of new settlers.

TRADE AND SETTLEMENT IN THE INTERIOR

The French and Spanish continued to dominate development in the interior of the continent. René Robert Cavelier, Sieur de La Salle, explored the Mississippi River from the Great Lakes to its mouth in 1682. In 1685, La Salle returned with a French commission to establish a colony at the mouth of the Mississippi River, which the French, attempting to render the native name, called the "Mischipipi." Spain and France were at war when he set out. Neither La Salle nor the Spanish mariners who soon began looking for his settlement to attack it could actually locate the mouth of the great river from the Gulf, because of the mud flats and many channels around it. La Salle built his small settlement on the Texas coast at Matagorda Bay. When a Spanish party finally located it in 1689, they found the fort had been destroyed by an Indian attack. Disease and dissension had rendered it miserable, and the disgruntled colonists had assassinated La Salle before the attack.

At the end of the century, Pierre LeMoyne, Sieur d'Iberville, did succeed in entering the Mississippi River from the Gulf. He created a tiny French settlement on Biloxi Bay (soon moved to Mobile Bay) and a fort near the great river's mouth in 1699. The Spanish also sought to control the Gulf shore. While the French were settling Mobile, the Spanish created a fort nearby at Pensacola, attempting to counter French thoughts of expanding eastward.

INDIAN WOMEN FROM LOWER MISSISSIPPI VALLEY, sketched by Dumont de Montigny in the early eighteenth century. The woman on the left is covered with tattoos, the one in the middle is wearing a feather cape, and the one on the right is pounding corn.

To the west in Texas there was a small community of Spanish settlers and Hispanicized Manso Indians at El Paso del Norte. Earlier, in about 1659, the Franciscans had begun to build their mission of Nuestra Señora de Guadalupe at the site of modern Ciudad Juárez.

Farther north around the Great Lakes, in the region the French called the *pays d'en haut* (upper country), a large number of people representing many Indian tribes as well as various European companies vied for a place in the rich trades. This "middle ground" drew people from the north, west, and east, and no one group could control the multifaceted exchange relationships that grew up there—although many Indian leaders as well as English and French emissaries tried to achieve control. Violence often accompanied these attempts at dominance. But new kinds of relationships emerged as well and many people, European and Indian, found themselves living in unexpected patterns in this land beyond the frontier. These novel frameworks incorporated both European and Indian ways of doing things, but the trade also tied the interior into the currents of the Atlantic trade world.

NEW ENGLAND TO FLORIDA: THE SETTLED COLONIES

NEW ENGLAND

New England experienced severe cultural strains in the later seventeenth century. Immigration into the region had slowed dramatically after the outbreak of the Civil War in England in the early 1640s, and it never became high again. Thus the great population growth stemmed from natural increase (more births than deaths), and New England was more cut off from new trends than other regions that continued to receive new migrants. Massachusetts Bay especially became inward-turned culturally, and the colony's leaders feared constantly that it was losing its special Puritan character.

One concern centered on the spiritual condition of the younger generations, especially those who had been born in the colony. They seemed to lack the spiritual intensity of the immigrants. Many were becoming adults and even parents without ever having come forward to ask for membership in the church. The very right for which the first generation had given up everything seemed to mean nothing to their children and grandchildren, and much anguish was expressed over this "declension" as the ministers termed it. Historians have suggested a different interpretation. Away from the tensions and fears of England, the younger generations may not have felt the particular kind of psychic crisis that their parents had experienced. Life was more placid, and they had grown up used to a Puritan structure rather than having to fight for it. Also the colony's mythology had so dramatized the lives of the founding generations that younger men and women, although they may have had genuine experiences of God's grace, might have felt that their feelings were too pale to be the real thing.

Whatever the reasons, the ministers saw a crisis looming over the status of the children that were being born to these younger men and women. The new parents had been baptized because their own mothers and fathers were church members. Now what would happen to these babies, who could not be baptized if their parents never became members? In order to solve this problem a meeting of the colony's ministers, termed a synod, in 1662 suggested a compromise that has become known as the Halfway Covenant. Under this compromise, those who had been baptized could be considered halfway members of the church, and their children could then be baptized. Many congregations adopted this plan; some did not. But all congregations experienced great turmoil over it and the need to discuss the problem at all made many fear for the future of their experiment.

Ministers contined to warn their congregations of the dangers of becoming lax and forgetting the true mission of the Puritans, creating a form of sermon so insistent and intense that it became known as a Jeremiad, after the Old Testament prophet. But what the ministers did not realize was that much of the "decline" they lamented was really growth and development. And this development would allow New England to continue to thrive in the eighteenth century.

Widespread concern over New England's spiritual decline, and particularly over the falling away of the younger generation, led to stirrings of new religious "enthusiasm" that would lead to a great movement of evangelical "awakening" in the eighteenth century. Ministers who detected these stirrings in their congregations directed and nurtured them. Samuel Parris in Salem Village interpreted the "fits" he witnessed in his daughter and her friends as the beginnings of cosmic struggle between God and Satan right in his own village. He was proud that even though young New Englanders were succumbing to worldliness in other places, in his congregation it was the younger generation that was leading the fight. The testimony of the "afflicted" girls as they resisted the Devil opened the way for their elders to confess their sins and come to terms with God. He seized the opportunity for a great drama of religious renewal.

Contributing to the sense of decline was the changing basis of economic life. Farmers occupied a declining role in the economy, as the rocky soil of New England began to give out after decades of overfarming. The merchants and their activities pointed the way to the future, but Puritan society had always been uneasy about them. The farmers, men and women who produced real products that one could see and touch from their own labor, seemed to be ideal for a Puritan society. Merchants, on the other hand, added cost to commodities by buying them up and moving them from place to place, but without really changing the product at all. One could not see and touch the value they added. Therefore the ministers and their congregations were rendered uneasy about the decline of farming and growth of commerce in New England's economy. This uneasiness rose to the surface in 1692: the accusing girls were from farming families and the accused were all somehow tainted by the tincture of commerce and greed. The scope and intensity of that crisis shows just how real these fears were.

NEW YORK

By the middle of the seventeenth century, Spain was no longer England's most important enemy. The Netherlands, England's fellow Protestant country, was now the focus of English enmity, and the cause was trade rivalry. The Netherlands was the greatest trading nation in the early seventeenth century and England was now trying to build its own power at sea. The English government had passed the first of its Navigation Acts, excluding Dutch ships from trade within the British Empire, in 1651, and this act led to the first Anglo-Dutch War in 1652–1654. The English passed a new Navigation Act in 1660 and the war was renewed. In the course of this second war, an English fleet seized New Netherland in 1664. The attention of the strong Dutch navy was focused elsewhere, and little New Netherland was too small and weak to offer any resistance.

The colony was renamed New York in honor of Charles II's brother James, Duke of York (the future James II), who became the plantation's proprietor. New Jersey was soon split off into a separate proprietorial colony. English settlers had been moving from Connecticut into the Dutch territory of Long Island under New Netherland's liberalized land-grant policies of 1640, creating English towns there. Thus, much of the eastern part of the colony was already English, but the rest of the colony remained Dutch in culture for most of the seventeenth century. As part of the settlement the English agreed that Dutch inhabitants would retain their rights and lands. In particular women under Dutch law had greater independent rights than English women. They could hold property, make contracts, and keep control of the dowry they brought to their marriage; none of these rights ordinarily belonged to English women, whose husbands or fathers controlled their property.

The Dutch briefly reconquered the colony in 1673, but the English quickly recovered control. Because New Netherland had been designed on different lines from the English settlements, James, the duke of York, saw the colony as a good place for experimentation with new forms of government. All land grants were called in for examination and had to be reconfirmed. Governor Richard Nicholls drew up a law code, called the Duke's Laws, in 1665. Under it the colonists had no elected assembly and no town meetings. Moreover, the government renewed, and even enlarged, the economic monopolies that had prevailed under the Dutch. English Long Islanders particularly resented these restrictions of their rights after their own country took control; they expected at least the same privileges that other English colonists had. New York did offer religious toleration, recognizing the great variety of creeds already present in the colony. There was a brief movement toward liberalization with the calling of an assembly during the early 1680s but the opening was not sustained.

New York occupied a crucial position between colonial empires. Tension between France and England was growing as the seventeenth century neared its end. The Iroquois League in northern New York—the Five Nations of Senecas, Cayugas, Onondagas, Oneidas, and Mohawks—occupied a controlling location in the fur trade between the French in Canada and the English in New York.[1] Although the Iroquois League was able to make use of its strategic location and superior organization, the Iroquois also found that the fur trade involved them in murderous and draining wars, especially with the Hurons to the north. The Iroquois also attempted to extend their influence westward toward the Great Lakes, the *"pays d'en haut."* Warfare increasingly was for the purpose of obtaining captives to replenish population lost both to warfare and to recurrent epidemics of imported diseases. These "mourning wars" involved the League members in a spiral of death.

Integral to the Iroquois League's balancing role was the problem of dealing with the two rival European empires, and many tribes split over the issue. Each empire thought it had won the loyalty

---

[1] *The Five Nations became the Six Nations in the eighteenth century when the Tuscaroras abandoned their location on the Carolina frontier and moved north to join them.*

NEW YORK COLONY SEAL. The seal's portrayal of beavers is a vivid presentation of the centrality of the fur trade to New York's economy.

of the tribes at various times, and therefore felt a sense of betrayal when Indians acted independently. In 1684 representatives of the Onondagas and Cayugas told Governor Thomas Dongan of New York: "We have put ourselves under the great Sachem Charles that lives over the great lake." They gave Dongan two deerskins and asked him to send them to the king "that he may write upon them, and put a great Red Seal to them." At the same time others, representing different political alignments, said to the French: "We are born free. We neither depend on Onontio [their name for the French governor] nor Corlaer [the English, originally their name for the Dutch]. We may go where we please, and carry with us whom we please, and buy and sell what we please." Finally the cycle of warfare was brought under control by the Grand Settlement of 1701 at Montreal, in which the Iroquois agreed to remain neutral in wars between England and France, and they withdrew from the area to the west.

THE CHESAPEAKE

Chesapeake society also underwent dramatic changes in the later seventeenth century. Most notable was the transition from European indentured servitude to slavery as the dominant form of labor. Whereas South Carolina was committed to slavery from its beginnings in the early 1660s, the Chesapeake continued to rely primarily on indentured servants until almost the end of the century. Slaves began to be imported into the Chesapeake colonies in fairly large numbers from the 1660s, but slavery began to dominate only after 1680. Why this transition took place when it did is unclear. Before 1680 planters seemed to prefer servants from England. Since most plantations were small and masters worked alongside servants, they may have wanted to have coworkers with whom they could talk and who shared their own cultural assumptions. After 1680 the economic situation began to improve in England and emigration seemed less attractive to young men and women than new opportunities at home, so planters may have turned to slaves in part because servants were less willing to come. On the other hand, slaves were more easily obtainable by the end of the seventeenth century because the slave trade had opened up. Also the disease environment in the Chesapeake seemed less bad, and planters may have been willing to pay the higher prices for slaves now because they expected them to survive. Thus a slave for life would be a good investment, especially as the slave's children would also belong to the master. All these reasons converged to underscore the move to enslavement of Africans, and soon the laws in the Chesapeake began to reflect the new labor system. Slavery was legally defined as a condition that pertained only to people of African heritage and was lifelong and inherited by their children. Masters of servants had owned their labor for a set period of years, but masters of slaves owned their bodies forever.

Another new element in the Chesapeake in the later seventeenth century was the growing creole (a person of European parentage born in America) presence. The children of those lucky former servants who had made it through servitude, had acquired their headrights, and found a marriage partner were beginning to come of age and have children of their own. As native-born people began to predominate in the population, it marked an enormous change in Chesapeake life. These young men and women occupied a privileged status. Immigrants from England had to serve long terms of servitude and then, often late in their twenties, began life with a fifty-acre headright and a few tools to clear it with. But the creoles, who often came of age at eighteen, started adult life with plantations already operating and slave forces already doing the work. They began with elite status and, with slavery established as the labor system, were able to keep adding to their holdings, whereas former servants were not able to amass the capital to acquire even one expensive slave. Increasingly it was creoles who were elected to office and who were considered the natural leaders of the colony. These men and women usually married within their class and thus they created a network of relationships.

As the elite came to dominate, both economically and socially, in the Chesapeake, it was less a "good poor man's country." Headrights, if they could still be had, were far out on the frontier and were less desirable. Maryland recognized this fact when it abolished the headright system in 1681.

The Chesapeake economy benefited from diversification in the later seventeenth century and early eighteenth century. Tobacco prices were very low in the last decades of the seventeenth century. Many planters turned to growing wheat, and the region became self-sufficient in food. Tobacco exports picked up in the early eighteenth century, and the now-diversified Chesapeake economy boomed. The population, both European and African, continued to grow, and settlers moved both north and south along the mountain ranges to the west.

FLORIDA

The Spanish in Florida continued to attempt to win converts to Christianity. By 1675 there were four missions, Guale (along the coast of Georgia), Timucua (along the east coast and in central Florida), Apalachee (along the Gulf coast), and Apalachicola (southern Georgia into Alabama). The Apalachicola Indians were known as the Lower Creeks to the English. Between forty and seventy Franciscans served in these far-flung missions at any one time, a far greater number of missionaries than the English colonists ever sent out. The priests claimed thousands of converts, about 10,000 new Catholics by one estimate, 26,000 by another. The missions originally extended up into South

PROCESSING TOBACCO. Tobacco was a labor-intensive crop, both as it grew in the field and in its later drying and packing. Here African-American slaves—men, women, and children—do the heavy work of bringing in and hanging the tobacco. White servants in the foreground do lighter work. The white servants are fully dressed in European style, whereas the slaves have little clothing.

Carolina, but these were withdrawn under Indian pressure, spurred on by the foundation of Carolina, after 1660. The Apalachicola mission was also quickly abandoned.

Some of these missions were supported by forts, but these, such as Fort San Luís near modern Tallahassee, were also abandoned at the opening of the eighteenth century. Only the small fort at St. Augustine remained, with its complement of about 300 married soldiers and their families, with a few priests and officials. All efforts to make the fort self-sustaining through introduction of crops and small-scale industrial activities had failed, and it continued to be dependent on an annual subsidy from the Spanish government, which saw the fort as a protection for Cuba.

COLONIAL WARS

A wave of frontier wars and rebellions swept over the colonies in the 1670s and 1680s, in part reflecting local concerns, and in part reflecting general developments both in America and in Europe. In the long-settled regions—Virginia, New Mexico, and New England—Indian resistance to European demands and expansion broke out in open warfare. The Pueblo Revolt in New Mexico (1680), Bacon's Rebellion in Virginia (1676), and King Philip's War in New England (1675–1676) all marked the end of an era of expansion.

THE PUEBLO REVOLT

New Mexico's plantations received tribute from the Indians under the system of *encomienda*, under which an *encomendero*, holder of a royal grant, was entitled to annual payment of goods from a specified group of Indians or pueblos. Sometimes *encomenderos* forced Indians to work directly for them, although this was not legal, and Indians taken into Spanish homes were often treated as slaves. Because New Mexico was so far removed from the centers of power and regulation in Mexico and in Spain, settlers were freer to bend the rules.

By 1680 times were hard for the Pueblos. Twenty years of drought and high temperatures had created harsh conditions: "a great many Indians perished of hunger, lying dead along the roads, in the ravines, and in their huts." Also, the Pueblos, whose homes were not moveable, were easy targets for Indian raiders from nomadic groups—Apaches, Navajos, and Comanches, who were mounted on horses.

In these times of hardship, Pueblos increasingly turned back to their native religion to try to right the balance of nature. The Franciscans punished such behavior savagely. In one case in 1675 three native priests were hanged and one committed suicide, as forty-three other priests were publicly whipped. The Pueblos decided that they must expel the Spaniards altogether to rid their country of the alien religion as well as the labor demands placed on them.

Popé, a priest who had been among those whipped in 1675, coordinated the planning for the Pueblo Revolt of 1680 from his headquarters at Taos. Although not all pueblos joined and some were split, the revolt involved more than twenty-four pueblos and 17,000 people. The Spanish numbered about 2,500. Outlying farms and villages were destroyed, and Santa Fe was besieged. When the town gave up, its inhabitants, including many refugees who had gathered there, were allowed to move back down to Mexico. About 400 Spanish were killed, and their churches were destroyed. Christian images were burned, and the Indians renounced their baptism and marriage within the church.

Although they rejected Christianity and Spanish culture, the Pueblos kept much of what the Europeans had brought. They continued to plant European crops and nurtured their livestock. And, although their victory was complete, it was not lasting. The Spanish set up their new capital at El Paso, but life was very hard. Then in the 1690s, a renewed effort in New Mexico was led by Diego de Vargas. Vargas succeeded in retaking Santa Fe and used it as a base from which to campaign against individual pueblos. All were eventually reconquered except for the Hopis, who were most remote from Spanish centers of power.

The renewal of native life and its aftermath had cost the Pueblos a great deal. Their population was in decline, and many had fled up into the plains or to join the Apaches and Navajos. But the Spanish had also suffered, and they never attempted to enforce discipline with the same strictness as before. The hated system of *encomienda* was not reestablished, but the Spanish did bring in *repartimiento*, under which Indians were required to provide labor on a rotating basis. In the eighteenth century the Spanish settlements would remain small and largely cut off from the centers of Spanish power to the south.

BACON'S REBELLION

War between Indians and colonists began in a different way in the Chesapeake, which saw the first example of a classic type of grievance in American history: resentment by people settled in the west against the governing elite in the east. By the 1670s the Virginia frontier had brought settlers uncomfortably close to Indians to the west, including many natives who had earlier been displaced from their traditional homes in the east. These settlers, often poor English men and women who had labored through long terms of

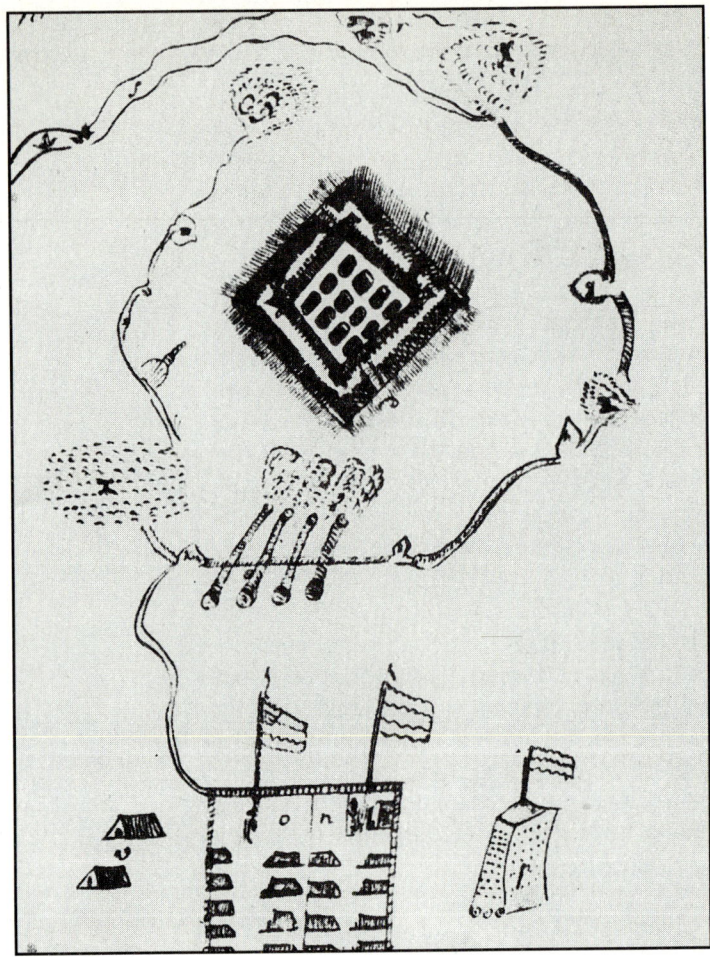

SUSQUEHANNOCK FORT. This picture of the colonists' attack on the Susquehannock fort in Maryland appeared in the report of a royal commission sent to investigate after Bacon's Rebellion. The illustration shows that the Susquehannocks, who were a powerful presence along the frontier, had built fortified villages and were formidable opponents.

servitude in order to gain land, found that the only land available to them was on the frontier. It was expensive and cumbersome to establish a farm there, because all the markets and sources of supply were along the coast. Access to the rivers, the only way to get from the coast to the interior, belonged to the great planters who owned the land along them. So the poor found their legitimate desire simply to live on their own constantly thwarted by the wealthy elite, who charged them high prices for every service.

Not only was life for these frontier people expensive, but they continually felt unsafe. A traditional warrior's path linking the great confederations in the north to those in the south carried Indians along the mountain chains in the west, and ex-servants attempting to farm in the region feared the presence of heavily armed Indians. Rumors of attacks circulated, and the settlers lived in constant fear. They expected the government to protect them. If not, they would take matters into their own hands.

For their part, the Indians were also simply trying to find a way to live in the dramatically changed circumstances. The tribes that originally met and challenged the Jamestown settlers were now much reduced by war and disease. Pushed into the lands of their traditional enemies, many had coalesced into new tribal entities. Many had long since made their peace with the settlers and, like them, wanted to live quietly. But their very weakness meant that they could not control the Indians that passed through the territory. And the line of English settlement kept moving west; no Indians could feel secure even on the reduced lands they held.

Virginia governor Sir William Berkeley wanted peace with the Indians, and believed that harmony could come if the colonists were restrained and the Indians knew they would not be threatened. He was even willing to create a limit to further settlement to reassure the natives. Such a policy seemed merely weak and self-serving to those in the west, who were forced to pay very high taxes and who demanded that the government act in their interest.

A series of incidents inflamed the frontier in the mid-1670s. Nathaniel Bacon, a young gentleman of a prominent family in England, had recently arrived in the colony but had not been accepted into the governing circles as he had expected. He put himself at the head of a growing group of angry settlers. The rebels attacked all Indians, those friendly to the colonists as well as those who had been hostile. They argued that the weaker friendly Indians could be used as cover by the warlike tribes; therefore, the planters felt they could not tolerate the presence of any Indians. As Bacon put it, the war was "against all Indians in general for that they were all Enemies."

Bacon and his followers went on to confront the government in Jamestown. For a time Bacon's forces took over the town and control of the government. Governor Berkeley had felt all along that his position was impossible: "How miserable the man is that governs a people where six parts of seven at least are poor, indebted, discontented, and armed." But as the summer of 1676 drew into autumn Berkeley's ability to draw on the resources of the English government became clear; rumors of the imminent arrival of large numbers of warships and troops made many rebels reconsider. And debilitating disease had spread through the forces. Nathaniel Bacon himself died of dysentery (what they called the "bloody flux") in October, and the rebellion collapsed. The most long-lasting effect of the rebel-

NATHANIEL BACON painted this picture of himself while he was a young man in England. He depicted himself as a young gentleman, very much in the way that Raleigh had been portrayed earlier.

lion was the entrenched enmity against all Indians felt by the settlers.

KING PHILIP'S WAR

At almost exactly the same time that frontier grievances and fears erupted in Bacon's Rebellion in Virginia, another frontier war was waged in New England, where the line of settlement was to the north as well as the west. Metacom, whom the English called King Philip, was a son of Massasoit of the Wampanoags, the chief who had worked to maintain good and mutually beneficial relations with the Plymouth settlers. Metacom was able to forge a confederation of many New England tribes who had been forced to relinquish their most desirable lands in the face of the inexorable advance of settlement. The fighting began in Plymouth colony in 1675, but quickly spread

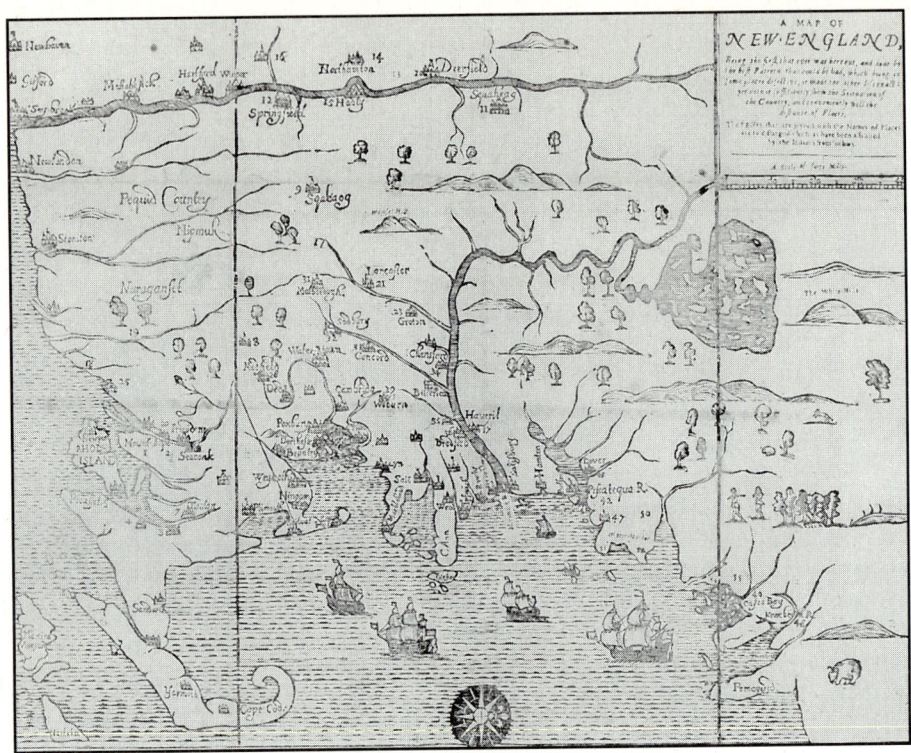

MAP OF NEW ENGLAND, in William Hubbard's *Narrative of the Troubles with the Indians in New England,* published just after King Philip's War in 1677. This map is turned to show off the author's points. The convention that maps should always have north at the top was not yet generally accepted.

throughout New England in the form of guerrilla warfare, hit-and-run raids on outlying hamlets.

Villages on the frontier of settlement were kept in a constant state of fear and uncertainty, not knowing when a band of fighters might swoop down on them. Some men and women from almost every attack were taken prisoner, and some captives were carried up into Canada. This war spawned a new type of literature, the captivity narrative, and some of these books became best-sellers. The first published narrative was Mary Rowlandson's story of her three months of captivity during which she actually saw and conversed with Metacom, who commissioned her to sew a shirt for his baby son. Mary, the wife of a minister, was ransomed and returned to her family, although some of her children died in captivity.

Rowlandson's narrative, although it was intended to show the savagery of the natives and the power of God's goodness to preserve her, actually demonstrated clearly how desperate the Indians were. The band that had captured her was constantly on the run and reduced to eating only what they could find in the depths of winter. Under these conditions, the Indians were defeated by the fall of 1676, and Metacom himself was captured and killed. The Indians paid dearly for their defiance, but the English settlers also were forced to change their ways as a result of the war, which had caused huge numbers of casualties on both sides. Many frontier towns had been abandoned during the war, and were not resettled; the frontier contracted after King Philip's War. Moreover, the northern frontier, where natives were supplied with weapons by

MARY ROWLANDSON'S *NARRATIVE*.
Rowlandson's thrilling narrative was published many times, and was read as novels would later be read. This title page is from the 1773 edition.

French allies, continued to be unsettled throughout the rest of the century.

GLORIOUS REVOLUTIONS

Frontier wars were not the only form of conflict in the later decades of the seventeenth century. In many colonies settlers also rebelled against what they saw as unwarranted restrictions or changes inspired by orders from London.

In New England colonists rose up against the imposition of a wholly new system decreed for them by King James II. Even before his accession to the throne in 1685, James and his advisors sought to sweep away the welter of different systems of government in the colonies and merge all the colonies into two great viceroyalties. This idea was partly inspired by the problems that were revealed as policy makers analyzed the causes of Bacon's Rebellion in the south and King Philip's War in the north. Sir Edmund Andros, governor of New York, had been directed to create the first of these new supercolonies, the Dominion of New England, which was to include New York and all colonies to the north of it. The capital was to be Boston.

With the Dominion of New England, King James, who had been the duke of York, attempted to spread some of the authoritarian aspects of New York's government to the hitherto self-governing New England colonies, a plan that confirmed the New Englanders' worst fears. All land titles were called in for inspection and possible confiscation, the town meetings were suspended, the assembly was restructured to cut off popular control, and the common lands were seized for distribution to the governor's friends and supporters. Moreover, religious toleration was decreed for the Puritan colonies, which were no longer to be allowed to operate their own exclusive system.

Hearing that the Roman Catholic King James II had been deposed and exiled in the Glorious Revolution in England in 1688, the outraged colonists in Massachusetts rose up (the news arrived early in 1689) and overthrew Governor Andros in their own Glorious Revolution. They were unable to resume their old system of government because Andros had confiscated the colonial charter on which it had been based. The great preacher Increase Mather went to England to negotiate with the government of the new monarchs, William and Mary, for a new charter, but it was not granted until 1691. During the period when they had no charter, the Massachusetts courts were not able to hold trials, and it was while the colony awaited Mather's return that the dramatic events in Salem erupted. Had the courts been able to meet and deal with the first few accusations as they were made, the outbreak might have been nipped in the bud and a sense of orderly procedures established, as had happened with all earlier accusations of witchcraft. As it was, the accusations spiraled out of control before the arrival of Increase Mather and the new charter in early summer of 1692 allowed the law to go to work.

Many in Massachusetts were disappointed in what Mather brought them. The new charter was less favorable to Puritan control than the original one had been. In part this change reflected changes within the colony, where diversity had made the old link between church membership and political participation less acceptable. Nevertheless the colonists had acted decisively in defense of their own ways and their voice had been heard.

In New York also the Glorious Revolution brought action against the Dominion of New England. The Dominion had been as unpopular in New York as in New England and in New York resentments were intensified by ethnic conflict. New York had a great many different religious and national traditions, all competing for a place in the colony's government. Governor Thomas Dongan wrote home describing the variety in 1687: "New York has first a Chaplain belonging to the Fort of the Church of England; secondly a Dutch Calvinist, thirdly a French Calvinist, fourthly a few Roman Catholics; abundance of Quakers preachers men and women especially; Singing Quakers; Ranting Quakers; Sabbatarians; Antisabbatarians; Some Anabaptists; some Independents; some Jews; in short of all sorts of opinions there are some; and the most part, of none at all."

Most prominent among ethnic groups vying for power were the Dutch and the English. Leisler's Rebellion, in 1689, was in part a revolt of the colony's displaced old Dutch elite. Dutch leaders naturally assumed that the new king, William of Orange, who was Dutch himself, would favor them. The rebels sought the reinstatement of their old community privileges and pointed to the great power of a small clique of leading merchants. The rebels were joined by many English colonists who had disliked the authoritarianism of the Andros regime. The rebel regime held power for almost two years, and called a popularly elected assembly, but Leisler

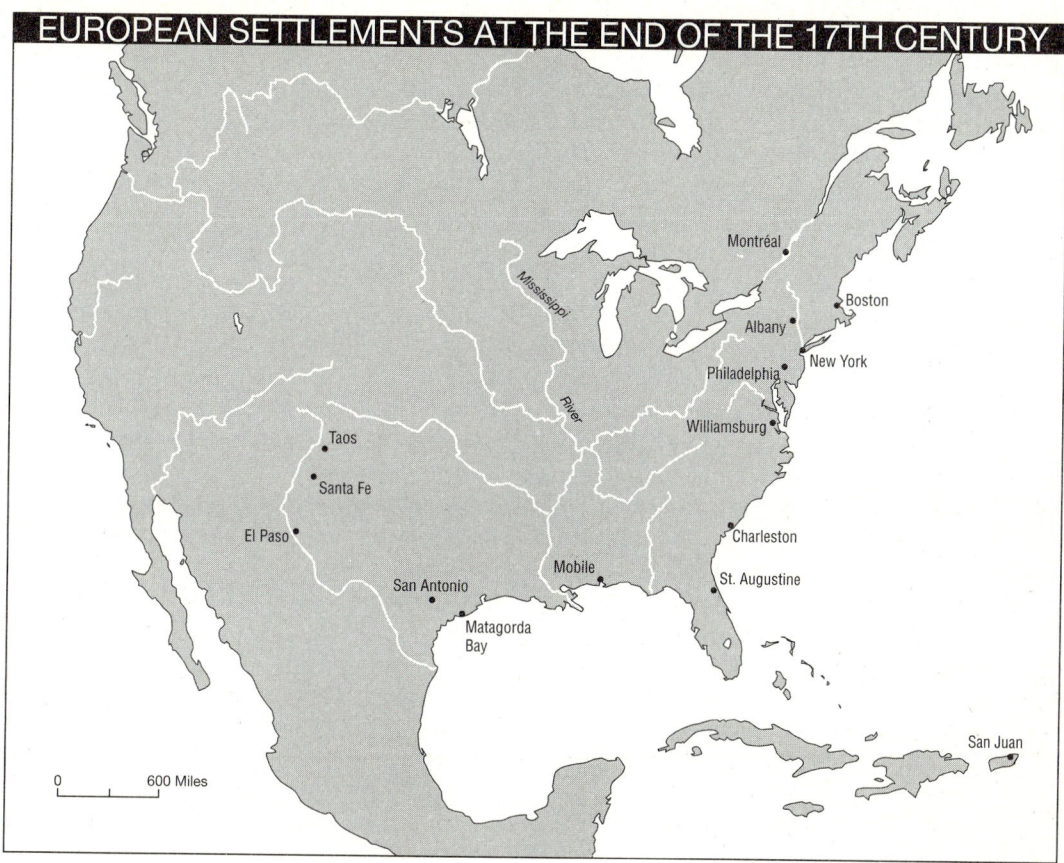

had miscalculated on his hope for royal approval. When the new governor arrived from England Leisler suffered the grisly death accorded traitors at that time. But the rebellion did have lasting effects. The power of the merchant elite was broken and New Yorkers were given a representative assembly. The coalition that had backed Leisler continued to operate as a political entity and influenced the development of New York.

Maryland also experienced a rebellion in 1689. Like Nathaniel Bacon and his lieutenants in Virginia a decade earlier, the leaders were members of the local county elites who had not been granted offices in the colonial government because they were out of favor with Lord Baltimore. They also claimed to speak for the Protestant majority in Maryland, and under their influence the assembly decreed that no Roman Catholic should be allowed to hold office. The rebellion ushered in a twenty-five year period of royal government by overthrowing the proprietorship.

PATTERNS

By the end of the seventeenth century settlement had grown from enclaves all around the coast. All the coastal regions saw some permanent settlement, and the future character of these regions and their people were beginning to be apparent. The long period of relatively weak oversight by England of its colonies was coming to an end with the close of the seventeenth century. The wave of rebellions and Indian wars at the end of the century had convinced the English government that much closer attention must be paid to the colonies in future and the Board of Trade was created in London in part to regulate colonial affairs. The strains created by British efforts to control colonial development would end in the American Revolution.

The colonies on the East Coast contained huge numbers of people by the end of the seventeenth century, probably 300,000. But the greatest wave of immigration was still to come in the eighteenth century. The patterns of life in the various regions were now set. In New England and the Middle Colonies, the typical family lived on a farm of a few hundred acres or less, growing much of their own food, but also producing for local and larger markets. There were extremes of wealth and poverty, but the relative distance between the poorest and the richest was not as great as in Europe. Towns, seaports, were well founded, and the economic life of the colonies was fed by international trade.

In the Chesapeake and in the northern and western parts of Carolina, as in the north, most families lived on modest farms, although extremely wealthy large landowners did exist, and the distance between the extremes of wealth and poverty was greater. These farmers produced primarily for the market, wheat and tobacco, with tobacco dominating as a cash crop. Their trade was through agents in Britain, whose ships came up the rivers directly to the plantations, and the region developed no real cities. By the end of the seventeenth century slavery, based on race and marked by total loss of rights, was the dominant labor system.

The tidewater and eastern parts of South Carolina saw a different pattern emerging, one based on large-plantation rice culture. This pattern would see slavery on a massive scale, with imported Africans outnumbering Europeans by ratios of three to one and even higher in the eighteenth century. These wealthy planters lived in the city, Charleston, and put their plantations in the hands of overseers, a pattern not seen in the rest of the South. Here elites would develop a style of life that seemed closest to that of aristocrats in Europe.

CHRONOLOGY

1651	First Navigation Act passed	1689	Glorious Revolution against the Dominion of New England;
1652–1654	First Anglo-Dutch War		Leisler's Rebellion in New York;
1660	Restoration of Charles II to the English throne		Maryland Rebellion
1662	Halfway Covenant in Massachusetts	1690s	Reconquest of New Mexico
1663	Carolinas founded	1691	North Carolina and South Carolina under separate governors
1664	New Netherland seized by English fleet, renamed New York	1692	Salem Village witchcraft outbreak
1676	Bacon's Rebellion in Virginia	1699	Mobile, New Orleans, and Pensacola founded on Gulf coast
1675–1676	King Philip's War in New England		
1680	Pueblo Revolt in New Mexico	1701	Iroquois Grand Settlement at Montreal
1681	Pennsylvania founded	1711	Tuscarora War in South Carolina
1685	LaSalle founds settlement on Texas coast	1715	Yamasee War in South Carolina

SUGGESTIONS FOR FURTHER READING

WITCHCRAFT AT SALEM VILLAGE

The best book on the Salem episode is Stephen Nissenbaum and Paul Boyer, *Salem Possessed: The Social Origins of Witchcraft* (1974). Alternative points of view are presented in John Demos, *Entertaining Satan* (1982); Carol Karlsen, *The Devil in the Shape of a Woman* (1987); and Chadwick Hansen, *Witchcraft at Salem* (1985). For students who like to work with original documents, Boyer and Nissenbaum have assembled a fine and substantial set in *Salem-Village Witchcraft* (1972).

NEW PEOPLES AND NEW PATTERNS IN THE LATER SEVENTEENTH CENTURY

For overviews of developments in the later seventeenth century and into the eighteenth, see the essays in Jack P. Greene and J. R. Pole, eds., *Colonial British America: Essays in the New History of the Early Modern Era* (1984), and Robert M. Bliss, *Revolution and Empire: English Politics and the American Colonies in the Seventeenth Century* (1990).

New Colonies

Colonization and development of the Carolinas are treated in Robert M. Weir, *Colonial South Carolina: A History* (1983), and Hugh T. Lefler and William S. Powell, *Colonial North Carolina: A History* (1973). On economic development see Peter A. Coclanis, *The Shadow of a Dream: Economic Life and Death in the South Carolina Low Country, 1670–1920* (1989).

On Quakerism and the founding and early development of Pennsylvania see Richard S. Dunn and Mary Maples Dunn, *The World of William Penn* (1986), and Gary B. Nash, *Quakers and Politics: Pennsylvania, 1681–1726* (1968, 1993).

Trade

For the development of the Atlantic trade routes and the interconnections that made them work see Bernard Bailyn, *The New England Merchants in the Seventeenth Century* (1955); Harold A. Innis, *The Fur Trade in Canada: An Introduction to Canadian Economic History* (rev. ed. 1956); and Alison G. Olson, *Making the Empire Work: The Development and Cooperation of London and American Interest Groups in the Seventeenth and Eighteenth Centuries* (1992). Robert Brenner, *Merchants and Revolution: Commercial Change, Political Conflict, and London's Overseas Traders, 1550–1653* (1993), and David Harris Sacks, *The Widening Gate: Bristol and the Atlantic Economy, 1450–1700* (1991) approach these connections from the English side of the Atlantic.

On trade in the interior, see Richard White, *The Middle Ground: Indians, Empires and Republics in the Great Lakes Region, 1650–1815* (1991),

The Settled Colonies

New England's development after mid-century can be approached through biography; see especially Michael G. Hall, *The Last American Puritan: The Life of Increase Mather* (1988). Changes and continuity in religious practice appear in David D. Hall, *Worlds of Wonder, Days of Judgment: Popular Religious Belief in Early New England* (1989) and Stephen Foster, *The Long Argument: English Puritanism and the Shaping of New England Culture, 1570–1700* (1991). On the Halfway Covenant see Robert Pope, *The Halfway Covenant: Church Membership in Puritan New England* (1969). On Connecticut see Bruce H. Mann, *Neighbors and Strangers: Law and Community in Early Connecticut* (1987).

New York's changing life under the transition from Dutch to English rule, including the rupture of Leisler's Rebellion, can be traced in Kammen, *Colonial New York* (from chapter two), and Donna Merwick, *Possessing Albany, 1630–1710: The Dutch and English Experiences* (1990); Thomas Burke, *Mohawk Frontier: The Dutch Community of Schenectady, New York, 1661–1710* (1991); David G. Hackett, *The Rude Hand of Innovation: Religion and Social Order in Albany, New York, 1652–1836* (1991); and Sung Bok Kim, *Landlord and Tenant in Colonial New York: Manorial Society, 1664–1775* (1978). On the relations between colonists and the Iroquois see Daniel Richter, *The Ordeal of the Longhouse*, and Matthew Dennis, *Cultivating a Landscape of Peace: Iroquois-European Encounters in Seventeenth-Century America* (1990).

Development of society and economy in the Chesapeake are the subject of Lois Green Carr, Russell R. Menard, and Lorena S. Walsh, *Robert Cole's World: Agriculture and Society in Early Maryland* (1991), and Lois Green Carr, Philip D. Morgan, and Jean Russo, eds., *Colonial Chesapeake Society* (1989). On Bacon's Rebellion see Morgan, *American Slavery, American Freedom* (from chapter two). Two older studies that provide opposing interpretations of the rebellion are T. J. Wertenbaker, *Torchbearer of the Revolution* (1940), and Wilcomb Washburn, *The Governor and the Rebel* (1957).

On New France see Louise Dechêne, *Habitants and Merchants in Seventeenth-Century Montreal* (1992), and the essays in Peter Benes, ed., *New England/New France, 1600–1850* (1992).

The best source for Spanish expansion in Florida and the Pueblo Revolt is David J. Weber, *The Spanish Frontier in North America* (New Haven, 1992). On the tensions that led to the Pueblo Revolt, see also Gutiérrez, *When Jesus Came, the Corn Mothers Went Away*, and John, *Storms Brewed in Other Men's Worlds* (from chapter two).

King Philip's War is treated in Douglas Leach, *Flintlock and Tomahawk: New England in King Philip's War* (1958, 1991), and Russell Bourne, *The Red King's Rebellion: Racial Politics in New England, 1675–1678* (1990). Mary Rowlandson's narrative is reprinted in William L. Andrews, et al., eds., *Journeys in New Worlds: Early American Women's Narratives* (1990). On the Glorious Revolution in New England and throughout the colonies see David S. Lovejoy, *The Glorious Revolution in America* (1972).

Chapter 4

The Eighteenth Century

Episode: Runaway Slaves and Spanish Florida

Expansion and Consolidation

New Areas of Settlement
The Settled East

The Episode: South Carolina was the most valuable of all England's mainland colonies. Slavery, and the crops the slaves labored to produce, created enormous wealth, but also fed great insecurity among Carolina planters. In 1739 slave rebellion and yellow fever combined to make colonists vividly aware of their vulnerability. The slaves' uprising had been inspired, they felt, by propaganda emanating from the Spanish colony at St. Augustine, encouraging English slaves to run away to freedom in Florida.

Georgia had been founded between Florida and South Carolina to act as a buffer, but the bleeding of slaves away from the rice plantations continued. Finally in 1740, the English determined to remove the Spanish from St. Augustine. The attack was a bitter failure, and the combined Georgia–South Carolina force blamed each other. But in assigning blame neither examined the true nature of war on the frontier, and the crucial roles of all the ethnic groups—African, Indian, English, and Spanish—in success or failure. No one could control all the circumstances and all the many rival interests sufficiently to bring full security.

The Historical Setting: Britain's mainland colonies began a new stage of maturity as the eighteenth century opened. American-born colonists assumed leadership roles and many of the earlier problems seemed settled. Economically, the colonies had found a niche within the British empire's vast trade networks. In the East, where the heirs of previous generations of settlers were established, life was becoming more comfortable as the rough conditions of earlier times gave way to a generally higher standard of living and greater extremes of wealth and poverty. The more comfortable they became, though, the more uneasy many men and women were about their own complacency and materialism. Great religious revivals swept over the colonies, as congregations sought to reawaken the fervor of the founding generations.

No part of the North American continent was free of European influence in the eighteenth century. Spanish soldiers and missionaries built permanent settlements in California and Texas, and the French built forts and trading posts in the continent's center. Men and women from all over Europe and Africa continued to pour, willingly or forced, into the eastern colonies throughout the eighteenth century. The mixing of people in the English colonies created rivalries, but also broke down insularity. Most people accepted the existing social order and their place in it, but challenges to authority could emerge in regions where different traditions clashed.

Life was dangerous for many of the newcomers, as for the Indians who were forced deeper into the interior by the progress of settlement. Colonists resented being drawn into the periodic great wars between France and England. Their economy was disrupted and their lives put in danger. The imperial rivals supplied arms to native allies, who, for reasons of their own, resisted the steady spread of new plantations and attacked the settlements. Colonists throughout America were constantly reminded that they lived within a great-power rivalry.

Runaway Slaves and Spanish Florida

Florida, with its Spanish colonists, was a constant sore spot for Britain's southern colonies, gnawing at their peace of mind and creating a deep sense of grievance. St. Augustine seemed only to play a spoiler's role. Spain never followed up that first colony with expansion into the eastern part of North America, but it did not, as the English colonists saw it, have the good grace simply to get out. Instead, the Florida authorities openly beckoned to slaves in South Carolina to flee and promised that, once in Spanish territory, they could be free. In 1693, shortly after the first arrival of a party of runaway slaves, the Spanish king approved "giving liberty to all . . . the men as well as the women . . . so that by their example and by my liberality others will do the same." A steady stream of runaways arrived in Florida in the eighteenth century. Carolina merchant Captain Caleb Davis saw his own slaves while he was conducting trade in St. Augustine, and wrote that they simply laughed at him when he tried to take them back. Formal expeditions of Carolinians attempting to recover their lost "property" were firmly turned away. Lt. Governor William Bull wrote that these rebuffs had "occasioned great dissatisfaction and Concern." As the slave population grew to outnumber the free in South Carolina, the colonists lived in constant fear of rebellion. It was unconscionable, they thought, that fellow Europeans should try to provoke alien Africans against them.

So serious was this fear that Carolinians actually gave up some of their territory so that Georgia could be placed as a buffer between them and the no-man's-land that led to Florida. Since slavery was forbidden in Georgia, any African found there could be presumed to be a runaway. Slaves could not be allowed to steal from their masters with impunity. And any slave who ran off was a thief because, since each slave was property, an escapee was stealing himself or herself. The escape often necessarily involved violence as well. The situation was intolerable and could not be allowed to continue, they argued.

Relations between the English and Spanish colonists were complicated by the terms of the Indian trade in the Southeast. South Carolinians had entered enthusiastically into the complex trade in deerskins, in which the Southeast's large Indian confederations maneuvered between French, Spanish, and English traders. The Carolinians distributed weapons to the Indians who hunted for them, making the competition more dangerous. The Indians were convinced that the Carolinians often cheated them in trade, giving less value in goods than the deerskins deserved. Moreover, Indians who had been given goods on credit often found that the skins they brought in were deemed insufficient to pay their debts, and they were thus caught in a cycle of indebtedness from which they could not win release. In 1715 warfare broke out between South Carolina and the Yamasee Indians on the colony's frontier over some of these issues, and the Yamasees became Spanish supporters. After the war, the Yamasees actively helped slaves escape to their new allies in Florida.

MOSE

In 1724 a party of slaves, including a man who took the name Francisco Menéndez arrived in Florida with the assistance of a Yamasee escort. After their dangerous and arduous journey, they were alarmed to find that St. Augustine's governor, Antonio de Benavides, denied them the liberty they had worked so hard for and sold them back into slavery. He claimed he feared retaliation by the Carolinians. Menéndez and his followers tirelessly worked to gain their freedom, and demonstrated their loyalty by fighting to defend St. Augustine. Menéndez learned to read and write in Spanish, and the band learned how to manipulate the Spanish legal system. They bombarded civil and religious authorities with petitions. Finally in 1737, Manuel de Montiano became governor and he soon freed Menéndez and his followers. Moreover, he offered freedom to any slaves who managed to escape to Florida.

The runaways were concentrated in the little fort at Gracia Real de Santa Teresa de Mose, usually referred to simply as Mose, just north of St. Augustine, which was intended to provide protection for St. Augustine. The freed slaves built the settlement themselves, with thick walls and a little stream running through it. The condition of their freedom was that they become Roman Catholics.

In running away from servitude, they had managed to preserve family ties, and many whole family groups made it to freedom in Florida. The original Mose group included Francisco Garzía, who was African, and his wife Ana, an Indian. Their daughter Francisca Xaviera married a free Black man from Carolina named Francisco Díaz, who served in the Mose militia. Juan Jacinto Rodríguez and his wife Ana María Menéndez also were in the group that set up Mose. Their son Juan married Cecilia, who was from Carolina, but remained a slave. Cecilia's godmother, María Francisca, married Marcos de Torres, who was a free Black man from the Spanish colony at Cartagena. Cecilia's parents were also at Mose, and she and her three children lived with them after Marcos died. Juan and Cecilia were godparents to the three children. María later married Thomas Chrisostomo, whose own wife had died. Thomas's godfather also lived in Mose.

Not only did these former slaves maintain close and dense family ties, despite the burdens of slavery and the uncertainty involved in their escape, they also were able to keep memories of African culture alive in their new homes. Modern archaeological work has discovered objects made in America that show African influence, such as a medal with St. Christopher on one side and a Kongo star on the other. They lived in poverty in Mose, but they also lived in freedom, and this freedom was the promise that drew runaways despite the risks.

The Mose inhabitants accepted their role as the first line of defense for St. Augustine and wrote to the Spanish king that they would be "the most cruel enemies of the English," and would give their "last drop of blood in defense of the Great Crown of

Spain and the Holy Faith." As more fugitives arrived, they were added to the Mose roster. Menéndez captained the militia for forty years, and served as the governor of the fort. The freed slaves provided skilled labor to the Spanish settlement, and were recruited into the militia. Their knowledge of the territory and of English and Indian languages and habits proved invaluable to their Spanish hosts.

SOUTH CAROLINA'S INSECURITY

For many reasons the South Carolinians were finding their situation increasingly intolerable as the 1730s came to an end. Uneasy Indian relations and continuing frontier skirmishes had fed insecurity on the western frontier and created further animosities. The creation of Georgia had not stopped the flow of runaways to Florida. And the slave system was changing. Not only was the proportion of slaves in the population growing, but many slaves were being trained in new skills. Slaves knew the terrain and the inland water system well. In fact, slaves often heard of the opportunities for freedom in

HERMAN MOLL'S MAP OF CAROLINA, 1729. This map, created before the settling of Georgia, shows South Carolina extending into Florida and clearly shows the land runaway slaves crossed to freedom. The legend argues that the land belongs to England because of the voyage of John Cabot under the direction of King Henry VII.

Spanish Florida while in St. Augustine serving their masters. Moreover, the denser population made for greater separation between Africans and Europeans, so masters were less sure they knew their slaves' opinions and attitudes, and they were much less convinced of their loyalty.

All this led to growing apprehensiveness among European-American planters. In 1734, Captain Philipp von Reck wrote a report that analyzed the situation. He wrote that the number of slaves grew by 3,000 every year:

> There are computed to be 30,000 Negroes in this Province, all of them Slaves, and their Posterity for ever: They work six Days in the Week for the Masters without pay, and are allowed to work on Sundays for themselves. . . . Being thus used, lays amongst them a Foundation of Discontent; and they are generally thought to watch an Opportunity of revolting against their Masters, as they have lately done in the Island of St. John and of St. Thomas, belonging to the Danes and Sweeds; and it is the Apprehension of these and other Inconveniences, that has induced the Honourable Trustees of Georgia, to prohibit the Importation and Use of Negroes within their Colony.

The sense of insecurity in which European Americans lived was massive. They feared poisoning by the slaves who handled their food. Reports of arson fires filled them with alarm. Most of all they feared the Spanish in St. Augustine, and rumors circulated constantly that the Spanish were trying to provoke outright slave rebellion.

But changing the system of slavery was considered impossible. As John Killpatrick wrote, "When we reflect that Rice, the chief Staple of Carolina is manufactured by Negroes, (European Constitutions being really unequal to the Culture of it in that Climate, or indeed to the general Culture of the Climate) it must be evident, that a great Number of Slaves are necessary to produce the yearly Quantities of that and other Commodities exported from that Province." In fact South Carolina saw a huge influx of slaves during the period 1735–1739, mostly from Angola. This meant that more than half the slaves in the colony were relative newcomers from Africa and therefore less accustomed to slavery. All this made the seditious rumors coming out of Florida almost intolerable. The planters feared, Lt. Governor William Bull wrote, "that their Negroes which were their chief support may in little time become their Enemies, if not their Masters, and that this Government is unable to withstand or prevent it."

During the summer of 1739, a great fever epidemic struck Charleston. The sickness, which doctors called "a yellow billious fever," killed ten or twelve people a day at its height. Even the environment seemed to be conspiring to make the English feel unwelcome and uneasy in their own homes. Many observers noticed that the fever was particularly "fatal to Strangers and Europeans."

Charleston's inhabitants were reeling from the epidemic's effect when their most horrible nightmare, slave rebellion, came true. The Stono Rebellion began on Sunday morning, September 9, 1739, with a company of twenty slaves led by a man named Jemmy. They broke into stores and plantations at Stono Bridge, seizing weapons and killing the European Americans they encountered. An innkeeper at Wallace's Tavern was spared, "for he was a good man and kind to his slaves," but other planters were killed and their houses burned. The rebels collected additions to their ranks as they moved over the countryside, and some slaves were forced to join so that they would not raise the alarm. About twenty-five European Americans were killed. The advance was stopped later that day and many of the rebels were killed, but others escaped and were hunted down over the next few days. A month later a letter reported that "the Rebellious Negroes are quite stopt from doing any further Mischief, many of them having been put to the most cruel Death." But even years later fugitives were still being brought in from hiding places in the swamps. Rumors of further uprisings spread over the countryside periodically, keeping families on the plantations in a state of alarm.

> On this Occasion every Breast was filled with Concern. Evil brought Home to us within our very Doors awakened the Attention of the most Unthinking. Every one that had any Relation, any Tie of Nature; every one that had a Life to lose were in the most Sensible Manner shocked at such Danger daily hanging over our Heads. With Regret we bewailed our peculiar Case, that we could not enjoy the Benefits of Peace like the rest of Mankind and that our own Industry should be the Means of taking from us all the Sweets of Life and of rendering us liable to the Loss of our Lives and Fortunes. With Indignation we looked at St. Augustine . . .

THE ATTACK ON ST. AUGUSTINE

In October 1739 the armed truce that characterized European international relations through the eighteenth century once again broke out in open war between Spain and England. The War of Jenkins' Ear was so called because an English mariner, Captain Thomas Jenkins, displayed to the English parliament his own ear, which he claimed had been cut off by Spanish authorities who had seized his ship on the high seas. The war was the latest hot phase in the alternating hot and cold war between the European powers in which the real issue was the British demand for freedom of the seas. James Oglethorpe, governor of Georgia, was eager to seize the opportunity to "annoy the Spaniards" in St. Augustine. Oglethorpe had already appealed to the Georgia trustees who were members of parliament and they had arranged for him to be appointed a major general with a regiment of 700 seasoned soldiers from England. He had also been named military commander of Georgia and South Carolina. Now that war was openly declared, Oglethorpe interpreted his mission gloriously, saying that Georgia "bridles the Spaniards in America and covers the English Frontiers."

The attack on St. Augustine, however, was a fiasco, and partisans have argued ever since over who was at fault for the debacle. The South Carolinians were angry that military command had been given to Oglethorpe after Georgia and South Carolina had been involved in bitter rivalry over the deerskin trade with Indians to the west. The Carolinians feared taking forces away at a time when the colony was weakened by smallpox and just after the Stono Rebellion. They assumed further slave uprisings were in store for them, so they debated long and hard over just how much support to give Oglethorpe, and they scaled back the amount of aid drastically. Oglethorpe and his supporters argued that South Carolina's delay had fatally weakened the expedition.

Oglethorpe had wanted to attack St. Augustine quickly before the Spanish had time to reinforce it from Cuba. He was frustrated by South Carolina's slowness and meagre appropriations, but orchestrated a stream of optimistic predictions of how easy

JAMES OGLETHORPE.

it would be to evict the Spanish. William Byrd of Virginia, under the influence of this optimism, said little effort would be required to "take the Nest of Pirates."

Every problem was a challenge to James Oglethorpe. Even the year before war broke out he had written ironically to a friend in England:

> I am here in one of the most delightful Situations as many man could wish to be. A great number of Debts, empty Magazines, no money to supply them, Numbers of People to be fed, mutinous Soldiers to Command, a Spanish Claim & a large body of their Troops not far from us.

While waiting for South Carolina's deliberations about aiding the expedition, Oglethorpe immediately got busy along the Georgia-Florida border, reconnoitering and seizing small outposts. Oglethorpe had ordered construction of a line of forts down into Spanish territory–on St. Simons Island, Cumberland Island, and at the mouth of the St. Johns River. He also made an expedition into the interior to enlist the support of Creeks and Cherokees.

Oglethorpe was an English gentleman, used to a life of privilege. He had studied at Eton, at Oxford University, and in Paris, and had served in the European wars as an aide-de-camp to Prince Eugene of Savoy. Yet he adjusted to the very different circumstances of frontier warfare with a zest that many of his lieutenants thought bizarre. Edward Kimber, writing of a later expedition, was repelled by the Indians clambering on board their little ship. He "found it very irksome, especially considering their Nastiness." But Oglethorpe slept on the deck among the Indians and required his officers to follow suit.

TOMOCHICHI AND HIS NEPHEW, TOOANAHOWI. Tomochichi and his nephew were painted by Willem Verelst in a New World setting and with such symbols of American strength as the eagle. Verelst also painted them as they were presented to the Georgia trustees in their formal London audience chamber.

Oglethorpe prided himself on his good relations with the Indian allies, and on his adaptability. The Indians nearest the site of Savannah, capital of Georgia, were the Yamacraws, who had split off from the Creeks. Tomochichi, their chief, became a firm ally of Oglethorpe and the Georgia enterprise, and Oglethorpe carefully cultivated the relationship. Tomochichi and his nephew and wife visited London along with other leading men and the company was received by the king and queen. They were lavishly entertained, but the Indians' chief concern was to set up official rules for the conduct of the trade in deerskins so that they would not be cheated by unscrupulous Englishmen. Dishonest trading had led directly to Indian wars in South Carolina, and Georgia officials sought to learn by their example. Tomochichi, back in America, died in September 1739 as the preparations for the St. Augustine attack were being made. Oglethorpe gave him a splendid military funeral and buried him in a Savannah square.

Oglethorpe carried his reputation for fair dealing and unself-conscious adaptation to Indian lifeways into the negotiations with the Creeks and Cherokees for their help in attacking the Spanish. In 1737 he had told the trustees that he could call on 7,000 warriors as allies. But despite his efforts, the expedition attracted only a few hundred Indian allies. Many potential friends were contemplating war against the French in the west instead. Others refused to be drawn into fights between Europeans. Americans were forced to learn the lesson that policy makers in England found difficult to grasp—Indian allies always operated in service of their own goals. They were never just puppets.

The Spanish governor of St. Augustine was also preparing for the attack, and the Spanish had learned from experience. Governor James Moore of South Carolina had attacked St. Augustine in 1702 and 1704. Moore's forces, composed of English, Creek, and Yamasee soldiers, had taken the town easily in 1702, but its 1,500 people had sheltered within the fort, the Castillo de San Marcos, which was besieged and bombarded for six weeks but held out. Finally the frustrated English forces burned the town and withdrew. In 1704 Moore returned and attacked outlying Franciscan missions. Indians unlucky enough to be caught within the missions were enslaved, and these deserted missions became the sites of Oglethorpe's string of forts.

After these attacks, the Spanish emptied the Florida interior of people and withdrew into St. Augustine. They rebuilt the town in stone and masonry, but the inhabitants lived in a much more restricted style as their ties to the rich land beyond St. Augustine were cut off. When Georgia was founded in 1732, the Spanish governor, fearing renewed attacks, ordered the Castillo de San Marcos rebuilt.

In the aftermath of his unsuccessful attack General Oglethorpe was to blame his expedition's failure on South Carolina's delays and parsimoniousness. Certainly the time for striking was lost while the other colony wrangled over exactly what contribution they would make to the effort. Oglethorpe had received his royal orders to attack St. Augustine in September, 1739, but the South Carolina assembly did not finally vote to send and equip troops until early April, 1740. The delay was fatal; on the day of the vote, April 3, six ships carrying nine-pound brass cannon arrived in St. Augustine. This meant that the possibility of taking the city with a swift assault was ended and that a long siege would be required. The window for action was small, because the British ships supporting the siege and blocking Spanish access to the city agreed to remain in place off the Florida coast only until July 5. After that date, the naval commanders argued, tropical storms made the location too dangerous.

Oglethorpe faced grave problems in coordinating his varied force, and his flamboyant style covered lack of command experience. He was hot-tempered and would tolerate no challenges. Earlier, when his election to parliament had been contested in a bitter fight, he had drawn his sword and wounded two members of the opposition. A month later he went to "a Night-House of evil Repute" after a night of drinking. Most of the clientele was of a far lower social station and Oglethorpe thought that one, a linkman (a torch bearer who could be hired to light people's way home along the streets), had stolen a gold piece from him. When the linkman hit him with his torch, Oglethorpe pulled out his sword and struck the man in the chest, killing him. The claim of self-defense and his high social station protected him, and Oglethorpe took his seat in parliament unpunished.

The arrogance and bravado bred in Oglethorpe by his upbringing and experiences blunted his ability to command in the field. He failed to keep officers under him informed of his planning, and he often took unnecessary personal risks. The professional soldiers from England mutinied shortly after their arrival. One of the leaders shot at Oglethorpe himself and, according to an observer, "he so narrowly escaped that the Bullet went through his Periwigg." Oglethorpe offered pardons and the mutineers gave in, but the incident did not bode well for the future. At another point in the campaign, the general ordered a forced march. Several of the men, all of whom were deeply fatigued and short of provisions, passed out. Oglethorpe ordered that stragglers be shot, an order which the officers, "out of Compassion," ignored.

The Carolinians also objected to Oglethorpe's conduct of the campaign, to which Oglethorpe's supporters replied that they were offended because he ignored their social pretensions and cared more for the welfare of the men than their comfort. They saw it quite differently. One of the South Carolina volunteers was Lieutenant Jonathan Bryan, the young son of an up-and-coming family, who had been a supporter of Oglethorpe from the beginning. He was said to have led the Georgia leader to the site of Savannah, and he offered the labor of his own slaves in the early days of clearing and settling. The first street in Savannah was named Bryan Street after Jonathan and his family. Jonathan Bryan became one of Oglethorpe's closest friends.

When Oglethorpe announced his intention to "annoy" the Spaniards in St. Augustine, Jonathan Bryan naturally signed on for the campaign. He and the other "gentleman volunteers" expected the expedition to rid the coast of Spanish influence, and they said they joined "only from a sincere Motive of serving their Country and of sharing somewhat in the Reputation of taking St. Augustine." The gentlemen were not to be paid in money, but in captured slaves and horses. The South Carolina volunteers, all men experienced in the ways of frontier warfare and the Indian trades, expected Oglethorpe to listen to them and to take advantage of their knowledge. Instead he seemed to disdain them and the customs of the frontier and seemed to want to conduct the attack by European gentleman's standards. The Carolinians were appalled when Oglethorpe seemed to go out of his way to offend the Indian allies. When the English forces seized the outlying post of Fort Diego, Oglethorpe berated Cherokee allies for killing some cows found there. The Cherokee leader complained to Jonathan Bryan, saying, "It was a strange Thing that they were permitted to kill the Spaniards but not their Beef." Oglethorpe decreed good treatment of prisoners, which the native forces interpreted as weakness.

Not only did Oglethorpe ignore the gentlemen volunteers' advice about the nature of frontier fighting, but he seemed to go out of his way to humiliate them. As they neared St. Augustine, the forces spotted a small group of houses, which the general commanded Bryan and a few volunteers to capture while the entire force looked on. Afterward, because some of the inhabitants had escaped, Oglethorpe rode up and said to Bryan, "Well, I see the Carolina Men have Courage but no Conduct." Bryan's defiant answer was, "Sir, the Conduct is yours."

On another occasion, Oglethorpe forced Bryan and his company of gentlemen to stay outside in a driving rain while the general and his officers stayed in a captured house that Bryan said was large enough to contain them all. When the sentinel at the door started to let the others in, the general told him "that he could not be guilty of a greater Crime, and that he deserved a thousand Lashes." The Carolinians' weapons were ruined by the rain, and they feared attack while they were rendered helpless with their powder wet. Most of the gentleman volunteers left the camp and returned to South Carolina, "disgusted by the General's usage of them," but Bryan, meeting another group of volunteers just arriving, decided to stay on.

In May 1740 the expedition of about 1,500 troops landed on the St. John's River and marched toward St. Augustine. In early June the force captured Mose, which contained about 100 inhabitants, and burned it. Governor Montiano was alarmed over St. Augustine's weakness, which constituted "a rebuff of His Majesty's sacred honor, a foul stain on his catholic arms." He withdrew all his forces, including the Mose refugees, into St. Augustine and kept watch. When Oglethorpe's troops began the siege of St. Augustine, the inhabitants of Mose were very active, venturing out repeatedly to reconnoiter and gain information.

Oglethorpe divided his forces between the mainland and Anastasia Island opposite St. Augustine. The South Carolina volunteers were put to work creating batteries and mounting guns on the island even though everyone knew that Anastasia was too far away for the artillery to reach the city. Bryan reported the disgust of the men as they saw the inhabitants of St. Augustine, who knew that the guns of Anastasia were no threat to them, freely moving into and out of the fort, driving their cattle before them. Oglethorpe marched his soldiers up and down trying to lure the Spanish out of the fort and into a fight, but the defenders, secure in their fort, refused to be drawn.

Oglethorpe sent Montiano a summons to surrender "in order to prevent the shedding of Christian blood and the evil consequences which may result from the unrestrained fury of the several nations when they capture a plaza by force of arms." In referring to "the several nations," Oglethorpe was using the "savage" reputation of his Indian allies to try to frighten the defenders. Montiano and the resident bishop replied "we are entirely prepared and resolved to shed Christian blood in defense of this fort and this plaza to the glory of the sacred name of God and the honor of the armed forces of the King of all Spains."

As the stalemate began to wear, Jonathan Bryan and the South Carolina volunteers consistently urged action. Bryan, with a party of three or four men, conducted a reconnaissance up to the city walls and captured three horses. He informed Oglethorpe that "the Town was in a great Tumult and Confusion, the Inhabitants screeching and

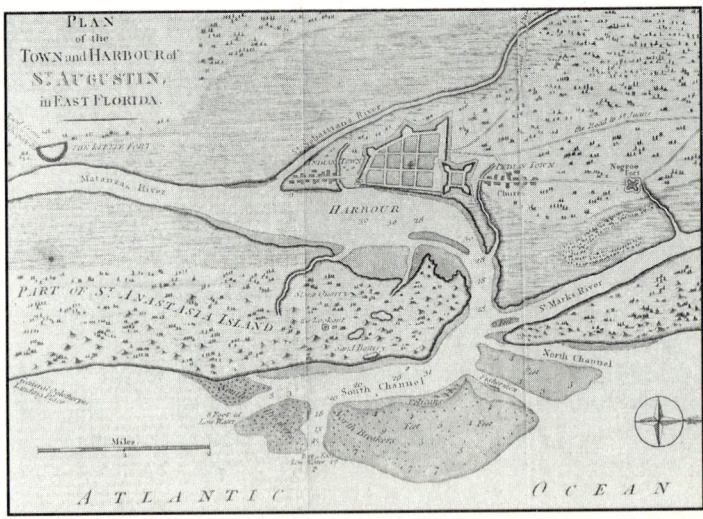

ST. AUGUSTINE, WITH THE "NEGROE FORT" two miles away. Anastasia Island is in the foreground.

crying." He implored the general to attack immediately but Oglethorpe refused, arguing that an attack would be unsuccessful and suicidal.

Then suddenly in the very early morning of June 15, a Spanish party emerged from the fort and surprised the contingent of English troops in Fort Mose. The soldiers had become complacent, lulled by the St. Augustine company's earlier refusal to fight. Many of the defenders were killed or captured and Mose was retaken. The few who escaped carried the shocking news that two badly wounded soldiers had been killed, and their heads and genitals cut off. This sudden reversal brought deep depression to the British forces.

The next day the commander of the South Carolina troops, Colonel Alexander Vanderdussen, visited General Oglethorpe's command on Anastasia and "found Things in a good deal of Distraction; Resolutions taken and not put in Execution." Vanderdussen reported that Oglethorpe was unable to plan a coherent strategy and carry it out, saying he "follows no advice." Vanderdussen tried in vain to create a winning plan with Oglethorpe's cooperation.

Oglethorpe compounded his mistakes by continuing to ignore the rules of cross-cultural alliances. Although he had made great efforts to recruit allies among the Creeks and Chickasaws, the Carolinians asserted that he did not treat them with respect once they had joined his expedition. Keeping the Indian allies committed to the project was essential. General Oglethorpe himself acknowledged that their decisions would be a major factor in its success or failure, saying, "much depends on the Nations." But he demanded that the Indians conform to his notions of proper conduct in warfare and censured them for following their own practices. James Killpatrick, putting the case of the disgruntled South Carolina troops, reported Oglethorpe's "Injustice and Imprudence" in his treatment of the allies. A band of Chickasaws killed a "Spanish Indian" and "bringing his Head in Triumph to the Camp after their Manner, presented it to the General, who rejected it with Indignation, calling them 'barbarous Dogs, and bidding them be gone.' Upon which they said, 'If they had carried the Head of an Englishman to the French, they should not be treated in that Manner.'" Squirrel, the Chickasaw chief, protested that if he had brought the head of one of Oglethorpe's men to the governor of St. Augustine, he would have been treated like a man, whereas the English general treated him like a dog.

South Carolinians understood the situation more clearly, and knew that the Indian allies had their own agenda and acted as independent forces. Killpatrick wrote that "These very brave People, dreaded by the French and Spaniards, and our constant Friends, came to fight and assist in good Earnest at the Siege." He also ridiculed Oglethorpe's fastidiousness in the midst of the slaughter of war: "nor could they be justly blamed, if it had been all a Joke, for having never been let into it, they could never have dreamt of such a warlike Refinement." The Chickasaws decided to go home and agreed to stay only when they were earnestly begged to do so by the South Carolinians.

Neither the ships nor the besieging batteries were able to prevent the arrival of a small convoy from Cuba bringing badly needed provisions for the deprived inhabitants of St. Augustine. Thus the siege was already ineffective at the time the Royal Navy ships supporting the expedition left as they had promised in early July, but with their departure the expedition collapsed. The volunteers, according to Charleston merchant

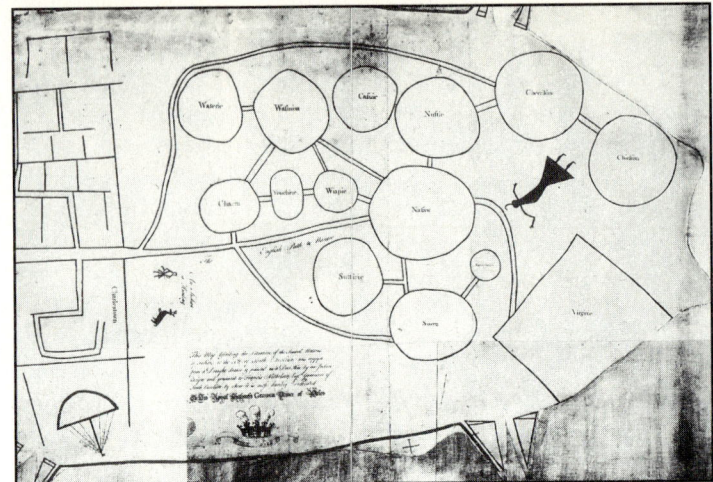

NATIVE MAP OF THE SOUTHEASTERN INDIANS, drawn by "An Indian Cacique" about 1724 on a deerskin. This map represents relationships rather than geographical features. Indian nations are all linked, and all are represented by circles, while the English settlements of Virginia and Charleston are presented as rectangles.

Joseph Wragg, were already deserting "as they see there is no prospect of Succeeding under such Mad conduct." The English withdrew on July 4. The Carolinian troops managed to carry off their cannon, but reported that General Oglethorpe "burnt a great Quantity of Provisions, Arms, &c. on his Retreat, notwithstanding there were two empty Boats at hand, which might have carry'd them off." Finally, "thus ended this most disgraceful and unfortunate Expedition."

AFTERMATH

After their return, Oglethorpe fell into a lingering sickness, which observers called "an extraordinary weakness." He had had the fever even during the siege of St. Augustine, but, according to Colonel Vanderdussen, then "his Spirits supported him under all Fatigue; but the Disappointment of Success (it is believed) now galled him, and too great Anxiety of Mind preyed upon him." Oglethorpe shut himself away and refused to talk to visitors.

Oglethorpe defended his record by saying that the delays and restrictions imposed by South Carolina and by the navy had cost the venture its victory. His associate Edward Kimber, praising the general's "great Qualities, and his indefatigable Zeal in serving his Country," wrote that "he was betray'd and neglected by the mean Carolina Regiment, and many of the Men of War." No one wished to confront the fact that all the English had underestimated the Spanish as enemies. The Carolinians, for their part, feared, as one wrote to an agent in London, "the consequence of abandoning the Siege of Saint Augustine will most certainly be the entire loss of the whole Province of Georgia." In response to Oglethorpe's charges of betrayal, the South Carolina assembly commissioned a complete investigation of the entire expedition. Jonathan Bryan testified that "all Things were carried on in the most dilatory Manner to general Dissatisfaction." The committee's report exonerated the South Carolina troops, and charged the general with incompetence, even cowardice. The assembly sent the complete report to London for printing, but Oglethorpe's sister, Anne, was able to block its publication.

Governor Montiano wrote the governor of Havana thanking him for the six ships that had been so important to the defense and saying he could not understand why Oglethorpe had given up so quickly when his force was so strong. He was especially amazed that Oglethorpe's men had left so quickly that they had abandoned a large stockpile of food supplies.

Montiano also wrote to the Spanish king, saying that he feared a second siege, reinforced by two entire regiments from London, more than 2,000 men. "Although I am persuaded that the rebuff he has suffered and his disgraceful flight can afford him nothing but universal disrespect, nonetheless, because of the influence that general can exert over personalities consonant with his restless and captious nature, I humbly beg Your Majesty to send me a reinforcement of men, ordnance, and warlike stores." Montiano's letter to the king included a special commendation of Francisco Menéndez, praising his valor and dedication in the fighting.

Menéndez was to be one of the first to feel the wrath of the English after he signed on to the crew of a privateering ship in 1741. Unluckily for him, the ship on which he sailed was captured by a British ship ironically named *Revenge*, and he was identified as "Signior Capitano Francisco," who had participated in the defense of St. Augustine. Menéndez was tied to a gun barrel and threatened with castration in retaliation for the two men mutilated by the Spanish. He frankly admitted that he had participated in the retaking of Mose, but denied that he had ordered atrocities. He was then given 200 lashes, and the English then "pickled him and left him to the Doctor to take Care of his Sore A-se."

When the *Revenge* landed in the Bahamas, its captain argued that Menéndez and the other captives should be reenslaved. He called Menéndez "this Francisco that Cursed Seed of Cain, Curst from the foundation of the world, who has the Impudence to Come into this Court and plead that he is free. Slavery is too Good for such a Savage, and all the Cruelty invented by man . . . the torments of the World to Come will not suffice." Menéndez was sold as a slave. The next chapter in his story is unclear, but by 1752 he was back in charge of the fort at Mose. How he managed his second escape is unknown. When Florida was handed over to the British in 1763 at the end of the French and Indian War, the Mose inhabitants went to Cuba, and Menéndez ended his life in Havana. When Spain recovered Florida in 1784, some of the former Mose people returned from their exile.

Meanwhile the garrison and citizens of St. Augustine continued to live cooped up in the fort, and cut off from their farmland and hunting for several years. The fort at Mose remained empty for twelve years until it was reoccupied in 1752. In 1741 the Spanish authorities began beefing up the garrison in St. Augustine, and the English noted great activity in Havana. Charles Pinckney of South Carolina wrote to the colony's agent in London that everyone was filled with fears for the future. They believed that Spain would now conquer Georgia, rendering South Carolina very fearful "with regard to our s—s." Pinckney refused even to spell out the word "slaves," so deep was his apprehension.

The attack did come in June 1742, exactly two years after the English failure to take St. Augustine. Montiano, commanding the Spanish troops, attempted to expel the English from Georgia. His attack was no more successful than the English expedition had been. The Spanish force landed at St. Simons Island and, although their force was larger and better equipped, they were "ambushed" at Bloody Marsh and defeated by the

Georgia forces under Oglethorpe. Montiano's expedition left after three weeks. Both the Spanish in Florida and the English in South Carolina and Georgia could make the life of the other uncomfortable and dangerous, but neither could expel the other. The *Boston Post*, mocking the danger in which both English and Spanish lived their lives, wrote:

> They both did meet, they both did fight, they both did run away;
> they both did strive to meet again, the quite Contrary Way.

The truth is that Georgia and Florida were on the front lines in the imperial struggles between the European nations, of which these colonies were only one insignificant part. War supplies came to the colonies unevenly and grudgingly. As one analyst wrote, "notwithstanding General Oglethorpe's good conduct and personal bravery, the preservation of that province was rather owing to the Ill management and disagreement of the Spanish commanders, than to any human means employed on our part for our defence." The colonies were always pawns in the dealings of the European powers. James Oglethorpe left Georgia for good in 1743, called home to answer an investigation into his conduct in Georgia. Twenty years later Spanish Florida was handed over to Britain in the settlement following the French and Indian War, only to be returned to Spain in the treaty ending the American Revolution.

In Georgia the future belonged to Jonathan Bryan and his circle. When the prohibition on slavery was lifted, men like Bryan moved into the southern colony with their huge labor forces, taking up and developing the land. Bryan, like others, sat on the governor's council in Georgia and used that position to acquire land near proposed roads and wharves. Bryan acquired over 32,000 acres of prime land, and owned a slave force of 250.

Bryan continued the pattern of commitments that had inspired Oglethorpe and the original Georgia trustees. He was a devout Christian, and a friend and supporter of George Whitefield, the greatest preacher of the eighteenth century. Bryan offered Christian baptism and preaching to his slaves, and was dedicated to leading a Christian life. He continued to be a patriot, and gave up his offices and influence in Georgia as the issues leading to the Revolution began to divide people. He dedicated his last years to the cause of independence and to the welfare of the new nation. Finally, during the Revolutionary War, Bryan urged an attack on St. Augustine, hoping finally to wipe out the shame of the 1740 failure.

Expansion and Consolidation

NEW AREAS OF SETTLEMENT

IMMIGRATION

America continued to be a magnet for Old World peoples in the eighteenth century. The opening land offered unparalleled opportunity for Europeans fleeing religious or economic adversity. Many such migrants were prepared to serve long terms of servitude in order to pay for their own passage and to bring over their families. Africans, involuntary immigrants, were brought in even larger numbers, and it was their labor that helped build the dreams of other immigrants. Their servitude would never end, and their children would inherit slave status. Opening opportunity for some and closing the door to freedom for others proceeded together throughout the century that would lead to the American Revolution.

Unparalleled growth transformed American life in the half-century before the Revolution. Because land was still available in the original grants, the settlements were able to perform a feat considered impossible: absorb huge numbers of new people without a drop in the standard of living. In fact, the population of the thirteen colonies doubled every twenty-five years in the century before the Revolution. Natural increase, more births than deaths, was the source of much of the growth, particularly in the healthy North, but immigration was the great provider of new Americans, increasing the population tenfold from about 200,000 in 1700 to almost 2 million by 1770.

Immigration from Germany, one major source of newcomers, peaked through the middle years of the eighteenth century, with 50,000 men and women flooding into America in this period. They were attracted by available land and religious toleration, and they fled war, conscription, persecution, and high taxation. But, despite the many reasons for coming, the servant flow began to grow only when the recruitment process became highly organized. Recruiters, often returned immigrants themselves, went through their old neighborhoods publicizing the opportunities available in America. Offering to arrange all the details of the passage, these recruiters worked with merchants in Rotterdam who carried the migrants across the Atlantic. Newcomers signed contracts that gave them a specified amount of time to pay off their passage, either by getting a relative already in America to pay for them or by working after arrival. The length of the term of servitude would depend on the skills the newcomer brought. The German migration was fam-

GERMAN IMMIGRANTS. The Salzburgers, persecuted Lutherans recruited to colonize the new colony of Georgia, are shown in this 1732 broadside. They were part of the flood of immigrants from all over Europe that flowed into Britain's American colonies in the eighteenth century.

ily-centered, and many newcomers did find support from relatives and former neighbors already in America.

The flow of settlers was most intense in the period between 1760 and the Revolution. Immigration from Britain contributed to the flood in those years. As many as 100,000 to 150,000 Scotch-Irish from northern Ireland came before 1760. And well over 100,000 Protestants from Ireland, plus Scots and others from the north of England, came in the decades before the Revolution.

The decision to emigrate always involved a combination of push and pull factors. All men and women who made the agonizing decision to leave their homes, friends, and families came partly because of hard times at home. But they also were lured to America by the organized recruitment that advertised the opportunities available across the Atlantic, the chance to build for a secure foundation for the future. The recruiters set up the organizations and connections that funneled Europe's discontented into the ports and ships that carried them to their new homes.

Enslaved Africans came in the largest numbers of all, but theirs was a forced migration. The mainland southern colonies had moved slowly and tentatively toward replacing the system of European indentured servants with slaves in the seventeenth century, although the number of enslaved Africans was still relatively small in 1700. In the eighteenth century, while indentured servants continued to arrive, there was a major shift to slavery as the preferred labor system, especially in the South.

Huge numbers of slaves, at least 250,000, were imported in the decades after 1700. These unwilling immigrants went through a series of terrifying and heart-rending experiences. At least one-fifth died at sea. Many were sick when they arrived and would die early in their enslavement. The captains were careful to load their ships with cargoes from different parts of Africa so that the captives could not talk together and plot rebellion at sea. In the eighteenth century most slaves destined for America came from Nigeria, the Bight of Biafra, and Angola. On their arrival, they went through the humiliating process of examination by prospective buyers. This poking, prodding inspection of their naked bodies might be repeated many times.

Then came transference to a plantation and unfamiliar work routines. Apparently, slaves fresh from Africa, faced with this overwhelming change, coped by denial, by running away repeatedly or by refusing to understand what was required of them. Edward Kimber, who visited the Chesapeake in 1747, described the planters' frustration: a "new Negro must be broke . . . You would really be surpriz'd at their Perseverance; let an hundred Men shew him how to hoe, or drive a Wheelbarrow, he'll still take the one by the Bottom, and the other by the Wheel." Such "ignorance" was the mode of resistance open to slaves.

SETTLEMENT OF THE FRONTIER IN THE EAST

Georgia, the last English colony, was created in 1732 on a plan different from any previous colony. The Georgia trustees were brought together by their concern about the plight of the poor in the growing cities of Europe. Their leader, James Oglethorpe, had served on a commission to study the hopeless situation of those imprisoned for debt in England, and had become convinced that the poor needed a place to make a new start. While they remained in the cities, they would never have the chance to get out of the endless cycle of debt and low wages. But if they could have land of their own in America the "deserving poor," those who had fallen into poverty through no fault of their own, could pull themselves back up into independence and respectability.

In line with these goals, the trustees decreed that each immigrating family would receive fifty acres. Slavery was forbidden, as was rum, and the immigrants were forbidden to sell their land for twenty-five years. Georgia was to be a colony of freeholders working their own land, not a land of large slave-run plantations. The plan was paternalistic and idealistic, and the trustees stipulated that they would receive no income from the colony. The plan attracted two of the greatest English religious leaders of their time: John Wesley, the founder of Methodism, spent two years in Georgia, 1736 and 1737, and when he returned to England, George Whitefield took his place. Whitefield, while carrying his evangelical message all over the colonies, continued to be committed to Georgia for the rest of his life.

Georgia's other purpose was to serve as a buffer between South Carolina, whose crops of rice and indigo made it the richest of the mainland colonies, and the Spanish colony in Florida. England sought to protect South Carolina from raids from the south, and also to cut the flow of runaway slaves into Florida. Thus the planters of Georgia, grateful for the second chance in life they had been given, were expected to repay their benefactors by a willingness to spring to the defense of South Carolina if that colony were threatened.

Although the colony drew large numbers of immigrants, the experiment rarely worked as planned. Most of the settlers sent to Georgia were from English cities and had little knowledge of how to farm, particularly in the unfamiliar soil and climate. Only the German religious migrants known as the Salzburgers stuck to the original plan. Other settlers quickly found ways to bring in slaves as "indentured servants" and leased their land out. In the early 1740s the restrictions were removed and larger plantations and slave labor became the rule. Georgia became a satellite of South Carolina, as men like Jonathan Bryan moved in.

The longer-settled colonies continued to draw new immigrants. New towns filled empty spaces in the already settled areas, but most of the immigrants went to the frontier, where huge numbers settled in the west of Pennsylvania, Virginia, the Carolinas, and Georgia. In some cases these new communities were created to realize the religious and social ideals of planners in Europe. The Moravians, a religious group from Germany, acquired land in Pennsylvania, Maine, and North Carolina on which they built "villages of the Lord." On these tracts Moravians could live and worship together and maintain their traditions. Their goal was to live "without interfering

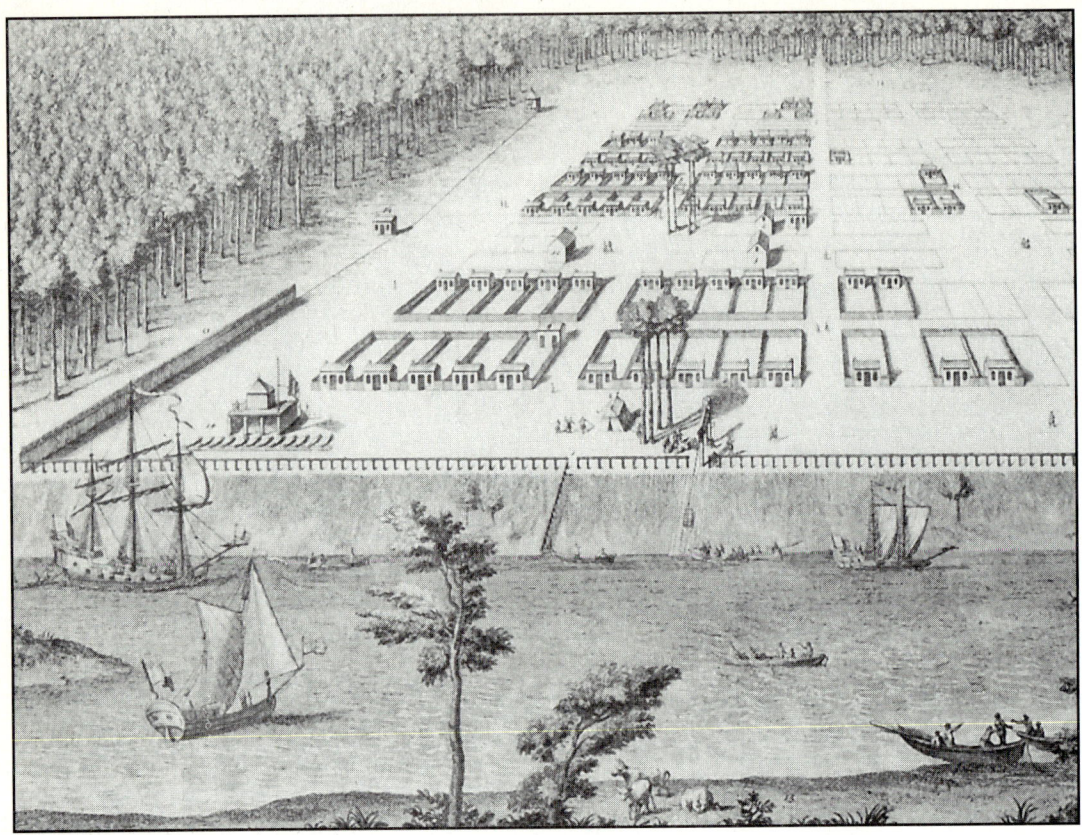

SAVANNAH. Oglethorpe was determined to lay Savannah out in open squares and regular streets, so that its inhabitants would not be undermined by the kind of squalid and twisted environment city dwellers in Europe faced. This plan presents Georgia and its capital as defying the forest in which it was set and creating order out of the "wilderness."

with others and without being disturbed by them."

Many others went to the frontier, usually accompanied by family and others from the same area in Europe, to take up the free land for which they had come to America. The numbers were enormous. On the day in 1769 when the land office at Fort Pitt began to open southwestern Pennsylvania to settlement, 2,790 people appeared to file applications; the rush into regions farther south was even greater. Settlement of the frontier was not the result of a haphazard outpouring of people onto the land. Huge grants of land were allotted to politically connected men in the East, and these grant holders then arranged to people their land with settlers and set up the county courts that would register deeds. These "undertakers" had strong personal reasons to see that the land was populated, and they valued the labor such settlers put into the land. As Virginia's lieutenant governor put it, the poorer people going out to the frontier would "seat themselves as it were under the Shade and Protection of the Greater."

Observers who traveled through the backcountry often ridiculed the settlers and their communities. The frontier people were seen as having degenerated into a kind of savagery, and their supposedly dirty, slovenly style of life was scorned by those who lived in the settled East. Some of these attitudes stemmed from old ethnic prejudices brought from Europe. The Reverend Charles Woodmason, who traveled through the backcountry in the 1760s, expressed contempt for the "Ignorant, mean, worthless, beggarly Irish Presbyterians, the Scum of the Earth, and Refuse of Mankind" who had settled on the North Carolina frontier. Observers from the long-settled East assumed that immigrants from groups that were looked down upon in Europe would be somehow better adapted to rough frontier conditions. But these same immigrants, whose labor was actively sought for developing new lands and who formed the front line in conflict, were ridiculed for their rough style of life.

Observers also misjudged the farming practices of the frontier people, seeing their farms as disorderly. In reality settlers had learned that practices developed for European conditions, where land was scarce and labor was plentiful, were not suited to the American frontier. Cattle and pigs were allowed to roam free, a sloppy practice by European standards, but one that made sense in Carolina's mild winters. Land was so fertile and labor so scarce that the intensive cultivation techniques used in Europe did not make sense. Instead, land was roughly cleared and crops such as corn that did not require plowing replaced wheat. Farmers in the backcounty were making creative adaptations, not degenerating.

Resentment grew over such characterizations, and especially over the neglect of the legitimate interests of families in the backcountry. In some frontier regions farmers organized to challenge the rule of the eastern elites. As in Bacon's Rebellion almost a century earlier, they demanded protection from Indians, and roads and other government services in return for the taxes they paid. They knew the easterners looked down on them as "white savages" and considered their problems unimportant, so the frontiersmen organized to "regulate" their own lives. In the North Carolina and South Carolina backcountry, the movements called themselves Regulators to signal their concerns in the 1760s. The causes were different in every instance, but many of the colonies, including New York, New Jersey, Pennsylvania, and Vermont, found such movements on their frontiers in the 1760s and 1770s. Such defiance and demands that backcountry rights and interests be respected helped set the scene for the revolutionary movement against Britain.

Increased interest in the backcountry in the eighteenth century stemmed in part from the activities of European powers and Indian confederations beyond the frontier. Imperial concerns fed the drive to expand the English-sponsored settlement beyond the narrow fringe along the east coast. French traders and settlers were becoming

PLAN OF AN AMERICAN NEWLY CLEARED FARM, showing the irregular fences and the fields studded with stumps characteristic of agriculture where land was plentiful and labor scarce.

AMERICAN LOG HOUSE, showing an isolated cabin in a rough clearing in the heavy woods.

increasingly active in the region between the Great Lakes and the Ohio Valley. New Orleans had been founded just at the end of the seventeenth century, and the colony was named Louisiana in honor of Louis XIV. In 1701 the Sieur de Cadillac founded Detroit. The French seemed to be positioning themselves to control the entire Mississippi River and the center of the continent. French, Spanish, and English traders competed for alliances with powerful Indian confederations and control of the lucrative deerskin trade throughout the Southeast.

AMERICAN INDIANS AND THE CLASH OF EMPIRES

Mighty Indian confederacies used the warrior's path along the Appalachian mountain chain. These nations raided each other for captives to replace members lost to war and to the ravages of European diseases, which continued to wreak havoc. Eastern leaders wanted the frontier settled by colonists under English government to avoid being squeezed out.

Indians were victims of the influx of Old World settlers. Absorption of huge numbers of immigrants from Europe and Africa was possible because of the decimation of Indian life east of the Appalachians. First devastated by European diseases to which they had no immunity, Indian populations were steadily reduced by war and expropriation, and even by enslavement in the South. Tribes or tribal remnants moved away from the pressure of the European Americans and their marauding animals. Often tribes that had grown too small to continue independently coalesced into new entities and great new Indian confederations were created.

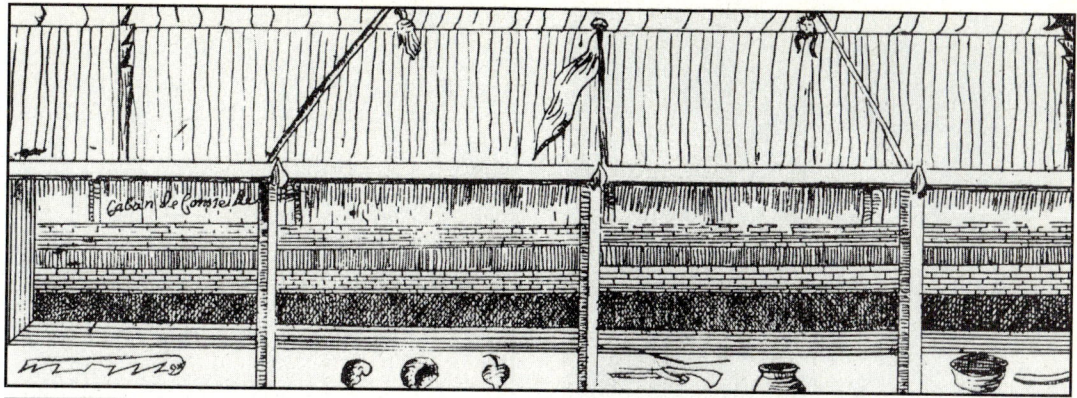

CREEK COUNCIL HOUSE, which hosted large meetings during the eighteenth century. The Creeks are called the Alibamons in this engraving.

The South held large, powerful nations. During the eighteenth century the Creeks withdrew from contact with the Europeans and worked through buffer tribes strategically placed between them and the colonists. Creek political structure was highly developed, based on a confederation in existence before the Europeans came. During the eighteenth century annual council meetings of the Creeks brought together 4,000 to 5,000 officials and as many as 12,000 people. The Cherokees, placed in closer contact with the English frontier and exposed to the unscrupulous tactics of many of the traders and frontiersmen, suffered during the eighteenth century.

In the North, the Iroquois League, consisting of the Oneidas, Mohawks, Cayugas, Onondagas, Senecas—and, after the murderous Carolina frontier wars in the early eighteenth century, the Tuscaroras—built a strong confederation. The League formed a series of relationships known as the Covenant Chain with other Indian tribes and with many of the colonies. The colonies signed treaties with the Iroquois League and thereby joined the Covenant Chain in order to streamline their Indian diplomacy. Rather than attempt to understand and work through the hundreds of different Indian political relationships, the colonial governments preferred to conduct Indian affairs through one agency: the Iroquois League.

This relationship involved give and take on both sides, and very subtle diplomacy. Several times representatives of most of the colonies met at Albany for great council meetings with the Iroquois that saw elaborate ceremony punctuated by exchanges of gifts. Indian diplomacy affected intercolonial relationships, because council sessions with the Iroquois were the only times representatives of the colonies came together for any joint purpose. Working through the Covenant Chain meant that the colonial govenments recognized Iroquois League sovereignty over and protection of many tribes and much of the territory in the Northeast. Often the Iroquois, caught between their obligations to their Indian clients and the pressure exerted by the ever expanding European frontier, forced Indians to give up land or were helpless to stop injustice. Ultimately the Covenant Chain broke down under this pressure.

The Ohio Valley appealed to displaced Indians. Many groups, tired of being pushed west in small moves every few years as the European frontier grew, decided to move far beyond the line of settlement into this fertile region. Here an unprecedented development took place. Indians who had formerly been hostile to each other came to see that they all shared a similar plight. A new spirit of pan-Indian sentiment grew up that promised concerted action in the face of the threat encroaching from the east.

MOHAWK CHIEF, identified in this 1710 engraving by John Verelst as Sa Ga Yeath Qua Pieth Tow, King of the Maquas (Mohawks).

Religious revivals swept through both Indian and European-American communities in the eighteenth century. The new sense of determination among Indians in the Ohio Valley grew out of a religious revival. Neolin, the Delaware Prophet, had had a mystical experience in which the path the Indians must follow was revealed to him. He taught that they had brought on their misfortunes by giving up their old ways. They must strictly avoid alcohol, wear nothing but animal skins, and throw away their guns and live by hunting with bow and arrow. All the old skills must be re-created, and the old rituals reinstated. Neolin was able to weave together many disparate Indian traditions, and he included some Christian elements, such as the idea of one great God. His was the first of many such revival movements that responded to the Indians' losses. Often, by giving Indians a sense of renewed purpose, they sparked off movements of armed resistance.

The restoration of native life called for by Neolin was not allowed time to develop. In moving beyond the frontier, Indians had hoped they would be able once again to take up their old ways, but the fertile Ohio Valley beckoned to the flood of settlers that soon filled the region east of the mountains. More importantly, the tribes found themselves in an arena of imperial conflict. Their fate was bound up in the policies of France and England and the continuing war between their empires.

THE WEST

French control of the Mississippi River and the center of the continent was threatening to Spanish authorities in the west as well as to English-sponsored colonies to the east. Spain decided to create a permanent presence in Texas to prevent French expansion. As one priest wrote, "They are slipping in behind our backs in silence, but God sees their intentions." San Antonio was founded as part of this determination. A series of missions was built in the eastern part of Texas, and four *presidios*, or forts. Outposts in East Texas, ironically, were always dependent on French Louisiana for food supplies. Legal trade was strictly controlled by the Spanish empire, and supplies could come legally only from Mexico at great cost. The result was that the beleaguered colonists resorted to smuggling. The Texas settlements lived in fear of Indian assault, and they blamed French traders for arming plains tribes. By 1760 a little over one thousand Hispanic people lived in Texas, many of them soldiers.

New Mexico also felt pressure from the activities of French traders on the central plains. Armed and mounted Indians who were French allies, especially Comanches and Pawnees, made life very tenuous. As New Mexico governor Antonio Valverde y Cosío wrote, the French were determined to thrust into the territory "little by

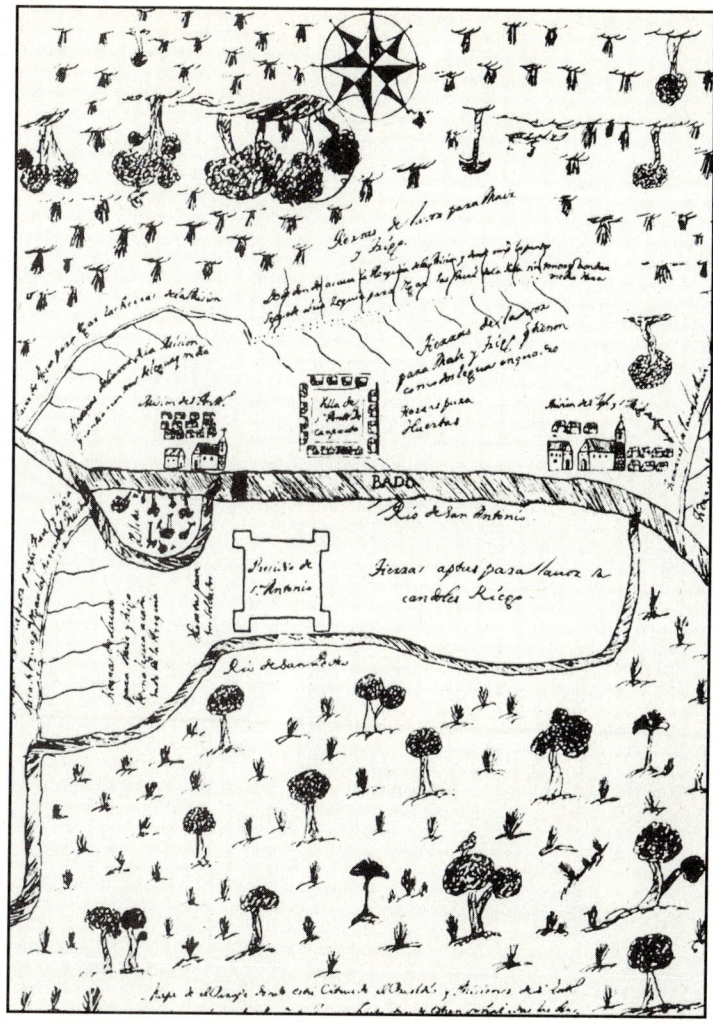

SAN ANTONIO in 1730. The settlement includes the villa, the presidio, and the mission.

little." Their fears were confirmed when a Spanish expedition into modern Nebraska, seeking to evict French traders living among the Pawnees, was soundly defeated and most of the party killed. The Spanish withdrew back into New Mexico and consolidated their holdings there. Spanish authorities were forced to live with the knowledge that, as one commander put it, "The heathen of the north are innumerable and rich. They enjoy the protection and commerce of the French; they dress well, breed horses, handle firearms with the greatest skill." New Mexico remained the front line for the protection of rich silver mines and ranches in northern Mexico.

Imperial planners in Spain, led by José de Gálvez, determined to secure Spanish control of the West by founding settlements in California. The idea that Spain should settle California had been proposed early in the eighteenth century by the Jesuit father Eusebio Francisco Kino, who saw rich possibilities for missionary work among the large Indian communities. In the 1760s the Spanish king decreed that the rich and powerful Jesuits, who almost seemed to rival the royal power, must leave America. Gálvez laid plans to carry the California plan to fruition, but as a secular rather than a religious enterprise. He quickly found, however, that missionaries were essential to winning the support of Indians among whom he proposed to place Spanish settlers.

The venture into California set out from the base in San Diego in 1769. It was led by Captain Gaspar de Portolá with Franciscan fray Junípero Serra as the religious leader. With the building of a presidio and mission at Monterey in 1770, New California was officially begun. Soon missions were also founded at San Gabriel and Santa Barbara. The colony's greatest problems lay in the difficulty of supplying soldiers and missions with food. Travel up the coast, by ship or by land, was extremely risky. Many ships disappeared without trace. Russian traders and soldiers were active along the coast and isolated communities feared for their ability to fend off attacks. The presidios remained tiny throughout the eighteenth century.

The native communities among whom the Spanish had settled soon grew unhappy with their presence. Soldiers, unaccompanied by Spanish women, formed liaisons with Indian women, some voluntary, but many forced. Fray Serra despaired over "the plague of immorality," and hoped to be able to keep the missions separate from the presidios. The soldiers attempted to keep the Indians overawed by a system of harsh retribution for any defiance. Soon undeclared warfare existed between the Indians and the newcomers. Conflict with Indians led to tension between the military, civilian, and religious authorities, with each group complaining back to authorities in Mexico or even to Spain about the other. Most of the settlers were of Spanish origin but had been born and raised in Mexico. The missionaries looked down on these "creoles," and considered them uncultured. They disliked the rough way the soldiers and settlers treated the Indians.

Many missionaries, cut off from Spanish communities, approached Indians in a more open way. One such man was fray Francisco Gárces, who possessed a phenomenal ability to adapt to Indian lifestyles and foodways. Others were fascinated and repelled by his flexibility, one Franciscan saying he "appears to be but an Indian himself. . . . God has created him solely for the purpose of seeking out these unhappy, ignorant, and rustic people."

But the colonists accused the religious men of holding the Indians in a kind of permanent dependent status at the missions. Fray Junípero Serra said of the converts that they were "our children . . . we look upon them as a father looks upon his family. We shower all our love and care upon them." The Spanish leaders, who wanted to integrate the Indians into Spanish life, countered that those living at the missions were in a situation "worse than that of slaves." Even the Franciscans admitted that Indians who gave up their native lifestyle and came to live at the missions had great trouble adapting: "They live well free but as soon as we reduce them to a Christian and community life . . . they fatten, sicken, and die."

Indian communities were caught between these competing authorities, and often rejected all of them. The Indian population of California fell from about 300,000 in 1769 to about 200,000 by the early nineteenth century.

Meanwhile the Hispanic presence grew slowly. In the 1770s, Hispanic women came to the presidios and life became more normal as the communities became self-sufficient in food production. San Francisco Bay saw creation of an agricultural town at San Jose as well as a presidio and mission at San Francisco. Founders believed that if San Francisco "could be well settled like Europe there would not be anything more beautiful in the world." Los Angeles, the second civilian town, was founded near the mission at San Gabriel in 1781, and Santa Barbara's presidio was built in 1782. Throughout the eighteenth century, however, the California settlements remained cut off from Spanish centers farther south by the arduous journey by sea or by land, and voluntary migrants remained a trickle. At the end of the century the Hispanic population numbered about 1,800.

Farther north and west new possibilities were revealed throughout the eighteenth century. In 1728 Russian explorer Vitus Bering had sailed

MONTEREY, SOLDIER AND HIS WIFE, drawn in 1791.

to the easternmost tip of Asia, and soon explorers knew of the existence of the *bolsháya zemlyá*, the "great land" to the east. Fur traders began to move into Alaska in the 1740s, but geographers continued to debate the nature of the revealed land. Was it a series of islands? More importantly, could ships find a passage through to Hudsons Bay? British explorers were mapping the coastline of Hudsons Bay in the 1740s, fruitlessly looking for the other end of such a passage.

By the 1770s the size of the lands to the north was more clearly understood, and many nations, including Spain, tried to establish claims in Alaska. In 1776 Captain James Cook, the most eminent explorer of the day, decided to conduct an expedition that would determine both the shape of the Alaska peninsula and whether a Northwest Passage existed. Parliament had offered a prize of £20,000 to the discoverer of the passage. Cook's previous voyages had revealed the true nature of the lands in the South Pacific, and he now proposed to do the same for Alaska. His ships sounded and charted the coast all the way from Oregon up to Alaska, but the Englishmen also met Russian traders who were there before them.

In traveling to Alaska, Cook stumbled across the Hawaiian Islands in January 1778. There he was honored as a great chief, and the natives valued highly the metal tools the English brought. As Captain Charles Clerke wrote, "This is the cheapest market I ever yet saw, a moderate sized Nail will supply my Ship's Company very plentifully with excellent Pork for the Day, and as to the Potatoes and Tarrow, they are attained upon still easier Terms, such is these People's avidity for Iron."

In returning from Alaska the expedition again stopped at Hawaii almost exactly a year after the first visit and this time relations deteriorated. The natives were not pleased to see the return of the English ships. As one mariner wrote, they were apprehensive about "our intentions; as fearing we should attempt to settle there, and deprive them of part if not the whole of their Country." The trade became more exacting. The Hawaiians were short of food and became very strict about what they required in exchange. When the natives took some tools they believed were owed to them for food they had provided, Cook ordered reprisals. The English attempted to take hostages among the leading men, the Hawaiians retaliated, and Cook and several of his men were killed in the ensuing fighting.

Although the Hawaiians acquired a reputation for violence as a result of Cook's death, the islands became a port of call for ships of many nations, where they took on food and fresh water. Some mariners stayed on, and a community of Europeans grew up at Honolulu. Hawaii quickly became involved in the flourishing fur trade between America's northwest coast and China. Thus by the end of the colonial period all the land of the future United States was the scene of activity by competing European agents, seeking to establish claims and create trading relationships.

THE SETTLED EAST

RELIGION AND COLONIAL ELITES

Anglo-American society had "matured" in some ways by 1700. For the first time, people of European parentage born in America outnumbered immigrants. An American consciousness was developing in the eighteenth century and religion played a major role in this new identity. Religion had always been important in the British-sponsored colonies; many had been founded as refuges for persecuted groups and had continued to emphasize that special mission. In the eighteenth century men and women fleeing persecution for religion came to the colonies from many parts of Europe. But some Americans, descendants of earlier immigrants, felt that the religious fervor in the more settled regions had waned. Religion had become routine, a part of the social order rather than a deeply felt sense of personal conviction. Growing prosperity had made people more concerned with taking advantage of new opportunities for amassing wealth than with the state of their souls.

Out of this concern emerged one of the most remarkable movements in American history, which historians have labeled the Great Awakening. It began with a series of small, local religious revivals as far back as the end of the seventeenth century in the Connecticut River valley, and these often began with a small number of

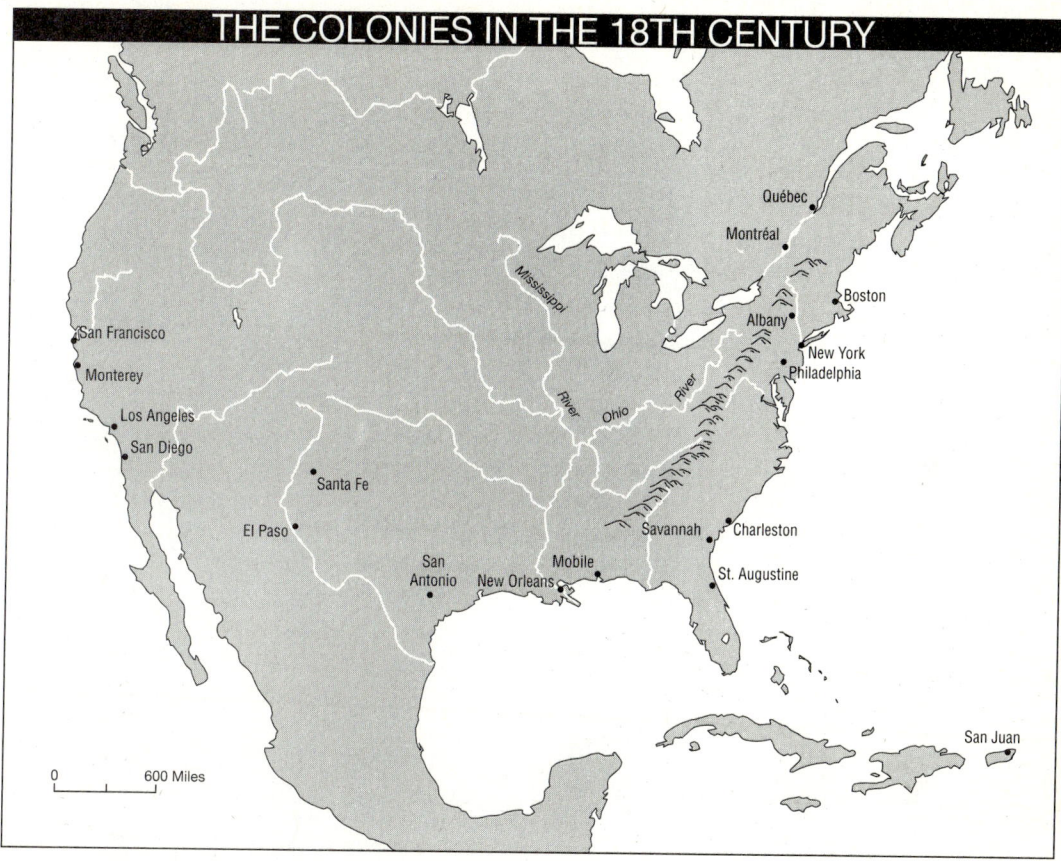

troubled souls seeking help. The minister's response channeled these apprehensions into a dramatic renewal of faith for the entire congregation. In fact, some historians have wondered whether the excitement generated at Salem Village in 1692, the sense of participating in a cosmic drama, might not have been turned into a revival if Samuel Parris, the minister, had shaped his response differently.

In the 1720s the Middle Colonies saw the beginnings of a series of revivals led by William and Gilbert Tennent, who worked primarily among Presbyterian Scotch-Irish congregations in New Jersey and New York. Jonathan Edwards, minister in Northampton, Massachusetts, led his congregation in a movement of religious renewal in 1734 and 1735. Edwards was a highly educated man who wrote extensively on the psychology of conversion and knew the work of the leading European philosophers of the day. He and his congregation became convinced that, though they had been going through the motions of a religious life, they had been spiritually dead. All the revivals stressed the *experience* of God's grace in daily life rather than adherence to specific doctrines.

Hundreds of Edwards's parishioners experienced the process of conversion, which began with devastating examination of their own souls, leading to despair of ever being worthy of God's grace. Just at the moment when despair set in, most experienced a sense of God's forgiveness,

GEORGE WHITEFIELD. This English painting shows the enraptured congregation listening to his powerful sermon, and the painter indicates the central role of women in the early eighteenth-century revivals.

of being flooded with light and grace. The movement spread to neighboring communities along the Connecticut River, but its excitement burned out by the end of 1735. Jonathan Edwards wrote a book about the revival, *Faithful Narrative of the Surprising Work of God*, describing how it affected "all sorts, sober and vicious, high and low, rich and poor, wise and unwise." Many people believed something great was about to happen.

Soon "it pleased God to send Mr. [George] Whitefield into this land." Whitefield, a charismatic preacher who was deeply committed to the Georgia experiment, traveled over the colonies spreading the revival from Georgia to Maine as he preached several sermons each day. Nothing like it had ever been seen. Wherever he went he gathered crowds too large for any building to hold, so he preached out in the open air. Nathan Cole, as he traveled to hear Whitefield preach in Middletown, Connecticut, in 1740

> saw before me a Cloud or fog rising; I first thought it came from the great River, but as I came nearer the Road, I heard a noise something like a low rumbling thunder and presently found it was the noise of Horse's feet . . . every horse seemed to go with all his might to carry his rider to hear news from heaven for the saving of Souls, it made me tremble to see the sight . . .

Thousands heard Whitefield in Charleston, Philadelphia, and New York. When he came to

Boston in 1740 his final sermon drew a crowd of near 30,000 people to the Common—and Boston's total population was half that number.

At first the ministers, who had been preaching to half-empty churches, were overjoyed and vied to attract Whitefield and other touring ministers to their pulpits. As Benjamin Franklin wrote, "it seem'd as if all the World were growing Religious." Franklin went to hear Whitefield preach in Philadelphia and was amazed because the "Multitudes of all Sects and Denominations that attended his Sermons were enormous." But soon enthusiasm turned to suspicion; many wondered what the effect of such outpourings of emotion would be. How could the emotion be controlled and channeled? Parishioners began to compare their own ministers to the Awakeners and called them cold and unconverted. The faculty of Harvard College pointed out that, because of Whitefield's example, "the People have been thence ready to despise their own Ministers."

Ben Franklin wrote that "the Clergy taking a Dislike to him, soon refus'd him their Pulpits and he was oblig'd to preach in the Fields." Closing the churches to Whitefield and other preachers who had adopted the Awakening forced people to choose. Many New England parishes split over whether they would follow the New Lights, as the Awakeners were called, or stay with the Old Lights, the established church. Old Lights pointed to the emotional nature of the conversion experience and doubted that it would outlast the excitement of the revivals.

To some extent the Old Lights were right. The fervor of the Awakening did fade. But the effects of the movement were long-lasting, and in some ways set the stage for the Revolution by breaking down habits of obedience. Just the experience of attending one of the Awakeners' sermons had its impact. Ordinary men and women used to sitting in the meetinghouse or church where every pew was assigned according to your wealth and importance in the community and where the minister preached a highly intellectual sermon suddenly found themselves in an open field where everyone jostled together and the preacher reached out to them in emotional everyday language. The Awakeners' message was: God wants *you* to be saved; *you* are important.

Conflicts between New Lights and Old Lights also produced important long-lasting effects. When parishioners chose the new churches over the old established church, they were also refusing to bow to the established order. Ordinarily such middling people would "know their place" and would never have challenged those in authority, but the Awakening gave them sufficient assurance to make that possible, even, as the Harvard faculty said, to "despise their own Ministers." It taught that the poorest and most ignorant may be chosen by God over the grandest Harvard graduate. Moreover, religious issues were important enough to risk challenging the social order because, where your soul was at stake, you could not stand by and duck responsibility.

The Awakening also had political effects, as churches in many communities split. In order to be recognized as congregations so that their taxes would go to their new churches, the New Lights had to have the approval of the colonial legislatures. Thus the Awakening led believers to challenge their traditional leaders for seats in the assemblies, and continuing political alignments were created.

The religious revivals became strong in the southern colonies in the 1760s, as lively Baptist congregations grew up to challenge the established Church of England. In the Chesapeake, where great planters lived ostentatiously in an aristocratic mode, the established church functioned as part of the social order. Church services, like all other public meetings, offered opportunities for display by men of high status. They rode to church on their elegant horses and entered only when all the lesser people were seated. It was "not the Custom for Gentlemen to go into Church til Service is beginning, when they enter in a Body, in the same manner as they come out." Everyone who attended church received a dramatic demonstration of the social hierarchy.

Now the Baptists offered an alternative. Instead of elegant churches, they met in rough surroundings. Where the established church offered restraint in sermon and music, the Baptist meetings featured heartfelt, emotional preaching and singing. Instead of reinforcing the hierarchy, they insisted that all were equal in the sight of God. In a breathtaking break with southern protocol, Baptists allowed slaves to join the church as equals. So outraged were the elite that they repeatedly tried to break up Baptist meetings with violence. Beatings were met with prayer and song, and ultimately only served to strengthen the new movement.

Women in all the eastern colonies were deeply affected by the revivals, which knew no distinction of age or sex. Many women experienced conversion and many of the new churches allowed them a greater public sphere. Nathan Bowen, a Marblehead, Massachusetts lawyer, was disgusted because now "women and even Common Negroes take upon them to exhort their Betters even in the pulpit before large assemblies." At the same time, women's roles in the home took on new meaning. Sects such as the Quakers in the Middle Colonies had long emphasized that women's child-rearing role was one of the most important functions of society. Children received their first knowledge of God and the world, as well as basic reading and writing skills, from their mothers. The future of the society was in the hands of women. Now, partly as a result of the revivals, child rearing received increasing emphasis, and moved to the center of women's lives. Though in the short run this new emphasis made women content with their place, it also, by enhancing women's dominance of their own separate sphere, made possible future claims to control.

ECONOMIC GROWTH

The great bulk of the population in the Anglo-American colonies lived by agriculture, which was a thriving, growing sector of the economy. Agricultural expansion allowed the colonies to be largely self-sufficient in food, and good incomes meant increasing importation of manufactured goods from England and from other countries.

Economic well-being led to a revolution in styles of life in the eighteenth-century East. The homes of even the wealthiest planters in the seventeenth century had been no more than large farmhouses. Now, although most people continued to live in one- or two-room houses, rich southern planters and city merchants began to build mansions with splendid downstairs rooms and great central halls and staircases. These homes were not only grander, they were designed for a new style of life, one centered on society and entertainment. Pine furniture was replaced by fine cherry and walnut imported from Europe and pottery dishes by china.

Though life in newly settled frontier areas was rough, the mid-century change in taste affected all levels of society in settled areas. Inventories, lists of possessions and their value, were taken when people died so that their estates could be divided up fairly. Inventories of humble farmers began to change about 1740 or 1750: families that had formerly eaten their meals from wooden bowls began to have pottery. Chairs began to replace benches in these lists, and furniture of all sorts became more plentiful. Life at all levels became easier and more genteel for colonists from Europe and their descendants.

Benjamin Franklin recorded this transition in his own family. After describing how his wife worked with him in his printing shop, and scrimped to make the business a success, he wrote:

> My Breakfast was a long time Bread and Milk, (no Tea,) and I ate it out of a twopenny earthen Porringer with a Pewter Spoon. But mark how Luxury will enter Families, and make a Progress, in Spite of Principle. Being Call'd one Morning to breakfast, I found it in a China Bowl with a Spoon of Silver.

Franklin explained that his wife had bought the bowl and spoon without his knowledge,

> for which she had no other Excuse or Apology to make, but that she thought *her* Husband deserv'd a Silver Spoon and China Bowl as well as any of his Neighbors. This was the first Appearance of Plate and China in our House.

Prosperity did not extend to everyone. In the oldest and largest cities, especially the seaports of Boston, New York, and Philadelphia, those at the bottom of the economic heap were becoming poorer in the decades before 1776. Unemployment was widespread, and those who acquired jobs usually found they were only seasonal. Real wages (purchasing power of income) dropped for the poor, and the cities faced demands for public relief. Both prosperity and poverty helped to break down habits of deference, because both could make colonists dissatified with a static social order.

SLAVERY IN THE EIGHTEENTH CENTURY

Other groups were left out of the general prosperity. Good times were partly built on the backs of enslaved labor. Slowly, the proportion of native-born slaves began to grow larger than those fresh from Africa, and the experience of slavery changed. African-American slaves responded to the demands made on them differently than did newcomers. Instead of denying the authority of the owners by running away or failing to understand orders, native-born slaves worked within the system to control it in their favor. In this they were able to have some success. The field hands worked in gangs of ten or twenty. If one of the gang were sick or old, the others would try to slow the work to a pace the weakest member could meet. While the master and his drivers literally held the whip hand, and beatings were common on the plantations, slaves had ways of frustrating the system's operation if they were driven too hard.

As the slave population became larger, slaves were more often housed in separate "quarters" away from the plantation's center. This separation allowed slaves to organize their own society centered on the institution of the family, with their own leadership. Almost all slaves faced the sale of family members to other plantations at some point in their lives and the support network of the quarters helped them over this trauma. While mothers were rarely separated from young children, other slaves in the quarter often acted as substitute father, uncle, grandmother, or cousin to bereaved families. Sometimes these networks extended to other nearby plantations and were bolstered by visiting back and forth. Slave women often formed the centers of such kin webs.

In many areas of the South, slave holdings remained small throughout the eighteenth century, with most owners having fewer than five slaves. This meant that owners and European indentured servants would have worked beside the slaves in the field. Many plantation techniques were learned from African laborers, such as the correct methods of rice cultivation in South Carolina. Even on larger plantations crops required very close attention and owners and overseers went into the fields daily. Planter William Byrd II compared his role to that of an Old Testament figure: "Like the patriarchs, I have my flocks and my herds, my bond-men and bond-women. . . . I must take care to keep all my people to their duty, to set all the springs in motion, and to make everyone draw his equal share to carry the machine forward."

Slaves also drew on Old Testament similes, as their songs and spirituals compared their lot to that of the Israelites enslaved by the Egyptians. European Americans who lived in close proximity with slaves often mistook the nature of their relationships. Eliza Lucas Pinckney of South Carolina worked assiduously as a plantation manager, but was dumbfounded when her slaves left her during the Revolution. In a letter to an English friend, she complained that her slaves had

An overseer doing his duty. This watercolor by Benjamin Henry Latrobe of a scene near Fredericksburg, Virginia, in 1798 is a graphic illustration of how the growing institution of slavery transformed southern society. Euro-American female servants did not do field work; slave women did. Here the overseer takes his ease while he watches the women work.

deserted her, and "my property pulled to pieces, burnt and destroyed; my money of no value, my Children sick and prisoners." The letter went on, "Such is the deplorable state of our Country from two armies being in it for nearly two years; the plantations have been some quite, some nearly, ruined—and all with very few exceptions great sufferers." Like many slaveowners, Pinckney had expected loyalty and found that slaves preferred freedom.

SOCIAL ORDER

At the opening of the eighteenth century, British American society was constructed on principles of deference. Deference rested on people's acceptance of their place in the social order. It meant that the "middling" and "poorer sort" of people normally deferred to, or accepted, the judgment of the wealthiest and most established among them. In politics deference meant that men from a few families were reelected to office again and again, in recognition of their natural right to lead. There were no secret ballots, and the voting was done in a body by show of hands, so men who were dependent on the patronage of those above them knew enough not to offend their "betters." Deference did not rest on fear, however. Much of the time, there seems to have been general agreement on who society's "natural leaders" were. All people were caught up in a web of relationships in which the more powerful looked out for the interests of their constituents and those lower on the social scale repaid them with support.

Because the majority of colonists were now born in America, they were also born into their roles in life. This "creole" society increasingly began to construct its own ways of doing things. Deference made elite officeholders confident in the rightness of their judgment, and the colonial assemblies began increasingly to enlarge the sphere in which they operated, sometimes even in defiance of the royal governor and his council. Samuel Shute, governor of Masschusetts, wrote angrily in 1732 that the assembly had usurped his powers: it was "in a manner the whole Legislative and in a Good measure the Executive Power of the Province." Colonial merchants, planters, and artisans began to develop their own markets and internal trade structures.

PHILADELPHIA, showing a settled city with impressive buildings in 1764.

In the family, deference also ruled, under a system historians call patriarchy. Fathers ruled their families. The flexibility of roles allowed women by the uncertainties of the seventeenth century had been submerged in a reassertion of male authority. Only very rarely did women have control of their own property, and public roles were largely denied them. There were some exceptional women, such as Eliza Lucas Pinckney, who ran her family's South Carolina plantation from the age of seventeen and was the first in the colony to develop cultivation and processing of indigo, which became a major cash crop for the colony. Another female entrepreneur was Betsy Ross of Philadelphia, whose upholstery shop saw several young men working under her direction. For most, though, women's sphere was the home, where female roles were enlarged by the addition of spinning wheels and other equipment. Women's contribution to the family economy was crucial, and in newly settled parts of the colonies women were still called on to do rough farm work at times. Despite the propaganda circulating in Europe, America was not a "Paradise on earth for women."

Deference was an accepted way of life in 1700. Yet, seventy-five years later these same Americans would rise up in an unprecedented shattering of deference. Not only would the colonists defy Britain, but within the colonies established elites were challenged by new groups dissatisfied with the way things were done. Over the course of that seventy-five years, a series of events and trends worked to break down deference and make possible the defiance of the American Revolution. The story of the eighteenth century in British America is largely the chronicle of that breakdown. As challenges to deference were played out, the Americans also developed an awakening consciousness of themselves as one people separate from Britain. Both were necessary to making the Revolution possible.

THE FRENCH AND INDIAN WAR

Britain's colonies in the East, like the Spanish colonies in the West, felt threatened and hemmed in by French activities in the continent's center. England and France were engaged in a worldwide struggle throughout the entire eighteenth century, and each nation headed a European alliance system delicately calculated to balance that of the other. Time and again, competition erupted into war as events in Europe temporarily gave one or the other an edge. Because Britain and France each held extensive territory in North America and the West Indies, the colonists, much against their will, were drawn into these imperial wars. The two nations vied for dominion of the region east of the Mississippi River.

The British colonists' resentment can be seen in the names they gave the conflicts. While they were known in Europe by names that pointed to the imperial concerns for which they were fought, such as the War of the Austrian Succession, the Americans named the wars after the British monarchs who had forced the colonists into their fights: King William's War (1689–1697), Queen Anne's War (1702–1713), and King George's War (1744–1748). The climax of this series was the French and Indian War, which began in America in 1754 and spread to Europe in 1756, where it was called the Seven Years' War. The war ended in 1763 and resulted in the expulsion of French control from the continent of North America.

In the middle of the eighteenth century, on the eve of the French and Indian War, France had looked much stronger in North America. Whereas the English colonies clung to the edge of the continent, France claimed the continent's center on the basis of early explorations. French fur traders moved throughout the vast interior of North America and French missionaries had converted many Indians, who became the French empire's staunch allies. Moreover the French controlled access to the Mississippi River, the continent's central artery of trade and communications.

France's advantages, however, were more apparent than real. Its territories were thinly populated, and supply lines to the interior could be cut off by capturing Quebec. The English, with heavy and growing concentrations of population, were stronger than they looked. Pressure of numbers meant the colonists increasingly looked to the fertile land of the Ohio Valley beyond the Appalachian mountain chain. It was here that the first clashes of the French and Indian War occurred after French agents began to build forts in the Ohio Valley to forestall English advance. A Virginia militia force, led by the young George Washington in 1754, failed to push the French out, so regular British troops under Major General Edward Braddock were sent a year later to teach both the French and the English colonists a lesson.

Indians in the Ohio Valley found themselves once again on the front lines. Tribes such as the Delawares had repeatedly been pushed back by the advance of European settlement and they knew that an English victory over France would accelerate that process. However, the English were generous with trade goods, and the Indians knew the value of being on the winning side. The Delawares, still a numerous tribe, approached General Braddock to offer support against France if he would guarantee their right to live in the Ohio Valley after an English victory. Braddock, arrogantly underestimating both his allies and his foes, said "No Savage Should Inherit the Land." The Delawares remained neutral, and Braddock, with most of his force, was slaughtered.

Meanwhile, representatives of six colonies, fully aware of the importance of Indian aid in the struggle against France, met with the Iroquois in a grand council meeting in Albany in 1754. Though the Iroquois were initially unmoved by colonists' appeals, the conference provided an opportunity for colonial representatives to discuss their mutual problems. Here Benjamin Franklin unveiled the first plan to bring the European Americans together in a union through which they would meet periodically and build a

THE BATTLE OF QUEBEC, 1759. English reports celebrated the victorious surprise attack on the supposedly unscalable Plains of Abraham above the city where the French army was lodged.

sense of common commitment. The plan did not immediately bear fruit, but it laid the foundation for future planning toward a sense of nationhood.

Braddock's defeat was followed by a series of British military failures in the Great Lakes and the northwest frontier that seemed to lay New York and New England open to French attack. At this point, British strategy changed dramatically. A brilliant politician, William Pitt, was called to head the English government in 1757. He decided to reverse the plan of previous imperial wars and make North America the main focus of operations, leaving his allies to oppose France in Europe. Unprecedented amounts of money were raised, and troops and supplies were poured into America. A series of victories was capped by the fall of the "invincible" fortress of Quebec in 1759. French bases in North America could now be "starved" into submission, as their access to weapons, ammunition, and other vital stores was cut off.

The Treaty of Paris, signed in 1763, recognized British control of all of North America east of the Mississippi River except for New Orleans, which went to Spain. Florida, the prize that had eluded Oglethorpe and his troops, now became a British possession. The territory of British America was increased manyfold, and the British empire achieved new heights of glory. Twenty years later, in 1783, that empire lay in ruins.

EFFECTS OF THE WAR

Signs of future trouble were evident even in the rejoicing of 1763, for the war had revealed to both the British and the American colonists that the empire had become in reality very different from what it was on paper. The British, believing the Americans unruly, had long sought to tighten the empire's control of colonial administration. Now, with the need to incorporate vast new territories into the colonies, and with the fear of France removed, such tightening would at last be possible.

The British government was desperately short of money. Not only had the war been tremendously costly, but George III, who had come to the throne in 1760 just after the Ameri-

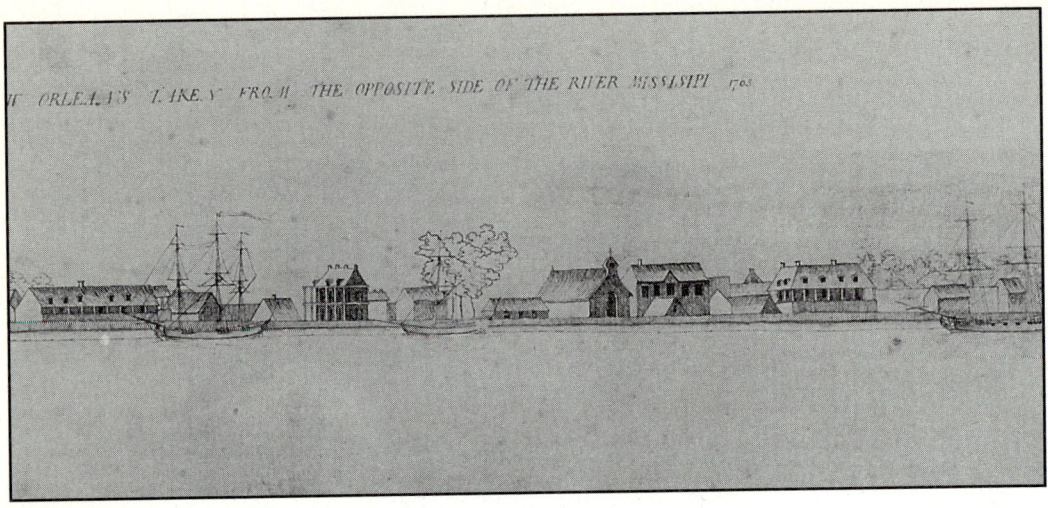

VIEW OF NEW ORLEANS, 1765, drawn by Philip Pittman, a British officer.

can victories, decided to keep an army of 10,000 men on the frontier to police the vast new territories acquired from France and to control the Indians and the French people who remained there. It seemed fair that the colonists pay part of the costs. After all, they were the beneficiaries of the war, and the army was for their protection. Moreover, the Americans were distinctly undertaxed. English citizens paid much heavier taxes.

Things looked very different from the American point of view. England's wars had meant nothing but trouble for the colonies. Many had suffered from Indian attacks on the frontier throughout the eighteenth century, and colonies had been called on time and again to provide troops and money for defense. Now that France would no longer be supplying weapons to allies in the interior, the 10,000-man standing army seemed unnecessary, and even potentially dangerous. English tradition held that a monarch who maintained an army in peacetime had tyranny in mind. The army could just as easily be turned against the colonists.

The first test of the army's usefulness came as colonists began to pour into the newly won area beyond the Appalachians, and Indians responded angrily to this encroachment. The frontier was inflamed in 1763 by a series of uprisings that together are known as Pontiac's War. Thirteen British posts were assaulted, and Forts Pitt and Detroit were besieged. The preaching of Neolin and other revivalists gave Indians a sense of mission in this defiance. Pontiac said that his actions were inspired by the "Master of Life," arguing that he "put Arms in our hands" and "ordered us to fight."

General Jeffrey Amherst, commander of British forces in America, considered the old Indian diplomacy with its rituals and gift giving a symptom of colonial cowardice. Rather than "bribe" the Indians, he would force them to obey his will, since they could no longer play off the French against the English. Amherst pursued a policy of "extirpation," ordering his men to "put to death all that fall into your hands." He introduced germ warfare by sending blankets infected with smallpox among the Delawares. The captain who delivered the blankets remarked, "I hope it will have the desired effect." He was not disappointed, as a violent epidemic struck the

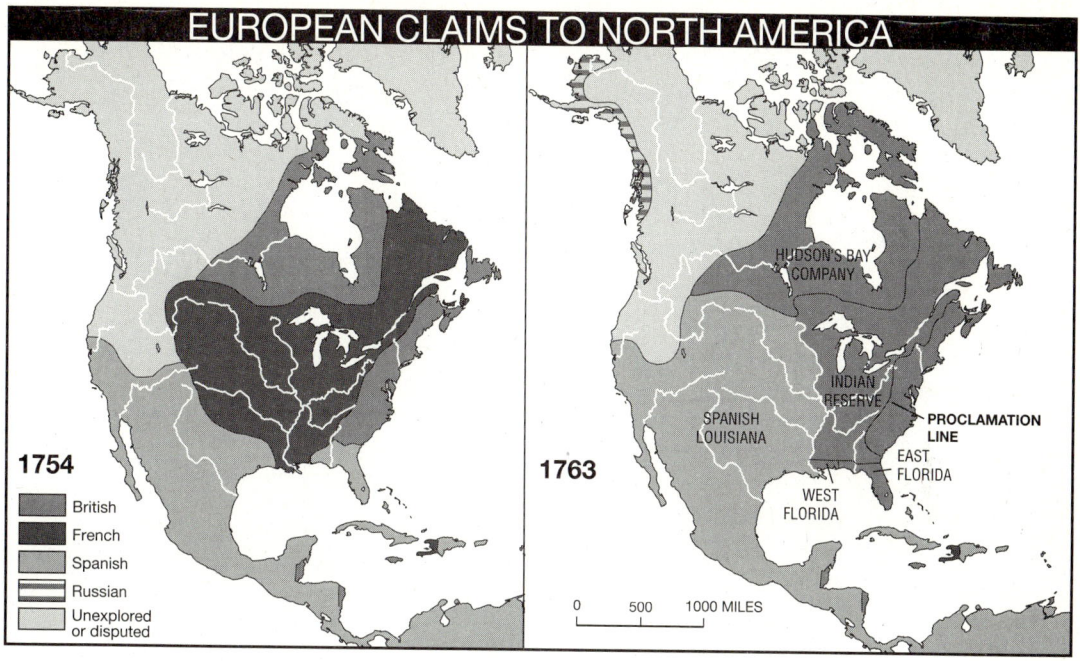

Delawares. Though the Indian uprising was put down, it inflicted great destruction on both sides of the frontier and caused many settlers to retreat to established areas.

The British government, alarmed by the Indian warfare and not wishing to have the new territories developed haphazardly as the thirteen original colonies had been, issued the Proclamation of 1763. This established a line of settlement, roughly equivalent to the edge of established farms and villages, beyond which the colonists were forbidden to go. It was meant to reassure the Indians and prevent expansion of the colonies until a fully thought-through policy was developed. With the issuance of the Proclamation of 1763, colonists saw the standing army in a different light: It seemed designed to prevent colonists from moving into the rich area they thought the war had won for them. The colonists wondered whose interests the British cared about.

The end of the French and Indian War in 1763 also brought changes in the feelings of the American colonists toward Britain. The colonists had been accustomed to thinking of themselves as British, and Americans looked to Britain for culture and trade. But the war brought individual Americans and Englishmen together, and the face-to-face meeting produced unexpected results. The British army was composed of aristocratic officers, who bought their commissions, and troops who were seen as the dregs of society. The troops were kept in line by a brutal system of discipline that prescribed the death penalty for relatively minor offenses and hundreds, sometimes even thousands, of whip lashes on the bare back for others. The Americans saw the officers as arrogant, brutal, and foppish, and the swearing, immoral troops disgusted the colonial militiamen who served with them. The revulsion Americans felt for the imperial army intensified when the troops were stationed in colonial cities, and culminated in the Boston Massacre.

For their part, the British came away with contempt for the Americans, who were seen as undisciplined, cowardly, and self-indulgent. Smuggling in wartime, sometimes even trading with the enemy, was seen as contemptible. Despite the victories of the recent war, each side saw the other's army as deeply flawed, a miscalculation that may have led to a willingness to go to war in 1776. Each side thought the other incapable of mounting a sustained campaign.

CHRONOLOGY

1701	Founding of Detroit	1754	Albany Congress; Franklin proposes Plan of Union
1718	Founding of San Antonio	1754–1763	French and Indian War, ended by Peace of Paris, 1763
1720s	Tennents lead New Jersey religious revivals	1760s	Baptist challenge to Church of England in the Chesapeake
1732	Founding of Georgia	1760–1776	Heaviest immigration into British America
1734–1735	Jonathan Edwards leads revival movement in Northampton, Massachusetts	1760s–1770s	Regulator movements on frontier
1739	Stono Rebellion in South Carolina	1760	Neolin begins preaching in Ohio Valley
1739–1740	George Whitefield begins first preaching tour of colonies	1763	Pontiac's War; Proclamation of 1763
1740s	Great Awakening	1770	Founding of Monterey, California
1740	Joint Georgia–South Carolina attack on St. Augustine	1778	Captain James Cook in Alaska and Hawaii
1754	Virginia militia under George Washington defeated by French		

SUGGESTIONS FOR FURTHER READING

The joint South Carolina–Georgia expedition against St. Augustine was the subject of controversy, and therefore several accounts were written at the time. Many of these have been made available in modern editions, including Anon. [James Killpatrick], *An Impartial Account of the Late Expedition Against St Augustine Under General Oglethorpe* (1742), ed. Aileen Moore Topping (1978), and Anon. [Edward Kimber], *A Relation or Journal, of a late Expedition to the Gates of St. Augustine, on Florida* (1742), ed. John Jay TePaske (1976). John Tate Lanning has edited the Report to the South Carolina General Assembly presented by the committee set up to analyze what went wrong. This has been published as *The St. Augustine Expedition of 1740* by the South Carolina Archives Department (1954).

On the escaped slaves and the situation from which they ran away see Jane Landers, "Gracia Real de Santa Teresa de Mose: A Free Black Town in Spanish Colonial Florida," *American Historical Review*, 95 (1990), 9–30, and Peter H. Wood, *Black Majority: Negroes in Colonial South Carolina from 1670 through the Stono Rebellion* (1974).

A varied picture of Oglethorpe as leader emerges from Phinizy Spalding, *Oglethorpe in America* (1977), Leslie F. Church, *Oglethorpe: A Study of Philanthropy in England and Georgia* (1932), and Amos Aschbach Ettinger, *James Edward Oglethorpe, Imperial Idealist* (1936). On Jonathan Bryan, see Alan Gallay, *The Formation of a Planter Elite: Jonathan Bryan and the Southern Colonial Frontier* (1989). The military aspects of the campaign are analyzed in Larry E. Ivers, *British Drums on the Southern Frontier: The Military Colonization of Georgia, 1733–1749* (1974). For St. Augustine's situation see David J. Weber, *The Spanish Frontier in North America* (1992).

POPULATION AND ECONOMY

Bernard Bailyn, *Voyagers to the West: A Passage in the Peopling of America on the Eve of the Revolution* (1986), is a definitive statement on the migration from Europe that peopled America during the eighteenth century. On the impact of the varied populations see the essays in Bernard Bailyn and Philip D. Morgan, eds., *Strangers Within the Realm: Cultural Margins of the First British Empire* (1991).

For challenging interpretations of the development of American society, and America's relationship to its European roots, see Jack P. Greene, *Pursuits of Happiness: The Social Development of Early Modern British Colonies and the Formation of American Culture* (1988), and David Hackett Fischer, *Albion's Seed: Four British Folkways in America* (1989).

The essays in Jack P. Greene and J. R. Pole, eds., *Colonial British America: Essays in the New History of the Early Modern Era* (1984), offer an excellent discussion of developing interpretation of American social, economic, and political relationships in the period before 1763. John J. McCusker and Russell R. Menard, *The Economy of British America, 1607–1789* (1985, 1992), is an encyclopedic, but very readable, overview of colonial economic and social development and its relationship to the Revolution. These two books make an excellent starting point for understanding Anglo-America in the eighteenth century. Another important book is Allan Kulikoff, *The Agrarian Origins of American Capitalism* (1992).

SLAVERY IN THE EIGHTEENTH CENTURY

In addition to Peter Wood's *Black Majority*, many recent studies have sought to understand the way in which slavery shaped American culture in the eighteenth century. Important studies include Mechal Sobel, *The World They Made Together: Black and White Values in Eighteenth-Century Virginia* (1987), Gary B. Nash, *Forging Freedom: Formation of Philadelphia's Black Community, 1720–1840* (1988), Betty Wood, *Slavery in Colonial Georgia, 1730–1775* (1984), and Daniel C. Littlefield, *Rice and Slaves: Ethnicity and the Slave Trade in Colonial South Carolina* (1981).

THE BACKCOUNTRY

The places and circumstances on and beyond the frontier where traders and Indians dealt with each other is a particularly exciting field of study. To pursue this subject see Richard White, *The Middle Ground* (from chapter three) and James H. Merrell, *The Indians' New World: Catawbas and Their Neighbors from European Contact Through the Era of Removal* (Chapel Hill, 1989), Gregory Evans Dowd, *A Spirited Resistance: The North American Indian Struggle for Unity, 1745–1815* (1992), Daniel H. Usner, Jr., *Indians, Settlers, and Slaves in a Frontier Exchange Economy* (Chapel Hill, 1992), and Peter Mancall, *Valley of Opportunity: Economic Culture Along the Upper Susquehanna, 1700–1800* (1991).

Frederick Jackson Turner, "The Significance of the Frontier in American History," in *The Frontier in American History* (New York, 1920) posed the most challenging interpretation of the frontier in American history. The backcountry and its settlement is once again attracting a great deal of scholarly attention. On this subject see Rachel N. Klein, *Unification of a Slave State: The Rise of the Planter Class in the South Carolina Backcountry, 1760–1808* (1990), Richard R. Beeman, *The Evolution of the Southern Backcountry: A Case Study of Lunenburg County, Virginia, 1746–1832* (1984), and Robert D. Mitchell, *Commercialism and Frontier: Perspectives on the Shenandoah Valley* (Charlottesville, 1977).

THE WEST

On expansion into California see Weber, *The Spanish Frontier in North America* (1992), Guttiérez, *When Jesus Came, the Corn Mothers Went Away* (1991), and Elizabeth John, *Storms Brewed in Other Men's Worlds* (1964). For the first contacts with Hawaii and Alaska, see Christine Holme, ed., *Captain Cook's Final Voyage: The Journal of Midshipman George Gilbert* (1982), and Gananath Obeyesekere, *The Apotheosis of Captain Cook* (1991), and Marshall Iahlins, *Islands of History* (1985).

THE SOUTH

Rhys Isaac, *The Transformation of Virginia, 1740–1790* (1982), Allan Kulikoff, *Tobacco and Slaves: The Development of Southern Cultures in the Chesapeake, 1680–1800* (1986), and T. H. Breen, *Tobacco Culture: The Mentality of the Great Tidewater Planters on the Eve of Revolution* (1985), together offer a brilliant, sometimes conflicting picture of the mature Chesapeake culture of the mid-eighteenth century. See also the older classic Charles S. Sydnor, *Gentleman Freeholders: Political Practices in Washington's Virginia* (1952).

On the lower South, in addition to the sources on the St. Augustine expedition see Joyce E. Chaplin, *An*

Anxious Pursuit: Agricultural Innovation and Modernity in the Lower South, 1730–1815 (1993), and Harold E. Davis, *The Fledgling Province: Social and Cultural Life in Colonial Georgia, 1733–1776* (1976).

THE EAST

On settled life in the older regions along the Atlantic coast, many illuminating studies have recently appeared. See especially Richard Bushman, *The Refinement of America: Persons, Houses, Cities* (1992), Stephanie Grauman Wolf, *As Various As Their Land: The Everyday Lives of Eighteenth-Century Americans* (1993), Richard D. Brown, *Knowledge Is Power: The Diffusion of Information in Early America, 1700–1865* (1989), and Jan Lewis, *The Pursuit of Happiness: Family Values in Jefferson's Virginia* (1983).

On religion, and especially the revivalism of the Great Awakening, see Harry S. Stout, *The Divine Dramatist: George Whitefield and the Rise of Modern Evangelicalism* (1991), Patricia U. Bonomi, *Under the Cope of Heaven: Religion, Society, and Politics in Colonial America* (1986), and Jon Butler, *Awash in a Sea of Faith: Christianizing the American People* (1990).

AMERICA AND THE WARS FOR EMPIRE

For an overview of the imperial wars, see John Ferling, *Struggle for a Continent: The Wars of Early America* (1993). On the experience of the French and Indian War and the changes in consciousness it wrought, see Francis Jennings, *Empire of Fortune: Crowns, Colonies, and Tribes in the Seven Years' War in America* (1988), and Fred Anderson, *A People's Army: Massachusetts Soldiers and Society in the Seven Years' War* (1984). For a moving and illuminating study of the impact of the imperial wars on one family, see John Demos, *The Unredeemed Captive: A Family Story from Early America* (1994).

CHAPTER 5

The American Revolution

Episode: The Boston Massacre

THE COMING OF INDEPENDENCE

Novel Taxation

Constitutional Challenges

The Townshend Acts, 1767

The Boston Tea Party and the Coercive Acts

The Continental Congress, 1774

First Shots

Tom Paine's *Common Sense*

The Declaration of Independence

War

Turning Point

Victory

THE EPISODE: American independence came about despite the best wishes of all involved. Eighteenth-century Americans viewed revolution with horror. They were proud of their membership in the great British Empire, whose government they saw as the most progressive on earth. Few believed that Americans could successfully defy Britain, or that a new nation could be forged to take a place among the nations of the world. These opinions persisted far longer than modern readers, knowing of the events of 1775 and 1776, believe. Despite Boston's defiance of the British army in 1770 that resulted in the Boston Massacre, and right up to the outbreak of fighting at Lexington and Concord and the signing of the Declaration of Independence, most Americans hoped the cataclysm could be avoided; yet eventually most came to feel that they had no choice but to fight.

THE HISTORICAL SETTING: Population growth contributed to Americans' sense of success, but immigration, both forced and free, drew on new sources in Europe and Africa. These new Americans had no automatic loyalty to Britain; many had suffered in the past from English depredations. They would have little hesitation about joining in defiance.

When the crisis came, it grew out of Britain's imperial concerns. Britain's long-running rivalry with France had reached a climax in the French and Indian War (1754–1763), which saw the end of French claims in North America. British-Americans greeted the news with joy, but the British government decided to forge a new colonial relationship. Imperial efforts to police the new territories, to force the colonists to pay their share of the costs of empire, and to tighten the administration of trade led to defiance. Americans viewed every action within an interpretive framework that convinced them the empire sought to place them under a tyrannical government. The interplay of events and interpretations led the Americans to war.

How and why the "rude rabble" of Americans was able to confront and defeat the greatest military power on earth is the subject of this chapter.

The Boston Massacre

March 1770. Boston was in the grip of ferocious cold. Snow and ice lay thick everywhere, the long winter subduing the people's spirits. Siege conditions prevailed in the city, which had been occupied by British troops since 1768. The inconceivable had come to pass: British soldiers were being used to control and spy on British subjects. Every passing day intensified the hatred between Bostonians and the "lobsterbacks" in their red coats. As the long winter wore on everyone's nerves, the situation was primed for an explosion.

All the elements for combustion were in place. Action built slowly at first, as mobs of young Bostonians pelted the marching units of British soldiers with snowballs wherever they went. The crowds taunted the redcoats, daring them to fire. For their part, the soldiers swaggered through the town as if it belonged to them, treating its citizens as if they were rude provincials of no account. Everything the soldiers did seemed deliberately calculated to offend the Americans. For both sides, tension was reaching the breaking point. That point was passed in late winter 1770.

Massachusetts had agreed with the other colonies not to import British goods while the empire sought to impose taxes Americans saw as illegal. Not all merchants cooperated with these agreements, however, and they bore the brunt of the colonists' wrath. Many in Boston honored the nonimportation agreements at great personal cost. Merchants lost business, and artisans in the shipping industry found work scarce. Yet they were willing to accept such privation in honoring the greater cause of American rights. They had nothing but scorn for those merchants who put personal gain first. Sometimes rough measures were used to make their displeasure clear.

Ebenezer Richardson was one man around whom suspicions gathered. He was known to have turned in Boston traders to the customs officials for monetary rewards. He had made clear his contempt for the cause so dear to most Bostonians. When he returned to his home about ten o'clock on the morning of February 23, he saw a sign in front of the shop of his neighbor, Theophilus Lillie, identifying Lillie as one who had broken the nonimportation agreements. A crowd had gathered to see that no one did business with Lillie: "The whole Street filled with People who would suffer no person to go to his Shop."

Richardson had boasted only the day before that he would see "a dust beat up" if he saw any more such signs, and said he hoped the soldiers would come and "cut up the damned Yankees." Gossip said he had also bragged that he was ready for the crowd, "for I've guns loaded." Richardson tried to pull down the sign in front of Lillie's shop, and the assembled people began pelting him with sticks and stones. Richardson fled into his house, saying to some members of the patriot organization, the Sons of Liberty, who had joined the throng, "By the eternal God, I'll make it too hot for you before night."

Richardson screamed to the people to disperse, but they knew they had every right to stand in the public street. He came to the door and shook a stick (many thought it was a gun) at the crowd, saying "By God! I'll make a lane through you!" A brickbat was thrown out of the house at the crowd. Before this, only fruit peelings and other soft items had been thrown at the building. Now the brickbat was thrown back through a window, and then a full barrage of rocks and sticks.

Suddenly, Richardson appeared with a musket at an upstairs window. He rested the weapon on the sill; everyone thought he was bluffing until he fired into the crowd. An eleven-year-old boy, Christopher Seider, lay dying with eleven pellets in his chest and abdomen. Seider, son of a poor German immigrant, became the symbol of the American people preyed on by a rapacious empire and its vicious toadies.

Samuel Adams took charge of events and staged the largest and grandest funeral ever seen in America for young Christopher Seider. Newspaper publicity called on patriots to turn out for the funeral. The *Boston Gazette* eulogized Seider as "a little hero." Those who knew him, the paper said, had "reason to think he had a martial genius and would have made a clever man. Young as he was, he died in his Country's Cause, by the hand of an execrable Villain, directed by others, who could not bear to see the Enemies of America made the Ridicule of Boys."

The procession began at 5 P.M. on Monday, February 26, at the Liberty Tree near Boston Common. Despite huge drifts left by a great snowstorm just two days before, the procession of nearly 3,000 people marched over half a mile to the Old Granary Burying Ground, where the coffin was interred. Many would have agreed with Samuel Adams's cousin John Adams, who said, "My eyes never beheld such a funeral." It meant, he wrote, "that the Ardor of the People is not to be quelled by the Slaughter of one Child."

Increasingly, crowd action had emerged as a weapon against the frustrations created by the army's presence in Boston; leaders such as Sam Adams scrambled to get ahead of the developing tactic so as to control and shape it. Many of the moderate leaders of the resistance had been reluctant to associate themselves with something so distasteful as mobs. Adams, under the pseudonym Populus, had written in the *Boston Gazette* in 1768 that there must be "NO MOBS—NO CONFUSIONS—NO TUMULTS." But it soon became clear that any direction over the resistance movement would be lost unless the crowds and the Sons of Liberty became allies.

Between the troops' arrival in Boston in October 1768 and the Boston Massacre of March 1770, Samuel Adams emerged as a principal leader of the city's struggle to force the imperial government to reconsider its new policies.

Samuel Adams is one of the most interesting men among the great revolutionary leaders. He is the first man in American history who thought of himself as a professional politician, and his reputation has risen and fallen as Americans have changed their attitudes toward politicians. Loyalists among the colonists saw him as the sinister manipulator of the crowds, characterizing the people as simple tools of the "Machiavel of Chaos," Adams. There is a small grain of truth in this mostly false characterization: Adams alone among the Boston elite could speak the language of the artisans and had won their respect.

Adams allied himself with leaders who had risen through the ranks, such as Ebenezer MacIntosh, a cobbler to whom Boston's workers had looked for leadership since 1765 and the Stamp Act riots. MacIntosh was passionately Protestant in religion and hated the Anglican, almost Roman Catholic, trappings that the empire was imposing on Boston. MacIntosh knew the poverty of the workers. He himself would be im-

Samuel Adams, painted by John Singleton Copley in the early 1770s.

prisoned for debt before 1770 was over. He despised the luxury and pretension of the great merchants and the army officers, and hoped that the radical movement would lead to a return to simplicity. He and his followers longed for the virtue and community solidarity of earlier times.

Proud of his descent from Puritan forebears, Adams saw the revolution as a chance to return to the virtue of the founders. Adams particularly liked the colonists' agreements not to buy or use British products, because these seemed to echo the covenants on which the early Puritan communities were built. He hoped that refusal to use imported products would bring back the simpler time before greed and acquisitiveness ruled everyone's lives. Far from being a rabble-rousing, power-mad boss, Adams was always content to work behind the scenes and let others take the glory; he remained a poor man till the day he died.

Adams was a politician in the sense that he believed in the political process. He had faith that the people, given a free choice, would choose wisely, and he hated any system that took away that freedom. He was also a politician in that he knew how to get things done, how to work with people and keep his attention focused on the main goal. Finally, he was a consummate politician in his use of publicity; he wrote effectively in the papers and was able to stage great public events, joyful or solemn as the occasion warranted, to focus attention on the resistance. The funeral of Christopher Seider was one such event.

As John Adams had predicted, the tensions did not die with young Seider. The shock and horror of wanton killing, particularly when the victim was so young, made many in Boston feel that the stakes had been raised at the end of February 1770. As the *Gazette* proclaimed on the day of his funeral, Christopher's blood "crieth for Vengeance, like the Blood of the righteous Abel."

An escalating series of incidents between townspeople and soldiers punctuated each day of the next week. The arrival of March did not lessen winter's grim hold on the city, and tempers were at the breaking point. On March 3 tension once again broke out into bloodshed. It began in a seemingly innocent way. An off-duty British soldier, Patrick Walker, came up to a rope and cable maker's looking for a job. The soldiers, whose pay was low, were allowed to "moonlight." By permitting off-duty work, the army could deflect pressure to raise salaries. William Green, one of the ropewalk workers, asked Walker whether he wanted a job. "Yes, I do, faith" was the reply. Green then retorted, "Well, then, go and clean my shithouse." "Empty it yourself" was Walker's reply.

The verbal sparring soon came to blows, and more of the workers got involved. Walker was humiliated when one man "knocked up his heels." He ran away, but soon returned with eight or nine other soldiers. The rope workers closed ranks and repelled the soldiers, who then returned with forty men armed with all sorts of clubs and weapons. The workers were armed with sticks used in rope twisting. Once again the soldiers were humiliated by the civilian ropemakers. Authority stepped in on both sides to stop the fighting from escalating further, but the warring parties vowed the conflict was not ended.

Why did Private Walker's request for honest work lead to Green's surly reply and a battle? The answer lies in the relationship between the townspeople of Boston and the British army. Many different groups had reason to hate the presence of redcoats in the city, and all these different reasons built solidarity among the citizens. Workingmen had special reasons for resenting the army's presence. Life was hard and becoming harder for those who worked in Boston's industries, such as the building and outfitting of ships. The colonists had chosen to fight the new taxes imposed by the British government by refusing to import British goods. This was a good tactic. Merchants in Britain found their livelihoods in jeopardy because of it. But nonimportation also meant that ships did not come to Boston regularly. Therefore, the repair and refitting shops lost business, and workers were let go or took cuts in wages. The soldiers compounded this grievance by taking jobs in their off-duty hours for lower wages than the Boston men. Thus the workingmen found themselves in direct competition with the soldiers. The army's presence threatened their livelihoods.

George Robert Twelves Hewes was, like Ebenezer MacIntosh, a poor shoemaker who was drawn to the radical cause. Gray's Ropewalk was just down the street from his own shop, and he remembered the events of that day vividly to the end of his life. Hewes was one of many Bostonians who had viewed the British army up close and did not like what he saw. Most British officers, men whose patrons had laid out huge sums to buy their commissions for them, were arrogant, swaggering through the town as if they were members of an elite corps before which the citizens must bend their knees. The mercantile leaders deeply resented this intrusion of an alien aristocratic system.

Rather than trying to adjust to the patterns accepted in Boston, the army made a display of flouting local custom. Traditional Sunday religious worship was disturbed by

British soldiers drilling on Boston Common outraged the citizens used to having the land for peaceful pursuits. This 1768 painting shows the Twenty-ninth Regiment in front of John Hancock's grand house.

the sound of army bands playing as the soldiers marched in formation. The redcoats raced their horses on the Common on Sunday afternoons, and the troops brought open drunkenness and prostitution to the town. Hewes, like many of his fellows, belonged to a strongly Protestant evangelical tradition. Radicals of all economic classes were united in their devotion to Boston's Puritan ways and hated the foreign intrusion.

The army made Bostonians feel like prisoners in their own city. Soldiers were stationed around the city at night to keep the peace. Citizens were stopped by sentries as they moved around their own streets on their own business. When challenged by a sentry to identify himself, a person was supposed to answer "Friend," but Bostonians found it increasingly difficult to make that reply. They felt the soldiers were an alien and unfriendly force in their midst who had no right to challenge them at all.

George Hewes solved the problem by carrying a bottle of rum and offering a drink each time he was stopped. But many Bostonians reacted with hostility. If the sentries, ignored or taunted, attempted to enforce what they thought of as their just authority, they sometimes found themselves hauled into court on a charge of assault, to be tried before a jury sympathetic to the citizen. Often, even the judges were openly hostile to the soldiers and the practice of posting sentries. Crowds attended the trials to see that justice was done.

George Robert Twelves Hewes painted near the end of his life in 1835 by Joseph G. Cole

For Boston's workingmen, the soldiers represented unwelcome competition in hard times, but the radicals also saw that the soldiers were victims of an unimaginably harsh system of military discipline. Many soldiers had deserted from the army. Some of the radicals encouraged such desertions to lower the troops' morale. As they learned of the life the soldiers led, their sympathy grew. George Robert Twelves Hewes brought charges against a soldier who had picked up a pair of shoes Hewes had made for his commanding officer, Captain Thomas Preston. The soldier, Sergeant Mark Burk, pocketed the money Preston had given him and took the shoes without paying for them. Hewes appealed to Preston, who paid him and told him to register a complaint against Burk. Burk was convicted at the military hearing and, to Hewes's utter horror, sentenced to 350 lashes on his bare back. Hewes stood up and told the court "that if he had thought the fellow was to be punished so severely for such an offense, bad as he was, he would have said nothing about it." Both groups suffered because of what they saw as the British empire's unjust practices. Yet the army's presence repeatedly threw these groups into competition or conflict, and the solidarity that might have grown up between them withered.

By early March 1770, it was clear the soldiers should never have been brought to Boston. English tradition held that a monarch who keeps an army in peacetime is planning some kind of tyranny because his intention must be to use military force against his own people. Now radical leaders saw their predictions coming true. When the Massachusetts governor felt a bit threatened, what did he do but immediately cry out for the support of the army? Military force was being used to prop up an unpopular governor. What was that but tyranny?

Commander in chief General Thomas Gage had sent the army into Boston in 1768 to deal with people he considered "mutinous" and "desperadoes." Now, early in 1770, he reflected on that mistake:

The People were as Lawless and Licentious after the Troops arrived, as they were before. The Troops could not act by Military Authority, and no Person in Civil Authority would ask their aid. They were there contrary to the wishes of the Council, Assembly, Magistrates and People, and seemed only offered to abuse and Ruin. And the Soldiers were either to suffer ill usage and even assaults upon their Persons till their Lives were in Danger, or by resisting and defending themselves, to run almost a Certainty of suffering by the Law.

Benjamin Franklin had earlier warned the British against sending troops among the colonists: "They will not find a rebellion; they may indeed make one." John Adams demonstrated just how prophetic his words were:

> My daily Reflections for two Years, at the Sight of those Soldiers before my door were serious enough. Their very Appearance in Boston was a strong proof to me, that the determination in Great Britain to subjugate Us, was too deep and inveterate ever to be altered by Us: For every thing We could do was misrepresented, and Nothing We could say was credited.

Law-abiding and loyal British subjects were radicalized by the army and the daily and constant affronts its presence generated.

All these feelings came to a head in the first week of March 1770. After the incident at Gray's Ropewalk on March 3, numerous small confrontations took place. Bostonians believed the situation was becoming increasingly serious. Rumors of an impending confrontation with the troops flew around the city. The soldiers also sensed a showdown was coming and prepared themselves for it. March 4 was a Sunday, and the city was quiet, but fears focused on the Monday.

About eight o'clock in the evening of Monday, March 5, an incident occurred that was to form the focus of that night's events. Small groups of civilians and off-duty soldiers patrolled the streets armed with clubs, and some minor altercations had already taken place. The *Boston Gazette* reported that "several soldiers of the Twenty-ninth Regiment were seen parading the streets with their drawn cutlasses and bayonets, abusing and wounding numbers of the inhabitants."

The main action was in front of the Customs House on King Street. A single private, Hugh White, was on guard at the corner of King Street and Royal Exchange Lane, but other, off-duty, soldiers were in the area. Edward Garrick, a young barber's apprentice, tried unsuccessfully to stop a passing officer, Captain-Lieutenant John Goldfinch, to collect an overdue bill from him. Garrick left, but later returned and began to shout that the officers of the Fourteenth Regiment were no gentlemen. Private White, outraged, rushed out of his sentry box to confront Garrick. When Garrick faced him, saying, "I am not ashamed to show my face," White hit him across the side of his head with his musket.

A crowd soon gathered, and Hugh White retreated from his sentry box to the steps of the Customs House, where he angrily fixed his bayonet onto his musket. White was nervous, but stood firm as the crowd insulted him, calling him a "damned rascally Scoundrel Lobster Son of a Bitch." The sentry held his gun level to keep off the crowd. Henry Knox, a bookseller who would go on to become a general in the Revolutionary War and Secretary of War in Washington's cabinet, warned him not to shoot. White answered, "Damn them, if they molest me I will fire." When snowballs, some packed with ice, began to rain down on him, he called for support from the main guard, which was stationed just down the block.

Paul Revere's engraving of the Boston Massacre made the deaths appear to be the result of a deliberate order to fire. This engraving, seen by many who knew little of the confusion of that night, was a powerful piece of propaganda.

The officer in charge of the guard, Captain Thomas Preston, who had been watching events with mounting concern, set out to rescue Private White about nine o'clock. He marched through the crowd at the head of a double file of six privates and a corporal, "the soldiers pushing their bayonets, and crying, make way!" The people parted to let them through, but once they had joined Private White in front of the Customs House, the rescue party found they were trapped there. With the threatening crowd in front of them, Preston ordered his eight men to form a semicircle with their bayonets and muskets pointed outward. He also apparently ordered the men to load their guns, though many in the street thought the muskets were loaded with powder alone to frighten the crowd, rather than powder and shot.

The atmosphere was charged with old hatreds. The civilians and the soldiers must have realized quickly that both the crowd and the little troop in front of them contained men who had been involved in the fight at the ropewalk two days before. Both sides felt there was unfinished business between them. The young men among the assembled townspeople, aware of the redcoats' predicament, taunted the soldiers. Some ran along their semicircle hitting the muskets with sticks, demonstrating that, despite their impressive uniforms and their weapons, they were powerless in this situation.

The church bells had been ringing since the trouble began. Since bells in the night usually meant fire, many men had come to help put out the flames. Others knew that this was a different kind of combustion and turned out to settle old scores. George Robert Twelves Hewes was there early: "I was soon on the ground among them," he later recalled. One of the soldiers, Matthew Kilroy, whom Hewes had caught and chastised when he mugged a Boston woman, struck Hewes on the shoulder with his musket as he passed. Samuel Gray and Nicholas Ferriter, both of whom had been at the ropewalk fight a few days earlier, hurried to the Customs House, not sure whether it was a fire or not. When told there was no fire but "it is the soldiers fighting," Gray replied, "I will knock some of them on the head."

Some men joined the throng to try to calm this very different kind of conflagration that threatened the peace of Boston. Captain Preston was well known in the town and had won the people's respect as a gentleman. Henry Knox, the young bookseller, had from the beginning tried to prevent bloodshed. As Preston marched out with his little troop to rescue Hugh White, Knox said to him: "For God's sake, take care of your Men, for if they fire your life must be answerable." Preston answered simply, "I am sensible of it." The risks were very great on all sides.

The firing began in confusion. The throng pressed so close that "you could not get your hat betwixt them and the bayonets." One of the privates, struck by a piece of ice, slipped and fell just as Preston's attention was diverted by a quiet warning from another concerned Bostonian, Richard Palmes. As the private stood up, he fired his musket into the crowd. Soon after, the rest of the guard also fired. Witnesses described Private Kilroy taking careful aim and bringing down Samuel Gray. Eleven men were hit, with three dead on the spot and two dying soon after.

As the troops, having reloaded, once again leveled their muskets, Preston ran along the line, pushing up the guns with his arm shouting, "Stop firing!" Even after the shooting was over, some citizens, still believing the guns had been loaded only with powder, did not understand that men had been hit. Joseph Hilyer later recalled that when he first saw the bodies, "I thought they had been scared and run away, and left their greatcoats behind."

Samuel Gray, one of the ropemakers who had fought the soldiers the previous Friday, fell dead with a hole in his skull as big as a man's hand. Before he died, he may have recognized the three soldiers from the ropewalk fight, Privates William Warren, Matthew Kilroy, and John Carroll, who were in the line before him. He certainly saw Kilroy taking aim at him. A young mariner who was in Boston to learn the art of navigation, Samuel Caldwell, died immediately of a bullet in the chest. Crispus Attucks, a tall, proud man who was variously said to be black or Indian and may have been of mixed descent, fell dead with two bullets in his chest. Samuel Maverick, a boy of seventeen, was hit by a ricocheting bullet; he was carried home to his mother, dying. Patrick Carr, an artisan from Ireland, was taken to his master's house, where he died a few days later.

The dispersing crowd carried news of what had happened all over Boston: "Language cannot describe the horror and indignation which was excited through the town by this dreadful event." More and more people began to gather. With the clamor of church bells throughout the city filling the air, the sense of crisis grew. Boston had no street lighting, and the moon was slender. Though the thick snow reflected what little

Boston in 1769, engraving by John Bonner showing the site of the events of March 1770. The Boston Massacre took place at the Custom House directly up the street from Long Wharf.

light there was, that reflection also created deep shadows. No one could be sure what was going on. Express riders had even gone to nearby towns, "and the inhabitants were called out of their beds, many of whom armed themselves but were stopped from coming into town by advice that there was no further danger that night."

John Adams, called to the scene by the firebells, went home convinced there would be no more violence. George Hewes gave a deposition the next day in which he told how he, like many of his friends, went home to arm himself. At about 1 A.M. he was back on the street carrying a cane. He met a troop of soldiers from the Twenty-ninth Regiment, all armed "with very large clubs or cutlasses." When one of the soldiers asked "how he far'd, he told him very badly to see his townsmen shot in such a manner, and asked him if he did not think it was a dreadful thing." The soldier, named Dobson, replied, "It was a fine thing" and that "you shall see more of it." When the soldiers tried to take his cane, Hewes told them, "I had as good a right to carry a cane as they had to carry clubs."

As crowds rumored to be in the thousands filled the streets, prevention of total disaster was up to Lieutenant Governor Thomas Hutchinson, in charge now that Governor Francis Bernard had returned to England. Concerned citizens appealed to Hutchinson, "For God's sake, . . . go to King Street," and warned that if something were not quickly done, "the town would be all in blood." Hutchinson responded quickly to the call. He first went to the scene of the massacre, despite the large and threatening crowd, and talked with Captain Preston. Hutchinson found Preston still backed by British soldiers in the street. "How came you to fire without orders from a civil magistrate?" Hutchinson demanded. Preston replied, "I was obliged to, to save my sentry." Hutchinson then countered, "These soldiers ought not to be here."

The crowd then began to push Hutchinson and the leaders with him toward the State House, the seat of the royal government on King Street. He addressed the crowd from the balcony, assuring the people that the law would see justice was done and imploring them to return to their homes. His words that night were the credo by which he lived: "The law shall have its course; I will live and die by the law."

Hutchinson then set immediately to work to see that the law did work. He began to take evidence that night. Witnesses were called, from their beds if necessary, to come and testify as to what they had seen. Though the evidence was conflicting, particularly on the source of the order to fire, Hutchinson issued warrants for the arrest of Captain Preston and his second in command, Lieutenant James Basset. By two o'clock in the morning, as news of all the soldiers' arrests spread, Boston became quiet and the people returned home. The barrel of tar that had been placed on Beacon Hill which, when lit, would have alerted the neighboring towns that their assistance was needed was carried away again.

Thomas Hutchinson's career forms a striking contrast to that of Samuel Adams. Both men were descended from the Puritan founders of New England (Hutchinson from the 1630s radical Anne Hutchinson), and each was devoted to his country. In different circumstances these men could have been allies, but the issues of the 1760s and 1770s divided them. Hutchinson, a merchant in a long line of merchants, had been involved in public service since shortly after his graduation from Harvard and had risen through the ranks of the colony's government. He had always been a strong supporter of the interests of Massachusetts.

In the 1760s, as Britain's new imperial policies aroused American defiance, Hutchinson felt divided within himself. He strongly opposed the new taxes, such as the Stamp Act of 1765, but he believed America's best interests lay in membership in the British empire. He was also a firm believer in the letter of the law. Therefore, though he wrote to England strongly objecting to the Stamp Act, for example, he felt that as long as it was the law it must be enforced.

When Thomas Hutchinson addressed the gathered people on the night of March 5, 1770, he, more than almost anyone else in Boston, had reason to fear the actions of an angry mob. From the events of five years before, he knew the destructive power of a populace that acted to defend rights it thought were being violated. Bostonians had not appreciated Hutchinson's fine distinctions about obeying the Stamp Act while applying through legal channels for its repeal. Many believed it was an illegal imposition and that to give in to it would only lead to further incursions on their rights.

Riots forcing the issue had erupted in Boston, and one of the crowd's targets was Hutchinson. One night in late August 1765, a mob attacked his townhouse, destroying what they could not carry away. So thorough were the rioters that, according to an eyewitness, they spent three hours hacking at the house's cupola before they brought it down. Governor Bernard's report said that next day the lanes leading from the house were littered "with money, plate, gold rings, etc., which had been dropped in carrying off." Hutchinson estimated his losses at £2,218, a fortune in those days. Among the losses that night was a massive archive of papers dealing with colonial New England that Hutchinson, who was an accomplished historian, had put together for the commonwealth.

Hutchinson was no coward; no riot could deter him from his duty. When colonial pressure succeeded in getting the Stamp Act overturned, he believed that success demonstrated that adherence to the law would bring true justice. He continued to serve in his posts of chief justice and lieutenant governor; his advice was especially needed as the governor, Francis Bernard, was a man of very limited talent. Hutchinson served because he believed Massachusetts needed a man of his experience and ideas. When Bernard fled, Hutchinson shouldered all the responsibility and brought his strict interpretation of the law to bear on the rising tension within Boston, a decision his Puritan ancestors would have understood. A more flexible man might have been more successful, but no one could have been more devoted to the good of the colony as he saw it.

Now, in 1770, the citizens were no more ready for fine legal distinctions than they had been in 1765. Boston was not satisfied with Hutchinson's demand that they allow the law to work its slow course. Until the troops were removed and the city was restored to full rights of citizenship, the people would continue to defy the empire and its representative, Thomas Hutchinson. A huge crowd, some said as many as 4,000 people, gathered in Faneuil Hall on the morning after the massacre and made their feelings clear.

Samuel Adams headed the committee that carried their demands to Hutchinson and his council in the State House. Adams reported the town meeting's insistence that all the soldiers be pulled out, and pointed to the large numbers of people all around Boston waiting to hear his reply and to force compliance with their will if necessary. Later, Adams wrote of the meeting with Hutchinson: "It was then I observed the Governor's knees to tremble. I thought I saw his face grow pale, and I enjoyed the sight."

The governor's council agreed that the army must leave: "Nothing can rationally be expected to restore the peace of the town and prevent carnage but the immediate removal of the troops." One councilor, Royall Tyler, warned that 10,000 men would come in from the countryside and force the troops out if they were not taken away. Delegates from Charlestown and Dedham confirmed this information. Hutchinson at first refused, saying he had no authority to command the troops to move, but finally gave in. The news gave "Great Joy to the Inhabitants," who had been waiting at the Old South Church for word of the governor's decision. The soldiers were removed to Castle William, on an island in the harbor. Technically, they were still within Boston, but three miles of water separated them from the city.

In the days immediately following the incident, each side took its case to the court of public opinion. Radical leaders took depositions from many witnesses, including George Hewes, and published them to show, as the Boston committee contended, that the soldiers had been "instruments in executing a settled plot to massacre the inhabitants." In terming the deaths of five men a massacre, the Boston leaders called up images of brutal, irresponsible use of force.

They spread their message via newspapers and broadsides, and those who supported the royal government also put their case in print. The publicity campaign shows that what people thought, how the public viewed the actions of the British, was important. By default, the imperial representatives had already conceded the most crucial point. No flat declarations that the empire had the right to do this or that would suffice. The people of America must be convinced. American resistance to British authority had already had its effect. Newspapers throughout America and in England printed sensational stories about the event. The massacre came to be a crucial milestone on the path to defiance.

Paul Revere made an engraving of a drawing of the massacre done by a young artist, Henry Pelham, and copies of this engraving were widely circulated. It was not an accurate representation of the event (it made the musket fire seem to be the result of a deliberate order), but it was an effective representation of Bostonians' feelings about the presence of the army. Revere also prepared a more accurate plan of the affair that was probably meant to be used in the trials, which was not published.

On March 8, the first four "unhappy Victims" were buried. The funeral processions began from each of their four houses, joined at King Street, "the Theatre of that inhuman Tragedy," and marched to the burial ground. Business came to a standstill that day, and the church bells of Boston and all the towns around tolled "a solemn Peal." The citizens of Boston were joined by an estimated 10,000 people from the countryside, all of whom walked in the procession. According to one report, "The aggravated Circumstances of their Death, the Distress and Sorrow visible in every Countenance, together with the peculiar Solemnity with which the whole Funeral was conducted, surpass Description." Another great procession gathered to take Patrick Carr to his grave when he died a week later.

John Adams, 1766, pastel by Benjamin Blyth.

THE TRIAL

All concerned in handling the proceedings against Captain Preston and his men were committed to the idea that justice must be done, and that the trials and verdicts be seen as fair. John Adams, a young cousin of Samuel Adams, took on the job of conducting the defense at the urging of the radical leaders, despite his anger at the army's presence in Boston. He later said that he instantly lost more than half his law business when his involvement in the case became known.

Adams took the assignment because he wanted to demonstrate that the resistance movement was not lawless and destructive, but that the Americans had acted in defense of the highest principles of English law. When asked to act for Preston, Adams answered, "If he thinks he cannot have a fair trial without my assistance, without hesitation he shall have it." Ultimately, he took on the defense of all the soldiers. He himself had not been involved in the events of March 5, but had come to the scene in answer to the firebell after the shooting and had seen the blood of the victims thick in the street.

Like his cousin Samuel and Thomas Hutchinson, John Adams was also a descendant of the Puritan founders of Massachusetts and shared their high sense of morality and dedication to duty. John Adams did not inherit family wealth and position. He fixed on the law as the avenue to the position of influence and importance he hoped for. After a stint as a schoolteacher, he began his legal studies and aimed to become the most learned and accomplished lawyer in Massachusetts.

Adams was always an awkward man; he never felt he really fit in, and he determined to work to make himself into a successful person. The campaign of resistance to Britain gave him his opportunity to shine on a large stage, and he made the most of it. From his beginnings as a provincial lawyer, he went on to the Continental Congresses, to important roles in the revolutionary period, and finally to the presidency of the United States. Sam Adams was always content to work behind the scenes; John, though he never felt completely at home there, liked center stage. Late in life he wrote: "I am but an ordinary man. The times alone have destined me to fame." This was only partly true, for it was John Adams's preparation and knowledge of what must be done that made him able to grasp opportunities.

All this was in the future. In 1770, at the time he ventured to defend the redcoats in the Boston Massacre, he was a young man in his mid-thirties, just starting out. The trials, originally set for April, were subject to repeated delays, making Bostonians distrustful of Hutchinson's motives. They were eventually opened October 24 with *Rex* (Latin for "king") v. *Preston*. Though they had acted as agents of the royal government, the soldiers were prosecuted by the Crown because they were accused of violating British law, which is the monarch's law.

John Adams faced the ethical problem of a possible conflict of interest between his various clients. Preston's best defense was that he had not ordered his men to fire, and was therefore not responsible. The soldiers, on the other hand, rested their defense on their duty to follow orders: They thought they had been commanded to fire. It would be hard for one man to argue both cases.

Testimony in Preston's trial revealed the same confusion as in the depositions taken the night of March 5. Many versions of what Preston was thought to have said were reported. Had he ordered his men to fire, or had he commanded, "Do not fire," or had the soldiers heard one of the many taunts from the crowd accusing the redcoats of being afraid to fire? Nothing was clear. Even Richard Palmes, the concerned citizen who had been talking to Preston when the firing began, was not sure. George Robert Twelves Hewes, interviewed many years later, remembered testifying at the trial on this very point:

> When Preston, their captain, was tried, I was called as one of the witnesses, on the part of the government, and testified that I believed it was the same man, Captain Preston, that ordered his soldiers to make ready, who also ordered them to fire. Mr. John Adams, former president of the United States, was advocate for the prisoners, and denied the fact, that Captain Preston gave orders to his men to fire; and on his cross examination of me asked whether my position was such, that I could see the captain's lips in motion when the order to fire was given; to which I answered, that I could not.

Clouding the whole proceeding was the widely shared conviction that, whatever the verdict, the king would see to it that Preston went free. In fact, Hutchinson had secretly been directed to ensure that no harm came to Preston until the king had a chance to issue a pardon. They need not have worried. The jury had been chosen from among men mostly sympathetic to the soldiers' cause, and Adams's summing-up was brilliant. Adams based his argument on the undoubted right of self-defense and the duty of an officer to protect his men if they appear to be in mortal danger, and he proceeded to tear apart the credibility of the Crown's witnesses. He pointed out that Captain Preston was standing between his men and the crowd and was therefore in danger of being hit by the musketballs if he had ordered the guns fired. Adams reminded the jury that the law preferred to free many guilty men rather than wrongly to execute one who was innocent. On October 30 the jury announced its verdict: Not Guilty.

The soldiers' trial began in late November; much of the evidence focused on the provocations by townspeople that night and other times that had made the redcoats jumpy. Several witnesses testified that large, sharp pieces of ice had been thrown at the semicircle before the Customs House. Others agreed that many in the crowd had been armed with large sticks. Others spoke of the roughness and arrogance with which the soldiers had treated townspeople, particularly laborers.

But Adams refused to ground the soldiers' defense on the charge that the townspeople had acted outrageously. He would not smear his own people. Rather, he placed the blame squarely on the British government. While admitting that the soldiers might have thought they were in danger, he pointed to the greater responsibility of Britain for placing them and Boston in such an impossible situation. "Soldiers quartered in a populous town will always occasion two mobs, where they prevent one. They are wretched conservators of the peace." The government had acted stupidly by asking the army to do a job it was ill-suited to accomplish and then had refused to admit its error in time, causing loss of life and suffering all round.

The jury deliberated two and a half hours before returning with its verdict. Six of the men were acquitted. The two convicted were deemed guilty of manslaughter, not murder. Only they had been proved to the jury's satisfaction to have fired their guns. When they were brought to court for sentencing December 14, both claimed Benefit of Clergy. This loophole in the law went back to medieval times, when anyone who could read was assumed to be a priest or monk. Since the government did not then have the right to take the life of someone under the control of the church, an accused person who could "prove" he was a priest by reading a selection from the Bible would be branded on the hand (this loophole could be used only once) and released.

The "neck verse," the passage that accused persons were asked to read, was Psalm 51:1, "Have mercy upon me, O God, according to thy loving-kindness: according unto the multitude of thy tender mercies blot out my transgressions." By colonial times, with the Bible translated into English and literacy much more widespread, Benefit of Clergy acted to allow many who had no official connection with the church to escape capital punishment. Though the law on the books was very harsh, such escape valves made its operation more lenient. The two soldiers were branded on the thumb by the sheriff and released.

Boston took the verdicts calmly; the great conflagration that many feared and some looked forward to was still in the future. The soldiers had been removed and, during the time that the trials had been pending, news of the repeal of all the Townshend Acts (which had imposed new taxes on essential commodities in 1767) except for the tax on tea had arrived. Colonists began to use imported products again, so business picked up and life returned to normal. Many people felt the crisis of the imperial relationship had passed for good.

Thomas Hutchinson's outlook was bleaker. He had been so shaken by his inability to control the situation that led to the massacre and his being forced to withdraw the troops that he had attempted to resign his post as lieutenant governor. He wrote to London that he was "absolutely alone." In his letter of resignation, he wrote, "I have not the strength of constitution to withstand the whole force of the other branches of government as well as the body of the people united against the governor." He could not uphold royal authority, and desired to retire to a more satisfying private life in his country house at Milton.

When the royal government begged him to reconsider, offering him the governorship in his own right, he agreed to shoulder the burden in a spirit that his Puritan ancestors would have approved. His insistence on observing the letter of the law would again cause trouble in the tea crisis of 1773. He did resign then, but the alternative of a quiet country life was no longer open to him. He lived the rest of his life as an unhappy exile.

Samuel and John Adams went on to roles of glory in the struggle that ended in the independence of the United States. John ever after remained proud of his role in defending the Boston Massacre soldiers, calling it "one of the most gallant, generous, manly and disinterested Actions of my whole Life, and one of the best pieces of Service I ever rendered my Country. Judgment of Death against those Soldiers would have been as foul a Stain upon this Country as the Executions of the Quakers or Witches, anciently."

George Robert Twelves Hewes lived on to 1840 to be celebrated every July 4 as one of the oldest survivors of the revolutionaries. After service in the Revolutionary War, he resumed his career as a shoemaker. He remained a poor man all his life, and died in Richfield Springs, New York. He was invited back to Boston for Independence Day celebrations in 1835. At ninety-three he was, briefly, a celebrated man and the center of all attention.

Every year March 5 was celebrated in Boston as a solemn day of remembrance. Orators recalled the day and drew its lessons anew. In the 1772 speech, Dr. Joseph Warren avowed:

> The fatal fifth of March, 1770, can never be forgotten—The horrors of that dreadful night are but too deeply impressed on our hearts—Language is too feeble to paint the emotion of our souls, when our streets were stained with the blood of our brethren—when our ears were wounded by the groans of the dying, and our eyes were tormented with the sight of the mangled bodies of the dead . . . our children subjected to the barbarous caprice of the raging soldiery—our virtuous wives, endeared to us by every tender tie, falling a sacrifice to worse than brutal violence . . .

Warren congratulated his fellow citizens on their restraint. The troops were removed, he reminded his hearers, "without one drop of blood being shed by the inhabitants."

Joseph Warren controlled his emotional picture of the horrors of March 5, 1770, by showing the Americans on the high ground of justice, refusing to meet violence with violence. As the crisis between the colonies and Britain again reached a critical point, the lessons drawn became more inflammatory. When Dr. Benjamin Church commemorated the massacre on its third anniversary in 1773, tensions were again rising to the boiling point. He told the crowd that "the sullen ghosts of murdered fellow-citizens haunt my imagination . . . the wan tenants of the grave still shriek for vengeance on their remorseless butchers."

Little did he know how fully that vengeance would soon be exacted, and how much more blood would be shed in the cause. Nine months after Church's oration, on December 16, 1773, patriots disguised as Mohawks dumped East India Company tea into Boston Harbor. The harsh punishment imposed on Massachusetts built colonial solidarity in reaction. All the colonies would soon feel the sense of outrage and fear for the future under British rule that the Boston Massacre had awakened and the commemorative celebrations had kept alive. John Adams, writing of the massacre in later life, reflected, "That night the foundation of American independence was laid."

The Coming of Independence

NOVEL TAXATION

The British government very quickly demonstrated its plans for the American plantations now that the French menace was eliminated. The colonies had been founded as mercantilist extensions of England. Their purpose had been to serve the needs of the parent country by providing raw materials and buying finished products. Mercantilism held that the country that could fill most of its needs without exporting money by buying essential products from other countries would be the strongest. Dependence on outside countries for essential commodities spelled weakness.

The Navigation Acts, the laws made by the British Parliament through which the empire regulated colonial trade and collected customs duties, were regularly evaded in America both by smuggling and by paying bribes. When military officers returned to England and described American disregard for the law, the government determined to tighten American administration and see that the Navigation Acts were enforced. Efforts to pass more effective laws and provide more efficient administration brought Parliament directly into conflict with the claims of the colonial assemblies. The first clashes were over taxation.

Though trade between Britain and America was strong and growing, the government saw the colonial system as hopelessly out of control. Determined to bring order and rationality to the system, the royal government began to pass new laws for the colonies. The three immediate goals were to gain revenue to relieve the hard-pressed English taxpayer, to provide a degree of independence for English officials in America, and to see that the laws, especially those against smuggling, were enforced.

THE SUGAR ACT

The Revenue Act of 1764, usually called the Sugar Act, sought to tighten up the customs service. To do so, it met one of the colonists' major objections: The Navigation Acts were such a tangle of regulations, and the duties so high, that if they were really enforced trade would stop altogether. The Sugar Act cut in half the tax on molasses, one of the staples of the New England–West Indies trade, and provided a new set of procedures to see that it was collected. Whereas earlier, higher taxes had simply been evaded, this one would be collected.

A swarm of officials entered the colonies to administer the new programs, and Americans increasingly felt the presence of the empire in their lives. Moreover, the tightening up of imperial regulation meant use of special vice-admiralty courts, in which judges made decisions without juries (colonial juries were notorious for refusing to convict smugglers), and the right of the accused to confront his accusers in open court was not honored. It seemed to colonists that the British government was setting up special procedures for Americans as if they were no longer full British citizens. Outraged colonists began an informal boycott of English goods in protest.

THE STAMP ACT

Soon news came that a new form of tax was to be imposed on the colonies: a stamp tax on all sorts of documents, from deeds and court papers to newspapers and almanacs. The British government, in deciding to impose this tax in the Stamp Act of 1765, pointed out that not only were Americans taxed much less heavily than the English, but British subjects had been paying this form of tax for decades. In American eyes that was not the point. The Sugar Act and the Stamp Act were both troubling for the same reason: they were novel taxes imposed for new purposes. The colonists argued that all former taxation had been for the regulation of trade, which the British government had the right to do. Now the government wanted to collect taxes in order to raise revenue, and colonial leaders believed this was illegal without the colonists' consent.

CONSTITUTIONAL CHALLENGES

New measures changing the colonial relationship forced the colonists to think about fundamental questions, especially about the place in the empire of the thirteen colonies and the governments they had evolved. In the changed situation after 1763, Americans began to develop a theory of their relationship to Britain that would fit the actual conditions of the 1760s rather than those of a century earlier. In this rethinking, colonial leaders drew on several English traditions concerning the British constitution and the rights of its citizens.

One of these was the English common law tradition, which guaranteed every British subject certain rights, such as the right to trial by a jury of one's peers in the district where the crime was committed. The colonists were firmly committed to the belief that they were full British citizens, although they lived across the ocean. Now it seemed that the king and his ministers sought to treat Anglo-Americans as less than citizens, to deprive them of some of those basic rights by the use of vice-admiralty courts, and by threatening to move trials away from sympathetic colonial juries.

Another fundamental tradition held that British citizens could not be taxed without the consent of their representatives. The British government recognized this right, but argued that the new taxes did not violate it. Parliament operated on the principle of virtual representation, which held that every member of parliament represented every British subject. This meant that even though most Englishmen and all women were denied the right to vote for members of parliament, all were virtually represented. Colonial experience had led to a different concept. The Americans argued for a theory of representation in which each member of the assembly represented the interests of a specific set of people who elected him. Therefore, the colonists could not consider themselves represented in the British Parliament. Their representatives sat in the thirteen colonial assemblies.

Over the previous half-century, the colonies had become used to a situation close to self-government. Most royal governors were controlled by colonial assemblies who paid their salaries. Colonial leaders had come to think of the assemblies as similar to the House of Commons. The Massachusetts Assembly declared in 1770 that it had "the same inherent rights in this province as the house of commons in Great Britain." Moreover, the assemblies were seen as directly answerable to the king. Now the actions of Parliament and the king combined to challenge colonists' conceptions of representation and the place of their assemblies in the structure of royal government.

As novel taxes were imposed, concerned leaders all over the colonies formed groups known as the Sons of Liberty to meet and correspond to interpret British actions. Under this examination, England's policies looked sinister. Interpretation of government actions was based on a third fundamental tradition that sprang from the constitutional battles of the English Civil War of the 1640s and the Glorious Revolution of 1688. This tradition, developed in eighteenth-century England by a group of dissenting commentators known as the Real Whigs, argued that a powerful government headed by a monarch is always dangerous because such governments have a strong, almost irresistible tendency to become tyrannical. The Real Whigs, especially John Trenchard and Thomas Gordon in their essays *Cato's Letters*, set up a series of signposts by which to judge whether a government was becoming tyrannical, and their writings were widely reprinted and avidly read in America.

One sure danger sign was the creation of a standing army in peacetime. Another was increased and novel taxation. A third was attacks on the right of free assemblies to meet. Another symptom was attacks on the freedom of the press. Colonial leaders seemed to see the Real Whigs' warning signs in every action of the royal government. The standing army, units of which were increasingly appearing in the East, in Boston and other cities, as well as on the frontier; the new taxes and regulations—especially the Stamp Act—all seemed to undermine basic rights. Why did the government, needing money, decide to tax newspapers with the Stamp Act, for example? Freedom of the press and the people's right to know what was going on seemed to be under attack.

Colonial leaders argued that the colonists had to make a stand because an important principle was at stake. If they appeared to concede that Parliament could levy new taxes without the consent of those taxed, then no property was safe. If they could add a tax of a penny, they could add a tax of a shilling or a pound, or take away citizens' property altogether. This is what colonists meant when they said the British aimed to make slaves of them.

THE STAMP ACT CONGRESS

Because such an important principle was at stake, colonial leaders, with the Sons of Liberty to coordinate activities, began to act. Representatives of nine colonies met in New York in October 1765. The Stamp Act Congress helped cement colonial resolve to resist. Americans were already boycotting English goods and had taken steps to force compliance from those who did not agree with the resisters' interpretation. Mobs had threatened the men, many of them prominent, who had been selected by the British to collect the stamp tax. In some cases houses were destroyed, as Thomas Hutchinson's was in Boston, and many collectors were hanged in effigy. Virtually all got the message and resigned their commissions. By the time the Stamp Act paraphernalia landed in America, the tax was a dead letter. No one would administer it and life went on as usual.

Many in England were outraged by this defiance, particularly since it involved mob action, but others were sympathetic to the colonists' arguments. British merchants in particular called on Parliament to reconsider because their trade had been drastically cut by the boycott. Benjamin Franklin was in England in 1766, and he told Parliament that the Americans were not disloyal, nor were they unwilling to accept their share of the burden. In attempting to calm the situation, he argued that colonists would willingly pay external

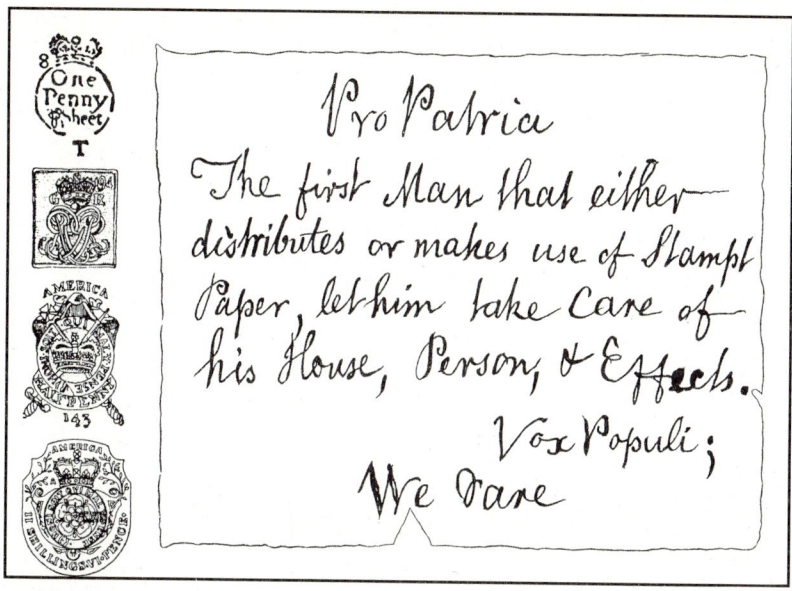

STAMPS USED BY THE ENGLISH GOVERNMENT IN 1765. The Sons of Liberty warning against allowing the stamps to be used was seriously meant, as men throughout the colonies discovered.

taxes, those collected as cargoes entered the country, but found the new internal taxes, collected inside the colonies, offensive.

The government accepted this distinction and, partly because of political changes in London that had nothing to do with America, repealed the Stamp Act in 1766. Repeal was accompanied by a Declaratory Act that stated Parliament had the right to legislate for the colonies "in all cases whatsoever," but the Americans felt they had won a great victory.

Other problems remained, however. In 1765 the government had also passed a Quartering Act, requiring the colonies to provide barracks for the British army in America or to accommodate soldiers in private homes, and to furnish some provisions. This was a new tax in another form, and added to the colonists' unease about the presence of the standing army among them. When New York refused to comply, the royal government punished that colony, in 1767, by refusing to allow the assembly to meet. Once again, the Real Whigs' warnings seemed to be fulfilled. The royal government took vengeance by canceling the right of the people's representatives to meet, an attack on fundamental rights. A meeting of Virginia freeholders denounced the forbidding of the New York Assembly as demonstrating "a fatal tendency . . . destructive of the Liberty of a free People."

THE TOWNSHEND ACTS, 1767

The British government was less effective than it might have been during the crisis period of the 1760s and early 1770s because of constant changes in leadership. Charles Townshend, a brilliant but erratic man, took control of the government early in 1767. He renewed the effort to make the colonies pay part of the expense of empire and to free British officials in America from control by colonial legislatures, who paid their salaries. He decided to take the colonists at their word, as given by Benjamin Franklin, and designed a new set of external taxes. These duties—on lead, paint, paper, glass, and tea—were to be collected at the point of entry into America and were to raise revenue that would be used to pay officials' salaries. The colonies presently paid officials, and the assemblies had been able to exercise a degree of control over their governors by the way they doled out the money. If the British now took over the payment of salaries through taxes collected in the colonies, the governors would become much more independent.

Now the trouble sown by Franklin's formula became apparent. The internal/external distinction had never been the colonists' concern. They objected to taxes for collection of revenue rather than regulation of trade. It was the new *purpose* of taxation rather than the way in which it was collected that mattered. Reaction to the Townshend Acts was surprisingly slow. Most colonists were reluctant to enter into opposition, and many hoped that merely petitioning the king and pointing out the acts' injustice would turn policy around. But as the new customs commissioners began to arrive in Boston, that city's radical leaders, Samuel Adams and James Otis, pushed a circular letter, to be sent to the legislatures of all the colonies, through the assembly. It did not suggest any particular program, merely that the colonies should once again prepare a joint reply. In response, the Virginia House of Burgesses sent around an even more radical letter calling for concerted action.

The year 1768 saw an outpouring of newspaper articles on resistance, and many popular demonstrations in Boston. Governor Francis Bernard, on orders from London, directed the Massachusetts legislature to rescind the circular letter. When they refused three times, he closed the assembly and called for troops to be sent to Boston to restore order, setting the stage for a new level of violence culminating in the Boston Massacre of 1770.

The immediate problem for colonial leaders was achieving repeal of the Townshend Acts. Failure to protest effectively would mean Britain could consider the principle of taxation for revenue to have been established. Agreements not to consume British goods were made fairly easily, but radical leaders wanted much more effective nonimportation codes. American merchants resisted, pointing out that importing and selling goods was their livelihood, but pressure grew until nonimportation became policy throughout the colonies. Local committees reinforced the agreements by seeking out anyone suspected of breaking them. Their names were published in the newspaper and their businesses boycotted. In extreme cases, offenders were tarred and feathered.

The nonimportation agreements were a rational use of economic power. American trade was important to Britain, and the colonists hoped to bring intolerable pressure on the government from injured merchants there. But there was more to the movement than that. Nonconsumption and nonimportation were used to build a new sense of purpose and of Americanness. British goods were associated with luxury and foolish chasing after fashionable "superfluities." Now Americans began to dress in homemade clothes made of homespun fabrics, and native food and drink replaced tea, wine, and other imported luxuries. Calls for the development of industries to free Americans of dependence on Europe echoed through the colonies. They were to be true to their own natures as sturdy, hardworking, independent citizens.

Women played important roles in this campaign. Most often they were the ones who coped with the problem of finding and preparing substitutes for imported goods. Women took up spinning and weaving as patriotic activities and made the boycotts work. Cloth production went up dramatically in the colonies as women, slave and free, devoted themselves to the tasks. Even though their activities were traditional, women saw themselves as acting politically, and were proud of their national contributions. Increasingly, women, both patriots and loyalists, became involved in the political debate. Patriot women's economic contribution was crucial to the resistance program, and women made informed choices as they took sides.

The boycott was successful, and it soon seemed that the colonists had won their point. In 1770 yet another new ministry, this time under Lord Frederick North, repealed the Townshend Acts, leaving only the tax on tea in effect. American rejection of British products had had an impact, but repeal also recognized that the law had been poorly thought through. To tax the products of British industry as they were exported into British colonies could only cut down on trade and revenue. In fact, the taxes had always cost more to collect than they brought in.

Most Americans, still loyal to the British system and proud of their membership in it, thought the crisis was now over despite the emotions stirred by the Boston Massacre in 1770. Nonimportation was given up and the tax on tea accepted for three years. There were some danger signs to disturb the general peace. One was that the goal of greater independence for royal officials, now paid from the tax on tea, had been achieved. Royal governors no longer feared they would have their funds cut off if they displeased colonial assemblies.

Another danger sign grew out of an attack on a customs ship, the *Gaspée*, by a Rhode Island mob in 1772. Though the culprits were not caught, the ministry made clear that in future they intended to take such offenders into Canada or even to England to be tried away from lenient colonial juries. This was such a fundamental assault on the jury trial system, which required accusers to confront the accused in open court in the place where the crime was committed, that in 1773 the colonies, led by the Virginia House of Burgesses, appointed Committees of Correspondence. If Britain acted against the colonists' rights and liberties, the committees would be ready to interpret such actions and call for defiance.

THE BOSTON TEA PARTY AND THE COERCIVE ACTS

The Committees of Correspondence soon had something to interpret: the Tea Act of 1773. The British government, seeking to bail out the East India Company, which had a huge surplus of tea, gave it a monopoly of the tea trade with America. Since the company could now sell directly to America and avoid the payment of taxes and middlemen's fees in England, colonists would actually be able to buy their tea at a lower price. Everyone would benefit, or so the ministry thought. The correspondents, already suspicious, fixed on the grant of a monopoly, however. They believed that elimination of competition meant, once again, the danger of enslavement. Eventually, the company could set the price at any level they chose and the Americans would have to pay. Today it was tea. Tomorrow it might be some essential commodity. The principle was important.

The colonial leaders agreed not to accept any of the East India Company tea, and the ships carrying it were turned away all along the coast. Only in Boston did this strategy meet a stumbling block in the form of the royal governor, Thomas Hutchinson. Although Hutchinson was a native-born Massachusetts man, he was completely out of sympathy with the radicals' methods of operation. He thought the tax on tea wrong, and had repeatedly argued to the British government for its repeal, but he was determined to enforce the law, which held that once a ship entered harbor, customs duties must be paid on its cargo before it could be allowed to leave. The owner of the tea ships begged Hutchinson to allow him simply to leave the harbor as ships had done elsewhere, but Hutchinson was adamant. The result was that in December 1773, a well-disciplined crowd of Bostonians, some "dressed in the Indian manner," boarded the ships and threw the tea into the harbor.

THE BOSTON TEA PARTY, from W. D. Cooper's *History of North America,* which was published in London in 1789. The proud British lion on the ship's prow occupies the center of the picture, but the Americans, many symbolically dressed as Indians, control the situation.

The tea was worth £10,000, a small fortune. Destruction of property on this scale took people's breath away on both sides of the Atlantic. Many Americans were deeply distressed and felt the owners should be compensated. Compensation would save the principle and make the action seem more legal. Other colonists drew back in horror. In associating themselves with the resistance movement, they had not expected such outlawry. In England even the friends of America were filled with revulsion and anger.

The royal government sought to take advantage of this feeling in punishing Boston for the tea party, and in doing so misread the nature of American public opinion. Realizing that a deep well of loyalist opinion existed, they began to visualize the radical movement as a kind of infection centered in Boston. If Boston could be cut off from the other colonies and fair punishment administered, the whole movement might simply die out. Lord North saw that the stakes were extremely high:

> We are not entering into a dispute between internal and external taxes, not between taxes laid for the purpose of revenues and taxes laid for the regulation of trade, not between representation and taxation, or legislation and taxation; but we are now to dispute whether we have, or have not any authority in that country.

When the punishment came, in a series of acts in 1774 known in England as the Coercive Acts and labeled the Intolerable Acts by the Americans, the extent of the ministers' miscalculation became clear. The acts were simply too extreme, and they came too long after the event. Rather than isolating Boston from more law-abiding colonies, the acts served to strengthen colonial solidarity. The cause of Massachusetts was seen as the cause of all.

The Intolerable Acts confirmed colonial suspicions that the underlying goal of the royal government was to do away with self-government and deny the colonists the rights of British subjects. The first act closed the port of Boston to all trade, a dire blow to the colony's economic life, which depended on commerce. The second took away two of Massachusetts's cherished rights of self-government by removing power to elect the governor's council from the assembly and giving it to the king, and forbidding town meetings, essential democratic institutions, except to elect town officials. The third act stipulated that any British official or soldier accused of a crime punishable by death could be sent to Nova Scotia or England for trial. Finally, the fourth act brought the army, removed after the Boston Massacre, back to the city. Not only were the troops back, but their commander, General Thomas Gage, was made governor. To colonists steeped in the Real Whig tradition, all the warning signs of tyranny were now present.

THE QUEBEC ACT

The colonies rose to Massachusetts's aid in the face of what the Virginia House of Burgesses called a "hostile invasion," sending relief supplies overland to feed and sustain the settlers. The outpouring of support was fueled partly by another act passed early in 1774 by the British Parliament: the Quebec Act. England had spent eleven years designing a government for France's American territories acquired in 1763. Now, intending an enlightened policy, the ministry planned a regime that would be acceptable to the former French subjects. Accordingly, the Quebec Act accepted French law in the region, which extended south to the Ohio River, and gave the Roman Catholic Church special status.

The colonists were horrified. Not only did the French system have no representative assemblies, the fundamental right to trial by jury was to be denied the territory's inhabitants. Added to these inroads on the rights of British subjects was recognition of the Roman Catholic Church, an institution that many of the colonists saw as going hand-in-hand with tyranny. Colonists who wanted to move into the rich Northwest Territory would do so at the expense of their liberties. No further proof that the British government intended to erect a tyranny in its American colonies was needed. Let the thirteen colonies beware.

THE CONTINENTAL CONGRESS, 1774

So serious had the situation become that the Committees of Correspondence proposed a meeting of representatives from all colonies to discuss the next move. The first Continental Congress in Philadelphia in September 1774 was a momentous event, and delegates were aware of that fact. Most of the men present had only heard about their counterparts in other colonies, and the first weeks were spent taking each other's measure. Only nine of the fifty-six delegates had been at the Stamp Act Congress, and they had much to learn about one another. At first glance, they seemed to represent extremely different societies. The aristocratic planters from South Carolina were attended by liveried slaves. At the other extreme was Sam Adams, whose friends had gotten together and bought him a new plain black suit so he would not disgrace Massachusetts by his shabbiness. Uppermost in most minds as they got acquainted was whether they would actually be able to work together. Could they trust each other?

Delegates were not thinking in terms of war. Most feared that alternative, believing America could never win, though many talked of it outside the formal sessions. Their concern in 1774 was to find a way to live within the British empire. They wanted to enunciate a set of principles that would give the king his due, including the right to regulate the empire's trade, and at the same time protect colonists' liberties. Many leaders had begun to hope for a situation in which the colonies would be directly under the king, with the assemblies acting as separate parliaments.

Governor Thomas Hutchinson of Massachusetts believed such a status was impossible. He had told the General Court in 1773, "I know of no line that can be drawn between the supreme authority of Parliament and the total independence of the colonies." Delegates to the Continental Congress hoped to be able to prove Hutchinson wrong. They, like the people they represented, still believed the British constitution to be the foundation of the best and freest government on earth, and one within whose laws they wanted to live. Moreover, they continued to think of themselves as orderly, law-abiding people.

The most pressing problem facing the Continental Congress was to overturn the Intolerable Acts. Spurred on by the Suffolk Resolves, passed by Suffolk County in Massachusetts and carried to the congress urgently by Paul Revere, the delegates voted not only a return to nonconsumption and nonimportation, but also a ban on exports. This was a hard commitment to make. Merchants would suffer, as they had earlier, and those colonies that lived by exporting their crops to England, particularly the southern agricultural colonies, would make a great sacrifice, but the congress agreed. Committees were to be set up in every village and town to see that the agreements were honored. The colonists continued to regard their self-denial as an exercise of virtue, an expression of their own special American strength of character. Where colonists took the loyalist position or did not accept this reasoning, dissent was crushed by the local committees.

The first Continental Congress dispersed in October 1774 with a sense of danger averted. John Adams confided to his diary as he left the city: "It is not very likely that I shall ever see this Part of the World again." Yet in a few short months the second congress was assembling in Philadelphia. Adams could not know that not only would the developing crisis bring him back to Philadelphia many times, but ultimately he would serve there as the president of the new nation.

FIRST SHOTS

With the army back in Boston as ordered by the 1774 Intolerable Acts, the situation there grew more tense every day. General Gage, seeing indisputable evidence of the American militia's growing preparations for resistance, sent desperate reports to London, begging that the Intolerable Acts be repealed and that the army be enlarged. He pointed out that he lacked the forces to put down a rebellion, and hoped that the most radical leaders would be undercut by conciliation offered to the moderate population at large. The ministry treated his messages with contempt, telling him his enemy was merely a "rude Rabble" and therefore "cannot be very formidable." Fearing that Gage's nerve had broken, they sent three generals to work under him: Major Generals Henry Clinton, William Howe, and John Burgoyne. Howe would take over as commander in chief in October 1775.

To strengthen his position, Gage decided to secure the munitions stores in Concord and Worcester. His earlier drive to seize ammunition and cannon from Charlestown and Cambridge in September 1774 had almost precipitated a crisis, with militiamen coming in defiance from as far away as Connecticut. Now his move toward Concord in April 1775 resulted in the first exchange of gunfire between colonial militias and the British army. Paul Revere had organized a net-

LEXINGTON AND CONCORD. Amos Doolittle did a series of engravings illustrating the British attempt to confiscate the arsenal at Concord and the resulting clashes with colonial militias at Lexington and Concord in April 1775. This plate shows the beleaguered soldiers leaving the scene of destruction and marching back to Boston through the sniper fire of expert colonial marksmen.

work of unemployed Boston artisans who followed every movement of the redcoats. Thus the militias in Lexington and Concord were forewarned. The British soldiers were forced back to Boston through sixteen miles of sniper fire and were badly shaken by their first encounter with the "rude Rabble."

News of the shots fired at Lexington and Concord spread over the colonies. Each town that received the information rushed it to the next. Written across the packet arriving in Charleston, South Carolina, was: "We send you momentous intelligence, this instant received." The British began to realize that their estimates based on colonists' conduct in the French and Indian War might have to be revised. General Gage wrote that "these people show a spirit and conduct against us that they never showed against the French, and everybody has judged them from their former appearance and behavior, which has led many into great mistakes."

The second Continental Congress, called before the fighting broke out, assembled as the news was being absorbed, on May 10, 1775. Despite all that had happened, it was to be more than a year before the subject of independence was formally broached there, for, despite the fact that war was on, the goals for which the colonists fought were still in doubt. Some new constitutional status within the British empire still seemed possible. Many still believed in the king, arguing that it was the ministers around him who persecuted the colonies. Accordingly, in July 1775 the Olive Branch Petition was sent to

George III affirming American loyalty and asking him to take charge of finding a constitutional solution. The king's answer was to declare the colonies in "an open and avowed rebellion."

WASHINGTON TAKES COMMAND

Meanwhile, the congress, still hoping for peace, prepared for war. A call for creation of an army went out, and on June 15, 1775, George Washington was named commanding general. As these decisions were made, violence once again flared up in Boston. General Gage decided to take and fortify the Dorchester Heights, which overlooked Boston and could render the city vulnerable. The Americans, hearing of the plan, decided to preempt him by seizing Bunker Hill and then moving to Dorchester Heights. When the two forces clashed, the British were successful, in that the Americans did withdraw, but the victory cost the redcoats dearly. This first full battle of the Revolutionary War resulted in 226 dead and 808 wounded on the British side, 140 deaths and 271 wounded among the colonial militia. One British general quipped that the "Americans' plan ought to be to lose a battle every week, till the British army was reduced to nothing."

George Washington arrived in Cambridge to take up his command on July 2, 1775, two weeks after the battle of Bunker Hill. He was conscious of the great problems facing the American side. The first necessary step was to whip the men besieging the British army in Boston into a recognizable military force. In a bold stroke, he and his men succeeded in taking Dorchester Heights.

General Howe had long hated having his army cooped up in Boston. He had already decided to make the colonies' midsection his base of operations, so when the Americans fortified the Dorchester Heights with heavy weapons taken by Ethan Allen and Benedict Arnold in daring attacks on British posts at Ticonderoga and Crown Point on Lake Champlain, Howe decided to depart. The British left in March 1776, hastily and in poor order. With the redcoats out of Boston, the first phase of British policy, the strategy of containing the infection of independence in Massachusetts, was over. At the same time, the Continental Congress was taking the first steps toward openly declaring separation from Britain.

TOM PAINE'S *COMMON SENSE*

Thomas Paine arrived from England in 1774; he established himself among Philadelphia's artisan community and began to write articles and editorials for newspapers. Probably because he had come in from outside, and because he had seen the operation of the English system as a tax collector before emigrating, he was able to cut through the slowly developing debate and convince the Americans that independence, not some new status within the British empire, was what they wanted. His book *Common Sense*, published in January 1776, was the great best-seller of the eighteenth century. It was so popular because its points were made clearly in the language of the people (John Adams thought the writing coarse and offensive), and its price kept low. More important, *Common Sense* crystallized popular thought. Paine made people see that independence was already in their minds, though not yet formulated.

Tom Paine knew his audience; he set the pamphlet up in the form of a sermon, which he knew would suit Americans. The first step in his argument was to disabuse his readers of the notion that the British system was something special, that they should want to continue as part of the empire. Moderates had been hoping the colonies could remain as thirteen dominions under the king, with the colonial legislatures as separate parliaments. Paine exploded this hope. He placed the blame for the colonists' troubles not on Parliament or the ministry but squarely on George III, the "Royal Brute of Britain." The English royal family was not ordained by God.

THOMAS PAINE. This mezzotint by James Watson is based on a painting by Charles Willson Peale.

Paine's genius was that he never forgot the practical concerns of his readers. While inspiring them with his vision of the American future, he also spoke to their needs. He argued that colonists need not fear being cut adrift if they became independent. They had already demonstrated that Europe depended on American trade. American products would always be in demand "while eating is the custom of Europe." America could have the best of the old relationship without the burdens of membership in the British empire.

From his vantage point in Pennsylvania, many of whose settlers were immigrants from Germany, Scotland, and northern Ireland, Paine was very aware that England was not the homeland of most Americans. All of Europe and Africa fed the colonial population. Moreover, not only did many of the flood of recent immigrants feel no special love for England, some, like the Irish, Scots, and Scots-Irish, had reason to hate that country for past imperial policies.

Rather, Paine argued, it came to the throne with the invasion of William the Conqueror in 1066. Thus the king owed his title to "a French bastard landing with an armed banditti . . . The plain truth is, that the antiquity of English monarchy will not bear looking into." Paine used history, reason, and the Bible to argue that not only was the British system corrupt, monarchy was a bad form of government. He used Old Testament examples to demonstrate that God did not favor kingship.

The second step was to shift people's focus away from fear of consequences to looking at how much could be accomplished. America was not to be a stepchild of Europe. Rather, this continent was to give birth to a whole new system. Europe was worn out and degenerate. The Americans were the wave of the future. In one of his most memorable phrases Paine argued that "freedom hath been hunted round the globe." Only the Americans still had the power to rescue liberty from encroaching tyranny and thus realize their own destiny: "We have it in our power to begin the world over again."

THE DECLARATION OF INDEPENDENCE

During the months after the publication of *Common Sense*, the Continental Congress came to share Paine's conclusions. In June 1776, Richard Henry Lee of Virginia moved: "That these United Colonies are, and of right ought to be, free and independent States." A committee was selected to draw up a statement. Thomas Jefferson wrote the first draft, and the Declaration of Independence follows his text closely. The Declaration, like *Common Sense*, places blame for the separation squarely on the king. There was a long list of specific accusations, many beginning with "He has."

The preamble to these charges is much more philosophical than Paine's work. Jefferson, a highly educated man, was very much aware of European intellectual currents. The Enlightenment of eighteenth-century Europe sought to examine the principles on which human society was erected. Rather than accept the notion that any particular government was ordained by God, these thinkers looked for natural reasons for government and tried to develop tests for judging whether a government was good. They argued that without government, human beings would be in a state of nature in which the strongest would rule, and there could be no progress because each family would be forced to devote itself to defense. Therefore, as the English philosopher John Locke (1632–1704) portrayed it, at some mythical time in the past, humans decided to form a government, to give it some rights over them, and to agree to abide by its decisions. Thus government is ordained by those who are governed, and its powers come from them.

Jefferson wrote these ideas into the Declaration of Independence. The truths in it were, he said, "self-evident" to human reason, not revealed by some mystical source. Government is set up to secure our rights, and this government derives its "just powers from the consent of the governed." It follows, then, that if a government does not offer the people protection but instead tramples on their rights, they have the right to change it. He said this would never be done lightly, but only after a "long train of abuses and usurpations." He then offered a lengthy list of "repeated injuries" that the colonies had suffered.

The Declaration of Independence shows how far the debate had moved along after the publication of *Common Sense*. Since 1763, Americans had been trying to convince England and its government of their sincerity and their suffering. In July 1776 the Continental Congress treated the special relationship with Britain as a dead letter. The Declaration was addressed not to England, but to "a candid world." And the arguments were not, as earlier, based on rights and privileges claimed under the British constitution, but on "the Laws of Nature and of Nature's God."

WAR

When General Howe moved his army away from hostile Boston in March 1776, they went to Halifax, Nova Scotia, and General Washington took advantage of the situation to move his troops to New York. In July, as the new states celebrated adoption of the Declaration of Independence, Howe moved his much larger and better-trained army to New York and ousted the Americans in a series of battles. Superiority at sea gave the British the capacity to move their army quickly along the coast. While the British established themselves in New York, the rebel army slowly moved in retreat across New Jersey to Morristown. British forces set up outposts at Trenton, Princeton, and New Brunswick, New Jersey.

Washington's concern, at this point and throughout the war, was to keep his army together and supplied. Many of the militiamen signed up for short periods, and even the regulars tended to drift away. Men would sign on to defend their homes, but might stay behind if the army moved on. Discipline was the heart of the British army regime. The men were trained to behave like automatons under fire. Such unquestioning discipline could not be achieved in the citizen army of the American forces. When Baron von Steuben, a Prussian soldier who volunteered to work with Washington, trained the troops in the Valley Forge winter of 1777–1778, he wrote to a European friend: "You say to your soldier, 'Do this,' and he does it, but I am obliged to say, 'This is the reason why you ought to do that,' and he does it."

In these circumstances, Washington was forced to conserve his troops, to choose the time and place of battle carefully. But the British were also concerned about conserving their armies. Highly trained soldiers were a precious commodity, and replacements were both far away and expensive to acquire. Howe might have been able to crush Washington's army in New York in the summer of 1776, but he chose to

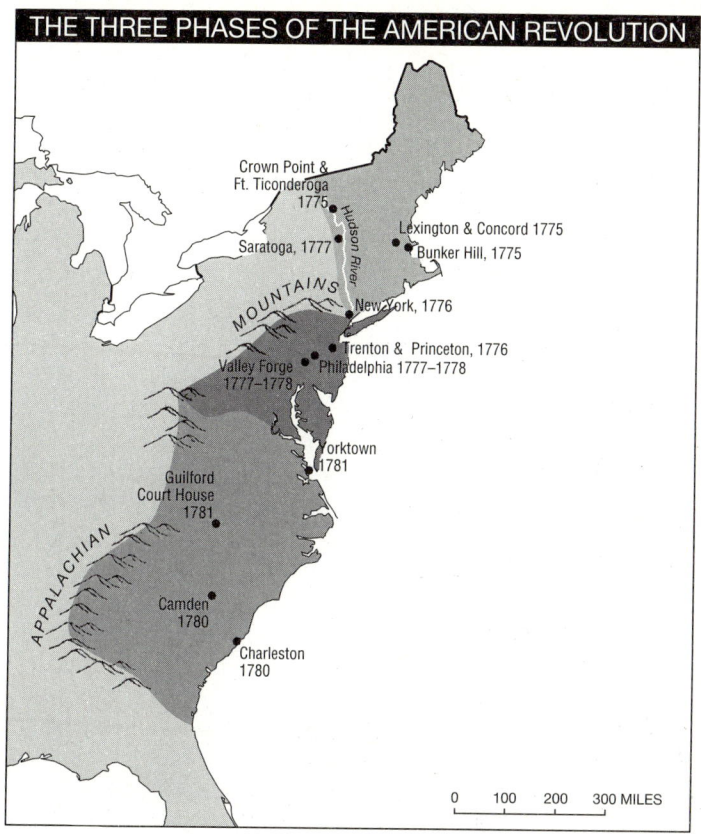

protect his force, giving the rebels time to slip away and rebuild. Many times throughout the war the British, by acting cautiously, allowed the Americans to garner the resources to continue resistance.

Because the British army was such a mighty force, and the rebels seen as an undisciplined rabble, any American success was psychologically important. Washington led successful surprise attacks on the British outposts at Trenton and Princeton at Christmas 1776, which helped build morale both for the troops and the citizens among whom the armies were encamped. Though neither site was strategically important, these victories reversed the impression of American weakness left by the retreat from New York. The British commanders could never get around the fact that, regardless of how great their victories were, their defeats counted more, as Washington pursued his strategy of attrition.

In the spring of 1777, the British adopted a new focus for the war effort. Howe decided to move his headquarters to Philadelphia, the rebel capital. His army moved by ship into Chesapeake Bay and marched up to the city. Meanwhile, British General John Burgoyne was to march his separate army from Canada down the Hudson Valley to meet Howe and the main force. This would have the effect of cutting the colonies in half and isolating New England. Once the Middle Colonies were firmly under control, then the

South could, imperial strategists thought, be brought quickly into line, and New England's resistance would collapse.

Crucial to this plan was the assumption that the Revolution was actually being foisted on an unwilling population. Most Americans, the British thought, were really loyal to the empire, but were intimidated by the local committees and the militia. If the redcoats were present to protect these loyalists at heart, they would make their true allegiance known and the revolutionary movement would die out. Historians do not know how most Americans felt in their hearts. One rule of thumb divided the population into thirds: one-third was probably devoted to independence, one-third was at least secretly loyalist, and one-third was somewhere in the middle.

Whatever the true figures, the British strategy could never work because the army was not a fit instrument for encouraging loyalist sentiment. Wherever the troops were sent, they created animosity. They tended to treat all the Americans with the contempt they thought rebels deserved. Even when they were strictly controlled, the fact that the armies lived off the land meant the people resented their presence. Even loyalists were disgusted. Sally Logan Fisher of Philadelphia initially welcomed the news that the British army was to make her city its headquarters, and looked forward to the arrival of Sir William Howe, "our beloved General." After just a few months, her opinion had changed completely. She was horrified by the army's plundering of Philadelphia citizens and the "wanton destruction" of the city.

Those with loyalist sentiments also soon learned that it was dangerous to trust in the protection of the British army. Sooner or later, the army would march on, and those who had publicly supported it were left to face angry neighbors. The great groundswell of sentiment in favor of reconciliation with the empire never materialized, but the British continued to hope for it.

INDIAN INVOLVEMENT

One key group of loyalists in the colonies on whom the British relied heavily was the many Indian tribes that sided with the empire. The large confederations such as the Iroquois League in the north and the Creeks and Cherokees in the south were courted by both sides. Indian leaders understood very well what was at stake in this contest. Many saw that an American victory would be disastrous for them; the colonists already looked greedily at the Ohio Valley, and the Indians who had settled there knew their land claims would not be respected.

It is not difficult to see why many Indians saw their future as brighter with a British victory. Whereas the American leaders urged the Indians to remain neutral, presenting the fight as a "family quarrel," the British sought active Indian participation. The Iroquois League first decided to remain neutral, hoping to play the Americans off against the British, but most eventually fought on the British side. The Creeks were able largely to continue their policy of neutrality, but the Cherokees, suffering depredations all along the line of settlement, attacked frontier settlements. In the north and south, the frontier was unsafe because of Indian warfare, and the Americans' military strength had to be divided to meet this challenge. Iroquois aid was an essential part of Burgoyne's plan as he marched through New York.

Though participation on the British side was a rational choice, all Indians suffered for that role after the war. The British were treacherous allies, circulating stories that presented the Indians as ferociously brutal fighters who slaughtered women and babies as willingly as men, many of which were wholesale inventions. The redcoats used such atrocity stories to frighten the Americans, and, like Oglethorpe in the siege of St. Augustine earlier, threatened to "unleash" their "savage" allies on rebel settlements. After the war, all Indians reaped the bitter fruits of such propaganda, as the new American government compared the natives to wild animals who had to be rooted out to make way for civilized settlers.

Moreover, the British abandoned their Indian allies at the treaty negotiations. The Iroquois took the perfectly sensible position that the British army had been beaten, but that the Iroquois forces were still in the field. To their shock, the British government signed over all the lands of their Indian allies, despite the fact that they had not been conquered, to the Americans and left the Indians to cope as best as they could. The Indians of the Northwest fought on until the Battle of Fallen Timbers in 1794 against the forces of the president to whom they had given the name "Town Destroyer," George Washington.

TURNING POINT

Even with Iroquois aid, the second phase of British strategy, based in New York and Pennsylvania and aiming to cut the rebel states in two, was doomed to failure. The generals never did the necessary planning. Burgoyne and Howe did not coordinate their activities, and direction from London was poor. "Gentleman Johnny" Burgoyne began his march south from Canada in June 1777 in great style as the American forces retreated before him and he reclaimed Fort Ticonderoga. As one of his officers remarked, "We had conceived the idea of our being irresistible." Burgoyne issued a series of proclamations offering to protect the Americans against the "tyranny" of the revolutionaries and predicting horrifying vengeance on those who held out.

The American forces, depressed at Howe's capture of Philadelphia, were soon heartened by the news that Burgoyne was in trouble, a situation that deepened as he moved farther from his supplies in Canada. Burgoyne's army was confronted and defeated at the battle of Saratoga in October 1777, an event many saw as the turning point in the war. For once, the Americans had met a major British force in a full-dress battle and won. The impact on American morale was tremendous.

FRANCE ENTERS THE WAR

The effect in Europe was equally momentous. France, still smarting from its defeat in 1763, had been aiding the rebels secretly with much-needed supplies. After Saratoga showed the Americans to be a formidable opponent for Britain, France, despite great misgivings about aiding rebels, openly allied itself with the United States. Now not only did the Americans receive war material, and the

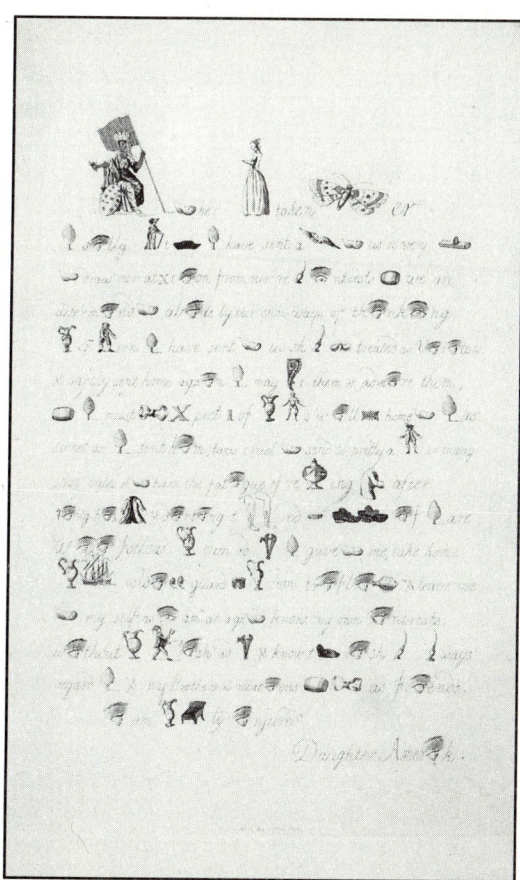

[AMERICA TOE] HER [MISS] TAKEN [MOTH] ER, a humorous comment from London on American defiance, 1778.

French navy challenged British superiority at sea. For the first time it looked as if the Revolution might succeed. Soon Spain declared war on Britain as France's ally, though it could never countenance befriending rebels. From this point forward, England was forced to fight all over the world as it sought to protect the empire from French and Spanish depredations.

The winter of 1777–1778 was spent garnering strength for the future. The British in Philadelphia saw another change in command, with General Sir Henry Clinton replacing Howe in May. The main American army spent the winter at Valley Forge, Pennsylvania, drilling and preparing for new engagements. General Washington also drilled the soldiers on the principles for which they were fighting and emphasized the necessity of sacrifice for the common good.

Washington was able to appeal to his soldiers' sense of commitment because the army genuinely thought in terms of a shared goal of great importance. Their dedication was grounded in the sense that they were fighting for their homes and families as well as for the principles of the Revolution.

THE HOME FRONT

These beliefs were shared by those on the home front. Men did the fighting, probably 200,000 in all on the American side, but women made the war effort possible. In doing so, they increasingly took on responsible public roles, running the farms and businesses of the absent men and providing the food and supplies the army required. Abigail Adams, wife of John Adams, ran the family farm so well that she aspired to have "the reputation of being as good a farmeress as my partner has of being a good statesman." Women gave up their own needs and collected money for the soldiers. The sums collected were large, and General Washington praised such "female patriotism." When the fighting came to their regions, women cared for the sick and wounded.

The home front often presented a scene of suffering as great as that in the armies. Dysentery and smallpox were carried by the armies to civilian populations. After dysentery had killed many, including her own mother and niece, during the siege of Boston, Abigail Adams wrote that "the Desolation of War is not so distressing as the Havoc made by the pestilence." Soldiers' looting and, sometimes, raping of women whose men were off fighting created terror throughout the civilian population. Nonetheless, American women affirmed their devotion to the cause and accepted deprivation willingly. Women throughout the colonies destroyed food supplies, even stocks on which they were dependent, rather than have them fall into the enemy's hands. Victory would not have been possible for the Americans without the contribution of women at home.

VICTORY

In the spring of 1778, the period of regrouping was over. General Clinton removed his army from Philadelphia to New York and prepared for the third and final phase of the war. British strategy was still based on the assumption that most Americans wished to be loyal to Britain. The focus in this third phase was on the South, which for several reasons was thought to be the most promising territory for the British. Not only were the southerners, with their more aristocratic society, thought to have a natural affinity for England, but strategists thought they could be more easily intimidated. The South contained vast numbers of slaves, in some areas much more than half the population, and the threat of a slave rebellion armed and abetted by the British would surely bring southerners around. There were also large and powerful Indian confederations, especially the Creeks and the Cherokees, who could be induced to ally themselves with the British.

This third phase of the war involved a plan for pacification of the countryside. The British would land in the far south and would then move north, sweeping the rebels before them and leaving the country in the hands of loyal self-defense forces. Accordingly, one force of redcoats seized Savannah, Georgia, in 1779, and Charleston, the key to the whole strategy, was besieged. The May 1780 fall of Charleston, the most important port in the South, marked the beginning of the pacification campaign.

Despite all the apparently favorable indications, British strategy failed here for some of the same reasons as earlier. Even if loyalist sentiment existed, luring it into the open was difficult. The plan called for the army to move north, and southerners knew that those who had been friendly to it would suffer when the troops were gone. Again, the soldiers made enemies by their seizure of food and supplies and by their rough manner.

More important, the southern strategy was based on fallacious reasoning. When the British appealed to slaves to rebel or leave, they offended white southerners and thus alienated potential loyalists. Slavery offered the ideological weak point of the American campaign. Historians have long pointed to the irony that Thomas Jefferson, while writing the stirring words "We hold these truths to be self-evident: That all men are created equal; that they are endowed by their Creator with certain unalienable rights; that among these are life, liberty, and the pursuit of happiness," actually owned some 200 slaves, who had neither rights nor equality. Some have argued, like the early nineteenth-century English visitor Sir Augustus John Foster, that slavery actually made high-flown democratic theories possible, because of "the mass of the people, who in other countries might become mobs, being there nearly altogether composed of their own Negro slaves." Slavery represented a kind of blind spot for the American leadership, a part of American life whose implications they agreed to ignore for the time being in order to achieve the unity of purpose needed for the war effort. But slavery could not be ignored in the conduct of the war, because fear of slave rebellion rendered the South vulnerable.

Slaves, like Indians, seemed natural loyalists. In 1775, even before hostilities were formally declared, John Murray, Lord Dunmore, royal governor of Virginia, offered freedom to any slave who succeeded in getting through to the British lines. Several thousand slaves did manage to escape to the redcoats during the war, including large numbers of women with children who took advantage of the opportunity for freedom despite the great dangers and hardships involved. The men manned a regiment of Black Guides and Pioneers. Many runaway slaves left America with the defeated army when the war was over. But any call to the slaves was sure to alienate white southerners, whose most fundamental fear was of slave rebellion.

The British southern strategy was badly misconceived. It was not really possible to sweep the revolutionaries out of the countryside. Many southern rebels waged a guerrilla campaign, striking at the British and then melting back into the population. An American force could be defeated and dispersed, but would coalesce again as soon as the British were occupied elsewhere.

The main American army in the South was first commanded by General Horatio Gates, whose incompetence was partly responsible for a massive defeat at Camden, South Carolina, on August 16, 1780. The rebels fared better when Nathaniel Greene took over and decided to conduct what he called a "fugitive war," one based on hit-and-run tactics. He was plagued by the necessity of constant supplication to the congress and the states for supplies. Meanwhile, the British army was suffering from sickness and the debilitating effects of the guerrilla activity. Far from finding a population filled with loyalists,

LORD CORNWALLIS SURRENDERS AT YORKTOWN, October 19, 1781. This painting by John Trumbull shows the French forces under Rochambeau on the left, with the Americans commanded by George Washington on the right. Lafayette and von Steuben are placed near Washington.

the redcoats confronted people so alienated that the British were starved of information about local conditions and about movements of the rebel armies, and ignorance cost them very dearly.

Even British victories, such as the bloody battle of Guilford Court House, North Carolina, on March 15, 1781, involved losses so devastating that they shored up American morale. Finally, Charles Cornwallis, commander of the British army in the South, decided to head for the Virginia shore, where he could once again be in touch with supply ships from home. His march led through Yorktown, where he confronted a large army of Americans and Frenchmen under Washington and the Comte de Rochambeau, backed by the French fleet in Chesapeake Bay under Admiral François-Joseph-Paul de Grasse. Cornwallis had begged General Clinton to bring the northern and southern armies together in Virginia in vain. Now surrounded by superior Franco-American forces, he surrendered his entire army in October 1781. As the redcoats marched out to turn over their weapons, the bands, reflecting the soldiers' feelings, played an English music hall song: "The World Turn'd Upside Down."

Britain could have continued the war. The major American ports were still in British hands and the northern army was still intact, but this long and costly war had lost support at home. Peace negotiations now replaced the study of war. It would be two years before the Peace of Paris officially ending the war was signed in 1783 and the world recognized the independent existence of the United States of America, which gained the land between the Ohio River, the Mississippi, and the Great Lakes. England retained Canada, Nova Scotia, and Cape Breton Island. Florida was ceded to Spain, and St. Augustine was once more in Spanish hands.

CHRONOLOGY

1764	Revenue Act (Sugar Act)
1765	Stamp Act and Quartering Act; Sons of Liberty organized; Stamp Act Congress
1766	Stamp Act repealed, accompanied by Declaratory Act
1767	New York assembly closed for failure to comply with Quartering Act; Townshend Acts
1768	Massachusetts assembly closed; British Army sent to Boston; Colonists form nonimportation and nonconsumption agreements to fight Townshend Acts
1770	Townshend Acts repealed; tax on tea remains in effect; Boston Massacre
1772	*Gaspée* attacked; British government announces that trials in such attacks will be held in Canada or England
1773	Committees of Correspondence formed; Boston Tea Party
1774	Coercive, or Intolerable, Acts, accompanied by Quebec Act; First Continental Congress; Nonconsumption, nonimportation, and nonexport agreements adopted
1775 (Apr.)	Shots fired at Lexington and Concord;
(May)	Second Continental Congress meets, calls for organization of army; Battle of Bunker Hill;
1775 (Cont'd)	
(July)	Olive Branch Petition; king declares colonies in rebellion;
(Nov.)	Lord Dunmore offers freedom to Virginia slaves
1776 (Jan.)	*Common Sense* published;
(Mar.)	British evacuate Boston;
(July 4)	Continental Congress endorses Declaration of Independence;
(July)	British forces take New York from American army;
(Dec.)	Surprise attacks on British forces at Princeton and Trenton;
1777	
(spring)	British forces under Howe occupy Philadelphia; General Burgoyne begins march down Hudson Valley;
(Oct.)	Burgoyne defeated at Saratoga;
(Oct.)	American army at Valley Forge
1779	British take Savannah
1780 (May)	Charleston falls to British;
(Aug.)	Americans defeated at Camden, South Carolina;
1781 (Mar.)	Battle of Guilford Court House, North Carolina;
(Oct.)	Cornwallis surrenders at Yorktown, Virginia
1783	Treaty of Paris recognizes American independence

SUGGESTIONS FOR FURTHER READING

THE BOSTON MASSACRE

See first Hiller B. Zobel, *The Boston Massacre* (1970). Zobel's study is criticized and set in context in Jesse Lemisch, "Radical Plot in Boston (1770): A Study in the Use of Evidence," *Harvard Law Review*, 84 (1970), 485–504. Dirk Hoerder, *Crowd Action in Revolutionary Massachusetts, 1765–1780* (1977), looks at the question of prerevolutionary violence from a perspective different from Zobel's. For the army's role as inciter of violence, see John Shy, *Toward Lexington: The Role of the British Army in the Coming of the American Revolution* (1965).

On men who took a leading role in the events of 1770, see Bernard Bailyn, *The Ordeal of Thomas Hutchinson* (1974), and "Butterfield's Adams: Notes for a Sketch," *William and Mary Quarterly*, 3d ser., 19 (1962), 238–256; Pauline Maier, *The Old Revolutionaries: Political Lives in the Age of Samuel Adams* (1980); Peter Shaw, *The Character of John Adams* (1976); and Alfred F. Young, "George Robert Twelves Hewes (1742–1840): A Boston Shoemaker and the Memory of the American Revolution," *William and Mary Quarterly*, 3d ser., 38 (1981), 561–623.

THE GROWTH OF AMERICAN RESISTANCE

The developing debate over English actions and their meaning for colonists is illuminated by Bernard Bailyn, *The Origins of American Politics* (1967); Pauline Maier, *From Resistance to Revolution: Colonial Radicals and the Development of American Opposition to Britain, 1765–1776* (1972); David Ammerman, *In the Common Cause: American Response to the Coercive Acts of 1774* (1974); and the essays in Alfred F. Young, ed., *The American Revolution: Explorations in the History of American Radicalism* (1976).

SOCIETY AND REVOLUTION

Gary B. Nash, *The Urban Crucible: Social Change, Political Consciousness, and the Origins of the American Revolution* (1979), analyzes urban development and its relationship to revolution. Robert A. Gross, *The Minutemen and Their World* (1976), and Richard D. Brown, *Revolutionary Politics in Massachusetts: The Boston Committee of Correspondence and the Towns, 1772–1774* (1970), discuss the coming of the Revolution in Massachusetts. See Edward Countryman, *A People in Revolution: The American Revolution and Political Society in New York, 1760–1790* (1981), Sung Bok Kim, *Landlord and Tenant in Colonial New York: Manorial Society, 1664–1775* (1978), and Eric Foner, *Tom Paine and Revolutionary America* (1976), for the Middle Colonies. For slavery in the revolutionary era, see Duncan J. MacLeod, *Slavery, Race, and the American Revolution* (1974).

WOMEN'S ROLES

Women's roles as they affected and were affected by the movement toward independence are the subject of two fine recent studies: Linda Kerber, *Women of the Republic: Intellect and Ideology in Revolutionary America* (1980), and Mary Beth Norton, *Liberty's Daughters: The Revolutionary Experience of American Women, 1750–1800* (1980). For an overall interpretation of changes in women's place, see Mary Beth Norton, "The Evolution of White Women's Experience in Early America," *American Historical Review*, 89 (1984), 593–619.

WAR

Robert Middlekauff, *The Glorious Cause: The American Revolution, 1763–1789* (1982), is a detailed history of the background and conduct of the Revolutionary War treated purely as a conflict between Britain and its colonists. Edward Countryman, *The American Revolution* (1985), is a shorter, very readable overview that incorporates more of the recent findings of social and intellectual historians. Charles Royster, *A Revolutionary People at War: The Continental Army and American Character, 1775–1783* (1979), and John Shy, *A People Numerous and Armed: Reflections on the Military Struggle for American Independence* (1976), discuss the military experience and its impact. For an illuminating reconstruction of the context see David Hackett Fischer, *Paul Revere's Ride* (1994).

Indians as a factor in both the cause and conduct of the American Revolution have attracted a good deal of recent scholarly attention. Barbara Graymont, *The Iroquois in the American Revolution* (1972); Francis Jennings, *The Ambiguous Iroquois Empire* (1984); Isabel T. Kelsay, *Joseph Brant, 1743–1807: Man of Two Worlds* (1984); and Anthony F. C. Wallace, *The Death and Rebirth of the Seneca* (1969), illuminate the position of the Iroquois League and its fate in the war and its aftermath. James H. O'Donnell III, *Southern Indians in the American Revolution* (1973), deals with the South. See also Francis Jennings, *Empire of Fortune* (1988).

CHAPTER

6

The Transition to Nationhood

Episode: George Washington, from General to President

THE MAKING OF THE AMERICAN CONSTITUTION

The Confederation Period
The Philadelphia Convention
The New Constitution
The Struggle for Ratification
Things Left Unsaid and Undone

THE EPISODE: When Charles, Lord Cornwallis, surrendered his British army to the combined American and French forces at Yorktown, the Revolutionary War was effectively ended. For many years, the leaders of the revolutionary movement had talked and acted as though the colonies had only one serious problem: British interference in their affairs. Now, most of them believed the thirteen states could go about their business in peace and harmony, tied together only by a loose bond of national government. But during the next few years, many political leaders became convinced that a much stronger framework of national government was needed if the country was to survive.

In this chapter, we follow one such leader, George Washington, through the steps that led him to this conclusion. Washington yearned for retirement from public life at the end of the Revolution. But his own experience seemed to teach him two things as time passed: that a new government ought to be created, and that he could not escape participating in this new government, perhaps even leading it. In some ways, Washington was a unique man. But the perceptions that led him to join the movement for a new constitution were far from unique. They typified the kinds of hopes and fears that would eventually lead the men Americans came to call their Founding Fathers to write the Constitution of the United States.

THE HISTORICAL SETTING: At the end of the Revolution, the United States was governed by the same Congress that had declared independence in 1776. Then it had been a voluntary assembly, legitimated only by its own declarations. Now it had a new kind of legitimacy in the first constitution, the Articles of Confederation. This document, which was finally ratified by all the states near the end of the Revolution, was written on the assumption that the states were willing to grant the national government only those powers they would once have been willing to see the British Parliament exercise over the colonies. They did not give the Congress certain crucial powers, such as the power to tax or the power to regulate foreign or interstate trade. Nor did the Articles provide for any executive or judicial branches; the national government was, in effect, only a national legislature.

This chapter examines the way the Articles of Confederation worked in practice and assesses the achievements of the Congress. It also explains the kinds of difficulties Washington and other political leaders came to believe could not be solved under the Articles. Then it analyzes the complex set of compromises the Constitutional Convention of 1787 reached in order to create a new frame of government. Finally, the chapter spells out how the process of getting the Constitution accepted by the states resulted in the creation of the Bill of Rights.

George Washington, from General to President

After he forced Charles, Lord Cornwallis, to surrender at Yorktown in 1781, George Washington had had more than enough of war. He wanted very much to go home to his beloved plantation, Mount Vernon. He did manage to spend a quick week there—his first time home in six years. But the Revolutionary War was not officially over. Not until April 1782 did American, French, and British representatives begin to negotiate a peace treaty in Paris. And there was still a British garrison in the city of New York. So Washington moved his army to Newburgh, New York, a short distance up the Hudson River, to keep a close watch over the enemy. A year and a half passed before the American Congress finally ratified the Treaty of Paris, in April 1783. But then Washington had to wait six more months, because the British did not begin to evacuate New York until November. At last, early in December, Washington decided that his war was finally over. He asked his officers to meet at a Manhattan tavern to say good-bye. One of them wrote this account of the moving scene of farewell:

> The time now drew near when the Commander-in-Chief intended to leave for his beloved retreat at Mount Vernon. On Tuesday, the fourth of December, it was made known to the officers then in New York that General Washington intended to commence his journey on that day.
>
> At twelve o'clock the officers repaired to Fraunces Tavern in Pearl Street, where General Washington had appointed to meet them and to take his final leave of them. We had been assembled but a few moments when His Excellency entered the room. His emotion, too strong to be concealed, seemed to be reciprocated by every officer present.
>
> After partaking of a slight refreshment, in almost breathless silence, the General filled his glass with wine, and turning to his officers, he said, "With a heart full of love and gratitude, I now take leave of you. I most devoutly wish that your latter days may be as prosperous and happy as your former ones have been glorious and honorable."
>
> After the officers had taken a glass of wine, General Washington said, "I cannot come to each of you, but shall feel obliged if each of you will come and take me by the hand."
>
> General Knox, being nearest to him, turned to the Commander-in-Chief, who, suffused in tears, was incapable of utterance, but grasped his hand, when they embraced each other in silence. In the same affectionate manner, every officer in the room marched up to, kissed, and parted with his General-in-Chief.
>
> Such a scene of sorrow and weeping I had never before witnessed, and hope I may never be called upon to witness again.

Washington rode south to Philadelphia, then on to Annapolis, Maryland, where Congress was in session. (After the Continental Congress was forced to leave Philadelphia, it had met in several towns for varying lengths of time. It held sessions in Annapolis for a year, beginning in November 1783.) The general-in-chief was by far the most popular and respected man in America. The new nation had a shadowy government, few traditions, and almost no leaders of national stature. Washington might have tried to claim political powers equal to the military powers he had held. Instead, he chose to renounce power, to resign, and to go home to Mount Vernon. He had come to Annapolis to turn in his commission as general of all Continental forces. In a draft of a speech to the Congress, he spoke of an "affectionate and final farewell" and of taking "ultimate leave" of public office.

For some reason, though, when Washington actually delivered the speech to the Congress on December 23, he struck out the words "final" and "ultimate." At the end of his address, Washington said only that he was taking "leave of all public employments." His farewell was only "affectionate"—not "final."

WASHINGTON'S FAREWELL. In this 1805 painting, Washington's tearful 1783 farewell to his officers in a New York tavern is given that combination of deep sentiment and dignified restraint that was thought to be part of the ideal character of a gentleman. This scene played an important part in remaking Washington's public image from that of the military leader to one as the civilian head of a republic.

The Washington who renounced power and resigned his commission was in many ways the simplest and most straightforward of men. Even his very few enemies recognized his almost perfect honesty and forthrightness. But Washington also embodied some important paradoxes of the American Revolution and the American situation in general. He was, to begin with, an aristocrat who (along with other aristocrats) had somehow led the first modern revolution, a revolution with many democratic overtones. Furthermore, history had placed Washington at the absolute center of the revolutionary stage. If he had been killed or captured or become ill, the Revolution might have collapsed very quickly. Washington was not, at heart, a dedicated revolutionary. He had been involved in the movement for revolution in Virginia almost from its beginnings in the 1760s. But he did not have the flaming philosophical dedication of the men whose words and ideas had been so important: Thomas Jefferson, Thomas Paine, Samuel Adams, and others like them. Before 1776, Washington had been a minor figure in the Virginia movement. Even during the war, he was often dismayed to find himself so constantly at center stage. When the war was over, he appeared to want nothing more than to return to Mount Vernon by Christmas Day 1783, and to stay there.

These paradoxes in Washington point to some larger problems of his country. In the last analysis, his power and influence had been military. He was not a great general in the tactical sense. But he was the only general, over the long haul from 1775 to 1783, whom everyone could trust. Now the fighting was over, the army broken up, and Washington back at Mount Vernon. The questions were as plain as they were important: Could Americans create a political unity to replace the fragile military unity that had won the Revolution? Would political leaders come forward who could unify the former colonies the way Washington had managed to hold the Continental Army together at Valley Forge? Would political institutions be developed to enable Virginians and New Yorkers, Carolinians and New Englanders, to act as one people?

When Washington rode home at the end of 1783, he had no wish to raise any such questions. Indirect or direct, they simply were not much on his mind. He was a public figure, and he knew it. From the time of the Revolution on, his life would always be full of public affairs. His days would be taken up with receiving distinguished visitors in his Virginia home. And an incredible amount of his time would always be absorbed with writing to important political figures, in both Europe and America. (His letters fill thirty-nine thick volumes.) But thinking about public affairs, entertaining important visitors, and keeping up a steady correspondence on the issues of the day—all these activities did not necessarily involve a direct participation in politics and government. What Washington wanted now was time—time to rest, time to tend his neglected plantation and to attend to the thousands of acres of land he owned in the West. He also wanted time for his wife, Martha, and the rest of his family, time for riding, fox hunting, and the other preoccupations of a leisured, slave-owning Virginia planter.

At first it seemed to work. Washington enjoyed his self-imposed retirement. Since it was winter, there was little farm work to supervise. The roads were bad, and not very many visitors came. The general seemed to believe he could turn himself into a gentleman planter again. To old military comrades he wrote: "The tranquil walks of domestic life are now beginning to unfold themselves. I am retiring within myself." He described himself as a wearied traveler, home at last after treading many a painful step with a heavy burden on his shoulders.

Turning inward had always meant Mount Vernon. This great estate was the center of Washington's conception of himself as a private man. It was his refuge and sanctuary, the visible, touchable focus of his private life.

But another focus—that of politics, revolution, war—had always pulled him away from Mount Vernon, out into the larger world of Virginian and American politics. When Washington resigned his commission in 1783, not only had he left the army, he had also returned home in a very special sense. He was fifty-one years old and healthy (except for the bad teeth that bothered him all his life). Yet he was on the downhill side of middle age. For all he or anyone else could tell, he had already reached the peak of his fame, public service, and involvement in politics. If he had never again left Mount Vernon, he probably would still have been known as the Father of His Country.

There were two flaws, however, in the peaceful picture Washington had of "retiring within myself." First, more than any other man in the country, he *was* the American cause. In an almost unique way, personal vanity and dedicated patriotism were the same emotion in him. He identified himself so closely with his new country that any ambition for it almost amounted to an ambition for himself—and vice versa. In an odd sense, Washington could have no private life.

The second flaw that threatened the "tranquil walks of domestic life" was that despite his land and his slaves, he was in some ways a poor man. He would have to build his fortune rather than retire on a fortune ready-made. The war had been expensive for him and his plantation. Slaves had been sold and crops had spoiled. Also, Washington had accepted no salary during his years as commanding general, though he had been reimbursed for his actual expenses. As he added up his accounts in 1784, he found himself short of money. At the end of the year he could not have put his hands on more than about $500 in cash. In slaves and land he was rich—at least on paper. Besides Mount Vernon, he owned well over 30,000 acres in the West, which he had bought before the war. Some of this land was just west of Pittsburgh. More was farther down the Ohio River, near the present city of Cincinnati. The land was a speculation, however, only a possible source of future wealth. It was worth very little at this time. Mount Vernon was a great plantation; but the land had become too poor for successful tobacco agriculture. The plantation was simply not a paying proposition in any substantial way.

Washington's wealth made him one of the richest men in America. But it was an odd form of wealth. Either it was impossible to turn into ready cash, like Mount Vernon itself or its slaves, or it was potential wealth, like the western lands. Washington's other assets—fine horses, clothes, furniture, and dogs—were all luxuries, not productive assets.

In many respects, Washington's financial future rested on the lands in the West. The value of those lands, in turn, depended on getting settlers there, improving road and water transportation, and extending orderly government into the Ohio Valley. In a very concrete way, then, Washington's future was tied to the nation's. He was not a particularly greedy man. But it was clear to him that he had a great personal stake in the new republic. If it prospered, so would he, as his Ohio lands became valuable real estate. And if the new United States became a respectable nation among nations, his work in shaping it would have been worthwhile and his reputation and honor secure.

THE HERO AT HOME. This painting is the only contemporary picture of Washington and his family at Mount Vernon. He is wearing his general's uniform. The two young people are Martha Washington's grandchildren, who grew up as part of Washington's household. The black man at the right bore one of Virginia's proudest names, Billy Lee, and had been the general's "body servant" during the Revolutionary War. The painting must have been made after 1791, because the map shows the site of the future capital in the District of Columbia. In the background is the Potomac River.

These kinds of concerns and reflections drew the retired general back toward public life. Mount Vernon could not be walled off from the world. Nor could Washington daydream for long on the "tranquil walks of domestic life." He had too much energy and too much of the habit of participation and power. These traits were reinforced by his great pride in himself and his country. When Washington's economic circumstances were added to such a picture, almost anyone could easily have predicted that his retirement would be either very short or very incomplete.

The most direct temptation to involvement beyond Mount Vernon led west, to the Ohio Valley lands. Several things were on Washington's mind. He was angry that land speculators were illegally offering his Ohio land for sale in Philadelphia and New York markets. Trespassers, or "squatters," were living on his land near Pittsburgh, without paying rent or recognizing Washington's title. Also, several Virginians, including Thomas Jefferson, were talking about opening up a trade route from the Chesapeake Bay area to the west. They planned to use the Potomac River and some of the branches of the Ohio for water transportation, possibly building canals or new roads across the short stretches between the eastern and western rivers. Washington was very interested in such schemes. They would help his state and the nation. And, obviously, opening the West for settlement and trade would also be to his own personal economic advantage.

All these concerns put Washington on horseback in early September 1784 for a trip west. He was accompanied by his nephew and an old friend and his son, plus three African-American "servants"—as planters liked to call their house slaves. The group started north along the Potomac toward the Allegheny Mountains and Pittsburgh. From there they planned to go by boat to the lands down the Ohio. On the way, Washington traveled over what was known as Braddock's Road, through territory he had scouted, surveyed, and fought in as a young soldier thirty years earlier, in the French and Indian War. Now the French were gone, the country was filling with farmers, and the British were surrendering the entire Ohio Valley to the Americans.

Washington traveled as the first citizen of the United States. But he traveled to argue with plain farmers who were living on his land and who were not ready to surrender what they thought of as their rights, even to the revolutionary general-in-chief. Trying to maintain a pace of five miles an hour, he finally reached his Pennsylvania land on September 18. In his diary, he kept a running account of his encounter with the squatter farmers:

> *September 19th*: Being Sunday, and the people living on my land apparently very religious, it was thought best to postpone going among them till tomorrow.
>
> *20th*: Went early this morning to view my land, and to receive the final determination of those who live upon it. Dined at David Reed's, after which Mr. James Scot and Reed began to inquire whether I would part with the land, and upon what terms. They did not conceive they could be dispossessed, but to avoid contention they would buy if my terms were moderate. I told them I had no inclination to sell. However, after hearing a great deal of their hardships, their religious principles, and unwillingness to separate or remove, I told them I would make a last offer: the whole tract at 25 shillings per acre. Or they could become tenants upon leases of 999 years.

The potential tenants discussed the question among themselves for a long time, while Washington sat gravely to one side. Then they turned back to him and said they would not buy. They would not pay rent. And they would not move off the land. Washington would have to sue them, they said. He made one last attempt to break up their united front by forcing them to confront him individually. But it did not work:

> They had a long consultation. They then determined to stand suit for the land. I told them I would receive their answers individually, and accordingly I called them by name as they stood. They severally answered that they meant to stand suit, and abide the issue of the law.

Washington had come face to face, on a very practical level, with a problem that was worrying many wealthy Americans who lived in the East: Would the settlers in the new lands beyond the mountains be subject to rules and laws made in the East? Could the frontier be governed? Or would the new areas be "lawless," and perhaps even separate from the United States? Theoretically, as educated Americans looked toward the

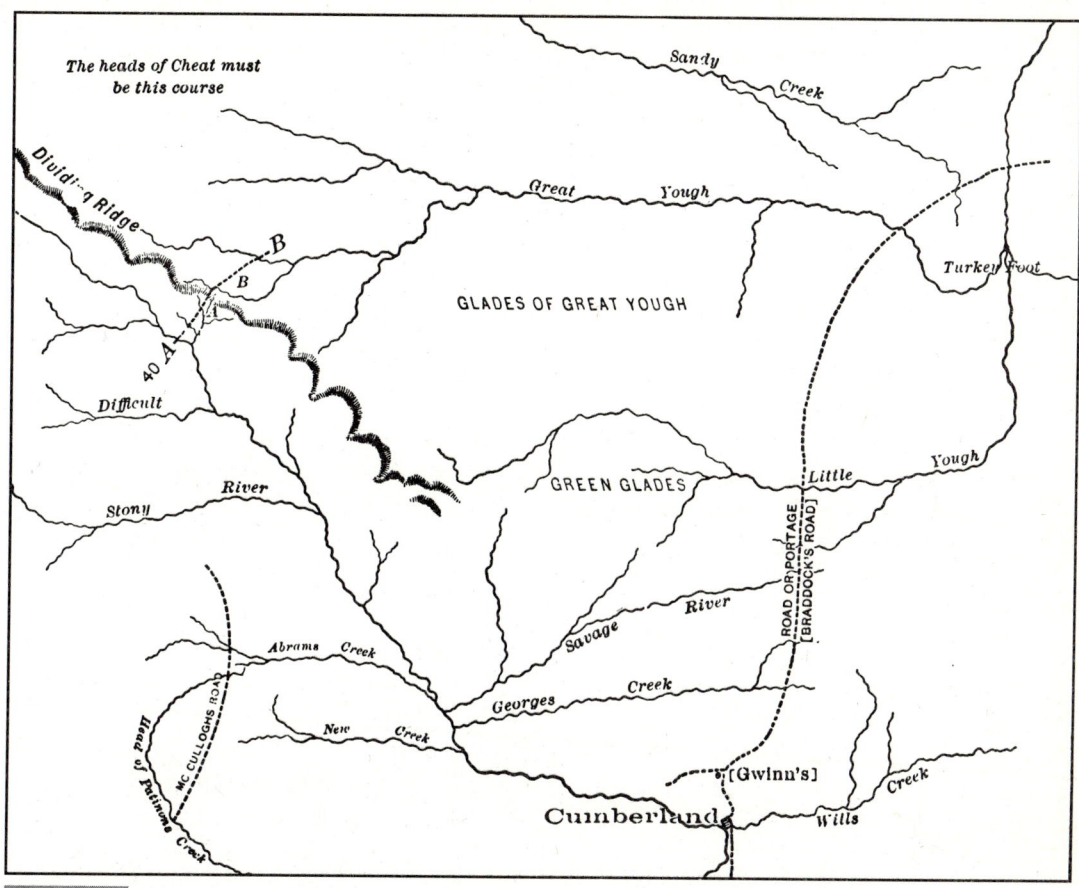

WASHINGTON'S WEST. On his trip to the West in 1784, Washington paid very close attention to the geography of the area, especially to the rivers and creeks that might provide a basis for a transportation system. When he returned home, he had this map printed. It shows Cumberland, Maryland, on the Potomac at the lower right. The "Glades of Great Yough" are in Pennsylvania. The general was particularly interested in passages across ridge lines, like the one he drew running north and east at the left of the map.

Mississippi River, the wilderness seemed to be both a tremendous opportunity and a tremendous problem. But Washington did not have to think on a theoretical level. (He was not much of a philosopher by nature, anyway.) He had already encountered the problem, and it had the most direct and worrisome kinds of consequences for him.

The question of government power and the western lands presented itself in yet another way on Washington's trip. The general had planned to go down the Ohio to look over his other lands, but every traveler he met coming east advised him to stay away. The Native Americans, they said, were on the "warpath." He was told over and over that it would be dangerous to travel much farther into the Ohio country. He decided to head for home, having accomplished almost nothing. Someday, he thought to himself and later wrote to his friends, the United States would have to deal aggressively with the Indians. The government would have to negotiate, make treaties, and, if necessary, use force. The problems and opportunities of westward expansion seemed always to demand more power and stronger government.

So far, Washington had met only disappointment. But his return trip had its rewards. He decided to head for home by a southern route up the Cheat River, a tributary of the Monongahela that cuts south into what is now West Virginia. From there he would cross the mountains to the upper reaches of the Potomac, looking for places to open connecting roads or canals between the two rivers. If such roads were possible, all the future produce of the Ohio Valley could come down the Potomac to Virginia instead of going north and east to New York or down the Ohio and Mississippi rivers to New Orleans. Virginia could become the commercial center of the new nation, taking trade away from Philadelphia, New York, and Boston.

Washington headed up the Cheat September 23. His trip took eleven days. Along the way he carefully noted every twist and turn of the rivers, every rapids, every stretch along which roads might be built or canals needed. The going was rough. The discomfort, however, was worth it, for Washington felt that he had found the key to the future of the West, of his own lands, of Virginia, and of the struggling economy of his young nation.

When Washington reached Mount Vernon on October 4, he went to work on a series of detailed reflections about his trip:

> *4th*: Reached home before sundown, having traveled on the same horses since the first day of September, by the computed distances, 680 miles.
>
> And, 'tho I was disappointed in one of the objects, namely to examine the land I hold on the Ohio and Kanawha, and rescuing them from the hands of land jobbers and speculators, I say notwithstanding this disappointment, I am well pleased with my journey.

Page after page in his diary he filled with his thoughts and calculations—detailed estimates of distance, of what rivers were navigable and how far, and where the lines of trade might eventually run.

He began with an analysis of river transportation in northern Virginia. All the rivers, taken as a network, could afford water transportation for all that fertile country between the Blue Ridge and the Allegheny Mountains. This filled Washington with proud confidence about the economic future of Virginia. But his thoughts ran well beyond the boundaries of his state, far to the west. The trade of western Virginia, great as it might become, was still "trifling, when viewed upon that immeasurable scale which is inviting our attention!"

Here was the key to the attitudes and actions of Washington—and many others like him—in the new nation. They had won independence. Now they were free to concentrate on the richest kinds of visions about the future of their country—especially on the possibilities of a new empire to the west. Part of Washington's mind may have been tied to Mount Vernon and plans for retirement. But he was also thinking of expansion.

Nor were his reflections vague and abstract. Washington rummaged among all the maps and papers in his possession and worked out in surprising detail a scheme for connecting the Ohio Valley to the Atlantic, preferably through Virginia—past his own great mansion, in fact—down the Potomac to Chesapeake Bay. Detroit, he calculated, would be the critical point in the Ohio Valley. It would control all the commerce of the

Great Lakes region—as far west, Washington figured, as the Lake of the Woods in northern Minnesota. According to Washington's estimates, the total distance from Detroit to Alexandria, Virginia, was only a little over 600 miles. The distances from Detroit to Philadelphia and New York were over 700 and 900 miles, respectively. So Virginia had the geographical advantage. It would not be Philadelphia, New York, or Boston that would become the economic and commercial capital of the republic. It would be Alexandria. (This city is just across the river from Washington, D.C. today—though Washington had no idea in 1784 that the District of Columbia would ever be created.)

All these calculations were of great importance for Washington. His mind ran in large and strategic channels:

> Hitherto, the people of the western country have had no excitements to industry; they labor very little. But let us open a good communication with the settlements west of us, and see how astonishingly our exports will be increased.

> No well-informed mind need be told that the flanks and rear of the united territory are possessed by other powers, and formidable ones too. It is necessary to apply the cement of interest to bind all the parts of the country together by one indissoluble band, particularly the Middle States and country back of them.

Washington had focused on a problem that would occupy him for a long time to come: how to apply the "cement" of economic interest—trade—to hold the nation together and make it powerful and stable. If the United States failed to achieve this unity, the West might very soon form a new nation and separate from the United States, or it might even fall into the hands of Spain or Great Britain.

As a result of this trip, Washington could see more clearly than before just how closely his own life was related to such large questions. His patriotism, which was intense and powerful, was not merely a notion or an ideal. It was also directly tied to his own stake in the future of the republic that he had done so much to bring into existence.

All these reflections led to a simple set of questions: Would Americans have the good sense to see how much was at stake and what had to be done? Would the governments of Virginia and the other states support projects to make the new commerce come to life? Would the central government be strong enough to maintain the unity of the nation and hold the West in line? The symbolic questions that had ridden with Washington from New York to Virginia in 1783 were gradually becoming more and more real.

For Washington himself, a chain of events had been set in motion that was to lead him eventually to join in overthrowing the existing government of the United States, creating a new constitution and government, and becoming the nation's first president. The chain led from the farmhouse confrontation with his Pennsylvania squatters in 1784 to the presidency five years later. One link in the chain was the observations he had made on the trip home. Another was his careful reflection on western trade. Now came the next link: an attempt to get Maryland and Virginia to cooperate in opening up the Potomac to trade.

⇥⊂⊃⇤

When Washington reached home in October 1784, he moved quickly from reflections on the West to practical action. He traveled to the new capital of Virginia at

Richmond to lobby for his Potomac project. It was clear that Maryland would have to cooperate, since the Potomac formed the border between the two states. So Washington was appointed commissioner to arrange for similar legislation in the two states.

It took him only three days to hurry to Maryland's capital, Annapolis, even though it meant missing his second Christmas at home since the war. Mount Vernon suddenly became a political clearinghouse. Washington was acting the politician in ways he had not practiced since he was a young man.

By the end of December everything was falling into place. Washington worked far past his usual nine o'clock bedtime on the project. As he wrote to his young friend James Madison on December 28, 1784: "It is now near 12 at night, and I am writing with an aching head, having been constantly employed in this business since the 22nd without assistance."

The "business" was complete by the first week in January. The legislatures of both Maryland and Virginia had appropriated money and joined in creating a joint-stock company to open up river transportation to the West. Washington was soon named president of the Potomac River Company, as it was called. Throughout the next two years he paid very close attention to its affairs. He fussed over the details of planning and surveying, and fretted when there were delays. He went about the project with such energy that Madison shrewdly observed, "The earnestness shows that a mind like his, capable of grand views, and which has long been occupied with them, cannot bear a vacancy."

Commissioners from Maryland and Virginia met several times, at least once at Mount Vernon itself. Then, in January 1786, just a year after the Potomac Company was formed, the Virginia legislature took a surprising step that would soon have even more surprising consequences: it suggested that delegates from all the states meet at Annapolis to discuss trade, taxes, and other matters of common concern. Such a meeting seemed innocent enough, but in fact it bypassed the existing national government completely. Washington thought carefully about the proposal. In many ways, it had grown directly out of his own work on the Potomac River Company. But the proposal raised large questions about the political future.

Washington was optimistic about the country. He wrote a French friend:

> The country is recovering rapidly from the ravages of war. The seeds of population are scattered far in the wilderness. Agriculture is prosecuted with industry. The works of peace, such as opening rivers, building bridges, etc., are carried on with spirit.

But despite the apparent prosperity, there was a problem of government, a problem that made Washington and many of his friends increasingly uneasy. During the Revolution the states had written a constitution, the Articles of Confederation, to bring a central government into being. This government was weak, Washington thought, too weak to fulfill his grand vision of empire. If the central government was weak, the states would constantly quarrel with one another. All during 1785, Washington's letters were filled with complaints:

> Contracted ideas and absurd jealousy are leading us from those great principles which are characteristic of wise and powerful nations, and without which we are no more than a rope of sand. The Confederation appears to me to be little more than a shadow without the substance. If we are afraid to trust one another, there is an end of the Union. We are

either a united people, or we are not. If we are not, let us no longer act a farce by pretending to it.

Because of these fears and doubts, Washington was intensely interested in the meeting at Annapolis, which was finally scheduled for September 1786. But the result of the meeting was only more anxiety. Only five states sent delegates. None at all came from New England. Here lay one source of Washington's frustrations. Out in the country, there was activity and opportunity. A great nation was waiting to be built, as it had waited in 1775 to be born. But the state governments, Washington felt, seemed to care nothing for the opportunity. Still, the few delegates who did come to Annapolis accomplished one thing. They recommended another meeting—a convention to begin in Philadelphia in May 1787—to consider what ought to be done to strengthen the Articles of Confederation.

Washington's reaction to the Annapolis Convention was a mixture of frustration and hope—frustration because more had not been accomplished, and hope for a more promising result in Philadelphia the following year. Other news soon burst in to trouble him further. An armed rebellion of some kind was under way in Massachusetts. Most of the rebels were farmers, who seemed to come mainly from the western part of the state. (They probably were men much like the squatters on Washington's Pennsylvania lands.) In September, bands of these men had kept courts from sitting in many sections of Massachusetts. Memories of 1776 crowded in on Washington. This time, however, it was an American government that was being threatened by mobs.

Friends sent Washington warped reports of the rebellion: It appeared to have a leader, a Revolutionary War captain named Daniel Shays. It was well organized and might even have foreign support (from old loyalists, perhaps). Shays and his followers believed in some kind of radical division of all private property. They wanted all debts canceled, all taxes abolished. They were threatening to raid the federal arsenal at Springfield. Then they planned to march on Boston and bring down the established government!

DANIEL SHAYS AND JOB SHATTUCK. This contemporary woodcut was part of a pamphlet published in 1787 that mocked Shays's Rebellion. The author gave Shays's rank as "General," and made Shattuck a "Colonel." The artist gives them uniforms, a flag, and artillery (none of which they had). The picture was accompanied by a poem saying, "Thro' drifted storms let SHAYS the Court assail / And Shattuck rise, illustrious from the Jail. / In coward Hands let legal Powers expire, / And give new subjects to my sounding Lyre."

These reports were wildly exaggerated, though Washington had no way of knowing it. Daniel Shays was not so much a leader of an organized movement as a surprised farmer who somehow found himself signing statements drawn up by the rebels. The farmers did not believe in abolishing private property, debts, or taxes. They were protesting more personal economic difficulties—namely, the seizure of their farms to pay their debts. The only time they threatened the Springfield arsenal, in January 1787, they were fired on by government cannon and ran away without returning a single shot. Once a body of the Massachusetts militia reached the Springfield area, it easily put the rebellion down without a real battle.

To Washington, however, and to most men of wealth all along the eastern coast, Shays's Rebellion was like a sudden thunderclap. Washington's informants were in near panic, and he shared their fears. The leaders of the revolutionary movement in the 1770s had always exaggerated the dangers of British actions, as though every new tax meant tyranny or slavery. Now Washington and many of his friends exaggerated the significance of Shays's Rebellion. A few hundred farmers turning out to close some country courts seemed to spell the eventual downfall of the whole federal republic.

On the last day of October, Washington sat at his writing table working on two long and important letters. The first was addressed to an organization of former Continental officers, the Society of the Cincinnati, of which he had been president for three years. They were scheduled to hold a general meeting and elect a president in May 1787 at Philadelphia. (The time and place were exactly those chosen for the new convention to revise the Articles of Confederation.) Washington's letter was a careful defense of his decision not to attend the meeting and not to serve again as president of the Society. He cited his heavy correspondence, his work on the Potomac Company, and problems with his health. All these increased his determination to pass the rest of his days in a state of retirement. More than anything else, the general said, he wanted tranquility and relaxation.

Washington's second letter was about Shays's Rebellion. It seemed to say that no matter how much he wanted retirement, Washington would not be able to stay away from politics:

> I am mortified beyond expression when I view the clouds that have spread over the brightest morn that ever dawned upon any country. You talk of employing influence to appease the present tumults in Massachusetts. Influence is no government. Let us have a government by which our lives, liberties and properties will be secured; or let us know the worst at once.
>
> These are my sentiments. Let the reins of government be braced and held with a steady hand. If the Constitution is defective, let it be amended, but not trampled upon whilst it has an existence.

Washington's canal project, and his hopes for the West, had made it clear to him that the Confederation had its problems. Shays's Rebellion pushed him over the line. To him, the rebellion proved that even in the older states the Confederation could not guarantee public order. How could such a weak government hope to make western expansion orderly and secure? Washington was now convinced that the Articles of Confederation were not workable. The central government was almost bankrupt, barely able to meet its current obligations. More important, it could not even begin to pay off the huge debts that Congress had run up while fighting the war—debts owed to foreign governments as well as to American citizens. And there was little hope that the debts would ever be paid, since the Articles did not give the central government the power to tax. It was very unlikely that this lack of taxing power would be remedied, either, since the Articles could be amended only with the agreement of every state.

※※※

There was another side to things, of course. Many people and political leaders believed that the problems of the Confederation could be solved in the course of time. They were confident that the West would be settled. They were equally sure that the roads and canals men like Washington dreamed of could be built. They knew that the sale of public lands would eventually bring in the money needed to pay off the debts. They were confident the governments of the states were strong enough to keep public order. (After all, Massachusetts had been able to handle Shays's Rebellion with ease.) People who thought this way believed that people's first loyalties belonged to their state and local governments, not to any national government, strong or weak. And there was always the possibility that a strengthened central government might turn out to behave like George III and his Parliament before the Revolution. Might not the liberties of the people depend on keeping power out of the hands of the national government?

Washington, however, thought otherwise. All his experience, his ambitions, and his interests conspired to convince him that nationalism was the solution. And if he had questions about America's future, many Americans had questions about his. He had more prestige than any man in America. No one else had anything like his reputation as a man of honor, good sense, and character. If he wanted a stronger national government, how could he hold back from sharing in the movement to abandon the old constitution and write a new one?

The Virginia legislature nominated Washington as a delegate to the Philadelphia convention. Some of his most faithful young followers, among them James Madison and Alexander Hamilton, kept urging him to join the movement. Others advised him to hold back, not to risk his flawless reputation on a venture that might prove an embarrassing failure. Month after month, Washington made excuses. Some were valid. He did have an aching rheumatism that forced him to go around the Mount Vernon farms with one arm in a sling. There were deaths in the family, financial troubles, and even a brief quarrel by letter with his mother. All these things reminded him that his life was full enough without involving himself in the creation of a new constitution.

In the end, though, Washington had no choice. The pressure from his friends was too powerful. His fears for his country were too strong. And, in the last analysis, he wanted to be part of a great event, to stand somewhere near the center of activity. In his letters of the spring, Washington referred often to his reputation. He was as close to being openly vain as he had been in twenty years. It may have been this vanity that provided the final tiny weight needed to tip the balance toward Philadelphia and away from Mount Vernon—though his rheumatism was better, too.

Philadelphia was miserable in May. It rained day after day. Most of the delegates were late in arriving. On the day the convention was set to open, only Virginia and Pennsylvania were represented. Gradually, enough delegates drifted into town to conduct business. To no one's surprise, Washington was unanimously elected president of the convention. Week after week he sat in the chair, presiding over the secret discussions, listening and wondering whether or not a new government could be created. Would the people accept this new Constitution? Would it work?

When the sections of the Constitution outlining the powers of the new office of president of the United States were being discussed, Washington must have listened with special care. Not a man in the room doubted that the office would belong to him if he would have it.

During the whole convention, Washington made only one speech. He had a talent for knowing when to be quiet and follow the lead of others who were quicker with words and ideas than he could ever be. Washington was always alert. He could follow a point in political theory or philosophy very well, but he made few points of his own. If he was a leader in Philadelphia, it was because other people trusted in his character, not because he led the way toward the new frame of government.

After the new Constitution had been created, Washington hoped for its ratification. Once more he did not actually lead. Younger men with more interesting minds—

THE FIRST INAUGURATION. This engraving is the only contemporary depiction of Washington's inauguration as president in New York, April 30, 1789. The artist, Peter Lacour, has paid more attention to the building than to the people, as though he were anxious to emphasize its grandeur. It had been renovated by Pierre Charles L'Enfant (who later designed the national capital). The image is dominated by the heraldic symbol of the eagle, above the clouds, with a sunburst behind, and holding the arrows of war in one claw and the olive branch of peace in the other. The capital would eventually move to the District of Columbia. But this view is from Wall Street, which would later be the center for a different kind of capital.

especially men like Madison and Hamilton—carried the burden of trying to explain the Constitution to an extremely suspicious public.

After a precarious struggle, the new Constitution was accepted by the required number of states. The Articles of Confederation were set aside. A presidential election was held, and Washington was, almost inevitably, given all the electoral votes.

The new president left Mount Vernon for New York City (which was the first capital of the United States) in mid-April 1789. From town to town—Alexandria, Wilmington, Philadelphia, Princeton—the citizens and the militia turned out for triumphant ceremonies. The trip took seven days. Finally, on April 23, Washington took a barge across the Hudson to Manhattan. There were more salutes, bells, and cheers as he reentered the city he had left six years before from Fraunces Tavern. A week later, Washington was inaugurated on an open balcony that looked down on a crowd in Wall Street. The judge who administered the oath turned to the cheering crowd and shouted, "Long live George Washington, President of the United States!"

The Making of the American Constitution

In 1799, ten years after taking his first oath as president, George Washington died. It was the middle of December, cold and wet, but he was back home at Mount Vernon. For eight years he had served as first president of the new republic, and then had come a brief and final period of retirement. Washington's health had been good almost to the end, and he died gently. "I am just going," he said to a friend. "Have me decently buried and do not let my body be put into a vault in less than two days after I am dead. Do you understand me?" "Yes, sir," answered the friend. "'Tis well," said Washington, and soon he was dead. His body had to be measured for a coffin, and the doctor recorded that he was "in length, six feet, three-and-one-half inches, exact."

Washington's height, which was unusual in a day when most men were much shorter than they are today, was in keeping with the gigantic reputation he had acquired. There have been times, during his lifetime and the centuries since, when he seemed more than human, when he seemed to rise above his surroundings just as his enormous monument does today. And Washington's last statement, "'Tis well," says a good deal about the kind of philosophical calm he seems to have won for himself during the long, difficult period between the Revolution and his death. About a month before he died, Washington heard from a friend about recent political troubles in the nation's capital. He would say nothing, Washington replied, because "the vessel is afloat, or very nearly so, and considering myself as a passenger only, I shall trust to the mariners whose duty it is to watch, to steer it into a safe port."

Washington had come a long way since he took command of the straggling little army outside Boston in 1775. Now, at the end of the century, the vessel was afloat. The Revolution had been won, difficult times had been endured, and the country had a government that looked promising. Washington had survived two presidential terms. John Adams, the second president, was now completing his term. The next year, the first year of the new century, a third president would be chosen. There had been two constitutions. There had been times when war with Britain, France, or Spain looked inevitable. But somehow the vessel had stayed afloat. And the man who had piloted it in the turbulent quarter-century was indeed entitled to congratulations at the end.

It had not been easy. At times it had seemed impossible. Every single year of the twenty-five years between Lexington and Washington's death had held out hope and fear. Washington and his political colleagues had acquired what amounted to a habit—hoping for the best and fearing the worst at the same time.

There had been plenty to fear. The Revolution might be lost, and its leaders might, as Franklin had joked, "hang separately." Or the Americans might win the Revolution only to lose their country. They might not be able to create a stable national government to hold the old colonies together. Or the new nation might be carved up by hungry European powers, just as all of North America had earlier been divided among several empires. Many people believed that they were living at a moment of profound historic significance. They thought they had a chance to create a nation built on the principle of liberty. They dreamed of a West where they might expand to fill half the huge continent that they thought of as "empty"—except for the Native Americans, who could surely be crushed and swept aside, as they had been for almost two centuries. They dreamed, too, of a new, more innocent world where the ancient tyrannies and corruptions of the Old World might be cast away. A new kind of nation, a republic, might be brought forth, whose people would be citizens and not subjects. There were even many Americans—some who had European roots, and some whose origins were African—who hoped that something might be done about the institution of slavery.

In the minds of most Americans who thought about their national future, the fears and the dreams were mingled. This mixture of anxiety and hope was the backdrop against which a critical period of history was acted out. There seemed to be only one real certainty in Washington's mind and in the minds of other citizens: The fate of America was being decided in the years after 1775. Some held an even more extravagant opinion: that it was not just the fate of America but the fate of humanity that somehow hung in the balance.

Debate about such matters was a major pastime of an entire generation during and after the Revolution. Gradually, in Congress, state legislatures, and the conventions at Annapolis and Philadelphia, debates grew more and more skillful. Painfully, voting Americans piled up experience in political theory. Their leaders became as sophisticated and adept as any generation of politicians in any nation's history. The questions were simple and classic: What form of government best preserves the liberties of its citizens? Can a national government exist without destroying individual states? How are powers to be divided among legislative bodies, executive officers, and courts? What is the relationship between a national constitution and the laws of the states?

The real problems may have been practical ones, such as Washington's problem with his western lands. But American political leaders had earned a generation's experience at translating practical problems into political theory and then retranslating the theory into practice through constitutions, treaties, and legislation. If Washington could relax somewhat at the end, it was because he and his generation of Americans had survived a revolutionary quarter-century with an astonishing mixture of stubbornness, skill, and plain luck.

THE CONFEDERATION PERIOD

The First and Second Continental Congresses were revolutionary governing bodies. They had no real legal standing. To the British, especially, they were little more than illegitimate collections of outlaws and traitors. But they were engaged in an act of frightening significance: creating a government where none had existed before. They exercised powers, such as making war, that usually belong only to established, or "legitimate," governments. Even before the Declaration of Independence was drawn up, the Second Continental Congress appointed a committee to draft a new constitution in order to give the government at least an appearance of legitimacy. The Congress debated the draft constitution until November 1777, when it agreed on the new Articles of Confederation, which would have to be approved by all thirteen of the states before it took effect.

In the meantime, the revolutionary government, the Continental Congress, simply kept on exercising power the way it had from the beginning. The arrangement was far from democratic, and a bit contradictory for people who were making war on the principle that governments are based on the consent of the governed. The Congress had no direct consent from the people, who had never voted to make a revolution in the first place. But there was a war on, and politics had to be adjusted to the shifting realities of the struggle. At last, in the spring of 1781, Maryland, the last state, finally ratified the Articles of Confederation. A new government had finally been officially created, bearing the name The United States of America.

GOVERNMENT UNDER THE ARTICLES

In most ways the new Articles simply confirmed the practices of the old Congress. The Constitution created a confederation of states, each of which was to retain its sovereignty, freedom, and independence. The states were the real political entities. The United States was, in the words of the Articles, "a league of friendship." The legislatures of the states would send delegates to the Congress, where each state would have one vote, regardless of its population. Small states such as Rhode Island and Delaware had as much legislative power as large states such as Virginia and Massachusetts. A state might choose to send as few as two delegates to the Congress or as many as seven. No matter how many delegates it sent, however, each state had its single vote.

The Congress had some of the powers that normally belong to "sovereign" states. It could declare war and raise an army and a navy. It could borrow money. It could coin money, issue paper currency, and operate a post office. It could send and receive ambassadors and negotiate treaties with foreign nations. In essence, the states gave the Congress the power to do all the things they had admitted the British government could do before the Revolution.

But the states kept for themselves powers they had refused to allow the king and Parliament: most importantly, regulating commerce and raising money through taxes. The Congress could not control the conditions of trade among the states or with foreign nations. And when the United States needed money—as every government does—it had to ask the states for it in a request called a "requisition." If a state did not pay its requisition, the Congress was powerless to force the issue.

The Confederation had been born in the midst of a revolution against the central authority of Parliament and the Crown. Most politically active Americans did not want to create a new central government that might subvert their "liberties" the way many Americans felt the British had tried to do. To the average American, his or her "country" still meant Virginia or Pennsylvania or Massachusetts. So Americans were ready to face the peace with the same kind of government that had conducted the war. This meant a government of states. They would work together to solve problems after they arose, but not before.

There was no permanent federal judiciary under the Articles and no supreme court to make final decisions about constitutional questions. The Congress had the power to settle disputes among states. This power was to work through a complicated system of arbitration, however, not through a national court. The state courts were expected to enforce federal law at the local level. There was no executive, either, although the Articles did provide for a number of secretaries who might eventually develop into a cabinet system like that of the British.

Obviously, there could be no separation of powers among legislative, judicial, and executive branches under the Articles. The colonists had long been familiar with the idea of separation of powers, for they had had ample experience in the conflicts between colonial governors and assemblies. All the new state constitutions had elaborate schemes of checks and balances—that is, the executive, legislative, and judicial departments were separated in function but balanced in power. At this time, though, the states thought of the Confederation as an instrument to be used only for certain very limited purposes.

Even the limited powers of the Congress were difficult to exercise. On all important questions, nine votes out of thirteen were necessary for passage of a bill. This meant a few small states could block any piece of legislation. It was almost impossible to amend the Articles. An amendment had to have the consent of every state. It was obvious that new states would eventually be admitted to the Confederation, which would make amendments even more difficult to ratify.

The Confederation did have one excellent possibility of making itself financially independent of the states. An energetic group of nationalists, led by Robert Morris, James Madison, and Alexander Hamilton, proposed in 1781 that the Articles be amended to give the Congress the power to put a five percent duty, or "impost," on imports. If it went into effect, the impost would easily pay off the Confederation's debts. But although twelve states were willing to approve the amendment, the approval had to be unanimous. So when Rhode Island rejected the proposed impost, it died. Morris and his supporters tried again in 1783, just as the peace treaty with Britain was ratified. General Washington himself published a passionate plea for the ratification of the impost. But this time the state governments were less willing to go along than they had been two years before. Again the impost failed. Morris quit politics. A dejected Madison retired to Virginia, to study the "defects" of the Confederation and to await the chance to change it. Hamilton, too, gave up on the Confederation and waited for better days.

ACHIEVEMENTS UNDER THE ARTICLES

Political leaders and historians have often dismissed the Articles of Confederation as a weak and ineffectual frame of government. After all, from Maryland's ratification in 1781 to the Philadelphia convention, the Articles lasted only six years. And, in retrospect, it seems obvious that the Articles had so many flaws that a new constitution was almost inevitable.

But when the question is put into proper perspective, and when the partisan opinions of victorious nationalists like Washington are set aside, it is equally obvious that the confederation system managed some remarkable achievements. For one thing, the Confederation was not actually born in 1781 but in 1775, with the Second Continental Congress. This means Americans were able, within the framework of a confederation, to declare their independence and conduct the war. They made a major alliance with France and wrote a treaty of peace with Britain. For a dozen violent and eventful years, internal peace and a reasonable level of cooperation among the states were maintained.

Most important of all, the Confederation was able to take control of the vast territory between the Appalachians and the Mississippi and to provide for orderly settlement and government there. In a series of laws, climaxed by the Ordinance of 1787—the Northwest Ordinance—the Congress established the basic set of rules under which new land could be organized into territories and finally become new states. A clear-cut survey system was created. Land in the territories—one thirty-sixth of the whole—was set aside for the support of a public school system. A General Land Office was formed to sell the remaining land. Finally, in what may have been its most significant action, the Congress prohibited slavery in the Northwest Territory—the area that eventually became the states of Ohio, Indiana, Michigan, Illinois, and Wisconsin.

Any assessment of the Articles of Confederation must take into account the fact that they were a product of history, not just of abstract political theory. For almost two centuries, each of the colonies had strained for a larger and larger degree of independence. Only when there was trouble—war with France, or with Native Americans, or with Britain—did the colonies admit their dependence on each other or on a central government. All this experience taught the same lesson: The real, day-to-day business of governing was a matter for the individual states.

Within the states, in fact, political leaders displayed great legislative and constitutional skill. Between 1776 and 1780, with no real help from the Congress, eleven of the thirteen states wrote new constitutions. (Rhode Island and Connecticut kept their old colonial charters with a few

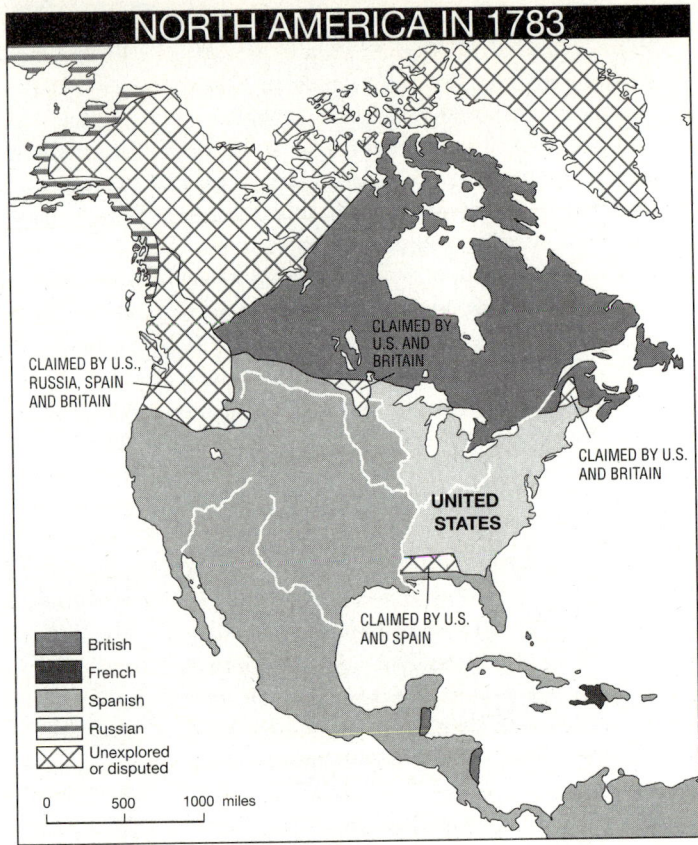

changes.) The methods varied from state to state, but some common characteristics emerged in all the constitutions. The powers of government were divided among executive, legislative, and judicial branches. Most of the new constitutions severely limited the authority of the governors, who were typically elected annually and could serve only one term. This was an echo of decades of contention with powerful and semipermanent royal governors.

The state constitutions also reflected the revolutionary preoccupation with "liberty" and the "consent of the governed." Explicit limits were placed on the powers of government. The rights of citizens were spelled out, sometimes in the constitutions themselves, and sometimes in separate "bills" of rights. The consent of "the people"—white, male property owners, at least—was recognized as the only ultimate source of governmental authority. But property qualifications for voting were kept, and women and blacks, slave or free, were systematically excluded from voting. (The only exception came in New Jersey, where a clause in the state's 1776 constitution provided that "all free inhabitants" could vote if they owned a certain amount of property. This allowed some women and free blacks to vote. This may or may not have been a political accident, but what certainly was not accidental was that the state stuck with its "mistake" for almost thirty years, not so much out of concern for the rights of women and African-Americans as for the political rights of property owners.)

In a number of the states, progress was even made in paying off the debts left over from the Revolution. By the time of the Philadelphia convention, Virginia, Maryland, North Carolina, and Georgia had repaid almost all of their state debts.

All in all, then—despite the restless impatience of critics like Washington—the Confederation period was one of rather spectacular accomplishment, both at the national level and within the states. A revolution had been won, and some of its principal results had been written into constitutions and laws. And all this had been gained despite almost overwhelming odds. Men like Washington might be shocked and frightened by something like Shays's Rebellion, but any partisan of the Confederation could point to the other side of the coin: the rebellion had been brief, and Massachusetts was able to restore order without the help of any powerful central government.

FIVE MAJOR PROBLEMS OF THE CONFEDERATION

The Articles of Confederation created a government that was equal to its immediate tasks, but there were other problems and opportunities that the Confederation could not handle efficiently. These were the problems and opportunities that had disturbed or excited Washington and many of his fellow participants in the Revolution—especially younger figures like Madison and Hamilton.

The first, and in a way the most severe, problem was public finance. During the Revolution, the Continental Congress had issued mountains of paper money. This paper currency was really a debt. It amounted to a vast number of promises by the government to pay off, at some future time and in "real" money, the dollar value of each bill. The states followed the same practice, so the country was flooded with paper money of all types. The real value of this paper money depended on the hope that the national or state government would eventually be able to pay off all or part of the debt.

The Congress simply could not meet its obligations. This meant the paper money of the United States was practically worthless. In 1783 and 1784 a United States dollar could buy about fifteen cents' worth of goods. The government was nearly bankrupt. There was no effective national currency in circulation. The states paid only about one-sixth of the requisitions made by the Congress. They were trying to pay off their own individual debts by buying back state-issued paper money. The result was a shortage of both money and credit. People found it difficult to conduct ordinary business.

Only a stronger government, with the power to raise money through taxes, could solve this problem. It was this realization, as much as any other, that moved political leaders in the various states to think of revising the Articles. The movement that led to the Annapolis convention, the Philadelphia convention, and eventually to a new government was fed by fear of financial anarchy and bankruptcy.

A second problem involved commerce. Under the Articles, the states were free to make most of their own trade regulations, both with foreign nations and with other states. Foreign trade, always extremely important in the American economy, depended, of course, on relations with foreign nations. The Revolution had not altered the basic economic relationship between America and Europe. Europe was still the principal market and manufacturing center. But the Revolution had removed the British government from the picture. Now the Americans were free from British restrictions—but they were also "free" from British protection.

Sensing American weakness at the national level, the British put restrictions on American trade that were more severe than those of the old colonial system. For example, they barred American ships from other British colonies in the New World, closing what had been some of the most important West Indian destinations of American shipping before the Revolution. Old patterns of trade were completely broken. New avenues of direct trade with nations like France and Spain did not take up the slack fast enough.

To those concerned about the nation's future, it seemed clear that the national government would have to be made strong enough to write new treaties of commerce with European nations, particularly with Britain. Otherwise, Americans would be ruined. They depended on European markets to sell their tobacco and other agricultural products. And they had to be able to buy European manufactured goods on a reasonable basis in order to survive.

A third difficulty was political stability. This was what people like Washington wanted most of all. If stability could be achieved, then Americans could seize the opportunities open to a new nation. The western lands furnished an important example. A stable political situation would allow people to move west, create new states, grow more crops, and import new quantities of manufactured goods. In doing so, they would be building a great new empire. But if stability was not gained, the British might try to hold onto their military posts in the Ohio Valley (which they did). The Spanish might try to break up American control of the Southwest by closing the Mississippi to American traffic (which they did). Frontier settlers might feel little loyalty to the nation and might even refuse to pay debts and to recognize eastern law and control (which they did).

Still another troublesome problem was the possibility of quarrels among individual states or different geographic regions of the country. Boundary quarrels had produced scattered armed conflicts between citizens of different states. Almost any law or treaty would have different effects on the North and the South, since one section depended heavily on commerce and the other was almost purely agricultural. Unless the states surrendered their sovereignty, sooner or later some issue would cause the nation to fly apart into competing regions.

Within the individual states, too, there were potential conflicts among groups that could tear state governments apart. Washington felt that Shays's Rebellion was frightening. It was even more frightening as an indication of what might happen in other states. There might be disputes between western farmers and eastern merchants or between religious groups or between political factions. If the country was to survive, it seemed essential to create a national government with enough power to settle problems among and within states.

Added to all these issues, in the minds of many political leaders, was what might be called the "problem" of democracy. The leaders of the Revolution were not democratic in the modern sense. That is, they did not believe everyone should participate directly in government. All the states had some kind of property or tax-paying qualification for voting. Only people with an economic stake in society could take part in government (and of these, only free white males almost everywhere). All the states had complicated barriers to popular control of any branch of the government. The political theory held by almost all the Founding Fathers taught that the people were sovereign only in an abstract sense; individuals were "equal," but only in theory. In practice, even political leaders dedicated to a republican form of government believed government ought to be in the hands of men of education and property.

In almost every state, however, there was a political faction that wanted more democracy—a broader suffrage, lower property qualifications for voting or office holding, more frequent elections, shorter terms of office for leaders. Such factions demanded laws that would protect debtors from their creditors. They tried to get the states to print more, not less, paper money. With more and cheaper money farmers could pay off their debts to bankers and merchants. These factions demanded equal representation in the legislatures for the farming areas outside cities like New York, Boston, and Philadelphia. They talked, in other words, of what Washington would have scorned as "democratical" government. To Washington—and to most of the wealthy, educated leaders who came from the eastern seaboard—such talk could lead only to anarchy. The inherent danger in the Articles was that in any given state a democratic faction might get control of the government. If this happened, there would be no national power to intervene in behalf of the state's "republican" government. There would be no national constitution forbidding the states to abolish debts, private property, or political privilege.

During the few years between the peace of 1783 and the Philadelphia convention, all these problems, domestic and foreign, gradually came together. The concerns might differ from person to person. John Adams might fear democracy more than Thomas Jefferson. Washington might be more concerned with western lands than Alexander Hamilton, whose principal worry was public finance. But sooner or later, in much the same way the revolutionary movement had built up in the colonies, the movement to revise or repudiate the Articles of Confederation grew. People in one state corresponded with their friends and relatives in another. Soon most of those who had led the Revolution were involved in a movement to make a second, peaceful revolution. They would throw off their government, just as they had done in 1776, and replace it with another.

Washington's interests, plans, and fears led him to Philadelphia in exactly the same way that dozens of other people were led by their interests, plans, and fears. Most of the delegates went to Philadelphia sharing the conviction that something had to be done. The Articles had to be drastically altered or else thrown out. If the Articles could have been amended more easily, the Philadelphia convention might well have simply changed them, leaving the government basically intact. But the delegates decided to start afresh, to draw on the experience of making state constitutions, and to build a new United States.

THE PHILADELPHIA CONVENTION

The fifty-five delegates who straggled into Philadelphia in the summer of 1787 were an extremely interesting group of politicians. As statesmen go, they were young. More were under thirty than over sixty. Together they represented an enormous amount of experience—in war, in the Congress, on foreign missions, and in state governments. Thirty-one had college educations—at a time when many people could not read, and only a tiny fraction of the population went to school for more than a few years. In fact, every delegate who actually spoke in the convention had attended college. Most of them were wealthy men, and they were more interested in maintaining social order than they were in social or political experiments. They were, in short, a political, economic, and social elite.

Perhaps the most interesting fact about the convention was that almost all its delegates had decided the main question before coming to Philadelphia. They were already committed to chartering a new and truly national government to replace the Confederation. Before the first hour of debate in the hot hall where they met, most of them had agreed on another point: their essential goal was to create a government that would operate directly on citizens of the United States, rather than on the states, as the old Congress had done. Since this goal was more or less taken for granted, the real questions involved practical methods, not constitutional theory. How would the interests of the small states and large states be reconciled? How would power be divided among various branches of government? How would the question of slavery be handled, or would it even be taken up? What sort of presidency would they create? What kind of court system?

For all its importance in American history, the Constitutional Convention spent much of its time in what might be called tinkering. The delegates' work was a kind of political carpentry, in which they arranged and rearranged parts to satisfy the most people.

All the tinkering had one principal objective. Delegates wanted to create a political structure that would not alarm the people, who were very much afraid of strong central government. They also wanted to avoid putting any particular state or geographic section of the country at a disadvantage. The Founding Fathers needed a consensus, a common acceptance of what they brought forth from their secret debates and discussions.

WASHINGTON PRESIDING. This rather crude contemporary engraving shows Washington and the delegates to the Constitutional Convention in Philadelphia. The artist has contrived the scene in a way that suggests Washington was much more active than he actually was. He is shown standing, though he usually sat. He is shown with parchment in one hand, and in the other the longest quill pen in sight, as though he were literally writing a constitution himself.

THE VIRGINIA AND NEW JERSEY PLANS

The convention spent much of its time discussing the virtues and faults of two different plans. The first, called the Virginia Plan (drafted by Virginian James Madison), would have allocated votes in the new national legislature on the basis of population. Virginia or Massachusetts, for example, would have had many more representatives than Rhode Island or Delaware. The second plan, the New Jersey Plan (proposed by delegate William Paterson of New Jersey), would have continued the system used in the Articles, giving each state the same number of votes.

There were several other important differences between the Virginia and New Jersey plans.

The Virginia Plan provided for an executive with a veto power over acts of Congress. In other words, it proposed creating a strong executive, with power balancing that of the legislature. The New Jersey Plan proposed an executive branch, too, but it would have been composed of several people elected by the legislature, like a cabinet, and it would have no veto power.

Both plans provided for a national judiciary, separated from and working in balance with the executive and the legislature. But there was an important difference. The Virginia Plan called for both a national supreme court and other, lower federal courts. The New Jersey Plan, in contrast, provided for a supreme court only.

Under this plan, therefore, the national court in most cases could act only on appeals from the state courts.

Though there were some exceptions, generally the delegates from the small states supported the New Jersey proposal, while those from large states favored the Virginia Plan. The reasons were obvious. The Virginia Plan would give the large states almost complete control of the national government. The New Jersey Plan would have made the states equal in Congress; it would have made Congress much more powerful than the other branches of government. No great principles of "liberty" or "democracy" were involved in this conflict. The issue was simple and practical. How could the new constitution be adjusted to give equal protection to the interests of both the large and the small states?

THE NEW CONSTITUTION

Out of the debate over the Virginia and New Jersey plans came a series of compromises, sometimes known as the Great Compromise. As with many compromises, the solution to the main problem was really very simple. The delegates fell back on their long experience with colonial and state legislatures. They devised a Congress that would consist of two houses. The "upper" house, which they named the Senate, would have equal representation, with each state sending two senators. In the "lower" house, the House of Representatives, representation would be by districts, apportioned according to population.

The Senate was essentially the kind of legislature proposed in the New Jersey Plan. It protected the interests of the small states. In fact, the convention provided that this feature of the Constitution could never be amended unless every state consented to have the number of its senators reduced. The House of Representatives, on the other hand, was a reflection of the large-state bias of the Virginia Plan.

There was, though, a nagging problem. Just how was population to be counted? Specifically, how were slaves to be counted? It was clear that they would not be able to vote, but should they be included in the census counts that would serve as the basis for representation in the House of Representatives? The delegates from states where slavery was common and important argued for including slaves in the political "population." Delegates from other states wanted to exclude them altogether. But even this disagreement produced no serious discussion of slavery in principle, or of the relationship between citizenship and representation. Instead the delegates worked out another simple and practical compromise. They simply fell back on a practice of the Confederation period, when Congress had apportioned its "requisitions" for funding according to the populations of the states. In this apportionment, each slave had been counted as three-fifths of a person. So the framers used this formula for determining how many representatives each state would be entitled to.

POWERS OF THE FEDERAL GOVERNMENT

Some of the powers given to the new Congress were about the same as those exercised by the old Congress under the Articles. Congress could declare war, coin and borrow money, and establish a post office. But two important new powers were added, powers whose absence had crippled the old Congress. The new Congress could raise revenues through taxation, and regulate commerce with foreign nations and among the states. And the new Congress was also authorized to make all the laws that might be "necessary and proper" to execute the powers that the Constitution gave the national government.

The Constitution also included a list of things Congress could not do. It could not pass a law that suspended the right of habeas corpus— the right of a person under arrest to a speedy hearing in a court of law. Congress could not tax exports—a protection that affected the southern states in particular. It could not pass any commercial regulations that favored one state over another. It could not grant any "titles of nobility."

And Congress could not regulate or interfere in any way with the slave trade before 1808.

A more significant revision of the old Articles was the creation of an executive branch, independent of Congress and on an equal footing with it. The chief executive would be called the president. (Everyone at the Convention assumed, as they drew up the article on executive powers, that the first president would be Washington.) The president's principal duty was to execute the laws passed by Congress, but he was also given some of the powers that the British king exercised: being commander in chief of the armed forces, for example, and conducting foreign policy.

The Constitution also provided for a judicial branch. There would be a Supreme Court with final power to enforce federal laws and interpret the Constitution whenever legal questions arose. In addition, Congress had the power to create other federal courts to ensure that federal law and the Constitution remained what the Constitution said they should be—the supreme law of the land.

CHECKS AND BALANCES

Among these three branches of the new government, there was to be a complicated system of relationships. Each branch was to have some independence from the others. That is, there was to be a separation of powers. The judges of the federal courts would serve for life. This would presumably make them independent. The president would owe his office to no other branch of the federal government but to the members of a complicated "electoral college." Senators would be chosen by state legislatures. Only members of the House of Representatives would be elected by their constituents. All the officers of the new government, in other words, would have separate bases of power and support.

These separations were far from complete, however. Judges were to be nominated by the president and approved by two-thirds of the Senate. They could be removed from office by Congress, through a process of impeachment. Nor was the presidency altogether separate. Obviously, presidential programs of almost every type would eventually require money. Funds would have to be voted by Congress. Also, presidential appointees, such as ambassadors or cabinet officers, would have to be approved by the Senate. Finally, as a last resort, Congress could remove a president from office through impeachment.

Despite the creation of the executive and judicial branches, the framers' minds were still dominated by their own experience. The legislature was, for most of them, still the basic, lawmaking centerpiece of the new government—as it had been in the states and in the Confederation. But the powers of Congress were subjected to new checks. The president was given the power to veto any law unless a two-thirds majority in both houses of Congress overturned a veto. The members of the convention assumed in their debates that the courts, especially the Supreme Court, would have the power to declare any act of Congress unconstitutional. (In the end, the Constitution did not explicitly give the courts this right, and a good deal of argument was to take place on the question of whether the courts actually had this ultimate power. In practice, however, no Congress and no president ever defied a Supreme Court ruling—at least not for long.) Still, within the constitutional limits of its powers, a two-thirds majority in Congress was given about as much freedom of action as Parliament had ever had in England.

In these and other ways, the powers of government were separate yet interdependent through a system of checks and balances. The idea behind this system was that no part of the government ought to become powerful enough to override the other branches or violate the Constitution. At any one time a strong president, a runaway Congress, or a determined Supreme Court might take the initiative on a policy question. But the other two branches would always be watching carefully—at least in theory. Each would thus protect its own powers and defend the basic structure of government as laid down in the Constitution.

Another division of powers was established between the states and the national government. The Constitution created a federal system of government. But the delegates did not attempt to solve any philosophical doubts about what federalism amounted to in the abstract. Rather, they maintained a discreet silence on some theoretical questions, and relied on specific provisions to settle practical questions that could not be avoided. Unlike the Articles of Confederation, the new Constitution said nothing about the "sovereignty" of the states. But it also refrained from using that powerful term to describe the national government. Nothing was said, one way or the other, about the right of a state to secede from the union.

But the Constitution did limit the powers that the national government could exercise. The states were guaranteed a degree of practical protection by retaining control over the processes of electing senators, congressmen, and the president. And the Constitution could not be amended without the consent of three-fourths of the states.

On the other hand, state courts were "bound" by the laws of the United States, which were declared to be the "supreme law of the land." States were forbidden to do some very important things. They could not engage in acts of war, or make treaties or agreements with other states or foreign governments; foreign policy was to be the exclusive domain of the national government. Like the national government, states were prohibited from granting titles of nobility. More importantly, they were prohibited from coining their own money or issuing paper money. They also were not to do anything that would "impair the obligation of contract." This provision meant that once private citizens or companies made agreements, the state could not alter the terms of the agreement in a way that benefited or damaged either party. (This provision was an echo of Shays's Rebellion, and of similar movements in other states to have governments pass laws for the "relief" of debtors.) Such provisions put fairly strict limits on what any state might do to try to significantly alter existing property relationships, even if a "democratical" faction got control of its legislature.

ATTITUDES TOWARD DEMOCRACY

The Constitution that came out of Philadelphia contained few guarantees of individual liberties. The right of habeas corpus was protected. The federal government—but not the states—was forbidden to set up any religious qualifications for holding office. Except for these provisions and one or two others, the Constitution was remarkably silent about the great question of liberty, the question that had rung out so loudly and clearly during the Revolution.

As for democracy, the Constitution had practically nothing to say. Only one group of officials in the new government would be elected by the voters directly: members of the House of Representatives. Even in this case the states were given complete control of qualifications for voting—which might include restrictions based on sex, age, religion, literacy, race, or the ownership of property. And those who were allowed to vote could express a direct choice only for members of the House of Representatives. Senators were to be chosen by the state legislatures. The president would be selected by an "electoral college." Justices of the Supreme Court and other federal judges would be appointed by the president (who had been chosen not by voters but by "electors"). Then judges would be confirmed by the Senate (chosen by state legislators).

Almost every member of the convention would have agreed that these provisions were much better than direct popular election. The people might rule in theory, but they would be allowed to rule only at a distance and through machinery complicated enough to slow down or stop any movement toward popular democracy at the national level. Furthermore, the federal government guaranteed each state a "republican" form of government. This protected the states from any attempt to establish monarchical governments. But it also meant that any move toward "anarchy"—like Shays's Rebellion—could be met by federal force.

Was there, then, no genius to the Constitution? Was it nothing more than political tinkering resulting from a desire to protect order from the "democratical" elements in society? Many of the delegates would probably have answered yes. They were practical, hard-bitten men who had been burned more than once by popular movements that threatened to get out of hand.

But for a few others, notably Madison, there was another aspect to the Constitution that not many people noticed at the time. The opening words of the document are "We the People." This Constitution, unlike the Articles and many of the state constitutions, would rest, in some sense or other, on the popular will. And it would operate directly on the people, with minimal intervention of state power. The new government could tax individual citizens. It could try them in its own courts under its own laws. The federal courts might even declare state or local laws unconstitutional—though this possibility was hardly discussed at all in Philadelphia. Finally (the most inspired maneuver of all), the Constitution would be ratified by specially chosen conventions in the states, not by the state legislatures. Thus the new government would be created, in principle at least, not by the states but by "the People."

THE STRUGGLE FOR RATIFICATION

The new Constitution was drafted and approved by a majority of delegates by mid-September. At this point, the delegates at Philadelphia must have felt somewhat uneasy. They had been told by their state legislatures and by the Congress to amend the Articles of Confederation. But they had scarcely considered this as a possibility. Instead, they had created a new government. They had held secret debates about a scheme that amounted to a coup d'état—though a quiet and cautious one. They knew they had only a slender chance of getting all the states to accept the new government, at least not for several years. So they proposed a radical idea: the new Constitution would go into effect as soon as nine state conventions had accepted it.

The proponents of the Constitution had some important advantages. For one thing, almost everyone agreed that *something* had to be done about the Articles. Another advantage was the prestige of men like Washington and Franklin. A third was the method of ratification. The state legislatures might have rejected the document in order to preserve their own powers, but a series of state conventions elected for the specific purpose of judging the plan would give it a better chance of adoption. As for the document itself, delegates argued that their complicated structure of checks and balances left little to fear from the new central government.

Despite all these advantages, ratification was an uphill fight. A shrewd observer of American politics in 1787 would probably have predicted that the Constitution would be rejected. There was opposition in the Congress. Why, some of its members argued, should that body roll over and play dead? Some members of the Constitutional Convention itself, alarmed by the final result, had refused to sign the document and were ready to mount opposition. Finally, there were the old traditional state loyalties to overcome. The Constitution, much more than the patriot leaders of the Revolution, much more than the Articles, asked people to think of themselves as Americans, not solely as citizens of a state.

Generally, those who favored the Constitution were more aggressive than its opponents. They were richer and better educated. They controlled almost all the nation's newspapers. They wrote more, spoke more, and lobbied more. Three young men—Madison, Hamilton, and John Jay of New York—produced a remarkable

ALEXANDER HAMILTON. One of the great leaders of the Federalist cause, and secretary of the treasury under the new government, was Alexander Hamilton. He was the author of more than half the essays in *The Federalist*. At the Constitutional Convention, Hamilton argued for an overwhelmingly powerful executive.

series of newspaper essays in favor of the Constitution. (The essays were later published as a book, *The Federalist*, and have become so much a part of history that they have frequently been used as evidence in Supreme Court opinions, to clarify the "intentions" of the framers of the Constitution.) Madison, Hamilton, and Jay also managed to acquire the name "Federalist" for their political faction, though "Nationalist" would have been more accurate and appropriate. This seemed to leave no name for the opposition but the clumsy and empty term "Antifederalist."

The first state convention to act, that of Delaware, did so swiftly. After that, the fight for ratification was close, tough, and full of bargaining. The decisions of the four largest states—Massachusetts, New York, Pennsylvania, and Virginia—were crucial. Theoretically, the Constitution could have been ratified without the participation of any of them, since only nine states were required. As a practical matter, however, the new government would have been crippled without all of them. Pennsylvania fell into line in December 1787. But when the Massachusetts convention first met, the vote on the Constitution was 192 against, 144 in favor. The prospects for ratification were also poor in Virginia and New York. Eventually, in February 1788, the Federalists managed to win in Massachusetts, by a narrow margin of 187 to 168. In Virginia the convention ended by supporting the Constitution at the end of June 1788, but only on a close vote of 89 to 79. Meanwhile, New Hampshire had ratified on June 21, becoming the ninth state to do so and thus officially putting the Constitution into effect. But New York still stood outside, along with North Carolina and Rhode Island.

The Antifederalists were very strong in New York, but Virginia's ratification helped turn the tide. With it, ten states had already ratified. Now the opponents of the Constitution had to argue that New York could stand alone, in the heart of a new federal union—a more difficult task than simply arguing against the Constitution on its merits. After several very tense weeks, New York finally ratified on July 26, just over a month after Virginia's decision. But the outcome was precarious; a shift of just two votes in the New York result would have reversed the decision. North Carolina and Rhode Island hung back until 1789 and 1790, respectively, but there was no need to wait for their decision once Virginia and New York had accepted the new union. The old Congress simply closed up shop and ordered elections for early in 1789.

THINGS LEFT UNSAID AND UNDONE

To Washington, Madison, Hamilton, and the other Federalists, it was clear that a crisis had been averted. They had acted with care and energy, they believed, and saved the nation from itself. The uphill struggle for ratification had been the final, critical stage, but they had won. The question now was, what had they won? The Constitution was only a skeletal frame of government. The nation's political future would be determined by the kinds of laws the new Congress passed, by the way Washington and future presidents executed those laws and conducted foreign policy, and by the way the new federal court system interpreted the laws and the Constitution.

Not only was the Constitution a just framework of government, but it carefully refrained from confronting directly what everyone knew were vital and thorny problems of American social and political life. In particular, the Constitution said nothing explicitly about political parties, and almost nothing about slavery. But in the decades to come, political parties would become the great shaping fact of American politics. And slavery would become the great issue that would finally threaten the Constitution itself.

POLITICAL PARTIES

The men who wrote the Constitution and worked for its ratification had lived intensely partisan political lives. They had organized a radical faction in the 1760s and 1770s to promote resistance to British "tyranny." They had taken the name of a British political faction—Whigs—for their party, and had labeled their opponents with another British party name—Tories. During the 1780s, they had formed another faction, and had worked to bring about another, peaceful, revolution, replacing the Confederation with a new national government. Then they had organized the movement for ratification in their states. Nothing was more familiar to them than political parties.

But the Founding Fathers were committed, more or less unanimously, to a political theory in which parties were regarded as dangerous, evil, and corrupting, something no gentleman could participate in. On this view, there were only two kinds of situations that justified a political party. One was to resist the attempt of a government to deprive people of their liberty, as they thought the British had done in the 1760s and 1770s. The other was to rescue a government that was too weak to prevent "anarchy," unable to protect the liberty of the people—as they insisted the Confederation had been. But in a society with a properly constituted republican government, which had the consent of the people and guaranteed liberty and property, there could be no excuse for a political party. In a truly republican society, parties could only be the instruments of ambitious and unscrupulous men, interested only in office and power, demagogues who manipulated the "democratical" mob.

Thomas Jefferson summed up this contempt for political parties when he said, in 1789, that "I never submitted the whole system of my opinions to the creed of any party. . . . Such addiction is the last degradation of a free and moral agent. If I could not go to heaven but with a party, I would not go there at all."

One of the main hopes of the men who wrote the Constitution was that they had created a system of government so remote from the voters that no national parties would be formed. This was one of their reasons for providing that senators would be chosen by state legislatures rather than by voters in statewide elections. There was only one national election that might bring national political parties into existence: the election of the president every four years. This was the reason the framers of the Constitution created their most complicated and mysterious piece of governmental machinery, the selection of the president and vice president by "electors."

The Constitution provided that the president and vice president would be chosen by electors. Each state would "appoint" electors—one for each member the state had in the Senate and House of Representatives. Each state legislature could decide how to "appoint" the electors. Each elector would then cast two votes for president (not one for president and one for vice president). Whoever received the largest number of electoral votes would become president—provided he got more than half the total votes cast—and the runner-up would become vice president. If no one won, the House of Representatives would choose the president from

THE NINTH PILLAR RAISED. After New Hampshire became the ninth state to ratify the new Constitution (by a narrow margin of 57 to 46), *The New Hampshire Gazette* celebrated with this woodcut. It represented each ratifying state as an independent column, but joined by a starry bond to the others, giving mutual support. Virginia, the tenth state, is being raised up by what would seem to be the hand of God. And three more stars, representing New York, Rhode Island, and North Carolina, wait at the lower right. "Fame," the *Gazette* trumpeted, "claps her wings and sounds it to the skies."

among the five men who had received the most electoral votes.

This "electoral college" (as it became known) was not created in a moment of perversity or playfulness. The men who created it thought they knew exactly what they were doing and why they were doing it. They were assuming that "appointed" electors, meeting separately in the states, would vote for a large number of individuals. (In fact, to prevent the number from becoming too large, they required each elector to vote for at least one person who did not live in the same state.) They expected the result in each state to yield a "list" of men who might become president. And they were content to have the House of Representatives, with each state casting one vote, choose a person who might have gained only fifth place on the final list to be president, even if he had gained only a small minority of the electoral votes.

The reason for this cumbersome and indirect method of choosing the president was actually very simple and direct. The Founding Fathers did not want the one truly national office in the government to become the subject of contests every four years between political parties. If they could prevent this from happening, as they meant to, then they might prevent the development of national political parties altogether.

On this point, of course, the framers did not accurately foresee the future. They did not even foresee their own personal futures. Within a few years after 1787, they themselves would take the lead in forming political parties and would contend in the most partisan ways for control of the presidency and the other branches of the national government. The organized efforts in favor of and against ratification began the process. But it went on with a vengeance in the 1790s. During the decades after 1800, there would be intermittent periods when the struggles between political parties were subdued. But in the long run, national parties became the most prominent and permanent fact of American political life. What Americans like to call the two-party system became an essential part of their political culture—but it was a part that the Founding Fathers would have regarded with fear and dismay, at least in 1787 when they were writing the Constitution.

SLAVERY

The Constitution said very little about another important feature of national life. The decision to count slaves as three-fifths of a person when allocating representation in the House of Representatives was certainly an implicit recognition of the importance of slavery. Congress was also forbidden to interfere with the slave trade before 1808. And there was a provision that any slave who escaped to another state could not be made free, but had to be "delivered up" to his or her owner.

But these clauses were like cracks in a constitutional surface that seemed determined to ignore slavery and the sorts of deep divisions it might bring about in the new nation. There was even something slightly furtive about the way the very concept of slavery entered the Constitution. The words "slave" and "slavery" were not even used. The three-fifths clause referred only to "free persons" and "other persons." The provision on the slave trade spoke abstractly of "the migration or importation of such persons as any of the states now existing shall think proper to admit." And the clause concerning "escaped" slaves referred to them not as slaves but as persons "held in service or labor."

The fact that the Constitution had little to say about slavery, and that its framers seemed almost embarrassed to have the subject even come up, was not the result of ignorance or carelessness. From its beginnings, the Revolution had brought slavery closer to the center of the American stage than it had ever been before. In 1779, two years before Yorktown, African Americans in New Hampshire petitioned the state legislature for emancipation, asking that "the name of slave may not more be heard in a land gloriously contending for the sweets of liberty." The same year, a similar petition in Connecticut asked how slavery could be allowed in a country committed to the "Cause of Liberty."

Vermont abolished slavery in its new constitution of 1777. In 1780, Pennsylvania passed a law that would gradually free all its slaves. In 1783, the chief justice of Massachusetts ruled that slavery was unconstitutional in that state because the state constitution "sets out with declaring that all men are born free and equal—and that every subject is entitled to liberty." The following year, Connecticut and Rhode Island established mechanisms for the (very) gradual elimination of slavery. And there were already strong movements against slavery in New York and New Jersey, though legislation did not finally come in those states until 1800 and 1804.

No southern states adopted any such laws, though several did make it a bit easier for masters to voluntarily free their own slaves. It was perfectly clear that the states in the North and the South were headed in different directions, and that in the long run their differences over slavery might threaten the union and the Constitution itself. But the framers of the Constitution deliberately chose to leave the question of slavery to history rather than allow it to become an issue that might defeat the constitutional consensus they were trying to create. In fact, slavery defined the limits of their nationalism. Except for the slave trade and the question of "escaped" slaves, they were unanimously agreed to leave the issue to the individual states to decide.

THE BILL OF RIGHTS

Another subject on which the Constitution was almost silent was "liberty"—all those rights that individuals claim against governments. This question was fiercely debated during the ratification process, and the Federalists responded by promising to add amendments spelling out the rights of citizens under the new government. The result of this promise was a series of amendments to the Constitution that quickly came to be known as the Bill of Rights.

The task of drawing up the amendments fell to James Madison. He sifted through a large number of recommendations, some proposing as many as forty different provisions. He also worked through precedents in the state constitutions, particularly the Declaration of Rights adopted in Virginia in the first year of the Revolution. Finally, Madison boiled the proposals down to seventeen. What finally emerged were the first ten amendments to the Constitution. The first eight contained the now familiar guarantees of freedom of speech, press, religion, assembly, trial by jury, and the right to "bear arms." There were also two general amendments that attempted to define the relationships among the new government, the people, and the states. The ninth amendment declared that there might be other rights, not mentioned in the Constitution or the first eight amendments. These unnamed rights were still "retained by the people." The tenth was a guarantee that any power the Constitution did not give the national government was "reserved" to the states or to the people.

The amendments were quickly ratified—though three of the original thirteen states did not get around to doing so until 1941. One of the main objections of the Antifederalists had been met, and the Constitution had at last some genuine claim to originality and historic significance.

CHRONOLOGY

1777	Continental Congress completes draft of the Articles of Confederation
1781	Maryland becomes thirteenth state to ratify the Articles of Confederation; Cornwallis surrenders his army at Yorktown, Virginia; Congress proposes amendment to Articles to allow duties on imports; Rhode Island rejects the amendment, causing it to fail
1782	Peace negotiations begin in Paris among representatives of France, Britain, and the United States
1783	Congress ratifies the Treaty of Paris, which recognizes the independence of the United States; Congress again proposes a five percent "impost" on imports and again it fails when New York rejects it; Washington resigns his commission as commander-in-chief
1784	Washington travels to Pennsylvania and the west
1785	Washington named head of the Potomac River Company
1786	Shays's Rebellion in western Massachusetts; Annapolis Convention meets to discuss revision of the Articles of Confederation
1787	The Confederation Congress passes the Northwest Ordinance; Constitutional Convention meets in Philadelphia; Hamilton, Madison, and Jay begin to publish *The Federalist Papers*; The first states ratify the new Constitution
1788	New York and Virginia ratify the Constitution
1789	The first federal elections; Washington inaugurated president; North Carolina ratifies the Constitution
1790	Rhode Island ratifies the Constitution; The first amendments to the Constitution, the Bill of Rights, approved by Congress and submitted to the states for ratification
1791	The Bill of Rights ratified by the necessary number of states

SUGGESTIONS FOR FURTHER READING

GEORGE WASHINGTON

A very readable introduction to Washington is Marcus Cunliffe, *George Washington, Man and Monument* (1958). Serious students will want to look into Douglas Southall Freeman's massive and adoring seven volumes, *George Washington* (1948–1959), and James T. Flexner's *George Washington*, 4 vols. (1965–1972). Washington's career as commanding general, both during and after the Revolutionary War, can be seen in context in Robert Middlekauff, *The Glorious Cause* (1982).

THE CONFEDERATION PERIOD

Gordon Wood, *The Creation of the American Republic, 1776–1787* (1969), is a fine place to start. Two books by Merrill Jensen, *The Articles of Confederation* (1940) and *The New Nation* (1950), are still essential reading for serious students. Jackson Turner Main, *The Sovereign States* (1973), is equally important. The functioning of the Congress can be followed in J. N. Rakove, *The Beginnings of National Politics* (1979). A particularly fine state study is Edward Countryman, *A People in Revolution: The American Revolution and Political Society in New York, 1760–1790* (1981). The economic and financial history of the Confederation period is treated in E. James Ferguson, *The Power of the Purse: A History of American Public Finance, 1776–1790* (1961), and Ronald Hoffman et al., *The Economy of Early America: The Revolutionary Period* (1988). For political and constitutional history at the state level, see Willi Paul Adams, *The First American Constitutions: Republican Ideology and the Making of the State Constitutions in the Revolutionary Era* (1980); Donald Lutz, *Popular Consent and Popular Control: Whig Political Theory in the Early State Constitutions* (1980); and Ann Withington, *Toward a More Perfect Union: Virtue and the Formation of American Republics* (1992).

THE CONVENTION AND THE CONSTITUTION

A long debate on the nature of the movements for and against the new Constitution was begun in 1913 by Charles Beard's *An Economic Interpretation of the Constitution*. Part of Beard's argument—that the Founding Fathers expected to benefit directly from the new government because they held large quantities of government securities—has been subjected to searching scrutiny by later historians, most aggressively by Forrest McDonald in *We the People* (1958). But Beard's more general point, that the Constitution was the product of a distinctive consciousness of the relationship between politics and social class, remains an important one. Fine examples of its continuing vitality are Jackson Turner Main, *The Anti-Federalists: Critics of the Constitution* (1961), and Gordon Wood, *The Creation of the American Republic* (1969). For an alternative approach, see Forrest McDonald, *Novus Ordo Seclorum: The Intellectual Origins of the Constitution* (1985), and Clinton Rossiter, *1787: The Grand Convention* (1973). There are a number of good modern editions of the essays of Madison, Hamilton, and Jay that became known as *The Federalist*.

THINGS LEFT UNSAID AND UNDONE

The best approach to the question of political parties is Jackson Turner Main's extremely careful study, *Political Parties Before the Constitution* (1973). On attitudes toward political parties, see the early chapters of Richard Hofstadter, *The Idea of Party: The Rise of Legitimate Opposition in the United States, 1789–1801* (1973). On slavery during this period, the indispensable book is David Brion Davis, *The Problem of Slavery in the Age of Revolution, 1770–1823* (1975). Arthur Zilversmit, *The First Emancipation* (1967), is a valuable study of the ending of slavery in some of the states. The later chapters of Winthrop Jordan, *White Over Black* (1968), are also relevant. Gary Nash, *Forging Freedom: The Formation of Philadelphia's Black Community, 1720–1840* (1988), is a superb study of one of the period's most vital and interesting black communities. Shane White, *Somewhat More Independent: The End of Slavery in New York City, 1770–1810* (1991), gets to the heart of an extremely complicated social and political story. A good introduction to the first amendments to the Constitution is Robert A. Rutland, *The Birth of the Bill of Rights* (1955). But students who like to use original documents will profit from Helen E. Veit et al., *Creating the Bill of Rights: The Documentary Record from the First Federal Congress* (1991).

CHAPTER 7

The Republic on Trial

Episode: Aaron Burr, Conspirator

DISSENT AND CONFLICT IN THE NEW NATION

Partisan Politics

Foreign Affairs

Territorial Expansion

THE EPISODE: *One of the most striking features of the movement that led to the American Revolution was that so many of its leaders were quite young men. And when the war for independence finally began, even younger men were catapulted from lives as farm boys, clerks, or students into positions of military authority. This sudden leap from obscurity to what they called "glory" led a whole generation of these young men to pursue very ambitious careers in public life after the war. From the end of the Revolution down to 1820, the United States was, in effect, governed by the cohort of youths that had declared and won independence.*

One such man was Aaron Burr, who at the beginning of the Revolution found himself a captain at the age of twenty. After the war, he became a lawyer—and a very good one, too. But, as for so many of his contemporaries, the law was only an aspect of his real career, politics. He helped form a political party, served as a senator, then became vice president of the United States in 1801. But then one of the most curious episodes in American history brought his spectacular career into crisis—eventually bringing him to trial for treason.

THE HISTORICAL SETTING: *The revolutionary generation had its heroes and its villains. The heroes—the Washingtons, Jeffersons, Hamiltons, and Franklins—are revered, and their faces adorn even our currency. The villains are less well known. Aaron Burr has become one of them, lost to the fame that might have been his. But our purpose is not to judge Burr; through understanding his career, we can understand the main forces at work in the history of the United States during its first decades.*

From 1790 to 1820, the new United States took shape. Its government became a reality rather than a constitutional projection. Its first political parties were formed. Its western lands began to be settled by European Americans. It confronted the strains of regional and sectional dissension. The new nation also had to find its way through a difficult thicket of foreign affairs, complicated by the French Revolution and the Napoleonic Wars in Europe. While trying to survive in this difficult international setting, the United States acquired a new territory in the west that doubled its size, fought an undeclared war with France, almost went to war with Spain, and fought a declared war with Britain. The forces at work in all these events were also at work in the rise and fall of Aaron Burr. In a sense, he was always on trial, from the time he became a revolutionary soldier to his formal trial for treason. But the new Republic was also on trial. And the nature and outcome of these twin processes, one individual and the other national, depended on the same kinds of historical realities.

Aaron Burr, Conspirator

Early on the morning of July 11, 1804, a pair of small barges carried two duelists across the Hudson River from New York City to the New Jersey shore. The two seconds for the duel, and the usual doctor, were also aboard. The five men clambered ashore at a deserted, level spot along the river. They cleared away some of the summer brush, and carefully loaded the pistols. The two adversaries took up the prescribed positions, ten paces apart. One of the seconds called out "Present!" The men raised their pistols, in a formal salute, similar to a fencer's "En garde!" Without any further ceremony or signal the two men fired, one a little after the other. One of them spun partly around and fell forward. The small, round lead ball had lodged in his spine, and he was bleeding internally. The other man started to rush forward, as if to help or offer a gentleman's regrets. But he was pulled away by his second and taken quickly back across the river to New York. The wounded man went home more slowly, lapsing in and out of consciousness. He lived with pain, doses of opium, and a grieving family, into the next afternoon. Then he died.

The dead man was Alexander Hamilton, a hero of the Revolution. He had been first secretary of the treasury, and he was a leader of the Federalist party. He had achieved a remarkable career in his forty-nine years. As he lay dying, his doctor released frequent public bulletins on his condition. After his death, the city of New York went into official mourning. Mass meetings demanded the arrest of the "murderer," who escaped from the city after a few days. Finally, in both New York and New Jersey, Hamilton's killer was indicted for murder. He fled first to Philadelphia and then south to Georgia and out of the country to Florida (still a Spanish possession). Much of the time, he traveled under an assumed name, like any ordinary fugitive from justice.

Sooner or later, however, this particular outlaw had to come out of hiding. For he was the vice president of the United States, Aaron Burr. He could afford to spend the late summer in the South, but Congress would go into session in the fall, and it was his constitutional duty to preside over the Senate. He was fairly certain that the murder charges would eventually be dropped. In the meantime, he would not be arrested if he stayed out of New York and New Jersey. Even though New York was his home, he had no reason to go there. His handsome house had already been sold at auction to pay off some of his debts, and his other creditors were howling for the rest of his money. So, on November 4, the vice president, over his head in debt and wanted for murder, boldly took his seat as the president of the Senate. One senator, shocked at Burr's display of nerve, wrote angrily to a friend, "We are indeed fallen on evil times!"

It was not really the Senate that had fallen on evil times. The main victim (aside from the dead Hamilton, of course) was Burr himself. He was a gentleman and had fought an honorable duel—still a custom among some gentlemen of the day, though it was illegal in most of the states. He had won the duel. But he had lost, too. His career as one of the Founding Fathers was threatened with a bleak ending.

Burr had enjoyed as spectacular a career as Hamilton. Like Hamilton, he had been one of the young heroes of the Revolution. A brilliant lawyer, he was said never to have lost a case. He was also a very shrewd and successful politician. He had already been a senator from New York before becoming vice president.

But now, in the fall of 1804, Burr was in disgrace because of the duel and his debts. His term as vice president was expiring. He had just been defeated in an attempt to become governor of New York—a defeat that Hamilton had helped bring about and that was one of the causes of their duel. Hamilton had been criticizing Burr privately for many years. During the campaign for governor, some remarks attributed to Hamilton were published, referring to Burr as "a dangerous man and one who ought not to be trusted with the reins of government." When Hamilton refused either to deny he had made the comment or to apologize for it, Burr had challenged him to the duel.

Burr was still in his forties, but it seemed his career might be ruined. Still, he never allowed himself to become visibly flustered, so he kept up an appearance of calm, both publicly and privately. In a letter to his married daughter, Theodosia, he even made a joke of the entire affair:

> You have doubtless heard that there has subsisted for some time a contention of a very singular nature between the states of New York and New Jersey. The subject in dispute is which shall have the honor of hanging the Vice President. A paper received this morning asserts, but without authority, that he has determined in favor of New York. You shall have due notice of the time and place. Whenever it may be you may rely on a great company, much gayety, and many rare sights, such as the lion, the elephant, etc.

To his daughter's husband, Burr hinted that the situation was more serious. The duel would not cost him a hanging, probably. But his career was a shambles, and so, he wrote, "I shall seek another country."

One thing was certain. During that winter the vice president's mind was not on Senate business. He was busy instead with mysterious maps and a dangerous partnership. An old friend of Burr's was in Washington that winter. He was James Wilkinson, the highest-ranking general in the army of the United States. The general also happened to be a spy. For years he had been Agent 13 on the Spanish espionage rolls. He was very much interested in the same sorts of maps and plans as Burr.

The vice president who was wanted for murder and the general who was a spy had known each other many years. In fact, they had been twenty-year-old captains together during the first year of the Revolution. Their paths parted when Wilkinson was forced to leave the army after joining a plot against George Washington. Burr went on to become a major on Washington's staff.

Like many others in trouble, Wilkinson had gone west. He made a career in politics in western Pennsylvania and Kentucky, and he began his secret occupation as a Spanish agent. In 1791 Wilkinson was able to reenter the army and fight against the

JAMES WILKINSON. General Wilkinson eventually testified against Burr in a treason trial. But the government prosecutors never quite trusted him. In the War of 1812, Wilkinson performed poorly, then retired to write a long and pompous autobiography.

Native Americans in the Ohio Valley. He rose rapidly in rank, and by 1796 was the highest-ranking general in the army.

From about 1794 on, Burr and Wilkinson had carried on a secret, coded correspondence. Now, together again in Washington in the winter of 1804–1805, they made new plans and copied maps of Spanish possessions in the Southwest and of the western territories of the United States.

At this time, Spain still ruled the American West and Southwest, as well as Mexico. ("Mexico" was generally used to refer to all these North American regions.) The Spanish also owned East Florida—the peninsula itself—and what was called West Florida—the panhandle area west of the peninsula, along the Gulf of Mexico. The United States had just purchased the territory known as Louisiana, the vast region between the Mississippi River and the Rocky Mountains (see map, p. 257).

In the area between the Mississippi and the Appalachians, change was the order of the day. So far, only Tennessee, Ohio, and Kentucky had been admitted to statehood. But from Michigan to Mississippi, settlers were on the move, driving out Native Americans and clearing land. If these western states and territories decided to secede from the union, there was little chance the federal government could use force to hold them.

Two very dangerous but exciting possibilities now filled the heated imaginations of Burr and Wilkinson. One was an invasion of Spanish territory. The other was an attempt to separate America's western lands from the rest of the union. If only one of the plans worked at first, then Burr and Wilkinson could still try the other at a later time. Either plan, obviously, was difficult and dangerous. A private attack on Spain would be a crime. Separation of the West from the rest of the United States by force of arms would be treason. But the result could be magnificent—a new nation stretching all the way from Ohio to Panama. The two plans had one very practical advantage: they required the same kind of preparation. If money could be found for it, a private army might be raised in the West. This army would travel downriver by way of the Ohio, the Cumberland, the Tennessee, and the Mississippi to New Orleans. Only then would a final choice have to be made between the conquest of Spanish possessions or the separation of the West.

Such outlandish schemes actually made a certain amount of sense in 1805. After all, the United States was a small and relatively weak nation. The government exerted little control over the states and territories west of the Appalachians. It had even less control over the enormous new territories west of the Mississippi. As for Mexico, it seemed only a matter of time before Mexico and the Southwest broke away from Spain in a revolution like the one the Americans had recently fought against Britain. The United States and Spain had been on the verge of war for some time. If war came, the conquest of Mexico and the Southwest would become a patriotic "duty." Burr and Wilkinson had influence and friends in high places. Some friends could be brought into the plan, and others could be tricked into helping. There was little need to fear the American army, even if Wilkinson had not been in command. Its strength consisted of only about 3,000 troops scattered along the Atlantic coast and through the West. Burr and Wilkinson had every reason to believe that one scheme or the other, Mexican conquest or western secession, could work. It was just possible that both plans might succeed, with thorough preparation, careful timing, and a run of good luck.

The first step was to obtain money and military support from some foreign power. When Burr fled New York after the duel with Hamilton, he sent a message to the British minister in Washington, Anthony Merry. Merry reported to his government that Burr had made an astonishing proposal.

> I have just received an offer from Mr. Burr to lend his assistance to his majesty's government in any manner in which they may think fit to employ him, particularly in endeavoring to effect a separation of the western part of the United States in its whole extent.

In late March of 1805, after a winter of planning with Wilkinson, Burr went to Merry in person. This time he had a more detailed scheme. Merry reported home in a dispatch marked Most Secret:

> Mr. Burr has mentioned to me that the inhabitants of Louisiana seem determined to render themselves independent of the United States, and that the execution of their design is only delayed by the difficulty of obtaining assurance of protection from some foreign power.

Burr wanted the British to station a squadron of ships at the mouth of the Mississippi in order to immobilize the American navy. And he wanted a loan of half a million dollars. Merry was hooked. His secret dispatch ended by recommending Burr in the most favorable terms:

He certainly possesses, perhaps in a much greater degree than any other individual in this country, all the talents, energy, intrepidity, and firmness which are required for such an enterprise.

The response from England was painfully slow, so Wilkinson and Burr went ahead on their own. They managed to persuade President Jefferson to appoint Wilkinson governor of the Louisiana Territory, which was formed in 1805. Wilkinson would make his headquarters in St. Louis. Burr, meanwhile, would take a "tour" down the Ohio River and "travel" for several weeks in Kentucky and Tennessee. Then he would go on down the Mississippi to New Orleans, making plans and enlisting support along the way.

Burr left Washington on horseback April 10, 1805. Three weeks later he arrived in Pittsburgh to begin his work. He embarked on the Ohio River in style, as he wrote to his daughter Theodosia on April 30:

> Arrived in good order yesterday. Find my boat and hands ready. My boat is, properly speaking, a floating house, sixty feet by fourteen, containing dining room, kitchen with fireplace, and two bedrooms; roofed from stem to stern; steps to go up, and a walk on the top of the whole length; glass windows, etc. This edifice costs one hundred and thirty-three dollars.

On this elaborate "ark," as he called it, Burr went everywhere and saw everyone of any importance. He visited the senators and congressmen he knew from his Washington days. He stopped at plantations and country houses. Everywhere he was treated as a celebrity. At each stop, the story was the same. There might be a concert or a traveling play. There was certain to be a dinner or two with the leading citizens. Most important, there would be at least one long and guarded conversation among the men only, flavored with whiskey, secrecy, and cigars. Then Burr would hint at his plans and sound out his hosts for their possible future support.

Burr left the Ohio River at Louisville, Kentucky, then rode south across the state and into Tennessee. He visited Andrew Jackson in Nashville. For four days he filled Jackson with the exciting prospect of a war against Spain, in which Jackson's hill-country militia could help drive the Spanish out of Florida and then off the entire continent. From Nashville, Burr went down the Cumberland on one of Jackson's boats to rejoin his own great "ark" on the Ohio River. He met Wilkinson at a small fort where the Ohio meets the Mississippi.

Wilkinson gave Burr a military escort (even though Burr was no longer the vice president) and another "elegant barge" for the trip downriver to Natchez and New Orleans. In Orleans Territory, as the future state of Louisiana was known, Burr continued to hint somewhat vaguely at his purposes and to seek out potential supporters. Then he headed north on horseback, through Nashville for another visit with Jackson. Then it was on to St. Louis, Wilkinson's headquarters, to report on the results of his trip. Burr made the hard, slow journey back east, arriving in Washington in November of 1805. Though only a little over a year had passed since Burr's duel with Hamilton, his life had taken on a new direction and new purposes. He really was prepared to "seek another country," though just what "country" it would be and how he would seek it remained in the realm of possibility.

The next year was frustrating. Minister Merry's appeal to the British government for funds got nowhere. With a new collaborator—Jonathan Dayton, a senator from New Jersey—Burr tried to trick the Spanish themselves into financing the secession of the West. But the Spanish minister was cautious and would provide only $1,500, hardly enough to finance an army. Wilkinson was strangely silent, perhaps sensing that the time was not ripe. Burr began to suspect his colleague of being fainthearted. Burr sent Wilkinson a coded letter complaining that "Nothing has been heard from Brigadier

[Wilkinson] since October." The bad news, Burr said, was that "the execution of our project is postponed till December; want of water in Ohio renders movement impracticable."

"Want of water in Ohio" was the plotters' code for lack of money. And without money they had no chance, unless there was a war with Spain. Unfortunately for the conspiracy, the administration of President Jefferson grounded its foreign strategy on the simple principle "Peace is our policy." But then, just as everything looked hopeless, the Spanish made a curious decision that almost led to the war Burr wanted so much.

When the United States bought Louisiana from France in 1803, its western boundary was left undefined. Technically, the United States could have claimed everything east of the Rio Grande. But the Spanish claimed the Texas region and sent in about 1,500 troops to occupy the area. Since Jefferson believed that Americans might never settle west of the Mississippi, he decided not to quarrel over Texas. Instead, he proposed to set the border with Mexico at the Sabine River. But the Spanish claimed that the border was east of the Sabine, along a small stream named the Arroyo Hondo (see map, p. 285). In the fall of 1805, while Burr was returning east from his trip, the Spanish moved a few troops—twenty-nine soldiers and one officer—across the Sabine. In February 1806 an American troop of sixty soldiers forced the Spanish to evacuate their post and return across the Sabine. These border incidents were small and not very dangerous, and Burr probably did not know about them. In fact, it took the government about six weeks to receive even emergency messages from the border.

The country between the Sabine and the Arroyo Hondo was virtually uninhabited, and either the United States or Spain could have given it up with no loss to national interest or security. But both sides suddenly became stubborn. Jefferson, when he finally learned of the problem, announced that he intended to hold the Sabine line, if necessary by force. The Spanish authorities in Mexico then reinforced their garrison and once more sent troops across the Sabine River.

The American commander in the area reported to his government that the situation was desperate. He had only 200 men fit for duty, six old cannon, and a shabby fort. The Spanish refused even to reply to his request to withdraw. Jefferson was determined. He ordered the frontier reinforced. Early in May the president told Wilkinson himself to move his headquarters to New Orleans and take personal command of the troops in the disputed area.

Now General Wilkinson was in an extremely awkward position. All along, he had been trying to juggle three roles: ranking general of the army, covert agent for Spain, and secret plotter with Burr. The problems on the border brought the three roles into painful conflict and put him in a predicament.

In a crisis, Wilkinson could choose to combine any two of his three roles, but at least one of them would have to be dropped. In case of war with Spain, he could be both commanding general and Burr's collaborator in the conquest of Mexico. The roles of spy for Spain and collaborator with Burr could work together if the goal were the secession of the West. Wilkinson's third option was to remain commanding general and spy for Spain. This would require him to keep peace with Spain along the Sabine but also to desert Burr and thus prevent either the conquest of Mexico or the secession of the West. The choices were extremely difficult. They depended on circumstances that Wilkinson could not completely control, such as the movements of Spanish troops and the aggressiveness of Jefferson. Faced with such difficult and risky choices, Wilkinson moved very deliberately. Jefferson ordered him to leave St. Louis in May. The general hung back until August, when he finally started downriver toward New Orleans.

Burr's problem, as he fretted through the spring of 1806, was just the opposite of Wilkinson's. Wilkinson had too many potential roles to juggle; Burr had no role and was trying to find one. During the months when it seemed there would be no war with Spain, Burr had been raising money among his friends and relatives. He had also decided to buy part of a huge land grant on the Ouachita River in what is now the state of Louisiana. If nothing else worked, he could bring in settlers and become a private prince. The preparations for the Ouachita plan—boats and armed men—were exactly the same as for the conquest of Mexico or the secession of the West.

When Burr heard the news of the border incidents on the Sabine River and learned that Jefferson had ordered Wilkinson to go to New Orleans, he made a fateful decision. On July 24 he sent a messenger west with a secret letter to Wilkinson written by Senator Jonathan Dayton. Dayton began by trying to convince Wilkinson that Jefferson was about to replace him as governor of the Louisiana Territory. He ended by urging Wilkinson to act:

> It is now well ascertained that you are to be displaced in the next session of Congress. Prepare yourself, therefore, for it. You know the rest. You are not a man to despair, especially when such prospects offer in another quarter. Are you ready? Are your numerous associates ready? Wealth and glory! Louisiana and Mexico!

The message was almost clear. Burr and Dayton were trying to get Wilkinson to commit himself. But to what? Dayton's words (which Burr probably dictated)—"You know the rest. Louisiana and Mexico!"—still left all the options open.

Burr had Dayton write another letter five days later, on July 29, in the code he and Wilkinson had always used. It was much more elaborate, but it still left the choice of destinations open. This letter tried to trick Wilkinson by falsely claiming that all the pieces had fallen into place and by implying that success was certain:

JONATHAN DAYTON. Senator Dayton (after whom Dayton, Ohio, is named) was eventually indicted for treason but was never put on trial. He may well have been the writer—though not the author—of the famous "cipher letter" that Wilkinson turned over to government authorities.

> Your letter postmarked 13th May is received. I have at length obtained funds and have actually commenced. The eastern detachments from different points and under different pretences will rendezvous on the Ohio, 1st of November.

The letter was exaggerating, and rather wildly. The "eastern detachments" did not exist, except perhaps in imagination. This exaggeration was small, however, compared to the lies that followed immediately:

> Every thing internal and external favors our views. Naval protection of England is secured. It [an English naval force] will meet us at the Mississippi.

The promise of English naval support was simply a lie. Minister Merry had not succeeded in getting a promise of help from London. The letter continued trying to excite Wilkinson's imagination:

> It will be a host of choice spirits. Wilkinson shall be second to Burr only, and Wilkinson shall dictate the rank and promotion of his officers. Burr will proceed westward 1st August, never to return. Our object, my dear friend, is brought to a point so long desired. Burr guarantees the result with his life and honor, with the lives, and honor, and the fortunes of hundreds of the best blood of our country.

Then came a few details of planned movements:

> Burr's plan of operation is to move down rapidly from the Falls [of the Ohio, at Louisville, Kentucky] on the 15th of November, with the first 500 or 1,000 men, in light boats now constructing for that purpose, to be at Natchez between the 5th and 15th of December, there to meet you, there to determine whether it will be expedient to seize on, or pass by, Baton Rouge.

After setting down these details, the letter hinted at the key to the entire scheme:

> The people of the country to which we are going are prepared to receive us; their agents, now with Burr, say that if we will protect their religion, and will not subject them to a foreign power, that in three weeks all will be settled.

What "country" did Burr, Wilkinson, and Dayton have in mind? The Louisiana Territory or Mexico? There probably were no "agents" of either Louisiana or Mexico with Burr at the time. Both areas were Catholic, so the protection of their religion would be a consideration in one as well as the other. The most important clue may be the timetable of three weeks. Burr could hardly have hoped to put together a fleet, sail across the Gulf of Mexico to Vera Cruz, and conquer Mexico in such a short time. On the other hand, "seizing on" Baton Rouge and then New Orleans, and proclaiming a new western nation probably could be done in three weeks, if Wilkinson did his part. What Burr probably planned to do was to gather his forces, meet Wilkinson at Natchez, and then decide whether to invade Mexico, try to take over New Orleans, or peacefully settle the Ouachita lands. The simple fact was that his future was in Wilkinson's hands, and those hands became more unsteady every day. The letter closed with a final, dramatic attempt to coax Wilkinson into action: "The gods invite us to glory and fortune; it remains to be seen whether we deserve the boon." A few days later, Burr set out for the Ohio, never to return—or so he believed.

Before he received the coded letter from Burr and Dayton, Wilkinson started south from St. Louis. He reached Natchez early in September and started up the Red River to the American fort at Natchitoches. He arrived there September 22 to find a

THE CIPHER LETTER. The most famous piece of writing ever attributed to Aaron Burr was this jumble of numbers. Burr may have written it, or he may have inspired it; it is much more likely that it was written by Jonathan Dayton. The code was a simple one: the numbers stood for entries in a dictionary owned by the writer and Wilkinson. The third paragraph reads: "Burr will proceed westward 1 August, never to return. With him go his daughter and grandson. The husband will follow in October with a corps of worthies." The letter refers many times to Burr, always as "Burr" or as "he." This may suggest that it was not written by Burr, though he could have dictated it.

small, unprepared garrison, with no cannon or horses ready for duty. For thirty hot, frustrating days the general bargained and hesitated and tried to reinforce his little army. At first he was tough. He wrote the Spanish military commander of Texas that his orders from Washington were "absolute": the border was going to be the Sabine River, and the Spanish must withdraw or face the consequences. But the Spanish commander was just as tough. His orders were to enforce the Spanish claim to the territory between the Sabine and the Arroyo Hondo, he said, and the choice of peace or war rested with Wilkinson.

While Wilkinson was engaged in this heady exchange of threats, he was also writing very excited letters to his American friends. For a crucial two weeks at the end of September and the beginning of October 1806, he was convinced that war with Spain was certain. The choice, in fact, seemed to be in his hands. And he was ready for much more than a squabble over the border. At last, his dream of conquering Spanish Mexico seemed about to come true. On September 26 he wrote to Senator John Smith of Ohio:

> I have made the last effort of conciliation. I shall be obliged to fight and flog them. Five thousand mounted infantry may suffice to carry us forward as far as the Grand River [the Rio Grande]. There we shall require 5,000 more to conduct us to Monterrey Mexico, and

from 20,000 to 30,000 will be necessary to carry our conquests to California and the Isthmus of Darien [Panama].

To another friend Wilkinson exulted, "A blow once struck, and away we go!"

It was at this critical point—with the Spanish refusing to retreat and war seemingly certain—that Wilkinson finally received Burr's coded letter of July 29. The letter had taken two months to catch up with him, and it hit him at an awkward moment. If a war did begin, Wilkinson would be pinned down in a land action in Texas. There was no way to control what Burr might do once he reached New Orleans. Wilkinson was convinced that Burr was bold enough to try almost anything. If Burr did have a thousand men on the Ohio, ready to start south, and if the British had really agreed to station a fleet off the Louisiana coast, then he could undoubtedly have his way at Baton Rouge and New Orleans, while the pitifully small American army contended with the Spanish forces along the border. Then Burr probably could mount some sort of attack on Mexico by sea before Wilkinson could get a respectable force assembled, much less advance to the Rio Grande. The moment had finally come when Wilkinson must choose. He received the crucial letter October 8. He waited and fretted for two agonizing weeks. He also drank even more whiskey than was his usual custom, for his situation was difficult indeed.

Meanwhile, Burr was in the Ohio country, having boats built and recruiting volunteers. Sometimes he told people that he was going to settle the Ouachita land grant. At other times he talked of raising a force of volunteers for the war with Spain that was sure to begin soon. He visited Cincinnati, Frankfort, Lexington, Nashville, and all the settlements in between.

Burr also established a base of operations. In the Ohio River near Cincinnati was an island owned by a wealthy Irish immigrant named Harman Blennerhassett, who had become involved with Burr during the winter of 1805–1806. He seems to have had a vision of himself as minister to England for the new government of Mexico that Burr would establish. Whatever the vision, Blennerhassett was willing to put himself into debt and danger to help Burr. According to the timetable, boats would be built at Blennerhassett Island and at other points along the river. Around the end of November, the fleet and the volunteers would start south.

All during September and October, preparations went fairly smoothly. Boats were completed. Dozens of volunteers were recruited, many of them the young sons of leading planters, politicians, and military men. In Kentucky, Ohio, and Tennessee, Burr's expedition—whatever its destination—was the main subject of gossip and speculation.

Some talk was good for Burr. Like any enterprise, his needed advertising. But the talk began to filter back to Washington. Jefferson's administration became first suspicious and then alarmed. Early in November a Kentucky district attorney even attempted to have Burr arrested for planning an invasion of Mexico. Most Kentuckians interpreted this action as a political move. The district attorney was a member of the Federalist party, and Burr was a Republican. In addition, the district attorney had so admired Hamilton that he had taken the name as his own legal middle name. Two sympathetic juries, one in November and another in December, found Burr innocent of any crime. Still, it was clear that Burr's preparations could not go on much longer without forcing the government into some kind of response.

As Burr won in court and completed his preparations, he did not know that he had already been betrayed. Wilkinson had decided to do whatever was necessary to make peace with the Spanish on the border. Then he would turn against Burr. He could thus gain credit with the Spanish for protecting their interests. At home he could claim he had saved his country from Burr's intrigues.

On October 20 Wilkinson put his plan in motion. He wrote President Jefferson two very strange letters. In the first, he enclosed an "anonymous" document—which he had actually written himself. In it Wilkinson sounded an alarm against "a numerous and powerful association" illegally organized for the invasion of Mexico. The general had to be careful not to appear involved. He claimed:

> It is unknown under what auspices this enterprise has been projected, from whence the means of its support are derived, or what may be the intentions of its leaders.

In the second letter (which he signed) Wilkinson again warned the president, and again tried to appear both innocent and confused:

> The magnitude of the enterprise staggers my belief. I have never in my whole life found myself in such perplexity. I am not only uninformed of the prime mover and ultimate objects of this daring enterprise, but am ignorant of the foundation on which it rests.

Wilkinson knew that when the president received these letters, he would have no choice but to move against Burr. This left only one nagging problem. If the Spanish insisted on starting a war, then Burr and his force might suddenly appear to be heroes on their way to fight the enemy. To cover this possibility, Wilkinson added an astonishing postscript to his second letter to Jefferson:

> Should Spain be disposed to war seriously with us, might not some plan be adopted to correct the delirium of the associates, and by a suitable appeal to their patriotism engage them in the service of their country? I do believe that I could accomplish the object.

Here was Wilkinson's escape hatch in case something went wrong. If war with Spain did come, he would simply rejoin Burr in the plan to conquer Mexico.

Now everything depended on the Spanish, and on this front Wilkinson had extraordinary luck. On October 23, three days after he wrote Jefferson, he mounted his troops to begin a slow, tense march toward the Sabine. He did not know at the time that the small Spanish force had already withdrawn west of the river. When he met no resistance, Wilkinson proposed a neutral zone between the Sabine and the Arroyo Hondo. No Spanish forces would cross the Sabine, and no American troops would cross the Arroyo Hondo. The Spanish accepted the agreement, and Wilkinson was finally free to confront Burr. He immediately headed east for Natchez and New Orleans.

Before marching east, Wilkinson sent a messenger to the Spanish authorities in Mexico asking for a payment to Agent 13 (himself) for keeping peace and stopping Burr's plan to conquer Mexico! The Spanish government refused to pay this audacious bill. But the resourceful Wilkinson did finally manage to get Jefferson to pay $1,500 for the messenger's "expenses" for the trip into Mexico.

Burr was now in deep trouble, though he did not know it. There was still a slender chance he might salvage something, but only if he moved quickly. Even by fast express, Wilkinson's letters to Jefferson would take six weeks to get to Washington. Burr thus had until early December before the federal government could begin to act. Wilkinson would also need several weeks to travel to New Orleans and put the city's defenses in any kind of order. If Burr could get to Natchez by his original deadline of December 15, he might still have a chance to trick or surprise Wilkinson. This meant that Burr and his collaborators had to get their boats into the water by the middle of November. Any delay would give the government time to act and Wilkinson time to prepare. News that there was to be no war with Spain would soon reach Ohio and Kentucky, and this would threaten every version of Burr's scheme. He did not know that Wilkinson had written to Jefferson, made peace with the Spanish commanders, and turned for New Orleans.

Burr's plans were certainly ambitious enough to attract intense suspicion. He was having fifteen boats built at Marietta, Ohio, near Blennerhassett Island. Andrew Jackson was building five more at Nashville on the Cumberland River. At least eight others were being bought or built in Pittsburgh and other settlements on the Ohio. These twenty-eight boats could carry at least a thousand men and their supplies—a force several times larger than the army Wilkinson would command in New Orleans. But the boat-building went more slowly than Burr had planned, and he showed no hurry to get into action.

The first four boats were launched in Pittsburgh December 4. By this time any hope Burr might have had was gone—though he did not know it. Ohio officials had been watching Burr's preparations for many weeks, and they now knew of Wilkinson's settlement with the Spanish. On December 9 they seized the fifteen boats at Marietta. Harman Blennerhassett and a few other men got away down the Ohio in four boats that had just arrived from Pittsburgh.

Burr knew nothing about these events. After his second trial in Kentucky he had gone to Nashville. He did not start down the Cumberland until December 22. By that time it was already much too late. Burr finally made his tardy rendezvous with Blennerhassett and the others on December 27, at the meeting of the Cumberland and Ohio rivers. There were only ten boats now, and fewer than a hundred men.

Burr would surely have quit at this point if he had known of Wilkinson's betrayal. But he still believed that a small force at New Orleans could accomplish a great deal if Wilkinson helped. Burr had learned that Wilkinson had made peace with the Spanish. He must have thought that either the peace would be temporary or that he and Wilkinson would capture New Orleans instead of Mexico. In any case, he went on down the river, completely out of communication with the rest of the world. On January 10, 1807, he pulled to shore at a small settlement just north of Natchez. A man quickly showed him a newspaper that told the story of Wilkinson's treachery. He also learned that President Jefferson had ordered his arrest. The former vice president was once more a fugitive from justice.

General Wilkinson had already declared martial law in New Orleans and had begun to arrest Burr's friends there. Burr decided to take his chances with civilian courts in the Mississippi Territory. There he hoped to be out of Wilkinson's grasp. But after a few weeks of legal maneuvering, Burr learned that Wilkinson had sent troops north to arrest him. He fled and hid with friends for about two weeks. Finally, on February 19, he was surprised and captured near Mobile. He was then taken east under military arrest for trial in Richmond, Virginia.

Burr's trial began March 30, 1807. It lasted five months and attracted more attention than any other criminal trial in America up to that time. Some of this attention was simply a result of Burr's prominent political position and the fact that he was charged with one of the worst of all crimes, high treason. But his trial also had great political significance. President Jefferson committed himself actively to prosecuting Burr, and so he became almost a party to the trial. Many Federalists, on the other hand, became partisans of Burr in order to align themselves against the Republican president. The trial was presided over by none other than the chief justice of the United States, John Marshall. He was a Federalist and a bitter enemy of the president. Jefferson, Burr, and Marshall had last been together on March 4, 1801. Then Marshall had administered the oaths of office to President Jefferson and Vice President Burr. Now all three were locked in ugly and curious political combat over whether the president's legal staff could force the chief justice to convict the former vice president of treason.

Almost everyone believed that Burr was guilty of something. President Jefferson had publicly declared that Burr was guilty before the trial even began. The question was, however, guilty of what? Before the Revolution, British law had made conviction in treason cases fairly easy. But the framers of the Constitution, in order to protect citizens from the power of the federal government, had defined treason quite narrowly. Only two things, the Constitution clearly said, were treasonable: giving "aid and comfort" to enemies of the United States and "levying war" against the United States. Since the country was at peace, it technically had no enemies. So Burr had to be convicted of "levying war." (What the expression "levying war" actually meant was one of the main issues of the trial.)

The Constitution contained another important provision. There had to be two witnesses to an overt act of treason. The government would have to prove that Burr had actually participated in an act of war against the United States—not just that he had planned, plotted, or encouraged it. And the government would also have to have at least two eyewitnesses to the specific act of "levying war."

Jefferson anxiously ordered the government's lawyers to do everything necessary to get a conviction. Still the prosecution had trouble putting a case together. At first, Marshall refused even to begin a trial for treason because the government could produce so few witnesses. The strongest witness would probably be Wilkinson, but weeks passed and he did not show up. One of Burr's lawyers pointed out, "In Europe, a general had been known to march the same distance at the head of his army in a shorter time than General Wilkinson has had to pass from New Orleans to this place." The court recessed, one hot June day after another, to wait for the general. The writer Washington Irving, who was covering the trial for a New York newspaper, commented sarcastically on the delay. Members of the court, he wrote, "used the opportunity to go home, see their wives, have their clothes washed, and flog their Negroes."

However the citizens of Richmond may have passed the time, they finally were treated to a sight of the general. On June 15 Wilkinson strode into court, as Washington Irving brilliantly described him, "booted to the middle, sashed to the chin, collared to the ears, and whiskered to the teeth." In a boastful letter to Jefferson, Wilkinson described his own courtroom appearance:

> I saluted the bench and my eyes darted a flash of indignation at the little traitor. This lion-hearted hero, with haggard eye, made an effort to meet the indignant salutation. But it was in vain. He averted his face, grew pale, and affected passion.

Washington Irving's newspaper story of the same meeting was a bit different:

> Wilkinson strutted into court and took his stand, swelling like a turkey-cock and bracing himself for the encounter of Burr's eye. Burr turned his head, looked him full in the face, and then coolly resumed his position. The whole look was over in an instant, but it was an admirable one.

Whoever won the exchange of looks, Wilkinson's pretrial testimony was enough—barely enough—to have Burr indicted for treason. The trial began August 3.

AARON BURR. This painting of Burr was done by a New York artist, John Vanderlyn. The painter was at pains to suggest a cool dignity and a repose that would surely not stoop to conspiracy. And the columns in the background are meant to associate Burr with the loftiest ideals of republican and Roman virtue.

The first task was the selection of a jury. Virginia was Jefferson country, and it was difficult, if not impossible, to get an unbiased jury. Even the ghost of Hamilton rose up to haunt Burr. Burr and his lawyers questioned one prospective juror very closely, and the man turned to the courtroom and said, "I am surprised that they should be in such terror of me. Perhaps my name may be the terror, for my first name is Hamilton." (He was excused.) Finally, Burr accepted an obviously biased jury, since he hoped to win on questions of procedure and law. These would be decided by the judge, not the jury.

The government lawyers received instructions directly from the president almost every day. Determined to prove that Burr had intended to make war, they held that he had assembled an armed force at Blennerhassett Island for this purpose. According to the prosecutors, this action was what the Constitution meant by levying war—raising an armed force for the purpose of committing an act of war.

The strategy of Burr's defense was to make the prosecution prove its accusation that anything that could be reasonably called "levying war" had occurred. As Burr sarcastically observed, Mr. Jefferson was having a great deal of trouble even finding a war:

> Our President is a lawyer, and a great one, too. He certainly ought to know what it is that constitutes a war. Six months ago he proclaimed that there was a civil war [between Burr's forces and the government]. And yet, for six months have they been hunting for it, and still cannot find one spot where it existed. There was, to be sure, a terrible war in the newspapers, but nowhere else.

Day after day, Burr and his lawyers tore holes in the government's case. The prosecution had proved only that thirty or forty men congregated at Blennerhassett Island in early December 1806. But Burr was not even present on the island at the time.

Burr's lawyers were brilliant and cutting in their cross-examination of government witnesses. Burr, acting as his own counsel, was even more brilliant and more cutting. One by one, the prosecution witnesses were broken. One had to admit, under Burr's questioning, that he had just been paid $10,000 by the government. Another ended by testifying for Burr; he admitted that, as far as he knew, Burr's force had been gathered for use only if the United States declared war against Spain. A third testified against Burr, only to have his own son follow him to the stand to swear that his father was "old and infirm, and like other old men, told long stories and was apt to forget his repetitions." Another witness, who knew Blennerhassett well, revealed that Blennerhassett was so nearsighted that it was ridiculous to imagine his participating in a military action.

The outcome depended on how Chief Justice Marshall defined treason. If he ruled that treason could mean participating in preparations whose ultimate purpose was to "levy war" against the United States, then the jury might find Burr guilty. But Burr's lawyers argued that the government would have to prove Burr had been personally present and had participated in an outright act of levying war. For days lawyers for the government and for Burr argued the point. On the last day of August, Marshall made his ruling. He decided in favor of Burr. To prove treason, he said, the government would have to prove by two eyewitnesses that Burr had been present and taken part in a specific act of war against the United States. Since the government had not made such a case, the jury had to deliberate only briefly. On September 1, Burr was found not guilty.

Burr had won the case, just as he had won his duel with Hamilton. But once again he seemed to lose in winning. He was still in legal trouble in several states, and he was now more deeply in debt than ever. Also, much of the public was convinced that Marshall, the Federalist, had let Burr go free just to embarrass the Republican administration. Burr's career was finished. Once more, he decided to "seek another country," and went to Europe in a self-imposed exile that lasted four years. In 1812 he came home to practice law in New York. Many years later, at the age of seventy-seven, he married a wealthy widow; she soon sued him for divorce (charging him with adultery!). The divorce became final September 14, 1836. Burr died the same day, at the age of eighty.

Dissent and Conflict in the New Nation

The strange career of Aaron Burr was understood by most of his contemporaries as the product of his peculiar, ambitious, and unpredictable character—the result of personality rather than of history. But personalities, no matter how bizarre, are shaped by history, and Burr's was no exception. His duel with Hamilton, his curious western schemes, and his trial for treason made sense as part of the larger history of his generation. The men who made the Revolution and the Constitution continued to govern the United States for decades after independence was achieved. The public lives of this generation were shaped by four main tendencies, all of them very important in the life of Aaron Burr.

First, the development of organized political factions—which everyone called parties—occupied the minds and energies of just about every politically active American during the period after 1789. Burr was, first and last, a politician and his political career was conditioned by the existence of parties. He was deeply involved in almost every partisan political struggle of the period, and carefully constructed a remarkable party organization in New York. In fact, partisan conflicts between Burr and Hamilton were what brought about the duel itself.

Second, the history of the United States during the decades after Washington's inauguration was tied very closely to foreign affairs. Relations with France, Spain, and Britain tended to dominate national and even local politics. Many leading politicians and military figures were involved in secret intrigues with one foreign power or another, just as Burr and Wilkinson were. Burr sensed this situation clearly, especially after his duel. His mind was filled with thoughts of war with Spain and secret arrangements with Britain.

Third, the years between 1789 and the 1820s were marked by rapid expansion of territory and population. During this period the territory of the United States doubled. Thousands of pioneer settlers pushed over the Appalachian Mountains into the valleys of the Ohio, the Tennessee, and the Mississippi rivers. Burr's thoughts ran west with this expansion, as did the thoughts of most of his contemporaries.

Fourth, the United States was involved in a serious test of whether the new federal system would work. Each section of the country had its own special interests and institutions. It was not clear whether the nation could survive. Would farmers in the West remain loyal to a government created and controlled by men of the seaboard? Would the question of slavery divide the North from the South? Would New England leave the union and try to go it alone? These questions were quite real and important, not just to Burr but to other leaders.

PARTISAN POLITICS

The framers of the Constitution thought of conflict between organized groups and factions as a normal feature of human societies. Differences of interest, real or perceived, would arise that could pit farmers against merchants, debtors against creditors, slaveholders against nonslaveholders, the rich against the poor. Such divisions in society would inevitably lead to factions, which would struggle for domination of state and local governments. These struggles could bring out people's worst failings: selfishness, intrigue, ambition, deceit, and demagoguery. In order to gain practical advantages, political parties and their leaders would typically try to mobilize popular support by appeals to fear and greed, and would attempt to replace a healthy republican patriotism by loyalty to a party.

To try to prevent the rise of parties at the national level, the authors of the Constitution tried to design a government that would be beyond the reach of such organized factions. They believed the system of checks and balances would make it impossible for any group to gain control of the whole federal structure. The president would not be the tool of a political party because he was chosen by the electoral college, not the people. Since federal judges were to be appointed for life, they would not depend on party support for their offices. If a party formed in the popularly elected House of Representatives, then surely the Senate would counteract it. (Senators, elected for long terms of six years, would be more independent than members of the House, who had to run for election every two years.) The Constitution forbade the states to do certain things, such as coin money and regulate interstate commerce, so the worst effects of party politics in the states could be controlled from the national capital.

The political history of the first forty years of the United States is, among other things, the story of the failure of these hopes. The national government did not prove to be above or beyond party. The presidency did become a party office. Control of the national government became the highest prize in the conflict between one party and another. Supreme Court justices, senators, and congressmen did become party men with party loyalties. In fact, the very men who had written the Constitution to guard against national parties became partisan leaders themselves. Even Washington, who had seemed in 1789 to stand loftily above all partisan conflict and ambition, was drawn into the struggle and made a symbol of party conflict.

DEFINING THE EXECUTIVE BRANCH

At first, Washington's reputation and personal dignity were the greatest assets of the new government, its principal claims on the loyalty of its citizens. His presence, more than anything else, could convince people that the power of the central government would not operate in favor of any section or class, but in a truly balanced and national way. He had been chosen by a unanimous vote of the electors—though in most states these electors were appointed by state legislatures rather than elected by voters.

Washington himself strained to create an appearance of dignity, even majesty, in the capital city of New York. He rode a white horse with a striking saddlecloth of leopard skin. He also had an elegant coach, bearing his crest and drawn by a matched team of six cream-colored horses. His house, fully staffed with servants, was one of the grandest in the city. He received visitors in a carefully staged, formal manner. Almost everything he did was calculated to give an impression of regal stateliness, far beyond anything that smacked of ambition or partisanship.

Some men in Congress wanted to put an official seal upon Washington's remote and dignified manner. Just after the first inauguration, Congress drew up a message of congratulations. There was a debate over how to address the president. The vice president, John Adams, proposed the title "His Highness, the President of the United States and Protector of Their Liberties."

Washington himself kept silent on the subject, and after a heated debate, men of simpler taste won the day. The letter was addressed to "George Washington, President of the United States."

One of the first things the new Congress had to do was to create and define the departments and officers of the executive branch. The three departments of the old Confederation were continued: War, the Treasury, and Foreign Affairs—renamed the Department of State. And a postmaster general and an attorney general were added. But the more important question was one on which the Constitution was silent. The men who would become the secretaries of those departments would be chosen by the president, with the confirmation of the Senate. But who could dismiss them? If the president could demand their resignations, then he could be in more or less complete control of the policies of an administration. But if the Senate had to concur in their dismissal, then the daily workings of the executive branch would be subject to congressional control. The struggle over this question in Congress was intense, but Washington's prestige probably determined the outcome: once confirmed, the officers of the executive branch would continue to serve only as long as the president wished. Washington, and subsequent presidents, would be able to control the workings of the executive branch.

In making his appointments to the new departments, Washington strove for balance. He chose men from different states and with different attitudes and political interests. He hoped his administration could be representative of the country at large. This was particularly important when he chose the men to fill the three most important offices in his first administration. The secretary of the treasury, Alexander Hamilton, was from New York. The secretary of state was a Virginia planter and slaveowner, Thomas Jefferson. The secretary of war was Henry Knox of Massachusetts. (Although Washington did consult regularly with the heads of his executive departments, they did not hold regular meetings. The "cabinet" as a formal institution did not develop until the beginning of the next century.)

HAMILTON'S FINANCIAL PROGRAM

One of the earliest items of business of the new Congress was to do what the old Confederation Congress had not been able to do: create a source of revenue through taxation. Under the leadership of James Madison, Congress put into law the "impost," or tariff, on all imported goods. It would give the government enough income not only to conduct its normal operations but also to do something about the debts left over from the Revolution and the Confederation. The questions now became: How much of the inherited debt would be honored? Would it be paid in full, or would a compromise settlement be made to take account of the fact that most of the people who held the debt had paid just a fraction of its face value for their "certificates"? Just how would the debt be paid, and to whom? And what, if anything, did the federal government have to do with the remaining unpaid debts of the states?

The man with the clearest financial program was Alexander Hamilton. When he took office as secretary of the treasury, his job was to try to make some sense out of a confused financial situation. The United States was more than $54 million in debt. For Hamilton, the existence of the debt was not the problem. The task was not, as he saw it, to pay the debt, but rather to give the government's "creditors"—private citizens and foreign governments—confidence that the debt would eventually be paid, fully and with interest. For Hamilton, this was what restoring "faith" in the new government meant.

Over the years since the Revolution, almost no one supposed that the government would ever pay back the entire debt, so the worth of the Confederation's certificates had declined. Speculators bought them for a fraction of their face value. For example, a soldier who held a certificate worth ten dollars might sell it to a speculator for one dollar, on the theory that a dollar in the hand is better than ten in an uncertain future. All over the country, millions of dollars in certificates had been bought up or taken in trade. The government theoretically owed the entire $54 million. But few people really expected it to pay back more than a few cents on the dollar.

Individual states had also printed certificates, and they were in debt, too. Some states had already paid off most of what they owed. Others had not.

Hamilton laid out his plan in a series of brilliant reports to Congress in 1790–1791. Concerning the federal and state debts, he made two unexpected proposals. One, known as "funding," called for the government to pledge to pay off the entire Confederation debt, and at its full, or "par," value. A certificate that was worth twenty dollars would be redeemed at twenty dollars, even if the person who held it had bought if from someone else for just one dollar. Hamilton's other proposal was termed "assumption." The federal government would take over (assume) the states' debts and pay them off at par.

Hamilton did not propose to pay off federal and state debts with cash. Instead, holders of certificates would receive newly issued government bonds, to replace the old Confederation and state certificates. In both cases, the new bonds would be issued to whoever actually held the certificates. The "original holders," many of them ordinary farmers or artisans who had fought in the Continental Army and the state militias during the Revolution, would get nothing.

Hamilton also called for two new taxes. One was a tax to be paid by distillers of alcoholic beverages—whiskey, mostly, but also rum. The other was a tariff on certain "enumerated" imports, which would not only raise money but also "protect" infant American manufacturing establishments from competition from cheaper English goods. Hamilton also proposed the creation of a national bank to help the government make all its financial transactions, and to create a stable national currency.

Taken as a whole, Hamilton's program amounted to a vigorous attempt to establish an economic basis for the nationalism that had triumphed in the Constitution. Politically, however, the immediate effect was to generate opposition in Congress to some elements of his scheme. Initially, the opposition centered on funding and assumption, and was led by James Madison. Madison tried to get Congress to divide repayment of the debt equally between present and original holders. And he opposed the assumption of the state debts, largely because Virginia and several other southern states had already paid their war debts and could hardly be expected to share now in the burden of paying off New York's or Massachusetts' debts.

Madison was able to mount a powerful opposition in Congress to both funding and assumption. He was soon supported by Jefferson, the influential secretary of state. But Hamilton had strong backing too. The standoff in Congress was finally settled by a classic political bargain. Madison and Jefferson promised to deliver enough votes in Congress to pass Hamilton's proposal. In return, Hamilton would deliver the votes of his followers for a measure providing that a new national capital would be created in the South rather than the North. The city would be called Washington, and it would be located on the Potomac River in a district that would bear the name Columbia. The funding and assumption measures were passed in July 1790 and were soon signed by Washington.

Hamilton also got his tax on whiskey, but Congress rejected the idea of protective tariffs and other subsidies for American manufacturing. And Hamilton very nearly failed to win on the question of a national bank. Congress did pass a bill creating the bank, but Washington hesitated to sign it. His problem was that the Constitution did not say that Congress had the power to create such a bank. Washington believed that a president ought to veto an act of Congress only if he thought it was unconstitutional. He asked Hamilton and Jefferson to submit opinions on the constitutionality of the bank.

The debate turned on the clause that gives Congress the power to make all the laws that are "necessary and proper" for the implementation of its constitutional powers. Hamilton argued that if Congress had a legitimate constitutional purpose, then any law that served that purpose was also legitimate (so long as the Constitution did not expressly forbid such a law, of course). Jefferson argued that the Constitution should be interpreted more strictly. Congress, he agreed, could do what was "necessary" to fulfill its constitutional obligations. But "necessary" did not mean "desirable" or even "effective." It meant indispensable. And a national bank was hardly indispensable to the execution of Congress's power to coin or borrow money, or any of its other specified powers. Washington hesitated, but then accepted Hamilton's argument and signed the act creating the Bank of the United States. But Hamilton and Jefferson had laid down two radically different ways of understanding the Constitution, two theories that could serve as a basis for partisan political conflict for a long time to come.

THE WHISKEY REBELLION

Hamilton's tax on distilled liquor had unforeseen and ominous consequences. The cheapest and most economical way for most western farmers to transport their grain crops to the East was to turn the grain into whiskey. From their point of view, a whiskey tax was not a "luxury" or a "sin" tax, but a very heavy economic burden.

Many farmers in western Pennsylvania resisted the tax. In the summer of 1794 they even mobbed tax collectors, much as Americans had attacked Stamp Act tax collectors a generation before. The Whiskey Rebellion was small, much smaller than Shays's uprising had been eight years earlier. But President Washington reacted with a series of steps that went well beyond what was needed. He called out 15,000 militiamen and marched them west toward Pittsburgh, with himself sometimes at their head. This excessive display of federal military power worked immediately. The rebels were totally intimidated, even before the militia reached the Pittsburgh area. In his zeal Washington revealed the depth of his old concern about maintaining law and order in the West.

After the rebellion had been easily suppressed, Washington delivered an address to Congress in which he condemned not only the rebels but a new kind of political organization called "Democratic" or "Democratic-Republican" societies. The societies, which eventually numbered about forty—had been formed in enthusiastic support of the French Revolution. But most of them were also the grass-roots bases of an emerging political opposition to Washington's own administration—though not to him personally. But to Washington's mind the sectional question that had been raised by the Whiskey Rebellion was closely tied to the question of political factions and opposition to the government. Anything that threatened national unity, whether it was a sectional uprising or an opposition political faction, was an evil to be dealt with quickly.

REPUBLICANS VERSUS FEDRALISTS

The increasingly bitter struggles over Hamilton's programs laid the groundwork for sustained conflict between two major political factions at the national level. From 1792 on, for two decades, every major decision on domestic and foreign policy caused a partisan quarrel. Jefferson and Madison, year after year, organized their supporters and strengthened their forces. They studied local and state elections throughout the country and supported candidates for Congress who they thought would be sympathetic to their views. Gradually, almost against their wills, they formed the beginnings of a political party.

The followers of Jefferson and Madison were mostly small farmers, artisans, and debtors. Many of them were former Antifederalists who thought Hamilton's program was a scheme to create a powerful federal government at the expense of states' rights. Gradually, this group adopted the name Republican (or Democratic-Republican). This term emphasized their avowed dedication to the interests of "the people" at large.

Hamilton's strongest supporters were mainly merchants, bankers, and entrepreneurs. They gradually began to call themselves Federalists. This proud name was derived, of course, from the term for supporters of the Constitution in 1788.

The grass-roots support for both factions was actually somewhat mixed. Only a small minority of Americans voted anyway, so both parties' claims to represent "the people" were exaggerated. In practice, voting support for the Republicans was only slightly more "democratic" than for the Federalists. But Jefferson was successful in creating the lasting myth that his was the party of the people against the rich and the well-born.

In 1792, President Washington still stood above party, and both sides joined in reelecting him. But in his second term, he gradually identified himself with Hamilton and the Federalists. He still talked of disliking parties more than any feature of government, but he was under constant pressure from Hamilton and his friends to support their positions. Bit by bit, Washington's second term took on the appearance of a real administration—that is, it was staffed by members of one partisan faction, with a specific political program.

When Washington finally approached his longed-for retirement, he prepared a Farewell Address that contained a severe condemnation of political parties. Paradoxically, however, the address was itself a highly partisan political action. It was published in September 1796—almost six months before Washington was scheduled to leave office. The Republicans claimed (rightly) that the timing was meant to influence the votes in the November presidential election. They also suspected (again, rightly) that Hamilton had a hand in both the content and timing of the farewell address. Still, what Washington had to say about political parties was bitter and eloquent:

> Let me warn you in the most solemn manner against the baneful effects of the spirit of party. This spirit serves always to distract the public councils and to enfeeble the public administration. It agitates the community with ill-founded jealousies and false alarms; kindles the animosity of one part against another; foments riot and insurrection. It opens the door to foreign influence and corruption.

In theory, at least, Madison and Jefferson might still have agreed. But by 1796 they had had six years of experience in opposition politics. And they had formed, like it or not, the nucleus of a political party. The Republicans in Congress nominated Jefferson for the presidency, to run against Federalist John Adams. Despite the short time available to mount a campaign, Jefferson was a close second in the electoral college. According to the awkward provisions of the Constitution, which had been designed to prevent the creation of party "tickets," the runner-up in the electoral vote became vice president. So for the next four years the United States had a Federalist president and a Republican vice president.

During Adams's term of office, party conflict reached a high pitch. Everywhere, Republicans were organizing for the election of 1800. The Federalists could sense the tide running toward Jefferson. In anger and desperation they managed to ram through Congress a series of laws designed to stifle political opposition. Three Alien Acts were directed against new immigrants from Europe (most of whom were becoming Republican voters once they gained citizenship). One of the acts increased the period of residence from five to fourteen years before an immigrant could become a citizen—and a Republican voter. More significant and controversial was the Federalists' Sedition Act of 1798. The Sedition Act made it a crime to publish any "false, scandalous and malicious writing against the government of the United States or either house of the Congress or the President." Under the Sedition Act, federal judges (appointed by a Federalist president) attempted to silence Republican criticism. A number of newspaper editors were prosecuted, and one Republican member of Congress was even sent to prison for speeches made against Adams during the campaign of 1798.

By and large, the Sedition Act backfired. Madison and Jefferson were able to use opposition to it to try to unite their party and the state governments against the Adams administration. Instead of trying to get a judicial solution from the Supreme Court—whose powers were unclear and whose members were staunchly Federalist anyway—the Republican leaders conducted what amounted to a political campaign.

WASHINGTON VS. JEFFERSON. This cartoon, published in 1795—the year following the Whiskey Rebellion—shows a determined but dignified Washington leading his volunteers out to put down rebels, who are the tools of French "cannibals." Jefferson, Madison, and one of their followers are vainly trying to hold back the chariot of republican order. In a French accent, Jefferson is shouting "Stop de wheels of de gouvernement."

Madison secretly wrote a resolution for Virginia's legislature and Jefferson drafted one for Kentucky's. These documents, which became known as the Virginia and Kentucky Resolutions, denounced the Sedition Act as unconstitutional. They held, too, that the states could resist any federal law they judged to be a violation of the Constitution. These resolutions drew the lines very clearly for the election of 1800, and they put the Republicans firmly on the side of "states' rights" against federal power.

THE ELECTION OF 1800

The Republicans organized an intense campaign in the summer and fall of 1800. New York was a typical and important state. The Republicans had to win there if they were to take the presidency from Adams and the Federalists. New York political affairs were in the hands of none other than Alexander Hamilton for the Federalists and Aaron Burr for the Republicans. In the state elections of 1799, Hamilton's party had won an im-

Party strife. The dignity of George Washington and the peaceful grace of Thomas Jefferson's Monticello represented Americans' best hopes for republican order. This fight in the House of Representatives, which took place in 1797, represented their worst fears. Roger Griswold, a Federalist from Connecticut, is attacking Matthew Lyon, a Republican from Vermont, with a cane. Lyon has grabbed the fireplace tongs to defend himself. In the Speaker's chair sits an amused Jonathan Dayton of New Jersey. The cartoon is clearly the work of one of many Americans who deplored the rise of political parties.

pressive victory. But Burr, Jefferson's candidate for the vice presidency, now went to work in the city of New York. He got Republicans to the polls by every means possible, and the result was a victory in the state legislature. Since the legislature in New York chose presidential electors, New York delivered all its electoral votes to Jefferson. Virginia, the largest state, also went to Jefferson. Although Adams held all the New England states, the Jeffersonians got more than half the votes in Pennsylvania.

The result should have been clear, but it was confused by the fact that the Constitution recognized no distinction between presidential and vice presidential candidates. Each elector was required to cast two votes, both for president. Every one of the Republican electors who voted for Jefferson carelessly voted for Burr, so there was, technically, a tie between two candidates from the same party. This meant the election would have to be decided by the House of Representatives.

Once the election was thrown into the House, the situation was even more confused. In the first place, voting was by states and each state was allowed one vote, no matter what its population. In the second place, the House was free to choose any of the candidates, even though Jefferson and Burr had both beaten Adams in the electoral voting. The voting quickly settled down to a contest between Jefferson and Adams. Burr stood rather coyly to one side, refusing to shift his support firmly and publicly to Jefferson. Thirty-five ballots were cast before Hamilton finally threw his support to Jefferson. Hamilton did this because, although he disliked Jefferson, he hated Burr. Hamilton's move settled the election. It also made the relationship between Burr and Hamilton impossible, and, together with events in New York, would lead the two men at last to the dueling ground.

JEFFERSON'S REPUBLICANISM

After the election had at last been decided, Jefferson tried publicly to soften party divisions—as Washington had always done. After one of the most bitter political campaigns in American history, he soothingly announced in his inaugural address that "We are all Federalists; we are all Republicans."

But privately Jefferson was convinced that nothing less than a political revolution had occurred—he called it the Revolution of 1800. And it was his task, he thought, to see that the revolution was completed. He believed the victory of his party over Hamilton, Adams, and the Federalists should bring about a basic reversal in the direction of American history. Jefferson told friends and colleagues that their ultimate purpose was to destroy the Federalists completely, to send them into the "abyss." This, he believed, would make it possible to realize the hope of the framers of the Constitution that there would be no national political parties.

Jefferson's conception of the good society rested on one fundamental opinion. As he put it, "Those who labor in the earth are the chosen people of God." Property-owning "yeoman" farmers, he thought, ought to be the backbone of any republican society. And the plain farmers ought to have as much political power as they had "virtue." They ought to control the government in a more or less direct and democratic way.

The national government should be devoted above all to republican simplicity. It should be small and relatively weak, so that it could not interfere with the liberties of the people. Power should be decentralized—that is, divided up among smaller authorities such as state and local governments. Then people could keep a close eye on their elected representatives.

It sometimes seemed that Jefferson's political philosophy was based on a conflict between two simple ideas: power and the people. Whatever contributed to governmental power injured people's control over their own private lives. Jefferson wanted a "government which shall restrain men from injuring one another." But government should do no more than this. It should leave men "otherwise free to regulate their own pursuits of industry and improvement."

Such a government ought to practice the strictest economy. The number of federal officers should be cut to the bare minimum—and they should all be good Republicans, of course. The national debt should be quickly liquidated. (It had ballooned from $54 million to about $83 million as a result of Hamilton's program of funding and assumption.) In fact, Jefferson promised to pay off the entire debt within sixteen years. To save on expenses, his administration reduced the army from 4,000 to 2,500 men. He cut the navy back sharply to a defensive force that would rely on coastal guns and small gunboats, rather than on big and expensive warships.

Jefferson's was a political program that promised not to do things: not to maintain a powerful government with a large standing army and a powerful navy; not to allow the federal government to become powerful at the expense of the rights of the states and the people; not to pursue a financial policy that would benefit only a small class of merchants, bankers, and speculators. The heart of Jefferson's idea of government was his belief that the American people—most of whom really were plain farmers—could build a great nation if only they were let alone by government. Jefferson himself was a cultivated aristocrat, a highly educated man, and a wealthy slaveholding planter. But his political philosophy was one of democratic simplicity and an almost religious faith in the good sense of the people.

In the long run, Jefferson and the other Republican presidents who followed him were the captives of history. They were forced to expand, not contract, federal power in order to meet emergencies and opportunities that came their way. Time and again, their ideas of strict construction of the Constitution and states' rights had to yield to the necessities of the situation. But their revolution was one of ideas, not actions. Jefferson and his successors made words like "liberty" and "democracy" the key terms of the political language of Americans. And, after 1800, a professed faith in "the people" became the most prominent and unique feature of American political rhetoric.

Jefferson continued to believe political parties were evil. True, he had helped build a party that had turned the Federalists out of office. But he had done so because he convinced himself that the Federalists were an evil party and that he and his party had saved the Republic.

After 1800 the Republicans were committed to making their party the only party, to driving the Federalists out of existence altogether. Jefferson was easily elected to a second term in

1804. Madison won the presidency in 1808 and 1812, and he was followed into office by another Virginia Republican, James Monroe, in 1816. By 1820 the Federalist party had collapsed and did not even run a candidate. Monroe was reelected by an electroal college margin of 231 to 1. Four years later, the destruction of the Federalist Party was so complete that the son of John Adams, John Quincy Adams, won the presidency—as a Republican.

After 1824 a new party structure would emerge, with new parties replacing the Republicans and the Federalists. But for the time being, it appeared that the Republicans had actually realized the hopes of the Founding Fathers by creating a unified government with no national political parties.

MARSHALL AND THE JUDICIARY

The triumph of Jefferson and the Republicans was incomplete, however. There was one branch of the national government over which they did not gain control. The federal judiciary remained a stronghold of Federalist nationalism, long after the "Revolution of 1800," and even after the collapse of the Federalists as a political organization.

The section of the Constitution that established the federal court system was much briefer than the sections on the presidency and the Congress. It was left to Congress to decide how large the Supreme Court should be, how many "inferior" courts were to be established, and to specify the relationships between state and federal courts.

In its first year, Congress passed the Judiciary Act of 1789, which defined the basic structure of the federal courts. The Supreme Court that the Constitution provided for would have a chief justice and five associate justices. Thirteen district courts and three circuit courts of appeal were established. And, most importantly, the Supreme Court was given the right to overturn state court decisions whenever the case involved a question about the constitutionality of a federal or state law.

MONTICELLO. This painting of Monticello shows how the leaders of the revolutionary movement tried in their lives, their writing, and their architecture to put together several seemingly contradictory principles. This grand mansion, planned and built by Thomas Jefferson, seems to argue that there was no incompatibility between his wealth and his principle that "all men are created equal." Greek grandeur is tucked into a simple, pastoral landscape. Geometrical order and child's play go together here, as do the gentleman's learned solitude and homey family closeness. Most of all, slavery is kept carefully offstage.

During its early years, the Supreme Court made few significant decisions. In fact, its most important early decision was soon defeated by a constitutional amendment. Under the Constitution, the Supreme Court was given jurisdiction over cases involving a state and a citizen of a different state. But did this mean that any citizen of one state could sue the government of another state? If so, this was an ominous fact for those who believed the states had kept their "sovereignty"; for it was generally believed that no "sovereign" power could be sued without its own consent. The question reached the Supreme Court in the case of *Chisholm* v. *Georgia* (1793), and the justices decided that the Constitution did indeed allow citizens to sue states in federal court. The outcry against the decision was so great, however, that a constitutional amendment, the eleventh, was quickly ratified to protect the states from such suits.

In 1796, in two related cases, the Supreme Court asserted two powers that were not definitely provided for in the Constitution. In *Ware* v. *Hylton* the Court for the first time declared a state law to be unconstitutional. In *Hylton* v. *United States,* the justices asked, for the first time, whether an act of Congress was constitutional. The Court upheld the federal law, but the justices had made it clear that they believed they had the authority to overturn any federal law they found "repugnant to the Constitution."

After the election of 1800, Federalist leaders understood at once that they could maintain a degree of control over the government, even in defeat, through the federal courts. In the last days of the Adams administration, the Federalists pushed through Congress the Judiciary Act of 1801. It created fifteen new district courts, which Adams was still filling with "midnight judges" down into the final hours before Jefferson's inauguration. The act also provided that when the next justice died or resigned, the Supreme Court would be reduced in size from six to five members—which would deny Jefferson the right to make a new appointment.

The new, Republican-controlled Congress quickly repealed the Judiciary Act of 1801. And the Republicans also counterattacked by removing one of the most blatantly incompetent of the Federalist district judges, John Pickering of New Hampshire, through impeachment. The House of Representatives then impeached—indicted—a Supreme Court justice, Samuel Chase, who had been a vigorous enforcer of the Sedition Act. The Republicans fell short of the two-thirds majority needed in the Senate to convict Chase. But they had made it clear that they regarded the federal bench as a major obstacle to the completion of their "Revolution of 1800."

But the figure the Republicans could not dislodge or control was John Marshall, the Virginia Federalist who was named chief justice by Adams early in 1801. For thirty-four years, Marshall managed to maintain effective control of the Supreme Court, even after Republican presidents had appointed all the associate justices. Marshall, who wrote most of the Court's decisions, held his fellow justices to a firmly nationalist line, and ensured that the Constitution and federal law would be the "supreme law of the land." His two most important decisions came in *Marbury* v. *Madison* (1803) and *McCulloch* v. *Maryland* (1819). In *Marbury,* the Court for the first time declared a federal law unconstitutional. In *McCulloch,* Marshall and his colleagues established the principle that if there was a conflict between a state law and a federal law, the state law was null and void. Marshall's court also gave a consistently broad and vigorous interpretation to federal powers, especially those that derived from the clauses of the Constitution concerning contracts and the control of interstate commerce.

FOREIGN AFFAIRS

During most of the twenty-five years after Washington's first inauguration, Europe was at war. Britain and France fought everywhere in Europe, around the Mediterranean, and in almost every other corner of the world. In the process, other European nations and the United States were drawn into the conflict.

Events in Europe had a profound effect on the United States in two fields. One was the economy. Americans imported most of their manufactured goods from England, and they in turn sold many agricultural products, like tobacco and cotton, in Europe. This transatlantic trade was crucial to farmers in the southern and western states. Merchants in eastern cities also depended heavily on a brisk trade across the Atlantic. European nations at war needed the American trade, but at the same time they tried to cut their enemies off from American shipping. By turns, the English and the French attacked American ships. They even kidnapped American seamen for service in their own navies and merchant marine, a practice known as impressment.

The other field deeply affected by European affairs was American politics. The conflict between Britain and France was an old one, going well back into the eighteenth century. Indeed, the Americans had fought their revolution against the British with French help. But there was a new element in the conflict after 1789. In that year the French began a revolution against their monarchy. They proclaimed France a republic in 1792, and from then on they fought their wars for ideological reasons, as well as for the more traditional military, political, and economic ones. In fact, the French aggressively proposed themselves the agents of "a war of all peoples against all kings."

In the beginning, many Americans favored the French Revolution. To them it meant another monarch deposed, another republic created. America's old ally, the Marquis de Lafayette, even sent Washington the key to the Bastille, the notorious Paris prison whose fall was one of the most dramatic events of the revolution.

Gradually, though, the French Revolution seemed to take a dangerous turn. At the height of revolutionary fervor, in 1793 and 1794, thousands of Frenchmen, including the king and queen, were guillotined. To many Americans (especially those with Federalist sympathies), this experience was a lesson in the "excesses" of democracy. But others—the political disciples of Jefferson—followed their leader in stubborn sympathy with the French Revolution and its democratic changes. Thus politics in America felt the impact of politics in Europe.

Out of this situation arose a crucial question: Could the United States remain neutral, since both its trade and its politics were tied so closely to the almost continuous wars of the British and the French? From George Washington to John Quincy Adams, American presidents and their administrations had to devote at least as much attention to foreign as to domestic questions. In fact, much of the time it was impossible to draw a line between the two.

This long episode in foreign policy involved almost every American political leader, from Washington, Hamilton, and Jefferson to men like Burr and Wilkinson. Burr's plans and intrigues were not the schemes of an isolated individual. Rather, he could claim the company of dozens of other public figures, all constantly involved in speculation, secret plans, and even spying. In the 1790s at least two cabinet officers were covertly working for European governments. Many senators, congressmen, and lesser politicians were so sympathetic to one European side or the other that they lost sight of American purposes and goals.

Thus, for twenty-five years, Americans had no real independence of Europe. They were tied to France, Spain, and Britain by every ship that left America for Europe, by developing systems of party loyalty, and by tough, troublesome issues of war and peace. Only after 1815, with the final defeat of Napoleon and general peace in Europe, did Americans find release from European entanglements and wars.

A SHAKY NEUTRALITY

Several forces pushed the United States toward renewed war with Britain during the early 1790s. Anger and resentment still lingered after the Revolutionary War. The British refused to evacuate their military posts in the Northwest Territory. They discriminated against American trade and harassed American shipping. They also refused to return American slaves whom they had freed during the Revolution. Many Americans sympathized with the French because of their aid during the war. In addition, there was the treaty of 1778, in which the United States pledged to come to the aid of France in case of conflict with Britain.

When France and Britain went to war in 1793, Washington's administration faced its first difficult decision in foreign policy. Partly under the influence of Hamilton, who despised the French for their democratic republicanism, Washington decided to ignore the alliance of 1778 and remain neutral. But the British made it very difficult for him. They used their position in Canada to incite Native Americans against American settlers. And British warships began to stop and even seize American merchant vessels trading with French islands in the West Indies.

But the French lost a chance to cement their relations with Americans by sending over a blundering diplomat, Edmond Genêt, who made the mistake of acting as though France and the United States were already allies. He did things that no representative of a foreign government can get away with for long. He set up French courts to take charge of captured English ships. He tried to talk a group of Americans into an armed attack on New Orleans (since Spain sided with Britain at the time). Worst of all, he interfered in domestic political matters. Even Jefferson, the ardent supporter of the French Revolution, could not stomach such behavior. Washington ended by demanding Genêt's recall to Paris.

In the meantime, despite Genêt's clumsiness, anti-British feeling was running high in America. There was real danger of war. Washington wanted to avoid it and settle old questions left over from the Revolution. He sent John Jay, a Federalist leader and a close friend of Hamilton's, to London to negotiate a treaty.

Jay returned home in 1794, bearing a document that became known as the Jay Treaty. In it, the British agreed to give up their northwest posts. They made a few other concessions of a minor nature. In general, though, the treaty was unfavorable to the United States and offered no real protection to American shipping. Like everything else during this period of party conflict, the Jay Treaty immediately became a political issue. Republicans opposed it and Federalists supported it. Even Washington, who wanted desperately to avoid a war, was reluctant to sign it, but he finally did so.

NEGOTIATIONS WITH FRANCE

The Jay Treaty made American relations with France more difficult, since the French believed that anything that helped the British hurt them. Late in Washington's administration and in the early months of Adams' presidency, the French began to intercept American shipping. Furthermore, they treated American sailors serving on British ships as pirates, to be hanged. Like Washington, Adams tried to meet the crisis by insisting on neutrality and opening negotiations. He sent a team of three negotiators to Paris to try to arrange a treaty recognizing American trading rights and somehow putting an end to the embarrassing alliance of 1778.

The American mission failed. The French foreign minister, a shrewd and corrupt man named Charles Talleyrand, demanded a bribe of $250,000 for himself. He never met the Americans. Instead, he communicated with them through three anonymous go-betweens known only as X, Y, and Z. Through these agents, Talleyrand also demanded that the Americans pay the government of France several million dollars as the price of peace and a treaty. Two of the three American commissioners returned angrily to America to report to a shocked president and Congress. For a time, war seemed inevitable.

Adams's position was delicate. Many members of his party wanted war with France—partly to discredit the Republicans and partly to solidify their own hold on the national government. Adams moved considerably in their direction. He called for a stronger navy, better coastal defenses, and the arming of American merchant ships. He also gave in to Hamilton's demands that the army be strengthened. The retired Washington even

LEWIS, CLARK, SACAJAWEA, AND YORK. Even before the purchase of Louisiana, Jefferson began to plan the exploration of the West. He chose his own private secretary, Meriwether Lewis, and William Clark to lead an expedition to the Pacific. For two years, their party made its way to the seacoast. They were helped enormously by a Native American woman, Sacajawea, who functioned as a guide, and by an African-American slave, York, an accomplished linguist who acted as interpreter. Nonetheless, the expedition has always been known by the name "Lewis and Clark." And in this painting, Lewis, standing, and Clark, armed, confidently hold center stage. A somewhat downcast Sacajawea and a somewhat anxious York are in the wings.

agreed to take charge of the army in case of war, with Hamilton as his second in command. For several years American and French ships fought an undeclared war in the Atlantic and the Caribbean, known as the Quasi-War.

But Adams was determined to avoid an unnecessary war, even if it hurt his position among the Federalists. In 1799 he sent another American mission to France with orders to negotiate an agreement. There the Americans found a new government in control. Its leader, Napoleon, was anxious to establish good relations with the United States. He agreed to end French interference with American shipping—a promise the French only partially kept. For the time being, at least, Adams had preserved American neutrality.

TERRITORIAL EXPANSION

One of the most obvious facts of life for the generation of Americans who lived after the making of the Constitution was national expansion. In 1790, at the time of the first census, there were fewer than 4 million Americans of European or African ancestry, and most of them lived on the eastern seaboard. Only about one person in every twenty-five lived over the mountains in Kentucky, Tennessee, or Ohio. But the spirit of expansion was everywhere. Every year, thousands of families set out for the West to make new homes. This growth and movement were very much on the minds of American political leaders. George Washington felt that strenuous efforts would have to be made to tie eastern and western peoples together. Burr, on the other hand, believed the federal government could not hold the loyalty of the western settlers.

By 1810 the population of the United States had almost doubled, to over 7 million. And by 1820 it was almost 10 million. As it grew, the population shifted steadily westward. In 1820 one of every ten citizens of the United States lived west of the Appalachian Mountains.

Everyone who looked carefully at the United States in the 1790s knew that the future lay in the West. Benjamin Franklin's calculations for the future always took for granted that the Ohio and Mississippi valleys held the key to the nation's destiny. Washington thought along similar lines, and so did Jefferson. After Hamilton's death had disgraced Burr, he simply followed what was becoming an American reflex: when in trouble or in doubt, look to the West for new opportunities and answers.

THE LOUISIANA PURCHASE

According to the peace treaty of 1783, the western boundary of the United States was the Mississippi River. This seemed to provide more than enough land to absorb the people and energies of the infant nation for decades to come. There was only one sore point. Spain still held most of the western half of the continent, and Spain controlled the Mississippi River and its outlet at New Orleans. Farmers west of the Appalachians depended almost entirely on the river to get their cash crops to market.

It came as a bitter shock when the United States learned in 1801 that Spain had given Louisiana to France in a secret treaty. Now New Orleans and the vast Mississippi Valley would be in the hands not of weak Spain but of powerful and ambitious Napoleon. In 1802 the Spanish—still theoretically in control of New Orleans—caused another shock when they declared that Americans would no longer have the right to use New Orleans as a port for their exports.

Jefferson summed up the horror of most Americans when he said there was "on the globe one single spot, the possessor of which is our natural and habitual enemy. It is New Orleans." As was his custom, Jefferson turned immediately to negotiation. He made Napoleon an offer to purchase New Orleans for $2 million. But the Americans were about to get much more than they expected. The American negotiator, James Monroe, was greatly surprised and pleased when the French offered to sell not just New Orleans but the entire territory of Louisiana, about 800,000 square miles of practically uninhabited land—at least as whites defined "uninhabited."

In April 1803, the Americans closed the deal. They bought all of Louisiana for $15 million—a price that averaged out at about $20 per square mile for one of the potentially richest areas in the world.

The purchase created some problems for Jefferson. He believed in a narrow, or "strict," interpretation of the Constitution. Basic to this constitutional theory was the idea that the president and Congress could do only those things that the Constitution expressly gave them power to do. The Constitution nowhere gave the president the power to acquire new territory. In contrast to Jefferson's position was "loose construction," favored by most Federalists. On this view, the government had not only those powers that were mentioned specifically by the Constitution but also other powers that were "implied." Thus, they would have argued, the power to make treaties implied the power to acquire territory, since acquisition was in the nature of a new treaty arrangement.

After some quarreling (mainly with himself), Jefferson gave up on what he called "metaphysical" questions. He asked Congress to appropriate the $15 million. The United States took formal possession of New Orleans in December of 1803, just seven months before the duel between Hamilton and Burr.

TROUBLE WITH BRITAIN

After his victory in the election of 1800, Jefferson began to dismantle the army and navy that Washington and Adams had expanded. Europe was temporarily at peace, and it looked as if the United States could achieve the promises of independence, freed from foreign involvements. In 1803, however, Europe again donned the familiar mask of war. The major player this time was the commanding figure of Napoleon. Over the next dozen years Napoleon's incredible ambition sent

French armies all over Europe and as far as Egypt and Russia.

The French emperor contemplated an invasion of England, and he even thought of moving some of his armies into North America. The British were locked in what they regarded as a deadly struggle for survival. For Americans the questions were the same old ones: Would they be able to carry on their vitally necessary trade with Europe? Would they be able to preserve their precious neutrality?

Beginning in 1805, British and French warships both began to intercept American merchant shipping again. The British controlled the seas, so they stopped more vessels. The British also followed one practice that the French did not. They would board American vessels, pick out men whom they suspected of being British subjects, and force them into service in the Royal Navy. This practice of impressment, which to most Americans seemed little short of kidnapping, added to the fury that gradually built up in the United States.

Jefferson was committed to peace, to a small army and navy, and to a policy of negotiation rather than threat and bluster. But between 1805 and 1807 the British seized about 1,000 American ships, and the French about 500. No administration, no matter how devoted to peace, could permit American ships and sailors to be treated like this.

Another crisis occurred in the summer of 1807. A British warship, the *Leopard,* fired three broadsides into an American frigate, the *Chesapeake,* within view of the Virginia shore. The *Chesapeake*'s guns were out of order, and it could return only one cannon shot. Three Americans were killed and eighteen wounded before the *Chesapeake* limped home.

Facing an aroused nation, Jefferson tried to ward off a war with Britain by a device used in pre-Revolution days. He asked Congress for a law, the Embargo Act, which simply prohibited any vessel from leaving an American port carrying cargo bound for any other nation. In short, the embargo was designed to halt foreign trade altogether. Jefferson was using an extremely "loose" construction of the Constitution's provision for the regulation of foreign commerce. But he hoped that the British need for American markets, plus the French desire to import American goods, would quickly force the two nations to behave more respectfully toward American commerce.

The embargo failed. It hurt Americans more than it hurt either the British or the French, because American farmers could not export their products. The law lasted until the end of Jefferson's second administration, when he happily left the capital for his plantation, Monticello. His successor, James Madison, then had to grapple with the problem. Madison's efforts at first were only modifications of Jefferson's policy. For the em-

THE BURNING OF WASHINGTON, 1814. The British burned a number of major government buildings in the capital on August 24, 1814, though they did not occupy the city for long. Their action was a retaliation for the American burning of the capital of Upper Canada, York (which was later renamed Toronto).

bargo, Madison substituted a modified policy of trade restriction with the Non-Intercourse Act of 1809. He reopened foreign trade with all nations *except* Britain and France. And he promised to resume commerce with either country if only it would respect American rights on the seas.

THE WAR OF 1812

The Madison administration experimented with one form of trade restriction or another for more than three years. Finally, Madison asked for a declaration of war against Britain, citing impressment and trade interference. Congress responded on June 18, 1812. Just two days earlier, the British had announced a favorable change in policy. But it was too late. By the time news of the British shift in policy reached the United States, war had already begun.

The War of 1812 produced frustrating and inconclusive results for the United States. There was a stalemate on what the Americans hoped would be the main front in the North. Then the British sailed almost unopposed into the Chesapeake and burned much of Washington. By the second year of the war, the British navy had total control of the North American coast. A final, spectacular American triumph in New Orleans came only after the treaty of peace had already been signed.

But the war did produce a couple of future presidents, several cherished slogans, a national anthem, and an important myth.

The Americans began with a shining confidence that they could quickly capture Canada. It was, Jefferson remarked, a mere matter of marching. But it was not to be. The Canadian front was divided by geography into three corridors. The first, in the east, ran up from Fort Ticonderoga across lakes George and Champlain, and on toward Montreal. The second lay across the Niagara River, between Lakes Erie and Ontario. The third ran eastward from Detroit, between lakes Huron and Erie.

In 1812 the Americans mounted assaults through all three corridors. All three failed miserably—two of them when New York militiamen simply refused to cross the border into Canada. The following year, the Americans again tried all three fronts. Once more, the result was defeat in the eastern and central corridors. But in the west, United States forces had a bit more luck. A young naval officer, Oliver Hazard Perry, sailed a small fleet of newly built ships from the eastern end of Lake Erie. Perry met and defeated the British at Put-in Bay, near Detroit. He reported his victory with one of the war's few lasting results, a slogan: "We have met the enemy, and they are ours."

Perry's victory made the position of combined British and Native American forces near Detroit untenable, so they began to withdraw into Canada. An American army under the command of William Henry Harrison—a future president who had already won a battle against Native Americans in 1811 at Tippecanoe, Indiana—gave chase and won the Battle of the Thames in October 1813. (One of the casualties of the battle was the great Indian leader Tecumseh, who had become a general officer in the British army.)

Meanwhile, the Americans had won a few victories at sea in engagements between single ships, most notably a string of victories by the frigate *Constitution* ("Old Ironsides"). And one American defeat gave rise to another slogan. When the U.S.S. *Chesapeake* was about to be taken by the British *Shannon,* the American captain, James Lawrence, supposedly uttered a famous dying order: "Don't give up the ship! Blow her up!" The order was not obeyed. The *Chesapeake* surrendered. But the slogan took hold of a public imagination badly in need of heroes and good news.

In the end, British naval superiority was overwhelming—800 warships against a few dozen vessels in the American fleet. By 1814 the British completely controlled the American coastline. This was an ominous fact. But it was joined to another fact even more ominous. In 1814, when Napoleon was defeated and sent into exile, crack British regi-

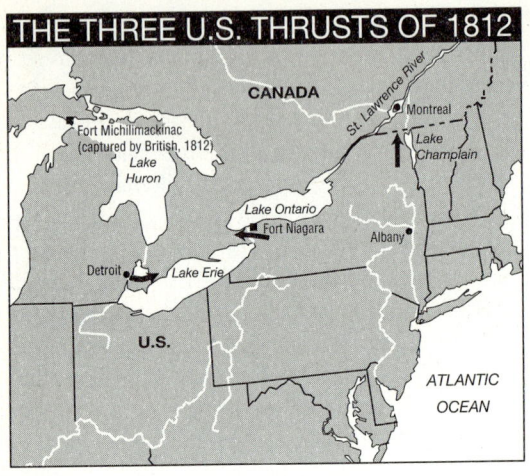

ments were freed to join the American war. The British now took the offensive.

Their first and largest assault came down the Lake Champlain–Lake George corridor from Canada. In the summer of 1814, about 10,000 British regulars began the attack. But they were turned back—as they had been in the Revolutionary War—by a desperate American victory on Lake Champlain, a victory managed by a skillful young officer, Thomas McDonough, in the battle of Plattsburgh.

The second British attack came in August, up Chesapeake Bay. The British easily captured Washington and burned most of its major public buildings, including the White House. Then they set out to raid Baltimore. But here they were stood off by the resistance of a well-placed American fortification, Fort McHenry. The British bombardment was watched by an American, Francis Scott Key, whose eyes searched the early light of the dawn for the American flag. He later set his thoughts to the tune of a bawdy British tavern song and gave the Americans a national anthem. With Washington in disarray, and Baltimore out of reach, the British could hope for little else in the Chesapeake.

Their third attack came in the South, at New Orleans. The Tennessee soldier-lawyer-planter-politician, Andrew Jackson, had marched an American force of militia down through the Mississippi Territory. He subdued the Creek Indians at the battle of Horseshoe Bend. Then he invaded Spanish Florida and captured Pensacola. Then on to New Orleans, where he threw together a force of pirates, vagabonds, militia, and free blacks (African Americans made up about 10 percent of his army) to defend the city against an invading force of British regulars.

The British commander, General Sir Edward Packenham, decided to throw his seasoned men in a close-ranked assault on the rough fortifications Jackson had built. The result was carnage. Jackson's well-placed artillery raked the British formations over and over again. Within about half an hour, some 500 British soldiers were dead, including Packenham, and about 1,500 others were wounded.

(Jackson's riflemen had also shot a few of the enemy. But these hunters from Kentucky received much of the credit for the victory. This reinforced the myth of the frontiersman with his rifle as the soul and sinew of the Republic and, incidentally, did more than anything else to make Jackson president in 1828. The myth of the rifleman was, clearly, much more attractive than the reality of a numerous and cunningly placed line of cannon.)

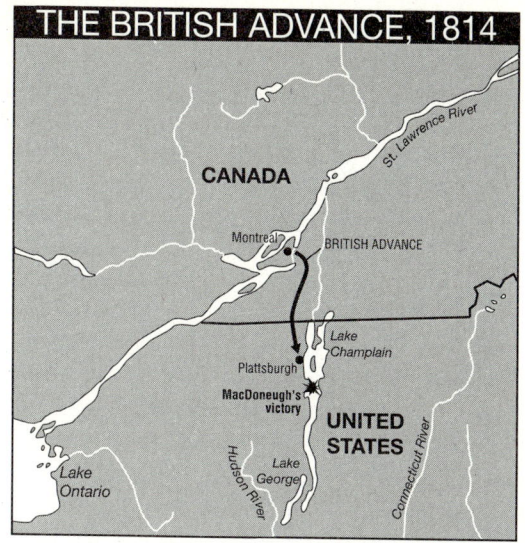
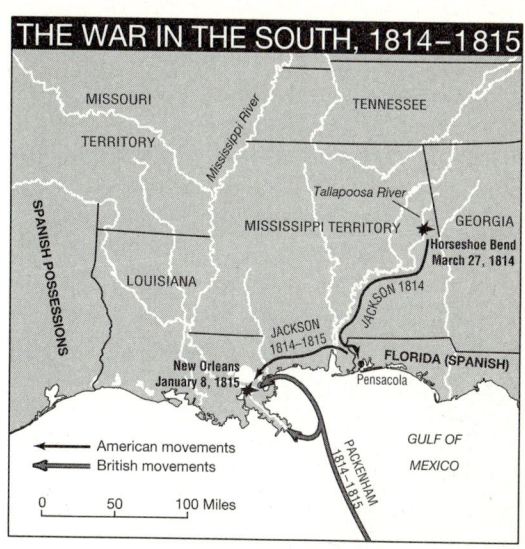

By the time Jackson defeated Packenham, the war was actually over. A treaty of peace had been signed in Europe, though news of it did not come until after the battle. But the flow of news was as important as the flow of events. Americans who heard first of Jackson's victory, and then of the peace treaty, were able to believe that the United States had won this inconclusive war.

The Treaty of Ghent provided only that the situation between Britain and America would remain just as it was in June 1812. No concessions or promises were made, and no territory changed hands.

The War of 1812 made little sense at the time, and it settled no real problems. Three years after it began came Napoleon's final defeat at Waterloo. From that time, Britain was not involved in a war with any Continental nation for a hundred years. If the Americans could have held out for three more years, British harassment of their trade would probably have stopped, and the war could have been avoided.

But at least the war was over, and the United States had not lost. In fact, many Americans, encouraged by Jackson's victory, thought of the war as a successful defense of American independence and neutral rights. They called it a Second War for Independence.

THE HARTFORD CONVENTION

The Louisiana Purchase had been approved in the Senate by a wide margin, twenty-four votes to seven. But the opposition was significant because it pointed toward a powerful and underlying problem in American life. Most of the opponents were from New England. People there realized that the westward movement would sooner or later result in a basic shift of people, economic power, and political control away from the East to the western territories and states. The Founding Fathers had worried about whether one government could control a nation as large as the United States. The future would be full of challenge to the American motto, *e pluribus unum*—"out of many, one."

Before the War of 1812, the New England states, which were tied closely to Britain by trade, had bitterly opposed Jefferson's embargo. New England opposed the war even more. In Congress the strongest voices for war had been those of the so-called War Hawks—congressmen from the frontier regions, and a few from the South, who wanted to invade and annex Canada, adding even more frontier territory at the expense of the East. Politicians and businessmen all over New England felt the government had betrayed them and was willing to sacrifice their interests to the war fever of the rest of the country.

In opposition to "Mr. Madison's War," New England resisted militia calls and wartime taxes and continued to trade with the enemy in Canada. In 1814 the New England governors called a convention in Hartford, Connecticut, to raise the same kinds of questions that the Annapolis Convention had raised about the Articles of Confederation in 1786. In calling the convention, the governors asserted that the Constitution had failed, that the New England states were not receiving equal rights and benefits, and that the frame of government would have to be seriously revised. A few members of the convention demanded immediate secession from the union. The convention drafted a series of proposed amendments to the Constitution—all of which would have weakened the federal government—and sent them to Washington to the next Congress.

Time, however, cured problems that might not have been solved otherwise. When the Hartford Convention proposal reached Washington, news of Jackson's victory had just arrived, and the news of the peace treaty was not far behind. As was to happen so often in American history, sectional crisis had been resolved by events and not by statesmanship. Despite its lack of effective results, the Hartford Convention had raised what was to become the basic political question for the next generation: Would the United States be able to resolve sectional differences, or would some crisis sooner or later divide one part of the country from the other? For the moment, however, all the Convention really achieved was the final defeat and demise of the Federalist party.

CHRONOLOGY

1783	Wilkinson forced to resign commission in army for plotting against Washington
1789	Washington becomes president;
	Judiciary Act of 1789
1790	Hamilton's proposal for funding, assumption, and national bank are adopted;
	District of Columbia created;
	Wilkinson rejoins the army
1792	Washington reelected for second term;
	France declared a republic
1793	The "Terror" begins in France;
	Washington demands recall of French ambassador Genêt
1794	The Whiskey Rebellion suppressed
1796	Wilkinson becomes highest ranking officer in the U.S. army;
	Washington publishes his farewell address;
	Adams defeats Jefferson in presidential election
1797	John Adams becomes president, Jefferson vice president;
	Adams tries to negotiate an end to the French Alliance of 1778;
	The XYZ Affair;
	The Quasi-War with France begins
1798	Alien and Sedition Acts;
	Jefferson and Madison write the Virginia and Kentucky Resolutions
1799	The Quasi-War with France ends;
	Hamilton's party defeats Burr's in New York elections
1800	Jefferson and Burr win the presidential election, but "tie" in electoral votes
1801	Congress passes the second Judiciary Act;
	John Marshall becomes chief justice;
1801 (cont'd)	Jefferson becomes president, Burr vice president;
	U.S. learns that Spain has given Louisiana to France in secret treaty
1803	War between France and Britain is resumed;
	Napoleon sells Louisiana to U.S.;
	Supreme Court decides *Marbury* v. *Madison*
1804	Jefferson elected for second term;
	Burr kills Hamilton in duel
1805	French and British navies begin to intercept American shipping;
	Burr approaches British ambassador with scheme to separate western states and territories, travels to New Orleans
1806	Burr expedition sets out for Louisiana
1807	Burr tried for treason, acquitted and goes to Europe;
	Jefferson imposes embargo on foreign trade
1809	Madison substitutes Non-Intercourse Act for embargo
1811	William Henry Harrison's forces win battle of Tippecanoe, in Indiana
1812	War declared on Britain
1813	Harrison's troops win battle of the Thames, in Canada
1814	Napoleon defeated and sent into exile;
	British forces burn Washington, D.C.;
	Federalist opponents of war meet in Hartford Convention
1815	Napoleon returns from exile, and is finally defeated at Waterloo;
	Peace negotiated between United States and Britain;
	Andrew Jackson's forces win battle of New Orleans
1819	*McCulloch* v. *Maryland*

SUGGESTIONS FOR FURTHER READING

AARON BURR

The best place to begin is still Thomas P. Abernethy, *The Burr Conspiracy* (1954). An attempt to clear Burr of the conspiracy charge is in the second volume of the biography by Milton Lomask, *Aaron Burr* (1982). Students who like to read original documents can follow Burr's trial in V. B. Reed and J. D. Williams, eds., *The Case of Aaron Burr* (1960). Perhaps the best way to see Burr's downfall, in the end, is as part of an interplay of monumental egos, as in J. Daniels, *Ordeal of Ambition: Jefferson, Hamilton, Burr* (1970). Anyone who prefers fiction to fact will find good summer reading in Gore Vidal, *Burr, A Novel* (1973).

THE DEVELOPMENT OF PARTY POLITICS

The best general survey of the political history of the early republic is Stanley Elkins and Eric McKitrick, *The Age of Federalism* (1993). A richly meditative book on the meaning of the early parties is Richard Hofstadter, *The Idea of a Party System* (1973). A beautifully written brief account of the development of the parties is Joseph Charles, *The Origins of the American Party System* (1968). Richard Buel, *Securing the Revolution* (1972), is a fine study of party ideology in the 1790s, as is Lance Banning, *The Jeffersonian Persuasion* (1978). An alternative view of Republican ideology—as basically capitalist and entrepreneurial—can be found in Joyce Appleby, *Capitalism and a New Social Order: The Republican Vision of the 1790s* (1984). A very useful treatment of economic notions is Drew McCoy, *The Elusive Republic: Political Economy in Jeffersonian America* (1982). Morton Frisch, *Alexander Hamilton and the Political Order* (1991), is very helpful. A fine account of the capital city is Kenneth Bowling, *The Creation of Washington, D.C.* (1991). Ronald Formisano, *The Transformation of Political Culture: Massachusetts Parties, 1790s–1840s* (1983), is a model state study. So is Alfred Young, *The Democratic Republicans of New York* (1967). The standard work on the Sedition Act is still Morton Smith, *Freedom's Fetters: the Alien and Sedition Laws and American Civil Liberties* (1956). Thomas Slaughter, *The Whiskey Rebellion* (1986), is the best account of that event. The Federalist collapse can be followed in David Hackett Fischer, *The Revolution of American Conservatism* (1965).

EXPANSION AND THE WAR OF 1812

A very readable place to begin is Felix Gilbert's fine little book, *To the Farewell Address* (1961). Jerald A. Combs, *The Jay Treaty* (1970), puts that affair into a comprehensible context. Alexander De Conde, *The Quasi-War* (1966), is a fine account of the undeclared war with France. A standard account of the diplomacy leading to the Louisiana Purchase is Alexander De Conde, *The Louisiana Affair* (1976). Jeffersonian foreign policy can be followed in Lawrence Kaplan, *"Entangling Alliances with None": American Foreign Policy in the Age of Jefferson* (1987). Reginald Horsman, *The Frontier in the Formative Years, 1783–1815* (1970), is a good general book on the West. The Ohio country is the subject of Andrew Cayton's excellent *The Frontier Republic: Ideology and Politics in the Ohio Country, 1789–1812*. Malcolm Rohrbough, *The Land Office Business* (1968), is the definitive account of the management of the public domain by the federal government during the early decades. The origins of the War of 1812 can be traced in Reginald Horsman, *The Causes of the War of 1812* (1962). A charmingly presented account of the impact of the war on Americans is in Marcus Cunliffe, *Soldiers and Civilians: The Martial Spirit in America, 1775–1860* (1973). The standard discussion of the arch-Federalist response to the war is James Banner, *The Hartford Convention* (1970).

Chapter 8

Beyond the Appalachian Barrier

Episode: The Trail of Tears—The Tragedy of the Cherokee Nation

EXPANSION AND THE MARKET ECONOMY

Osceola and the Seminole Wars

The Expansion of Southern Agriculture

The Expansion of Northern Agriculture

The Expansion of Market Agriculture

THE EPISODE: On October 1, 1838, about 13,000 people set out from their homes in the southeastern United States. Most of them were on foot for their journey, which would not end until they had crossed the Mississippi River, hundreds of miles to the west. They were joining a westward trek that thousands of European Americans were also making to new homes on the frontier. But these were not ordinary pioneers. They were escorted by units of the United States Army, and most of them did not want to go where they were going. They were members of the Cherokee tribe, and their land had been taken from them. The state of Georgia had declared that the tribe was extinguished. Now they were setting out on the path they would come to call "The Trail Where They Cried" or The Trail of Tears. By the time the last group of Cherokees reached the area known to white people as the Indian Territory (now Oklahoma), thousands of them had perished of cold, exhaustion, and disease. Their terrible travail had taken many months, and they got to their destination in the midst of winter.

The Cherokees' forced march to Indian Territory was the culmination of a long story that had begun toward the end of the eighteenth century. It was the outcome of a bitter struggle to protect their homes and farms against the mounting and relentless pressure of white settlement. In this episode the story of that struggle is told.

THE HISTORICAL SETTING: The Trail of Tears was a tragic event with its heroes and villains, but it cannot be understood only as the outcome of heroism and villainy. It did not result only from some particular individuals' choices, actions, or personalities. It was part of a larger history. The removal of the Cherokees has to be understood as one moment in the history of a closely related process: an astonishing expansion of the market economy in European-American society during the first decades of the nineteenth century. This chapter explains how the systematic removal of the Indians during this period, otherwise known as "westward expansion," would not have taken place without the equally rapid expansion of the market economy. It provides the context within which the tragedy of the Cherokee people can be understood and judged.

This is the first of two chapters that analyze American society during the period between the 1810s and 1840s. In this chapter, the emphasis is on the relationship between Indian removal and economic development. In the chapter that follows, the emphasis will be on the development of a new political system. Taken together, the two chapters provide the basis for a clear understanding of the way a profoundly new culture was taking shape in the United States.

The Trail of Tears—The Tragedy of the Cherokee Nation

Cherokees received their permanent names only after they reached adulthood. They were named for some aspect of their behavior or appearance that seemed characteristic: Thick Legs or Woman Holder. So when one young Cherokee warrior told his friends that he always returned home from the hunt by walking along the top of the mountain, it was only fitting that he began to be called Kahnungdaclageh, or The Man Who Walks on the Mountaintop. Later, when Kahnungdaclageh became well known to many white people, they called him simply The Ridge.

Now, as a young chieftain of thirty-six, The Ridge was about to commit a murder. It was August 1807—while Aaron Burr, hundreds of miles away, was on trial for treason. With an accomplice, The Ridge waited in a Georgia tavern for the arrival of his intended victim, an important Cherokee chief known as Doublehead. It was well after dark when Doublehead finally arrived and sat down to drink. A candle burned nearby; according to plan, someone moved it closer to Doublehead. The Ridge quietly approached the table and blew out the candle. Then, while Doublehead was startled and momentarily unable to see, The Ridge drew a pistol, shot him in the face, and quickly left the tavern. But, although the bullet had smashed through Doublehead's jaw, he was not dead. All night The Ridge and his accomplice searched the area for Doublehead, but it was not until daybreak that they finally found the house where he was hiding. The pair rushed in, yelling war whoops, and aimed their pistols at the wounded man. Another failure: this time their guns misfired. With a strength born of desperation, Doublehead leaped at The Ridge with a knife, and the two men struggled. Finally, the murder was done: The Ridge's accomplice reloaded his pistol, shot Doublehead, and finished him off with a crushing blow to the head with a tomahawk. The Ridge had to place his foot on the dead man's head and pull hard with both hands before the tomahawk could be removed.

Later, in the words of a white official of the United States government, The Ridge "addressed the crowd who were drawn together by this act of violence, and explained his authority and his reasons." But there was only one reason that he thought really mattered: Chief Doublehead had betrayed the Cherokee Nation.

It was under Doublehead's leadership that the Cherokees had surrendered ever-larger portions of their territory to the United States, in four separate treaties signed between 1798 and 1806.[1] Doublehead himself had profited handsomely from each of

---

[1] The Cherokees had already had to cede much of their land to the United States after the Revolutionary War, in which they supported the British side.

THE RIDGE. The Ridge began his career as a hunter. By the time this portrait was painted in 1834, he had become every inch the southern gentleman. But he never learned to speak English.

these treaties: he had received tracts of land from the government, and he had begun to purchase thoroughbred horses and black slaves. By 1802 Doublehead was addressing the government's agent (through a translator) as his "friend and brother," and requesting the gift of a large boat "for the purpose of descending the river to New Orleans" so that he could "open up a trade with the western wild Indians." By 1806 the United States secretary of war was so sure that Doublehead could be bought off that he instructed federal agents to negotiate specifically with him for the immense tract of land that the tribe would cede later that year. In 1807 still another land cession was in the works. Because of Doublehead's murder, the deal fell through. It would be almost ten more years before the Cherokees yielded any more territory.

In the meantime, the tribe was deeply troubled, and their problems were further complicated by Doublehead's death. Like all Native Americans east of the Mississippi, the Cherokees were caught up in a process as old as European expansion and as relentless as white progress. For over a century they had been trading with whites—mostly in animal pelts, and often in return for alcohol. Increasingly, the tribe had come to depend on this trade, and white traders—often with official encouragement—had taken advantage of their dependence. After the American Revolution, the federal government continued the same policy. President Thomas Jefferson, for instance, instructed federal agents to lure the Indians into debt and then to offer to take their land as payment. A vicious cycle of poverty, alcoholism, and corruption had been set in motion, and the Cherokees had either to break the cycle or die as a tribe.

In 1811 an Indian chieftain from the north named Tecumseh urged all the Native Americans in North America to join together in an unprecedented alliance against the power of the United States. Such an alliance might well mean war—and Tecumseh darkly hinted that he spoke "in the name of the British." Tecumseh found ready ears among the Creek tribe to the south of the Cherokees (especially among those Creeks who were known to whites as Red Sticks, after their practice of staking a red pole in the ground as a declaration of war). But when Tecumseh's spokesmen, known as "prophets," came to organize the Cherokees, they met more resistance—a resistance that was finally led by The Ridge himself.

When a local "prophet" brought Tecumseh's message to a responsive Cherokee audience, and threatened that the Great Spirit would strike dead anyone who denied Tecumseh's words, it was The Ridge who took up the challenge. He said to the crowd:

> My friends, the talk you have heard is not good. It would lead us to a war with the United States, and we should suffer. It is false; it is not a talk from the Great Spirit. I stand here and defy the threat that he who disbelieves shall die. Let the death come upon me. I offer to test this scheme of imposters!

The Ridge survived. And when the United States went to war with Britain the next year, he and his friends persuaded the Cherokees to side with the Americans, even though that meant fighting against the neighboring Creeks, many of whom had heeded Tecumseh's call and attacked American citizens.

At The Ridge's urging, the Cherokee tribal council sent soldiers to support the United States against the Creek Red Sticks. Early in 1814 a Cherokee regiment under the command of General Andrew Jackson played a key role in the crucial battle of Horseshoe Bend, a bloody clash that ended in the death of some 800 Creek warriors—more Indian deaths than in any other battle in the history of Indian-white warfare.

The Ridge distinguished himself at Horseshoe Bend, and he hoped his role and that of his fellow Cherokees would make their lands safe forever. But it was not to be. First, General Jackson forced the Creeks (not only the Red Sticks but even those who had remained neutral) to cede more than 20 million acres of territory—an area encompassing most of what would soon become the state of Alabama plus a large part of southern Georgia. Then, after he had disposed of his Creek enemies, Jackson proceeded to turn upon his Cherokee allies. He forced the tribe to sign two disastrous treaties in 1816 and 1817, surrendering more than 3 million acres for a token price of about twenty cents an acre.

The Cherokees did what they could to resist these cessions. They reminded Jackson of their previous loyalty and service to him. They tried to boycott the meetings at which he pressed his demands. They even sent delegations to Washington to argue their case. But to no avail. In the face of Jackson's barrage of patriotic pleading, threats, and bribery, Cherokee resistance withered.

First, Jackson would cajole the Indians:

> Receive the offering of your beloved father the President of the United States Madison. Give him proof that you return his love and that you wish to join hearts and heads and live like our people, one family in peace and friendship.

Then Jackson would turn ugly and warn the Indians what might happen if he—or other white men—should become "irritated" with them: "Look around," he would say, simply and tellingly, "and recollect what happened to our brothers the Creeks." Finally, Jackson would dispense bribes with a free hand to any influential Cherokee who would accept them. He reported these bribes tersely enough to his white friends: "In concluding the treaty with the Cherokees, it was found both well and polite to make a few presents to the chiefs and interpreters." In fact, the "few presents" amounted to more than $5,000 in 1817 alone.

Jackson's ultimate purpose, even at this time, was the complete removal of the tribe. "The cession of land obtained is not important," he wrote of the 1817 treaty, "but the principle established leads to great importance." The "principle" was removal. The 1817 treaty promised the tribe, in return for the 2 million acres it ceded, an equivalent amount of land west of the Mississippi. Each Cherokee who chose to move to the new territory would receive one rifle and ammunition, one brass kettle, or, in lieu of the brass kettle, a beaver trap. To be sure, nothing in the treaty required individual Cherokees to move west, but Jackson was confident that the pressure to emigrate would soon become too powerful to resist. The inevitable course of white expansion would surely, Jackson wrote to a friend, "give us the whole country in less than two years."

Only Jackson's timing was off the mark. While the Cherokees did make one final territorial cession in 1819, it would take not two years to remove the tribe, but twenty-one. And during eight of these years, Andrew Jackson would again play a central role—this time as president of the United States.

The delay stemmed from new and effective forms of Cherokee resistance. Between 1817 and 1827 the Cherokees devised a new form of tribal government. It was modeled on the government of the United States, and it undercut the old clan-based leadership that had made the tribe so vulnerable in its treaty negotiations. The new government replaced the traditional tribal council of local chiefs and headmen with a two-house legislature. Members of the lower house were elected on a geographic basis, and they in turn designated thirteen men to serve as members of the upper house. It was this group of thirteen, known as the National Committee, that assumed ongoing

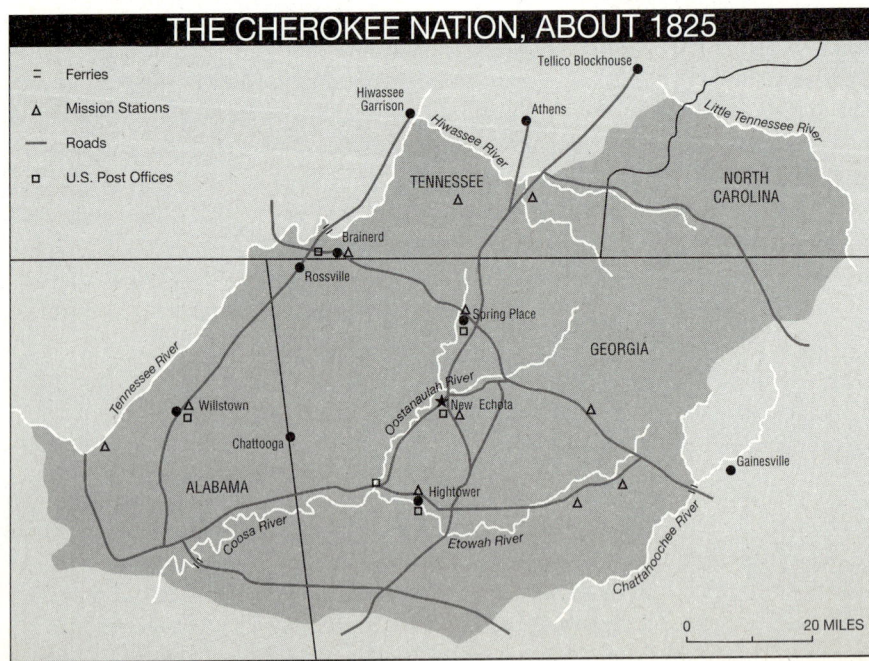

responsibility for most tribal affairs (including negotiations with the United States). Its members were chosen to serve the tribe as a whole, and not the clans to which they belonged. Many of them were able to speak English. A system of courts and salaried administrative officials completed the new arrangement.

The Cherokees had been transformed from a tribe into a republic. The climax came in 1827, with the adoption of a written constitution, which resembled the Constitution of the United States. It provided for universal male suffrage and made the principal chief of the tribe (elected by the legislature to a four-year term) the Cherokee "president" in all but name.

This political transformation might have come about even if the Cherokees had not been trying to protect themselves from the incursions of the whites. Many Cherokees had come to adopt the manners of white "civilization." By the beginning of the nineteenth century, there were no longer enough game animals left in Cherokee country to permit the tribe to continue living on the fur trade. "Their hunting was nearly over," one Cherokee remarked, and the Indians were now "scratching after every bit of raccoon skin that was big enough to cover a squaw's —."

In place of the fur trade, the Cherokees had established a thriving agricultural economy. An 1825 survey of Cherokee property listed the results: 22,000 cattle, 7,600 horses, 46,000 pigs, 2,500 sheep, 762 looms, 2,488 spinning wheels, 172 wagons, almost 10,000 plows, 31 grist mills, 10 sawmills, 62 blacksmith shops, 8 cotton gins, 18 schools, and 18 ferries.

These economic changes were inevitably accompanied by cultural ones. Christian missionaries of several denominations, especially Congregationalists from New England and Methodists from the South, established schools within tribal territory. A portion of the tribe, including several prominent chiefs, became converts to Christianity, and a few even went on to become missionaries themselves. In 1824 the tribal legislature proposed the establishment of a Cherokee National Academy, complete with classrooms, library, and lecture hall, to serve as an educational and cultural center for the Nation. The legislature also planned to erect a museum designed to display artifacts of Cherokee history and craftsmanship. (The Ridge himself donated an old ceremonial pipe to the proposed museum.) In 1825 the legislature resolved to build a permanent capital city, New Echota, complete with municipal square, main street, and impressive government buildings. The new capital even contained a printing press, which, after 1828, published a bilingual national newspaper, the *Cherokee Phoenix*.

To be sure, much of this transformation touched only a minority of the tribe. The handsome frame houses and government buildings of New Echota were probably never seen by most Cherokees, who continued to live in log huts and who never learned the language or the customs of white Americans. In fact, the lavish reports of astonishing Cherokee "progress" were part of a deliberate campaign by tribal leaders and their white supporters to arouse sympathy for the Cherokee cause among the American public.

Still, for an important minority of privileged Cherokees, the transformation was very real—and very comfortable. And it meant something more than becoming "civilized" in some vague sense. It meant that they modeled their lives on one particular group of privileged white Americans: the southern ruling class—the plantation gentry,

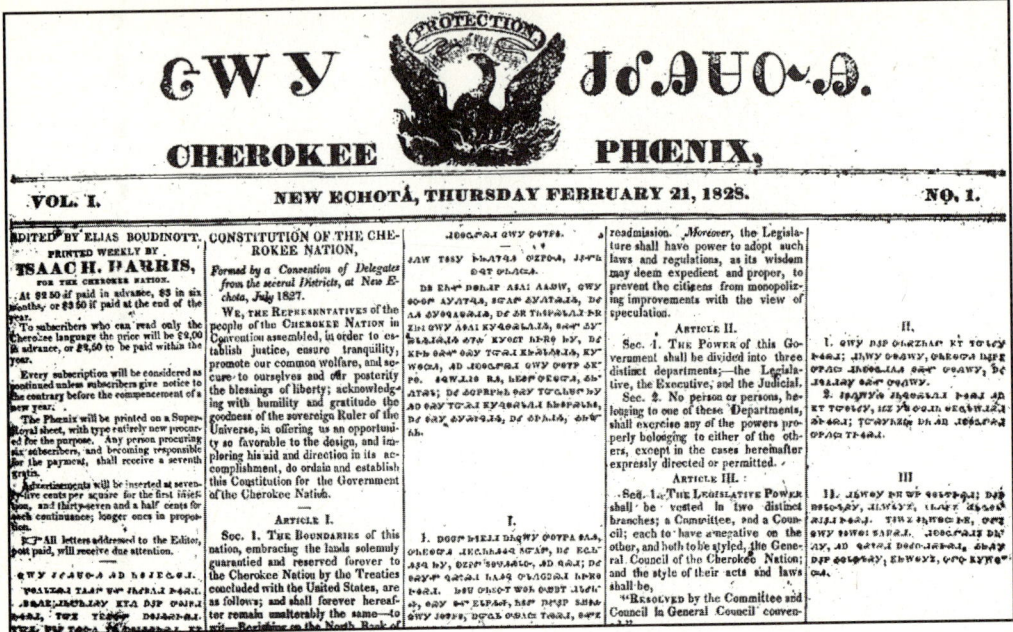

THE CHEROKEE PHOENIX. *The Cherokee Phoenix,* a bilingual newspaper edited by Elias Boudinot, used the alphabet (or "syllabary") devised a few years earlier by a Cherokee named Sequoya. The left-hand columns were printed in English; the right-hand columns in Cherokee. The paper was intended partly to appeal to the tribe's white sympathizers. This first number contains the Cherokee constitution of 1827.

complete with its racehorses and its black slaves. And one man who adopted this style was The Ridge himself.

It had been sometime around 1800, as a young man, that The Ridge had made the shift from hunting to farming. By the 1820s he was prosperous enough to erect an elegant two-story "mansion," built for him by a white carpenter from Tennessee. The house boasted four brick fireplaces. All eight of its rooms were finished with hardwood floors, panels, and ceilings. Its thirty windows were set in walnut frames, and one of them, a large arched triple window, overlooked the commercial ferry that The Ridge owned on a river nearby. Behind the house were outbuildings that included two kitchens, a smokehouse, and a pair of stables. Then there was a group of cabins that housed The Ridge's thirty black slaves. These slaves labored in eight separate fields that produced corn, tobacco, wheat, indigo—and cotton. The slaves also worked on the plantation's vineyard, its ornamental garden, and its extensive orchards (which contained more than a thousand peach trees alone). The Ridge even gave his plantation a name: he called it Chieftains.

One element of white culture that The Ridge never did absorb was the English language. But he made sure that his family acquired the white education he lacked. He sent his son (who was known as John Ridge), along with one of his nephews, to a mission school on tribal territory. Then, when the two boys became teenagers, he sent them off to distant Connecticut, where Congregationalists had recently started a school in the small town of Cornwall, "to educate the male aboriginees of all nations." There

John Ridge. Son of The Ridge, who sent him to be educated at a mission school in Connecticut, John Ridge impressed one New England girl as a noble youth, beautiful in appearance, very graceful, a perfect gentleman everywhere. He returned to the Cherokee Nation and eventually took his father's place as a tribal leader.

the two boys completed their adjustment to white culture in triumphant fashion. The Ridge's nephew, who had come to Cornwall with the Cherokee name Gullageenah, soon came to call himself Elias Boudinot, after a wealthy white man of that name who had made a $500 donation to the school. Young Boudinot proved such a brilliant student that after his graduation he was sent on to receive advanced training at Andover Theological Seminary in Massachusetts. (Boudinot would later serve as editor of the *Cherokee Phoenix* and single-handedly translate the New Testament into the Cherokee language—from the original Greek.)

John Ridge and Elias Boudinot triumphed socially as well as academically in New England. To one Cornwall girl, they were "so graceful and genteel that the white pupils appeared uncouth beside them." And when the two young men returned to the Cherokee Nation in the mid-1820s, they brought with them the white women from Cornwall they had married. Both wives were members of locally prominent families; Elias Boudinot's new father-in-law was even a graduate of Yale.

In the Cherokee Nation, intermarriage between Indians and whites had been taking place for nearly a century, and the mixed-blood offspring were accepted as full members of the tribe. The Ridge himself had married a half-blood Cherokee woman, whose father was probably a local white judge—so that his son John Ridge was himself partly white.

In fact, as a full-blooded Native American, The Ridge was a rarity among the new Cherokee leadership. By the 1820s the tribe was coming to be dominated, politically and economically, by mixed-blood Cherokees who were able to speak English and who were known by names like Joseph Vann, George Lowery, and Elijah Hicks. The white ancestors of these leaders had come to America in the eighteenth century, mostly from Scotland, moved west to make their fortunes by trading in furs and other goods with the Indians, and often married Indian women. Prosperous to begin with, the children of these traders found it easy to adjust to the change from hunting to agriculture when the supply of game ran low. They built large farms, generally near navigable rivers so that they could sell their produce in white markets. Many of them also ran stores and taverns that allowed them to profit from the trade of their poorer full-blooded fellow tribesmen. They became, in short, a Cherokee upper class.

Usually, these mixed-blood Cherokees were not traditional clan leaders or headmen. But they were the most prosperous members of the tribe. They already knew about farming and marketing when the rest of the tribe was just turning from the hunt to agriculture. They were able to operate easily in the white people's world at the very point when the Indians desperately needed leaders who could understand the fine print in white men's treaties and who could hold their own—if any could—against men like Andrew Jackson. And they were accepted, by Cherokee law and tradition, as full members of the tribe. It was only natural, then, that these men came to win political power in the Cherokee Nation in the years after 1815. When the Cherokees began to reorganize their government in 1817, it was the mixed-bloods who initiated the move; from the start, it was they who dominated the National Committee that took

ELIAS BOUDINOT. Both John Ridge and his cousin Elias Boudinot married white women from Connecticut. The day before Boudinot's wedding, an enraged white mob burned him in effigy. Even the Reverend Lyman Beecher, the most prominent New England minister of his day (and father of Harriet Beecher Stowe), protested the marriage. The scandal was so serious that the mission school closed the very next year.

charge of tribal affairs. And it was one of them—the "whitest" of them all—who was chosen president of the National Committee, who wrote the Cherokee constitution in 1827, and who was elected the following year as the principal chief of the tribe. His name was John Ross, and he proved to be the key figure in the struggle of the Cherokees.

John Ross was only one-eighth Indian. He was a Scotsman with only a touch of Cherokee ancestry. His maternal great-grandfather had immigrated from Scotland in the mid-eighteenth century, become a trader with the Cherokees, and married a Cherokee woman. The half-blood daughter of this couple married another Scottish immigrant in 1769. During the 1780s their quarter-blood daughter married still another Scotsman, Daniel Ross; he, too, was an Indian trader among the Cherokees. It was to this couple that John Ross was born in 1790.

Until he was in his mid-twenties, John Ross gave no hint that he would become a champion of the Cherokee Nation, or even that he would identify himself as an Indian at all. He was educated at a white boarding school in Tennessee and received his business training with a wealthy white merchant and planter there. (To the end of his life, Ross remained unable to speak or understand the Cherokee language with any fluency—he was forced to use an interpreter whenever he addressed his own people.) In 1813, as a young man of twenty-three, Ross left Tennessee to follow in the footsteps of his white father, grandfather, and great-grandfather: he moved to Cherokee country

CHIEF JOHN ROSS. Although he was only one-eighth Indian by blood and never even learned to speak the Cherokee language, John Ross was universally accepted as a member of the tribe and as its principal leader. In general, Indians were not concerned with ancestry or skin color but with loyalty when there was a question of tribal membership.

and became an Indian trader. The War of 1812 was under way, and Ross quickly managed to win lucrative government contracts to supply food and blankets for the Cherokee regiment that fought under Andrew Jackson at Horseshoe Bend. After the war, he set up a store and ferry on the Tennessee River at the edge of the Cherokee Nation and established there a flourishing trade. (One of his ventures—an especially ironic one, in light of his later role—involved selling supplies to those Cherokees who decided to move to the West.) Ross speculated in Tennessee land on the side. As late as 1817 he was asking the federal agent to the Cherokees to award him a certain contract on the grounds that it would be "more satisfactory to the Indians" if they were dealing with him rather than with some other merchant, because he was a man "they could confide in." This was the language of an Indian trader—not of an Indian.

From these beginnings, John Ross came slowly, during the 1820s, to assume a new identity as a member and a leader of the tribe he initially regarded as a source of financial profit. He may have sensed there was greater opportunity to win lasting success and glory as the political leader of an independent nation—a patriotic "chief" in every sense of the word—than as a private merchant. (That was exactly what happened to another Tennessean, the son of a Scottish immigrant, who also started as a planter and land speculator—Andrew Jackson.) In any case, in 1827 Ross abandoned his thriving business at the edge of the Cherokee Nation and built an elegant new house at its very heart, just a few miles from the new national capital at New Echota. The same year, he began to receive instruction in the oral traditions of the tribe. Despite the color of his skin and his white man's clothing and manners, John Ross soon came to receive the unquestioning support and adulation of the great mass of ordinary Cherokees. They knew he had staked his life on their interests, and they were right. He had come along in the nick of time.

Armed with their new tribal structure and "civilized" leadership, the Cherokee Nation squared off against the whites with real success during the 1820s. Andrew Jackson was no longer a military commander, and he was not yet president. Until the end of the decade, most of the pressure on the tribe to cede its remaining territory came from the land-hungry state of Georgia, which claimed most of what remained of the once-extensive tribal lands.

From the white point of view, there was a semblance of legality to Georgia's claims. Back in 1802, when the state had ceded its extensive western lands to the United States, the federal government had promised Georgia to "extinguish the Indian title to all lands lying within the limits of the State." The time limit on this promise had been left deliberately vague (in part because it conflicted with existing federal treaty obligations to protect the Cherokees against outside intruders). All that the government had agreed to do was to give Georgia the land "as early as [it] can be peaceably obtained upon reasonable terms."

During the 1820s the government of Georgia began to press the government of the United States to make good its promise. In the face of this pressure, Presidents James Monroe and John Quincy Adams each appointed agents to try to wring further concessions from the Cherokees. These agents resorted to the traditional techniques—

private persuasion and bribery—but the new leaders like John Ross were able to resist these tactics and even to make them backfire against the whites. On one occasion, John Ross received a letter offering him $2,000 if he could persuade the tribal council to make a cession and assuring that "nobody shall know about it." Ross made a dramatic gesture: addressing the tribal council, he not only refused the bribe, he even recited the offending letter aloud to the assembled council. The episode sealed John Ross's prestige among the Cherokees and enhanced the tribe's growing unity and pride. It was Ross who wrote what soon became the Cherokees' standard answer to the periodic white attempts to win territorial cessions: "It is the fixed and unalterable determination of this Nation never again to cede one foot more of land."

But the Cherokee leaders knew it would take more than pride and determination to protect their borders. They sent brilliant young Elias Boudinot, fresh out of theological school, on a tour of the United States to lecture about the tribe's "progress"—and to display himself as its prime example. They circulated their bilingual newspaper, the *Cherokee Phoenix*, through white America. And almost every year during the 1820s they sent delegations to Washington to lobby with federal officials—and to impress influential whites with their "civilized" manners. John Quincy Adams, serving as Monroe's secretary of state in 1824, recorded his amazement at a four-man Cherokee delegation that included both John Ross and The Ridge. The Indians, Adams confided to his diary, "dress like ourselves" and behave like "well-bred country gentlemen." The Ridge especially—dressed in a satin-collared overcoat, buff vest, and silk cravat—made a great impression on Washington society with his "fine figure and handsome face."

While The Ridge impressed Washington society with his physical appearance, John Ross handled the serious negotiations with the federal government. And he did well. After several meetings, President Monroe publicly acknowledged that the United States government was under "no obligation to remove the Indians by force." John Quincy Adams, who succeeded Monroe as president, proved even more reluctant to apply strong federal pressure against the Cherokees.

As the decade went by, the Georgians became increasingly impatient. And when the Cherokees went so far as to adopt their written constitution in July 1827, the Georgians correctly interpreted the move as a blatant assertion of Cherokee sovereignty. If the tribe could get away with this move, it might become an independent nation in fact as well as in name. In December 1827 the Georgia legislature resolved that the land on which the Cherokees lived belonged to Georgia alone. The "Indians are tenants at her will," and the state had "the right to extend her authority and her laws over her whole territory and to coerce obedience to them from all descriptions of people, be they white, red, or black, who may reside within her limits." The resolution closed with a veiled threat that the state would use violence to secure its rights if peaceful means failed. The legislature set no time limit, but the federal government had been put on notice to act. Two years later, when nothing had been done, Georgia finally set a deadline: June 1, 1830. On that day the Cherokee Nation, with all its laws and institutions, would cease to exist. The tribal land itself would be formally annexed to Georgia—new county lines were already drawn—and it would be opened to white settlement.

By this time the Georgians had finally found themselves a powerful friend in Washington: in the election of 1828, Andrew Jackson had been chosen president of the United States—and many people had voted for him partly because they knew he would take a hard line on Indian removal. As president, Jackson was at last in a position to finish the job he had set out to do a dozen years earlier. Within weeks of his inauguration, the new president notified the Cherokees that he would not tolerate the existence of a "foreign and independent government" within the boundaries of an existing state, and he all but invited the Georgians to take over the Cherokee Nation by letting them know he would not stop them. Jackson flatly denied that the 16,000 Cherokees were entitled to hold the land they continued to inhabit. These unsettled people had no right to claim lands as their own "merely because they have seen them from the mountain or passed them in the chase."

But even Andrew Jackson had to operate within the framework of United States law. Before the Indian removal program could proceed, he needed Congress to authorize him to negotiate with the Cherokees and other tribes to "exchange" their existing homeland for land west of the Mississippi—land as yet unsettled by whites. Early in 1830 he submitted to Congress a bill that would allow him to do just that.

Jackson's Indian Removal Bill became one of the most controversial questions to come before Congress in 1830. Many legislators were already sympathetic to the Cherokee cause, and others were prepared to oppose the bill simply because they disliked Andrew Jackson. The opposition to removal was led by such prominent politicians as Daniel Webster and Henry Clay. Even the famous frontiersman Davy Crockett, who was serving in Congress from Jackson's home state of Tennessee, spoke out against the injustice of Indian removal. A senator from New Jersey argued for three days in behalf of the Native Americans. "Do the obligations of justice change with the color of the skin?" he asked.

> As the tide of our population has rolled on, we have added purchase to purchase. The confiding Indian listened to our professions of friendship: we called him brother, and he believed us. Millions after millions he has yielded to our importunity, until we have acquired more than can be cultivated in centuries—and yet we crave more. We have crowded the tribes upon a few miserable acres on our southern frontier; it is all that is left to them of their once boundless forests: and still, like the horse-leech, our cupidity cries, "give! give!"

But the proposed bill had powerful support, and, in a very close vote (102 to 97 in the House), it was approved. Jackson signed it into law immediately, on May 28, 1830.

The Indian Removal Law, like the treaties Jackson had forced on the Cherokees in 1816 and 1817, did not actually require the Indians to leave their homeland. It would take a new treaty to do that—a removal treaty, duly signed by Cherokee leaders, which would create the illusion that the migration was a free act. "This emigration should be voluntary," Jackson piously assured Congress. But in his very next sentence, Jackson made clear what freedom of choice would really amount to for the Cherokees: "They should be distinctly informed that if they remain within the limits of the States, they must be subject to their laws." In plain words, Jackson would let the Georgians do the dirty work while he himself posed as the Cherokees' friend and protector.

Georgia had already launched into the task with enthusiasm. The state law that "extinguished" the Cherokee Nation and placed its land and people under Georgia's control was due to go into effect June 1, 1830—just four days after Jackson signed the

Indian Removal Bill. But months earlier, Georgians had already begun to move in large numbers onto Cherokee territory. Confident that they were acting with the support of both the state and federal authorities, some white families even occupied houses that had been abandoned by fleeing Cherokees.

The Indians made a desperate attempt to resist. For one last time, The Ridge daubed himself with war paint and led a raiding party of some thirty Cherokees to force the white intruders out of the houses they were occupying. As they came to each house, the raiders permitted the white occupants to leave, then burned the structure to the ground. But although The Ridge's men carefully avoided hurting anyone (even the war paint was a purely symbolic gesture), the raid proved to be a mistake. The Cherokees had neither the means nor the will to make war. And the Georgians, for once, were able to get some favorable publicity. One newspaper sarcastically pictured "the enlightened leader of the Cherokee Nation, Major Ridge, dressed in his buffalo's head and horns, brandishing his tomahawk over suffering females and children."

Meanwhile, during the spring of 1830 Jackson pressed the tribe with all the power of the presidency. He ordered the removal of the federal troops that had long been stationed on Cherokee land (according to treaty) to protect the Indians from white intrusion. He told his agents to withhold from the Cherokees the $6,000 that the government owed the tribe each year in payment for its previous land cessions. And, ominously, he invited the Cherokee chiefs to meet with him privately that coming summer at his Tennessee plantation in order to discuss the terms of their removal.

A Cherokee chief. Although he chose to wear native tribal costume when his portrait was painted, this man (like John Ross) was partly of Scottish ancestry. His name was George Lowrey, and he served under Ross as assistant principal chief of the Cherokees at the time of their removal.

But the tribe would not yield. They refused to meet with Jackson, and they drafted an appeal for support directly to "the good people of the United States." Finally, they decided to take their case to the one branch of the U.S. government that might still protect them: the Supreme Court. The Court was controlled by men who were hostile to Jackson. The old patrician John Marshall, who had led the Court during the conspiracy trial of Aaron Burr, was still chief justice. And Marshall had privately let it be known that he was sympathetic to the Cherokee cause. In addition, a prominent anti-Jackson politician and lawyer named William Wirt offered his legal services to the tribe. (Wirt would run for president against Jackson in 1832.) He proposed a test case that would challenge the right of Georgia to extend its laws over the Cherokees.

For a brief moment, the strategy even seemed to work. Early in 1832 the case of *Cherokee Nation* v. *State of Georgia* was heard by the Supreme Court. And Chief Justice Marshall issued a ringing decision in favor of the Cherokees:

> The Cherokee Nation is a distinct community, occupying its own territory, in which the laws of Georgia have no right to enter. The acts of Georgia are repugnant to the Constitution, laws, and treaties of the United States.

"It is glorious news!" wrote Elijah Boudinot. But the glory was short-lived. John Marshall's words did nothing to help the Cherokees, because both Georgia and President Jackson simply refused to put the Supreme Court judgment into effect. (According to one of Jackson's opponents, the president said: "Well, John Marshall has made his decision: now let him enforce it!") The Cherokees had plenty of sympathizers in white America, but by the 1830s those sympathizers had lost national political power.

Meanwhile, in the absence of a removal treaty the Georgians continued to move into the Cherokee Nation and to dismantle its institutions. The tribal government was forced to abandon its bustling capital of New Echota and to meet at a makeshift site called Red Clay across the state line in Tennessee. And the Georgia government ordered a survey of Cherokee land so that it could be divided into 160-acre parcels. In October 1832 the state began to distribute these parcels by lottery. First, numbered cardboard tickets were sold; then the spin of a gambling wheel determined the lucky winners. Displaying their winning tickets in place of title deeds, hundreds of white Georgians began to take "legal" possession of Cherokee farms and houses. Many of them evicted the resident families without notice; some even demanded back rent from the Indians. The luckiest ticket holders won title to opulent plantations like that of Chief John Ross, who arrived home late one night from one of his thankless visits to Washington to find his house, fields, and ferry in the hands of a stranger, and his family turned out. (Ross moved with his family into a two-room log cabin in Tennessee, where he remained until the final removal of the tribe.) By 1835 there may have been as many as 40,000 white intruders living in the Cherokee Nation—well over twice the number of Indian residents.

These white invaders may have been thinking only of themselves as they claimed their new homesteads, but, back in Washington, Andrew Jackson was using them as part of a larger plan. It was Jackson's strategy to make life so intolerable for the Cherokees that they would finally agree to give him what he still needed: a formal treaty that would legalize removal by clothing it in the garb of a free contract. Congress had passed Jackson's Indian Removal Bill with a guilty conscience, and only on the assurance that the federal government would not "compel" the Indians to leave their homeland. Without a treaty, Jackson would have to rely on the piecemeal migration of demoralized or displaced Cherokees—not the mass migration he had in mind. And the Cherokee leaders knew that their last, faint chance of keeping their ancestral land lay in holding out collectively against a treaty until Jackson finally left office. Even after the president was elected to a second term in November 1832 (defeating Henry Clay, who had helped lead the opposition to the Indian Removal Bill), the Cherokee National Committee continued to resist. Visiting Washington early in 1833, John Ross defiantly told Jackson that his people remained "unshaken in their objections to a removal."

But Ross was wrong. Now, for the first time, he was not speaking for a united Cherokee leadership. The heavy blows that had fallen on the tribe had finally broken down its hard-won unity. A small group of important Cherokees had reluctantly concluded that removal was inevitable. Even as Ross was arguing with Jackson in Washington, one of the members of this group wrote Ross a letter that pleaded with him to reconsider his position: "We all know that we can't be a nation here. I hope we shall attempt to establish it somewhere else! Where, the wisdom of the Nation must try to find."

This letter must have been particularly discouraging for Ross, for it was signed "John Ridge." And young Ridge was speaking not only for himself but also for his distinguished father and for his cousin Elias Boudinot. These three men were highly respected within the tribe, and, except for Ross himself, they were its most influential spokesmen to white America. Boudinot now proposed to use the *Cherokee Phoenix* as a forum for arguments in favor of a removal treaty.

Ross was alarmed. He was sure Boudinot and the two Ridges were speaking for only a small minority of the tribe. But he also knew that the *Phoenix,* which was printed in English as well as in Cherokee, was the tribe's main channel of communication with white supporters everywhere. Ross pleaded with Boudinot to back down, at least in public. "On all important questions," he wrote, "the sentiments of the majority should prevail. The duty of the minority is to yield." When Boudinot refused to yield, Ross forced him to resign from the *Phoenix,* and the animosity between the opposing groups intensified. Soon, each side was openly accusing the other of self-interest, demagoguery, even treason.

That was just what Andrew Jackson had been waiting for. From his agents and spies, the president learned that John Ross continued to command the unquestioning support of almost the entire tribe, and that the protreaty Ridge faction was limited almost exclusively to a small minority of mixed-blood Cherokees. But this information did not discourage Jackson. It had always been his practice when dealing with Indians to lure a handful of chiefs into accepting his demands and then to deal with them as if they represented the tribe as a whole. And Jackson also knew that the Cherokees' white supporters thought of John Ridge and Elias Boudinot as the tribe's official spokesmen. If he could get a treaty with the Ridge faction and confirm it with even the flimsiest appearance of tribal support, he knew the Senate would ratify it and the American public would accept it as a legitimate agreement.

Early in 1834 Jackson decided the time was ripe. He authorized his secretary of war, John Eaton, to enter into secret negotiations with the protreaty Cherokees. When word of these negotiations filtered back to the Cherokee Nation, the bitter animosities between the two factions finally exploded into violence, and a member of the negotiating team, a mixed-blood named John Walker, Jr., was murdered. (Back in 1829 the tribe had passed a "blood law," which provided that any Cherokee who engaged in unauthorized negotiations with the whites would become an outlaw, and "any citizens of this nation may kill him, in any manner most convenient, and shall not be held accountable for the same.") When Jackson learned of the murder, he dashed off an angry letter to his agent:

> I have been advised that Walker has been shot and Ridge and other chiefs in favor of emigration threatened with death. The government of the United States has promised them protection. It will perform its obligations to a tittle. Notify John Ross and his council that we will hold them answerable for every murder committed on the emigrating party.

For the present, there would be no more murders. (In any event, John Ross was personally committed to nonviolence.) But while the federal government promised to protect the Ridge faction against physical attack, the Georgia authorities assisted them in other ways. The governor of the state made sure that their property was kept out of the state land lottery, and he ordered his mounted police to "assure Boudinot, Ridge, and their friends of state protection under any circumstances." It was clear that the Ridges had now become collaborators with their former enemies.

Toward the end of 1834 the pace of events quickened. In November eighty-three members of the removal faction met at the comfortable home of John Ridge and organized themselves into a "Treaty party." Early in 1835 two rival delegations arrived almost simultaneously in Washington: one was headed by John Ross, the other by John Ridge. The "National party," as Ross's antitreaty forces were now known, was received politely enough by Jackson. But it was with Ridge's Treaty party men that the administration negotiated. By March a provisional treaty was drawn up. It provided 13 million acres of land across the Mississippi in the Indian Territory (modern-day Oklahoma), along with $4.5 million in cash and various additional benefits—in exchange for the entire Cherokee Nation.

John Ridge was pleased with the treaty. It was financially "very liberal in its terms," he wrote to his father, and it would permit the tribe "to enjoy our own laws in the west." By agreeing to such a generous settlement, he added, "Gen. Jackson has demonstrated his ancient friendship and truly paternal benevolence to the Cherokees." (When John Ridge's Connecticut-born wife bore a son in 1835, the couple gave him a name that demonstrated the sincerity of his new outlook: they called the baby Andrew Jackson Ridge.)

But even now, before the removal treaty could go into effect, it had to be approved—somehow—by the Cherokee tribal council. John Ridge knew that Chief Ross would do everything in his power to block that approval. "The Ross party," Ridge warned Jackson, "will try to mislead the poor ignorant Indians, and may for a while succeed." He wrote to his father and their allies:

> Ross has failed before the Senate, before the Secretary of War, and before the President. He tried hard to cheat you and his people, but he has been prevented. In a day or two he goes home—no doubt to tell lies. But we will bring all his papers, and the people shall see him as he is.

And Ridge wrote to the governor of Georgia: "John Ross is unhorsed in Washington, and you must unhorse him here."

But it proved easier to "unhorse" John Ross in Washington than among his own people. When the tribal council met in May 1835, it refused even to consider the treaty that John Ridge had brought with him from Washington, and it unanimously passed a vote of confidence in Ross, giving the chief "full power to adjust all difficulties in whatever way he might think most beneficial to the people."

Once again, a snag had developed in Jackson's plans. But a solution was quickly proposed by the president's newly appointed agent on the scene, a minister named John Schermerhorn—a particularly sleazy character whom Ross's followers called, in an obscene reference to his habit of fondling Cherokee women, The Devil's Horn. The Reverend Schermerhorn pointed out that no tribal elections had been held for almost seven years. (In fact, there was no way elections could have been held, since they were now prohibited by Georgia law.) Schermerhorn concluded that under the terms of the Cherokee constitution of 1827, John Ross was technically no longer the chief of the tribe. There was no chief. Any Cherokee could call a council meeting.

John Ridge took Schermerhorn's hint: he called for a special council to assemble that July at his own house. Ridge expected John Ross to order a boycott of the meeting. That would allow members of the Treaty party to approve the pact in the name of the whole tribe. But instead, Ross had the meeting packed by his own followers, and once again the treaty was defeated. It was voted down still a third time at the regular annual meeting of the tribe in October 1835.

Undaunted, Schermerhorn personally announced a fourth meeting, to be held in December at the former Cherokee capital of New Echota. Elias Boudinot translated Schermerhorn's announcement into Cherokee and had it posted around the Nation. The announcement ended with an ominous warning: Any member of the tribe who stayed away from the meeting would be counted as voting in agreement with whatever might be decided there. Early in November, John Ross was arrested by Georgia authorities and jailed for more than a week, and after his release his movements were carefully watched. Ross was on his way to Washington to lodge a protest when the council assembled at New Echota late in December. For whatever reason, the fateful meeting was attended by only 300 or 400 Cherokees, many of them mixed-bloods or white men who had married into the tribe.

The serious negotiations at New Echota were performed by a Cherokee committee of twenty, chaired by The Ridge himself, that met with Schermerhorn at the house of Elias Boudinot. The treaty was signed by both Schermerhorn and the committee at midnight on December 29, 1835, and it was ratified by the "tribe" the following day by a vote of seventy-five to seven. Schermerhorn, exuberant at his success, wrote to Washington:

> I have the extreme pleasure to announce to you that yesterday I concluded a treaty. Ross, after this treaty, is prostrate. The power of the Nation is taken from him as well as the money, and the treaty will give general satisfaction.

But the military official whom President Jackson had appointed to superintend Cherokee removal was so outraged by what Schermerhorn had done that he angrily wrote this account of the proceedings to the secretary of war:

> Sir, that paper is no treaty at all, because [it was] not sanctioned by the great body of the Cherokee and made without their participation or consent. I solemnly declare to you that it would be instantly rejected by nineteen-twentieths of them. There were not present at the conclusion of the treaty more than one hundred Cherokee voters, although the weather was everything that could be desired. The Indians had long been notified of the meeting, and blankets were promised to all who would come and vote for the treaty. Mr. Schermerhorn's apparent design was to conceal the real number present. The delegation taken to Washington by Mr. Schermerhorn [in March 1835] had no more authority to make a treaty than any other dozen Cherokee accidentally picked up for the purpose.

The Ridge was the first to put his mark to the treaty. He said simply: "I expect to die for it."

The United States Senate approved the treaty of New Echota on May 16, 1836, thirty-one to fifteen—only a single vote more than the two-thirds required for the ratification of any treaty. The last legal barrier to Cherokee removal had been crossed.

It would still be two and a half years before the people of the Cherokee Nation would leave their homeland. The treaty itself allowed two full years from the date of ratification before the tribe had to be gone. John Ross used much of the time to continue his lobbying efforts in Washington and around the country. He refused to acknowledge that the treaty was legally binding, and he made no effort to prepare the Cherokees for their inevitable departure. Ross's opponents accused him of leading the tribe to destruction. Elias Boudinot wrote in despair:

> [Ross] says he is doing the will of the people. The will of the people! This has been the cry for the last five years, until that people have become a mere wreck of what they once were: all their institutions and improvements utterly destroyed; their energy enervated; their moral character debased, corrupted, and ruined.

But one federal agent who was on the scene insisted that Ross was indeed expressing the will of his people:

> Were he to advise the Indians to acknowledge the treaty, he would at once forfeit their confidence, and probably his life. Opposition to the treaty among the Indians is unanimous and sincere. It is not a mere political game played by Ross for the maintenance of his ascendancy.

When the official deadline, May 23, 1838, finally came, only some 2,000 Cherokees had left. The rest, close to 16,000 in all, simply went about their ordinary business. It was becoming obvious that the federal government would have to use coercion, perhaps actual violence. In the middle of May, General Winfield Scott arrived in the Cherokee Nation to take charge of the removal operation. The general immediately made his intentions known:

> The full moon of May is already on the wane, and before another has passed away, every Cherokee man, woman, and child must be in motion to join their brethren in the far west. I come to carry out that determination. My troops already occupy many positions in the country that you are to abandon; thousands and thousands are approaching from every quarter, to render resistance and escape alike hopeless. Will you, then, by resistance, compel us to resort to arms? God forbid! Or will you, by flight, seek to hide yourselves in

mountains and forests, and thus oblige us to hunt you down? I am an old warrior, and have been present at many a scene of slaughter; but spare me, I beseech you, the horror of witnessing the destruction of the Cherokees.

General Scott's threat proved unnecessary: John Ross had always preached a nonviolent form of resistance, and no violence occurred now. Nevertheless, Scott had his troops construct a series of twenty-three concentration camps, scattered around the Nation—stockades built of logs that had been split, sharpened, and set in the ground. In these camps the Cherokees would be held until their departure. Beginning May 26, 7,000 soldiers fanned out across the Nation to round up every Cherokee man, woman, and child.

The roundup was completed with impressive efficiency. Almost 15,000 Cherokees were captured in just twenty-five days and impounded in the concentration camps. Because of summer heat and drought, General Scott agreed to postpone the tribe's departure until cooler weather arrived. Crowded into the stockades, the Indians were easy prey to disease. As many as 500 may have died over the summer.

John Ross returned from Washington in mid-July to find his people in despair. At last, he too was forced to accept the fact that further resistance was useless. With the approval of the federal government, Ross now decided to take into his own hands the terrible responsibility of organizing the migration. He became the official "superintendent of removal and subsistence"; it would be his job to arrange for transportation, food, and other supplies. All against his will, Ross became once again just what he had been at the beginning of his career—an Indian trader.

The migration got under way October 1, 1838. There were thirteen separate groups altogether, each about 1,000 strong, departing at irregular intervals throughout the month. Twelve of the groups made the 800-mile journey by land; the thirteenth, Ross's own, went by boat via the Tennessee and Arkansas rivers.

THE TRAIL OF TEARS. On the surface, this wagon train is reminiscent of many others that carried migrants westward in the middle of the nineteenth century. But the presence of armed soldiers in this twentieth-century artist's rendering hints at the difference.

The trip was a disaster. For most of the march, neither roads nor lodging was available. Most of the Indians traveled on foot and without shoes. Few had tents or any other form of shelter. November brought hard rains; December, blizzards; and January followed with bitter cold. The Mississippi River was covered with ice that proved too thick for boats to break and too thin for people to walk on. One unfortunate group of Native Americans was forced to camp out on its exposed bank for more than a month, while hundreds of people lay sick or dying on the ground, with only blankets for protection.

When the travelers did encounter people along the route, they proved as unpredictable as the weather—and often as cruel. Many of these white pioneers were not willing to let the Indians stay on their land, or even to cross over it. (One marcher recorded in his diary: "Sunday, very cold—Jason Harrison, a mean man—will not let any person connected with the emigration stay on his property.") Other white landowners collected outrageous tolls for permitting the caravans to cross their land—$40 on one occasion. The Cherokees had to purchase most of their food and supplies from some of these same men, and often at prices double or even triple what the goods were worth. "They rob us in open daylight," one participant lamented; "they know that we are in a defenseless situation."

Once in a while, there was unexpected hospitality. One farmer let the passing Indians sleep in his barn; he fed them fresh eggs and even entertained them with a pet dog that had been trained to "sing, dance, and talk." This time, at least, the Cherokee children "talked and laughed all night."

But joking and laughter were not often heard on the long march. A far more frequent sound was crying, brought on by pain and hopelessness. One Cherokee later remembered how first his father, then his wife, and later his mother collapsed in the snow and died of exposure. ("She speak no more; we bury her and go on.") By the end of the trip, this same Indian had lost his brothers and sisters as well:

> One each day, and all are gone. Looks like maybe all be dead before we get to new Indian country, but always we keep marching on. Women cry and make sad wails. Children cry, and many men cry, and all look sad when friends die, but they say nothing and just put heads down and keep on go towards west.

In Cherokee society it was a terrible humiliation to cry in public. But the survivors came to refer to their tragic winter's journey as "The Trail Where They Cried"—or "The Trail of Tears."

The Indians finally arrived in the Oklahoma Indian Territory between late January and March 1839. They had buried some 1,500 on the trail; perhaps another 1,500 were missing. All told, including the summer of internment that preceded the march, close to 4,000 Cherokees—almost one-fourth of the tribe—may have died.

It was the white people who were responsible for everything that had happened, but the embittered Indians were able to vent their rage only on their own brethren. On June 22, 1839, in the Indian Territory, three more Cherokee leaders died—this time at the hands of assassins. John Ridge was hauled from his bed by masked intruders and, in the presence of his wife and children, stabbed twenty-five times. A few hours later, four strangers accosted Elias Boudinot as he was directing the construction of his new house. One of them stabbed him in the back, another drove a tomahawk into his skull.

At about the same time, The Ridge himself, now almost seventy years old, was ambushed on the road by gunmen who riddled him with bullets. The three murders were committed after a secret "trial" under the blood law of 1829, which called for the execution of any Cherokee who gave up tribal land to the white man. Thirty-two years earlier, The Ridge had killed Chief Doublehead for the same offense.

    The murderers were never identified, and no evidence was found that John Ross was in any way responsible for them. At no time had Ross advocated violence against anyone, white or Indian. He would remain as principal chief of the deeply divided Cherokee Nation until his own death twenty-seven years later, in 1866. Ross died in bed, of natural causes. His death occurred in Washington—where he had gone to lobby against still another treaty that the United States was trying to impose on his divided tribe.

Expansion and the Market Economy

OSCEOLA AND THE SEMINOLE WARS

The Cherokees fought against removal with almost every weapon at their disposal, from legal petitions and court challenges to alliances with influential whites and the creation of an effective propaganda network. One weapon they did not employ was violent resistance. Neither did three of their neighboring "civilized" tribes: the Creeks, the Choctaws, and the Chickasaws were all peacefully dispossessed of their lands by the late 1830s.

But one of the "civilized" southern tribes did turn to violence as a last resort. The Seminoles fought the U.S. government between 1835 and 1837, in what became the single most expensive war ever fought against the Native American population. Nearly 1,500 U.S. soldiers died in this war, and the cost to the federal government came to nearly $20 million. But when the war ended, Seminoles were still living in their Florida homeland.

How did the Seminoles prevail? Why did they resort to arms while neighboring tribes chose not to do so? To answer these questions is to tell something of the history of this tribe. It is to say, for example, that the Seminoles were not really a distinct "tribe," and that its members were not even all "Indians." The Seminoles came into being only in the eighteenth century, as a mixed group of Creeks and other Indians who had been living in the unsettled territory that later became Georgia, many of whom crossed the border into northern Florida, then controlled by Spain. (There had been native groups in this area, but these had been almost destroyed in the early eighteenth century.) The Indians made this move because there was less population pressure from the Spanish than from the English to their north. They were joined by another sort of immigrant group: escaped slaves who were lured to Florida by the prospect of winning their freedom, promised by the Spanish government (their story was told in Chapter 4). This new "tribe" gradually came to adopt two Indian languages (Muskogee and Miccosukee), and to take on a mixed culture involving Spanish, Indian, and African elements.

With the end of American Revolution, Spain regained control of Florida, but it could no longer offer much protection to the Seminoles living there, or to those who remained in the no-man's-land of southern Georgia. The fertile land of this region soon attracted the attention of white settlers, and in addition the fugitive slave population attracted the attention of southern planters, who began to send slave-catchers into the area to "recapture" runaway slaves who had joined up with the Seminoles.

These pressures intensified after the War of 1812, which resulted in a catastrophe for the Creeks—the forced cession of most of their land. Nearly a thousand Creek warriors and their families, mostly those who had fought valiantly against Andrew Jackson (the so-called Red Sticks), now migrated to southern Georgia and Florida and joined the Seminoles, in a move that tripled the tribe's population. Among these warriors was a Red Stick named Osceola.

By 1820 there were several dozen "Seminole" towns comprised of Indians of Creek origin. In addition, there were several affiliated towns settled by escaped African-American slaves and their descendants. These black villagers had learned to speak the Seminole languages and had also adopted other aspects of Seminole culture (and agriculture). Some of the escaped slaves married Seminoles. The "black Seminoles" had, if anything, even more reason than their Indian allies to fear the incursions of the United States. These blacks would soon become the backbone of the resistance to the tribe's removal.

The U.S. government declared war on the Seminoles in 1817, in what would later be referred to as the First Seminole War. Two years later, American troops under General Andrew Jackson drove the Seminoles south out of Georgia. Jackson made incursions into Spanish Florida as well (and, without any clear authority, he ordered two British subjects there to be hanged). After Jackson's victory, in 1819, Spain surrendered Florida to the United States. But Seminoles continued to wield effective control of the territory and to raid U.S. military installations as well as the homesteads of white planters.

Under constant pressure, in 1823, the Seminoles (through most but not all of their chiefs) agreed in the Treaty of Moultrie Creek to "trade" their possession of 30 million acres of prime farmland in northern Florida for 5 million acres of sandy marshland in the central part of the territory. The United States carefully chose this area in an effort to cut the Seminoles' access to the coast—and thus deny the possibility of alliances with (and weapons from) European powers.

By 1830, when Congress passed the Indian Removal Act, whites had settled all the Seminoles' former land in northern Florida—and land pressure was still mounting. In 1832, the Seminoles were in line for removal to the west, and their leaders were divided on what to do. Andrew Jackson was now president, and he exploited this division among the Seminoles just as he would afterwards do with the Cherokees. The tribe agreed to send a group of seven Seminoles west to the Indian Territory to evaluate the region. But while these representatives were in the west, they actually signed a treaty (the Treaty of Fort Gibson) agreeing to removal—with absolutely no tribal authority to do so. (Some of the signers may have actually accepted the necessity for removal, but even these men were probably misled about the actual terms of the treaty: the interpreter who translated the treaty into the native language may have been bribed to misrepresent it.) In any event, when the seven signatories returned to Florida, most Seminoles were outraged at what they had done. Four of the seven whose marks appeared on the treaty denied that they had even signed it; one said they all knew the treaty would not be binding on the nation. But the U.S. agents insisted they had made it clear exactly what was being signed.

It was at this point that Osceola, the former Creek Red Stick, emerged as a leader of the antiremoval forces (he was not a hereditary chief). Four other leaders favored migration. Among them was a hereditary chief called Charley Emathla, one of the men who had signed the removal treaty.

The Seminoles had been given a deadline of January 1, 1836, to prepare for their removal. Most of them actually spent this time preparing for war. At one crucial point Osceola had a violent encounter with Charley Emathla, the proremoval leader. Charley Emathla was preparing to lead a group of about 450 Seminoles to the West. He had just sold his cattle to federal agents in preparation for the removal, and was carrying the money he had received in return from them. The two men fought, and Charley Emathla was killed. In a powerful gesture, Osceola proceeded to throw the money onto the ground. The Seminoles responded with an equally powerful gesture of support for Osceola: Charley Emathla's money would remain on the ground untouched, along with his body, for two full years. Osceola had discredited the estab-

OSCEOLA. Not a hereditary tribal chief, Osceola became a leader of the Seminoles through personal courage and charisma. While he probably had a white father (in his early years he was known as "Billy Powell"), Osceola considered himself to be a "pure-blooded" Indian—and he married a woman who was the descendant of an escaped slave.

lished tribal leadership. After his act, no Seminole sold any more livestock to federal agents, and proremoval leaders moved to safer places.

In December 1835, anticipating the coming removal deadline, the Seminoles launched a military offensive against federal troops. Thus began the Second Seminole War. The Seminoles were badly outnumbered. They mustered a fighting force of at most 800, facing at least 5,000 American troops. Once the war started they had no access to gunpowder or weapons except for what they captured. And they were forced to endure the horrible hardship of hiding in the Florida swamps. Furthermore, they had no organized central leadership, because the tribe—like most Native American tribes—was really an alliance among a variety of diverse bands. (The Cherokees, with their centralized form of government, were exceptional in this regard.)

The Seminole advantage was terrain. The standard procedure in fighting against Indians was to build an overwhelming force of forts and roads into their territory, then to bring in large numbers of white troops and their Indian allies, and surround whatever pockets of resistance existed. That couldn't work in Florida, most importantly because the territory itself was still unmapped and the marshy terrain was extremely difficult to penetrate.

The Seminoles had another advantage: their African-American allies. Initially, the U.S. government had promised to allow these "black Seminoles" to accompany the rest of the tribe when it moved west. But the white planters in southern Georgia and Florida were unwilling to permit these blacks (whom they still considered "their" slaves) to slip away into freedom. Ominous signs appeared that the federal forces were planning to allow southern planters to take away any ex-slaves they could find. This new situation sealed the commitment of the black Seminoles to resist to the end. Osceola's fighting bands were largely black.

For the first year of the war the Seminoles were on the offensive. But in December 1836, General Thomas Jesup took command of a U.S. Army that now numbered as many as 10,000 troops. Jesup embarked on a "scorched-earth" campaign, destroying crops, burning villages, and taking women and children captive. The campaign worked. By March 1837 some Seminole leaders had become convinced that the costs of continued resistance were simply too high, and they began to show interest in negotiating a settlement. Several times in 1837 groups of Seminoles sent representatives to negotiate with the United States. On October 25, 1837, Osceola himself and a group of his men arranged to meet with a group of federal officers under a flag of truce. But in the course of the meeting, General Jesup had Osceola and his men surrounded and taken prisoner. Osceola died in jail of malaria several months later.

After Osceola's capture, General Jesup began a campaign designed to put an end to all further resistance, sweeping his troops down through remaining Seminole strongholds in Big Cypress Swamp and the Everglades. More than half of all the soldiers in the regular U.S. Army were now in Florida, and they were assisted by militia units from neighboring states, and also by volunteers. On Christmas Day, 1837, 1,000 men under Colonel Zachary Taylor confronted 400 Seminoles in the biggest battle of the war, northeast of Lake Okechobee. By early 1838 the U.S. Army had succeeded in putting more than half the Seminole fighting force out of commission. Perhaps 400 warriors had been killed, and almost 2,000 Indians captured and forcibly sent west.

But even so, there was no real end to the war. Seminole guerrillas continued to hide in the swamps, conducting guerrilla campaigns. By 1842 about 4,000 Seminoles had been removed, but about 500 more were still in Florida, retreating ever deeper into the Everglades. In 1842, the U.S. government, in frustration, finally agreed to a settlement that allowed the remaining Seminoles to stay in Florida.[2] Although they paid a heavy price, the tribe had accomplished what none of the other eastern tribes had been able to do: They fought the United States Army to a draw.

There was nothing new about the removal of the southern tribes. For more than two centuries, Indians had been killed, subdued, displaced, and even enslaved by the white invaders. It could even be argued (in fact, it was argued) that Cherokee removal was carried out with unprecedented humanity and compassion—with no war and very little violence, at federal expense, and with generous provision for economic compensation. As President Jackson himself pointedly asked, "How many thousands of our own people would gladly embrace the opportunity of removing to the West on such conditions?"

Still, there was something different about the whole tragic episode—something that has etched it on the conscience of many Americans at the time and since. During the colonial period, the slaughter of Indians had generally been carried out in a haphazard, often informal manner, without any plan. In those days, the point had been to subdue Indian populations until they posed no further military threat to white life or property, and then to allow the Indians to live—their territory reduced, their morale shattered, their culture destroyed—on the edges of white settlement or even in its midst. And in the past, the authority of the government had often been applied as a restraining influence to counteract the impulsive violence of the whites. But now, in the Jacksonian period, five tribes—some 60,000 people in all—were displaced from their territory and systematically transported to land a thousand miles away. And the entire process was conceived, organized, and carried out by the military and bureaucratic machinery of the federal government. There was relatively little violence, to be sure. But the systematic relentlessness of the enterprise was something quite new. It was a massive undertaking, and one that could not have happened any earlier than it did. In a sense, the removal of the southern Indians between 1815 and 1840 was the first large-scale peacetime undertaking of the government of the United States. And it reveals a great deal about what was happening to American society in the Jacksonian period.

THE EXPANSION OF SOUTHERN AGRICULTURE

WAR

Indian removal did not take place before the War of 1812 for a very simple reason. Before the end of that war, much of the area west of the

---

[2]There was one more battle after this. In 1855, white surveyors in the Everglades who trampled the garden of a Seminole chief named Billy Bowlegs were attacked. The U.S. Army attempted one last time to remove all Seminoles from Florida. In 1858, Billy Bowlegs and 162 people agreed to move west. But the rest simply retreated still farther into the swamps.

Appalachians had been constantly threatened by European powers—the English, the French, and the Spanish. And the Indian tribes—especially the relatively powerful ones like the Creeks—had been able to retain some vestige of independence by threatening to forge military alliances with one or more of these European powers. It was this strategy that the great Tecumseh had attempted just before the outbreak of the War of 1812.

But with the end of the war, and with Andrew Jackson's conquest of East Florida in 1819, the European nations lost their influence in the area—and the Indians lost their last strategic advantage, their last remaining room for maneuver.

By themselves, without the possibility of European support, the southern Indians were finished. They lacked the numbers, the weapons, even the unity of the whites. The ending of the War of 1812 made it possible to remove them from the area with little risk to the white population. The lands they still inhabited—the future states of Alabama and Mississippi, along with the western part of Georgia—were now available for white occupation. Mississippi became a state in 1817, just two years after the end of the war, and Alabama followed two years later.

LAND HUNGER: THE RISE OF "KING COTTON"

One of the excuses white Americans used to justify taking Indian lands was that there were simply too few Indians living on too much land—and too many whites living on too little land. The white population of the United States increased by nearly 10 million between 1810 and 1840, and the increase was accelerating all the time. In 1790 virtually all the white (and black) people of America had lived on a thin ribbon along the east coast. But by 1840 one-third of them lived in states west of the seaboard. And by 1860 the figure had risen to one-half.

Until the 1830s, the four western states that grew fastest were Alabama, Mississippi, Tennessee, and Kentucky. And most of the people who moved into this region came from the crowded seaboard states of Georgia, the two Carolinas, and Virginia. Andrew Jackson himself was a case in point: he was born in North Carolina in 1767 and moved west to Tennessee when he was twenty-two. For Jackson as well as for thousands of other Americans, the seaboard had become too crowded.

The land itself was causing problems that intensified the sense of overcrowding in the coastal states. Many of the farms in the region had been cultivated for a century or more, and the soil had become exhausted. In the headlong drive to grow as much as possible, and as fast as possible, farmers had neglected to rotate their crops or to rest their fields every few years. In many cases, they had seen their topsoil disappear by constant erosion, the result of plowing and planting in straight lines, often up and down hills, ignoring the contours of the land. The once-prosperous tobacco fields of Virginia and North Carolina and the rice plantations of South Carolina had come to yield small, stunted crops. Ineffective farm management reduced three early Virginia presidents—Jefferson, Madison, and Monroe—to embarrassing debt and near-poverty in their old age.

North Carolina was particularly hard hit. By 1815 the state contained as much land that had been abandoned to weeds as was still under cultivation. All along the seaboard, land was decreasing in value. In Georgia, more than in any other state, people were farming their land intensively and carelessly for a few years, then selling it or simply abandoning it in order to move on—to the West.

And in the West were Indians. It was a favorite argument of whites that the Indians did not "use" or "improve" their lands. Even when some did become farmers (as the Cherokees and the other southern tribes had done), the Indians

COTTON GIN. The magazine artist has drawn the cotton gin in operation on a rather idealized southern plantation. A young girl slave is tending the machinery, and a male slave standing in the loft gathers the cleaned cotton. An even younger girl and a boy are watching the process with curiosity. The baskets on the floor lie empty, and the ropes are neatly coiled. The work seems easy, even relaxed. All in all, the artist has deliberately conveyed a misleading impression that the cotton gin made the life of a slave easier and more pleasant.

had left vast areas out of cultivation. They did not exploit the land with the same intensity as the increasingly desperate whites now pressing upon them from the east. But to many whites this attitude of the Indians was only one more argument for their removal. Land-poor whites were moving west; what was wrong with urging land-rich Indians to do the same?

The western lands, fertile and unspoiled, were alluring and valuable for yet another reason. It had suddenly become incredibly profitable to raise a single crop on these lands. This crop was cotton. Before about 1800, cotton had not been grown on a large scale in the United States because it was slow and difficult to separate the valuable fibers from the worthless seeds so that the fiber could be spun and woven into cloth. But in 1793 Eli Whitney and others had developed a simple mechanical device, the cotton gin (short for "engine"), which permitted one person—generally a slave—to clean as much cotton in a day as several people had previously been able to do.

Suddenly, there was a new use for the new land. By the 1820s the United States was producing more cotton than any other nation, and by

1850 more than two-thirds of the world's cotton came from American farms and plantations. Most of it was grown in the very places that had been Indian land barely a generation earlier: western Georgia, Alabama, Mississippi, and eastern Texas. It was the removal of the southern Indians that was directly responsible for the rise of the "Cotton Kingdom," the rich belt of large plantations, worked by black slaves, that was the heart of the new South.

Cotton did not become "king" simply on account of the invention of the cotton gin. The invention of various other machines—machines that could spin the cotton fibers into thread, weave the thread into cloth, and cut and sew the cloth into garments—contributed to its ascent. These new machines in turn depended on the need and ability of large numbers of people to purchase the manufactured cloth and clothing. The value of cotton lands ultimately depended on the existence of a technology to process the cotton, and of a ready market to consume it. And both these elements were present.

In the beginning they were British. It was British textile mills that first purchased most of the raw American cotton, and British consumers who bought most of the finished clothing. It was also British capital that provided American planters with most of the credit to begin producing cotton on the new western lands. But from the 1820s on, New Englanders increasingly competed with the British for southern cotton, by building their own factories and providing their own customers.

One final ingredient was needed: efficient low-cost transportation that would enable cotton farmers to get their bound bales to market in ports like New Orleans and New York. Here they were fortunate in two ways. First, unlike food crops such as wheat or corn, cotton did not spoil easily, so it did not have to be harvested and shipped to market in a very short time. Second, the South was blessed more than any section of the country with many navigable rivers along which goods could be shipped. This was a matter of utmost importance at a time when there was no such thing as a paved road, and—for the time being—no railroads. To be sure, it was difficult for sailboats to navigate the intricate turns of these rivers, but this problem was neatly solved in the 1810s with the invention of the steamboat. Within a few years, steamboats were proudly plying the Mississippi and other rivers, carrying cotton and other goods below decks and passengers above.

But no matter how fast southerners converted virgin land into fields of cotton, they were unable to supply enough of this miracle crop to keep pace with the ever increasing demand. As a result, the price of cotton kept going up, and so did the price of slaves, and of land itself. (This was at a time of little general inflation, when the price of most goods remained generally stable.) Hundreds of British and New England capitalists got rich investing in southern agricultural expansion. Thousands of southerners got rich growing cotton.

Thousands of others got rich without even growing cotton, just by speculating in land and in slaves. Both land and slaves had, along with cotton itself, become commodities to be traded for profit. These men were land speculators and slave traders.

Indian removal, westward expansion, cotton production, technology, population growth, and the slave market—these were all bound together in an interconnected system. It was this system that produced the land-hungry Georgians who descended on Cherokee lands in the 1830s. It was this system that produced Andrew Jackson himself. The system was market capitalism, of a distinctively American type.

The struggle for Indian removal was a struggle between two dramatically different attitudes toward living on—and off—the land. By the end of the War of 1812, the Cherokee Nation had become for white people a tremendously valuable piece of real estate; it was worth a great deal of money in the marketplace.

But the Cherokees held so steadfastly to their land not because of its exchange value but simply because it belonged to them and they belonged to it. They farmed and hunted in order to feed, clothe, and shelter themselves and because their ancestors had done much the same. The land was designated for their use, and not for its cash value in the market. In this sense, the struggle for Indian removal was not simply a racial struggle between whites and Indians: it was a conflict between a market system and a nonmarket system. This is what distinguishes the events of the Jacksonian period from earlier episodes in the long history of conflict between European Americans and Native Americans.

THE EXPANSION OF NORTHERN AGRICULTURE

In some ways, the North changed in a very different fashion from the South. It eliminated black slavery. It developed industry, not plantations. Without question, the North and the South were far more distinct from each other in 1850 than they had been in 1815; the Jacksonian years represented an era of clear new regional identities—new identities that would make it possible for the two sections to go to war with each other in 1861.

Still, the North was responding in its own way to pressures that were similar or even identical to those that characterized the South. Like the South, the North in 1800 was a farming area along a thin coastal strip whose agricultural potential was not sufficient to sustain its growing population. The problem here was not soil depletion but the fact that, except for a few fertile valleys like that of the Connecticut River, most of the land in New England and in much of the Middle Atlantic states was too hilly, rocky, and infertile to support farming at anything much above a bare subsistence level. West of the Appalachians, on the other hand, in the Ohio Valley, the land was invitingly flat and clear, with deep topsoil.

TECUMSEH, WILLIAM HENRY HARRISON, AND THE DEFEAT OF THE NORTHWESTERN INDIANS

Of course, there were Indians there, too. But as it happened, they were forced out of the area a full generation earlier than the southern Indians—by the end of the War of 1812. The Indians who dominated the Ohio Valley were the Shawnees, a traditionally nomadic, mobile warrior tribe with a reputation for ferocity. Shawnee tradition refused to recognize any rights in land, whether individual or even collective forms of ownership. The very concept of a "homeland" was alien to their culture. In fact, groups of Shawnees often moved into the homelands of other more settled tribes, using warfare to carve out hunting space for themselves. In the middle of the eighteenth century, the Shawnees were at the height of their power and prosperity. They controlled most of the present-day state of Ohio, and their hunting grounds extended east into Virginia and Pennsylvania, south into present-day Kentucky, and west into what is now the state of Indiana.

In the French and Indian War the Shawnees allied themselves with the French, and in the Revolutionary War they fought on the British side. Even after the end of that war, the Shawnees continued to fight sporadically against the Americans. After they were decisively defeated by General Anthony Wayne at the battle of Fallen Timbers in 1794, the Shawnees and their allies finally made peace with the Americans in a treaty signed at Greenville, in western Ohio, in 1795. In this agreement, negotiated by older leaders, the Indians ceded most of their homelands, and the treaty restricted them to the northwest quarter of what the United States now regarded as the state of Ohio.

A group of younger Indians refused to accept the Treaty of Greenville. Among these was a Shawnee known as Tecumseh. Tecumseh (the name is best translated as "Panther Lying in Wait") was born about 1768. As a boy, he had fought against the American side in the Revolutionary War. His father and older brother were both killed by the Americans. By the 1790s he had become a war leader (like many other militant young Indian leaders, he was never an actual chief). Tecumseh refused even to participate in the negotiations at Greenville—not simply because he knew the Indians would lose much of their land, but also because he refused to accept the idea that land could be owned in the first place, by Indians or anybody else. Tecumseh's adamant position in 1795 enhanced his reputation and added to his following. Soon afterward, he led a small band to settle in the eastern part of the Indiana Territory.

It was actually Tecumseh's younger brother, Lalawethika, who helped transform Tecumseh's defiant resistance into a mass movement. Up until 1805, Lalawethika was a ne'er-do-well and an alcoholic. One day in 1805 he collapsed into a stupor so deep his family believed he was dead and were actually preparing his funeral when the dead man awakened, reporting that he had undergone a supernatural experience in which it had been revealed to him what the source of the Indians' degradation was, and what they had to do to restore their dignity and power. Over the next few weeks he experienced several similar trance experiences. From that time on, he would no longer be known as Lalawethika but as Tenskwatawa, the "Open Door." In English, he would be called The Prophet.

The Prophet soon began to receive visitors who wished to hear his message, first among his own Shawnees, but soon from members of neighboring tribes as well. His message was about the restoration of traditional Indian values, and the systematic rejection of the white culture that so many Indians had come to adopt, a culture that had corrupted and degraded them to the point that they were too weak to resist white leaders.

The Prophet told whoever would listen that Indians should stop dressing like whites and accumulating private property. They should reject white technologies, even white foodways—to stop eating domesticated meat and bread and using metal utensils, even to replace the rifle with the bow and arrow when they hunted. Above all, they should give up drinking alcohol. If the Indians did all this, The Prophet promised, they would prosper again, and the Americans would disappear. The Prophet's religious teachings found a ready ear, and not just among Shawnees.

In 1805 Tecumseh and his brother established a community at Greenville, Ohio—the very site of the treaty that Tecumseh had rejected ten years earlier. Shawnees and others began to leave their own native villages in order to join them, attracted by the new Indian "religion." It was becoming clear to the more conservative Shawnee chiefs that the Greenville community represented the growth of a rival organization that posed a challenge to their leadership. On one occasion, The Prophet even accused "Americanized" Indians of being witches, and collaborated in burning four of them at the stake. The Prophet's reputation spread still further when he accurately predicted a solar eclipse (his enemies insisted that he had merely gotten his information from someone with access to an almanac).

In 1805, leaders of eight tribes in the area all signed treaties giving up part of their land. These treaties were made by the official "government chiefs" who had by this time become little more than mediators between their people and the United States. Once again, many Indians became disaffected with their official leaders and were ready to turn elsewhere. Many of these disaffected Indians moved to join Tecumseh at Greenville. For the first time these included, in addition to local Shawnees, Wyandots, Miamis, and Delawares, members of other tribes from the area around the Great Lakes, farther to the west: Ottawas, Ojibways and Potawatomis, Menominees and Winnebagos from Wisconsin, and Sacs and Foxes from northern Illinois.

TECUMSEH. Tecumseh impressed everybody he met with his eloquence, his unbreachable integrity, and his extraordinary intelligence. Many whites thought he looked like a Greek god. The name "Tecumseh" is best translated as "Panther Lying in Wait."

In 1807, Tecumseh used his enhanced status to stake out a new political position. He and his followers now agreed to accept the 1795 Treaty of Greenville, and not to drive settlers out of former Shawnee territory—but they would not allow any more territory to leave Indian hands. This new position involved another compromise on Tecumseh's part, a tacit recognition that land could be "owned" after all. But even on this point Tecumseh was evolving a new idea: the remaining Indian land belonged to all Indians and could not be sold without the consent of them all. No single tribe had the right to sell what was really the common property of all tribes. And any whites who ventured into Indian lands would be risking their lives.

With his new political position, along with the cultural message of his brother The Prophet, Tecumseh now began to fashion the idea of a pan-Indian alliance, a unified military federation of all Indian peoples. He began a series of journeys to actively recruit new followers. (Tecumseh was not the first Indian leader to conceive of such an intertribal alliance, but his efforts were the most well organized.)

Meanwhile, the settlement at Greenville was becoming too crowded. It was also vulnerable to attack. So, in 1808, Tecumseh and some 500 of his followers left Ohio and moved westward to the neighboring Indiana Territory, richer in game and fish, less accessible to Americans, and closer to the tribes in Illinois and Michigan whose support Tecumseh was wooing. There, on the bank of the Wabash River, just below the mouth of the Tippecanoe, he and his brother constructed a model village. The new community was called Tippecanoe (though many called it "Prophetstown"). It was laid out in symmetrical house-lots, more like a midwestern American town than a typical Shawnee village. But Tecumseh planned to make Tippecanoe more than a residential town; it was also to be a great capital city, with a large log structure that could hold more than 500 people (this would serve as a political center) and a medicine lodge intended to serve as a great spiritual temple, presided over by The Prophet. The expected visitors would be housed in a large hotel, the "House of Strangers."

As Tecumseh developed his plans, he found himself coming to confront the governor of the Indiana Territory, William Henry Harrison, the man who would finally bring him down. Harrison (1773–1841) had been born to a genteel southern family; his father had once been governor of Virginia. After studying medicine in Philadelphia, he joined the army in 1791 and was sent to the Northwest Territory, where he fought in the battle of Fallen Timbers. Thereafter Harrison rose rapidly: in 1798 he was named secretary of the Northwest Territory; a year later he entered the U.S. House of Representatives; and in 1800 he was appointed governor of the new Indiana Territory, a position he would hold until 1812. At the time when Tecumseh and his brother were developing the settlement at Tippecanoe, Harrison was dealing with pressure from the white settlers who were also streaming into Indiana, and who were demanding more land—Indian land.

William Henry Harrison decided to negotiate a new series of land sales with the Indians. He was convinced that Tecumseh's movement was not powerful enough to block the sales. Harrison brought together several influential chiefs from among the Miamis, Delawares, and Potawatomis (who had never even occupied any of the land in question), and bribed them to sell the land to the United States. In 1809 they signed the Treaty of Fort Wayne, giving up almost 3 million more acres along the upper Wabash River. Harrison was right: Tecumseh was unable to stop the Fort Wayne treaty. But the episode convinced many more Indians that his ideas were right, and that only an intertribal confederacy would stop the incursions. This was especially true because the Treaty of Fort Wayne brought into the front lines of defense tribes that had previously been protected before by groups to their east.

Before the Treaty of Fort Wayne, Tecumseh had probably been secondary to his brother The Prophet, but now he emerged as the more important leader. Tecumseh impressed everybody he met with his eloquence, his integrity, and his extraordinary intelligence. Many whites thought he looked like a Greek god. And Tecumseh made effective use of his reputation as an invincible warrior. Tecumseh spent much of the two years between 1809 and 1811 in visiting other tribes, trying to persuade them to join his pan-Indian alliance. He met several times with William Henry Harrison, too, and he also kept in close touch with British officials posted in Canada. Tecumseh was a shrewd politician. When he spoke to Indian groups, he would hint that he had received promises of British support in any struggle against the Americans. But when he dealt with whites—both British and American—he claimed that he had the unquestioned backing of all the western Indians. Neither claim was really true, of course, but by making them Tecumseh was able to enhance the credibility of his promises—and his threats.

What Tecumseh was attempting was, in its own way, strikingly similar to what Aaron Burr had attempted just a few years before in the same region of the continent: to play different nations against each other, using promises, threats, and subterfuge, all in a concerted effort to create a great new nation located just west of the United States. (A philosopher once remarked, in another connection, that when history repeats itself, it does so the first time as tragedy, the second time as farce. In this case, however, the farce had come first.)

By the summer of 1811, most of the Indians in the Northwest had been drawn into Tecumseh's proposed alliance. Now the Shawnee leader launched a campaign to enlist the southern tribes as well. For the first time in his life, he went south to meet with the Cherokees, the Creeks, and the other "civilized" tribes. If Tecumseh could succeed in the difficult task of gaining their support, he would have assembled a vast Indian federation that faced the United States along its entire western flank.

Tecumseh was away on his southern journey for almost five months, leaving his younger brother The Prophet in charge of matters in Tippecanoe. Tecumseh met with only limited success in the South. He received little support among the Cherokees, the Chickasaws (who had been traditional enemies of the northern tribes), or the Choctaws (who were the most pro-American and anti-British of the southern tribes). These tribes had opted for assimilation as the best form of resistance. But Tecumseh did find considerable success among the "upper" group of Creeks, the more traditional portion of their tribe, who resented the Americanized customs of the "Lower Creeks." It was among this group of Upper Creeks—Osceola's group—that the so-called Red Stick movement emerged.

Back in Tippecanoe, Tecumseh's absence turned out to be a lethal mistake. While he was on his southern trip, Governor Harrison decided it was a good time to attack the village called Prophetstown. A successful attack could put an end to Tecumseh's hitherto-untested reputation for invincibility, and thereby break up his emerging confederation before it had a chance to go into operation. Harrison wrote to the U.S. secretary of state that Tecumseh's absence "affords a most favorable opportunity for breaking up his Confederacy . . . I hope [that] before his return that that part of the fabric which he considered complete [i.e., the federation of northern Indians] will be demolished and even its foundations rooted up."

But it was actually Tenskwatawa, The Prophet, who decided to launch a preemptive attack of his own. Tenskwatawa had a vision promising an Indian triumph and a rout of the American forces. Harrison himself would be killed, and his troops "would run and hide in the grass like young quails." Thus before dawn on the morning of November 7, 1811, was fought the battle of Tippecanoe. The battle was a draw—about fifty Americans were killed, along with perhaps forty Indians. But it was the Indians who withdrew, and they proceeded to abandon the Tippecanoe settlement (partly out of disillusionment with The Prophet, whose vision had been discredited), and the village was entered and partially destroyed by Harrison's men. Harrison was able to claim he had won a major victory at Tippecanoe (indeed, it would give him the nickname with which he would run for President of the United States almost forty years later). And the battle proved devastating to Tecumseh's organization and strategy. Almost certainly, if Tecumseh had been present, his followers would never have attacked the Americans.

At this point, Tecumseh had little choice but to follow a strategy of open alliance with the British. When war broke out in 1812, Tecumseh's forces fought against the Americans in the Great Lakes region until they were finally abandoned by the retreating British in Canada. It was there, in Ontario, that Tecumseh himself died in 1813, in another battle led by William Henry Harrison (now a brigadier general in command of the U.S. army in the Northwest). The rest was anticlimactic. In 1814 Harrison supervised a final round of negotiations with the Shawnees and their allies, negotiations that led to their removal from the entire area.

LAND HUNGER: THE RISE OF WHEAT

By the end of the War of 1812, the Northwest was essentially free of Indians—at least, of Indians who might pose a military threat. In the South, Andrew Jackson's massacre of Creeks at Horseshoe Bend in 1814 marked only the beginning of massive Indian removal. But in the Northwest, the battle of Tippecanoe virtually ended Indian resistance. Northern farmers quickly swarmed west out of New England and the Middle Atlantic states, first into upstate New York, then into Ohio and on west toward the Mississippi. The new state of Indiana entered the union in 1816, and Illinois followed in 1818.

Like the southerners, the new northwestern farmers soon found a valuable cash crop—

wheat—that was suited to the soil and climate and also found a demand in the marketplace. A better-quality wheat could be grown in the new lands than along the seaboard, and it could be grown more cheaply.

GETTING TO MARKET: THE ERIE CANAL

There was only one thing that could hold back the rapid development of the Northwest: for all its advantages, the farmers who moved into this area lacked convenient access to markets on the coast and in Europe. Unlike the South, the Northwest did not contain a system of navigable rivers leading to the Atlantic. For those farmers who lived in the lower Ohio Valley, the long way to market lay down the Ohio and Mississippi rivers to New Orleans. For those who lived in upstate New York and northern Ohio, it lay across the Great Lakes and down the St. Lawrence River to Montreal. Each of these routes was difficult. Both threatened to shift the commercial benefits of the Northwest away from New England and New York and into the hands of the South—or worse, into the hands of a foreign power, British Canada.

It was no accident that, in the North, the War of 1812 was seen primarily as a war for Canada—and thus for access to the trade of the Northwest. The Americans had mounted six separate invasions of Canada in the course of the war; all of them failed (see pp. 287–289). What followed the failure to conquer Canada was an even more massive enterprise, this time a purely economic one: to deny the British the fruits of the western trade. It was the Erie Canal, begun in 1817 (just two years after the end of the war) and completed eight years later. The Erie Canal was just as daring a venture as the battle of New Orleans, and its success proved as important to the North as Indian removal was to the South.

Early in the nineteenth century, the mayor of New York City, DeWitt Clinton, described a vision: "The trade of almost all the lakes in North America," he wrote,

would centre at New York for their common mart. This port would be left without a competition in trade, except by that of New Orleans. In a century its island would be covered with the buildings and population of its city. Albany would be necessitated to cut down her hills and fill her valleys in order to give spread to her population. The harbor of Buffalo would exchange her forest trees for a thicket of marine spars.

But in order for this to happen, the canal would have to reach west all the way to Buffalo, a distance of 364 miles from the Hudson River at Albany. (A shorter canal to Lake Ontario would have been much easier to construct, but such a canal would only have continued to divert most of the western trade to Canada.) The technological problems were extreme. Lake Erie is fully 565 feet higher than the Hudson River at Albany. That meant building a set of stairs, a series of eighty-three locks that would raise and lower boats. At one point, at a town aptly named Lockport, there were five of these locks in a row, rising sixty feet, like a huge, watery escalator. At other places, construction of the canal meant cutting deep into the hills that formed an obstacle to its passage—and occasionally blasting through solid rock. The most difficult of these deep cuts went through "seven miles of limestone, thirty feet thick and harder than a tax collector's heart." At eighteen other places, the canal had to be raised above valleys and streams. Here, the canal literally became a series of bridges that crossed over the rivers in its path on elaborate viaducts that resembled modern overpasses.

Construction of the Erie Canal obviously involved a massive and systematic application of technology, labor, and money. The money—over $26,000 per mile—was put up by the government of the state of New York, on the assumption that the canal would pay for itself within a few years and then bring a steady profit to the state. Contracts for the construction were given on the basis of low bids to private entrepreneurs, who assumed responsibil-

LOCKPORT, NEW YORK. The town of Lockport owed its existence to the Erie Canal. This picture, drawn eleven years after the canal opened, shows a barge leaving the series of five locks that raised boats by a total of sixty feet.

ity for short sections of the canal. Contractors hired laborers at the average rate of fifty cents a day. They worked in gangs under close supervision. Many of these laborers were young men who lived near the areas where they worked, but since western New York was still sparsely populated, it became necessary to import workers from New York City and even from Ireland.

The technology of the construction, while ingenious and innovative, was entirely preindustrial in nature. Most of the work was done by hand (in this sense, the gangs of workers who dug the canal resembled the gangs of slaves who picked cotton in the South). The explosives that excavated the rocky areas were simply a modified variety of gunpowder provided by E. I. duPont of Delaware. The "machines" that removed tree stumps and rocks from the canal pathway involved levers and pulleys pulled by the same horses and oxen that worked the upstate farms.

The canal was completed and opened in several separate sections between 1819 and 1825. It was 364 miles long (the longest canal in America before this had been only 27 miles!), but it was only 40 feet wide and a mere 4 feet deep. Only small boats could travel the canal, pulled by horses or mules that trudged along towpaths constructed on the canal's edges. The boats were able to move at a speed of only four miles per hour, and it could take a full week to travel from Buffalo to New York City.

But, primitive as the canal may seem today, it was a staggering improvement at the time. A ton of wheat could now be shipped from Buffalo to Albany at a tenth of the previous cost and in a third of the time. Travelers themselves could make the same trip in a mere four to six days at the rate of only four cents per mile, meals included.

The Erie Canal opened up the Ohio Valley to agriculture, commerce, and industry, and it ensured that New York City would win the benefits of that prosperity. Struggling farmers from the hill towns of New England filtered west during the 1820s and 1830s. In 1817, as canal construction was starting up, Rochester was an isolated village of barely 300 people; by 1828 it was a city of 13,000—the most rapidly growing city in the entire country, in the middle of the most fertile wheat-producing area. Its ten flour mills had already made it the flour-milling center of the nation. Buffalo grew from 2,000 in 1820 to 42,000 in 1850.

THE EXPANSION OF MARKET AGRICULTURE

In 1800 most Americans lived on farms, and most of their work involved producing food and other goods that never left the farm—or at least the community in which they lived. In fact, about three-fourths of their produce was untouched by the market. It was outside the economy, for their own subsistence or that of their neighbors. By the middle of the century, the situation was reversed. Roughly three-fourths of the productive work that Americans did had now entered the market economy. Labor, shoes, cotton cloth, passage on a steamboat—all were now for sale in the market. The family farm, on which most Americans lived as late as 1840, had formerly been a largely self-contained operation, raising (whatever its size) a variety of grains, livestock, and timber, which fed, clothed, and even housed its members. But now farms began to specialize. A farmer in Georgia might grow only cotton, while his counterpart in Kentucky might plant nothing but corn; a third farmer in upstate New York might grow only wheat, and a fourth in the hills of Vermont might do nothing but raise sheep.

Specialization meant that farmers no longer raised crops for their own use and that of their neighbors but rather for sale in the market economy. Most southern planters had to devote all their land and energy to raising cotton—they could not afford to do otherwise. Farmers in New York's Genesee Valley, along the Erie Canal, grew wheat right up to their doorsteps—wheat they had to sell to merchants in Rochester, to be milled and shipped to New York City. The clothing they wore was no longer homespun. It was woven in Massachusetts factories (or British ones) from cotton grown in Alabama or Georgia—probably on land recently seized from the Cherokees or some other Indian tribe. The sheep raised by a farmer in Vermont were probably of a specialized breed imported from Spain, the Merino, which grew an especially heavy coat of wool—but their meat was tough and tasteless. The Vermont farmer might therefore have to buy most of his meat—perhaps pork shipped from Cincinnati (or "Porkopolis," as it was jokingly known). The commercialization of agricultural production meant that many people devoted all their labor to the production of a single item, intended for sale rather than for use. It meant, also, that they were forced to buy an increasing number of goods that they had formerly made for their own use.

Market agriculture demanded new levels of efficiency and productivity. A new cast-iron plow, for example, cut in half the labor required to prepare the soil for planting. Before seedtime, a farmer increased his productivity by treating his fields with fertilizer—a largely new development. At harvest time, the automatic reaper (invented by Cyrus McCormick in 1831) made it possible for a single farmer to cut twelve acres of crops each day—about twenty times as much as he could have harvested with a traditional hand-held scythe. All in all, agricultural productivity increased 10 percent per capita in the period 1800–1840, and perhaps another 20 percent in the 1850s alone.

A revolution was under way. Farming had always had two purposes. People grew food and fiber for their own use or for sale. But now the balance had tilted dramatically, from use to marketing. It was a worldwide revolution. And in the

United States, it was combined with something distinctive: westward expansion. Commercial agriculture and the conquest of the frontier went hand in hand. Together they redefined the shape and style of American politics.

In the quarter-century between 1812 and 1837, America developed a political culture that reinforced both the freedom and the limitations of the economic marketplace. The Cherokees' Trail of Tears was a single link, but a crucial one, in a chain of events that connected the expansion of southern slavery, the growth of northern commerce and industry, and the emergence of national democracy. Taken together, these developments shaped the experience of an American generation dominated by the looming figure of Andrew Jackson—the Jacksonian era.

CHRONOLOGY

1793	Cotton gin invented	1825 (cont'd)	Erie Canal completed
1797	Andrew Jackson elected to the U.S. Senate from Tennessee	1827	Cherokees adopt a written constitution; Georgia's legislature resolves to take over all Cherokee lands in 1830
1798	Jackson resigns from U.S. Senate		
1806	Cherokees cede land to the United States	1828	John Ross elected principal chief of the Cherokees; *Cherokee Phoenix* begins publication;
1807	The Ridge murders Chief Doublehead		
1811	U.S. victory over Indians at Tippecanoe; Chief Tecumseh tries to forge an alliance of all Native Americans		Andrew Jackson elected president
		1830	Indian Removal Bill becomes law on May 28; Georgia takes legal control of Cherokee land June 1
1812	War of 1812 begins; Louisiana joins the union		
1815	War of 1812 ends; Jackson wins battle of New Orleans	1831	Cyrus McCormick invents the automatic reaper
1816	Indiana joins the union; James Monroe elected president;	1832	Supreme Court decides *Cherokee Nation* v. *State of Georgia* in favor of the Indians; in October, Georgia holds lottery for Cherokee lands;
	Cherokees cede land to the United States		
1817	Cherokees cede land to the United States; the tribe begins to reform its government		Jackson reelected president
		1833	Emergence of a proremoval faction among the Cherokees
1817	Mississippi joins the union; construction of Erie Canal begins	1834	Jackson enters into secret negotiations with the proremoval faction
1818	Illinois joins the union;		
1819	Alabama joins the union;	1835	A removal treaty concluded with the proremoval faction—rejected three times by the tribal council; in December the treaty is "ratified"
	Cherokees cede land to the United States;		
	Panic of 1819		
1821	Sequoya invents written Cherokee alphabet ("syllabary")	1836	U.S. Senate approves the removal treaty
		1838	Forced Cherokee removal begins—the Trail of Tears
1824	John Quincy Adams elected president (Jackson wins the popular vote);		
	Cherokees establish National Academy	1839	Surviving Cherokees arrive in Indian Territory; in June three prominent pro-treaty Cherokees are murdered
1825	Cherokees begin to construct a capital city, New Echota		

SUGGESTIONS FOR FURTHER READING

THE TRAIL OF TEARS

The story of the Cherokees is told in great detail in a series of books by William G. McLoughlin: *Cherokees and Missionaries, 1789–1839* (1984), *Cherokee Renascence in the New Republic* (1986), *Champions of the Cherokees: Evan and John B. Jones* (1990), and *After the Trail of Tears: The Cherokees' Struggle for Sovereignty, 1839–1880* (1993). For the removal of the southeastern tribes, see Anthony F. C. Wallace, *The Long Bitter Trail: Andrew Jackson and the Indians* (1993). One of the best accounts, Thurman Wilkins, *Cherokee Tragedy* (1970), tells the story from the perspective of the Ridge family. Also useful is Dale Van Every, *Disinherited: The Lost Birthright of the American Indian* (1966). Grace Woodward, *The Cherokees* (1966), is a more general history of the tribe. R. S. Cotterill, *The Southern Indians* (1954), describes the world of the Cherokees and the other four "civilized tribes" before their removal. A good account of United States government actions toward all the Native Americans in the West is Ronald N. Satz, *American Indian Policy in the Jacksonian Era* (1975). Mary Young, *Redskins, Ruffleshirts, and Rednecks: Indian Allotments in Alabama and Mississippi* (1961), analyzes the distribution to white pioneers of lands that had once belonged to Native Americans. Finally, *The Papers of Chief John Ross* (1986), provides two thick volumes of original English-language documents.

SEMINOLES AND SHAWNEES

The story of the Seminole wars is told in James W. Covington, *The Seminoles of Florida* (1993), John K. Mahon, *History of the Second Seminole War 1835–1842* (1967), and J. Leitch Wright, Jr., *Creeks and Seminoles* (1986). For the life of Osceola, see William and Ellen Hartley, *Osceola, The Unconquered Indian* (1973). A book that places Tecumseh in the context of other Indian efforts to achieve intertribal unity is Gregory Dowd, *A Spirited Resistance: The North American Indian Struggle for Unity, 1745–1815* (1992). The best books on Tecumseh himself are R. David Edmonds, *Tecumseh and the Quest for Indian Leadership* (1984), and Bil Gilbert, *God Gave Us This Country: Tekamthi and the First American Civil War* (1989), which goes into some depth about Shawnee history and culture. Allan W. Eckert, *A Sorrow in Our Heart: The Life of Tecumseh* (1992), is a long, partly fictionalized account. Tecumseh's brother Tenskwatawa is the focus of R. David Edmunds, *The Shawnee Prophet* (1983). A fascinating analysis of a parallel "revitalization" movement among an eastern tribe, written by an anthropologist, is Anthony F. C. Wallace, *The Death and Rebirth of the Seneca* (1969).

THE ECONOMY, NORTH AND SOUTH

An ambitious recent interpretive history of this period is Charles G. Sellers, *The Market Revolution: Jacksonian America, 1815–1846* (1991). A good overview of the emergence of a market economy can be found in W. Elliot Brownlee, *Dynamics of Ascent* (1974). The transformation of agriculture in all parts of the nation is described by Paul W. Gates, *The Farmers' Age: Agriculture, 1815–1860* (1960). Caroline F. Ware, *Early New England Cotton Manufacturing* (1934), remains the best account. George R. Taylor, *The Transportation Revolution, 1815–1860* (1951), is a classic. The construction and operation of the Erie Canal is the subject of Ronald E. Shaw, *Erie Water West* (1966). An extremely valuable analysis of the railroad and canal system is Christopher T. Baer, *Canals and Railroads of the Middle Atlantic States, 1800–1860* (1981). Paul Johnson, *A Shopkeeper's Millennium* (1978), examines some social and institutional consequences of the development of the canal system and the growth of commerce. Christopher Clark, *The Roots of Rural Capitalism: Western Massachusetts, 1780–1860* (1990), illuminates the complex efforts of rural folk to harness capitalism to preserve their traditional culture. It is well matched with Laurel Thatcher Ulrich, *A Midwife's Tale* (1991), which brilliantly evokes a slightly earlier rural world substantially untouched by capitalism.

Chapter 9

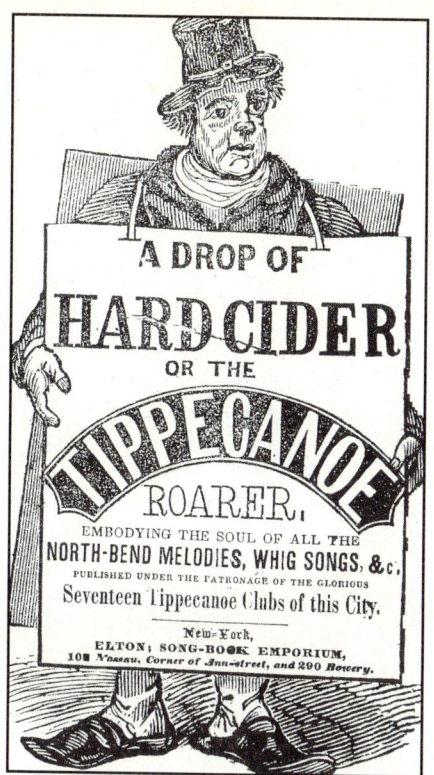

The Age of Party

Episode: 1840—The Log Cabin Campaign

DEMOCRACY AND A NEW POLITICS

Political Parties

The End of the Dynasty

The Election of 1828

The New Politicians

A New Theory of Party

The Politics of Sectionalism

The Bank "War"

Jackson and His Party

And Tyler Too

Government "By the People"

THE EPISODE: *The history of American politics has been punctuated by crucial elections that marked turning points. The election of 1800 that brought Thomas Jefferson and the Republicans to power, and the election of 1828 that began what some historians call the Age of Jackson, are two examples of such turning-point campaigns. Another example was the election of 1840—but for reasons quite different from those that made the outcomes of the campaigns of 1800 and 1828 memorable. In conventional terms, neither candidate in 1840 was a great political leader. Martin Van Buren, the Democrat, and William Henry Harrison, who ran as a Whig, had no striking new ideas or programs. As politicians go, they were quite run-of-the-mill. Indeed, the winner of the election would live to serve for only one month as president.*

But the election was an important event, nonetheless, and for reasons that had little to do with either candidate. It was the first presidential election in which the American two-party system was fully and energetically set into motion. The riotous exercise that became known as the Log Cabin Campaign was the first in which both contending parties publicly agreed that the normal situation in a democratic election was to have (1) two highly organized parties, (2) run by professionals, (3) competing for votes among masses of men, (4) using every possible means of persuasion. This election, in other words, established many of the practices that would govern national politics in the United States for the next century and a half.

THE HISTORICAL SETTING: *The significance of the election of 1840 is that it finally laid to rest one of the great failed hopes of the authors of the Constitution. The framers had deplored political parties and had tried to create a constitution that would prevent their emergence in national politics.*

There had been party struggles in the 1790s, but both parties—Federalist and Republican—publicly agreed that having two political parties was a bad thing; the purpose of each was to destroy the other, a purpose the Republicans achieved by 1820.

Then, in the 1820s and 1830s two new parties, Democratic and Whig, were shaped. But this time the parties' leaders worked their way to a novel conception of party. Political parties, they decided, were a sign of health in a democracy. This principle generated a new political logic. It justified new kinds of practices by new kinds of politicians. And the new political parties would depend for their support on a voting public that was much more democratic than the Founding Fathers had ever envisaged. Universal manhood suffrage (for whites), combined with a new two-party "system," provided much of the basis for the confidence of most Americans that what made their society unique was its political democracy.

1840—The Log Cabin Campaign

Everyone knew something strange was going on in American politics. All over the country, people found themselves swept up in a new and different kind of presidential campaign. The Whig party's most popular campaign song best captured what was happening:

> *What has caused the great commotion, motion, motion, our country through?*
> *It is the ball a-rolling on.*
> *For Tippecanoe and Tyler too—Tippecanoe and Tyler too,*
> *And with them we'll beat little Van, Van, Van.*
> *Van is a used-up man,*
> *And with them we'll beat little Van.*

When it was all over, no one seemed very clear about what the commotion added up to. But Democrats and Whigs alike agreed that there never was anything like it. Former president and Whig statesman John Quincy Adams thought the election betokened some deep and mysterious revolution in "the manners and morals" of the American people. The losing candidate, Martin Van Buren, thought the election had been a political "debaucheries" in which "reason and justice" had taken flight. But however anyone looked at it, no matter how strange and bewildering it might appear, one thing seemed clear: the campaign of 1840 had created a new political culture. With it a new kind of mass politics, a politics Americans might embrace or condemn as a new style of democracy, had moved to the center of public life.

At the center of the campaign was an unlikely figure, a sixty-eight-year-old retired general and gentleman farmer, William Henry Harrison, the Tippecanoe in the Whig campaign song. Historical myth has it that Harrison was an obscure figure with no known political views. According to the myth, a bunch of wily Whig politicians turned him into a presidential candidate and sold him to a gullible public as a hero cast in its own image. There is some (but not much) basis for this myth. It is true that in 1835, when Harrison's name was first put forth as a presidential candidate, he had fallen into relative obscurity. But in fact, he was one of the Ohio Valley's most respected and best-known citizens and had enjoyed a long and successful public life.

He was the son of a Virginia gentleman who had been one of the signers of the Declaration of Independence. Harrison had first come to the Ohio country in 1792, when he was only nineteen, to take command of the garrison at Fort Washington that protected Cincinnati. Like many younger sons of well-to-do Virginia planters, he decided to settle in the western territory. He married the daughter of a local official, bought a farm, and entered public life.

There was a lot of room at the top in the West, and Harrison made his way there rapidly. In 1800 President John Adams named him first governor of the Indiana Territory, a post he held for twelve years. He spent one term in the House of Representatives, and in 1827 was elected to the Senate. He left the Senate in 1829 to become minister to Colombia. But (as with Andrew Jackson) it was as an Indian fighter and as a victorious general against the British in the War of 1812 that Harrison became a national figure and a hero of the West. He led the troops that defeated The Prophet at the battle of Tippecanoe in 1811.

In 1835 Harrison had been retired from active public life for nearly five years. His farm at North Bend on the Ohio River proving insufficient to support "his numerous family," his friends secured him the clerkship of the Cincinnati Court of Common Pleas as a kind of pension to support him in retirement. It was, Harrison wrote a friend, "a humble office indeed but still honorable and lucrative." He was only fifty-eight when he retired but seemed content with his standing as a respected elder statesman from the early days of the Republic, presiding at Fourth of July and other patriotic celebrations.

Ironically, it was *Democratic* party maneuverings that first brought Harrison back into the public eye. Democrats were worried about holding on to the White House when Andrew Jackson stepped aside after the customary two terms in office. Some of them began to promote Colonel Richard Johnson, a veteran of the War of 1812 and now a senator from Kentucky, as the successor to Jackson. Johnson's backers did not think he had much chance of gaining the nomination (and some of them did not actually want him to be president). But building Johnson up as a candidate would make him a good running mate for Martin Van Buren, an unheroic easterner, who as Jackson's designated heir was almost certain to be the presidential candidate. As another westerner with military credentials, Johnson might well help the Democrats hold the West.

A Van Buren brooch. Political parties in the nineteenth century, like their modern counterparts, used all of the "media" available to them. Instead of television spots, they put out articles like this mass-produced brooch showing a gentlemanly Martin Van Buren, the Democratic party candidate for president in 1836. The artist has transformed Van Buren's baldness (which might have damaged his "media image") into an asset by using it to emphasize an impossibly high forehead—a suggestion of statesmanlike wisdom.

But the ploy had one unforeseen consequence. It helped turn Harrison into a serious candidate for the Whig nomination. Puffing up Johnson involved rewriting western military history at Harrison's expense. Johnson's backers prepared campaign materials giving Colonel Johnson equal if not the major credit for General Harrison's victory in the battle of the Thames. They also claimed that Johnson rather than some anonymous soldier had killed Tecumseh. Harrison's friends rushed into print with refutations of these claims. And when Harrison was invited to celebrate what was dubbed "the victory by the American forces under Gen. Harrison and Col. Johnson," he used the opportunity to answer the Democrats' "misrepresentations and slanders." He declined the invitation with a long letter setting the record straight and exposing the political motives behind the Johnson boomlet.

But Harrison also shrewdly sent a copy of his letter to Hezekiah Niles, editor of *Niles' Weekly Register*, one of the most influential and widely distributed Whig newspapers. Niles promptly printed the letter along with an editorial praising Harrison. Almost immediately a Pennsylvania newspaper extolled "Old Buckeye" as a match for "Old Hickory." And some western Whigs began "circulating political knowledge favorable to the election of the people's candidate for presidency—William Henry Harrison." Harrison's candidacy quickly began to take hold.

It did so largely because of the confused state of the opposition to the continuation of Democratic rule. After nearly eight years in office, the Jacksonians had accumulated a lot of opponents. Even though many of these opponents had taken to calling themselves Whigs, as revolutionary leaders had called themselves sixty years before, they did not yet constitute a rival political party. In reality, the opposition was an incoherent mix of organizations and candidates. It had few views in common and no obvious candidate around whom to unite to defeat Van Buren. None of the most prominent opponents—Senators Henry Clay of Kentucky, Daniel Webster of Massachusetts, and John Calhoun of South Carolina—could provide a rallying point for a Whig victory. They all wanted to be president and were as much rivals of each other as they were of Van Buren. And besides, each was too controversial, had too many opponents of his own, and was too regional in appeal to muster the national support needed to wrest the presidency from the Democrats.

For these reasons, Whig politicians began to turn to the hero of Tippecanoe and the battle of the Thames as the champion who might lead them to victory. They copied the "Hickory Clubs" that had first promoted Andrew Jackson as a presidential candidate, organizing "Tippecanoe Clubs" that conducted lavish celebrations of each of Harrison's military exploits. And they staged popular conventions of supposedly ordinary citizens who would proclaim Harrison their nominee for president. But Harrison was not simply a tool in the hands of politicians. He was an active candidate and a proud man who thought himself just as well suited for the presidency as Andrew Jackson. He sent out numerous letters judiciously expounding his views on the "true nature of republican government" and embarked on carefully arranged tours of statesmanlike public and ceremonial appearances.

As Harrison took hold as the "people's candidate," Whigs in a number of states turned to him as an essential part of the closest thing to a national strategy that they could muster. The Whigs had no way to select a single candidate. They had initially condemned the Democrats' use of a national nominating convention as an illegitimate usurpation and centralization of power, leaving each state free to nominate its own candidate. Now all they could hope to do was divide and conquer. Harrison would run well in the North and West. Hugh Lawson White of Tennessee, an anti–Van Buren, renegade Democrat might carry some southern states. Daniel Webster could expect to hold on to a few New England states. If all this happened, maybe Van Buren could be deprived of a majority of the electoral vote. That would throw the election into the House of Representatives, where it might be possible to defeat Van Buren.

The strategy failed. Van Buren won only slightly more than half the popular vote, but he won the electoral vote by a margin of 170 to 124. He actually carried more of New England (four states) than Jackson had in 1832. He won New York and Pennsylvania. And he held on to enough Democratic votes in the South and West to blunt the Whig challenge in the regions that had given Jackson his greatest support. Still, General William Henry Harrison had done very well. He won 73 electoral votes, carrying states in every region except the South. He was a candidate to be reckoned with.

Defeat in 1836 taught the Whigs an important lesson. National organization and unity had elected Van Buren. Without comparable organization and unity, the Whigs would not dislodge the Democrats from national office. The Whigs proved to be quick learners. At a convention held on the Fourth of July 1837, the Whigs of Ohio adopted resolutions calling for a national convention that would enable them to concentrate their energies on a single candidate in the election of 1840. More to the point, even though the convention declared its clear preference for Harrison, it pledged support for any man the Whigs nominated at a national convention. This commitment to unity became even stronger as an economic panic and depression made Van Buren ever more vulnerable. If the opposition could only agree on a candidate, victory would be theirs. In May 1838 the opposition in Congress issued a call for a national convention to be held in Baltimore, Maryland, in December 1839. The group asked Whigs in the various states to resist the temptation to hold state nominating conventions and to pledge to support the nominee of the national convention.

But who should that be? Henry Clay of Kentucky fully expected to be the choice. He was the best known of the opposition leaders. He had worked hard to build a broad base of national support. He seemed the best bet to undercut Democratic strength in the South. Clay adopted a statesmanlike stance of aloof detachment from active campaigning—all the while working tirelessly to make sure that the prize he so coveted would not elude his grasp. But, shrewd as he was, Clay misjudged the determination of his political enemies and underestimated Harrison, who was now a very well-known public figure, especially popular in the North and West. And Harrison had few political liabilities. In his 1836 campaign he had carefully avoided taking controversial stands. Instead, he had presented himself to the voters as a statesman who had always been fervent in support of "the rights of the people, in the councils of the nation, and in the field, their faithful and devoted soldier."

Harrison's political task was a simple one. All he had to do was protect his standing as a statesman above petty politics and keep his name before the public. His friends sponsored popular meetings that declared their preference for him. Men of affairs from across the country made well-publicized visits to his North Bend farm. And Harrison himself made a few timely and well-publicized speaking tours. It was a strategy calculated to strengthen Harrison's best political card—the idea that he could be elected, and that, deserving as Clay might be, Clay could not.

It proved to be the high card. Thurlow Weed, a young political wizard from New York who was unalterably opposed to Clay, used it to undercut Clay in New York. He arranged for local leaders from across the state to circulate letters declaring Clay unelectable and extolling Winfield Scott—recently in the news as a hero in a border skirmish with Canada—as someone who might serve as a new general around whom the Whigs could rally.

Still, as the delegates gathered in Harrisburg, Pennsylvania, on December 4, 1839, for the Whigs' first national convention, Clay remained confident of victory. He had more support among the individual delegates than either the old or the new general. But the Harrison and Scott forces pushed through a "unit rule" that gave a state's whole vote to anyone receiving a simple majority of the state's delegation. This worked against Clay, since in his states he had large majorities, while Harrison and Scott had only narrow majorities in the states where they were strong. Thus even though Clay led at the end of the first tally, with 103 votes to 91 for Harrison and 57 for Scott, he was stopped short of the majority he needed.

Two adroit maneuvers finally threw the nomination to Harrison. Weed convinced a number of delegates that Clay's greatest strength lay in states the Whigs probably could not win in the general election, while Harrison and Scott were strongest in states like Ohio, Massachusetts, Pennsylvania, and New York—states the Whigs had to carry in order to win. Then Thaddeus Stevens of Pennsylvania, a firm Harrison supporter, "accidentally" dropped in front of some southern delegates a letter Scott had written to curry favor with New York abolitionists. This caused Scott's candidacy to collapse, and the convention closed ranks behind Old Tippecanoe. Henry Clay went into a drunken rage when he learned of his defeat, shouting that he was "always run by my friends when sure to be defeated, and now betrayed . . . when I, or anyone, would be sure of an election." But even Clay submerged his bitterness in the greater interest of Whig victory. He was somewhat placated by Harrison's vow to step aside after a single term and the tacit promise that, next time around, the nomination would indeed belong to Clay.

The Whigs emerged from their first national convention full of confidence. They had finally united behind a single presidential candidate. And they had moved to offset Harrison's major electoral weakness, the South. Harrison had strong support in New England, the Middle Atlantic states, and the West. But Van Buren was also strong in New York and Pennsylvania. To be sure of victory, the Whigs had to make enough of an inroad among southern voters to enable them to carry a few southern states. Southerners were uneasy about how sound Harrison really was on the slavery issue, so the Whigs selected as their vice presidential candidate John Tyler, a fifty-year-old former governor of Virginia who had served as senator from that state from 1827 to 1836. It was a shrewd move. Tyler would be unlikely to hurt Harrison in the North and West. He was relatively uncontroversial and had been out of national office for four years. Besides, the vice presidency was an office without any power to worry about. But Tyler could be expected to attract to the Whig ticket southern Democratic voters who did not like Van Buren. In fact, Tyler was a states' rights advocate who had begun his political life as a Jeffersonian Democrat, and he had only finally broken with the Democrats in 1836.

The signs seemed to point to a Whig victory. All they needed was a winning strategy. There seemed no lack of situations the Whigs might turn into political capital. For nearly eight years a whole range of issues had agitated American politics: tariffs, banks, "hard" and "soft" money, expansion, abolition, internal improvements. One strategy might be to carve a winning program out of at least some of these issues.

But this time the Whigs resolutely rejected such a strategy. Instead, they waged the campaign almost as if these specific issues did not exist. (Of course, they did not have to be very specific in invoking "hard times" as an issue.) They decided Harrison should avoid taking any position on any controversial issue, and initially kept him from making any public comments at all. His campaign managers handled all questions about where he stood. They insisted that since Harrison was a well-established national figure, his position on issues of the day was already known and referred inquirers to his previous statements (knowing full well, of course, that even in those statements Harrison had not taken any clear-cut stands). And the committee only sent him into public to counter the Democrats' ridicule of Harrison as General Mum and to undercut the charge that Harrison was being kept out of the public view because he had become feeble and senile. (Harrison was, at sixty-eight, the oldest man to be elected president until 1980, when Ronald Reagan was elected at age sixty-nine.)

In the end, the Whig presidential campaign deliberately *suppressed* the positions that most of the politicians who now called themselves Whigs, and who had united behind Harrison, had taken on the various issues of the day. By selecting Harrison, a public figure who was not identified with a firm position on any measures, and then having him keep mum about all controversial issues, the Whigs directed attention away from all the Whig views that the Democrats had so successfully attacked in previous elections. But the strategy had an even more important effect. It kept the focus of the campaign just where the Whigs wanted it—on the "character" of Harrison as an American hero.

The Whig strategy was well designed for a complex political situation. In the first place, there was the problem of the size, diversity, and structure of the American political universe. The presidential electorate was spread out over almost half a continent, and located in states and regions with very different and often conflicting interests and concerns. This problem was compounded by the peculiar features of the American electoral system. Even though the presidency was itself a national office (it and the vice presidency are the only national elective offices in the American system), there was not a single, national electorate. This meant that even though the election for president was a national contest, it really consisted of a set of twenty-five separate state elections. To win the presidency, a candidate had to win enough of the separate state elections to capture a majority of votes in the electoral college. This was a double-edged problem. It required selecting a candidate and putting together a campaign that would not inflame the local jealousies of so many states as to make it impossible to win an electoral majority. But it also required figuring out a way to attract voters in the various states in spite of their different interests.

There were two ways to solve the problem: to focus on the party or to focus on the candidate. Van Buren's triumph in 1836 had been a triumph of party. What had originated in 1828 as a political organization held together by commitment to Andrew

Jackson had by 1836 become the Democratic party, held together by loyalty to the party itself as an instrument for gaining national power and furthering the ideals and programs it professed.

The Whigs could not follow a party strategy for a very simple reason. Even though the Whigs had united around Harrison and adopted a common label, there was still no established body of voters that identified itself as Whig in the way that so many voters had come to think of themselves as loyal Democrats. The Whigs' only real option was to copy what the Democrats had originally done—find a "champion" whose character and exploits transcended local differences, a man who could attract the broad following that victory in the electoral college required.

The Whigs cloaked their champion in familiar heroic garb. As an Indian fighter and victorious general in the War of 1812, even in the style of his political nickname, Harrison was presented to the public as a Whig Jackson. After failing in various attempts to find a way that could offset Jackson's heroic appeal, the Whigs had turned to Harrison precisely because he seemed to be someone who could capture that appeal for the Whigs, once Jackson himself was no longer a candidate.

But Harrison was not simply a Jackson clone. The Whigs went back beyond Jackson to another general and president, George Washington, for the full heroic mold in which to cast their hero. They invoked the classical image that had first been used to turn Washington into the godlike Founding Father of the American Republic. They portrayed Harrison as another Cincinnatus, the noble Roman citizen who had taken up arms and office not out of a thirst for personal power and glory, but because his country was in danger. When the task was done, Cincinnatus had voluntarily surrendered the instruments of power and returned to farming and the quiet civilian life.

This portrait of Harrison placed him in a kind of heroic succession, next in a line of American heroes that extended back to the Revolution itself. But the portrait reached even more deeply into American political culture than that. Presenting Harrison to the public as a latter-day Cincinnatus turned the election into a familiar kind of political melodrama—a contest that pitted "virtue" and "liberty" against "corruption" and "tyranny." Casting Harrison as a Cincinnatus also involved casting Van Buren as a special kind of political villain.

The drama the Whigs presented to the voters went like this: Van Buren had gone into office as the pretended "friend of the people" and protector of their liberties. But power, as was its inherent tendency, had corrupted him. He had become a "usurper"—"King Mat." He had turned the government into an instrument of faction and a threat to the sacred liberties of the American people. This was the danger from which Harrison would deliver the American people, just as the first American Cincinnatus, Washington, had saved the country from the corruption and tyranny of King George. Like Cincinnatus and Washington, Harrison had put aside his plow, not because he coveted office and power but out of patriotism and love of liberty. And, again like Cincinnatus and Washington, Harrison would take power reluctantly. He even pledged to surrender it after just one term in office, once his task was complete. This script, of course, was wholly familiar to the American public. In fact, it was a version of the basic script that had shaped political rhetoric at least since the Revolution. And that was precisely the point. The Whigs were trying to lay claim to the na-

THE HERO'S HOME, TWO VERSIONS. The 1840 campaign engraving (top) shows William Henry Harrison at the plow—like the legendary Roman Cincinnatus, ready to be called to the service of the Republic. Behind him are the other two essential symbols of his campaign, the cider barrel and the log cabin. Below is a drawing of his actual house at North Bend, Ohio. It may have exaggerated the grandeur of the house a little, but not nearly so much as the political drawing exaggerated his rustic simplicity.

tion's most cherished values, to establish their champion as the champion of American liberty.

This was the "Old Tippecanoe" the Whigs presented to the American public as they began their campaign. But almost immediately they grafted a new and very different kind of symbol onto the campaign, the log cabin. Again, the Democrats were partly responsible. On December 11, 1839, a newspaper correspondent printed his own facetious answer to a Clay supporter's exasperated question about how to "get rid of Harrison." The reporter (himself a Democrat) printed this as his answer: "Give him a barrel of hard cider, and settle a pension of two thousand a year on him, and my word for it, he will sit the remainder of his days in his log cabin." Some Democratic editors, trying to exploit the idea that "Old Granny" Harrison was nothing more than a tool in the hand of cynical Whig managers, reprinted the taunt.

This was the opening the Whigs had been waiting for. Again and again the Democrats had won election by presenting themselves as the party of plain and ordinary folk, of the common man, all the while condemning the Whigs as aristocrats and friends of wealth and privilege. Now the Whigs could turn the tables. In early January 1840, the *New York Daily Whig* replied to the supposed insult that had been leveled against the Whig champion. Only "pampered office-holders" who "sneer at the idea of making a poor man president" would consider "log-cabin candidate" a term with which to "reproach" General Harrison. Within a week, other Whig papers joined in. The editor of the Whig paper in Galena, Illinois, told his readers that "Gen. Harrison is sneered at by the Eastern office-holders' pimps, as the Log cabin candidate." But those who live in log cabins "have a way of taking care of themselves, when insulted, which has sometimes surprised folks."

On January 20, a Harrisburg, Pennsylvania, rally took the next step in the transformation of the Whig campaign. The Whig managers openly presented Harrison to the rally as "The Log-Cabin Candidate." They prepared a huge transparency of what was purportedly Old Tip's log cabin (his original "cabin" had long since been expanded into an impressive sixteen-room house) and placed it next to a barrel of cider and a woodpile. Borrowing from Davy Crockett, they pinned a coonskin cap on the wall.

Whigs all over the country followed suit, and from then on no Whig rally was complete unless it had a display of the log cabin symbols. By May the log cabin had become the official symbol of the campaign. Horace Greeley, chosen by Thurlow Weed to edit the major Whig campaign paper, named it the *Log Cabin*.

Recasting Harrison as a homespun farmer of simple tastes and manly virtues also meant recasting Van Buren as the point-by-point opposite. The Whigs ridiculed the president as a foppish, effeminate dandy, given to extravagant, aristocratic tastes. Davy Crockett in 1836 had already fashioned some potent material for Whig "slang-wangers" (orators whose specialty was slanderous, farfetched ridicule). Crockett had written a scurrilous and largely ghostwritten "biography" of Van Buren, which the Whigs now hastily reprinted for service in the 1840 campaign. Crockett portrayed Van Buren as "so laced up in corsets, such as women in town wear, and, if possible, tighter than the best

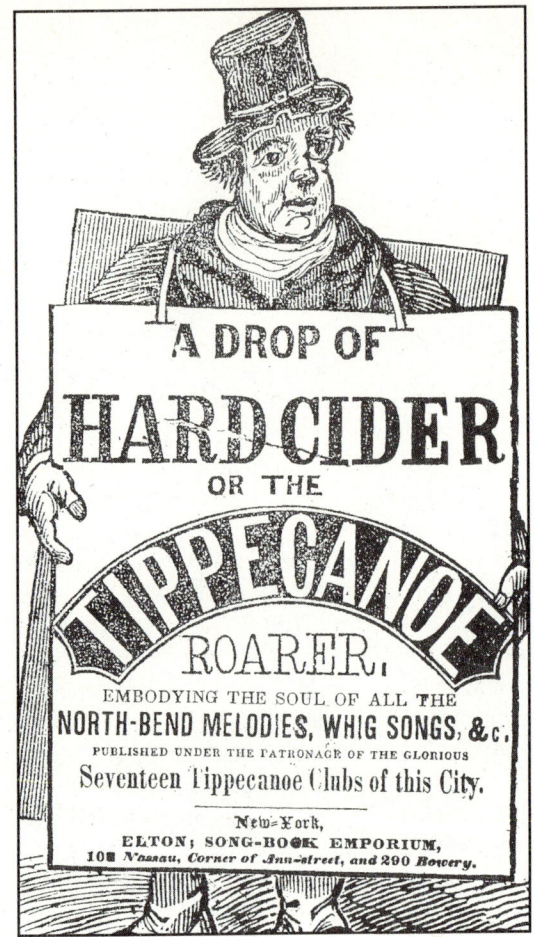

THE TIPPECANOE ROARER. This collection of Whig campaign songs was printed in New York's Bowery section. The man wearing the sandwich board is a stereotypical Irishman, and the songbook was part of a Whig effort to make a dent in the Democrats' hold on the votes of New York's immigrants.

of them. . . . It would be difficult to say from his personal appearance, whether he was man or woman, but for his large red and gray whiskers."

But it was a Pennsylvania congressman, Charles Ogle, who put the finishing touches on the image. Van Buren had asked Congress for an appropriation to improve the White House. For three days in the House, Ogle painted a humorous but lurid picture of Van Buren pandering to his dandified and luxurious tastes while his countrymen suffered under hard times. Ogle took his listeners on a long verbal tour of the "Regal Splendor of the Presidential Palace," a palace he said was already "as splendid as that of the Caesars, and as richly adorned as the proudest Asiatic mansion." He described lavish furnishings and adornments—"silk tassels, gallon, gimp decorative braiding, and satin medallions." The landscaping, with its hills, was designed, Ogle insisted, "to resemble an Amazon's bosom, with a miniature knoll or hillock on its apex, to denote the n-pple." He was especially scornful of four large mirrors purchased for $2,400. What, he wondered out loud, "would frugal and honest Hoosiers think were they to behold a democratic peacock, in full court costume, strutting by the hour before golden-framed mirrors, nine feet high and four feet and a half wide." The Democrats (and a few Whigs who were offended by its affront to the dignity of the presidential office) condemned Ogle's wildly exaggerated portrait as an "omnibus of lies." But to no avail: the dandified Van Buren became a staple of Whig slogans and songs. One observer later insisted that Harrison was sung into the office with ditties like:

> We've tried your purse-proud lords
> Who love in palaces to shine.
> But we'll have a ploughman
> President of the Cincinnatus line.
>
> Let Van from his coolers of silver drink wine,
> And lounge on his cushioned setee,
> Our man on a buckeye bench can recline,
> Content with hard cider is he.

The campaign of the "ploughman of North Bend" against the "democratic peacock" immediately took hold, generating a "great commotion" that took even the Whigs by surprise. Each succeeding rally seemed to top the last—Democrats conceded that in state after state they had never before "seen such a state of things." To John Quincy Adams the campaign seemed to generate "a state of agitation . . . never before witnessed in the American Republic." A Democratic editor said that "every man, woman, and child [seemed] to prefer politics to anything else."

The "great commotion" was a measure of how well the Whigs had learned their political lessons from the Democrats. They whipped up the commotion by appropriating all the techniques that other reform and political groups—especially the Democrats—had invented to appeal to and win the support of the people. The Whigs based their campaign on a series of lavish conventions, celebrations, and rallies. In fact, they turned almost the whole election year into one long Whig rally. They staged a rally of one sort or another at every possible opportunity—to commemorate Washington's birthday and simultaneously ratify Harrison as the people's candidate, to mark the victories at Tippecanoe and the Thames, to nominate local Whig candidates, and, finally, as conventions of "the people" to promote "Tippecanoe and Tyler Too."

A full-blown rally was usually held in a centrally located or principal town or city and drew people from all the outlying towns, and often across state boundaries. Like fair days, these days were set aside as special. As a Whig editor put it, describing a rally in St. Louis, "The city itself bore, in some respects, the remarkable character of a Sabbath day. By the Whigs, and even among the Democrats, there was little work done. The doors of all places of business were closed and nothing was thought of on this carnival day" but politics and fun.

Planning began weeks in advance. There would be smaller conventions and rallies in all the outlying communities to select numerous "delegates" to the big convention. As the day approached, the delegates were given a rousing send-off. They then made their way to the convention city with the nineteenth-century version of parade floats—wagons mounted with log cabins and canoes, with banners and "campaign balls" pasted with the latest slogans extolling Harrison and slurs lampooning "Van, Van the used-up man."

Convention day really was a kind of political carnival. Cannon and bells announced the dawn of the big day, calling forth the formal procession to the site where the speechmaking and banqueting would take place. The procession often numbered several thousand people and stretched out for a mile or two: a dozen or more bands, ranks of dignitaries, veterans who had fought with Old Tip, citizens with banners, on horseback and in carriages, displays of Fort Miegs and other scenes of Harrison's heroism, innumerable canoes, several log cabins, wagons loaded with barrels of cider, other wagons carrying representatives of the various crafts—blacksmiths, for example, with forge and bellows and a banner declaring "We strike for our Country's Good"—and delegation after delegation with banners and the various symbols of the Log Cabin campaign.

No Whig procession was complete without paraders, dressed up in lavish and hilarious costumes, who lampooned Van Buren and the Democrats. And the spectators along the parade route were as much a part of the ritual as the marchers. They cheered and heckled and usually themselves fell into line at the end of the official parade, following the procession. Often, the line of march passed through floral arches and past balconies and embankments filled with "the fairest part of the population" wielding banners and liberty poles inscribed with slogans such as "Harrison Our Protector" and "Harrison: He saved us from the savage tomahawk; may he be the highest in office, and

A WHIG RALLY. One of the main features of the 1840 campaign was the mass rally. This etching shows a Cincinnati rally held in October. For the occasion, the Whigs built an arch of triumph across the main street. In the background, over a store on the right side of Main Street, is a gigantic cider jug topped by a waving flag and pennant.

the first in the hearts of his countrymen." One marcher in a Boston rally reported balconies filled "with women with bright eyes and pounding bosoms, waving handkerchiefs, exhibiting flags and garlands, and casting bouquets of flowers upon us."

The procession ended at the "grounds," where a kind of multi-ring oratorical circus would be staged. At the center was the main platform, from which the most prominent speakers (often Whig giants like Henry Clay or Daniel Webster or even Harrison himself) addressed crowds that sometimes numbered in the tens of thousands. At the corners of the grounds were the smaller stands, from which various orators simultaneously harangued the crowd. On one stand, local Whig candidates might take turns holding forth, while at another a local citizen (often a veteran from one of Harrison's victories) would extol the virtues and exploits of Old Tip. On still another platform there might be a rising young Whig politician like thirty-one-year-old Abraham Lincoln of Illinois, who had a reputation as an especially effective stump speaker.

One of the platforms on such occasions would feature one of the folk orators, who rarely used the classical political rhetoric of a Webster or Clay. They spoke in the words and accents of ordinary farmers and workingmen, delivering "straight hits from the shoulder." John W. Bear, the best known of these homespun orators, gave over 300 speeches in over a half dozen states. Bear, soon dubbed the "Buckeye Blacksmith," would mount the platform with blacksmith garb and tools. Claiming to have some "dirty work" to do, he would pick up the local Democratic newspaper with his tongs, ridicule it, drop it onto the platform, wipe his feet on it and then wash the "dirt" from his tongs. Once when charged by a heckler that he was not really a blacksmith, Bear quickly hammered out a horseshoe on his anvil. He held it up and, to the great glee of the audience and the chagrin of the heckler, shouted that he would "like to nail it on the jackass who just said I was not a blacksmith."

Such gigantic rallies and conventions were the most dramatic spectacles of the campaign. But they were not the whole of it. Smaller towns had scaled-down versions of them, and villages and hamlets of every size had log-cabin raisings. Almost everywhere the people were subjected to a steady, almost unrelenting stream of Whig oratory. But it was the Whig press that wove all the individual and scattered rallies, speeches, and cabin raisings into a single national commotion. Most newspapers of the day were avowedly political in their affiliations, and consciously partisan in the "news" they chose to print (they often simply ignored the statements of opposition officeholders) and how they printed it. But the Whigs in 1840 went one step beyond journalistic custom. They set up a series of new papers, like Horace Greeley's *Log Cabin*, that were exclusively campaign newspapers. Their sole function was to provide Whig editors with political stories from all across the country. Local Whig editors sent Greeley copies of their own papers, which were filled with lavish accounts of local Whig rallies and speeches. Greeley, in turn, reprinted much of it in the *Log Cabin*, which was itself sent back to the same local editors, who used it to tell their readers about what Whigs in other parts of the country were saying and doing.

The Whig press had found a way to spread word of new campaign techniques, new slogans and songs, and new put-downs of "Little Mat" to Whig organizers across the country. In addition, the Whig press deliberately and very effectively created a sense of unstoppable momentum, inflating figures far beyond plausibility and then circulating those numbers to Whig papers across the land. (The Whig press reported a crowd of 100,000 at a rally in September in Dayton, Ohio, a city of 6,000.) As the campaign progressed, this kind of momentum became the essential "news" story the Whig press told—each rally was reported as the largest that had ever been held in that particular place, and each succeeding rally was reported as exceeding all those that had come before. Thus the campaign press was the essential medium that created a national Whig campaign, the essential instrument by which the crowds at a Whig rally in Kankakee, Illinois, or Barre, Massachusetts, or Little Rock, Arkansas, came to feel they were participants in something far larger than a local event, that they were part of a great national commotion by which "the people" would elect the nation's president.

A Whig almanac. In this cartoon, Harrison is shown offering "true Hospitality" to well-dressed and well-behaved supporters in front of his Log Cabin. A sneaky Van Buren is trying to bore a hole in the barrel, foppishly telling Andrew Jackson, "I shall Endeavor to stop the supply." And old General Jackson, hiding behind the cabin's open door, is urging him on, saying "Do so, Matty, for by the Etarnal it's cursed Sour." The viewer is being assured that Van Buren failed, for there are plenty more barrels where this one came from.

But the "great commotion" was not simply a triumph of technique. It was equally a matter of content and form. The Whig campaign as a whole integrated three quite distinct popular rituals. First, the various Whig rallies and commemorations fully appropriated symbols and forms that had long characterized ceremonies at presidential and gubernatorial inaugurations, at dedications of monuments marking great events in the nation's history, and on the Fourth of July—which by 1815 had emerged as the "political sabbath" of the Republic. It was already a well-established practice for different political groups to hold separate, competing Fourth of July celebrations, claiming that they were the true carriers of the nation's revolutionary heritage. But what the Whigs did in 1840 was construct the presidential campaign—with its constant evocation of Harrison as a latter-day Cincinnatus, the protector of the nation's liberties and hearths, and the true heir of the spirit of '76—as a yearlong Fourth of July, a continuing national ceremony that celebrated all the grand themes and sacred political values of the American Republic.

Second, the Whig campaign was a ritual of popular political participation that exemplified what seemed to be the full sovereignty of a democratic people. Here again, the Whigs adopted and dramatically extended devices invented by others. The Whigs had originally opposed the use of conventions to select candidates for public office. But in this election they called for "conventions" (rallies) at every possible opportunity. And they used their innumerable conventions to establish the idea that Harrison was in fact "the people's choice" (rather than a candidate selected by scheming, self-interested political bosses or undemocratic political caucuses). In addition, the Log Cabin campaign itself—culminating, of course, in the act of voting—was a ritual enactment of a new, far more democratic conception of the relationship between the people and their leaders.

Third, the campaign was also an elaborately staged contest. In fact, many of the forms and much of the language of the campaign were direct imports from the sports and competitions of the day. A common event at many rallies was an actual wrestling match between a Whig and a Democratic "champion." (For some reason, the Whig wrestler always seemed to win.) Many Whig songs and slogans (operating much like the cheers at modern-day athletic contests) incorporated the chants that crowds at log-rollings, plowing contests, horse and foot races, wrestling matches, and cockfights used to urge on the combatants:

> *Mum is the word boys,*
> *Brag is the Game;*
> *Cooney[1] is the emblem of Old Tip's fame.*
> *Go it then for cooney*
> *Cooney in a cage.*
> *Go it with a rush, boys*
> *Go it with a rage.*

As Whig and Democratic orators, debaters, and slang-wangers vied with each other for the support of the crowds that gathered around them, they were engaging in a form of intellectual sport. It borrowed from court days, when crowds would press into local courthouses to watch rival lawyers go at each other. The new sport also imitated popular tale-swappings, in which storytellers would try to outdo each other with ever

---

[1]*Cooney* is a reference to raccoons that were the object of "baiting," a popular "sport" of the time.

taller tales. The politicians also incorporated the competitive exchange of toasts Americans often practiced at festivals and banquets. Victory, not truth, was what the competing orators sought. And what the spectators cheered was the contest itself, the struggle of wit and skill between the combatants as they tried to best each other by ridicule, a more telling argument, a clever, unanswerable put-down, a more elaborate pun. They tried, in the language of the day, to "use up" their opponent.

The partisan political press reported these campaign contests as though they were wrestling matches or horse races. In reporting on the debates between Abe Lincoln, the Whigs' champion, and John McClernand, the Democratic champion, a Democratic editor in Springfield, Illinois, insisted that McClernand was routinely "using up A. Lincoln." A Whig editor immediately denounced this as "too simple a lie to tell. Abraham Lincoln used up by John A. McClernand, Bah." And another Whig editor, reporting on some debates between Lincoln and yet another Democratic opponent, asserted: "Mr Lincoln is going it with such a perfect rush that all the Democratic nags have come off the field crippled or broken down."

Try as they might, the Democrats were never able to offset the Whig momentum. From beginning to end, Whig rallies dwarfed Democratic efforts. At the Fourth of July celebrations in Barre, Massachusetts, for example, the Democratic champion, George Bancroft, drew a crowd of 600, whereas more than 5,000 turned out to hear Daniel Webster address the Whig celebration. The Democrats' attempts to put down Harrison as Old Granny or General Mum never took hold. And whenever the Democrats tried to counter Whig ridicule of Van Buren, the Whigs simply "used him up" with another song or slogan.

In the end, the Whig campaign song proved prophetic. The Whigs had "caused a great commotion" that swept Van Buren and the Democrats out of office. The commotion drew a million more people to the polls than had voted in the 1836 election. This was more than 80 percent of the eligible voters (58 percent had voted in the 1836 election). Van Buren in defeat actually got 400,000 more votes than he did in his victory four years earlier. But nearly two-thirds of these million new voters cast their ballots for Old Tip, carrying him to a decisive victory—234 electoral votes to Van Buren's 60. When all the votes were counted, Harrison and the Whigs had won nineteen of the twenty-six states. They carried the crucial Middle Atlantic states of New York and Pennsylvania and swept the Ohio Valley. They even won most of the South.

An embittered Van Buren never became reconciled to what had happened to him. To the end of his life, he remained convinced that the election of 1840 had been some terrible perversion of the democratic politics he himself had done so much to create. But it was the editor of the *Democratic Review* who best summed it up when he sadly lamented, "We have taught them how to conquer us."

Democracy and a New Politics

The election of 1840 gave Americans ample proof that a new kind of political system had been taking shape for two decades. This new politics was a radical departure from some of the most cherished purposes of the Founding Fathers. The deep change that took place in American political life in the years that led up to the Log Cabin campaign of 1840 was quiet and nonviolent. But it put national politics on a footing that the authors of the Constitution would have found shocking, deplorable, and truly revolutionary.

POLITICAL PARTIES

The Constitution had been written by men who hoped to place the national government above and beyond the turbulent struggles of political factions and parties. To the Founding Fathers, this meant keeping elected federal officials (the president and members of Congress) from being chosen by political parties. The clanking, complicated machinery of the electoral college had had one main purpose: to prevent political parties from conducting campaigns for the presidency. The framers of the Constitution had also supposed that the electoral college (and thus the president) would be chosen not by voters but by state legislatures. This too, they hoped, would prevent the presidency from becoming a great political plum that might cause politicians to organize factions in support of candidates. The Constitution further provided that senators would be chosen by state legislatures, not voters. If it all worked, no federal election would involve voters in an area larger than a single congressional district. The system was designed to keep the federal government beyond the reach of what George Washington called "the baneful influence of party spirit."

When Thomas Jefferson and James Madison had set out in the 1790s to found an opposition party, they seemed on the surface to be rejecting this antiparty attitude. But their Republican party was what might be called an antiparty party. So was the Federalist party of John Adams and Alexander Hamilton. Republican and Federalist leaders both assumed that only their own party was legitimate, and that the other party was a danger to the health of the Republic. Both Republicans and Federalists had looked forward to the day when their party would triumph, and the other party would be driven out, forever.

It took them a while, but the Republicans achieved their goal. The Federalist opposition gradually became more and more limited to New England, and after the War of 1812 it disappeared. In the election of 1820 the Federalists did not even field a candidate for president. The incumbent, James Monroe, was reelected by an electoral college count of 231 to 1. The men who cast that electoral vote had been chosen not in a roughhouse party campaign but in a calm and decorous way, not by voters but by state legislatures. Little wonder that Monroe could boast that the nation had entered an "Era of Good Feeling." Everything seemed to be working just as the Founding Fathers had planned.

POLITICS AND THE PANIC OF 1819

James Monroe was the last American president who had participated in the American Revolution—and he was the last to wear one of the symbols of the eighteenth-century gentleman, a wig. He had made it the main business of his presidency to promote national unity and to drive the last nails into the coffin of political parties. He chose John Quincy Adams, the son of Jefferson's old antagonist, to be secretary of state—which was assumed to be the natural stepping-stone to the presidency. Monroe also appointed a number of Federalists to other important offices. Surely, he said in 1822, "our government may go on and prosper without the existence of parties."

One measure of the success of the Republicans in creating a political consensus was the degree to which Monroe and Adams were able to survive a severe economic crisis, the Panic of 1819.

The booming expansion of the market economy (see Chapter 8) had been fueled by risky credit arrangements and risky monetary policies. There was not a single stable national currency, but a crazy quilt of state and local currencies, almost all of them based on credit rather than on gold and silver. For most people, "real" or "hard" money took the form of *specie*, coins of gold or silver. But there was not nearly enough specie to enable the expansive economy to function, especially in boom areas like the Southwest.

In place of hard money, there emerged a set of shaky arrangements that produced a kind of pseudo-currency, made up mostly of "soft" money. Almost any group of men could set up shop as a bank, get a state charter, and issue notes that could pass from hand to hand as money. Many of these banks were completely unregulated. At any one time, literally hundreds of competing brands of money were circulating in the United States. In 1817, for example, different currencies were issued in Pennsylvania by forty-eight legal banks, twenty-two nonlegal ones, and thirty-nine private citizens.

Bank notes could be exchanged for hard cash at the bank of origin—at least in theory. In reality, most banks issued notes in amounts that were far, far greater than what they could pay out in hard cash on any given day. People knew that, and so a five-dollar bank note might actually be worth much less than five dollars in specie.

In 1819, the currency bubble collapsed. One after another, banks were unable to redeem their notes, and had to close their doors. Each bank failure only put more pressure on the remaining banks. Men who were in debt could not pay their creditors because the money they had on hand was suddenly worthless. Prices, particularly the prices of agricultural commodities, fell suddenly and sharply. A man who had borrowed, say, $1,000 before the panic could have repaid the loan by selling about a ton and a half of cotton at thirty cents a pound. But when the price of cotton dropped to less than ten cents, the debtor suddenly saw his real debt tripled. He still owed the same number of dollars, on paper, but now he would have to sell almost five tons of cotton to pay his debt. From the point of view of the lender, such a result was a splendid windfall—provided he could collect the money or take the property that had been promised as security for the loan.

The panic put landowning debtors in a terrible bind, especially in the West. Farmers began to agitate for "relief" legislation to protect them from foreclosure on their property. Typically they wanted their state governments to enable them to use soft paper money at face value to pay off

BANK NOTE. This five-dollar note resembles modern money, but it was privately issued by the Mt. Kean County Bank in Pennsylvania. The small line of print at the bottom even gives the name of the private company that printed the note. A well-stocked lumberyard is pictured at the left, and at the right is a fashionably dressed woman holding a dove. Taken together, the two pictures suggest commercial prosperity and domestic comfort—just the kind of situation a bank would have an interest in presenting.

debts. The simplest way to do that would have been for the states to issue their own paper money. But the U.S. Constitution prohibited states from issuing their own money. Still, the debtors knew there might be a way around that prohibition: the states could charter official banks, and the banks in turn could issue their own notes—lots of them. Those notes would be "soft" money, to be sure, but with the authority of the state behind them, they would be legal tender (meaning that a creditor would be legally obliged to accept them at face value, as if they were actually specie).

Questions of money and banking were suddenly heated by the panic into fierce political issues. Creditor and debtor factions were organized in state after state. These efforts were particularly powerful in Kentucky. There, the debtor faction was able to push through the legislature a state bank, the Bank of the Commonwealth, which printed paper money whose real value was only about half what hard money, based on gold, was worth. But the state provided that creditors would have to accept the soft money, thus reducing the value of outstanding debts in the state to about half their face amounts. The Kentucky courts eventually declared the law unconstitutional in 1823.

The Panic of 1819 also focused attention once more—and sharply—on the Bank of the United States. As part of their embrace of important elements of the old Hamiltonian system, the Republicans had chartered the Second Bank of the United States in 1816. Now, during the panic, the Bank responded by demanding payment, in hard money, for all the state bank notes it held (and it held a lot). This demand forced state-chartered banks to call in their loans to farmers and businessmen, and so accelerated the rate of foreclosures and bankruptcies.

A number of state and local banks failed as a result. The net effect was to make money scarcer, to send farmers and businessmen into bankruptcy—to make a bad situation even worse. And many western politicians discovered that attacking what they called the "monster Bank" was a powerfully effective way to appeal for votes. Thomas Hart Benton, a senator from Missouri, summed up the antibank sentiment perfectly when he told his supporters, "All the flourishing cities of the West are mortgaged to this money power. They may be devoured by it at any moment."

Some states even tried to tax the Bank of the United States out of existence. Maryland passed a heavy tax on the Bank. The Bank refused to pay, so the state sued the Bank's cashier, James McCulloch. The resulting case, *McCulloch* v. *Maryland*, was decided by the Supreme Court in 1819, in one of John Marshall's most significant decisions. The United States, he ruled, had a right to establish the Bank of the United States, even though the Constitution did not expressly say so—for the simple reason that the government could do whatever was necessary and proper to achieve the general results the Constitution aimed at. If such a federal action was legitimate, Marshall reasoned, then no state could be allowed to place any tax or restriction on the Bank, because "the power to tax involves the power to destroy." The decision was the first case in which the Supreme Court had actually decided that a state law was unconstitutional, and this fact alone was enough to make the very existence of the Bank of the United States a raw political issue for the next two decades.

It is something of an axiom of modern American politics that incumbent presidential administrations will take the blame for economic recessions or depressions. But James Monroe and his heir apparent, John Quincy Adams, were almost completely untouched by the Panic of 1819. And one important reason for this is that there was no opposition party, no surviving Federalist faction at the national level, to point the finger of blame. The Era of Good Feeling seemed able to survive even an extremely severe economic crisis. At the state level, especially west of the Appalachians, the panic had made questions of money and banking into fiercely partisan issues. The question was, would increasing political factionalism in the states be translated into a revival of political parties at the national level?

THE REPUBLICAN CONSENSUS AND DIPLOMACY

An essential feature of Monroe's attempt to mold a national consensus was an aggressive foreign policy, guided by a continental—even hemispheric—vision. Monroe and Adams set out to extend and secure the boundaries of the nation, and also to project American power into the "vacuum" created by the end of Spain's empire in Central and South America.

Adams followed up on Andrew Jackson's 1817 incursion into Florida by threatening Spain with further conflict. The Spanish backed down. In the Adams-Onís Treaty of 1819, Spain surrendered the Florida peninsula. All the United States had to do was to assume responsibility for $5 million in claims by American citizens against Spain, and to settle the disputed border between Louisiana and Spanish Texas. Spain also agreed to accept a northern limit to Mexico, at about the latitude of Washington, D.C. This meant that once disputes with Britain over the Oregon Country could be settled, the United States would extend to the Pacific Ocean.

That clear line to the Pacific depended in part on the British. Monroe and Adams took two of three giant steps toward completing the United States as a continental nation, secure in its boundaries. In 1817, the Rush-Bagot agreement demilitarized the border between the United States and Canada by requiring that all military vessels be removed from the Great Lakes. The next year, in the Convention of 1818, the United States and Britain agreed that the border between Canada and the western United States would lie along the 49th parallel—at least to the Rocky Mountains. Adams wanted to extend the line all the way to the Pacific, thus settling the Oregon question. Instead, the United States and Britain agreed to hold the Oregon Country "jointly" for the time being. But Adams could be satisfied, for the Convention of 1818 had given the United States much of what today are Minnesota and North Dakota.

The external horizons of Monroe's administration were soon expanded dramatically, to take in the entire Western Hemisphere. In 1822, the United States became the first nation to recognize the independence of a number of new nations that had won independence from Spain. But there was a chance that other European powers might try to replace Spain's imperial presence in the Americas. To try to prevent this, Britain proposed a joint U.S.-British declaration against European interference in any of Spain's former colonies. Adams rejected this friendly proposal, and instead drew up what became known as the Monroe Doctrine. This 1823 policy statement was presented to the world in the form of a message from Monroe to Congress. In it, he called for an end to European colonization of the Americas, and said that the United States would not accept European intervention in the affairs of any independent state in the Western Hemisphere. In return, he promised only that the United States would not "interfere" in the affairs of Europe.

THE END OF THE DYNASTY

To have any real effect, the Monroe Doctrine probably depended on the willingness of the British to use their navy to enforce it. Still, the pronouncement was enormously popular domestically, for it seemed to be a vigorous foreign-policy outcome of the apparent end to political parties and the successful building of a nonpartisan national consensus. For a national government that had nearly been torn apart by factional strife during the War of 1812, this seemed to be a grand achievement.

But any appearance of political consensus was an illusion. Monroe's winning every state in 1820, and his attempt to "go on and prosper without the existence of parties," might have been comforting to the revolutionary old guard. But four years later the Era of Good Feeling was a shambles.

In its complete control over the federal government, the Republican party had no disciplinary control over its own leaders—especially not over men with a strong following in a particular state or region. As the election of 1824 approached, the old, unwritten rules of succession appeared to entitle John Quincy Adams to the presidency. He had worked his way through the executive branch to the conventional jumping-off point, as secretary of state. But the rules broke down. There were too many new and ambitious men on the scene, too much awareness of conflicting interests and regional identities to allow the one-party system to function smoothly.

The strongest signal that the rules had failed came when the usual caucus of congressional Republicans met to nominate the party's candidate. Only about one-third of the congressmen even took the trouble to show up, and most of those who did were the supporters not of a party position but of a man. They nominated the secretary of the treasury, William Crawford—a Virginia-born Georgian who had the support of old Thomas Jefferson himself. But there was no party discipline. In effect, there was no party. And so several other men went to their state legislatures for nomination as candidates. Adams would run, not as the heir of Monroe, but as a northern candidate. John C. Calhoun, another member of the Monroe cabinet, was the candidate of South Carolina. Henry Clay had strong support in his native Kentucky and in neighboring Indiana and Ohio.

Crawford, Calhoun, Adams, and Clay had one thing in common. They were members with full standing in the Republicans' Washington establishment—three of them cabinet members and Clay the Speaker of the House of Representatives. Each of them might reasonably expect to reunite Jefferson's party, to make it last another generation as the national political party. But Calhoun withdrew just before the election because he was certain he could become vice president, and so set the stage for a conventional run for the presidency in 1828 or 1832. Crawford suffered a stroke during the campaign, and ended up getting the electoral votes of only Virginia and Georgia.

As for Clay and Adams, whichever of them lost would probably join the other's cabinet, hoping to become the next figure in the Republican dynasty. They even agreed in general on a strong program of national economic development supported by the federal government—including tariffs, internal improvements, and a powerful national bank. This program, which Clay had dubbed "The American System," was reminiscent much more of Alexander Hamilton than of Thomas Jefferson. It was possible, in short, that a new dynastic generation of presidential leadership could be founded—by the party of Thomas Jefferson on the principles of Alexander Hamilton.

But there was a spoiler in the wings: Andrew Jackson. The Tennessee legislature nominated him for the presidency late in the election year and with little expectation that he could win. But his campaign caught fire. He took no political positions and announced no program, but he did inspire intense personal loyalty among his supporters. And his fame as "the Hero of New Orleans" guaranteed him a strong popular following in those states where presidential electors were chosen directly by the voters.

The election of 1824 was not a campaign of party against party but a bitter and nasty contest of factions loyal to individual men. There were few significant differences, other than those of personality, among the candidates. They all used the same party label, with slight variations. And faction was only as strong as the determination of a candidate's supporters to elect him. Despite the serious stroke that Crawford suffered during the campaign, his friends kept working for his election. They were driven partly by loyalty to a party label or a sectional program, but mainly by loyalty to their man. On the other hand, the factions were so ill-defined that politicians could move gracefully from one to another, or even straddle. Calhoun proposed himself as a candidate for vice president, and campaigned to serve with either

JACKSON STATUE. This great statue of Jackson, which stands in Jackson Park in New Orleans, captures the fascination that military prowess and machismo held for Americans of the mid-nineteenth century. It is difficult to imagine a sculpture more determined to emphasize aggression and stereotyped masculinity.

Adams or Jackson, if either of them won. A strong and workable conception of political party would have prevented both the Crawford faction's stubborn insistence on their man and Calhoun's straddle between Jackson and Adams. What had looked in 1820 like one-party politics had suddenly become no-party politics at the national level.

The Founding Fathers would not have been pleased. A new generation of ambitious political leaders had come forward, ready to mount vigorous campaigns for office. Their campaigns were turbulent because a striking new element was being added to presidential elections. Eighteen of the twenty-four states had now decided that presidential electors should be chosen by the voters instead of state legislatures. So candidates were appealing to masses of voters directly. For the first time there was something approaching a popular vote for president.

The outcome of the combination of a new method of voting and a multiplicity of candidates was a confusion unique in the electoral history of the United States. Jackson had won 42 percent of the popular vote, but his support was heavily concentrated in the South, where he won several states by very large margins. He had 99 electoral votes to Adams' 84. But it took 131 to win.

As the strategists for the candidates studied the results, they confronted a curious mess that left only a few points clear. The decision would have to be made, for the second time, in the House of Representatives, where each state would cast one vote. When the candidates and their strategists counted by states, Jackson's situation was plain. He had won in ten states out of the twenty-four; if they remained loyal, he needed only three more. Crawford had won in three states, and so had Clay. But the sick Crawford had no real control over his supporters in the House. The key man was obviously Clay. He could not only deliver his own states but might be able to use his influence as Speaker of the House to shake loose some of Jackson's or Crawford's. Clay held important cards, and he played them with skill. He was courted by all factions, but he finally threw his support to Adams, who in turn named Clay his secretary of state—a political deal that seemed to mean Clay would be the next president after Adams. Jackson's supporters tagged this arrangement "the Corrupt Bargain"— though it was a bargain they would have been willing to make with Clay if they had been offered the chance.

JOHN QUINCY ADAMS

In practical terms, the election of 1824 was significant primarily as part of the stage scenery for the next round, 1828. The presidency of John Quincy Adams resembled nothing so much as a four-year campaign between him and Jackson.

In this lengthy jockeying for position, Adams operated at a serious disadvantage, one he inadvertently created for himself. He steadfastly refused to act as a party man. Like all his predecessors in the presidency, John Quincy Adams believed political parties were evil, a symptom of some deep flaw in the American social fabric. Perhaps naively, he thought that "the baneful weed of party strife" was being uprooted.

So Adams took a calculated gamble. He continued Monroe's policy of appointing some old-line Federalists to high office, but he took that policy to an extreme. Adams refused to use his patronage powers to punish his personal opponents or even to reward his supporters. "I shall exclude no person for political opinions or for opposition to me," he said. "My great object will be to break up the remnant of old party distinctions and bring the whole people together in sentiment as much as possible." In his entire term, he removed only twelve men from office.

As president, Adams acted as if he stood not just above party politics but above the people themselves. (Here, too, he was only taking to an extreme an idea of political authority he shared with all his predecessors.) In his inaugural address, Adams recommended to Congress a vigorous program of federal action that he knew would be politically unpopular. But he urged Congress to support his proposals anyway—and not to be "palsied by the will of our constituents." But on other matters, Adams called for a policy that would make unprecedented use of federal power and money to develop the nation's economy and culture.

His program would have involved building a national system of roads and canals, a national university, even a national astronomical observatory. The program resembled Henry Clay's American System, but it went beyond anything even Clay had proposed. Adams devoted much of his administration to the pursuit of his program. To a certain extent, he succeeded—particularly with internal improvements. But many Americans remained deeply suspicious of such aggressive use of federal power. And Adams's own refusal to appoint his friends to political office meant he never created a political base of loyalists he could count on in 1828.

In some respects John Quincy Adams was the best-prepared man ever to become president. The son of a president, he was a Harvard-educated lawyer who became a skilled diplomat in Europe, a senator, and then secretary of state. But in one crucial way he was not prepared at all: he sorely miscalculated the changing temper of American political culture. Adams may have thought he was attempting to unite the nation. But, as one of his opponents noted, he succeeded in uniting it only in opposition to him.

THE ELECTION OF 1828

If Andrew Jackson had a campaign issue in 1824, it was simply that he was the outsider, a man of only limited contact with a Washington establishment his followers labeled "aristocratic." Jackson and his supporters emphasized the fact that the Old Hero was a "man of the people," of humble origins. His talk was marked by plain common sense, instead of Adams's Greek quotations and struggles for eloquence. The image was completed by dramatic use of the 1824 election, when the people's choice had been turned back by an unholy alliance between "luxury" and "corruption." Jackson's supporters argued that the true, manipulative face of Adams's aristocratic pretensions had been revealed in the "Corrupt Bargain." This, in turn, had been supported in a Congress dominated by what Jackson's party workers called King Caucus.

To kick off the election year, Jackson attended a giant celebration in New Orleans on the anniversary of the battle there. The crowds were given miniature hickory sticks, and over and over he was toasted with the line that became the refrain of his campaign and his career as president: "Andrew Jackson—his Party is the People!"

What this amounted to was nothing less than a political language, a rhetoric, that pitted the homespun against the refined, the people against a conspiratorial elite in Washington, and the people's leader, who now called himself "Old Hickory," against the "aristocratic" Adams.

But Jackson was as good a politician as he was a general, and he knew perfectly well that it had been cannon, not just songs and slogans, that had won for him in New Orleans. It would be political organization, not campaign rhetoric, that would win for him in 1828. So he and his circle of supporters set out to build a national political party.

A study of the election map of 1824 bore home several lessons. If Adams could hold on to what he had won then, he would need to pick up only a few more electoral votes to claim the presidency. If Adams could win in Pennsylvania and add just a couple more states like New Jersey and Ohio, then the "man of the people" would lose again. And so Jackson and his strategists set out to build the party organization that, in the end, would be their major political accomplishment.

New York was an obvious key, so Jackson courted Martin Van Buren and John Van Ness, one of Van Buren's lieutenants. A central committee was formed in Washington to coordinate state efforts, with Van Ness as its chairman. Newspapers were founded to support Jackson—eighteen in the crucial state of Ohio alone, and many others elsewhere. To hold the South in line, Jackson chose Calhoun as a running mate. And to angle for votes in the West—particularly in Clay states like Ohio and Kentucky—Jackson's "friends" in Congress went to work on the issue of the tariff. They helped push through what became known as the Tariff of Abominations. In it, they conceded limited tariff support to New England manufacturers of cotton and woolen cloth, and of hemp rope. But they gave higher tariff barriers to the people who raised the sheep and the hemp (people who happened to live in crucial states like New York and Ohio). The South opposed the tariff vigorously, as always, but Jackson and his supporters knew the South would never turn to Adams.

It all worked. Jackson not only held Pennsylvania but won more than half the electoral votes of New York away from Adams. Twice as many people voted as in 1824, and Jackson had the support of 56 percent of them. The ingredi-

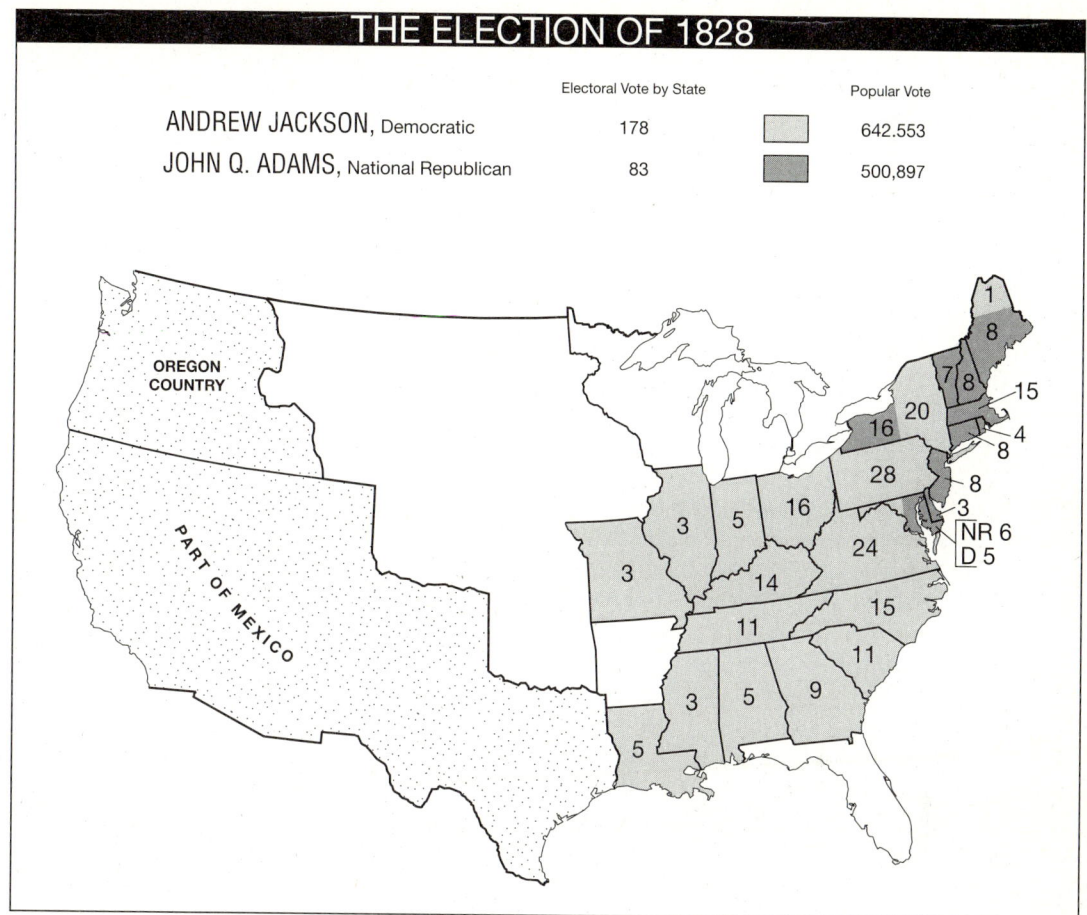

ents of victory had been obvious: an expanded electorate; direct election of the presidential electors (only South Carolina still chose them in the legislature); democratic slogans and rhetoric; and a party organization carefully built and controlled by professionals like Van Buren.

Jackson swept into the White House on a wave of democratic feeling combined with his fame as the Hero of New Orleans. On inauguration day, he even threw open the White House to a brawling, muddy-booted crowd that shocked old Washington hands who had grown accustomed to the decorum of the Republican dynasty. But it was difficult to predict what his policies would be. In the campaign, he had taken soft stands on every question and had confined his efforts to building the party and attacking Adams.

THE NEW POLITICIANS

Whatever Andrew Jackson might actually do as president, he and his supporters had already completed their most historic accomplishment before election day. They had built a political party, which they chose to call the Democratic party. During the coming years, their opponents would form another party, and reach back to the vocabulary of the American Revolution for its name, the Whig party. And so by the election of

1840, a new party system would come into being, one that historians refer to as the second party system. By 1840, most Americans would take it for granted that there were two national parties, the Democratic and the Whig, and that each of them would unite behind a single candidate for the presidency. But more was happening than the creation of two political parties. Political men set out to redefine the very *idea* of political parties. In the process, they also redefined the nature and meaning of democracy in America.

The new party system was the creation of men who a generation earlier would have had little chance of gaining high office. One of the results of the American Revolution had been a modest but real democratization of politics. Before the Revolution, most men who held political office at all levels had had wealth, education, social standing, and family connections. After independence, there were many more men in local and state government who had what would have been called a "middling" status: tavern-keepers, artisans, farmers, small merchants, and petty lawyers. But such men tended to advance no further than sheriff or alderman or state legislator. The men who claimed the higher offices in the state and national governments continued to be those with wealth, education, and extensive connections. All the early presidents, from Washington through John Quincy Adams, had the clear markings of a social and economic elite.

In the decades after the War of 1812, though, men of modest and even humble origins began to elbow their way into national politics at the highest levels. For them, political careers were not the result of having wealth and prestige. On the contrary, their political careers were the *means* for getting wealth and prestige. They were not political leaders because they were rich and powerful. Instead, they became rich and powerful because they gained important positions in government and in political parties.

Andrew Jackson's own career is a striking case in point. He was a self-made man, the first president who did not inherit wealth and status. He was born in the Carolina backcountry in 1767, the son of poor Scotch-Irish immigrants. Jackson left home at the age of seventeen. Four years later, in 1788, he moved farther west to Nashville, Tennessee, which was little more than a stockaded frontier village of log houses. Young Jackson became, in short order, a lawyer, a district prosecutor, a congressman, and (in 1797, when he was barely thirty years of age) a U.S. senator. He resigned this last position just a year later and returned to Tennessee, only to be elected to a state judgeship. In 1802 he resigned this position too in order to devote all his energy to the economic empire he had managed to accumulate.

Jackson's hard work led to wealth from virtually the moment he set foot in Tennessee. As a new lawyer, he specialized in collecting debts. (In his first month of legal practice, he issued almost seventy writs to delinquent debtors.) With his earnings, he began to speculate heavily in sparsely settled Tennessee lands, and he was able to use the public offices he held to befriend some of the wealthiest and most influential men in the state. On his plantation near Nashville, worked by more than a hundred slaves, he built one of the greatest mansions in the United States, which he named the Hermitage. Even before Jackson left private life once again in 1812 to assume the military command that would win him national fame at New Orleans, he had become a great southern "aristocrat."

Andrew Jackson was the first self-made man to become president. His successor, Martin Van Buren, would be the second. (He was the son of a tavern-keeper in the little town of Kinderhook, New York.) In the Log Cabin campaign of 1840, Harrison became the first president to *pretend* to be a self-made man. The carefully cultivated myth that he had been born in a log cabin was proof that humble origins had become not only acceptable but almost essential to political success.

It was not just presidents who were—or sometimes pretended they were—self-made men. Henry Clay, whose supporters called him "Harry of the West," went to Kentucky in 1798, at the age of twenty-one. He started more or less from scratch, though he did have good legal training. He made an advantageous marriage, and when only twenty-nine, he was appointed to fill a va-

A Napoleonic Clay. If a political leader could not be depicted as a military hero, there were several conventional alternatives. One was to show him as a Napoleonic figure. In this portrait of Henry Clay, the artist has used his hair to suggest a resemblance to images of Napoleon that were very widely circulated at the time. His right hand is not thrust into his coat, as Napoleon's often was; but it is in about the same position. And the paper he is holding is an 1821 House of Representatives resolution supporting independence for Spain's Latin American colonies. This also had Napoleonic overtones, because Napoleon had taken his armies into half the nations of Europe saying he was going to bring French *liberté* to their people.

cancy in the U.S. Senate caused by a death. Then, in 1810, he was elected to the House of Representatives and was immediately chosen Speaker of the House, though he was only thirty-four and had never been a congressman before. Daniel Webster, who eventually would become a towering Whig presence in the Senate, was the son of a modest New Hampshire farming family. Abraham Lincoln, the active young Whig from Illinois who spoke to so many rallies in the campaign of 1840, was from a very poor family. In the end, he would become the legendary model of a politician who had educated himself, reading books by firelight in a rude cabin after a hard day splitting logs for fence rails.

The popular idea of the self-made man had much more reality in political life than in the spheres of commerce, manufacturing, and finance. Most of the wealthy bankers, businessmen, and entrepreneurs of the nineteenth century were born into comfortable or rich families. This has caused historians to be puzzled over how the myth of the self-made man came to be so widely believed. An important part of the answer to the puzzle lies in the new political styles and practices that took shape in the period after 1820. In the new political parties, there really *was* an abundance of prominent men whose social origins were very modest. The politicians of the day liked to believe that their rise from poverty or obscurity was the realization of a uniquely American dream; and they worked hard to get their supporters to believe it, too. To many people, the fact that a poor boy actually could grow up to be president was proof that, in America, the same boy might have grown up to be a wealthy merchant or manufacturer.

POLITICS AND THE LAW

A part of the explanation for the emergence of political leaders from poor backgrounds (real or pretended) had to do with changes in the legal profession. In the early nineteenth century, it was easy to become a lawyer. Standards for admission to the bar dropped sharply. The change was most pronounced in western states like Jackson's Tennessee, Clay's Kentucky, and Lincoln's Illinois. But the change also occurred in older states like Van Buren's New York and Webster's Massachusetts.

In the past, most men who became lawyers already belonged to elite families. As a career, the law had been a path for the sons of the educated and the wealthy. Now the law was becoming a path *to* wealth and prominence, and one that did not require much education. There were no law schools. Lawyers usually had a minimal amount of training—a few months studying as a clerk to some local practicing lawyer. This short apprenticeship was typically concluded by a brief, oral bar examination that was likely to be no more than a sociable gathering of small-town good old boys, lubricated with whiskey.

At the same time, the tie between law and politics was becoming closer. The expectation of most young men who became lawyers was that the career might well lead them to public office, to fame, and even to dizzying heights of power. But this would depend, at the local and state levels, on their making connections with the right circle of men, the right factions, and the right party organizations. As a result, at the same time that Monroe's presidency seemed to have ended party politics at the national level, politics in the states, counties, and towns was becoming highly organized and partisan. To men who pursued the career of lawyer-politician, loyalty to party was supremely important—much more important than any issue or program. For many, like the Van Burens and the Clays and the Lincolns, politics was their real profession. The political parties were the institutions through which that profession could be pursued.

A NEW THEORY OF PARTY

The new professional politicians had to come to terms with the American past. They understood very well that their chosen institution, the political party, was something the Founding Fathers had regarded as a kind of prostitution of republican government, an instrument of corruption and demagoguery.

So they began to work out a new theory of politics and parties. No single man made the theory. No single book or speech or magazine summed it up. But gradually, out of the day-to-day and election-to-election practice of the professionals, a new conception of the political party developed. It involved ideas about three basic relationships: (1) of parties to each other, (2) of parties to the constitutional institutions of government, and (3) of parties to the people.

THE TWO-PARTY IDEA

During the presidential campaign of 1824, the *Albany Argus*, a newspaper that ardently supported the New York Democratic party, which Martin Van Buren was working hard to build and discipline, commented on the history of party in the United States:

> From the first organization of the government, this country has been divided into two great parties. We cannot admit that the majority of either have been actuated by any other than the purest, the most patriotic, and the most disinterested motives.

To a modern ear, this sounds perfectly normal, if somewhat pious. Today it is a breach of political good manners for a candidate for president to openly question the patriotism of an opponent. But to the ears of the Federalist and Republican leaders of the revolutionary generation, the *Argus*'s analysis of party would have sounded downright evil.

But the *Argus*—speaking for Van Buren—was talking about a new idea: that having two parties, both presumed to be full of virtuous, patriotic men, was actually healthy in a free society. According to the new political logic, one-party government was a bad thing. A single dominant party would always break up into factions, as the Republican party had in 1824. These factions would be tied to the individual personalities of their leaders. Eventually, some leader would be able to build his faction into a party that was strong enough to control the government. Then the whole cycle would have to be repeated, again and again, from one party to many factions, then back again to one party.

The only way to prevent this alternation between one-party and no-party politics was to have two permanent parties. Both would be loyal to the Republic. They would compete. Sometimes one would win, sometimes the other. No party could afford to take extreme positions, because

A ROMAN VAN BUREN. Martin Van Buren had what a campaign manager today might call "an image problem." He was not a military hero. And it would have been very difficult to make him look Napoleonic—an alternative to a military pose that was used by some politicians. A second alternative was to look Roman, the choice that Van Buren and his artist agreed on when this picture was made in the 1840s. The cloak is handled like a Roman toga, and the columns and the balustrade are meant to create a setting suggestive of the ancient republic.

that might risk defeat in the next election. The result would be that politics would be kept stable and moderate, in the hands of sound men.

What this meant, in turn, was that professional politicians would have to learn that the wild rhetoric of campaigns like the one of 1840 was just a part of the election business. The suggestions that Harrison was a drunkard or Van Buren a man of uncertain sexual identity were only a kind of political theater. No holds were barred, but the lurid charges and countercharges could be forgotten as soon as the campaign ended and the results were in.

The truth, as professionals like Van Buren and Clay and Webster understood, was that the two parties might compete, but they really depended on each other. Democrats did not campaign for a program, they campaigned against Whigs, and vice versa. Without opposition, no party could survive. There would be no party discipline, no party loyalty. There would be no need for the arts of coalition and compromise that were the career politician's stock-in-trade. Wrestling matches and horse races staged in the rallies of 1840 were symbolic: in the conception of party, there could no more be a campaign without parties than there could be a one-horse race or a one-man wrestling match.

PARTIES AND THE GOVERMENT

The new political logic tied the administrative machinery of the federal government directly to party. When either party won control of a house of Congress or of the presidency, it could be expected to reward loyal supporters with patronage appointments that would in turn strengthen the party organization. In his inaugural address of 1825, John Quincy Adams had said the national government ought to be above patronage. It ought to give office only to men of talent and virtue. Washington ought to be a capital city where "the most distinguished men from every section of the country meet to deliberate." Four years later, in his first inaugural, Andrew Jackson made a quite different statement: "The duties of all public officers are so simple that men of intelligence may readily qualify themselves for their performance. No man has any more intrinsic claim to office than another." In 1832, one of his New York supporters, Van Buren's close associate Senator William Learned Marcy, put it more simply: "To the victor belong the spoils."

Jackson seemed to be talking about democracy, and Marcy about corruption. But in reality they both were talking about the same thing: the use of patronage as a way of enforcing party discipline and rewarding party loyalty. They could talk this way because they knew that to function, the parties needed organization. To organize, they needed people. But most men would work for a party only if they could expect some kind of reward, and since there were not enough elective offices to go around, appointments had to be the currency of party politics. The idea of political spoils was not a new one. What was new was the idea that political patronage was legitimate, that it was a good thing that every office from cabinet secretary to local postmaster should depend on party loyalty.

The new logic of party also made the president the leader of his party in Congress. The one-party assumptions of Monroe and John Quincy Adams had meant they had almost no influence over voting in the House and Senate. But a president who clearly identified himself with a party, and assumed that there would be an opposition in Congress, could use patronage and other forms of influence to enforce voting along party lines. So the new conception of political parties involved a new conception of the way the separation of powers ought to work in practice. The framers of the Constitution had separated the executive and legislative branches in the belief that each would act as a check or a balance on the other at times. The idea that a president ought to exert control over members of his party in Congress was a recognition that it was parties, not branches of government, that would provide the checks and the balances.

PARTIES AND "THE PEOPLE"

The Whig and Democratic parties both assumed that voting was, and ought to be, universal (at least among white males). They also assumed that one of the main purposes of a political party was to mobilize support among the voters. These two parties were the first truly modern political parties in the world in several important ways. They were permanent organizations, from Washington down to the grass roots. They were staffed by professionals. They went after voters aggressively, using the most up-to-date techniques and media—huge picnics with cider and whiskey; newspapers, signs, and handbills; mass-produced banners, engravings, buttons, and gimmicks; wagons carrying blaring bands and mass meetings with as many as five speakers talking at once.

In fact, the parties helped produce an information revolution that was as dramatic as the one brought about in our own time by television and computer technology. In 1790 there were only 75 post offices—one for every 50,000 people. By 1830 there were more than 8,500 post offices—one for every 1,500 people. The result was a flood of mail. In that flood, nothing was more important than newspapers. Between 1790 and 1840 the number of newspapers in the United States increased from 92 to more than 1,400. This meant that during the Log Cabin campaign the number of copies of newspapers printed equaled the number of eligible voters. Almost every one of these newspapers was a party paper, whose columns were devotedly Whig or Democratic.

One of the main causes of this information revolution was the simultaneous revolution in the nature of the American electorate. Most of the new states in the west adopted universal manhood suffrage (for whites, at least) in their first constitutions. Political leaders in the older, eastern states also worked to abolish their states' property qualifications for voting. By the election of 1828, the United States had come much closer to electoral "democracy" than any nation in Europe.

(To be sure, this new "democracy" was a restricted one. Outside New England, the only people eligible to vote were adult white males. In fact, in five northern states that originally had permitted black men to vote if they met property qualifications–Ohio, New Jersey, Connecticut, New York, and Pennsylvania–that right was taken away, at the very time it was given to propertyless white men. And not a single state that entered the union after 1819 permitted African-Americans to vote. In 1807 women lost the franchise in New Jersey, the one state where they had once held it.)

The professional party leaders understood very well that if they were going to appeal to a great mass of voters, they had to be careful. They could not afford to do or say anything that might alienate the voters or the newspapers or

A New Theory of Party

NEWSPAPERS were so important to political campaigns that they were sometimes founded just for an election season. These two were published during the elections of 1840 (the lower) and 1848. They endorse not only the presidential and vice presidential candidates, but state and local candidates as well. "Old Rough and Ready" was the nickname of General Zachary Taylor, the Whig candidate of 1848. He is shown leading a heroic charge, mounted on a white horse. (Note that this issue was published in January, almost a year before election day; the campaign was already in full swing.) North Bend was the name of Harrison's town in Ohio—a far cry from Worcester, Massachusetts, where this newspaper was published.

George Caleb Bingham's The County Election (1854) captured much of the essence of the political culture that emerged between the 1830s and the Civil War. His Missouri voters—all white and male—are mostly plain farmers and artisans. Some are obviously quite drunk. But a candidate stands at the top of the stairs, smiling, half-bowing, and tipping his top hat. This eager appeal from a gentleman to a much poorer man who is not even wearing a jacket and tie would have astonished and appalled the Founding Fathers. But the banner proclaims the central premise of the new political logic: "The Will of the People The Supreme Law."

their own party workers. Thus they were reluctant to take clear stands on any issue that might involve serious controversy. Sometimes, as with Harrison in 1840, it meant not taking a stand on any issue. One of Martin Van Buren's proudest memories was of a speech he had made on the tariff, not because he had changed anyone's mind but because he had been warmly congratulated afterward both by men who opposed the tariff and men who supported it.

Occasionally, a party might gamble that taking a position on some single question might pay off at the polls. But typically parties tried to keep attention focused on the personal "character" of their candidates. In order to win a presidential election, a political party needed the votes of northerners and southerners, city people and farmers, workers and businessmen, poor people and rich, immigrants and old-stock Americans. Putting together a coalition that was diverse enough to win an election required an appeal that would alienate no potential voter. This was another consequence of the new logic of party and democracy.

THE POLITICS OF SECTIONALISM

In order to function successfully at the national level, any political party had to be able to deal with—or evade—the problem of slavery. Parties could function very well in most states by taking a strong stand on slavery and on divergent interests and attitudes of North and South. But national parties existed primarily to win the presidency. And in a national election, no party could hope to win without carrying some states in both the North and the South. It was in the interest of any national political party to keep slavery off the political agenda altogether.

THE MISSOURI COMPROMISE

Whatever touched the interests of the northern and southern states in different ways touched slavery, even if politicians preferred to keep silent on the problem. If a system of internal improvements diverted western grain shipments away from New Orleans to New York, the economy of the South would suffer. And the plain fact was that slavery had become so central to southern life that there was no problem—whether it was the tariff or the Bank question—that was not somehow connected to that "peculiar institution." It was urgent for southern political leaders to be able to have at least an equal voice in the national government, and this would depend on the fate of slavery in the new states that would be formed west of the Mississippi.

The settlement of the West had brought one new state after another into the union without controversy, though some were obviously slave states and others free. Louisiana joined in 1812, Indiana in 1816, Illinois in 1818, and Alabama in 1819. There was almost a pattern to it: one new slave state, one new free state. As long as an equal division of slave and free states could be maintained, hardly anyone noticed.

It was a shock, then, when the admission of Missouri to the union suddenly flared into a political crisis in 1819 and 1820. With no opposition party to contend with, Monroe's Republicans were able to take any position they wanted on any question, and still claim to be loyal to their party. When a bill to admit Missouri came to the floor of the House of Representatives for what everyone expected would be routine approval, Congressman James Tallmadge of New York proposed a startling amendment: that no more slaves could be brought into the state, and that any child born into slavery in Missouri would become automatically free at the age of twenty-five.

The response of the southerners in the House was immediate and outraged. Thomas W. Cobb of Georgia yelled across the floor: "You have kindled a fire which all the waters of the oceans cannot put out, which only seas of blood can extinguish." After bitter debate, the House actually passed the Tallmadge amendment by a slender margin. But no one doubted what the Senate—always the secure nest of southern power—would do: it defeated the amendment just before the spring adjournment.

This meant the House and Senate versions of the Missouri Bill had to be brought into agreement before Missouri could become a state. Clay, the Speaker of the House and anxious to bury the slavery question for all time, found the solution. The northeastern part of Massachusetts, luckily, had applied for admission to the union as the state of Maine. Missouri plus Maine: this would preserve the precious balance of slave and free states. Further, Clay proposed simply to split the Louisiana Purchase along the line of latitude of Missouri's southern border, at 36°30'. Slavery would be prohibited forever north of that line.

The compromise worked, though the Missouri controversy sent a thrilling shock through the political system. But the settlement—which became known as the Missouri Compromise—seemed to prove that the slavery question could be avoided and might even resolve itself peacefully in the long run. In fact, the compromise established that slavery was not going to be an explicit issue in Jacksonian politics but would be carefully kept below the surface. It would influ-

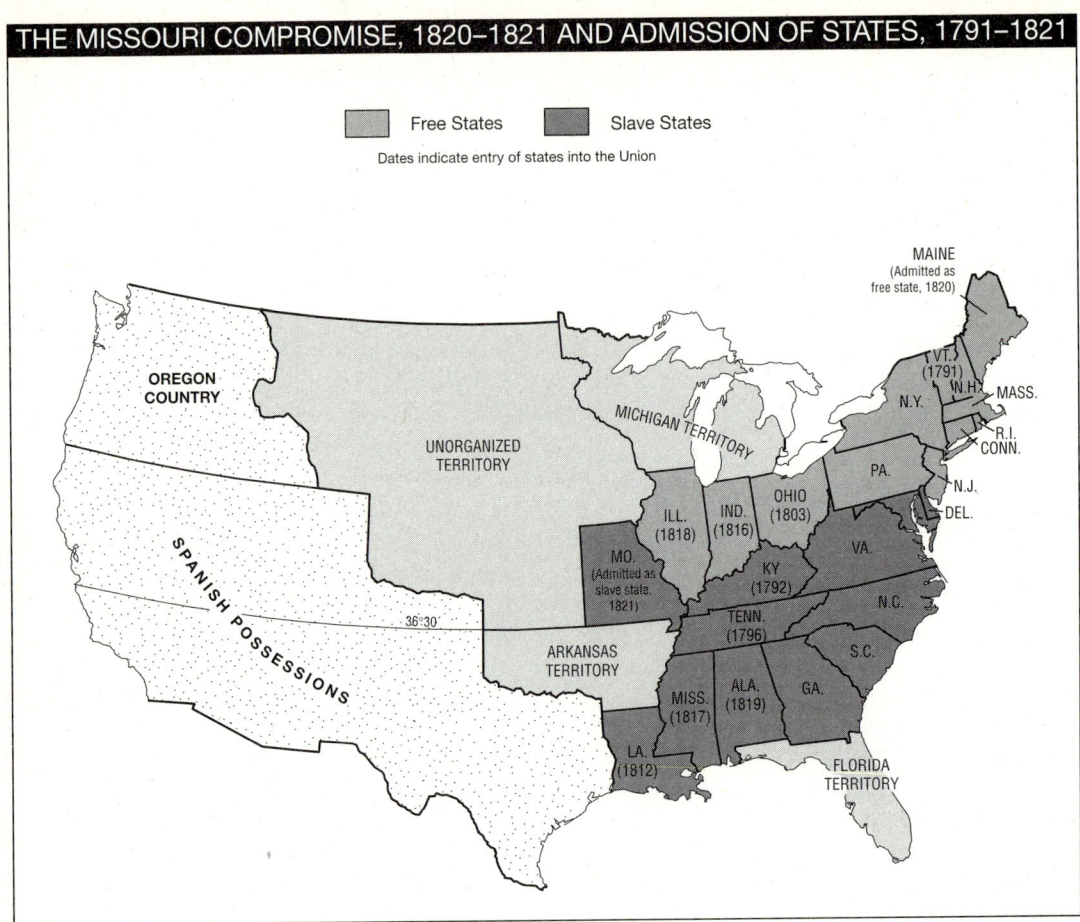

THE MISSOURI COMPROMISE, 1820–1821 AND ADMISSION OF STATES, 1791–1821

ence everything indirectly—tariffs, money questions, internal improvements, and much else—but it would not be a subject of debates in national elections, of bills in Congress, or of presidential speeches and actions. Once more, as in the Constitutional Convention, the problem of slavery had been kept over the political horizon, like some dark and incomprehensible landmark that receded as the country approached it but never went away.

THE NULLIFICATION CRISIS

The tacit agreement among professional politicians that slavery and sectional tension ought be kept out of national politics nearly broke down late in Jackson's first term. The issue was not, immediately, slavery, but the tariff. Still, the tariff was an issue on which there had always been a definite southern position. The slave economy depended on exports, and on the free flow of returning imports of manufactured goods. High tariffs on imports were a threat to the South's expansive market agriculture—and so ultimately to slavery.

During the election of 1828, Jackson's supporters had pushed through the so-called Tariff of Abominations, in an obvious attempt to gain political support in states like Ohio and New York. It had worked; but now, as president, Jackson faced a severe challenge. Already, in 1828, the South Carolina legislature formally denounced the tariff. Such a denunciation was not unusual, but the legislature went further. It published an *Exposition and Protest*—written anonymously by Jackson's own vice president, John C. Calhoun.

Calhoun argued that a state that is convinced a federal law is unconstitutional has the right to "nullify" the law within its own boundaries. If the federal government tried to enforce such a law, the state could go even further and "interpose" state power to protect its own citizens from the exercise of federal authority.

For four years, all the state of South Carolina did was talk and publish. But as the election of 1832 approached, it was clear that Calhoun and Jackson had broken for good. Martin Van Buren was chosen as the Democrats' vice presidential candidate (and presumed successor to Jackson). Now South Carolina acted dramatically. The legislature called a special convention in Charleston. The convention formally nullified the federal tariff of 1828 and warned that if the president tried to enforce the law, the state might secede from the union.

Jackson met the South Carolina Ordinance of Nullification with a ringing proclamation that insisted on the supremacy of federal law. South Carolina had acted in a way that was "incompatible with the existence of the Union, contradicted expressly by the Constitution, unauthorized by its spirit, inconsistent with every principle on which it was founded and destructive of the great object for which it was formed." But while he thundered, Jackson also offered gifts—as he had always done in making Indian treaties: he actually asked Congress to lower the tariff rates.

When the South Carolinians scorned his methods, Jackson went to Congress to ask for a Force Bill, giving him the power to use federal troops to collect the tariff in South Carolina. But he continued to offer compromise on the tariff itself. The result was a little comic (except that it foreshadowed a similar and more devastating confrontation a generation later). Congress, on the same day, passed the Force Bill and a new tariff that lowered rates gradually over a nine-year period. The compromise had been supported by both Jackson and Calhoun. Ten days later, South Carolina repealed its nullification of the existing tariff law. But it added one gesture of defiance: it nullified the Force Bill—a law that was a dead letter anyway.

THE BANK "WAR"

During the election of 1832, the crisis over nullification was overshadowed by an intense struggle over the status of the Bank of the United States.

The Bank issue was an old one—as old as the Republic itself. It had become heated during the collapse of credit and banking during the panic of 1819. Now it came to center stage because of party politics. Jackson's opponents were beginning to organize the Whig party, and were looking for an issue. The Bank of the United States was not scheduled for recharter until 1836. But the opposition in Congress, led by Clay and Daniel Webster, decided to push through a recharter bill in 1830. They believed they could trap Jackson. If he approved the bill, he would appear to desert "the people," accepting an institution clearly identified with an eastern commercial elite. If he vetoed the Bank, on the other hand, he could be accused of bringing on economic confusion—maybe even another panic. The Bank did help bring some order to the economy, mainly by regulating the amount of credit that state-chartered banks could grant. It had the power, within limits, to either expand or contract credit, thereby promoting speculation or stability.

Jackson accepted the challenge and made a definite political gamble. He vetoed the bill to recharter the Bank. In a passionate veto message, he accused the Bank (and its powerful, lordly president, Nicholas Biddle) of being the servant of the rich, the enemy of the poor. And he presented himself and his party as the only ones who could protect the people from Biddle and his "monster." The gamble—and the patient party organization that the Democrats had been pursu-

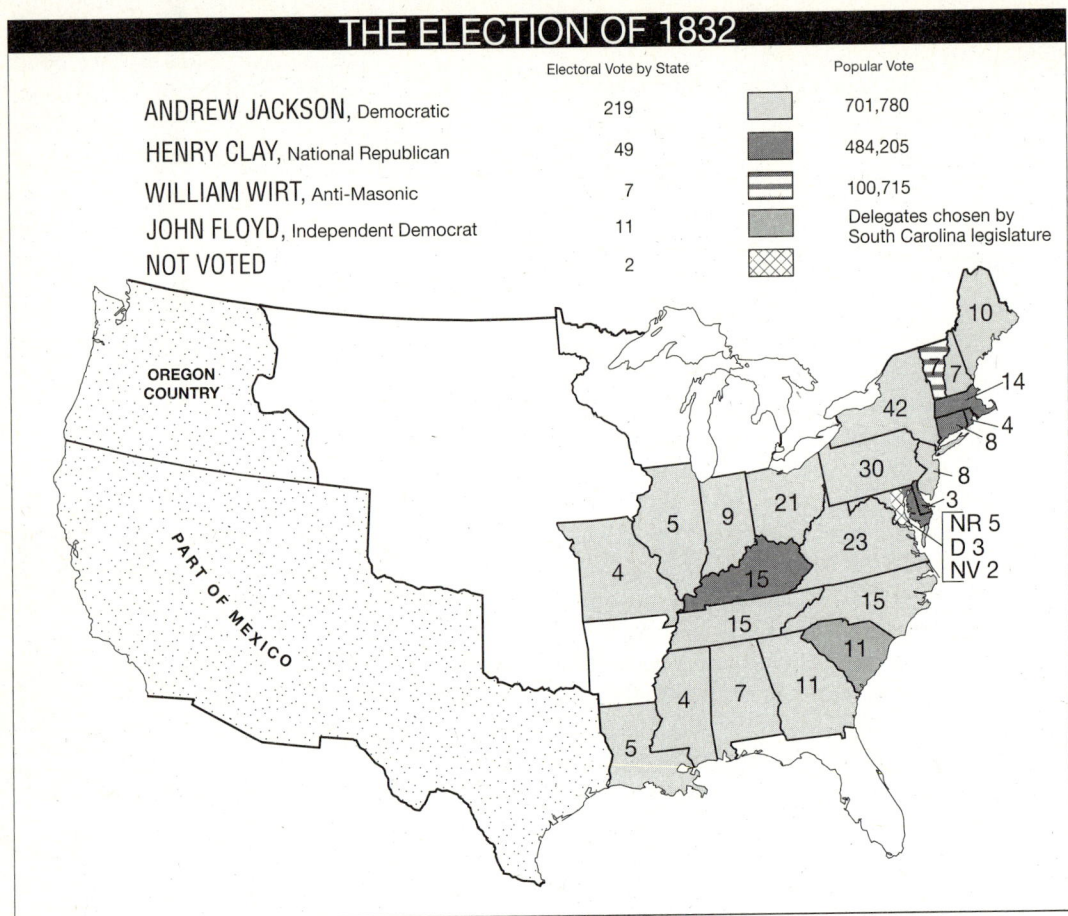

ing for years—paid off. Jackson won a crushing electoral victory (though by a narrower popular margin than in 1828).

The main business of the second Jackson administration became to liquidate the Bank of the United States. The president withdrew federal deposits from the Bank, and issued a "Specie Circular," an executive order providing that only gold—not the notes of the Bank—could be used to pay for public lands. The other principal task was to prepare to pass the presidency and the leadership of the Democratic party to his successor, Van Buren.

JACKSON AND HIS PARTY

The role of Andrew Jackson himself in the development of the new system of political parties was uncertain and contradictory. The Democratic party wanted to claim him as its great leader. He was, after all, the Old Hero who had defeated the British at New Orleans in the War of 1812. He took on the "monster" bank and defeated it. For Democratic candidates for political office in most parts of the country, identifying themselves with Old Hickory was a distinct political advantage.

But for Andrew Jackson, politics was intensely personal. His fame was older than the Democratic party. He had a stubborn personal pride—arrogance, his enemies would have said—that could override any professional politician's arguments about what might be best for the party.

Whenever Jackson met opposition, he had a tendency to regard it as a personal challenge, and to respond in ways that sometimes ignored his party's interests. Midway through his first term, for example, he provoked a terrific shake-up in his cabinet over just such a personal issue. Peggy O'Neale Eaton, wife of the secretary of war, John Eaton, happened to be the daughter of a tavern keeper (a signal that not only might the new breed of politicians have modest origins, but that their wives might also). There were rumors that she had had an adulterous affair with her current husband before they were married. When Jackson learned that the wives of other cabinet members were snubbing Peggy Eaton socially, he made an issue of it at a cabinet meeting and forced the resignation of most of the cabinet. A good party man would never have risked party unity over such a trivial social question. Martin Van Buren's loyalty during the quarrel over Peggy Eaton cemented Jackson's personal loyalty to him.

The Eaton affair, probably more than deep political differences, also drove a deep wedge between Jackson and his vice president, Calhoun. Jackson blamed Calhoun (and, even more, Calhoun's wife) for Peggy Eaton's social distress. When Jackson discovered that Calhoun, way back in 1818, had recommended punishing him for his military incursion into Spanish Florida, the break was complete. This probably helped account for Jackson's ferocious response to the nullification movement in Calhoun's South Carolina. When Jackson threatened to hang the nullifiers from the highest tree, he risked alienating Southerners who were committed to the Jeffersonian notion of states' rights. This would be bad for the party, but Jackson's determination had more to do with people than with party.

Jackson responded more or less the same way to the gathering Whig opposition in Congress (at first a coalition with nothing to hold itself together except a dislike for the president). He vetoed their bank and campaigned for reelection with this veto as the main issue. A good party man would probably have let the bank die a slow death until its existing charter expired in 1836—just in time for another election. But Jackson was aroused, and he defined the contest not as a party issue but as a personal struggle to the death between the monster bank and himself. "The bank," he said, "is trying to kill me. But I will kill it." Then, instead of leaving the bank alone, he decided to stop depositing federal funds in it. This may well have been illegal. It was certainly against the cautious advice of many professional party men. His own secretary of the treasury refused to go along, and Jackson had to replace him.

Jackson's professional supporters talked a great deal about using the patronage system to distribute offices to loyal Democrats, but he was actually quite restrained in his replacement of Adams's appointees in federal positions with members of the Democratic party. He was much more likely to demand the resignation of a good Democrat who had committed some kind of personal affront to his own sense of dignity. So the "spoils of office" came more slowly than the party professionals would have liked.

In the final analysis, it is probably more correct to say that the Democratic party unified around the figure of Andrew Jackson than to say that Andrew Jackson unified the party. Jackson was a soldier, but he had spent very little time in the ranks. He had been a field commander, often operating with either no orders or only vague instructions from civilian authorities. He had the habit of imposing his will on other men, in military campaigns, as the master of many slaves, and as a veteran of the dueling grounds. He was also an *old* soldier, older than most of the working

THE EATON AFFAIR. In this unfriendly drawing, made in 1834, Peggy O'Neale Eaton is being introduced to President Jackson. This tavern keeper's daughter is quite elaborately dressed and on her toes, perhaps demonstrating a ballet step. The members of the cabinet all look pretty grim, except perhaps for Van Buren, at the right, who is using a lorgnette to get a better look. (Library of Congress)

politicians who surrounded him. He still tended to think of political struggle the way Jefferson had in 1800, as a total struggle, and of any form of opposition as disloyalty.

The truth, as party leaders like Van Buren understood, was that in Jackson the party had found an ideal candidate for the new political age, an "outsider" with no career in the federal government, with few political enemies and no political record. Such a man could be promoted by aggressive, well-organized party campaigns. If the candidate had a colorful past and a vigorous personality, as Jackson did, he could be presented by his organization as the "champion of the people." This was the formula the Whigs learned so well in 1840 with Harrison. The same formula would be tried again and again by Whigs and Democrats in the years to come.

AND TYLER TOO

The second party system was not going to be perfected by a man like Andrew Jackson, but by a generation of comparatively featureless politicians and bureaucrats. Indeed, the office of president would not be occupied by a man of Jackson's force of personality until Abraham Lincoln. Between Jackson and Lincoln would come a succession of one-term presidents, alternating between Whig and Democratic parties with great regularity. Two of these presidents did not live to serve a full term. This sequence of presidents is difficult to memorize, and some of them, like Millard Fillmore, have become the answers to trivia questions, or standing jokes. But these seemingly unimportant men did an extremely important thing: They cemented the two-party system into place with such skill and effectiveness that many Americans are tempted to believe that no nation without such a system can possibly govern itself properly.

THE TRAVAIL OF MARTIN VAN BUREN

The Whig opposition knew it would be difficult to defeat the Democrats in the election of 1836. President Jackson's personal popularity would help his chosen successor, Van Buren. And the Democratic organization was too powerful to confront in a direct contest. So the Whigs settled on a diversionary strategy that looked back to the election of 1824 as its model. They decided to run three sectional candidates: Hugh Lawson White of Tennessee for the South, Daniel Webster of Massachusetts for the Northeast, and William Henry Harrison of Ohio for the Northwest. They hoped the result would be that no candidate would win a majority of the electoral votes, so the election would be thrown into the House of Representatives, as it had been in 1824. There, with each state casting one vote, the Whigs might have a chance of winning.

The popular vote was close—762,000 for Van Buren and 735,000 for all his opponents combined. But the Democrats carried every large state except Virginia, and won the electoral victory, 170 to 124.

The new president took office at a troubled time. A new financial crisis, known as the Panic of 1837, was already under way. The beginnings of the collapse lay in a decision by the Bank of England, the most powerful financial institution in the world, to tighten credit late in 1836. The impact on the American economy was direct and swift. The normal practice for cotton buyers in England was to borrow money to buy American cotton. Now, unable to borrow easily, they did not place their usual orders. The price of cotton fell drastically. Many American brokerage houses went bankrupt and could not pay their large debts to banks. Banks, drained by these failures, were not able to redeem their notes in specie. In May 1837, New York banks suspended specie payments, and other major banks around the country soon followed suit. This meant outstanding bank notes were suddenly worth much less than their face value. In effect, there was a sudden collapse of the supply of both money and credit. Without money and credit, what had been a long spiral of growth and speculation suddenly became a deep depression.

The causes of the panic had little to do with the actions of the Democratic administration, but the new logic of political parties made everything a partisan issue. The Whigs were quick to blame Van Buren's Democrats for the troubles. Whigs argued it was no coincidence that the panic came after Jackson's assault on the Bank of the United States. They made much of the fact that just before the election of 1836, the Jackson administration had issued the Specie Circular. This effort to get some control over wild speculation in western lands had required that all payments for public lands be made in gold or silver. This had made bank notes less valuable, since they could not be used by speculators to buy land. In 1837, the sale of public lands shrank to less than one-tenth of the sales of 1836.

Van Buren attempted to meet the crisis with a policy that was designed to tighten the supply of money and credit even further. He proposed a new system of public finance that had two main features. First, a system of Independent Treasuries would be established in the large cities. These would hold all federal deposits and conduct government transactions. This would mean that federal funds would not be deposited in any banks, and could not be used as the basis for issuing bank notes. Second, the government would adopt a severe hard-money policy and accept only specie for all taxes, customs duties, or land sales.

In effect, Van Buren was trying to get his party to commit itself to a definite policy on an important question. But the nature of the new parties quickly became clear. The national parties had only one fundamental purpose: the election of presidents. Van Buren had no success getting his program through (and it would not have cured the depression anyway). The Independent Treasury Bill was not passed until the summer of 1840, when the Log Cabin campaign was already under way, and it was repealed a few years later. The provision that the government would accept only specie payments never went into effect.

The economy rebounded slightly in 1838–1839 but went into an even steeper decline after 1839. Prices for most commodities fell by an average of about 50 percent, and stayed low until well after the election of 1840. This meant the Democrats entered the campaign of 1840 as the first political party to be saddled (unfairly) with the blame for a depression. In this kind of economic setting, the Whig charges—that Van Buren was a man with a taste for expensive wines who wasted money redecorating the White House—

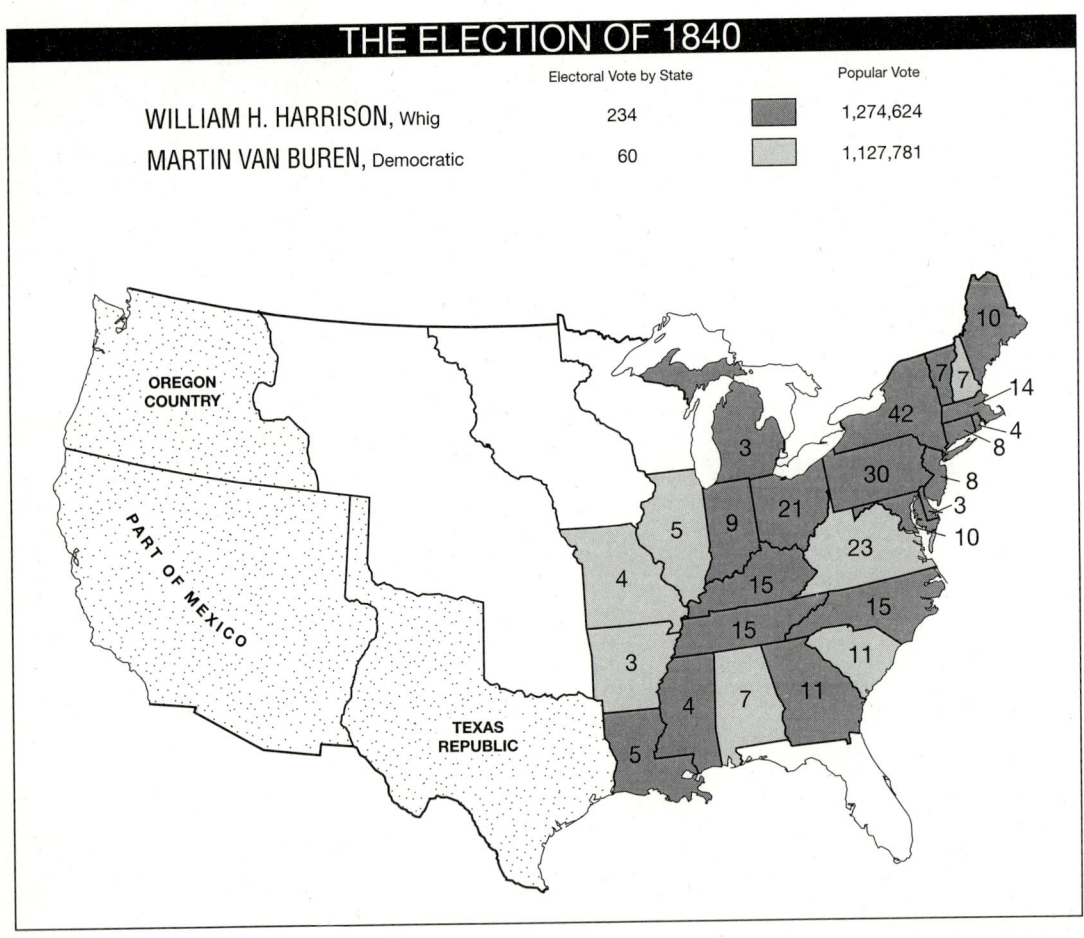

had a bite they would not have had in prosperous times. And the claim that Harrison was a simple farmer who was happy with his homemade cider had a strong appeal. Neither candidate really fitted the picture his party drew. And neither party really had a plan for curing the depression. But the new political logic gave little or no weight to the truth. Van Buren and his party went down to defeat in 1840 as the victims of new methods of party organization and campaigning that they themselves had brought into being. Well might the *Democratic Review* complain, after the election, "We have taught them how to conquer us."

THE WHIG SPLIT

The Whig victory was an empty one. The sixty-eight-year-old Harrison died after only a month in office. The political logic that had dictated the choice of "Tyler Too" quickly took its toll on the party. John Tyler had been one of those political choices designed to unite different factions of the party long enough to win an election. He was a states' rights advocate of the Calhoun stripe and was opposed to the high tariffs and internal improvements that were dear to the hearts of Henry Clay and the supporters of the American System.

Tyler kept all of Harrison's cabinet appointees—mostly Clay men, along with Daniel Webster as secretary of state. But then Tyler began to veto legislation that had the support of most Whigs in Congress—particularly two bills that attempted to create a new version of the national bank. The result was a rift between Tyler and Clay, and a split in the Whig party. A caucus of Whigs in Congress put out a manifesto declaring that the president did not represent his party. All the members of the cabinet, with the exception of Webster, resigned. Clay himself quit the Senate in 1842 to begin a successful two-year campaign for the 1844 nomination as Whig candidate for the presidency, fully expecting to run against Van Buren in a politics-as-usual campaign (for the election of 1844).

GOVERNMENT "BY THE PEOPLE"

The political landscape of the three decades after the War of 1812 was in some respects dull and disappointing. The kinds of leaders that emerged with the new party system seemed to be primarily interested in office for the sake of office. Or they were, like Jackson, much more intriguing as personalities than as political leaders. As for the parties, they were perhaps more given to humbug, confidence games, and hoopla than ever before or since. They were certainly more interested in keeping fundamental questions—particularly the question of slavery—out of politics than they were in adopting positions and finding solutions to social or economic problems.

Little wonder, then, that Abraham Lincoln—who was very much a product of the second-party system—would stand at Gettysburg in 1863 and give all the credit to the Founding Fathers for having created a government "of the people, by the people, and for the people." But for all the eloquence of his statement at Gettysburg, Lincoln was making a historical mistake. The generation that made the Revolution and the Constitution had not actually created a government "by the people." Specifically, they had not wanted presidential elections to be determined by the direct votes of the people—not even the votes of white males. It had been the two succeeding generations of politicians—roughly, Van Buren's and Lincoln's—who had really made national politics democratic. For all their faults, the political parties that were shaped during the 1830s and 1840s were perhaps the most important instruments in this process of democratization.

The Whig and Democratic parties would continue down to the middle of the 1850s to be very much as they were established to be: very practical organizations, run by men of limited capacities and aims. The parties did not have very definite programs, and their primary reason for existing was to win elections. They very seldom addressed basic, difficult social or economic questions. But the politicians of the period did have one principle and did set themselves one steady goal. The principle was that the meaning of democracy is centered in the way politicians ought to gain power—by winning mass popular support in open, hotly contested elections. The goal was to make American politics into the most democratic electoral system the Western world had ever known.

The individual motivations that lay behind this principle and this goal were mostly selfish, shortsighted, and petty. But the historical result was nothing less than a remarkable transformation of American politics. Electoral democracy became the distinctive political fact of American life not, as Lincoln would say at Gettysburg, "four score and seven years ago." The transformation happened during Lincoln's own political lifetime, during the quarter-century that followed the election of 1824. The men who made it happen were not Lincoln's "our fathers"—the makers of the American Revolution and the authors of the Constitution. They were, instead, his own contemporaries, the professional politicians who had been his colleagues and competitors. And they did it not through lofty means and high purposes, but through rough-and-tumble, pragmatic practices like those that were finally perfected in the rambunctious Log Cabin campaign of 1840.

CHRONOLOGY

1810	Henry Clay elected to Congress, becomes Speaker of the House	1836	Jackson issues Specie Circular; Martin Van Buren (Democrat) elected president
1820	James Monroe elected president with electoral vote of 231–1;	1837	Banks suspend specie payment in financial panic;
	Missouri Compromise		Depression begins
1824	Five major candidates compete for presidency, none receives electoral majority;	1839	Whigs hold first major-party presidential nominating convention, Harrison chosen over Clay;
	Albany *Argus* endorses idea of two competing political parties		Depression worsens
1825	John Quincy Adams chosen president by House of Representatives	1840	Harrison (Whig) elected president;
			Number of newspapers reaches one for every 400 persons eligible to vote
1827	William Henry Harrison becomes U.S. Senator	1841	Harrison inaugurated, dies after one month in office;
1828	Andrew Jackson (Democrat) elected president; "Tariff of Abominations"		John Tyler (Whig) becomes president;
1830	Number of post offices reaches one for every 1,500 people		Struggle begins between Tyler and Clay factions for control of Whig party
1832	Jackson vetoes rechartering of Second Bank of the United States;	1842	Clay resigns from Senate to begin campaign for presidency
	Jackson reelected;	1844	James K. Polk (Democrat) elected president
	South Carolina Nullification Crisis		

SUGGESTIONS FOR FURTHER READING

1840: THE LOG CABIN CAMPAIGN

R. G. Gunderson, *The Log Cabin Campaign* (1957), is a sprightly account of the election of 1840. Harrison needs a new biography, to replace Freeman Cleaves, *Old Tippecanoe: William Henry Harrison and His Time* (1939). Some useful material is in David Durfee, *William Henry Harrison, 1773–1841: Chronology, Documents and Bibliographical Aids* (1970). The first volume of Arthur M. Schlesinger, Jr., ed., *History of American Presidential Elections* (1971), includes a short account of the 1840 campaign.

A NEW THEORY OF PARTY

The best place to begin is with Michael F. Holt, *Political Parties and American Political Development From the Age of Jackson to the Age of Lincoln* (1992). Another fine general study is Richard P. McCormick, *The Second Party System* (1966). It can be supplemented with the same author's *The Presidential Game* (1982). An excellent biography is *The Life of Andrew Jackson* (1988). It can be supplemented by Richard B. Latner, *The Presidency of Andrew Jackson* (1979). The political theory of parties is neatly laid out in the final chapter of Richard Hofstadter, *The Idea of a Party System* (1970). There are old and powerful traditions among historians, traditions that attempt to see the two parties of the ·1830s and 1840s as the political institutionalization of deep ideological divisions. Arthur Schlesinger, Jr., *The Age of Jackson* (1945), argued that the Democrats were the party of the new industrial working class. Marvin Meyers, *The Jacksonian Persuasion* (1960), was an attempt to show that the Democrats really had an ideology, a set of shared social and political beliefs and attitudes. Daniel Walker Howe, *The Political Culture of the American Whigs* (1979), tries to do the same thing for the Whigs. An extremely useful study of three giants of the period is Merrill D. Peterson, *The Great Triumvirate: Webster, Clay, and Calhoun* (1987). A thorough treatment of Clay is Robert Remini, *Henry Clay, Statesman for the Union* (1991). The most recent book-length studies of Webster are Sydney Nathans, *Daniel Webster and Jacksonian Democracy* (1973), and Maurice G. Baxter, *One and Inseparable: Daniel Webster and the Union* (1984).

Charles Sellers, *The Market Revolution: Jacksonian Democracy, 1815–1846* (1991) is an attempt to relate politics to economic development. For a more suspicious account of the nature of the new political culture, and its relationship to social and economic change, see Edward Pessen, *Jacksonian America: Society, Personality, and Politics* (1979). Ronald Formisano, *The Transformation of Political Culture: Massachusetts Parties, 1790s–1840s* (1983), and *The Birth of Mass Political Parties: Michigan, 1827–1861* (1971) are both excellent studies at the state level. The standard account of the expansion of the suffrage is Chilton Williamson, *American Suffrage: From Property to Democracy* (1960). Lawrence Frederick Kohl, *The Politics of Individualism: Parties and the American Character in the Jacksonian Era* (1989), is an interesting attempt to put the party system into a cultural context. Morton J. Horowitz, *The Transformation of American Law, 1780–1860* (1977), lays the groundwork for a good understanding of the relationship between law and politics. The aftermath of the "Bank War" in state politics is nicely treated in James Roger Sharp, *The Jacksonians Versus the Banks: Politics in the States after the Panic of 1837* (1970).

AND TYLER TOO

James C. Curtis, *The Fox at Bay* (1970), is a careful study of Van Buren's administration. A more general analysis is available in John Niven, *Martin Van Buren: The Romantic Age of American Politics* (1983), and D. B. Cole, *Martin Van Buren and the American Political System* (1984). The administrations of Harrison and Tyler can be followed in Norman Louis Peterson, *The Presidencies of William Henry Harrison and John Tyler* (1989). William Cooper, *The South and the Politics of Slavery, 1828–1856* (1978), contains a thorough discussion of the role of the South in the Tyler administration.

CHAPTER

10

A New North

Episode: The Garrisons—An Antebellum Family

THE SELF-MADE SOCIETY

Economic Growth and Transformation

The "Self-Made Man"

Middle-Class Evangelism

A New Model of Family Life

A Feminist Alternative

An Age of Reformers

Workers' Movements

New Artists, New Ideas

THE EPISODE: William Lloyd Garrison eventually became famous as an abolitionist. In 1831, he began to publish the most radical antislavery journal in the United States, The Liberator, in which he demanded the immediate and unconditional end of slavery. But before he was famous, and before he was an abolitionist, he was, like everyone, part of a family. This chapter begins by exploring his family's history.

The Garrison family was not important, as historians usually judge importance. The father deserted his wife and children, and the family group was completely broken up by deaths, by "vice," and by economic depressions. The family produced three girls, who all died young, one boy who grew up to be a hopeless, drunkard, and William Lloyd Garrison. But, like other families of the period, it was subject to the powerful impacts of social change. Our purpose in looking so closely at the Garrisons is to set the stage for an examination of what amounted to an economic and social revolution that was taking place in the United States during the period between the 1820s and the beginning of the Civil War.

William Lloyd Garrison eventually became a radical. And radicals are often treated by historians as though they were simply born to be different. Our purpose is to show how Garrison's career was the product not of some mysterious quirk of personality, but of history.

THE HISTORICAL SETTING: The Garrison family history was a product of deep changes in the ways people produced and exchanged goods and services. An accelerating industrial revolution dramatically increased the impact of the development of the market economy that was discussed in Chapter 8. These changes, in their turn, brought about very significant redefinitions of social class. A new middle class took shape, with new institutions, new kinds of organizations, new ideas about what a family was and how it ought to work, new sexual and religious practices, new social expectations and morals, and new culture.

To some extent, the entire United States was transformed by such changes. But in this chapter, we concentrate on the North, where the transformation was much more rapid and pronounced. In the South, the institution of African-American slavery was molding an increasingly divergent economy, society, and culture. (In the following chapter, we will discuss the history of the South and slavery during the same period.)

We have twin purposes in this chapter: to show how the most unusual individuals—like William Lloyd Garrison—are products of the most common social institution, the family; and to show how explaining the lives of the most insignificant-seeming families—like the Garrisons—can bring about an understanding of social and economic change.

THE GARRISONS—
AN ANTEBELLUM FAMILY

William Lloyd Garrison, journalist and reformer, sat up late into the morning of October 14, 1842, keeping a death watch over his brother James. At about three o'clock in the morning James died. As William Lloyd told it in a letter a few hours later, James "threw off his mortal habiliments" so gently that at first he seemed only to have dropped off into a quiet sleep. The watching brother took half an hour, at least, to discover his "error."

Then came that rush of relief that sometimes softens grief. James Garrison's "release from the flesh" seemed a "consolation" rather than a sorrow. He had suffered long enough. He had been approaching death, almost courting it, for a long time. A few years earlier, he had tried to commit suicide. He had, in William Lloyd's curious word, been "habitancing" toward this final peace for much of his forty-one-year life. Finally, in this dim room in Cambridgeport, just outside Boston, the end had come.

As William Lloyd saw it, James died bravely. In the last hours he had found (at least it seemed so) something that had always escaped him in life: a measure of control over himself. James Garrison appeared to look death steadily in the face, to meet this last struggle as he had met no other before, "with all possible fortitude." He had never been able to master his own weaknesses, and so life had mastered him. But his brother could now see in James Garrison's death a novel triumph of will; finally, there was something to praise: "Death had no power over his spirit."

James had been viewed by all the Garrison family as a hopeless disgrace for years; they called him "Crazy Jem." And he had accepted the role of the family disgrace. In fact, at the end it was this role that provided him with his only real sense of identity: as an almost perfect contrast to his brother.

The career that had led James Garrison to his early death in Cambridgeport had been a fantastic series of defeats and failures. He had been a sailor on every imaginable kind of ship: in the coasting trade from the Caribbean to the maritime provinces of Canada, on a British man-of-war, and on American ships of battle. Along the way, he had been in prisons on both sides of the Atlantic—in Cuba, Portugal, France. A dozen times and more, he had waked up owning only the tattered clothes he was wearing. Sometimes he did not even have those, but was simply naked and alone. Almost every house of "ill fame"—prostitution—on the eastern seaboard had taken his money and watched him stagger away the next day, sick and broke. He had had girls in some ports, men and boys in others. He had been a deserter and a thief, a prisoner and a patient. Finally, he had crept back to Massachusetts, too sick to serve in the navy any longer. His brother William Lloyd had taken charge and had sent him to dry out on a small farm in Connecticut owned by relatives. After an uncertain recuperation, James had come to live with William Lloyd. But then had come a final fantastic binge along the Boston docks. And now, death.

Little wonder that William Lloyd Garrison's waking instinct, on the morning after his brother's death, was to plan the funeral as an occasion for making the moral clear:

> I intend that the funeral arrangements and ceremonies shall be as plain, simple and *free* as possible. Liberty of speech shall be given to all who may attend. I shall probably have a testimony to bear against the war system, the navy, intemperance, &c. in connection with James's history.

A few months later, Garrison described the funeral, and added, almost unnecessarily, "My remarks were very pointed."

The brother who lay in the coffin and the brother who made pointed remarks over him could hardly have been more different. William Lloyd Garrison had carefully managed his life, making himself into almost a model of piety and virtue. He had learned to control every weakness, to deny every temptation, to be always the master of himself. James, in contrast, had been mastered—by drink, by women and men, by poverty and illness, and by captains and lieutenants whose cruelty had left him scarred and frightened. Both brothers had been in jails. But William Lloyd always went there because of virtuous stands in virtuous causes; James went for his weaknesses and sins. William Lloyd was a radical in the service of reforms: pacifism, temperance, free speech, antislavery—plus an imposing list of others. James was a radical of vices: drunkenness, thievery, desertion, promiscuity, and licentiousness—plus an imposing list of others. William Lloyd was a drastically upright man; James was just as drastically corrupted.

These contrasts between the Garrison brothers were real, important, and obvious. But there was a veiled similarity in their two lives, less obvious but no less real. The two men, each in his own way, lived lives that were very mobile and uncertain. Both challenged powerful men and institutions—one as a reformer, the other as a chronic misbehaver. For their passions, both men took enormous risks, placing their bodies and their lives in peril. Both had their circles of intimates and friends: one his fellow reformers, the other his shipmates and occasional lovers. But both confronted society at large in angry and provocative ways. As a result, both found themselves branded as outlaws and outcasts. And these lives of uncertainty, opposition, and isolation grew out of an enormous preoccupation with the self that the two brothers shared. Their self-awareness knew almost no limits; nor did their belief that the self was something the individual could make (or destroy) at will. Both were, in short, radical individualists.

The Garrison family took shape in the eighteenth century after the English conquest of Canada during the Seven Years' War. New land was available in Canada for Englishmen to claim and settle. This chance was taken primarily by families that moved up from Massachusetts—families that brought with them the legacies of Puritanism, congregational religion, disciplined lives, and evangelical piety. There were also a few settlers who came directly from England, among them a certain Joseph Garrison, who was alone and ready to start a new family. He married the daughter of one of the Massachusetts immigrants in New Brunswick, and they settled down to the task of having and rearing nine children. Among these nine was Abijah, born in 1773.

Abijah Garrison grew into a tall, strong, ambitious, red-bearded, balding man with a fatefully restless personality. He went to sea and became a pilot in the coasting trade, faring from Newfoundland to the Caribbean. According to family legend at least, he was a skilled navigator and expert seaman. One thing is certain. He somehow managed to educate himself, and he even developed a taste for fancy writing. His letters were artful and contrived, full of the excessive sentimentality of the period—full, too, of pretentious language like "a Tempestuous Sky and Enraged Ocean." He could also summon up the rhetoric of religious piety when the occasion seemed to call for it, praying for "a Ray of Divine Light from the Throne of God and Lamb."

This mixture of sentimental romance and religion found a new object in the 1790s. She was a tall, handsome young woman named Frances Maria Lloyd, the daughter of another New Brunswick sailor. Abijah Garrison and Frances Lloyd met for the first time at a religious meeting, a gathering of New Brunswick Baptists. Frances Maria Lloyd—Fanny, as she came to be called—was a woman of great energy and almost desperate faith. She was as literate as Abijah Garrison, and capable of some of the same literary flourishes as he. But her capabilities and her flourishings ran to religion more than to romance.

When she met Abijah, she had already suffered for faith. Her father was a Church of England man, an Anglo-Irish immigrant, and a loyal Englishman. He watched in distress in the 1790s as the Anglican establishment in New Brunswick suffered from the energetic efforts of traveling preachers—Baptists, especially—to convert the province to the kind of religion that dominated the newly independent American states down the coast. The threat entered his own house, found his favorite daughter, Fanny, and made her a convert. Her new birth of faith broke the ties of her first birth of the flesh; her father expelled her from his house. Abijah Garrison had found a woman who determined to live in her religious faith, no matter what the price.

Fanny and Abijah were married in 1798 or 1799 and began a series of moves from place to place in New Brunswick and Nova Scotia. Their first child, a girl, died in infancy. The second, born in 1801, was named James Holley; this was the boy who would grow up to be "Crazy Jem." In the first years of the nineteenth century, Abijah Garrison found the going rough. The Napoleonic Wars were making ocean trade difficult and precarious for ships sailing under the British flag. To try to escape what he called "the Ravages of War and the stagnation of business" in Canada, he decided to go to Massachusetts. He chose Newburyport, a prosperous and growing trading and shipbuilding town. He found work readily available, prices cheap, and goods plentiful. As for Fanny, she found Baptists in large numbers, and a couple of rented rooms big enough for her, Abijah, James, and a two-year-old daughter, Caroline. She also found herself pregnant with the child born in December 1805 and named William Lloyd. Jemmy had a trumpet, a toy fife, and a penknife; his father proudly wrote back to New Brunswick that the boy could "Sing a Great many tunes." Things, in short, were good. Wherever he sailed, to Virginia or to Guadeloupe, Abijah Garrison would write home to Fanny: "May God bless you, preserve you in health is the prayer of your affectionate Husband."

Then, at the end of 1807, history closed in on the Garrisons. The Jefferson administration clamped its embargo on all foreign commerce. Newburyport, like the rest of New England's trading towns, suddenly found itself in a profound depression. Abijah Garrison could no longer find voyages. Fanny, late in 1807, became pregnant again. And Abijah—like millions of other frustrated, unemployed men of all generations—began to spend his time in taverns, drinking with his friends. Sometimes he brought the friends and the drinking home. In the summer of 1808, five-year-old Caroline died. It was all too much for the pregnant Fanny Garrison. One day, when Abijah was at home with some of his mates, she lost her pious temper and shouted the men out of the house. The birth of another daughter in July was not enough to hold the family together—or may have been enough to break it up. Abijah fled, leaving Fanny with James, seven, Lloyd, three, and the infant Maria Elizabeth. Abijah also left behind his sailor's hourglass, with his initials carved into the bottom. But that was all.

For the next three or four years, Fanny Garrison stayed on in Newburyport, working occasionally as a nurse, somehow managing to hold her family together. Then, at about the time the United States finally entered the European wars in 1812, she moved to Lynn, a few miles away. She took James with her, but left Lloyd and Maria Elizabeth with two different families in Newburyport. (Abijah, meanwhile, returned to New Brunswick, where he became an anonymous casualty of the uncertain age. He did write to a cousin in 1814, referring mysteriously to "the Whirl I have taken in the World." But whatever the "Whirl" may have involved, it did not include his family. Fanny and the children never saw him again.)

For the next few years, Fanny Garrison's life took on an unquiet rhythm, alternating between hope and depression. James was troublesome almost from the beginning of the years in Lynn. He was bound out as an apprentice to a cordwainer—a shoemaker who worked with cordovan leather. In the cordwainer's shop, it was the custom to pass a heavy drink of rum mixed with molasses. Soon James was a confirmed drinker. He began a pattern of "sinning," begging his mother for her forgiveness, promising to sin no more, and being encouraged by her to make a new beginning:

> I had never tasted liquor, but was persuaded by my fellow apprentices and likewise my master, to drink a little as it would not hurt me. I took a drink, and it was sweet, and from that fatal hour I became a drunkard.
>
> I soon got so I could take my glass as often as my master, and in a little while it required double that quantity to satisfy my appetite. I was now a confirmed drunkard. It soon reached my mother's ear, that her darling boy, one in whom she had placed strong hopes that he would be a comfort and support to her declining years, one who she had so often prayed to her heavenly father to guide and direct, had fallen before that monster Rum. I went, but with feelings I can not describe. She received me kindly, and pointed out in an affectionate and kind manner the path I was pursuing, what the consequences would be to my health, my reputation in this world, the many sufferings it would cause her, and the eternal damnation of my soul in the world to come. I promised to do better, and drink no more.

But the promises failed, and James was soon spending time at a "house of ill fame" just outside Lynn, "a sink of infamy and vice," where "many, many a poor young girl has lost her reputation."

As if money worries and James's unsteadiness were not problems enough, Fanny Garrison was always "tired with slavish work." Things looked up a little in 1814 when she was able to bring William Lloyd, now nine, to Lynn and apprentice him to a shoemaker. And things looked even brighter the next year when another Lynn shoemaker decided to take a group of workers to the city of Baltimore to open a shoe factory. He invited Fanny and her two boys to join the enterprise.

But the factory failed. By January 1816 Fanny was complaining in letters back to Newburyport that "I walk the streets of Baltimore and feel myself alone." James was "a great trial." William Lloyd was "homesick." Finally, James and William Lloyd both deserted their mother. James went to sea after a frightful sequence of jobs, fights, and drinking bouts; Lloyd went back to Newburyport. Fanny took up nursing again, working in the suburban mansions of people she called "the Quality," and was proud of "being treated like a lady," for a change.

For the next few years, Fanny Garrison played out a lonely and pathetic drama. She had to put Maria Elizabeth out to work as a servant in Baltimore (where she died). She complained constantly of illness and fatigue. She started a diary to record her sinking, gloomy anxieties, her record of blood coughed up from the tuberculosis that flared from time to time, her thoughts of death, dreams of death, and premonitions of death. She also started a prayer group for Baptist women in Baltimore. But even the comforts of the church were denied her. In 1816 she became involved in some sort of controversy by mail with a member of the church in Newburyport where she still kept her membership. She lost, and in 1818 the church voted to deny her the privileges of membership for at least four years. Alone, sick, tired, and afraid, Fanny worked out a simple analysis of her life, which pictured her experience as one of progressive decline and alienation:

> At an early period of life, I was surrounded with every comfort that was necessary, nurtured with peculiar care and tenderness in the bosom of parental affection, blessed with the friendship of an extensive acquaintance, and beloved by all my relations. I had enough to attach me to this world. Gay and thoughtless, vain and wild, I looked forward to nothing but pleasure and happiness.

Her conversion by the Baptists, her marriage, and her migration to Massachusetts had all conspired to spoil the picture:

> But alas! have not my subsequent years taught me that all was visionary? How has the rude blast of misfortune burst over my head, and had it not been for an overruling Providence, I must have sunk under their pressure.

But if she had to learn that this world held only pain, she had also learned that there was a consolation:

> I was taught to see that all my dreams of happiness in this life were chimerical; the efforts we make here are all of them imbecility in themselves and illusive, but religion is perennial. It fortifies the mind to support trouble, elevates the affection of the heart, and its perpetuity has no end.

The ideas were conventional—even clichés—but they fitted. And they were deeply felt. As it happened, there was, finally, only one other human object on which the feelings could really be fastened: the distant, small son in Newburyport, Fanny Garrison's last real hope in what she called "this world."

Whatever the eventual fate of his soul might be, it was very much "this world" and not the next that William Lloyd Garrison set out to master at the age of ten, when he went back to Newburyport, to live in the house of the Baptist deacon who had taken him in when Abijah Garrison had disappeared. He attended a grammar school for a few months, but his last hours in a classroom came in his eleventh year. Most of his education was religious. He sang in the choir, read sermons and tracts, and faithfully attended Sunday school and church. Then he took up his second apprenticeship, this time to a cabinetmaker in the nearby town of Haverhill. There was a rebellious streak in William Lloyd—a streak he shared not only with his father and brother but with hundreds of other young apprentices of the day. After only six weeks, he ran away from his master, home again to Newburyport. The master kindly released him from the apprentice's bond. Then, by a stroke of what Garrison always regarded as a "Providence," an apprentice's place opened up at a local newspaper, the *Newburyport Herald*. He won the job and settled down quickly to a seven-year apprenticeship.

These years were full of work, learning, ambition, and success. Garrison was able to make himself over from a poor, semi-orphaned waif into a man on the threshold of what he believed would be a great career. He read tirelessly, despite being very nearsighted: Shakespeare, contemporary novels and poetry, political books and speeches. He even learned some Latin from a fellow apprentice. He joined a local Franklin Club, where he and other young men of ambition would gather for "improving discussions." He began to dress well, even elegantly. He spent hard-earned apprentice's dollars to have his portrait done in oil at twenty, with his hair arranged in a curling, Byronic style, wearing a high, stiff collar and an elegant shirt; his eyes shown in the brooding, slightly mysterious, insinuating Romantic style so popular in gentlemen's portraits of the period.

Garrison still attended church faithfully, trying to be what his mother had hoped he would be, a "perfect Baptist." But there was a straining, worldly ambition in him, a vague determination that he would somehow earn fame. The ambition and the acute preoccupation with the self were not traits that belonged to Garrison by some sort of genetic mystery. He had absorbed them from his society. The ideal of the self-made man was becoming almost an official part of the creed of middle-class young men in America and England. And Garrison, as a member of the Franklin Club (and, like Franklin, a printer), could hardly have failed to adopt the ideal and the ambition that went with it. He also developed an open-ended sense of possibility, a sense that any man could make himself over into whatever he chose, forsaking parental models, starting from scratch, building whatever type of personality and career he chose.

When he (mistakenly) thought he was twenty-one, in 1824, Garrison wrote a fervent celebration of his maturity, full of excessive rhetoric in praise of his own "Spirit of Independence," entitled simply "Twenty-One." He saw himself as a young success, destined to fame, free of obligations and involvements. Such a man, he wrote, would al-

GARRISON AT 20. Garrison paid hard-earned money to have this portrait painted in Newburyport, Massachusetts, in 1825. He was about to finish his apprenticeship at the local newspaper. He was still quite poor, but dressed himself as a gentleman in anticipation of the great career he already was dreaming of.

ways defy the world, defy wealth, might and power, even defy "lank poverty" or "threatening clouds of dark oppression."

When he was just twenty-three, in the midst of a newspaper quarrel with another journalist, he proclaimed in print to all the world:

> If my life be spared, my name shall one day be known so extensively as to render private inquiry unnecessary; and known, too, in a praise-worthy manner. I speak in the spirit of prophesy, not of vainglory—with a strong pulse, a flashing eye, and a glow of the heart. *The task may be yours to write my biography.*

But all this celebration of the free individual and all the blustering about independence could not cut the one tie that still bound him to the memory of real poverty and shame. During his years of apprenticeship, although he lived alone in the home of his master, there was still the persistent tug of his mother. And the tug was in an opposite direction, away from worldly ambition, away from success, away from reputation and fame, from oil portraits and elegant clothes. William Lloyd Garrison viewed his own life as a progress toward self-mastery. His mother saw her experience as a progressive decline, a virtual sinking. And she tried, from Baltimore, to impose at least some of her pathetic religious version of things on her son.

To begin with, while he was still very young, there were gloomy, mothering cautions:

> Only let me hear that you are steady and go not in the way of bad company, and my heart will be lifted up to God for you, that you may be kept from the snares and temptations of this evil world. Be a good boy and God will bless, and you have a Mother, although distant from you, that loves you with tenderness.

Fanny Garrison even wrote in 1819 that she was glad he could *not* join her in Baltimore because "you might be led astray by bad company." And James's "fall from Grace" was a concrete and powerful example of what bad company might cause.

Then, as time passed and Fanny Garrison became ill, she introduced the theme of death's approach. Once, when she sent William Lloyd a small trunk full of old clothes, she added a note saying that this might be the last token of love that she would be spared to send. Whenever she wrote him, she detailed her own symptoms and sufferings and described the ravages of epidemics of disease in Baltimore. She signed her letters "Your Mother until Death," or "Adieu, my dear, for I am tired."

When William Lloyd showed the first real signs of worldly ambition and success, such cautionings and lamentings came to a sharp focus. He proudly sent Fanny his first newspaper contributions, which he signed "A.O.B." for "An Old Bachelor." Her first response was to express guarded pleasure: "I am pleased, myself, with the idea, provided that nothing wrong should result from it." Her second was to joke (wittily enough, but with an edge that the seventeen-year-old must have felt): She wondered whether A.O.B. might not in fact signify "Ass, Oaf, and Blockhead."

The humor went out of her letters a bit later, after Garrison had sent more pieces—verbal explosions on Latin America, Europe, national politics, and even a fictional account of a shipwreck—all written with obvious energy and efficiency in a short period of time. Fanny Garrison was appalled. She drew for Lloyd a clear line between worldly ambition and the demands of religious piety, and she fretted aggressively about what would become of him if he continued to stray across that line:

> Next, your turning author. You have no doubt read and heard the fate of such characters, that they generally starve to death in some garret or place that no one inhabits. Secondly, you think your time was wisely spent while you were writing political pieces. I cannot join with you there, for had you been searching the scriptures for truth, and praying for direction of the holy spirit to lead your mind into the path of holiness, your time would have been more wisely spent, and your advance to the heavenly world more rapid. But instead, you have taken the Hydra by the head, and now beware of his mouth; but as it is done, I suppose you had better go on and seek the applause of mortals. But my Dear L., lose not the favor of God; have an eye single to his glory, and you will not lose your reward.

This reprimand was plain enough to someone who had published his little essays with an almost trembling hope for the "applause of mortals." But it was driven home in the last written words Fanny Garrison ever addressed to her son:

> Now, my dear, I must draw to a close and say that I love you as dear as ever, especially when you consider your dear mother and are trying by your good behavior to soothe her path to the grave.

She asked him, gently, to bring his work for her to see, and signed her full name: "Your affectionate Mother, Frances M. Garrison." Two weeks later, Garrison set out for Baltimore, to make an often-delayed last visit. He found her broken and emaciated and stayed two or three weeks. In a few more weeks she was dead, probably of cancer. Garrison himself wrote and set the type for her obituary in the *Newburyport Herald*:

> DIED. In Baltimore, after a long and distressing illness, which she bore with Christian fortitude and resignation, Mrs. Frances Maria Garrison, relict [widow] of the late Capt. Abijah G., formerly of this town.

This obituary and a couple of short poems were all that Garrison published for the next year. He wrote no more pieces, as though he were trying to reassure his dead mother that he would not become worldly and unsteady. As for his father, Garrison had promoted him to "Capt." and then symbolically killed "Abijah G." off with the words "relict," and "late,"—though he had no idea, in truth, whether his father was dead or alive. Maria Elizabeth was dead, and Caroline too. James was somewhere, drowning in rum or salt water, God only knew which. Garrison was alone with his printer's trade, his oil portrait, and his ambition.

But he had the company, too, of the memory of Fanny Garrison. Years after she died, when Garrison was courting the woman he was to marry, he wrote his fiancée a remarkable letter about his mother:

> You speak of "a mother's love." An allusion like this dissolves my heart, and causes it to grow liquid as water. I had a mother once, who cared for me with such a passionate regard, who loved me so intensely. How often did she watch over me—weep over me—and pray over me. "O that my mother were living!" is often the exclamation of my heart.

The letter invented a childhood that never had been. For most of the years after Abijah Garrison deserted his family, William Lloyd had not lived with his mother. She

HELEN ELIZA BENSON GARRISON. In 1834, Garrison married this daughter of a Connecticut antislavery man, George Benson. During their courtship, he wrote her letters and poems about his mother. During their long and happy marriage, she would share his commitment to reform. As shown in this daguerreotype, made about twenty years after the marriage, she is an almost perfect combination of middle-class respectability and uncompromising principle.

did not care for him with "passionate regard" or "watch over" him. But distortion of memory was not his only problem. He added to his letter some lines of poor poetry that revealed a more serious ambiguity:

> *She was the masterpiece of womankind;*
>   *In shape and height majestically fine;*
> *Her cheeks the lily and the rose combined;*
>   *Her lips—more opulently red than wine;*
> *Her raven locks hung tastefully entwined;*
>   *Her aspect fair as Nature could design;*
> *And then her eyes! so eloquently bright;*
>   *An eagle would recoil before their light.*

The overt purpose of the poem was to reinforce the picture of his mother as a thing of gentle, caring beauty. But the real effect—an effect that Garrison could hardly have been aware of—was to present a picture of intimidating power: a woman of "majestic" height (Garrison himself was only a few inches over five feet) and vivid aspect, colored in lurid shades of red, white, and black, with "entwining" locks and with eyes whose light would frighten even an eagle. Little wonder that when Garrison was much older, he would still tell his own children that "I always feel like a little boy when I think of Mother."

⋅⇒◉⇐⋅

When he completed his apprenticeship in December 1825, Garrison's life was a mixture of conflicting purposes and self-images. The center of experience for him was his career. He had mastered his trade. But the trade of printing was only the beginning. His task now was to transform a craft into a vocation—to become not just a printer but an owner and editor, a man of affairs. The most likely path that lay before him was an entrepreneurial one. And since the journalism of the day was very closely associated with party politics, his vocation would lead naturally to political involvement, almost as naturally as the careers of lawyers did. Garrison had chosen a calling that was on intimate terms with what his mother fearfully called "this world." And if his life followed the normal pattern, he could expect to deal constantly with the fearsome "Hydra" of worldly realities: political parties, issues of foreign policy and elections, the pragmatic facts of commerce and legislation, as well as with the economic realities of publishing.

But, always, there was the conflicting pull of his mother's disdain of the world, her suspicion of power, her mistrust of success, her conviction that the Christian life is, in essence, a life of sacrifice and suffering. In such a world, the only real security and consolation lay in faith, and in the world to come. The issue of Garrison's life was simple: Could the ambitions of the self-made man be reconciled with Fanny Garrison's sacrificial piety? It took Garrison about ten years to come to terms with his dilemma, ten years of movement, frustration, and danger.

His first step was economic. With the help of a loan from his former master, he bought a recently founded newspaper in Newburyport, which he renamed the *Free Press*. He spent about half of 1826 editing and publishing the paper, writing mostly about party politics. His motto was the motto of Massachusetts Federalism: "Our

Country, Our Whole Country, and Nothing But Our Country." And in the pages of the *Free Press* he adopted an almost desperately conservative Federalist line, even though the Federalist party was no longer a viable political organization. Already, while still an apprentice, he had written a number of political pieces damning Andrew Jackson, whom Garrison saw as a dueling, gambling, drinking, slaveowning planter.

But Garrison's attachment to Federalism went well beyond fear of General Jackson. He resented all the political compromises of the 1820s, the adoption by John Quincy Adams of the loose principles of the Jeffersonians. Even when Jefferson died, while most other newspapers in New England were willing to forgive the ex-president in a quick flurry of bereaved patriotism, Garrison was unbending. For him, Jefferson was still an "infidel," and the only acceptable politics was the good, old, true Federalism of the 1790s. So Garrison committed himself to a lost political cause. It cost him subscribers; after six months, his first venture had failed. His choice of his first battleground was political. But in a deeper sense he had been true to his mother's wishes. He had defined politics in moral terms and taken an uncompromising position on the highest principles, regardless of penalty. He had courted the world's rejection, and his courtship was successful.

The next year, Garrison stepped into the tide that was taking thousands of other young men of ambition into the cities, and moved to Boston. He had been to the city at least twice before—once on the way to his deathbed visit to his mother in Baltimore, when he became hopelessly lost and confused; a second time, later, when he had walked the forty miles to the city and arrived with raw and bleeding feet, only to turn around the next day and take the stagecoach back home to Newburyport. This third time, in 1827, he came on a mission, in quest of his own career. He went from one printing establishment to another, ready to hire himself out as a journeyman to any master. But it was several months before an opportunity came his way. He took a position on a struggling newspaper devoted to the cause of temperance, the *National Philanthropist*.

During his months on the *National Philanthropist*, Garrison made a delicate and important transition. He began to write about "the slothfulness and bane of party spirit"—echoing Washington's Farewell Address of 1796. He now wrote on issues that he thought went beyond questions of party politics: drunkenness, militarism, gambling, dueling, Sabbath-breaking, and a dozen other disorders in American life. Everywhere he looked, he saw depravity, a host of evils threatening to "subvert the purity of our institutions." And the way to survival, he now saw, lay not through politics but through Christian reform.

What was happening to Garrison was simple: He was becoming a social reformer. Like many other Americans, he was being converted to a new type of alternative to the normal channels of political parties and government institutions. To be sure, Garrison still wanted to influence politics. But preserving "the purity of our institutions," he now decided, demanded something that was *prior* to politics: the reformation of the national character. If men could be saved from drunkenness, kept from prostitutes, exposed to the saving influences of evangelical religion, then (and only then) might they be trusted to elect others to political office. The task of reform was nothing less than the salvation of the national soul, a task well beyond the capacities of party politicians.

Reform, as Garrison saw it in the late 1820s, was a difficult and dangerous undertaking. He, and other reformers like him, would have to confront public ridicule and would risk their reputations and their honor. But Garrison was willing to dare it. More than willing, he was delighted. He could now confront the world in a combative spirit. He would be called on for sacrifice. He could view himself in lonely but heroic terms:

> While there remains a tyrant to sway the iron rod of power, or chain about the body or mind to be broken, I cannot surrender my arms. While drunkenness and intemperance abound, I will try to reclaim the dissolute, and to annihilate the progress of vice. I will reprove, admonish and condemn. My duty is plain.

Being a reformer had several advantages for Garrison. As a reform editor and publicist, he could appeal to a constituency that was not local. He would not have to compromise with the prejudices of small towns like Newburyport. He could appeal to a selective audience of people like himself—people of Christian piety and principled energy. Among them, he could find a fame that did not require him to satisfy the demands of "this world." And if triumph came, in time, then it would be honorable. In the meantime, the formula was simple: Take positions that were radical enough to be dangerous (but also radical enough to gain fame) and persist in the faith that the odds could be overcome, the triumph achieved.

Garrison sometimes talked and wrote as though there were only two parties to the reform struggle: on one side was the whole world, full of its disorders, vices, and tyrannies; on the other side was the lone individual, defiant, daring, almost self-created. It was as though the self-made man stepped forth into the world to find a reality so alien to his own virtue that it could be met on no other terms than hostility. But, in truth, something stood between the individual and the world. Reform organizations gave meaning and extension to individual experience. Garrison did not invent reform to solve his vocational problem. He found it. When he came to Boston, new benevolent organizations and societies were being formed in the city at the fantastic rate of one a month.

This organizing fever dated back to the Revolution. But the fever reached its highest pitch just at the time Garrison began his adult career. And, as luck would have it, he chose Boston, the city more in the grip of reform activity than any other in the United States. Garrison lived in a boardinghouse full of reformers and Baptist "city missionaries." It was in this boardinghouse that he met the man who had founded the *National Philanthropist*. A steady stream of reformers came to talk to the boarders. Wherever Garrison went to listen to sermons, ministers preached the necessity of reform. If he chose to be a radical, he did so in a movement that was gathering strength, power, and organization.

Garrison sometimes succumbed to the temptation to romanticize himself, to see his role as that of the radical individual facing a series of corrupt powers with only his words as weapons. But this picture was distorted. He became a reformer as a way of *joining*, of gaining membership in an organized community of like-minded people. As a

A BOSTON MOB. In 1835 William Lloyd Garrison was mobbed in Boston. He escaped only when he was placed under arrest for his own protection. The crowd is shown accurately as a combination of (mostly) gentlemen, with some sailors and stereotyped Irishmen. To the right is another abolitionist, William Thompson, who is escaping in a woman's clothing.

radical reformer, he could be both victim and victor. He could resolve the central difficulty of his young life by satisfying the claims of ambition and piety together.

However spiritually rewarding the *National Philanthropist* may have been, it did not satisfy Garrison. He decided to become editor of the *Journal of the Times,* in Bennington, Vermont, where he would give newspaper support to John Quincy Adams in the election of 1828. Garrison's editorials for Adams were lukewarm (despite his very intense fear that Jackson might win). But he made the *Journal of the Times* unusual among the small-town newspapers of the day by devoting a great deal of space to the three nonpolitical reforms he had decided were most important: peace, temperance, and antislavery. His months in Bennington amounted to a temporary and partial relapse into party politics. But in the meantime, he was restlessly preparing to define himself as a radical reformer in even more pointed terms.

Garrison was peculiarly vulnerable to other reformers. While he was still in Newburyport, a leader of the pacifist movement gave a lecture there; overnight, Garrison was a pacifist. Every new society in Boston for the suppression of vice caught his attention easily and roused him to the most optimistic kinds of hopes. He was a man in search of movements, a publicist in search of causes, a moralist in search of outrages.

So it was with the issue of slavery. Garrison had had little or no direct contact with the institution of slavery. He had never seen a plantation. He had seen very few slaves. But slavery was, in the end, to be his cause. He never lost his interest in universal reform: he kept alive his hopes for evangelism, for women's rights, and for peace. But slavery became, after about 1828, his primary public concern.

Garrison's conversion to antislavery came in 1828 in the same quick way his earlier conversion to pacifism and other reforms had come. Benjamin Lundy, a young Quaker from Ohio, came to Boston to lecture on slavery. He spoke first to an earnest group at Garrison's boardinghouse. Garrison was urgently moved. He made slavery one of the concerns of the *National Philanthropist* and the *Journal of the Times*. After Jackson's victory in the 1828 election, Garrison was out of work and broke; when Lundy invited him to come to Baltimore and serve as coeditor of Lundy's antislavery newspaper, the *Genius of Universal Emancipation,* Garrison jumped at the chance.

When Garrison went to Baltimore, he was in his mid-twenties. He had been a marvelously "steady" boy, and he might have expected to become more successful with the passage of years. But he had failed in his first publishing venture. He had moved through two other editorial positions rapidly and unprofitably. Economically, he was a failure. His financial unsteadiness was more than matched by his growing attraction to unpopular causes and unprofitable reforms. Even before he reached Baltimore, he had decided that Lundy's antislavery position was too cautious. Garrison quickly announced in the *Genius* a radical demand for immediate, unconditional emancipation, by whatever means, at whatever cost, and with whatever consequences. Slavery was a sin, and he would not accept any slow and incomplete solution. He had already reached similar conclusions about drinking and war: he had demanded total prohibition of alcohol, a total end to war. Now he applied the same logic to slavery. Within a few months he was in jail.

Garrison's first imprisonment was connected, by slender threads of history, back to his youth. In the fall of 1829 he printed in the *Genius* a pair of brief items accusing a New England merchant of cruelty and greed. The merchant, who happened to be from Newburyport, and who was engaged in the same coasting trade that Abijah Garrison had plied, had transported some eighty slaves from Baltimore to New Orleans for sale. The venture was entirely legal and commonplace. But Garrison singled the man out for a bitter (and somewhat inaccurate) attack. The result was a suit for libel brought by the merchant against Garrison and Lundy, who were both found guilty and fined. Garrison would not pay his fine, and so was sentenced to a six-month jail term.

He was happy. The jail was large, old-fashioned, and relaxed. He could wander around it and eat his meals comfortably with the warden and his family, and he had time to write a pamphlet giving *A Brief Sketch of the Trial of William Lloyd Garrison*. But his relaxation, his sense of harmony—almost of ease—were not a result of the physical comforts of jail life, or of the pleasure of writing about his own victimization. Garrison was delighted primarily because all the elements of a new image of himself had at last come neatly together. He had worked out, over the past few years, the main outlines of

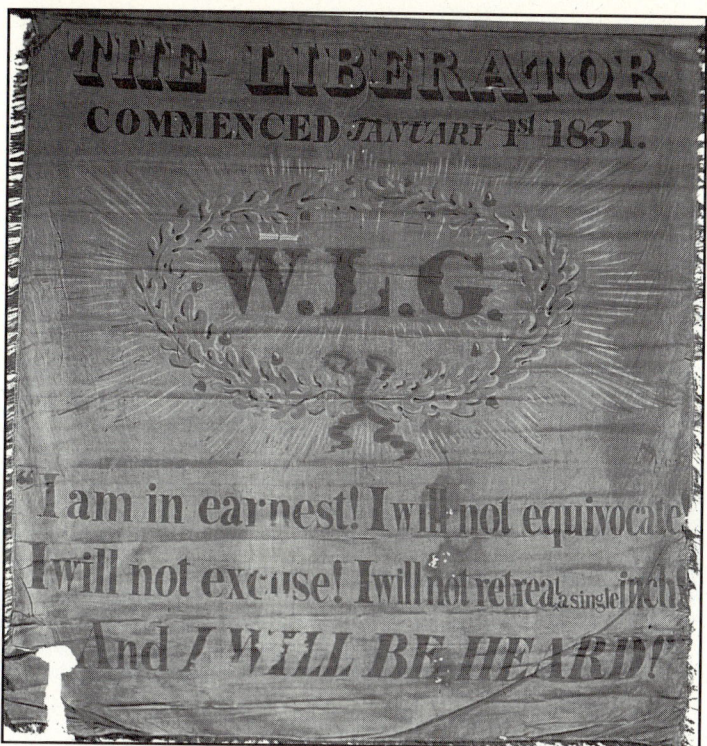

LIBERATOR BANNER. This fringed banner was hand-lettered to celebrate the beginnings of *The Liberator*. It captures something of Garrison's extreme preoccupation with the self by placing the initials W.L.G. within a conventional wreath and sunburst, and by quoting the thundering sentences that all begin with "I." The designer did not plan the second line very carefully and initially omitted the second *t* in "retreat."

a new identity. Now, in jail for the first time, these outlines came into dramatic focus, almost as though his life had, for a few weeks at least, an unambiguous dramatic script.

The central theme of the drama was not really slavery, or even reform in general. It was Garrison's realization of his own freedom. As he put it in a joking letter that he proudly dated "Baltimore Jail—May 12, 1830": "I pay no rent—am bound to make no repairs—and enjoy the luxury of independence divested of its cares." He had, in fact, divested (literally, undressed) himself of a good many cares. He had sloughed off, one by one, the protective layers of social identity that men and women ordinarily have. He had no family, no job, no property, no protection of law, no control even over his own body. He had transcended every tie of kinship and institution. He had become, or so it seemed to him, the ultimate master of his own fate and soul. Like many fictional prisoners of his romantic age, Garrison scratched a sonnet onto the wall of his cell, a rhymed celebration of his own transcendent spiritual independence:

> High walls and huge the BODY may confine,
>   And iron gates obstruct the prisoner's gaze,
> And massive bolts may baffle his design,
>   And vigilant keepers watch his devious ways:
> Yet scorns the immortal MIND this base control!
>   No chains can bind it, and no cell enclose:
> Swifter than light, it flies from pole to pole.

In a curious way, this kind of freedom had been the unacknowledged quest of the whole Garrison family for two generations. Abijah's desertion was his way of claiming liberation. James's debauches were his more desperate assertions of freedom. Fanny Garrison's yearnings for the release of death and the perfections of heaven were her version of the search for individual immunity from the world. William Lloyd Garrison found what his brother and parents had failed to find: a way of giving freedom an organized focus in *this* world and not the next, a way of deserting social institutions instead of a wife and children. He could break laws, as his brother did, but his criminality was pious and spiritual, not drunken and fleshly.

Armed with this final sense of his own freedom, his total immunity from the "rude blast of misfortune," Garrison could easily accept the gesture of a wealthy New York merchant who paid his fine after forty-nine days in jail; only his body was dependent on the charity. He could press his radicalism to its logical limit. He had a confident identity now. The old conflict between ambition and piety was laid to rest. He could leave the Baltimore jail and return to Boston to found a new antislavery journal, *The Liberator,* whose first issue appeared on New Year's Day 1831. And in it he could thunder his defiance of the whole world, with a sure sense of who the "I" of the sentences was, and with the words "I will be" set in italics by his own hand:

> *I will be* harsh as truth, and as uncompromising as justice. I am in earnest—I will not equivocate—I will not excuse—I will not retreat a single inch—AND I WILL BE HEARD.

The Self-Made Society

William Lloyd and James Garrison were curious, idiosyncratic men. Their lives seem to be made up of individual choices and accidents. They do not seem to be typical of anything whatsoever. But the life stories of all the Garrisons were products of the same processes of change that were touching the lives of every American during the first half of the nineteenth century. Both William Lloyd and James Garrison would have been regarded as social freaks by most of their contemporaries. But the two brothers were really mirrors, in which the "normal" characteristics of American society can be clearly seen.

At bottom, the life of the Garrison family can be understood as the result of half a dozen processes of change that were transforming American society. The first was an accelerating change in the ways Americans produced, bought, and sold goods and services. The second was an equally drastic change in the ways Americans thought about mobility, about the ways individuals and families moved across the landscape and up or down a ladder of economic and social status. The third change was the spread of another wave of religious revivalism that altered the face of American Protestantism. Fourth, both in practice and in theory, the family became a different kind of social institution. The fifth change was the development of a new sense of the power of people to control and reform their society. Thousands of groups were created whose purpose was to stamp out one kind of social "evil" or another. Finally, in literature and in art, a new set of ideas about the individual and society was shaped by a remarkable generation of intellectuals and writers.

All these developments need to be understood together, for they were in fact closely related. Taken together, they help make sense of the odd, even freakish, experiences of William Lloyd Garrison and his family.

ECONOMIC GROWTH AND TRANSFORMATION

To many Americans who lived during the first half of the nineteenth century, an economic miracle seemed to be happening. Their numbers increased dramatically, from 5 million in 1800 to 31 million in 1850. Their cities mushroomed and multiplied. Everywhere, there were new machines and new ways of doing things: an engine, or "gin," for removing the seeds from cotton; a mechanical harvester for wheat; canals and railroads; steamboats and textile mills. For most people, there was more to eat, more to wear, bigger houses with bigger rooms. The world seemed to explode with chances and choices: to go west and take up a farm in Ohio or Michigan or Oregon; to invent a machine; to become an educated white-collar worker instead of an illiterate farmer like your father; to marry whomever you chose and live wherever you wanted. "Freedom" for many Americans was more than an abstract principle of the Declaration of Independence. It seemed to be everywhere, in the concrete details of life. And it seemed to go hand in hand with economic well-being.

There was another side to the coin, though. If there was more wealth every decade, it was owned by fewer and fewer people. In 1800, 10 percent of the families in America owned somewhere between one-third and one-half of all the land and buildings, and other tangible property. But by 1870 the share that belonged to the richest 10 percent had increased to about two-thirds. And if their other property—stocks, bonds, and other intangibles—was added in, their share of the national pie was even bigger. In the cities, the unequal distribution of wealth was even more striking. In New York in 1845, 4 percent of the people owned 80 percent of the property. In Philadelphia in 1860, 5 percent owned 90 percent.

Yet the evidence is overwhelming that many of the other 90 percent—the 90 percent who owned less than one-third of all the wealth—were convinced that the economy was good to them, and that their society was opening up, not closing down, opportunities.

The solution to the puzzle lies in growth. As measured by economists, at least, the American economy was growing so rapidly that most of the people did earn more and own more as time passed. The economy could sustain both a growing concentration of wealth in a few rich hands and a generally improving situation for a majority of the free population. And the 10 percent who owned two-thirds of the wealth represented many more people in 1850 than it had in 1800—half a million in 1800, over 3 million in 1850. This meant some people did go from poverty to riches. And for every man or woman who made it, there were thousands of others whose dreams were fed on the successes of a few. When William Lloyd Garrison, poor and practically orphaned, daydreamed about owning a newspaper and being a gentleman. When he bought an oil portrait of himself as a kind of forecast of his future status, he was only hoping the hopes of his generation.

The economic growth that fed the dream of success and prosperity was part of the industrial revolution that had been changing the entire world for at least two centuries. The term "industrial revolution" conjures up a picture of huge factories and complicated machines, but this is not an accurate way of seeing the economic growth of the first half of the nineteenth century.

Most production still took place in small shops and in homes. Much of the change had to do not with machines but with scale. In Cincinnati in the 1840s, a shop for butchering hogs was built. It used no complicated machinery. Its construction was of traditional materials—mostly wood with a little iron. But the work was laid out in an assembly-line fashion, and the result was that a hog could be slaughtered, cleaned, butchered, and barreled in only one minute. Similarly, pictures of the construction of the Erie Canal show workers using hand tools and very primitive wood and rope devices. But there were thousands of them, organized into efficient gangs by professional engineers, and the result was a striking increase in efficiency. Hat manufacturers in Danbury, Connecticut, continued to use the traditional "putting-out" system—sending work into rural households to be done by hand, then collecting the results, finishing the hats, and marketing them. But the system could now be organized on a larger and larger scale. The hats could reach bigger markets in shorter times. And the profits would return sooner to Danbury, where they could finance even more systematic organization and marketing. Everywhere, but particularly in the northern states, the organization of economic activity on a larger scale, designed to function at high speed, turned out more and more goods and profits.

THE RISE OF CORPORATIONS

Both the scale and the speed depended on the spread of other forms of organization—of methods of gathering capital, borrowing, and paying. Economic activity became corporate activity. By the time of the War of 1812 the states had already issued almost 2,000 corporate charters. And by the 1820s the state of Massachusetts alone had more corporations than all of western Europe.

After the 1830s, the pace of incorporation became even faster. Before then, in most states it took a special act of the legislature to create a corporation. But after 1830, the states all began to adopt general incorporation laws, which made incorporation a relatively simple clerical process that required no legislative approval.

The advantages of corporations—from the point of view of those who owned them, at least—were basically two. First, the corporation could, by selling shares of stock or bonds, create a large pool of capital. Second, the corporation limited the liability of any single shareholder. If an individual went bankrupt, he might lose everything—house, furniture, horses, even clothing. But if a corporation failed, the investors would lose only the value of the stock they held. They would not be liable for any of the unpaid debts of the corporation.

THE ADVENT OF THE RAILROAD

The large-scale corporations depended heavily on the capacity of producers to get their goods to market rapidly. The Erie Canal, its dozens of imitators, and the steamboats on the Ohio and the Mississippi provided the basic transportation network. But after the 1830s the water and road systems were supplemented by a new invention, the railroad. The workability of the steam locomotive was proved in England in 1829. Within just a few years, the idea caught on in the United States. Short lines were built to connect cities like Charleston or Boston with their surrounding countryside. Then, in the 1840s, a number of major cities were connected not just to the countryside but to each other. In the next decade, rail mileage increased 400 percent, and by 1860 the United States had a total of 30,000 miles of rail lines (about ten times the total canal mileage).

Building the transportation network required corporations, of course. In fact, railroads were among the first truly large corporations in American history. But something more was needed. There was not enough private capital in the country to build the railroads and canals. The crucial missing portion was supplied by governments. The states were especially generous patrons of the canal and railroad companies. All in all, the states went into debt almost $100 million to help finance the construction of rail lines. And what state governments did on such a huge scale, local and county governments imitated wherever they could. Local governments may actually have financed as much as one-fifth of all the rail mileage in the United States before 1860. In 1850 the federal government entered the picture. Congress voted to give almost 4 million acres of land to the Illinois Central Railroad to help it pay for building a line from Illinois to Alabama. By 1860 the federal government had granted away a total of 22 million acres of the public's land to railroad corporations.

POPULATION

All these changes demanded people—people to produce the goods, to get them from place to place, and to buy them. The population of the United States increased about 600 percent between 1800 and 1860. Some of this increase was the result of a high birthrate, particularly in rural areas. But the overall birthrate was actually declining, and by the 1840s only a new wave of European immigration could keep the rate of population growth as high as it had been. In the 1840s and 1850s a stream of Irish and German immigrants joined the continuing British immigration. Most of the immigrants were young. And this fact, coupled with the high birth rate of earlier decades, created a population that was dramatically younger than that of western Europe. By the middle of the century, seven Americans out of every ten were under thirty—as compared to six out of ten in England and five out of ten in France.

The population was both young and mobile. In five towns in western Massachusetts, nine

An early locomotive. This machine, named the *Atlantic,* was the first steam locomotive to enter Washington, D.C. It was operated by the Baltimore and Ohio Railroad and was built in 1832. To the modern eye, the engine seems frail and even slightly comic. But to the men and women of the 1830s, it was an imposing symbol of power and technological progress.

out of ten people who were between the ages of sixteen and twenty in 1850 had left their communities by 1860. The Garrison family's nomadic life—from Canada to Massachusetts, Maryland, and Vermont—was typical of the experience of their contemporaries. And it was typical in another way, too. Most of the people who moved around the country were poor or unskilled, looking for work or for land, and providing a ready pool of cheap labor for commercial and manufacturing enterprises.

On the other hand, the economy also needed a pool of skilled workers. Someone had to design and build the boats and engines. Someone had to add up the columns of figures, keep track of the inventories, pay the bills, and file the receipts. These needs were met by governments, mostly state and local, through the school system. Although public schools had existed in America since the seventeenth century, the first true public school law was passed in Massachusetts in 1837, and it was quickly imitated by a number of other states. Most of the schools were only at the elementary level, but most of the people in the northern states attended them and at least learned to read and to do simple arithmetic. For some others, there were more years of school ahead. In 1860, 300 high schools and 137 colleges in the United States were turning out the managers, the accountants, and the engineers needed to tend the new economy.

URBANIZATION

Skills and education led people more often than not into towns and cities. During the eighteenth century, four port cities had contained more than half the urban population of the nation: Boston, New York, Philadelphia, and Baltimore. After about 1820 the pattern began to change. Boston, Philadelphia, and Baltimore continued to grow, but less rapidly than the population as a whole. Only New York outstripped the national growth

IRISH IMMIGRANTS. This detail from an 1847 painting shows an immigrant ship being emptied in New York. The Irish immigrants are of both sexes and all ages. In the lower center, a portly gentleman (not an immigrant, his dress and cane suggest) may be negotiating a job with one of the immigrants, who is shown hat-in-hand. At the lower left, another gentleman, in a dandified white waistcoat, is studying a woman, perhaps with a different sort of transaction in mind. The mass of people still on deck suggests how overcrowded the immigrant ships were.

rate to become, by the middle of the century, the dominant city. The Hudson River and the Erie Canal gave New York crucial access to the fastest-growing section of the United States, the trans-Appalachian interior.

The same reasons that explain the spectacular growth of New York also explain the rise of hundreds of new towns and cities, from the coast to the Mississippi. Where in 1800 there had been only villages or wilderness, new cen- ters like Cincinnati, Rochester, Louisville, Pittsburgh, St. Louis, and New Orleans sprang into life. In 1800 the United States contained only thirty-two cities of the second rank—less than 50,000 inhabitants. By 1860 there were ten times as many. The opening of the agricultural West was an important development, and Americans tend to look to that frontier experience for their myths and their heroes. But migration to the cities was in fact larger than migration west-

BROADWAY. This 1834 print shows Broadway, in New York City, looking north from the corner of Canal Street. This is the preindustrial city at its peak of development. Animals are almost as numerous as people. There are hardly any machines in evidence. And the four-story facades are practically uniform, all the way up the long avenue.

ward during the first half of the nineteenth century. Like the rates of growth of the population and of economic productivity, the increase in the pace of urbanization was more rapid during the decades before 1860 than it had ever been before or would ever be again.

TECHNOLOGY, GROWTH, AND THEIR EFFECTS

Here, then, was an incredibly rich economic mixture: enterprises of large scale, using corporate organization and efficient techniques; the most effective system of transportation the world had ever known; a pool of workers who were mobile and willing to work because they were poor and young, or able to work because they were skilled and educated; governments that helped underwrite ventures for which private capital was unavailable; and cities, old and new, where production and marketing could be concentrated. It was into this mixture that new technological developments were introduced.

Taken by itself, a new machine could have only a limited effect. But combined with all the other ingredients of economic growth, an invention could pay enormous dividends. Robert Fulton demonstrated a steamboat in 1807, but it would not have had such an impact if it had not been for things like the assembly-line hog butchering firm in Cincinnati. Samuel F. B. Morse's invention of the telegraph in 1840 would have had much less importance if there were not a multitude of inter-city commercial messages waiting to be transmitted.

A FACTORY TOWN. Much of the early industrial revolution took place not in great cities but in smaller manufacturing villages, especially in New England. This factory for making scales, in St. Johnsbury, Vermont, was originally built on a river for water power, but it has been transformed by the development of steam power. The artist is also at pains to emphasize the presence of railroad transportation.

The most spectacular technological changes occurred in the textile industry. Inventions—mostly British—made it possible to spin thread and yarn, and to weave cloth, at rates that were dizzying compared to traditional hand methods. Between the end of the War of 1812 and 1833, the cotton industry produced 16 percent more cloth each year than it had the year before.

The largest textile corporation, the Boston Associates, assembled capital of $600,000 to build cotton mills in Massachusetts towns like Waltham and Lowell. They used new machines as fast as inventors could turn them out. But they also used other, nonmechanical methods: they tapped a cheap labor pool by hiring young girls from rural communities as their primary labor force. (Later, the Irish and other immigrants would largely replace the mill girls. They would work even harder for the same low wages.) The Boston Associates also led the way for other corporations by establishing their own national marketing organization. And they engaged in a program of national advertising that would set a pattern for later large-scale corporations.

The results of this kind of large-scale, high-technology enterprise were spectacular. Lowell—known as the "city of spindles"—grew from a town of 2,500 people in the 1820s to a manufacturing city of more than 30,000 in just twenty-five years. In 1820, New England's cotton mills produced about 13 million yards of cloth. By

1860, production had reached well over 800 million yards. This astonishing output represented about 25 yards of cloth for every man, woman, and child in the United States.

The economic change that resulted from all these elements—plus the abundance of land and natural resources—was remarkable. It raised the average standard of living of American workers and their families. On the whole, they probably ate more than any other large population in the world.

But the changes were not all beneficial. The 90 percent of young people who left their Massachusetts towns may not have wanted to go and often did not better themselves when they did move. The skilled shoemaker who lost markets to factory-produced shoes was unhappy. Nearly half the workers of Garrison's Newburyport in the 1850s could testify that their children did not attend the public schools. Skilled workers were better off, to be sure, and there were more of them. The same was true of the shareholders of the new companies. But more numerous were the unskilled workers whose lives had not been improved by economic growth at all. And for the immigrant poor, most of whom stayed in the cities, the death rate was more than twice as high as for rural, native-born, white Americans.

But beneficial or not, economic change reached into every family and into every individual's life. The Garrison family's elation when they first arrived in Massachusetts, where there was plenty of work and low prices, was offset by the economic disasters that broke up the family a few years later. But it would have been difficult to identify an American family that had *not* been touched just as deeply by economic change—whose world would ever be the same again—for better or for worse.

THE "SELF-MADE MAN"

The effect of economic growth on people's lives was very often dramatic. Some men whose fathers had been poor became rich. Women whose mothers had minded farmhouses found themselves in cities, married to clerks, or working in mills or shops themselves. Irish peasant boys became saloon keepers in New York or worked on canal boats on the Erie Canal. A few boys who had been poor and even orphaned as children actually did grow up to become president of the United States.

As a result, it began to seem to many people that there was no limit to the way a man—though seldom a woman—could make himself into a "success." All the restrictions imposed by tradition—poverty or the custom of following a father's trade or being bound to his farm—seemed to drop away in the new rush of opportunity. The popular notion of the "self-made man" supposed that success was everywhere to be had, that opportunity was boundless, that the world was usually fair and rewarded those who deserved success.

The idea of the self-made man found expression in hundreds of books, pamphlets, poems, newspaper articles and editorials, and speeches. But its classic statement was the autobiography written by Benjamin Franklin when he was an old man, published in full only in 1818. Thousands of boys practically memorized Franklin's account of his simple origins. They studied his picture of himself arriving in Philadelphia at seventeen, dressed in old clothes, munching the rolls he had bought with his last money. Then they learned how he had disciplined his character by practicing the virtues of industry, frugality, and sobriety. Franklin's message was plain: if he could do it, there was no reason any other man could not.

The boys and young men who pored over Franklin's life story found the same message in the books they were given to read in the public schools. The idea was reinforced by the fame of Andrew Jackson, the first American president whose lowly beginnings were ever pointed to with pride. And when the boys grew up, they founded Franklin clubs and Franklin societies in almost every town. No American but Washington had more places named after him than Franklin.

If Washington was the father of his country, then Franklin was its kindly ideological uncle, dispensing the advice and encouragement needed by young men on their way up. Garrison's joining the Franklin Club in Newburyport was not an isolated action. It was part of a wave of enthusiasm for enterprise, a faith that anyone could break free of the past, start from scratch, and become rich or famous—or at least respectable.

The ideology of the self-made man was not universal. Many people who belonged to families with old wealth saw it as a threat and complained bitterly about the *nouveaux riches*. The idea of being self-made meant little to most women—except through their husbands' or sons' careers. It meant less than nothing to millions of slaves, for whom the most certain thing of all was that history could *not* be escaped. Poor farmers or immigrants were untouched by it. And the notion of being self-made was bitterly ironic to the thousands of traditional artisans and craftsmen who saw their ways being eroded by the currents of the new economy.

The idea of the self-made man appealed to only a segment of the society. But it was a powerful segment. They could vote, and they did. They clustered in the towns and cities, now clearly the centers of power in the northern states. They had money, and more of it with every passing year. They bought the newspapers and magazines, the novels and poetry. This class of Americans—and there is no more accurate name for it than the middle class—paid the salaries of the ministers and the lecturers. They supported the public schools and sent their children there. In short, they dominated the popular expressions of attitude and opinion. There were other attitudes, of course, and other opinions, but they tended to be voiceless or to express themselves in acts rather than in written words and pictures.

The attitudes of this new middle class seemed utterly confident, even boastful. But there was another side to things. The idea of success implies the possibility of failure. Change could be seen as a gain, but it concealed the threat of rootlessness. Escaping from history or ancestry might be a good thing, but it could also lead to a world without customs and standards, a world where every man was as good as the next man, but where every action, good or bad, was equally appropriate—if it worked.

One task of the new middle class was to find ways of getting *control* of change, both in their own lives and in their society. They needed to develop new sources of discipline and order. And so they devised new ideas and practices in religion, in their family patterns, and in thousands of clubs and associations they organized to "reform" themselves and other people, to make the world safe for opportunity. Their religion was a new kind of revivalism. Their ideal family was an instrument of restraint and discipline. Their reform movements were designed to turn people whose lives were out of control—slaves or slaveholders, criminals, the insane, drunkards, prostitutes, children—into orderly citizens or, if that failed, into orderly inmates of some well-managed asylum or prison.

MIDDLE-CLASS EVANGELISM

Evangelical revivals had always been part of American life. The seventeenth century saw frequent "quickenings" and "awakenings." In the mid-eighteenth century, a greater wave of the "outpouring of God's grace" had produced the Great Awakening. In the 1780s and 1790s had come another revival. Older denominations like the Congregationalists and the Presbyterians seemed revitalized, and newer denominations like the Methodists and the Baptists experienced rapid and sustained growth. The energies of Protestantism were so powerful that the movement seemed to deserve the title of the Second Great Awakening. Still, the rate of religious conversions remained so high down through the first half of the nineteenth century that it became difficult to separate one religious "awakening" from another. American religious experience appeared to be one sustained evangelical revival, stretching across more than a century, enduring revolution and war, party shifts, and every other change.

But the evangelism of the 1820s and the following decades was a religious movement of the new middle class, and it had some new and distinctive features. Much remained the same, of course. The vocabulary of salvation was still "sin" and "damnation," "grace" and "salvation." But ministers and their congregations, revivalists and their audiences, began to talk and behave differently. And the differences were all related to the hopes and the anxieties of the new social groups that had been generated by economic change.

CHARLES GRANDISON FINNEY

Social movements seldom have precise beginnings. But a symbolic beginning for the new evangelism was the conversion, in 1823, of Charles Grandison Finney, who was to become the most spectacularly successful American preacher of the period. He had been born into a farming family that moved out onto the New York frontier at about the time the Erie Canal was begun. In 1823 Finney had moved to a small town not far from Buffalo and was struggling to become a lawyer, hoping, like so many others, to catch the wave of self-made success.

One day he went into the woods, worried about his soul and determined to wrest salvation from God that day or to die a sinner. After hours of struggle, in which he set his will against God's as though in a contest, Finny surrendered. He accepted his damnation as God's will. But the moment of surrender was miraculously transformed into the moment of grace. No sooner did he give up than he was visited by "wave upon wave of liquid love."

The experience altered his life forever, and he began to preach, informally at first, then as a licensed Presbyterian. The conversions he brought about in his little town were spectacular and numerous. He kept to no pulpit but traveled wherever an audience could be assembled. Finally, in 1831 he was invited to Rochester, a booming flour-milling town. The result was a revival that made Finney famous everywhere. From Rochester, the road led to New York, and then out again into whatever communities summoned Finney to save them.

Well before the Rochester revival, other ministers were learning the same strategies. Some preachers, especially in the older denominations, resisted Finney's "New Measures," but most of them gradually became convinced by the most practical test of all: the New Measures worked.

Finney's message, and the New Measures of evangelism, were partly theology, partly pulpit technique, and partly organization. What Finney had learned in his own conversion experience, he thought, was that grace came only when he had given up hope, when he had been willing to deny his own selfish interests and recognize the overriding power and claims of God. Once this had been done, he became free to exercise enormous power as a preacher. Surrendering the self ended by making the self strong, not weak.

The same paradox was part of every conversion, Finney and his associates believed. They demanded that the men and women who came to them become humble and recognize that they were hopelessly damned. But the result, when they truly believed, was that the humble became high, the damned, saved. An evangelical conversion experience was an exercise in religious mobility, in which the converted man or woman could become a kind of self-made Christian. God's help was necessary, of course, but God's help was offered at every moment to every person. Grace was somewhat like success in the ideology of the self-made man: it was there, waiting for anyone who was willing to acknowledge his or her spiritual rags to earn spiritual riches.

TRACTS AND MISSIONARIES

Finney and his colleagues communicated their message in language and gestures that were simple, passionate, impatient of theological technicalities, and careless of denominational lines. They were out to reach the largest possible audiences. And they were technologically up-to-date.

In important ways, they were adapting the newest methods of manufacturing and marketing. Their sermons were not hand-crafted for local consumers, but were made like interchangeable parts that would work as well in Indiana as in New York or Kentucky, and as well on Baptists as on Methodists or Presbyterians. The evangelists traveled, like the "agents" who were beginning to represent manufacturers in regional markets, or "territories." They advertised and promoted, and they measured their success—as entrepreneurs did—by the volume of the conversions they brought about.

The new evangelism, like the new world of corporate enterprise, was based on organization. A number of new, interdenominational organizations were founded. The most important were the American Tract Society, which distributed the mass-produced Evangelical Family Library, and the American Home Missionary Society, which sent its missionaries into almost every part of the North and West. By the 1850s, the Home Missionary Society had about 1,000 full-time "agents" in the "field." The Tract Society had over 600 full-time "distributors."

In theory, the revivalists and their powerful organizations wanted to convert everyone. But in practice, their source of strength was the new middle class. In the Rochester revival of 1831, Finney's converts were mainly in the families of lawyers, merchants, manufacturers, and master artisans. Among the poor and the unskilled he was much less successful. And this remained the primary pattern of revivalism throughout the North. Only in periods of economic depression, or in areas where workers were losing jobs to Catholic immigrants, did evangelism make much headway among the poor and the unskilled.

Evangelism made great strides, too, in the West, but its success there was peculiar. To the preachers, the West was a distant problem. It had to be saved not from within, and not by its own people, but by the East, by the missionaries who would carry the evangelical word, distribute the tracts, and record the conversions. In fact, the revivalists tended to look at workers and westerners in somewhat the same way: as populations that needed restraint and discipline.

The new evangelism was also different from the old in the much heavier emphasis it gave to the role of women. Many of the supporters of the missionary and tract societies were women, and the conversion of wives and mothers was often preached as an essential step toward the conversion of entire families. In fact, women were described frequently as being instinctively more virtuous than men. They were pictured, at the most extreme, as the only Christianizing influence that could restrain a society as competitive, as subject to material temptation, and as much in flux as the United States.

Revivalism fitted nicely with the ideology of the self-made man. It emphasized the possibility that people could change themselves, and it also seemed to provide a means for quieting anxieties generated by change. It held out hope, but it demanded self-denial, self-control, and self-restraint.

A NEW MODEL OF FAMILY LIFE

Wherever industrialization has taken place, whether in the United States, Europe, or other parts of the world, the ways women, men, and their children live together have been deeply altered. In the nineteenth-century United States, a new model of the family began to take shape. It did not emerge in full detail until the twentieth century, and it was as much an ideal as a reality. But the same kinds of people that adopted the idea of the self-made man and provided the memberships for the tract and home missions organizations gradually started to redefine what it meant to be a man or a woman, to bring up a child or manage a home.

In objective terms, the most striking development was a decline in the birthrate among native-born white people. The United States entered the nineteenth century with one of the highest birthrates in the Western world—a fact

AN IDEALIZED FAMILY. This 1840 painting captured the new conception of family life rather well. The husband in the picture is its geometrical center. But in other respects he is almost out of it. Looking off to the side, he is not touching either his wife or his children. The emotional center of the family is the wife, who is holding one child and being grasped by two others. The eldest, a boy, is posed in a way that suggests he will soon become like his father—detached from the home, interested in other things. The elaborate furniture, draperies, and carpet, used to suggest the family's solid economic status, were all mass-produced in factories.

that reflected the easy availability of land more than anything else. Where land was plentiful and cheap, people continued to marry early and to have large numbers of children. But in older, more crowded rural areas, family size began to shrink. And in the towns and cities, it went down even faster. The net result was a reduction, between the beginning of the century and 1860, of almost 30 percent in the number of children for each woman between the ages of sixteen and forty-four.

But the change was not evenly spread through the society. Immigrants continued to have large families. So did people on the frontier. So did many of the poor everywhere, especially in the South. The decline of 30 percent was a national figure. Among the well-off, the educated, and the city dwellers, the drop was even more dramatic.

Some of the reasons for the change are clear. Poor farmers and workers could think of their children as potential economic assets, who could be put to work and needed little or no education. But for well-off town families, who did not expect their children to go into the fields or into shops and mills, children were a costly burden. And there were other, more subtle reasons. New standards of space and privacy in the home made children a greater problem. More and more women were active outside the home, busily taking on roles in clubs, churches, and reform groups. Their time, more than for most women in earlier centuries, was at a premium. Even geographical mobility probably helped cut the birthrate (though it is difficult to tell whether people did not want children because they were on the move, or were on the move because they did not have so many children to take along).

CHANGES IN THE ROLE OF WOMEN

It is easier to determine why the new middle class might want fewer children than it is to know how they accomplished their purpose. A part of the explanation lies in the fact that the better-educated simply tended to marry later, and even to remain single. There was some publicity about contraception—though very little. It seems clear that one method was simply to reduce the frequency of sexual intercourse. And with this practice came a striking new set of ideas and attitudes about sex.

The little poem "Sugar and spice, and everything nice; / That's what little girls are made of. . . . / Snips and snails, and puppy dogs' tails;/That's what little boys are made of," first became popular on both sides of the Atlantic during the 1820s and 1830s. It captured the essence of a new way of thinking about masculinity and femininity. What the poem implied was made clear in hundreds of pamphlets, lectures, and magazine articles: men were by nature suited to the rough, competitive world. Their nature was tough, their passions more "base," even "animal," than women's. Women, on the other hand, were "naturally" tender, innocent, and purer than men. They were the prime carriers of religious sentiments. They shrank from whatever was "base." And if some did not, there was some kind of deep flaw in their nature. By the middle of the nineteenth century, much of the middle class had probably reached the conclusion that women did not naturally enjoy or want sex.

Starting with such assumptions, the role of women in the home, and of home in the lives of children and husbands, could be radically revised. The most popular manual on home life was written in 1841 by Catherine Beecher. Its title, *A Treatise on Domestic Economy,* suggested one of its main arguments. There was an economy of the home as important as the economy of the world. In the world, all was effort, competition, and flux. But the ideal home was a place of refuge and order, a place where men might retreat from their fevered struggles and children might be protected from evil influences.

Within this home of Beecher's—and of the many other writers who imitated her—women were to be the central figures. What she proposed was nothing less than a new kind of division of labor. Men made forays into the world of business or industry; women managed the household—deciding on diet, decoration, and the training of children, on religious questions and social practices.

Beecher put heavy emphasis on organization and efficiency. Even more emphatically, she laid down rules for avoiding tempting "stimulations." In fact, everything that might stimulate was to be rigorously suppressed. Food should be bland and served at a moderate temperature, since spices or food that was too hot might stimulate. Clothing should be loose; tight garments were "stimulating." Coffee, tea, and alcohol were dangerous stimulants. So was sleeping late. Visiting, entertaining, and other kinds of sociability should be kept to a minimum.

The picture of woman as a domestic figure, whose proper place was in the home and whose main role seemed to be repression, was not an idea invented by men to keep women in their "place" (though it could be used that way). The idea belonged to a new social class and was welcomed by both its men and its women. In fact, for some women it was a way of claiming a place where they could be supreme and independent, at least in theory. The "sphere" for women was small. It hardly passed the boundaries of church and home. But by comparison with most of their eighteenth-century grandmothers, nineteenth-century women were making a strong bargain: They would leave politics and business to men, in return for a more powerful role in family life.

A SCHOOL FOR YOUNG LADIES. This daguerreotype, made around 1855, shows a classroom in Boston's Emerson School for Young Ladies. It was founded by George Barrell Emerson (not related to Ralph Waldo Emerson) and was considered a model school. Sending daughters as well as sons off to such schools was a convenient thing to do for middle-class women whose lives increasingly involved active membership in religious, civic, and social organizations. But higher education for women was still extremely rare.

Oddly, dozens of women like Catherine Beecher made professional careers *outside* the home as the publicists of the ideal of domesticity. Women's magazines with large circulations made their first appearance. Women's clubs invited women speakers and writers to lecture. An enormous amount—perhaps even most—of magazine writing, sentimental novels and poetry, and other forms of popular literature was produced by women, for women readers. The idea of women's essentially domestic nature became the stock-in-trade of a new group of women who were either unmarried—as was Catherine Beecher—or who played limited roles in their own homes. Women spoke, wrote, and organized to promote the idea that women were *not* suited to public careers. When Garrison began his career as a reformer, he understood what every other reformer and evangelical preacher understood: the pathetic, suffering figure of Fanny Garrison was being replaced by women for whom moral and religious questions demanded organization, even action.

A FEMINIST ALTERNATIVE

A majority of middle-class women seemed happy enough to embrace the new notions of woman's special nature and mission. To many, in fact, this set of ideas was a distinct advance over the old situation, when women were regarded simply as inferior creatures, with no special attributes or special sphere of activity.

But a determined minority of middle-class women was gaining experience as reformers in fields such as abolition, education, and temperance—the same reforms promoted by men like William Lloyd Garrison. And it was inevitable that such women would sooner or later turn their attention to the plight of women themselves and to developing a feminist movement.

This path was illustrated by the careers of Lucretia Mott and Elizabeth Cady Stanton. Both were active in the antislavery movement; Mott was famous as an effective speaker at abolitionist rallies. In 1840 the two women met in London, where they had gone to attend the World Anti-Slavery Convention. To their shock, the convention refused to seat women delegates, and they had to sit in the balcony.

From that point on, both were feminists as well as abolitionists. In 1848 they organized a meeting in Seneca Falls, New York, where Stanton lived with her husband and children. The meeting attracted a variety of reformers, male and female. And it issued the most ringing declaration of women's rights ever made in America.

Mott and Stanton, who drafted the declaration, took the Declaration of Independence as their model. They used its organization; a preface consisting of a statement of general principles, followed by a list of the "long train of abuses" of George III. But in the Seneca Falls Declaration, the inalienable rights became the "rights of men and women." The tyrant was no longer George III of England but men. And the long train of abuses was transformed into a list of "repeated injuries on the part of man toward woman, having in direct object the establishment of an absolute tyranny over her."

The declaration could be ridiculed—as it was in most of the press. But for anyone who came to it with a sympathetic mind, or for any woman who was ready to be drawn into feminist activity, it was both convincing and exciting.

As writing, the declaration worked because it took the tone of the most hallowed American document of all and changed very little of its stirring language. It began with the same words: "When in the course of human events . . . ." And it went on in (almost) familiar language: "We hold these truths to be self-evident: that all men and women are created equal; that they are endowed by their Creator with certain inalienable rights; that among these are life, liberty and the pursuit of happiness."

This much could be accepted even by a woman who was committed to the doctrine of women's separate and special sphere. She could argue that women were entitled to the pursuit of happiness in an equal, though *separate* realm.

But the "train of abuses" set the feminists very much apart from the proponents of middle-class domesticity. The abuses included every law and restraint that made women's status any different from men's. It began with the right to vote. But it went on to claim equality of women's rights in divorce and the rights to hold property, to sue and be sued, to obtain an education, to pursue a career in any profession. Finally, it attacked the new morality of domesticity. Men, it charged, had "created a false public sentiment by giving to the world a different code of morals for men and women."

AN AGE OF REFORMERS

During the last half of the eighteenth century, and especially after the Revolution, Americans had begun to form large numbers of societies and associations to solve the problems of the world. After about 1820, their efforts redoubled. Just as revivalism seemed to develop continuously from the eighteenth century into the nineteenth, so did the impulse to reform everything and everyone in sight. But again, as with evangelical revivalism, there were important differences that separated the reformers of Garrison's lifetime from those of the revolutionary period.

Reformist organizations before the 1820s had tended to address practical problems. During the 1820s the focus began to shift from solving practical problems to reforming *persons*. Reformers began to treat every question as though it could be solved only by changing the *character* of the needy or the oppressed.

The new reformers' efforts to rescue or discipline the *lost* people in their society took a bewildering number of shapes. For every social evil, a dozen organizations promoted a solution. But the solutions and the organizations all had some basic things in common.

Nineteenth-century reformers divided the world more or less simply into two kinds of people. On one side were those individuals who were reasonably well-off, literate, white, and Christian, and whose character was marked by discipline, restraint, and a capacity for self-control. Such men and women could be trusted to be citizens in a free society. On the other side were vast numbers who could not be trusted because they were morally crippled and dependent. They might be insane. They might be drunkards like James Garrison, hopelessly lost in their dependence on alcohol. They might be children, who had not yet developed the adult character traits essential to moral citizenship. Or they might be criminals or prostitutes, caught in the grip of systems of vice. They might be women, reduced by dependence to childlike, frivolous moral cripples. They might be slaves, whose enslavement made them incapable of self-control. Every reform movement defined a group of victims in some sort of "bondage."

The reformers agreed that most types of bondage could be broken, most victims rescued and made over into alert, honest, and disciplined citizens. The insane—most of them anyway—could be treated in "asylums," rather than being shut away in misery. Criminals could be taken off the streets and put into institutions where they could become penitent (and the redeeming institutions could then plausibly be called "penitentiaries"). Women could be educated and trained to accept the social responsibilities that would teach them good character instead of the nervous frivolity that governed their captive lives. Even blacks, whom most reformers still regarded as racially inferior, could be freed and sent back to their native Africa—the solution favored by many early antislavery reformers.

The new reformers almost always agreed that the final cure lay within the victim. It would do no good simply to break some form of bondage, unless the liberated individual learned to control himself or herself. For many of the reform movements, this implied the creation of a place of asylum where the handicapped, the depraved, or the childlike could be taught. Societies to rescue "fallen" women created "homes" for "wayward" girls. Prison reformers persuaded state legislatures to build model prisons, the most famous of which was at Auburn, New York. For educational reformers like Massachusetts' Horace Mann, the public school was just such a place of asylum, where children could be made over into mature candidates for responsibility and respectability. For a family reformer like Catherine Beecher, the family itself was an asylum from what she called the "sordid" passions of the world.

The places of asylum and training promoted by the reformers were all fundamentally alike, whether their inmates were children, prostitutes, the insane, or the deaf. Their main preoccupation was with order, regularity, and habit. The idealized schoolroom of the day pictured straight-backed children sitting on benches spaced with geometrical perfection, being put through mechanical paces. The perfect prison, for the proponents of the Auburn system, was one in which every foot of space and every hour of time was perfectly organized, so that the criminal could be habituated to regularity in every feature of life and thus made safe for reentry into the world. The same efficient organization governed Catherine Beecher's model home.

All these common elements made it possible for many men and women to be active in a great variety of reform movements, with no sense of discontinuity. For a woman like Dorothea Dix, whose primary cause was to improve the treatment of the insane, there was no essential difference between that effort and the temperance movement or the "rescue" of prostitutes. William Lloyd Garrison could move easily from temperance to antislavery to pacifism to women's rights and back to slavery, confident that the various middle-class crusades all shared the same basic concerns and techniques.

But for all the similarities among reform movements and their leaders, there were important differences that tended to deepen with time. For the more cautious reformers—men like Charles Finney and Horace Mann—the initial assumption was that society was basically healthy; the problem was to find ways of treating its unhealthy parts. Such reformers could use the institutions already available: churches, schools, governments, and the like. Their reform organizations and their missionary societies were designed to supplement the established order.

But as time passed, an activist minority of people—people like Garrison—reached the conclusion that the disease was deeper than had at first been thought: society itself was the real problem. For such reformers, a solution more radical than creating better prisons and schools had to be found. This logic created a paradox: men and women whose personal lives were characterized by a preoccupation with self-discipline, order, and restraint could begin to seek radical alternatives and find themselves treated as dangerous prophets of disorder and confusion. A few years after Garrison began to publish *The Liberator,* he was attacked by a mob in the streets of Boston. Garrison once publicly burned a copy of the Constitution of the United States, and he often used similar provocations, courting abuse and welcoming the publicity that might make converts out of a daring few.

UTOPIAN COMMUNITIES

But for most of the men and women who decided that social problems demanded radical strategies, the solution was not confrontation, but withdrawal. The outcome was the creation of dozens of communal societies. Almost every such community was utopian—convinced that its scheme could become the model for the salvation and perfection of the world the members had left behind.

Some of the utopian communities, like New Harmony in Indiana, focused on creating "rational" relationships of production. Others, like villages planned by the Shakers, concentrated more attention on religious piety and asceticism. Some communities, like Oneida, New York, experimented with sexual practices like intercourse without orgasm, and multiple marriage. Others, like Brook Farm in Massachusetts, were built by intellectuals around philosophical notions or cults.

Whatever their tone, the utopian groups all emphasized some scheme of order, planning, and disciplined self-denial. They were willing to be viewed as cranks by their former neighbors and relatives, but their crankiness ran not toward anarchy but toward order. The communities were, in fact, simply taking the most cherished beliefs of the new middle class to a logical and uncompromising conclusion. Within their walls, their own notions of industry, temperance, and self-control reigned supreme.

THE MORMONS

The most famous and successful community of radical withdrawal was the Church of Jesus Christ of Latter-Day Saints, or the Mormons. This first original American religion was founded in the 1820s by a rural New Yorker named Joseph Smith. He was convinced that he had been given a divine revelation, which he wrote down as the Book of Mormon. It taught that the world as it was presently constituted was thoroughly "anti-Christ," and thoroughly doomed.

The true solution for Christians was to leave the world behind and make their own, purified society. Smith's converts, under his leadership, migrated from New York to Ohio. Then they moved on to Missouri. By 1839 they had moved again—always under pressure from their neighbors—to Illinois. There, on the Mississippi, they founded a community they named Nauvoo. But in 1844 Smith was killed by an armed mob, and the Mormons were driven out of Nauvoo.

Under the guidance of a new leader, Brigham Young, the Mormons moved on, this time to a place of expansive emptiness. Out in the Great Basin, they tried to found a new state, Deseret, covering much of what is now Nevada, Utah, Arizona, and southern California.

Largely because of their practice of polygamy, the Mormons were objects of scorn and fear.

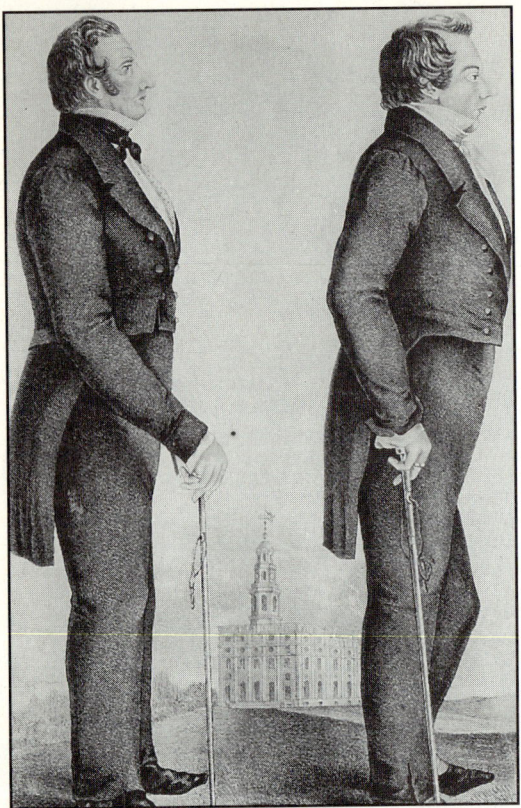

THE SMITH BROTHERS. Hyrum and Joseph Smith, leaders of the Mormons, were both killed in 1844 in a mob attack on the Mormon settlement in Illinois. In the background is an exaggerated sketch of the Mormon temple of Nauvoo. The artist has tried to make the Smiths look as proper, elegant, and restrained as any middle-class "gentlemen" of the period.

Beecher would have found much to approve of, such as the exclusion of hot drinks, alcohol, and tobacco.

WORKERS' MOVEMENTS

Evangelical religion and middle-class reform movements did not make much headway among the men and women who worked as mill hands, or in manufacturing shops, or on the countless construction and shipping jobs that made economic growth possible. For them, economic and social change was full of threats and dangers. This was especially true if they were unskilled workers in the manufacturing sectors that were making a transition from skilled labor to mass-production techniques that used mostly unskilled (and easily replaceable) workers. For them, the individualistic values of middle-class culture had little to do with the concrete conditions under which they lived and worked. And many of them chose to try to use union organization to protect themselves from the threats posed by entrepreneurial capitalism.

In New England's textile mills, for example, most of the work was done by native-born young women. They entered the mills at an average age of sixteen, and they typically kept their jobs for only about five years. Most of them expected to save a little money, marry, and return to their outlying towns and villages.

But their lives in the mills were not easy. Typically, they worked more than sixty hours a week—and at a pace much more relentless than the one they would have been used to on their home farms. More importantly, they were vulnerable to their employers' obvious desire to maximize profits. In the famous cotton mills of Lowell, Massachusetts, for example, the number of spinning and weaving machines tripled between the 1830s and the 1850s; but the number of workers to tend the machines increased by only 50 per cent. This meant that the amount of cloth each worker produced doubled (and with no corresponding increase in wages).

But they shared with all the other utopian experiments of the period—and indeed with most orthodox reformers—an intense concern for order and discipline within their world. One of their leaders, Orson Pratt, summed up the Mormon condemnation of the world in language a Finney or a Garrison might have used: "Wickedness keeps pace with the hurried revolutions of the age. Gross immoralities, drunkenness, whoredoms, robbing, murdering, have engulfed the nations in a deathly ocean of filth." And in Mormon households, a popular writer like Catherine

The women of the mills did try, from time to time, to assert their own collective power, and in ways that violated middle-class notions of woman's "proper place." In 1834, when they were threatened with a 25 percent wage cut, 2,000 workers in Lowell went on strike, and a Boston newspaper reported that "one of their leaders . . . made a flaming speech on the rights of women and the iniquities of the 'monied aristocracy.'" But such strikes almost always failed. And it became even more difficult to mount any sort of labor organization among textile workers after the 1840s, when native-born women were gradually replaced by immigrant workers, mostly Irish, who had little choice but to accept whatever wages and working conditions the mill-owners offered.

Unions of skilled male workers had somewhat more success. The demand for construction workers, particularly carpenters, was high, and their skills were still essential. Construction workers in major cities managed to create stable trade unions. In many cities, they struck successfully for a standard ten-hour day to replace the traditional sunup to sundown workday—which could last thirteen or even fourteen hours during the summer months. Philadelphia developed a particularly strong tradition of trade unions. There, in the late 1820s, skilled workers organized a general union, the Mechanics' Union of Trade Associations, and even founded a political organization, the Working Men's Party. Similar trade unions were created in other cities, and in 1834, many of them became federated with the first (and fragile) attempt at a national union, the National Trades Union. This effort failed, but several national unions were formed by men who pursued particular crafts—painters, shoemakers, iron molders, and machinists.

Shoemakers, a group whose traditional skills were threatened by new manufacturing methods, were very prone to radicalism, particularly in the manufacturing towns of the Northeast. In 1830, the shoemakers of Lynn, Massachusetts, formed a strikingly militant organization, The Mutual Benefit Society of Journeymen Cordwainers. They produced a radical analysis of the way the new economy had altered the relationships between workers and their employers: "Labor now becomes a commodity, wealth capital. . . . Capital and labor stand opposed."

The shoemakers' stark analysis may have been correct. But their goal, the triumph of labor over a "monied aristocracy," was beyond their immediate grasp. Several factors made it very difficult for workers to organize successfully. Capital was being concentrated in fewer and fewer hands with every passing year. Technological innovation was occurring at a dizzying pace, and each new invention threatened to make some workers' skills obsolete. An increasing flow of immigration from Europe gave employers a growing pool of "replacement" workers, men and women they could hire instead of a union activist. Many states had laws that made it a criminal "conspiracy" for a union to demand the "closed shop"—an agreement that every employee in the workplace be a union member. Worst of all, the panic of 1837 and the long depression that followed produced so much unemployment that workers were forced to accept whatever wages and working conditions the "market" dictated. The depression of 1837–1843 also seems to have made working people much more open to the messages of evangelical revivalism than to talk about the opposition between labor and capital.

NEW ARTISTS, NEW IDEAS

During the first half of the nineteenth century, the United States produced a remarkable generation of writers, who created what Americans began to celebrate as their own, "new" national literature.

This literary explosion began during the first two decades of the century with the work of Washington Irving: first with his comic *Knickerbocker History of New York* (1809) and then, in 1819, with the *Sketch Book*—particularly its tales of Rip Van Winkle and Ichabod Crane. During the 1820s James Fenimore Cooper began to write the novels about his frontier scout, Leatherstocking, that would make him the most successful American writer of his age. The series included *The Last of the Mohicans* (1826), and eventually ran to five novels, each of which only added to Cooper's fame in Europe and in the United States.

Then, between the presidencies of Jackson and Lincoln, a group of even more gifted writers appeared. In the 1830s Ralph Waldo Emerson began to publish lectures and essays that would eventually become part of most middle-class libraries. In the 1840s his friend Henry David Thoreau managed to turn a two-year experiment at living alone in the woods into the masterpiece *Walden, or Life in the Woods*. Their acquaintance Nathaniel Hawthorne published classic novels like *The Scarlet Letter* (1850) and *The House of Seven Gables* (1851). His friend Herman Melville completed the momentous *Moby Dick* in 1851. A poet with whom some of these writers would develop a distant and tentative acquaintance, Walt Whitman, published in 1855 the first edition of *Leaves of Grass*. A young woman who was utterly unknown to all these intellectuals, Emily Dickinson, started at the end of the 1850s to write the powerful poems that were to make her (after she died) at least Whitman's equal in literary reputation and influence.

Thus in about half a century a group of literary monuments had sprung into existence. And these monuments throw some interesting light on the kinds of economic, social, and ideological changes that Americans were undergoing.

The writers experienced the same sorts of change that touched the lives of other Americans. They did not simply observe, in detachment, the emergence of a market economy or the myths and realities of the self-made man. Instead, intellectuals now found themselves in the market, part of the new economy, and with the same kinds of possibilities of success and failure that every other entrepreneur faced.

Beginning late in the eighteenth century, an explosion of literacy caused a dramatic increase

NATHANIEL HAWTHORNE. This oil portrait of Hawthorne was painted in 1840, before he completed his most famous novels. Hawthorne's first published story was titled "The Gentle Boy," and he quickly became known as "the Gentle Hawthorne." But as he aged, his tales took on a bite and a gloom that seem at odds with this painting, which depicts a young man at peace with both himself and his world.

in the size of the potential audience for novels, essays, and poems. Literacy went hand in hand, in the new middle class, with increasing incomes. In short, the market for literature expanded at least as dramatically as the market for shoes or stoves. The first recognizably modern publishing companies appeared. And they used innovations—like the steam press and aggressive marketing methods—just as other entrepreneurs did.

The result was that newspapers, magazines, and books poured into the new market at much cheaper prices.

For talented men (and women as well), this meant that for the first time it was possible for many people to have a successful—even a lucrative—career as a writer. A new kind of intellectual career had opened up, a career that could put intellectuals in touch with a larger public. Writers could become self-made men, or women. They could win fame, recognition, even wealth—all as a result of their own individual efforts, talent, and will. Or they could fail.

It is not surprising, then, that the main preoccupation of American writers—themselves "self-made" or ambitious to be—was the free individual. The typical central figure of their novels, poems, and essays was the singular man or woman whose life was undergoing some sort of radical transformation. In general, American writers portrayed society as a network of customs, laws, and other restraints, against which the individual struggled to win freedom. In fact, the classic American literature of the period often seemed to be a simple celebration of individual freedom and solitude, against the demands of the community and its order.

In Rip Van Winkle, for example, Irving pictured a man who was trapped by his marriage, by his farm, by the web of social custom. Irving had this character undergo a radical transformation. Alone, in nature, Rip encounters a band of sailors, the ghosts of Henry Hudson's Dutch crew. He drinks a mysterious liquor they offer him and sleeps for twenty years. The end result is that Rip Van Winkle returns to his community as a "free" man. He now has no wife, no farm, no obligation to work. He can be what he always wanted to be, an idler and a storyteller. On his own terms, Rip is a success, and he owes his success to no one. Cooper's Leatherstocking figure was, like Rip Van Winkle, an individual defined by solitude in the woods. Cooper's novels are about the ways the solitary frontiersman evades the traps set for him by civilization, with all its restraints.

THOREAU'S CABIN. The title page of the 1854 edition of *Walden* shows Thoreau's house at the pond. The line from the book promises that Thoreau will not dwell on "dejection," but will brag "lustily" about the possibilities of living outside the system of property, custom, and law. The cabin pictured is a bit more snug and permanent-looking than the building Thoreau describes in the book.

In the essay that probably had the greatest influence on other intellectuals, *Nature* (1836), Emerson precisely sketched out the rules for authentic experience: A person's truest self was to be found only in solitude and only in nature. Thoreau's *Walden* was an even clearer declaration of individual independence from the social order. Its prescription was simple: Only by freeing themselves from society could individuals gain true insights into nature and the self. In society, men could only lead lives of "quiet desperation." Walt Whitman was just as pointed: The longest section of *Leaves of Grass* was the poem he labeled "Song of Myself." And Emily Dickinson's poetry had only one principal subject: the inner experience of the self, the figure she always called simply "I." In the world of her poems—if not in her actual life—society seemed hardly to exist at all.

RALPH WALDO EMERSON. Emerson, shown here as a young man, coined the term "transcendentalism" to explain the preoccupation with the self that dominated much American thought in the 1840s and 1850s. His essay *Nature* was extremely influential among intellectuals of this period. It urged self-study in solitary, unspoiled surroundings, removed from the social order.

Emerson summed it all up neatly when he said that "the present age" was "the age of the first person singular." And Emerson gave a name to the preoccupation with the free individual, "transcendentalism." The term was adopted by a number of New England intellectuals, like Thoreau and the founders of the utopian community at Brook Farm. The cumbersome expression meant simply that it was possible for any individual to transcend—literally, get beyond—the social and historical conditions of his or her life. Men and women could transcend all boundaries, customs, and restraints. As a result of this liberation, they could put themselves in spiritual touch with a sublime reality that some people called Nature, others God.

For all their subtlety, writers like Emerson and Thoreau shared much with the celebrators of the self-made man, and with the evangelical revivalists. But (like the ideas of the self-made man and evangelical revivalism) the radical individualism of American writing had another, darker side of doubt. Rip Van Winkle's "freedom" had an enormous price: he had to surrender twenty years of his life. Cooper's scout, no matter how virtuous and skilled he was, was doomed to fail in the long run. It was clear to Cooper and to his readers that "civilization" and "progress" would be the inevitable winners, and that Leatherstocking and his Mohican companions belonged only to the past. At the end of Whitman's "Song of Myself," the "I" of the poem dies. Emily Dickinson's "I" repeatedly suffers and dies in her anguished lyrics. In Emerson's *Nature*, the moment when the solitary individual finally achieves mystical union with nature is the moment when he disappears. "I become nothing," Emerson said. "I see all."

Here was a curious contradiction. The same writers who insisted on individual freedom as the essence of life seemed to be saying that freedom led nowhere, or even to death. In fact, the writers of the period seemed to fear the liberated self as much as they celebrated it. But the monumental works of art were only expressing the same contradiction that underlay the idea of the self-made man, evangelical religion, and the reform movements of their day. Both in popular culture and in the work of people like Emerson or Dickinson, the assertion of the self went hand in hand with a deep dread of truly "free" individuals.

The solution to the contradiction, both in popular culture and in great literature, was to combine freedom with *inner* restraint. Like the ideal self-made man, the heroes of the novels and poems were men and women of rigid self-control, even asceticism. Thoreau, in *Walden,* wanted little or nothing in a material way. In fact, his description of life at the pond bore a considerable resemblance to the lifestyle laid out by Catherine Beecher in her *Treatise on Domestic Economy.* Emerson's model individual was equally self-denying. Cooper's Leatherstocking wanted no wealth, no property, no sex, no income, and no civilized luxuries. For all his brash language, Whitman's poetic "I" was a man of almost monastic habits of self-denial. Emily Dickinson's poems were filled with repudiations of pleasures of every kind, from money to sex.

And when American writers dealt with liberated individuals who did *not* exercise self-control and restraint, they treated them as tainted men or women, who had to be punished or destroyed. Hester Prynne, the heroine of *The Scarlet Letter,* was a woman who had defied Puritan society by committing adultery. The novel is about her gradual and heroic recognition that she *has* sinned and must pay her social debt with a long life of industry, frugality, modesty, and temperance. In *Moby Dick,* Melville drew the same moral lesson, but in more violent terms. Captain Ahab, who commands the whaling vessel *Pequod* is obsessed with revenge against the mysterious white whale that has cost him a leg. Because of his obsession, he is determined to break all the social and economic rules, to pervert a commercial whaling enterprise into a voyage of private vengeance. His individual freedom, which is radical, has become dangerous. It knows no boundaries or inner restraints. And the outcome is that Ahab brings disaster and death not only upon himself but upon his crew.

EMILY DICKINSON AT SEVENTEEN. Emily Dickinson grew up to be a great poet. Here, however, she was photographed as a very conventional schoolgirl of seventeen, a student at a female seminary in South Hadley, Massachusetts. The photographer has posed her in a rigid way, managing to suggest that she is like any well-brought-up middle-class girl, familiar with books but closer to flowers, passive, and rigidly self-controlled. Years later she would write her most famous sentence of self-description: "I am small, like the Wren, and my Hair is bold, like the Chestnut Bur—and my eyes, like the Sherry in the Glass, that the Guest leaves."

When William Lloyd Garrison took up writing as a career, a path to success, he was acting on the same assumptions as an Irving or a Cooper. His assertion of the determined self against all of society was earlier than Thoreau's, and just as powerful. He suffered through his mother's warnings about the fatal dangers of worldly success. But he did so in terms that an Emerson or an Emily Dickinson would have understood at once. Garrison's individualism was at bottom a radical version of the tamer individualism of the new middle class. It promised success, morality, and progress, but it feared excess, cynicism, and disorder. And so it demanded rigid self-control and self-denial.

CHRONOLOGY

1805	William Lloyd Garrison born	1837	First true public school system created in Massachusetts
1807	Robert Fulton demonstrates the first steamboat	1841	Catherine Beecher publishes *Treatise on Domestic Economy*
1818	First full-length English publication of Benjamin Franklin's autobiography	1844	Mormons driven out of Nauvoo, Illinois; migrate to Utah
1826	James Fenimore Cooper publishes *The Last of the Mohicans*	1848	Seneca Falls Convention on women's rights
1829	First workable steam locomotive tested in England	1849	Nathaniel Hawthorne publishes *The Scarlet Letter*
1830	Garrison jailed in Baltimore	1850	Federal government makes first large railroad grant to Illinois Central
1831	Garrison begins to publish *The Liberator*; Charles Grandison Finney conducts Rochester revivals	1851	Herman Melville publishes *Moby Dick*
1835	William Lloyd Garrison mobbed in Boston	1854	Henry David Thoreau publishes *Walden*
1836	Ralph Waldo Emerson publishes *Nature*	1855	Walt Whitman publishes *Leaves of Grass*

SUGGESTIONS FOR FURTHER READING

THE GARRISONS

Two modern biographies of William Lloyd Garrison are John Thomas, *The Liberator* (1963), and Walter M. Merrill, *Against Wind and Tide* (1963). But the best approach to the family may still be the four-volume account by Garrison's children, *William Lloyd Garrison, 1805–1879: The Story of His Life as Told by His Children* (1885–89). For students who like to work with documents, the six volumes of *The Letters of William Lloyd Garrison* (1971–1981), edited by Walter M. Merrill and Louis Ruchames, are a careful and valuable resource. The most fascinating reading on the family is the autobiography of "Crazy Jem" Garrison, written shortly before his death and edited by Walter M. Merrill as *Behold Myself Once More* (1954).

ECONOMIC GROWTH AND TRANSFORMATION

Douglass C. North, *The Economic Growth of the United States* (1961), is a serious and thoughtful survey. So are the relevant chapters of Elliott Brownlee, *The Dynamics of Ascent* (1985). Albert Fishlow, *American Railroads and the Transformation of the Antebellum Economy* (1965), examines the impact of railroads on economic growth. A detailed study of the railroad and canal system is Christopher T. Baer, *Canals and Railroads of the Middle Atlantic States, 1800–1860* (1981). Anthony F. C. Wallace, *Rockdale: The Growth of an American Village in the Early Industrial Revolution* (1978), has stirred considerable debate about the ways that the coming of mills and factories transformed smaller towns and villages.

TECHNOLOGY, GROWTH, AND THEIR EFFECTS

Stephen Thernstrom, *Poverty and Progress* (1964), was a ground-breaking study of social mobility. David Montgomery's superb essay, "The Shuttle and the Cross: Weavers and Artisans in the Kensington Riots of 1844," *Journal of Social History* (1972), is an excellent introduction to the working-class experience of the period. Among the most valuable books on work and workers are Herbert Gutman, *Work, Culture, and Society* (1976); Alan Dawley, *Class and Community: The Industrial Revolution in Lynn* (1977); and Bruce Laurie, *Working People of Philadelphia, 1800–1850* (1980). Two fine studies of urban development and its consequences are Paul Boyer, *Urban Masses and Moral Order* (1978), and Sam Bass Warner, *The Urban Wilderness* (1972). Paul Johnson, *Shopkeeper's Millennium* (1978), makes a strong case for an intimate relationship between the growth of commerce and industry and the new revivalism. It can be supplemented with Michael Barkun, *Crucible of the Millennium: The Burned-Over District of New York in the 1840s* (1986).

THE SELF-MADE MAN

Irvin G. Wyllie, *The Self-Made Man in America* (1954), is a very readable introduction to the subject. It can be supplemented with John G. Cawelti, *Apostles of the Self-Made Man* (1965), and Daniel T. Rodgers, *The Work Ethic in Industrial America, 1850–1920* (1981).

MIDDLE-CLASS EVANGELISM

K. J. Hardman, *Charles Grandison Finney* (1987), filled an important gap. W. G. McLoughlin, *Modern Revivalism* (1957), is still a useful survey, with early chapters that address the Finney period.

CHANGES IN THE ROLE OF WOMEN

Women in the industrial labor force are discussed in Thomas Dublin, *Women at Work: The Transformation of Work and Community in Lowell, Massachusetts, 1826–1860* (1979). Nancy Cott, *The Bonds of Womanhood* (1977), attempts to assess both the costs and the rewards of the ideology of separate spheres for women in New England. The ways that growing up has changed during the course of history is the subject of Joseph Kett, *Rites of Passage: Adolescence in America* (1977). Carl Degler, *At Odds: Women and the Family in America From the Revolution to the Present* (1980), is a readable survey that adequately summarizes the work of many scholars.

AN AGE OF REFORMERS

A good place to begin is Ronald G. Walters, *American Reformers, 1815–1860* (1978). C. S. Griffen, *The Ferment of Reform* (1967), is a very thoughtful essay on the ways historians have tried to explain the surge of interest in social problems during this period. Lewis Perry, *Childhood, Marriage, and Reform* (1980), is an interesting interpretation. Stephen Nissenbaum, *Sex, Diet, and Debility in Jacksonian America* (1989), is a fascinating study. Good places to begin reading on the beginnings of feminism are K. E. Melder, *The Beginnings of Sisterhood* (1977), and Catherine Clinton, *The Other Civil War: American Women in the Nineteenth Century* (1984). An original and provocative interpretation of feminism can be found in William Leach, *True Love and Perfect Union: The Feminist Reform of Sex and Society* (1980). The temperance movement is well treated in I. R. Tyrrell, *Sobering Up: From Temperance to Prohibition in Antebellum America* (1979). Lawrence A. Cremin's excellent survey, *American Education: The National Experience, 1783–1876* (1980), has a wealth of information on literacy and educational reform.

NEW ARTISTS, NEW IDEAS

The classic study of American writers of the antebellum period is F. O. Mathiessen, *American Renaissance* (1941). Other significant works on writers and intellectuals include Perry Miller, *The Life of the Mind in America* (1965); Henry Nash Smith, *Virgin Land: The American West as Symbol and Myth* (1951); R. W. B. Lewis, *The American Adam: Innocence, Tragedy, and Tradition in the Nineteenth Century* (1955); Leo Marx, *The Machine in the Garden* (1965); Quentin Anderson, *The Imperial Self* (1971); and R. Jackson Wilson, *Figures of Speech: American Writers and the Literary Marketplace, From Benjamin Franklin to Emily Dickinson* (1989). Anne C. Rose, *Transcendentalism as a Social Movement, 1830–1850* (1974), is a good attempt to place Emerson and his colleagues in a social context. A good study of literary nationalism is Larzer Ziff, *Literary Democracy: The Declaration of Cultural Independence in America* (1981).

CHAPTER 11

A New South

Episode: Nat Turner's Rebellion

SLAVERY AND SOUTHERN SOCIETY

    Slavery and Market Capitalism

    Slavery as a Social System

    Slaves' Responses to Servitude

    The Social Structure of the South

    The Proslavery Argument

THE EPISODE: The labor of millions of African-American slaves enabled some white people to live lives of a comfort that shaded into luxury with a confidence that shaded into arrogance. But behind the comfort and the confidence, the luxury and the arrogance, there was always a haunting fear that the slaves might rise up and wrathfully strike for their freedom.

This white nightmare came true on an August morning in 1831 in Southampton County, Virginia. A slave who became known as Nat Turner led a band of rebels into bloody insurrection. Panic-stricken and enraged white people struck back, brutally murdering African Americans without knowing whether they had taken part in the revolt. Nat Turner himself was able to hide out for two months, but then he was captured, tried, and put to death—asking, poignantly, "Was not Christ crucified?"

THE HISTORICAL SETTING: Nat Turner's rebellion was not the first slave revolt in North America, but it was the largest and bloodiest. It came at a key moment in the history of American slavery. In the three decades following the American Revolution more and more southern slaves had been able to gain their freedom by purchasing it or through voluntary manumission by their masters. In fact, by 1810, there were almost 135,000 free blacks in the South (8.5 percent of the black population). But by the early 1820s, this pattern had reversed itself: in 1830, the percentage of free blacks in the South was actually less than it had been in 1810.

As they saw the opportunity for emancipation diminish, some blacks became more vehement in their opposition to slavery. In 1822, Denmark Vesey, a former slave who had purchased his freedom, organized a slave revolt in South Carolina that was thwarted only at the last minute when authorities got wind of his plot. And in 1829, David Walker, a North Carolina free black who had moved to Boston, published a passionate appeal to blacks to rise up against slavery.

The retreat from manumission as well as the angry response of blacks to it was a symptom of changes taking place not only in slavery itself but in the place of slavery in Southern life and society. In almost every way—economically, socially, politically, and ideologically—slavery deepened its hold on the South after 1830. By 1850, slavery was no longer a "peculiar institution" that happened to exist in the South; the South itself had become a slave society. Its economy revolved around forms of large-scale agriculture that depended on slave labor; its society was organized around a system of caste and class in which the divide between slave and master, black and white, was fixed and immutable; its politics centered on the defense of its "peculiar institution" against any and all perceived threats; its ideology extolled slavery, not as a necessary evil, but as a "positive good," the foundation of a noble civilization.

Nat Turner's Rebellion

The voice of the spirit had told him the sign would appear in the sky. Now, as Nat Turner looked at the sun on the morning of Saturday, August 13, 1831, he knew this was the signal he had been waiting for. It was a strange phenomenon, one that many people on the east coast of the United States were noticing that day, even though it did not mean to them what it meant to Nat Turner as he worked in the fields of Southampton County, Virginia. First, the sun grew dim in the cloudless sky. Then it began to change colors—turning green, then blue, finally almost white. By the afternoon the sun was looking almost like a silvery mirror. Then, as Nat stared in fascination, on the solar surface appeared a single black spot.

Nat Turner thought he knew exactly what it all meant. The sun had become a mirror of what was about to happen on the earth. Just as a black spot had passed across the sun, so black men would rise up and move across the earth. This was the signal Nat had been waiting for—the signal the spirit had promised him. He knew the time for delay had passed. The massacre must begin. The white people of Southampton County must be killed or put to flight.

Nine days later, fifty-five whites lay slaughtered—forty-two of them women and children. Most were hacked to death with axes. Many had been decapitated. Then vengeful whites struck back. The luckier blacks were captured alive and held for trial; others were simply killed outright by enraged and terrified white men. It was by far the bloodiest uprising in the long history of American slavery. Nat Turner himself managed to evade capture for more than two months, far longer than any of his fellow conspirators. He was finally taken in late October, duly tried and convicted, and publicly hanged on November 11, 1831. It was less than a year after William Lloyd Garrison had begun publishing *The Liberator*.

After Nat Turner had been captured, he recounted his life to a white interviewer in the prison where he was being held, and the interviewer published his recollections as *The Confessions of Nat Turner*. (That is the name by which he is known to us today. But he was probably never called Nat Turner during his lifetime, by either black or white people. Like all slaves, he had only a given name—Nat. Slaves normally received last names only when they became fugitives or embroiled in legal proceedings. Turner was nothing but the surname of a white man who once happened to "own" him. At most, he would have been spoken of as "Turner's Nat." To call him Turner here would be to identify him as a piece of property. It is possible that he had an African name,

TURNER'S NAT. The poster that offered a $500 reward for the capture of Turner's Nat described him as between 30 and 35 years old—five feet six or eight inches high—weighs between 150 and 160—rather bright complexion but not a mulatto—broad-shouldered—large flat nose—large eyes—broad flat fleet—rather knock kneed—walk brisk and active—hair on the top of the head very thin—no beard except on the upper lip and tip of the chin. A scar on one of his temples produced by the kick of a mule—also one on the back of his neck by a bite—a large knot on one of the bones of his right arm near the wrist produced by a blow.

which white people did not know then and we do not know now. We have chosen to call him Nat here.)

Nat was about thirty years old at the time of the massacre. Even in his earliest years, though, he had felt himself to be no ordinary slave but someone who was marked for greatness—or, as he put it, "called to superior righteousness." Nat had taught himself how to read—his parents were both illiterate—and he seemed to "remember" things that had happened before he was born. Around the farm on which his parents worked, his abilities soon became a "source of wonder." More than once Nat had overheard his mother and father tell each other that he was "intended for some great purpose." Even the white man who owned the farm, pious Benjamin Turner, took to displaying the talented young slave to his white friends, and Nat heard them all agree that he was too special to be "of any service to anyone as a slave."

Nat Turner grew up with great expectations and, much like the young William Lloyd Garrison, with a determination to make something of himself. He played with the white children around the farm. His mind was restless. He read every book that came his way. He performed experiments with everyday materials, devising things like paper and gunpowder. When he reached his teens, he decided to adopt a life of "austerity": never to touch alcohol or tobacco, and "studiously" to avoid any kind of carousing with his fellow slaves. Through this program of self-improvement and self-discipline, Nat Turner tried to show others something of his great promise and to prepare himself for the rewards it would bring.

What happened was a bitter disappointment. He hoped to be emancipated at the death of his master. But when Benjamin Turner died, ten-year-old Nat was simply handed on to Turner's son Samuel, who was just setting himself up on a nearby farm of his own. Within a few years, Nat found himself laboring in the fields alongside the half-dozen slaves Samuel Turner used to work his 360-acre farm. For the first time it occurred to him, as a teenager, that he might have to spend his entire life as a field hand. When Nat reached his twenty-first birthday, his future had become clear: "I had arrived to man's estate," he recalled, "and was a slave." The prospect was unbearable.

In his frustration, Nat ran away from his owner. For an entire month he hid in the woods. But for some reason he changed his mind. At the end of the month he voluntarily returned, to resume the drudgery of field work.

But still he held his ambition. It was about this time that Nat discovered his hopes might be fulfilled through religion. His mind fastened on one verse he had read in the Bible: "Seek ye the kingdom of heaven, and all things shall be added to you." The words seemed to promise that if Nat would only concentrate his energy on spiritual matters—the kingdom of heaven—everything else would follow. In order to win the world, he must look to heaven. But what did that involve?

One day, while working alone behind the plow in one of his owner's fields, Nat heard a voice intoning the biblical passage he had been pondering. He was sure the voice was the spirit of God, speaking directly to him as He had spoken ages before to the biblical prophets. From that time on, the divine spirit addressed him regularly. And this confirmed Nat's belief that he was "ordained to some great purpose."

But there were worldly disappointments. About 1822, Nat's young master, Samuel Turner, died, and Nat was sold outside the Turner family, to a neighboring farmer named Thomas Moore. What made this event even more unsettling was the fact that Nat had recently married a slave woman on Samuel Turner's farm, and the couple was now forced to live apart. All in all, it was a vivid display of Nat's inability to control the ordinary course of his life. But he had decided to focus his attention elsewhere. He fasted, he prayed, and he avoided contact with his fellow slaves. And through it all the spirit continued to talk to him, to reassure him that "something was about to happen that would terminate in fulfilling the great promise that had been made to me."

For the time being, though, Nat did not know just how his "great promise" would be fulfilled, and he awaited further revelations. First, the spirit gave him secret understandings of the natural world around him: "knowledge of the elements, the revolution of the planets, the operation of the tides, and changes of the seasons." In essence, Nat was resuming his old program of self-improvement in the only way still open to him—through mystic revelation instead of white men's books.

Little by little, through fasting, prayer, and revelation, Nat sensed that he was being "made perfect" in "true knowledge" and "holiness." At length, he began to speak about his powers to other slaves in the neighborhood, and his strange dignity brought many of them under his spell. On one occasion, Nat's charismatic influence even reached across racial lines to touch a white man. Nat would later recall the incident with pride:

> I told these things to a white man, Ethelred T. Brantley, on whom it had a wonderful effect—and he ceased immediately from his wickedness, and was attacked immediately

with a cutaneous [skin] eruption, and blood oozed from the pores of his skin. And after praying and fasting nine days, he was healed.

The spirit even told Nat to baptize this white man. To the shock of other whites, the man agreed:

> And when the white people would not let us be baptized by the church, we went down to the water together, in the sight of many who reviled us, and were baptized by the Spirit. After this, I rejoiced greatly, and gave thanks to God.

But that was to be the only time Nat would achieve even this much impact in the white world, the only time that he would stop a white man's blood from flowing.

One day in 1825, Nat had his first vision of racial violence:

> I saw white spirits and black spirits engaged in battle, and the sun was darkened—the thunder rolled in the heavens, and blood flowed in streams. And I heard a voice saying, "Such is your luck, such you are called to see, and let it come rough or smooth, you must surely bear it."

Was race war, then, the "great purpose" for which Nat was chosen? It was a shocking prospect. Nat decided not to tell this terrible vision to his fellow slaves, and for several years he even withdrew from associating with them in order to ponder it, and to understand more fully what he was expected to bear.

Nat looked everywhere for signs—in the sky, in the woods, even in the crops he worked for his master. And slowly, with the aid of his spirit voice, he came to discover strange connections—between heaven and earth, between religious salvation and slave rebellion, between Jesus Christ and Nat Turner.

He learned that what people called the Milky Way was really "the lights of the Savior's hands, stretched forth from east to west, as they were extended on the cross on Calvary for the redemption of sinners." One day, at work in the corn field, Nat found "drops of blood on the corn, as though it were dew from Heaven." And the spirit explained to him that the Milky Way and the blood on the corn were both symbols of Christ's sacrifice:

> The blood of Christ had been shed on this earth, and had ascended to heaven for the salvation of sinners, and was now returning to earth again in the form of dew.

Searching the night sky once again, Nat saw that the stars were arranged to form pictures of men in different poses. Then, walking in the woods, he discovered certain leaves that contained the very same pictures, along with mysterious hieroglyphic markings—all marked in blood. Once more the spirit explained the meaning—the ominous meaning—of this strange discovery:

> As the leaves on the trees bore the impression of the figures I had seen in the heavens, it was plain to me that the Savior was about to lay down the yoke he had borne for the sins of men—and the Day of Judgment was at hand.

The signs were beginning to become clear. Nat was finally putting together the diverse elements in his life: religion, self-improvement, the promise of greatness, and the bitter, incomprehensible frustration. But what did it all mean for Nat himself? What was his personal role in the tremendous mystery he was coming to unravel? Finally, the answer to that question began to emerge. On May 12, 1828—he would always recall the exact date—Nat heard a loud noise in the heavens. Then, in fateful language, the spirit spoke again:

> The serpent was loosened [let loose], and Christ had laid down the yoke he had borne for the sins of man, and I should take it on, and fight against the serpent—for the time was fast approaching when the first should be last, and the last should be first.

Finally, it was all fitting into place: the patterns in the leaves and the stars, the blood on the corn, the vision of race war, and the abiding question of Nat's own great purpose in life. Christ had not simply laid down his burden of suffering, he had passed it on, to Nat Turner himself. By taking up the cross, Nat would fulfill both Christ's purpose and his own burning ambition.

The "serpent" in Nat's vision was of course the white man, and by doing battle against him, Nat would "redeem" his own black race in both a religious sense and a political one—freeing them simultaneously from the bonds of both sin and slavery. The final result would not be race war but a more just reordering of society—"the first should be last, and the last should be first." Nat himself might die in the struggle, but his death, like Christ's, would only seal his triumph. When a white man visited Nat in jail after the rebellion and asked him whether his approaching execution did not prove his visions had been false and his rebellion useless, Nat was able to respond, simply: "Was not Christ crucified?"

The Day of Judgment was nearly at hand. All that now remained was to discover the details. And even these the spirit promised to reveal. "By signs in the heavens," Nat would learn exactly when to begin his "great work." At the appearance of the first of these signs—but not a day before—he was to reveal to a handful of other slaves the nature of the plan. Until then, he was to keep the project to himself.

The promised signs took almost three years to appear. In the meantime, Nat's owner, Thomas Moore, died, and Moore's widow married a local wheelwright named Joseph Travis. Once again, Nat was forced to change one master and one home for another. Travis was a decent fellow, but that was hardly the point. (When the rebellion finally did get under way, he was the first man to be slaughtered.)

Finally, in February 1831, there was an eclipse of the sun. Nat determined this to be the promised sign—the sign that removed "the seal from my lips." He now revealed his intentions to four trusted black friends who had fallen under the influence of his personality. The four men soon agreed to participate in his great work. The time had come "to slay my enemies with their own weapons," to plan strategy, to convert a private religious vision into a political and military operation.

First, it was necessary to decide on a date to begin the slaughter. Always sensitive to symbols, Nat first proposed July 4—Independence Day—and his friends agreed. But there agreement ended. Up to this time Nat had dealt with private visions, not public strategy, and on these practical questions, the spirit failed to address him.

The questions to be answered were numerous and difficult. How many slaves should be told about the plan? Where should the operation begin? What route should their army follow? How would they get weapons? Should they spare anybody from the slaughter? How could they protect themselves against capture by the white troops who were sure to arrive? Above all, what was to be their practical goal? To escape, perhaps into the Great Dismal Swamp some thirty miles to the east? To capture the county seat, Jerusalem? To establish a secure free state in Southampton County? To spread rebellion throughout the South?

Through the spring months of 1831, the five men engaged in long debates and formulated any number of plans. But they could come to no agreement. "The time passed," Nat later recalled, "without our coming to any determination how to commence." Nat himself was so disturbed by this turn of events that he fell ill.

So July 4 came and went, and nothing happened. The conspirators were "still forming new schemes and rejecting them." It was at this confused and discouraged point, on August 13, that Nat was finally jolted into action by a sign too clear to be ignored. This was, of course, the day the sun grew dim and changed colors, and the black spot appeared on its surface. Now Nat knew that the Day of Judgment could be delayed no longer.

Eight days later, on Sunday, August 21, Nat's four associates gathered at a secluded pond in the neighborhood: Hark, Nelson, Sam, and Henry. Hark (his full name was Hercules) brought a pig he had filched from his master. Henry brought some brandy. There were also present two new conspirators, slaves who had not previously been part of the group. Both were well known to the original four. The pig was killed and cooked.

Nat himself did not join this last meal until the middle of the afternoon. The seven men ate and drank (though Nat himself, true to his temperance principles, refused to touch the brandy). After the food was finished, the group continued to sit around the pond and debate their plans—for even at this late hour they had not formulated any clear strategy. There was, however, general agreement that the group could delay no longer—that very night they had to rise up and "kill all the white people."

Jack, one of the newcomers, objected that the scheme was impractical—"their number was too few." Jack's objection seemed reasonable. How could seven unarmed slaves mount a general insurrection? Surely they would be captured and killed before they could accomplish anything.

But Nat was ready to answer this objection. It was not through carelessness, or visionary fanaticism, that he had failed to spread advance word of the rebellion to the slaves in the county. It was hard political calculation. He had carefully weighed the two options available to him, each involving great but different risks. First, he might try to organize the rebellion in advance. He could inform a large number of slaves of his plans, giving them time to prepare emotionally and tactically to murder their masters and join his army. But Nat knew that to do so was to risk betrayal—there was bound to be at least one slave who, out of fear or loyalty, would betray the conspiracy. Nat was aware of the fact that earlier American slave insurrections had been uncovered and stopped in just this fashion before they could even get under way.

Nat was determined above all to maintain secrecy. Until the moment of the actual onslaught, only seven men knew what was going to happen. And these seven were closely related to each other by ties of friendship or kinship. Jack was Hark's brother-in-law. Hark and Nat both worked for the same white man, Joseph Travis. And both Sam and Will were the property of Nathaniel Francis, who was Joseph Travis's brother-in-law. Among such a tight-knit group, the risk of betrayal was minimal.

But by ensuring secrecy, Nat was forced to take the second of his options—and risks. He had to give up the possibility of systematic recruitment and effective organization. He would have to recruit his forces in spontaneous fashion as the group moved on from one farm to another. Their numbers would increase as they went along, he argued. The places Nat planned to attack were all familiar to him. He had lived his entire life in the neighborhood, and his party of insurrectionists was well known to many of the slaves in the region. When these slaves saw their owners actually lying dead, and felt themselves masterless, they would surely join the liberating army. And since the slaves in Southampton County outnumbered the whites, the county would belong to them.

So Nat argued, as he and his six friends sat by the pond, watching afternoon turn to dusk, and dusk slip into darkness. Finally, then, it was agreed: that very night they would begin. They would head to the house of Joseph Travis, the master of Nat and Hark. There they would stop and "kill all the white people." Then they would collect weapons and horses, recruit other male Travis slaves—slaves now without a master—to join them, and march on to other farms and plantations. There the scene would be repeated, and their army of recruits would swell to overwhelming proportions. At first, they would spare no white person in their path, whether man, woman, or child—that much was necessary in order to "strike terror and alarm" through the countryside and cause the remaining white people of the county to flee for their lives. Within a day, if all went well, the black army could march unopposed and triumphant into the county seat—a town whose biblical name, Jerusalem, could not have escaped Nat's notice.

The killings had to be brutal, to intensify the general terror. The heads of some victims were to be severed, and the bodies of others dismembered. But Nat also insisted on clear limits: there was to be no torture, no rape, and (except for necessary supplies) no looting. There was no room for indulging in simple revenge or personal gratification. Furthermore, the slaughter would not continue indefinitely. Nat later told a white questioner that "indiscriminate massacre was not their intention after they obtained a foothold. Women and children would afterward be spared, and men too who ceased to resist."

The seven slaves waited at the pond until sometime after midnight. Then they walked the half-mile to the Travis house. But still they hung back. To fortify themselves for the awful things that had to be done, they retreated to an outbuilding that housed the family's cider press, where all of them drank—all except Nat. Then, finally, they returned to the house. It was now about 2 A.M. Nat reported what happened next:

> On returning to the house Hark went to the door with an axe, for the purpose of breaking it open, as we knew we were strong enough to murder the family even if they were awakened by the noise. But, reflecting that it might create an alarm in the neighborhood, we determined to enter the house secretly, and murder them whilst sleeping. Hark got a ladder and set it against the chimney, on which I ascended, and hoisting a window, entered and came downstairs, unbarred the door, and removed the guns from their places.
>
> It was then observed that I must spill the first blood. Armed with a hatchet, and accompanied by Will, I entered my master's chamber. It being dark, I could not give him a death blow; the hatchet glanced from his head, he sprang from the bed and called his wife. It

was his last word—Will laid him dead with a blow of his ax, and Mrs. Travis shared the same fate as she lay in the bed.

The murder of his family, five in number, was the work of a moment. Not one of them awoke. There was a little infant sleeping in a cradle, that was forgotten until we had left the house and gone some distance, when Henry and Will returned and killed it.

In military formation, the troop now marched a few hundred yards to the property of the nearest neighbor, Salathiel Francis. Nat sent Sam to knock on the door and announce he had a letter for Mr. Francis. As soon as the door opened, Francis's head was smashed with hatchets and clubs. Quickly now and silently, the army moved to the next house, the home of a widow, Piety Reese, and her son William, who was Jack's master. This time the door was not locked. The men entered quietly and killed the widow Reese in her bed. But the noise woke her grown son. "Who is that?" he called out. These were his last words. Finally, the killers turned on the Reeses' overseer, whom they mistakenly left for dead—the first white to survive the terror. Before they left, Jack celebrated his liberation by putting on his dead master's socks and shoes. It was a gesture that would be repeated several times in the hours to come.

At dawn—about 5:30—the troop reached the farm that had belonged to Samuel Turner, Nat's former master. This time, Nat abandoned stealth and trickery and simply stormed the farmhouse. Will broke open the door with an axe, and quickly the list of the dead was lengthened by three: Mrs. Turner, a female visitor, and the white overseer. Nat was well known among the Turner slaves, and here, if anywhere, he could expect new recruits. He did get a few. One man celebrated his liberation by putting on the clothes of the dead overseer. Another was less elated, and seems to have joined only under a threat of death from Nat's men. It was a bad sign. Four raids had netted only six recruits. If this was the result at Turner's, then what could Nat expect at other farms where he was less well known? He could take some comfort in the fact that his army now had nine horses and a few guns to go with their precarious arsenal of axes, swords, and hoes.

Nat now moved his mounted men on northward, headed toward Barrow Road, which led to the town of Jerusalem. The next farm north belonged to another widow, Catherine Whitehead, and was the largest farm Nat had yet attacked. Here for the first and last time, Nat Turner killed.

Out in a field near the main house, the rebels found Mrs. Whitehead's son, a young Methodist minister. Will finished him with an axe. Then the army moved on the main house, where they quickly slaughtered three of Mrs. Whitehead's daughters, a young grandchild, and the old mistress herself.

Nat waited outside as these murders were finished. But, like it or not, he had his own desperate baptism to perform: he had to come face to face with slaughter. One of the Whitehead daughters, Margaret, had been able to sneak out of the house and hide herself. Nat saw her, and she ran wildly into a nearby field. He chased her down and began to swing at her with a small sword he was now carrying. For some reason, the sword would not finish off the screaming woman, and he had to pick up a fence post and finally club her to death.

The Whitehead farm had twenty-five slaves, and Nat could reasonably hope for some recruits. But his luck was even worse here than it had been at Turner's. Three of the adult male slaves ran away to the woods, and Nat could persuade only two of those who remained to join his campaign of terror. One of the slaves, an old house servant, had even managed to save the life of a fifth Whitehead daughter by hiding her under a mattress and convincing Nat's men that she was not at the house.

The August dawn had now become full day. It was a Monday, and every farm family in the neighborhood would be awake and at work. Before the day was over, Nat Turner would know the answer to two very crucial questions: How many of Southampton County's 10,000 blacks would join him? and Would the county's 6,000 white people flee, or would they resist? The answer to the first question would depend on Nat's ability to persuade. The answer to the second would hang on the success of his deliberate, calculated tactic of terror. He knew one thing for certain. He had to get scores, even hundreds, of recruits. The only alternative was collapse.

Already there were ominous signs of failure. The very next house Nat raided was empty. The family had been warned by its own slaves—who in turn had been told what was happening by slaves from the Travis place, site of the first killings. And there were few recruits. Months later, after the rebellion had been crushed, a local white man summed up the problem accurately enough:

> They did not find one dozen efficient recruits along their whole route of slaughter. They certainly made many more than twelve, but instead of being of any service, most of them had to be guarded, by some two or three of the principals [rebel leaders], furnished with guns—with orders to shoot the first men who endeavored to escape.

If Nat Turner's few guns and the precious energies of his lieutenants had to be put to such uses, his chances of success were frail indeed. And if he came upon more empty houses whose white occupants had been warned, could a force of mounted and well-armed whites be far away? Sadly, from his point of view, the first whites to flee had not even seen the bloodied and headless bodies he was counting on to generate terror. He had almost reached the road leading east to Jerusalem. But a terrible burden of fatigue and uncertainty had to lie behind the flat and understated judgment Nat remembered making at this point: "I understood, then, that the alarm had already spread."

It had been spread first by slaves. A boy had run all the way from the Travis farm—the first that had been attacked—to warn Travis's brother-in-law, Nathaniel Francis. Francis, not convinced, had decided to ride off to see for himself. His mother had followed. When Nat's men arrived at about 9 A.M., they killed an overseer, a female visitor and her child, and two young Francis nephews. One of these boys, a three-year-old, had innocently run from the house to greet the advancing army. He was immediately decapitated by Will. His older brother had a chance to scream before he was killed, just as quickly. Only Nathaniel Francis's wife, who was eight months pregnant, escaped. One of her slaves hid her in an upstairs room and told the troops that she was gone.

And so it went at the next farm, where the whites had been warned by their slaves, and had all left. At the next, the troops managed to kill only the owner, an old man who was out working alone in the fields.

At each of the farms, however, Nat had been able to recruit a few slaves—not many, but enough to give him a little sense of momentum. As he reached the end of

Barrow Road, Nat was "still determined on starting for Jerusalem—Our number amounted now to fifty or sixty, armed with guns, axes, swords and clubs." They had left twenty-eight dead whites behind them. Down the road, about three hours' march, lay the town. They could be there by noon if they moved swiftly. But Nat's tactics required a slower pace. He had to send more and more shock waves of terror ahead of him as he moved. And there was still the all-important task of recruitment to be performed from house to house along the way.

Nat Turner was experiencing some of the problems of command. His men were calling him "General" and were addressing Hark as "Captain." But discipline was a problem. The men drank—every farm they raided had a still or at least a cider press. And they tended to get strung out along the line of march, since not all had horses. Nat had devised a rather simple strategy. He would send a force of cavalry ahead with one standing order: to kill every white they found. He would then bring up his "infantry," regroup, and give a new order to "Go ahead." The tactic was makeshift, but it worked well enough for the time being.

Before the advance guard of cavalry reached Levi Waller's homestead, a man rushed up, shouting, "The Negroes have risen, and are murdering the whites, and are coming." The warning may have cost the lives of ten young children. Waller sent his son to a school, about 500 yards away, to warn the schoolmaster and to bring back several of Waller's own children. The schoolmaster soon came, bringing several other children as well. Waller shouted to him to go to the house and load the guns, but before the schoolmaster could get ready, the terrorists' cavalry rode up.

Waller hid behind a fence, crouching in deep weeds, and watched while his wife was slashed to death and one child after another was decapitated. One young girl escaped by climbing up a dirt chimney. Two of Waller's sons and the schoolmaster managed to get away in the confusion. All in all, four males and one little girl had survived—she with no help from anyone. One woman and a total of ten children had been killed. It was the bloodiest single raid of the campaign.

Waller himself could only stare in horror and disbelief. He testified that his own slave, Davy, came out now, "dressed clean," drank with Nat's men, and "rode his master's horse off in good spirits—was called brother Clements [i.e., Mercy] by one of the company—left in great glee."

It was almost the end of the terror. Nat's men would hurl themselves at only three more houses containing unsuspecting whites—fourteen victims, all but two of them women or children. But from this point on, most of the farmhouses they found were empty (or they contained only one or two poor whites, whom Nat decided to spare because they "thought no better of themselves than they did [of] the negroes"). With fifty-five whites now dead, word was out. Nat could not have known it, but two bands of white horsemen were even now tracking his party. One group came upon the heap of children's bodies at Waller's before the blood was quite dried, in time to witness the last few minutes of life of a little girl who was still breathing when they got there. Ahead, near the crucial bridge that led across the river and into Jerusalem, reinforcements were gathering.

By the time Nat reached the intersection of Barrow Road and the highway into Jerusalem—less than three miles away—a complicated mixture of emotion and ideas flooded up in him. First, there was some mild conflict between him and a few of his men. He wanted to make all haste across the bridge and into the town. But some of the men insisted on "calling" first at the house of James Parker, who lived about a half-mile south and west of the intersection. He let them go to the house while he waited on the road, irritated with their slowness and their tendency to drink cider or brandy at the farms they attacked. He knew, from the number of deserted houses he was finding, that most of the whites in the area would have been warned.

But this knowledge was mixed with satisfaction at his progress so far. He had developed a good tactic: he would send his horsemen ahead to house after house, riding as fast as their horses could move, to bring death to the whites. Then he would arrive. This meant that he had not killed again, or even witnessed a murder, for hours: "I sometimes got in sight in time to see the work of death completed," he told a white man later, "viewed the mangled bodies as they lay, in silent satisfaction."

But Nat's experience was about to take a new turn. His systematic campaign of terror was about to become a more conventional military operation, complete with an organized enemy, march and countermarch, and plans for maneuvers of retreat and flanking. After waiting on the road, Nat went to look for his men. He formed them up and started back toward the road. Then he saw his enemy: about eighteen whites, armed and advancing, commanded by a local militia officer. The white men were advancing across a field of low, sparse corn, with their officer in front, under orders not to fire until they had come within about 100 feet of the blacks. Nat formed his men up—he had been trying to drill some of them in marching formations from time to time during the day—and ordered them to stand fast. A decisive moment had come. Who would break discipline first, the fresh whites, each with a loaded and primed gun? Or the exhausted blacks, many of whom had only an axe or a club?

The answer was not long in coming. A white man discharged his musket long before the white line had reached an effective shooting range. The leading officer's horse bolted and ran straight toward the black line. A second white officer's horse also stampeded and carried him into woods. The astonished whites broke ranks. Most ran back through the corn. A few stood their ground until Nat and his men had come within 50 yards—still too great a distance for an effective volley. The white men fired and then retreated, looking for a few precious moments to reload. But Nat was too quick for them. "Charge!" he ordered. His men rushed their horses at the whites, swinging their axes and using their guns as clubs. They chased the whites about 200 yards. Then Nat saw white reinforcements, fresh from Jerusalem. Now his men panicked a little. The whites fired. Hark's horse was shot from under him. It was time to retreat.

Nat decided on a guerrilla tactic. He headed his troops south through some thick woods, toward Cypress Bridge over the Nottoway River. This would take him into Jerusalem from the rear. It was a risky maneuver, for crossing the bridge would box him into a triangle formed by a fork in the river. But he knew now that he badly needed guns and ammunition, and that Jerusalem was his best chance.

As he moved through the woods, he tried to collect his men into a disciplined group, realizing, as he later said, that they were "dispersed in every direction." Even worse, as he approached Cypress Bridge, he could see from the woods that the whites had anticipated his next move: the bridge was heavily guarded. What was he to do? He could not attack; his force was too small and disoriented. He needed time, and he needed men.

There was only one way to get them now. Nat Turner had not yet confronted the institution of slavery at its sensitive and powerful center. He had attacked relatively small corn and cotton farmers, but he had not sent his men onto a large plantation. On a great plantation, surely, the slaves would be more numerous and more relentlessly worked. There, by one logic, he would find men who had very little contact with white families, little or no reason to be "loyal" to their masters. On a great plantation he might find men who were used to working in gangs, driven harder by their overseers than he or Hark or Nelson had been. But there had been another logic at work in Nat Turner's strategies. He had gone to the smaller farms where he or his lieutenants were known, where they had brothers or sisters or cousins. Even that morning, as he had sent his horsemen ahead down Barrow Road, he had decided not to turn a few miles north, not to attack the plantations of Thomas Ridley, who owned about 150 slaves—the third-largest holding in the county.

Now, in desperation, Nat decided to attack Ridley's two plantations after all. All through the long afternoon, he held his men together—about forty of them, now—back north, back across Barrow Road. At dusk Nat and his forty men reached woods near the main buildings of the plantation, only to find that white militia had already come to barricade the place—having chosen to protect one of their great, half-industrialized centers of agricultural production.

What of Ridley's slaves? Only four of them made their way to join Nat's group. The rest held back in their rough cabins. Here was a key fact: unlike Nat and his core of lieutenants, for whom almost daily movement and contact from farm to farm was a habit, these slaves lived and worked on a more or less self-contained plantation and had few if any kin or friends on neighboring estates. They had little or no reason to trust Nat or his men.

For the moment, Nat decided neither to attack nor to retreat. He chose instead to post guards and allow himself and his weary troops to lie down among the trees and sleep. Rest came hard, though. His men were more than tired; they were also shaken and demoralized. And so a mistaken alarm that white militia were attacking was enough to send some of his men fleeing. While Nat slept, other men slipped away through the woods, to reappear at their own farms the next morning, hoping their masters would not suspect them. When Nat Turner woke early on Tuesday, he found only twenty men still around him.

In the morning, Nat made a risky guess. He supposed that other white families near Ridley's had all fled to the big plantation. This would mean that another sizable farm, belonging to Dr. Thomas Blunt, who owned about sixty slaves, might be deserted by the whites. There Nat might find the additional men he so badly needed. And so he headed toward Blunt's place.

Nat's guess, however shrewd, had been wrong. The whites were there. One opened fire from an upstairs window with a shotgun. Another began to shoot from the porch. One of Nat's men fell dead, and his friend Hark was badly wounded, then captured. According to stories told later by whites, Blunt's "loyal" slaves joined in the battle, rushing against Nat's scattering troops with clubs and pitchforks. Blunt himself claimed he had given his slaves a choice during the night to help him or go over to the rebels. He did not say what he had offered to do to the slaves who chose not to remain "loyal."

There was little Nat could do now. Without Hark and with only a few men left, he headed back south. He had not gone far when he met still another party of white militia. It took only a few shots, and three of his remaining few men fell dead, including Will, the most tireless of his killers. Only Nat and four others escaped this time, including two of the late recruits from Ridley's plantation. Nat ordered the four to go out looking for his men, or for new recruits, and to meet him back at the pond where it had all begun on Sunday. Now he was alone, and the struggle was over. All that was left was hiding and capture, immediate death for some and short trials later for the rest.

Nat made his way, somehow, back to the Travis house—his house—now completely deserted. He swiped a few provisions and waited all day for some of his men to show up. None came. "On this," he quietly reported later, "I gave up all hope for the present."

Then Nat went, literally, underground. He found his way to a pile of rough-hewn fence rails in a field. With the same sword he had used with poor success trying to kill Margaret Whitehead, he began to scratch out a hole under the pile of wood. By Thursday evening, he had completed a crude cave, just big enough for his body.

Now it was the white man's turn. By Thursday, when Nat went into his cave, local and state militia had been joined by federal troops in Jerusalem, where some 400 white women had also taken refuge. The troops fanned out through the countryside. They had orders to capture or kill any "insurrectionists." But Nat's men had worn no uniforms. No one could tell who had been part of the terror and who had not. There were even rumors among the whites that a huge slave army of more than 1,000 was still moving around the county. The whites' fear and rage had few limits. Blacks were murdered at random, all over the county and even down into North Carolina. Some were lynched, others shot or beheaded. Many were tortured and mutilated. One company of cavalry killed forty blacks in two days, then put the heads of fifteen on poles— "as a warning to all who should undertake a similar plot."

It took days for order to return. On Sunday, August 28, a week after the rebellion had started, the general commanding the militia announced that "there no longer exists any cause of apprehension for the public safety or the security of individuals." It remained only to hope for the quick capture of "Nat, the fanatical desperado who led the band."

But the capture did not come quickly. Three weeks later, with Nat Turner still at large, the governor offered a $500 reward for him. He was still in his cave near the Travis house, where he did little but lie quietly during the day. He moved about only at night, and then just far enough to get water. Then, as weeks passed, he began to move around more in the dark, taking food from nearby farms and even daring to "eaves drop the houses in the neighborhood." He was hoping, still, to pick up some "intelligence" about his men.

In this fashion, he evaded capture for fully eight weeks. He was not taken until October 30. Before Nat's trial and hanging, a white man took down his story of the capture in these words:

I know not how long I might have led this life, if accident had not betrayed me. A dog in the neighborhood, passing by my hiding place one night while I was out, was attracted by some meat I had in my cave, and crawled in and stole it, and was coming out just as I returned.

A few nights after, two negroes having started to go hunting with the same dog, and passing that way, the dog came in again to the place, and having just gone out to walk about, discovered me and barked. I spoke to them to beg concealment. On making myself known, they fled from me. Knowing then they would betray me, I immediately left my hiding place and was pursued almost incessantly until I was taken a fortnight afterwards by Mr. Benjamin Phipps, in a little hole I had dug out with my sword, for the purpose of concealment, under the top of a fallen tree.

The capture of Nat Turner. After the revolt, Nat hid out in the woods for almost two months, settling at last in a cave near the Francis farm. He was captured by a local farmer who had come upon Nat by chance. Benjamin Phipps tied Nat's hands and then fired his gun into the air to summon attention.

On Mr. Phipps's discovering the place of my concealment, he cocked his gun and aimed at me. I requested him not to shoot and I would give up, upon which he demanded my sword. I delivered it to him, and he brought me to prison.

I am here loaded with chains, and willing to suffer the fate that awaits me.

Fifty rebels had already been tried and nineteen hanged. Ten others would be transported out of the area. Even outside Southampton County, there had been twenty or thirty trials and executions of black men and women who had supposedly been involved in a nonexistent conspiracy.

But these others died without the triumphant solace that remained with Nat Turner until the end—his confidence that he had been destined for this fate. In jail, he could remember all the signs. And all the identification of his mission with that of Christ came back. He had done something, as he said, that would end by "fulfilling the great promise that had been made to me." Perhaps only his death could really redeem the promise. He remembered the voice telling him five years earlier: "Such is your luck, such you are called to see, and, let it come rough or smooth, you must surely bear it." It had been the rough, not the smooth. But he could bear it. It all came down, now, to one last question, the question he asked in jail as he waited for the end: "Was not Christ crucified?"

Slavery and Southern Society

On the day Nat Turner's rebellion began, a group of sweaty riders galloped into Richmond, the state capital, with the news. Shouting, they rushed to the mansion of the governor, John Floyd. He immediately put the militia of the entire state on alert and sent companies of cavalry and artillery off to Southampton County, with bugles blaring and guns at the ready. Floyd and many others in Virginia were convinced that a massive uprising of slaves had begun. Roadblocks were put up around many towns, and black slaves were arrested everywhere, for little or no reason.

In the days that followed, the governor calmed down a little, and so did other white Virginians. Then, ten days after the rebellion, Floyd made a remarkable entry in his diary: "Before I leave this government, I will have contrived to have a law passed gradually abolishing slavery in this state." And if he could not accomplish that, he would at least get a law that would prohibit slavery west of the Blue Ridge Mountains—more than half of Virginia. For a brief moment, it seemed that the outcome of Nat Turner's rebellion might be the end of slavery in Virginia, the oldest and still the most important slave state of all. It seemed possible, briefly, that Nat Turner had been able to win freedom for his people.

Floyd was not the only Virginian who wanted to be rid of slavery. Many members of the legislature shared his wish. Some of them were gentlemen whose dream was of a modern commercial and industrial South; they were convinced that slavery kept them in bondage to economic underdevelopment. And there were others—mostly from the western part of the state, where slavery had not yet become important—who feared it, although not for moral reasons or out of any concern for blacks. Like most other Americans, they were racists, and they simply did not want African Americans living in their midst, either as slaves or as free people. These westerners also disliked slavery because they were convinced it inevitably brought with it aristocracy, an extreme social division between wealthy planters and ordinary white people. Both antislavery groups, the gentlemen interested in economic development and the westerners, agreed on one thing. If slavery actually ended, the freed slaves would have to be transported out of the country and "colonized" in Africa. The South could then become white, democratic, and prosperous.

The question was, did the opponents of slavery in Virginia have enough power to overturn the rule of the eastern planters who had always run the state? John Floyd, for one, was determined. Just before the legislature met in Richmond in December, he said, "I will not rest until slavery is abolished in Virginia." And a number of the legislators were equally determined. They began a debate that was the most serious and important discussion of slavery ever to have occurred in a southern state.

In their debate, the Virginia legislators talked about the economic benefits and drawbacks of slavery, and its general political consequences. But the very specific and terrifying fact of the rebellion hovered in the background and occasionally broke the surface. One legislator drew a conclusion that was clearly in the minds of many Virginians: every slave was a potential Nat Turner. Could a "deluded and drunken handful" of rebels like Nat Turner's band possibly have created panic throughout Virginia? this legislator asked. "No," came his answer." It was the suspicion eternally attached to the slave himself, the suspicion that a Nat Turner might be in every family, that the same bloody deed could be acted over at any time in any place, that the materials for it were spread through the land, and always ready for a like explosion." The only solution, he argued, was to abolish slavery and send the freed slaves far away.

The debate was exciting to Virginians. People flocked to the galleries to listen, and a Richmond newspaper published the entire proceedings from week to week. As the paper's editor described it, "We now see the whole subject ripped up and discussed with open doors, and in the presence of a crowded gallery and lobby. And nothing else could have prompted it, but the bloody massacre in the month of August."

The debate wore on through January and into February 1832. Antislavery legislators won no important vote. In the end, they lost key votes in the Virginia House and Senate by about the same margins. In the lower house, fifty-eight members, almost all from the western part of the state, voted in favor of a bill that provided for gradual emancipation, money compensation for slaveholders, and colonization. But seventy-three voted no, and the bill lost. In the Senate, a later vote was eighteen to fourteen against even *considering* any sort of antislavery measure. In the end, the legislators decided to accept the judgment of one of the proslavery speakers, that slavery "is our destiny, and the moment has never yet been when it was possible for us to free ourselves from it." Philosophical arguments had made little dent in the hard realities of southern life. The members from the west, who cast forty-nine of the antislavery votes, owned only 102 slaves. The eastern members, who provided sixty-seven of the proslavery votes, owned a total of over 1,000 slaves.

The slender and fleeting chance that Virginia might actually abolish slavery passed quickly. The state and the South settled firmly into another generation of slavery. But Nat Turner's rebellion and the ensuing debate had revealed what now became a crucial fact. A point of crisis had been reached, and white southerners had to choose which way to turn. If they did not do something to end slavery, they had to do something to make it more secure and profitable. The choice was made without much hesitation: the white South fastened slavery on the African Americans—and on themselves—much more firmly than ever before.

The very same Virginia legislature that had considered ending slavery now turned to the alternative and passed new laws to make certain that if the blacks could not be gotten rid of, they would be more severely yoked and harnessed. These laws strengthened the militia system and provided for regular "patrols" throughout the state. But they were aimed less at making whites vigilant than at securing black submission. The new code made it a crime for a black—free or slave—to preach or to hold any kind of religious meeting, on pain of thirty-nine lashes on a bare back. No free black was allowed to own a weapon. No slave could sell or buy liquor. No more free blacks could enter the state.

SLAVERY AND MARKET CAPITALISM

To some extent, the new Virginia slave code was a response to Nat Turner's rebellion. It was also a reaction to growing Northern criticism of slavery (Governor Floyd filed copies of the most radical abolitionist newspaper, William Lloyd Garrison's *The Liberator* with material related to Nat Turner's rebellion). But the causes of the new laws went deeper, and they operated all over the South, not just in Virginia. The nature and status of slavery in the South were changing rapidly and profoundly. And it was these changes, not just a single rebellion or Yankee agitation, that were altering both the experience of the slaves and white ways of looking at and dealing with their "peculiar institution."

At the time of the American Revolution—just half a century before Nat Turner's rebellion—slavery had been a national institution. It was, even then, mainly southern. But 15 slaves out of every 100 lived in the North. Every state recognized slavery as legal, and there were slaves in every one of them. To be sure, Virginia had about 200,000 slaves—almost 40 percent of the total number. But New York had its 25,000, and even little Rhode Island had about 4,000.

By 1820, though, slavery had become a sectional fact. All the northern states had abolished slavery or provided for gradual abolition. So except for a few aged slaves left over from the old days, slavery was strictly a southern affair. In the South, however, the direction of things was precisely the opposite. Slavery was clamping itself onto southern life in ever more tenacious ways.

Since the eighteenth century, slavery had been the basis of the fortunes and lifestyle of a southern planter class that thought of itself as an aristocracy. It had been this planter class from which most of the presidents of the United States were drawn during the first three decades of the Republic. But by the end of the eighteenth century, many of these planters were convinced that slavery was not only a moral evil but an economic and social disaster. Many slaveholders, especially in Virginia, believed slavery would die out as planters realized how uneconomical and inefficient it was. In fact, during the last quarter of the eighteenth century a number of planters did voluntarily free their slaves.

But slavery did not die out at all. It took on renewed and increasing importance, instead. And in the process, it changed. It was no longer simply a labor system designed to sustain a planter in an "aristocratic" style. Along with the rest of the nation, the South was entering more and more into the world of international market capitalism. As this happened, agriculture became more aggressive, more governed by a concern for productivity, efficiency, and profit than ever before. The planter might still like to think of himself as a leisured aristocrat, but by the 1820s he was clearly a capitalist as well. Slaves were part of his capital. And like other capitalists, the southern planter sought to expand his holdings, make them more productive and more profitable.

Historians have argued about whether slavery was an economically workable and "rational" system, or a system that was maintained primarily for cultural or emotional reasons. In fact, a number of historians have stated that slavery was not a viable and profitable system and that, as a consequence, the Civil War itself was an unnecessary "blunder." Sooner or later, they claim, slavery would have fallen of its own dead weight. Emancipation would have come peaceably, as Jefferson and others had hoped and as it did in other countries—most notably in Brazil—in the Western Hemisphere.

But the evidence today points in a different direction. Slavery seems to have been both viable and profitable all the way to the Civil War. From an economist's point of view, the viability of an investment in slaves is little different from the viability of an investment in cattle or sheep, or any other asset that has to be maintained. The question of the economic viability of an investment in slavery comes down to this: Were the costs of breeding and maintaining slaves equal to or less than the market price they could be sold for? The

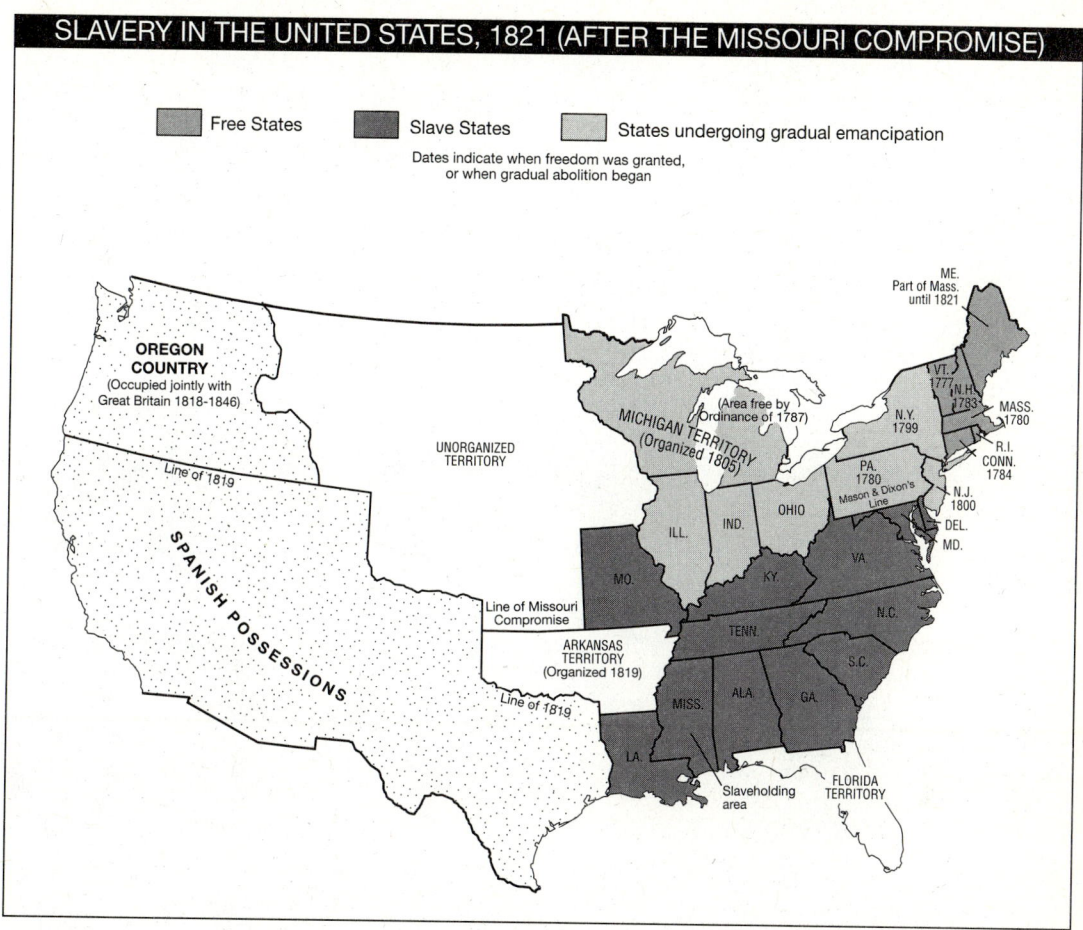

difference (market value minus the cost of food, clothing, and shelter for the slaves) equals what economists call economic rent.

The economic rent on slaves in the South *increased* during the crucial period between the 1820s and the Civil War. By the 1850s a planter who had brought a slave to maturity could sell him or her for well over twice the money he had spent feeding and sheltering his "property." Slavery was not only viable, it was increasingly viable.

It was also a profitable way of investing money. A planter who bought and maintained slaves, not to sell again but to use as a labor force, could realize a profit from this investment. The net rate of return on slaves, male and female, seems to have averaged about 10 percent a year. This was not true every year, and it was not true when the land itself was poor (hence the pressure to find new, good land). But it was true on average all across the South. More important, this rate of return on investment was equal to any other major investment the planter might make in railroads or canals, or even in one of the spanking new Yankee cotton mills in Massachusetts. Slavery was not only viable, it was as profitable as any other capital investment of that period.

SLAVERY AND COTTON

The South had already developed a strong export economy in the colonial period. Its cash crops—mainly tobacco, rice, and indigo—had all used

THE SLAVE AUCTION. This detail of a painting by an antislavery artist depicts an auctioneer calling for bids on a mother and child. Slaves were sold for many reasons—as punishment, for profit, or to pay taxes and settle debts left at a planter's death. They usually were sold at auctions in which buyers would inspect the slave goods, which were then sold to the highest bidder. Many slaveholders accepted the auction as a necessary part of the system, but antislavery critics considered it to be the ultimate symbol of the degradation visited upon the slave.

slave labor. But it was the dramatic growth of cotton as the South's most important cash crop that stamped slavery so firmly on the southern economy and society. In 1790 only slightly more than 3,000 bales of cotton were produced. By 1830, production had expanded to nearly 1 million bales. By 1860, cotton production exceeded 4 million bales and accounted for an astonishing two-thirds of all United States exports.

As noted in Chapter 7, several things lay behind this dramatic growth. First, Eli Whitney's invention of the cotton gin in 1793 made it easy to separate the cotton seed from the fiber. The end of the Napoleonic Wars opened up a booming international market for American agricultural produce after 1815. By the 1830s both England and New England had developed a textiles industry that was capable of producing enormous quantities of cheap cotton cloth. Finally, rich new land in Georgia, Alabama, Mississippi, and Louisiana was opened up to cotton cultivation, as the Native American populations were systematically removed to the West.

All these cash crops, and especially cotton and sugar (which became important in Louisiana in the 1840s), depended on slave labor for their profitability. They were all crops that benefited enormously from what economists call "economies of scale": the larger the plantation and the greater the number of slaves in the labor force, the higher the rate of profit. By 1850, for example, the productivity of slave labor in the cotton and sugar economy—the value of the crops produced in relation to the cost of slave labor itself—was almost eight times what it had been at the end of the eighteenth century, when slaveholders had complained of how uneconomical the institution was and had begun to talk of getting rid of it.

Fluctuations in the price of cotton also led southern planters to an ever greater reliance on increasing numbers of slaves. Cotton prices nearly tripled between 1831 and 1836. Southern planters rushed to increase their production and take advantage of the enormous profits. They pushed into Alabama, Georgia, Mississippi, Arkansas, Louisiana, and Texas, where the soil was rich and land was plentiful and inexpensive. But when cotton prices declined, the pressures to expand production only increased more. Falling prices demanded even more land and more slaves if profit was to stay high. Planters pushed all available land into cotton production and intensified their search for new lands. By the late 1840s, in fact, many planters in the states of the lower Mississippi Valley found that it was more profitable to import corn and wheat for their slaves' food than to take any of their own land out of cotton cultivation.

The dramatic growth of cotton as the South's major cash crop and the nation's leading export had several important consequences. It fostered a mystique among southern planters and politicians about the importance of cotton to the nation and the world. "King Cotton," many came to believe, was the foundation of all the progress of the modern world: it sustained the prosperity and civilization of the South. Northern merchants and manufacturers depended on it for their wealth. It fueled the industrial revolution in England and France. In all, then, it fostered the absolute conviction among planters and politicians that continued prosperity depended on the continuing expansion of cotton production. From the 1830s on, southerners constantly sought ways to find new lands for cotton cultivation. And if the production of cotton had to expand, so did the slave system it depended on.

The slave system had become just as important to southern market capitalism as the textile factories were to the emergent industrial system of New England. The planters now had to calculate the possibilities of profit and loss in larger and more precise terms. The pressure to produce more efficiently and more consistently bore down on them heavily—and, through them, onto their African-American labor force. It became more important than ever that slave labor be disciplined and submissive.

There were variations in the South between old tobacco areas and new cotton-producing areas, between upland regions, where agriculture centered on grain and livestock production, and the lower South of single-crop production for export. But through all the variations ran a consistent thread. The large plantations—rice, cotton, or sugar—that produced for external markets were the plantations that had to function most efficiently. And on them, slavery was at its most brutal. In one southern state after another, the need for a disciplined and submissive slave labor force produced slave codes even more severe than the one passed in Virginia just after Nat Turner's rebellion. These codes prohibited slaves from owning property, going about at night, assembling in groups, preaching, traveling without a written pass, or bearing arms. In most places after 1830, it was even against the law for whites to teach blacks to read or write.

SLAVES AT WORK. This photograph by G. N. Barnard shows slaves returning from the cotton fields. The vast majority of American slaves were field hands. During the planting, growing, and harvest seasons, most of the men, women, and youths over the age of twelve spent long twelve- and sixteen-hour days tending the crops.

SLAVERY AS A SOCIAL SYSTEM

Nat Turner's rebellion, the Virginia debate, the cotton boom, the slave codes—all pointed to the same fact. Slavery was not just a labor system, it was a *social* system that involved the legal status of the slave and the master; the organization of labor; patterns of landholding and land use; and religion, both white and black.

This complex and all-inclusive character is what has caused so much dispute about slavery—dispute that has lasted for more than a century since the emancipation of blacks during the Civil War. In particular, historians have argued vehemently about how masters treated their slaves.

Some have argued that slavery was a cruel and brutal system—though admitting the existence of some humane masters. They point to the meager cotton dresses, shirts, and pants, the crude huts and furnishings, and the protein-poor diets masters gave their slaves. Most of all, they point to the often sadistic and brutal forms of punishment—whipping, chaining, branding, maiming, and killing—to which some masters subjected their slaves.

Other historians have argued that in actual practice slavery was relatively mild—though admitting that there were plenty of abuses. They suggest that whippings were relatively infrequent, and that many masters did not resort to whipping at all. They argue that many slaves were better off than many southern poor whites, and better off than much of the working class of industrial Europe and the North. They point out that slave housing was at least as good as that of most poor whites, and that the slave diet, especially when it was supplemented by produce from the slaves' garden plots and by game and fish, was considerably better. They argue that on many plantations, children, the sick, and the elderly were better taken care of than were the children, sick, and aged in the working classes of free society.

VARIETIES OF SLAVE EXPERIENCE

In practice, slavery differed considerably according to the size of the plantation or farm, the nature of the crop work, and the place the slave lived. Slavery in the older, eastern states of Virginia, North Carolina, and South Carolina, and in border states like Maryland, Kentucky, and Tennessee often had a milder character than slavery on the generally larger, more efficient, and more productive cotton and sugar plantations of Alabama, Mississippi, and Texas. There, work was often harder, and both the heat and the treatment more brutal. In fact, masters in the eastern and border states used "sale down the river" as both a threat and a punishment for slaves they considered disobedient or unruly.

On small farms where there were only a few slaves, they might do a wide variety of jobs—much like hired hands in the free states. Like Nat Turner, they might move from farm to farm and belong to a series of owners. But a majority of slaves belonged to large, essentially self-contained black communities on a single plantation, to which their families might be attached for generations. Many of the slaves on the Cameron family's plantations in North Carolina in the 1850s, for example, were descended from slaves who had been in the family since the 1770s.

But in spite of the numerous guises slavery could take, all slaves had one thing in common. They were chattel—property. Like horses or land, they could be bought and sold, claimed for payment of a debt, transferred, and inherited. The law, at least in theory, offered slaves some protection. It was a crime for a master wantonly to maim or kill a slave. Still, slaves had no legal standing as persons. They had no access to the courts. They could not charge whites with a crime, bring a suit, or testify in court against whites. Slave marriages and families had no legal standing or protection. Like Nat Turner's marriage, they could be broken up simply by a master's decision to sell one of his slaves.

In formal, legal ways, slavery in the American South was harsher and more complete than anywhere else in the Western Hemisphere. But in actual practice, it could often be considerably milder. Many of the prohibitions were loosely or only sporadically enforced. Some slaves were taught to read and write, and some, like Nat Turner, continued to teach themselves. Slaves were sometimes able to gather in their own religious, familial, and festive ceremonies. Many had a small garden plot and a few animals to tend. Most probably had some personal possessions beyond the clothes, shelter, and rations provided by masters. Still, they had no rights in any of these things. A master could always confiscate their possessions, and slaves who were sold usually had to leave everything behind. The only rights, finally, were the masters' rights in their slave property.

Slaves engaged in a number of different kinds of labor and worked under all sorts of conditions. They served as valets and personal maids, wet nurses and nannies, cooks and butlers, grooms and coachmen. Some slaves were artisans—seamstresses, shoemakers, blacksmiths, carpenters, bricklayers. Slaves worked in mills and occasionally even in factories and were often "hired out" as skilled craftsmen. The vast majority of slaves, however, were field hands, who did the hardest and most menial forms of farm labor.

Their work was organized in various ways. On farms with only a few slaves, masters might work alongside slaves. On small plantations, owners might directly supervise the slaves' work. But on large plantations, owners hired overseers (usually whites from a lower social class) to manage the day-to-day work of the plantation. The overseers used "drivers," trusted slaves, to supervise work in the fields. The most common arrangement of labor on large tobacco, sugar, and cotton plantations was the gang system, in which the field hands were divided into groups, each of which was directed by a driver.

The day-to-day relations between slaves and masters varied enormously. On the larger plantations, field hands and masters lived in separate worlds; the master was a remote figure with whom few field hands had much direct contact. These slaves worked in the fields all day, under the supervision of black drivers, and spent the rest of the time in the quarters, where the master rarely came. Drivers and "mammies" (who were the household equivalents of the drivers) lived in both the black and the white worlds. They were the master's agents, responsible for getting the other slaves to do the work the master wanted done. At the same time, however, they were also agents of the slave community. They could provide their fellow slaves with information about the master and his family, and they could give advice on how to deal with masters and overseers. Other slaves often relied on them to use their influence with mistress or master to modify treatment or improve conditions, or to convey complaints against the overseer—often the most hated figure on the plantation.

The personal servants of the master's family had the most complicated relationship of all. A personal servant was often attached to a member of the planter's family when both were children and stayed with him or her for the rest of their lives. Personal servants lived in the "big house" and were in close, constant attendance on their masters and mistresses, at their immediate beck and call. Within the social system of the plantation itself, personal servants held a privileged position. They ate better, dressed better, and were treated better than most of the other slaves on the plantation. A personal servant often ranked higher in his or her master's esteem than did the white overseer. Many personal servants and their masters or mistresses established enduring bonds of trust, loyalty, and affection. It was partly this kind of loyalty that saved the lives of a few white people during Nat Turner's rebellion.

But privilege often had its price. The personal servants inhabited their master's world and had little physical or psychological space of their own. They were expected to cater at once to their owner's whims and desires. They were subject to his or her changing moods and absolute authority, within easy range of verbal, psychological, and even physical abuse. It is no wonder that they often developed a complex set of poses—"puttin' on ole massa"—to mask their own feelings and cushion themselves against the arbitrariness of their master's changing humor.

THE MASTER'S POWER

Trying to figure out what slavery was really like by drawing up a balance sheet between cruelty and humaneness—as historians sometimes do—misses an essential point. The common thread that ran through slavery in *all* its variety and complexity was the absolute and arbitrary power of the master over the slave. It could be exerted for reasons, in ways, and at times that lay totally within the master's whimsy. Most masters, most of the time, probably did not abuse, mistreat, or (one of the cruelest things a master could do to a slave) sell most of their slaves. But many masters at some time did punish or sell at least some of their slaves. Even more to the point, master and slave alike knew that the power was there and available, and that little could or would prevent masters from exerting it if they wanted to. Even "good" masters came down hard on anything—especially running away—that seemed to defy their authority or undermine the spirit of submission they expected of their slaves.

Neither the law nor the planter's white neighbors were likely to interfere with a master's "right" to punish or instill obedience and subordination in his slaves. The master's sovereignty was nearly complete on his own plantation. In 1829 Justice Thomas Ruffin of the North Carolina Supreme Court spelled out the ultimate logic, which seemed to dictate that "the power of the master must be absolute to render the submission of the slave perfect." He recognized the "harshness of the proposition" and agreed that as a private "moral principle" a good man "must repudiate it." Still, he argued, so long as slavery existed there was no getting around it. "Absolute power and perfect submission belong to the state of slavery. They cannot be disunited without abrogating at once the rights of the master and absolving the slave from his subjection. It constitutes the curse of slavery to both the bond and the free portion of our population. But it is inherent in the relation of master and slave."

SLAVE RESPONSES TO SERVITUDE

The slaves themselves responded to their servitude in a number of ways. Bondage often exacted a heavy toll. Many were scarred physically and psychologically. It was humiliating to be whipped publicly, or to be forced to stand by helplessly when fellow slaves or family members were whipped or sold. Bondage was also demeaning even in its milder forms. When in the presence of masters or whites, slaves were expected to pay continual homage to their master's authority and to the whites' "superiority."

RESISTANCE

But slaves were not simply passive victims of bondage. They resisted slavery in various ways. Some stole. Others committed sabotage. Punishment itself can be seen as a partial index of resistance: slaves who defied their masters and seemed to refuse to submit to authority were probably the ones most often whipped or sold. Running away, of course, was the most common form of overt resistance to slavery—and the act slaveholders were most anxious to prevent and quick to punish.

The slaves shielded themselves against the effects of bondage in other ways as well. Some were able to use special skills or hard work to earn the praise and esteem of their masters and partially immunize themselves against harsh treatment. (Many plantations contained slaves whom their masters thought of as "exceptional.") There was also a good bit of dissembling, playing dumb to avoid punishment or excessive work. By conforming to stereotyped notions that they were inherently lazy, slaves could exert at least some control over the rhythm of work.

The notion of slave contentedness could also be used to advantage. Some planters used fear and punishment to extract as much work as possible from their slaves. But by the 1840s it had become a widely held maxim that contented slaves worked best. And there were a number of ways discontented slaves could disrupt the smooth operation of the plantation. Masters often noted the disarray that followed when they or their overseers whipped or sold a slave, imposed unusually heavy work schedules, or took away festival and holiday times.

THE SLAVE FAMILY

One of the most important buffers against the effects of bondage was the slave family. Slave and master both attached great importance to the families the slaves created—though for very different reasons. Many planters and defenders of slavery argued that such families were a testament to how well slavery had civilized the slaves and elevated them out of the supposed degradation of their African past. In addition, they considered the family as a way to control slaves: in a family state, slaves seemed to be less "wild," more content, and better workers. Besides, it was be-

HARRIET TUBMAN; FREDERICK DOUGLASS. The two most famous fugitives from slavery were Harriet Tubman and Frederick Douglass. After she escaped from slavery, Tubman became one of the most effective conductors on the Underground Railroad. Nineteen times between 1850 and 1861, she returned to the South to lead nearly 300 slaves north to freedom. During the Civil War she helped gather intelligence for the Union forces; after the war she turned her farm into a refuge for black orphans and aged ex-slaves. Shortly after his escape in 1838, Frederick Douglass enlisted as an antislavery orator. With the 1845 publication of his powerful *Narrative of the Life of Frederick Douglass: An American Slave,* he became the leading black abolitionist. As the best known fugitive, he provided the logical cover for the abolitionist song composed after the passage of the Fugitive Slave Act in 1852.

lieved, firm family ties made them less likely to run away.

This was not the way the slaves saw it. Masters might extol the slave family as a mechanism for domesticating the former Africans to bondage. But slaves cherished their families for just the opposite reason—as a barrier against the incursions and influences of the master's world. The slaves' families connected them to their past, helped them forge personal identity and esteem, and brought them into a community of mutual support and protection. Here slave children picked up the skills they needed for adulthood and to cope with their lot as slaves. Here they were taught the special values and sense of mutual identity and obligation by which the slave community sheltered itself against the harshest features of bondage. Because of this, not because their masters wanted it, slaves created their own families and clung to them so tenaciously.

Slave families could never escape the reach of the master's power and were never free of the threat of disruption through sale, migra-

A SLAVE FAMILY. Slave families had no legal recognition or protection. They endured in the face of the threat of disruption by the sale of family members, and they lived under crude and overcrowded conditions. Nevertheless, most slaves developed and maintained firm familial bonds and identities.

In certain ways, slave families resembled those of nonslaves. Like their masters and most free Americans, most slaves belonged to discrete families that centered on monogamous couples. Even the sexual divisions within slave families were similar. Slave fathers were at least the symbolic if not always the actual head of their families. They never did the household chores considered "woman's work," and they furnished their sons with clear models of manhood. Although slaves depended on their masters for their basic shelter, clothing, and food, slave fathers often helped provide for their families by hunting, fishing, and making goods for the cabin.

Slave mothers did double duty. The vast majority worked in the fields with the men. Usually they could leave the fields to nurse their babies, but often babies were brought to the fields for nursing. In addition to their plantation work, slave mothers had to cook for their families, nurture, rear, and protect their children, wash, sew, tend a few animals, and keep a small garden. "My mammy," one former slave recalled in an interview conducted by researchers in the 1930s, "work in the field all day and piece and quilt all night. I never see how mammy stand such hard work. She stand up for her children though. The old overseer he hate my mammy, because she fought him for beating her children." In fact, slave mothers often resisted and resented separation from their children so vehemently that it was a commonplace among planters and slave traders that the sale of her children ruined a slave mother as a good slave.

The similarities between slave and nonslave families went only so far. Masters considered the slave family a flawed imitation of their own institution. But as with so many slave practices, appearances could be deceptive. Beneath the surface similarities, the slave family had form and meaning that masters scarcely saw or that they misunderstood. Most free whites equated the unit made up of parents and their dependent children with "the family." But the slave "family" extended

tion, or inheritance. Slave wives and husbands often belonged to different owners and lived apart, meeting in secret or only when the husband had a "pass" to visit his wife. But in spite of such obstacles, the slaves created a remarkably durable familial order. They often managed to keep ties between husbands and wives and parents and children alive even under the most difficult circumstances. They tried desperately to keep track of distant spouses, children, parents, and siblings and, whenever an opportunity seemed to arise, tried to unite with them. (Masters, in fact, first looked for runaways in the neighborhoods of the family members from which they had been separated.) And when emancipation finally did come after the Civil War, tens of thousands of slave couples, many of whom had been separated for years, came forward to have their informal slave marriages finally sanctified by law.

well beyond spouses and their children. It brought a vast array of real and fictive kin—people with no blood or marital ties who were still thought of as family—into the circle of mutual obligation and protection that slaves associated with the idea of a family. Although sale often separated immediate family members from one another, this broader family was remarkably durable and readily extended its care and protection to anyone who needed it. Many a slave child was reared by a grandmother, adult sister, or aunt, whether real or fictive. Many a brother or uncle guided boys with absent fathers safely along the path to adulthood.

This larger kin structure was almost totally unnoticed by the slaves' masters. In fact, only in the last few years have historians uncovered it and come to appreciate its importance. Similarly, whites often misinterpreted the quickness with which slaves often took a new spouse after separation from a husband or wife, regarding it as proof that slaves had weak family affections—and hence did not suffer as much from separation as whites would. But such practices could also be interpreted as a sign of the importance slaves attached to the family, of their deep reluctance to remain outside its benefits and protections. Most baffling to whites were the slaves' sexual mores. To the whites, monogamy and marital fidelity were inseparable from ideas of general sexual self-discipline and chastity, especially among "decent," Christian women. But the slaves seemed to combine premarital promiscuity and unashamed tolerance for premarital pregnancy with strict codes of marital fidelity. As one planter's wife wrote with some wonderment, "slave women have a chance that women have nowhere else. They can redeem themselves—the impropers can. They can marry decently, and nothing is remembered against them." What few whites could understand was that slaves valued families not as agencies for fostering the planter's brand of morality but for the human support and protection they provided.

SLAVE CULTURE

The slaves' most effective counter to their servitude was the community and culture they built around their family order. The slaves on the largest plantations in Southampton County had been least sympathetic to Nat Turner's appeal. Slaves on such plantations lived a highly communal existence. They worked in groups and spent most of the time when they were not working in various social and ceremonial gatherings. Most slaves lived in small huts or cabins placed in a single location usually referred to as the quarters, which many masters respected as the slaves' special domain. Here blacks developed a life and culture of their own. In the quarters, slaves found a protective and supportive community and developed a deep sense of solidarity and mutual obligation. It was in the quarters that slaves traded lore and information about how to cope with overseers and masters, learned what was going on at other plantations and in the outside world, and helped each other in times of trouble and sorrow. Most of all, the community of the quarters worked to maintain some autonomy, to preserve the space the slaves needed for their own culture.

Their culture gave many blacks a sense of hope and dignity that transcended their bondage. It drew on four main sources—survivals from the African past, customs and beliefs brought in by slaves imported from the Caribbean, tales developed under a century of slavery, and Protestant Christianity. Black culture was expressed in a number of oral and communal ways. The slaves' sorrow songs, work songs, and nonsense songs expressed the joys and trials of love, labor, and death. Mostly, however, slave culture expressed slaves' feelings about bondage, and their hopes for release from it. The slave tales told over and over around fires and in cabins were often both humorous and serious. Br'er Rabbit always used boastful cunning to outwit larger, more powerful animals. In the "John tales," the slave hero provided a coded commentary on the cruelty or the gullibility of masters.

SLAVE RELIGION

Religion was at the core of the slaves' culture. Slaves, like their masters, were Christians, but they practiced and professed their own brand of Christianity. The special nature of black religion did not lie in its "superstitions." Like Nat Turner, many blacks trusted signs and portents. But so did many white people. Black religion was different because, first, it was clandestine, and, second, it had a special message.

Slave religion has been called the "invisible institution" largely because slaves went to great lengths to keep it hidden from whites. In fact, slave religious ceremonies were often secret gatherings, carried out at night in hush harbors, off in the woods or swamps. Even when masters provided religious services, slaves usually held their own and did not dwell so much on the scriptural command that slaves obey their masters.

The slaves' Christianity was above all else a religion of deliverance: It had inspired Nat Turner to think himself chosen by God to release his people from bondage. It portrayed life as a pilgrimage through the travail and sorrow of this world to a triumphant new life in the heavenly kingdom. As the spiritual put it:

> And it won't be long, And it won't be long,
> And it won't be long, Poor sinner suffer here.
> We'll soon be free.
> The Lord will call us home.

Christ (who cared especially for the lowly, despised, and weak) and Moses (who led his people out of bondage into the Promised Land) were the two most important figures in the slaves' religion. Over and over, spirituals and preachers stressed the better day to come, the day when slaves would cross over to that "distant shore," where families would be reunited, and their trials would be over, and there would be no masters and slaves.

These were common Christian themes, but they had special meaning for the slaves. They fostered a continuing sense of hope and a promise of freedom. The Canaan the slaves sang of could be the promised land of heaven, but it could also be the promised land of freedom to the North:

> O Canaan, sweet Canaan!
> I am bound for the land of Canaan.
> I thought I heard them say
> There were lions in the way.
> I don't expect to stay
> Much longer here.
> Run to Jesus, shun the danger.
> I don't expect to stay
> Much longer here.

As slaves gathered to pray and sing, hear their preachers, and proclaim the joy of salvation, they could even experience a powerful sense of themselves as a special, chosen people. Their masters might own their bodies, but their souls belonged to the Lord. Though lowly slaves in this life, in God's eyes they were surely superior to the whites who kept them in bondage.

THE SOCIAL STRUCTURE OF THE SOUTH

More than two-thirds of the white families in the slaveholding states were not slaveholders at all. Moreover, all white southerners had many things in common with white northerners: They had a common history, voted in the same political parties, worshiped in the same denominations, read many of the same things in their books and newspapers, and did many of the same kinds of work. They also shared the same social and political values. Still, the South in the 1840s and 1850s was increasingly a slave society—"the peculiar institution" touched all other institutions and all people. So powerful, in fact, was the presence of the institution that by the 1850s most white southerners, whether they owned slaves or not, had begun to think of themselves as belonging to a society that was very different from that of the free states.

The antebellum South was a hierarchical society. At the top were the few thousand great planters who cultivated 1,000 or more acres and owned at least fifty slaves. Below them were the middling planters who farmed at least 350 acres and possessed ten or more slaves. Closely allied to these planters were merchants, manufacturers, and professionals, many of whom were sons of planters and some of whom owned plantations of their own. In 1850 there were about 6,000 great planters. There were another 35,000 planters with between twenty and fifty slaves, and approximately 75,000 more who owned between ten and twenty slaves. On the next social rung were the 275,000 whites who owned fewer than ten slaves; they were not really planters at all, but farmers. The overwhelming majority of southern whites owned no slaves and had little direct contact with the institution of slavery. Small-scale, independent farmers, they lived lives very similar to those of their counterparts in the North.

Beneath these property–owning classes were three other groups. The slaves, permanently fixed in bondage, were at the bottom of the social hierarchy. But there was also a second underclass, the poor whites. Contemptuously referred to as "white trash," "crackers," or "sand-hillers," these people lived degraded, disease-ridden lives, surviving largely by hunting and fishing, and often living as squatters on poor lands in the hills or pine barrens.

Finally, there were about 250,000 free blacks. A few had purchased their freedom, but most were descended from slaves who had been freed before southerners came to view slavery as a positive good. Though not slaves, the free blacks were only minimally free. They were confined to segregated neighborhoods, restricted in employment, denied most civil rights, and curtailed in their freedom to move about or assemble. White southerners feared and distrusted the free blacks; their very presence seemed to be a threat to the institution of slavery. By the 1840s many states had passed laws that either prohibited manumission altogether or required all newly freed slaves to leave the state. There were even attempts to reenslave some of the freed blacks.

The class system of the antebellum South was more fixed than the class system in the rest of the country. Some great planters were descended from the "older" gentry of colonial Virginia and South Carolina and thought of themselves as almost a hereditary aristocracy. (One element in the myth of the Old South was that the planters, unlike the New England Puritans, were descended from the nobles of seventeenth-century England.) In fact, the planter class was open to rapid invasion from below, especially in the cotton states of the Mississippi Valley. Most of the cotton lords of that region, in fact, were nouveaux riches who had risen from more obscure and ordinary ranks. They built grand manor houses and quickly adopted the manners and style of life of the "southern gentleman."

PLANTER RULE

Although the planter class constituted little more than 1 percent of the population of the South, it dominated southern politics and society far more than the merchant or manufacturing elites dominated northern society. An overwhelming majority of nonslaveholding whites readily accepted planter rule. There were several reasons for this. The planter class and its allies had the wealth and leisure to pursue politics. Southern culture still retained some of the older styles of deference, in which people of the lower orders deferred to the judgment and rule of their social "betters." Moreover, few nonslaveholding whites saw themselves as exploited or harmed by planter rule. In fact, there was little in planter rule that seemed to them to go against the interests of the small-scale independent farmer. Many actually looked to the planters to protect their interests for them. In addition, many small farmers aspired to the planter class. Like the "common man" in the rest of the country, they wanted to rise above their circum-

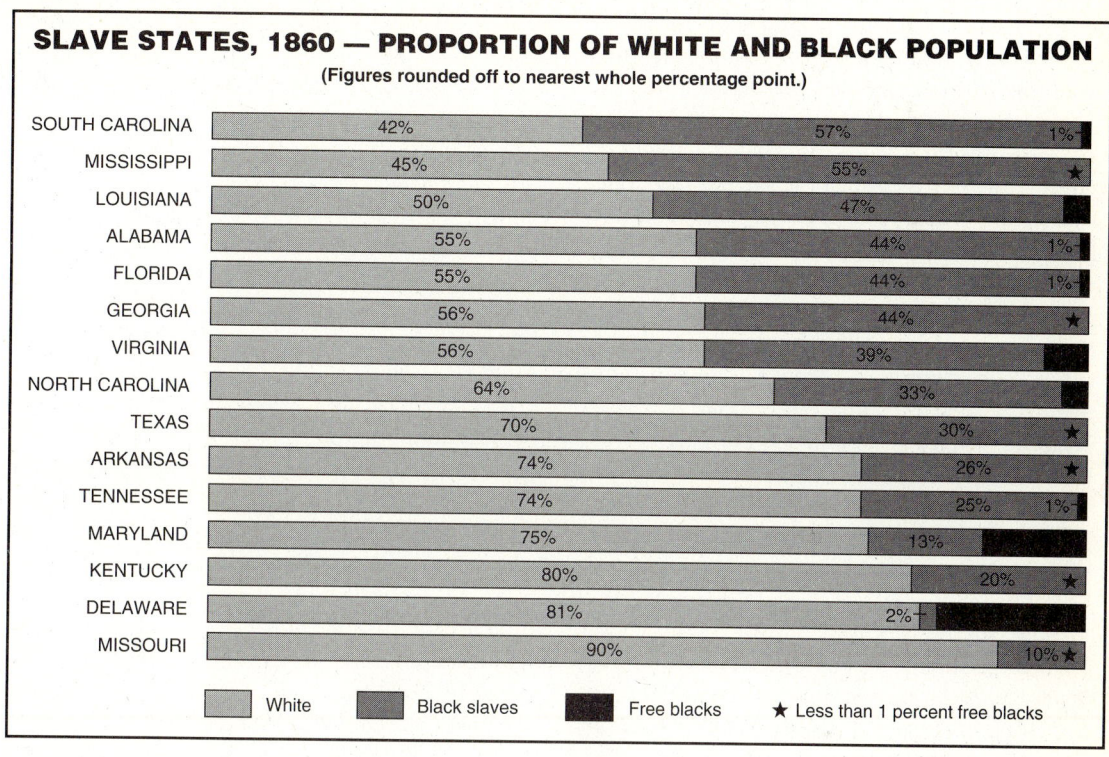

stances and often hoped to become slaveholders themselves.

Most nonslaveholding whites in the South were also firm supporters of the institution of slavery. To them, slavery was less a labor system than a system of race relations that gave them status and guaranteed them a sort of freedom. Slavery gave all whites, even the most lowly, social standing above the black slave. White racial solidarity seemed to cut across the social and economic gulf dividing planters and ordinary whites. All whites considered blacks to be an inferior race. As long as blacks were strictly tied to the lowliest forms of labor, even the poorest whites could believe themselves "free" and "independent," people whose lives and labor belonged to themselves. It was this belief, as much as anything else, that unleashed the fear and rage with which slaveholding and nonslaveholding whites alike had wrought their bloody revenge for Nat Turner's rebellion. The same belief, in 1861, would lead them to fight for southern "independence" and the preservation of the South's way of life, its slave society.

THE PROSLAVERY ARGUMENT

The heart of the old southern critique of slavery— the critique made by many of the leaders of the Revolution—had been economic: slavery was just not efficient or profitable. But this argument had been made by men whose objection to slavery was not so much economic as it was moral and philosophical. Now, after the 1830s, this situation was reversing itself. Slavery was profitable to most planters, much more profitable than it had been for the generation of Washington and Jefferson. And the arguments were turning the other way, too, toward the view that slavery was far from a moral evil; it was a positive good. The paradox was real, and has a somewhat bitter edge. In a generation of philosophical men and Founding Fathers, the principal argument was that slavery was not profitable. In a later generation, which profited more from slavery, the argument was that slavery was honorable.

The proslavery argument began to fall into place soon after Nat Turner's rebellion—and soon after the first publication of Garrison's *The Liberator*. In fact, one of the men responsible for the argument was John Floyd. After the failure of the antislavery movement in the Virginia legislature, Floyd became a convert to the opposite idea. He decided that slavery was not an evil after all, nor even a historically determined fate for the South. It was a positive good. Floyd persuaded Thomas Dew, a professor at the College of William and Mary, to write a systematic *Review of the Debate of the Virginia Legislature in 1831 and 1832*. In 1826, Thomas Cooper, the president of South Carolina College, had published a tract defending slavery. But Dew's treatise was the earliest full-dress rehearsal in America of the defense of slavery as a great human cause.

Dew argued that only slavery permitted high civilization. At their peak, Egypt, Israel, Greece, and Rome had all been slave societies. And they were great societies not in spite of slavery but because of it. Second, Dew argued that slavery was good for blacks. It rescued them from paganism, barbarism, and disease. It introduced them to a higher, Christian civilization. It took them from under cruel chieftains and placed them with benevolent masters. Finally, Dew claimed that slavery promoted democracy among whites. It brought all white men (he did not discuss women) as close to "one common level" as possible. Blacks performed all the "low and menial tasks," he said, and this removed from whites the usual causes of "the distinction of ranks of society."

As the grip of slavery tightened on southern society during the 1830s, 1840s, and 1850s, its defenders elaborated the themes and arguments Dew had made. They may have hoped to convince some northerners or Europeans, but they seemed most anxious to convince those who needed no convincing, the slaveholders themselves.

From the early 1830s on, abolitionists pictured slavery as an unbroken series of atrocities. The defenders of slavery knew they had to counter this portrait. So it was important to make the point that most masters were kind, and that those few who were not were repudiated by white society. But it became apparent that the proslavery argument needed more than this, and more than routine references to biblical justifications of the institution. Gradually, too, the defenders of slavery realized that it was increasingly difficult to promote slavery as long as the argument stayed within standard and simple democratic assumptions. Armed with these realizations, proslavery apologists had by the 1850s devised a thorough defense of "the peculiar institution." But they had done something else in the process. They had defined the South itself as a superior, unique, aristocratic, and potentially separable society.

Some writers challenged the notion of democratic equality and began to talk of their society as a special kind of aristocracy. Senator John C. Calhoun, for example, argued that liberty should not be considered a natural right that belonged to all men equally. Rather, he argued, it was a privilege that had to be deserved and earned. South Carolina planter and politician James Hammond argued that all great civilizations had to have a "mudsill"—a lower social order that did all the hard, menial, and unpleasant work.

The apologists for slavery insisted that the enslaved blacks were inferior to whites, that they were well suited to their status and to no other. Their racial arguments varied—some attributed the alleged inferiority of blacks to their African past; others argued that blacks were not variants of a common human species but a different species altogether. Whatever the particular form, these racist arguments all projected a stereotyped image of the slaves as a docile, happy-go-lucky people, loyal and affectionate, perfectly content to live a life free of all the anxieties that perplexed white adults.

This slave base, the argument ran, enabled the South to create an aristocratic civilization far finer than the aggressive, materialistic Yankee society of the North. Graciousness, nobility, and refinement of character, habits of command and leadership—these were the true fruits of slavery. If these traits of character were "peculiar to the Southern gentleman," D. R. Hundley, a southern planter and proslavery apologist, insisted, it was

> doubtless owing to his habitual use of authority from his earliest years; for while coarser natures are ever rendered more savage and brutal by being allowed the control of others, refined natures are perfected by the same means. Their sense of responsibility and its incident obligations teaches them first to control themselves before attempting to exact obedience from the inferior natures placed under their charge.

It was for this reason, Hundley alleged, that "the South has furnished us with all our great generals, from Washington to Scott, as well as most of our leading statesmen, from Jefferson to Calhoun."

The proslavery apologists also insisted that the slave society of the American South was more humane than the free societies of the United States and western Europe. George Fitzhugh, a Virginia lawyer, planter, and publicist, mounted this argument in its fullest form in two books, *Cannibals All: Or Slaves Without Masters* and *Sociology for the South: Or the Failure of Free Society*.

Fitzhugh portrayed free society as a war of all against all, in which the powerful few reduced the weaker masses to "wage slavery." In a so-called free society, factory owners exploited their workers thoroughly, robbing them of the fruits of their labor and then discarding them when they were disabled, sick, or too old to work. These masters, Fitzhugh and others argued, were free from any need to care for their wage slaves. Indeed, the economic laws of a free society demanded that workers be exploited as fully as possible. Thus the ordinary people of a free society were free only to slip into poverty and misery. But under slavery, the apologists argued, the situation was very different. The master's economic interest forced him to treat his slaves well. Slaves were valuable property and represented a large investment of capital. The slave had to be cared for and protected for the master to realize the best return on his investment.

The apologists for slavery did not rest their case for the well-being of the slave solely on the economic necessity and self-interest of the master. They argued that southern slavery fostered deep bonds between master and slave. They pictured the well-run plantation as a large, harmonious family, bound together by mutual affection. Paternalism was the glue, according to this argument, that held the plantation together as a human institution and gave it its humane and smiling face. The "good" planter cared for his slave "children" as any adult of noble, refined, and unselfish character cared for those who depended on him.

All the patriarch of the plantation required was obedience. This, the apologists insisted, the planter's grateful and loyal slaves were happy to give. The institution of slavery "gives full development and full play to the affections," Fitzhugh insisted, because "a state of dependence is the only condition in which the war of competition ceases and peace, amity, and good will arise." Indeed, he went on, the slaveholder's "whole life is spent in providing for the minutest wants of others, in taking care of them in sickness and in health. . . . Is not," he asked rhetorically, "the head of a large family almost always kind and benevolent? and is not the slave-holder the head of the largest family?"

THE IDEAL OF SOUTHERN WOMANHOOD

The plantation mistress figured as prominently as the master in the idealization of plantation culture. Southern apologists, no less than northerners, cherished the ideal of the pure woman in her "sacred sphere." "A Southern matron," one wrote, "is ever idolized by her dependents, and beloved by her children, to whom no word ever sounds half so sweet as mother and for whom no place possesses one half the charms of home." But as with so much else in southern life, slavery endowed the southern idea of pure womanhood with meanings it did not have in the North. Southerners also eulogized the planter's wife as an exquisite aristocrat. Distinguished by moral purity as well as by grace and beauty, she was seen as an ornament of her husband and her culture.

Of course, this image bore little resemblance to the lives most plantation wives actually led. They in fact were as essential to the smooth running of a plantation as their husbands. They tended the sick, taught the young, and oversaw the operations of a vast and complicated household. And when their husbands were away on business or politics, they often took over full management of the plantation and oversaw agricultural production as well. Still, even if the aristocratic ideal did not fully describe reality, it did serve to elevate the southern lady above her northern counterpart.

The southern ideal of true womanhood combined the ideas of sexual and racial purity. Northerners and southerners alike considered pure womanhood to be both the source and the symbol of morality and civilization. According to the ideology, the absence of sexual passion distinguished true womanhood. The true gentleman, in turn, worshiped this purity and held his own sexual drives in check. But in the South, race and servitude complicated the issue. Southern white men paid elaborate homage to the ideal of female purity. They envisioned the southern lady as the counter not only to male sexuality but to black sexuality as well. She was viewed as the direct opposite of the slave woman, who was looked upon as a sensual and lustful being whose passionate nature was simply one more mark of her inherent racial inferiority. While a gentleman was expected to discipline his passions when dealing with women of his own race and class, it was not necessary for him to exert the same control when it came to the slave women under his dominion. As one woman stated, "Violations of the moral law made mulattoes as common as blackberries." And another bitterly declared that "every woman is ready to tell you who is the father of all the mulatto children in everybody's household, but those in her own she seems to think drop from the clouds."

It was partly because of this fact that southerners held so firmly to the notion of white female purity. Indeed, it is one of the cruel ironies of the situation that while many white men had few reservations about sexual relations with black women, they punished, often brutally, any suspicion of similar relations between black men and white women. For these reasons, the ideal of pure womanhood did double duty in the South. It was the ultimate symbol of both the racial purity and the moral superiority of white southern culture. In her own nature and in her capacity to inspire the white men around her to true nobility and morality, the southern lady, it was argued, elevated southern culture to a high moral plane. And she stood as an equally powerful token of the superiority of white culture and the unbridgeable gulf between the masters and their slaves.

The South the proslavery apologists defended was, of course, a mythic creation. But for the planter class to which it was directed, it was a powerful myth. It gave the planter a welcome counter to the abolitionist portrait. It provided a

THE DAVIDSON FAMILY OF POYDRAS PLANTATION. The great planters of the antebellum South, like eighteenth-century gentry and the great merchants and manufacturers of the North, commissioned paintings that portrayed them as they most liked to think of themselves. This painting, centered on mother and children, represents the idealization of southern womanhood that was so integral a part of the planter class's portrait of itself as noble and aristocratic.

flattering image of himself as at once a noble aristocrat, a benevolent father to his slaves, and a masterful capitalist—a man who combined nobility of spirit with humanity and forcefulness of character. It presented an image of the slave that legitimized keeping blacks in bondage but also brought the slaves within the ideals of domesticity and family order that all of American society honored. Finally, it promoted an image of southern society that let slaveholders embrace slavery not as a matter of self-interest but as an act of benevolence. Slavery had become, oddly, the mainstay of a fine and superior civilization.

When John Floyd was changing his mind, deciding that slavery was a good thing after all, he confronted a special Virginia problem. There was such a deep sectional division between east and west that perhaps the best solution was simply to split the state. Floyd reported that on the last day of the 1832 debate, a legislator from a western county

> said to me that the eastern and western people were not all the same people, that they were essentially a different people, that they did not think alike, feel alike, and had no interests in common, that a separation of the state must ensue, and rather than have the subject of abolition again debated he would be glad for a separation. Both sides seem ready to separate the state if any one would propose it. I think that event from appearances highly probable.

The event, as it turned out, was highly probable. But not imminent. Only in the 1860s, in the midst of a civil war, did Virginia become two states.

But Floyd's logic was impeccable. The more certainly slavery fastened itself on the South—the more the South became slavery, instead of just containing it—the more likely it was that other people would agree that slave state and free state could not "think alike, feel alike." Half a lifetime after Nat Turner's death, not only Virginia but the union itself would become "a house divided."

CHRONOLOGY

1800	New Jersey begins gradual elimination of slavery, the last northern state to do so
1801	Probable birth of Nat Turner, slave to Benjamin Turner
1810s	The first American textile mills are constructed in New England;
	Nat Turner begins to have religious visions
1811	Benjamin Turner dies, his son Samuel inherits Nat Turner
Early 1820s	Nat Turner runs away, but returns voluntarily, he marries;
	Samuel Turner dies and Nat is sold to Thomas Moore
1820s	Nat Turner seen as possessing special spiritual gifts, preaches to both blacks and whites.
1822	Denmark Vesey "plot" for a slave uprising in South Carolina is discovered
1825	Nat Turner's first vision of racial violence
1828	Nat Turner has a vision that he has inherited the mission of Jesus Christ;
	Thomas Moore dies; Nat is sold to Joseph Travis;
	David Walker publishes his *Appeal*, calling for slaves to rise up and throw off their bondage
1830s	Cotton prices nearly triple between 1831 and 1836;
	Slavery becomes much more profitable for white planters
1831 (Jan.)	William Lloyd Garrison begins publication of *The Liberator*
1831 (Aug.)	Nat Turner's rebellion
(Nov. 19)	Turner executed
1831–32	Virginia legislature debates the abolition of slavery
1832	Virginia legislature rejects abolition, passes stringent legislation controlling slave behavior and making it a crime for slaves to preach or hold religious meetings;
	Thomas Dew publishes his *Review of the Debate of the Virginia Legislature of 1831 and 1832*, an extensive defense of slavery as a "positive good"
1830s and 1840s	Slavery expands rapidly into the lower South
1840s and 1850s	Southern leaders elaborate the ideal of southern womanhood as the mark of the superiority of southern civilization;
	Increase in runaway slaves
1845	Frederick Douglass publishes his *Narrative of the Life of Frederick Douglass, an American Slave*, the first "slave narrative"
1850s	The productivity of slave labor in the cotton economy is now almost eight times higher than it was in 1800;
	Southern intellectuals complete the construction of the defense of slavery as a positive good;
	Harriet Tubman, an escaped slave, conducts ninteen trips into the South to help nearly 300 slaves escape

SUGGESTIONS FOR FURTHER READING

NAT TURNER'S REBELLION

Thomas C. Parramore, *Southampton County, Virginia* (1978), contains a definitive and trustworthy account of the rebellion and its aftermath. An engaging book-length treatment is Stephen B. Oates, *The Fires of Jubilee: Nat Turner's Fiery Rebellion* (1975). An intense controversy over the event was set off by William Styron's 1967 novel, *The Confessions of Nat Turner*. The controversy can be followed in John Henrik Clarke, ed., *William Styron's Nat Turner: Ten Black Writers Respond* (1968), and John B. Duff and Peter M. Mitchell, eds., *The Nat Turner Rebellion: The Historical Event and the Modern Controversy* (1971). Henry Tragle has edited a fine collection of documents, including *Turner's Confession: The Southampton Slave Revolt of 1831* (1971).

SLAVERY

The classic traditional account of slavery from an explicitly racist, white southern point of view was U. B. Phillips, *American Negro Slavery* (1919). Kenneth Stampp, *The Peculiar Institution* (1956), is still well worth reading, as is Clement Eaton, *The Growth of Southern Civilization* (1961). Peter Kolchin, *American Slavery: 1619–1877* (1993) is a superb, readily accessible treatment of slavery that pays needed attention to slavery in the eighteenth century as well as comparing North American slavery to slavery elsewhere. The book also contains an extensive bibliography. Ira Berlin and Philip D. Morgan, eds., *Cultivation and Culture: Labor and the Shaping of Slave Life in the Americas* (1993) is a collection of important recent essays. Robert William Fogel and Stanley L. Engerman, *Time on the Cross: The Economics of American Negro Slavery* (1974), set off a commotion among scholars, which can be followed in Paul A. David, ed., *Reckoning with Slavery* (1976), and Herbert G. Gutman, *The Numbers Game: A Critique of Time on the Cross* (1975). Slavery in nonagricultural settings is the subject of Robert S. Starobin's fine *Industrial Slavery in the Old South* (1975). The starting point for the modern study of the psychological and social lives of slaves is Stanley Elkins, *Slavery: A Problem in American Institutional and Intellectual Life* (1959).

Elkins's argument was that American slavery, in its setting of market capitalism and a laissez-faire state, was much more brutal and total than the slave systems of Latin America. As a result, the system tended to break down the slaves' personalities and to make maturity, autonomy, and resistance difficult if not impossible to achieve. Among the more notable books that argue that there was a rich and dense social and cultural life among slaves are Eugene D. Genovese, *Roll, Jordan, Roll: The World the Slaves Made* (1974); Herbert G. Gutman, *The Black Family in Slavery and Freedom* (1976); Lawrence W. Levine, *Black Culture and Black Consciousness* (1977); Albert J. Raboteau, *Slave Religion* (1978); Vincent Harding, *There Is a River: The Black Struggle for Freedom in America* (1981); and John Blassingame, *The Slave Community: Plantation Life in the Ante-Bellum South* (1972). George P. Rawick, *From Sundown to Sunup: The Making of the Black Community* (1972), and Thomas L. Webber, *Deep Like Rivers: Education in the Slave Quarters* (1978), are very informative. The travail of free blacks, North and South, is the subject of Leon Litwack, *North of Slavery* (1961), and Ira Berlin, *Slaves Without Masters* (1974).

THE SOCIAL STRUCTURE OF THE SOUTH

Gavin Wright, *The Political Economy of the Cotton South* (1978), is the most challenging account of the economics of the southern system. Eugene Genovese, *The World the Slaveholders Made* (1964), is an important study of the slaveowning class. A different view of the plantation elite can be found in James Oakes, *The Ruling Race* (1982). William R. Taylor, *Cavalier and Yankee* (1961), is a superb analysis of the shaping of the plantation myth. The ways white southerners acted out the myth is the subject of Bertram Wyatt-Brown's *Southern Honor: Ethics and Behavior in the Old South* (1982). Ira Berlin, *Slaves Without Masters* (1974), and Frank L. Owsley, *Plain Folk of the Old South* (1949), deal with southerners who were neither slaves nor slaveholders. The role of women on the plantations is the subject of Catherine Clinton, *The Plantation Mistress: Woman's World in the Old South* (1983).

Chapter 12

Expansion and the Crisis of the Union

Episode: Uncle Tom's Cabin

SLAVERY, THE WEST, AND THE FATE OF THE REPUBLIC

"Manifest Destiny"

The Mexican War

Slavery and Expansion

The Resumption of Expansion

The Rise of the Republican Party

The Rush to Disunion

THE EPISODE: *The dramatic episode we have chosen for this chapter is not a type that historians usually have in mind when they talk about an event. It is a work of fiction, Harriet Beecher Stowe's novel* Uncle Tom's Cabin.

Nevertheless, an enormous number of Americans who lived through the 1850s and 1860s would have said that the publication of Uncle Tom's Cabin *was an event of enormous significance. During the Civil War, Stowe visited Abraham Lincoln in the White House, and he is supposed to have said that her book had been one of the causes of the war. Hundreds of thousands of other people would have agreed, saying that reading* Uncle Tom's Cabin *had changed their attitudes toward the great issue of slavery.*

This chapter examines the novel not just as a piece of literature, but as part of the history of the greatest crisis the union has endured. All of Stowe's most legendary characters are here—Uncle Tom himself, the beautiful and daring Eliza, the consummately cruel Simon Legree, the pathetically angelic Little Eva. But our purpose is not just to understand how Stowe's story worked as a novel. The historian's problem is to understand what it was about the book that caused so many people to read and reread it with such passion and to believe that a work of fiction might actually have changed the course of history.

THE HISTORICAL SETTING: *The astonishing popularity of* Uncle Tom's Cabin *was not caused by the contents of the book itself. It resulted from a deep change in the attitudes of white Americans, North and South, toward slavery. For many decades, most northerners had considered slavery to be a southern matter. They knew full well that it was a dangerous and potentially divisive matter. But for more than half a century—from the debates in the Constitutional Convention of 1787 to the early 1850s—political leaders had managed either to suppress the question of slavery or to find acceptable compromises when the question did reach the surface of politics.*

But in the 1850s an increasing number of northerners became determined to do something about slavery. If they could not eradicate it in the states where it already existed, then they would try to prevent it from spreading into the territories west of the Mississippi. And for an increasing number of people in the South, pushing slavery westward became a purpose so urgent that they would leave the union rather than give it up.

These changes in attitude set the stage for the explosive success of Uncle Tom's Cabin. *This chapter analyzes why millions of free Americans changed their minds about slavery, became convinced that the union could not remain half slave and half free, and were ready to risk cruel and bloody war to settle the issue. The grapes of wrath had been stored, the vintage made ready, and the terrible, swift sword waited not far ahead.*

Uncle Tom's Cabin

The two men were talking business when a beautiful young woman walked into the room. Conversation stopped; one of the men, a coarse-looking individual, looked her over. The woman blushed deeply as the coarse man's eyes moved quickly from her rich, silky hair and her darkly beautiful face to her delicate hands and shapely figure. Embarrassed and frightened, the young woman quickly left the room.

The business conversation resumed, but now it turned to the young woman. The coarse-looking man's interest in her was not sexual—it was economic. The woman, despite her light skin and European features, was an African-American slave, and the property of the other man in the room, a gentleman farmer in whose Kentucky home this conversation was taking place. And the coarse-looking man, Haley, was a slave trader. "By Jupiter, there's an article, now!" he exclaimed to the woman's owner. "Capital, sir—first chop! Come, how will you trade about the gal?—What shall I say for her? What'll you take?"

She is not to be sold, the owner answered. "I say no, and I mean no." Eliza Harris, the beautiful young woman whom Haley wanted to purchase, was the personal servant of the gentleman farmer's wife, and he explained that "she would not part with her for her weight in gold." In fact, he did not want to sell any of his slaves. He was a kindly man, and he had always treated them well. But he had succumbed to the lure of financial speculation; his investments had failed, and he was deeply in debt. His notes of indebtedness had fallen into the hands of the slave trader, and now he had no choice but to give in to Haley's demands. Already he had agreed to sell one of his best slaves, a strong middle-aged farmhand named Tom, right-hand man on the farm and a beloved figure. But now Haley insisted on adding another slave in order to satisfy the debt. And because the gentleman farmer would not part with his wife's beautiful servant, Eliza, Haley finally accepted a substitute: Eliza's five-year-old son. He realized the child would fetch a good sum from one of his regular customers, a man who "buys up handsome boys to raise for the market."

"I would rather not sell him," the gentleman farmer argued halfheartedly. "I'm a humane man, and I hate to take the boy from his mother." But Haley assured him that it was possible to avoid an unpleasant scene of separation. "These yer screechin' screamin' times are mighty unpleasant," he agreed, "but as I manages business, I generally avoids 'em, sir." The trick was simple—just "get the girl off for a day, or a week, or so. Then the thing's done quietly—all over before she comes home. These critters an't like white folks, you know; they gets over things, only manage right." The trader assumed a confidential air as he discussed his business techniques.

"Now, they say that this kind o' trade is hardening to the feelings; but I never found it so. Fact is, I never could do things up the way some fellers manage this business. I've seen 'em as would pull a woman's child out of her arms, and set him up to sell, and she screechin' like mad all the time. Very bad policy—damages the article—makes 'em quite unfit for service sometimes. . . . It's always best to do the humane thing, sir; that's been my experience."

So it was settled: Haley would take the farmhand Tom and Eliza Harris's little boy.

These two slaves could not have been more different. The boy looked just like his mother: His skin was almost white, and his silky hair hung in pretty curls around his dimpled face. The other slave, Tom, had glossy black skin, woolly hair, and African features. He was a large man, powerfully built and accustomed to manual labor. And he, too, was an exceptional slave: he was deeply religious, and completely trustworthy. He carried a pass that permitted him to travel freely. In fact, he had recently been entrusted to go by himself on a business trip to Cincinnati, a trip on which he carried home $500 in hard cash. Cincinnati was in the neighboring state of Ohio—a free state—and when Tom was offered the opportunity to remain there with the money and thus gain his own freedom, he had refused. "Master trusted me, and I couldn't" was his only explanation.

Tom cried when he learned he was to be sold and separated from his family. But once again, he refused to escape. "No, no," he sobbed,

"I an't going. If I must be sold, or all the people on the place . . . , why, let me be sold I s'pose I can b'ar it as well as any on 'em. Mas'r always found me on the spot—he always will. I have never broke trust and I never will."

But Eliza Harris, whose son was to be taken away, felt differently. She was determined to run off with her child before the boy's new owner could take him from her. Even pious Uncle Tom approved her decision. "It's her right!" he exclaimed. "T'aint in natur for her to stay."

Eliza scrawled a hasty note to her mistress:

O, Missis! dear Missis! don't think me ungrateful—don't think hard of me. I heard all you and master said tonight. I am going to try to save my boy—you will not blame me! God bless and reward you for your kindness!

And she was on her way. Before dark, the mother and child had walked all the way to the Ohio River—the border between Kentucky and free Ohio.

But as night approached, the two refugees were forced to pause at the edge of the river. There was no bridge, and even the ferry had canceled its usual run. It was late February, and the water was high and turbulent. Even worse, large cakes of ice were shifting to and fro in the water, forming a great, undulating raft that extended almost—but not quite—to the bank near where Eliza was waiting. The river surely could not be crossed.

The sky was almost dark when Eliza spotted a familiar man approaching. It was Haley, the slave trader. The most important moment in Eliza's life had come, and her reaction was quick and instinctive:

She caught her child, and sprang towards [the river bank]. The trader caught a full glimpse of her just as she was disappearing down the bank, and throwing himself from his horse, he was after her like a hound after a deer. In that dizzy moment her feet scarce seemed to touch the ground, and a moment brought her to the water's edge. Right on behind her [Haley] came; and, nerved with strength such as God gives only to the desperate, with one wild and flying leap, she vaulted sheer over the turbid current by the shore, on to the raft of ice beyond. It was a desperate leap—impossible to anything but madness and despair, and Haley instinctively cried as she did it.

The huge green fragment of ice on which she alighted pitched and creaked as her weight came on it, but she stayed there not a moment. With wild cries and desperate energy she leaped to another and still another cake—stumbling—leaping—slipping—springing upwards again! Her shoes are gone—her stockings cut from her feet—while blood marked every step; but she saw nothing, felt nothing, till dimly, as in a dream, she saw the Ohio side, and a man helping her up the bank.

Eliza was in Ohio now, on free soil. For the time being she was safe. The trader could not possibly follow her until the next day. In the meantime, a sympathetic man directed Eliza and her child to a nearby house. "Go there," he urged; "they're kind folks. That's no danger but they'll help you—they're up to all that sort o' thing." "The Lord bless you," Eliza answered. She picked up the little boy and walked rapidly toward the house—and freedom.

―――※―――

It was all fiction, of course—the first eight chapters of *Uncle Tom's Cabin,* a novel that was to outpace its author's modest expectations, both for its length and for its popularity. *Uncle Tom's Cabin* finally ran to forty-five chapters, appearing weekly in an antislavery magazine over a ten-month period between June 1851 and April 1852. Within three weeks of its publication in book form in March 1852, 20,000 copies were sold. The printer was desperately running three power presses around the clock, and he hired 100 bookbinders—all in a vain effort to keep up with the unexpected public demand. Within a year, more than 300,000 copies had been sold—an unprecedented figure for an American book. By the end of the decade, *Uncle Tom's Cabin* had been set to music and had been published in a special children's edition. Pictures of its characters and its scenes (including Eliza's escape across the ice) were sold in the form of lithographs, playing cards, and even on dishes and wallpaper.

But *Uncle Tom's Cabin* had a political impact as well as a literary and commercial one. In fact, its publication did as much as anything that happened during the 1850s to help reshape the political consciousness of the North. In 1850 most northerners thought of slavery merely as an unfortunate fact of life about the South. Ten years later, they had come to feel it to be an intolerable stain on the entire nation. And many of them looked back on their reading of *Uncle Tom's Cabin* as the event that had changed their feelings. When the author of the book visited Abraham Lincoln in the White House during the Civil War, he is said to have greeted her with the words, "So this is the little lady who made this big war."

The extraordinary literary success and political impact of *Uncle Tom's Cabin* took the "little lady" who wrote it as much by storm as it did the rest of the country. In 1851 Harriet Beecher Stowe was forty years old; she had published only a single, obscure volume of stories. And her earlier writings had not been about slavery, or any other controversial question. They had been entertaining pieces of New England local color,

THE BOOK THAT TOOK THE NATION BY STORM. The title page of an early edition of *Uncle Tom's Cabin*. The book was a huge and immediate success. Within a year of its publication, an unprecedented 300,000 copies had been sold.

based on the author's memories of her Connecticut girlhood. Stowe had never written about the South before. Indeed, except for a single one-day excursion into northern Kentucky sixteen years earlier, she had not even been in the South. It would have been hard to imagine a less likely author of *Uncle Tom's Cabin*.

Yet everything Stowe did in this novel, deliberately or otherwise, was exactly right. In a way, her lack of direct personal experience turned out to be a major asset. Because she had no firsthand knowledge of slave society, Stowe was free to spin the book out of her own fantasies. She covered these fantasies with a thin but highly effective veneer of literary realism. It was Stowe's good fortune, and a part of the political history of the 1850s, that these fantasies struck home for hundreds of thousands of other Americans.

Stowe's initial problem was to win the sympathy of her readers for the slaves. Most of the people who read *Uncle Tom's Cabin* were racist—even in the North, and even those people who found slavery itself to be distasteful. In fact, many northerners who were hostile to slavery were even more hostile to African Americans. One of their main objections to slavery was simply that it had brought blacks to America.

Many antislavery tracts had been published during the twenty years since William Lloyd Garrison had started *The Liberator* in 1831. These books were filled with impassioned arguments about the evils of slavery and with graphic pictures of its relentless brutality: slaves who were chained, whipped, sold, and killed. The innocent black slaves were portrayed as victims of vicious brutality. But they were faceless, anonymous creatures who were introduced only to be mistreated. In a perverse way, the fact that they were shown being brutalized even managed to confirm the stereotype that they were "brutes" to begin with. There was a large group of people in the United States ready to sympathize with the plight of "primitive" races in their attempt to resist exploitation by whites—that much had become clear twenty years earlier, in 1830, when many Americans had sided with the Cherokee Indians in their struggle against Andrew Jackson's removal policy. But these people had sympathized with the Cherokees not simply because they were being mistreated but because they appeared to be "civilized," to resemble middle-class white people in their appearance and manner. It was for this reason their fate could seem so tragic.

Uncle Tom's Cabin did the same thing for black people. While it showed that slaves were treated brutally, it also showed that they were not brutes to begin with. Eliza Harris was virtually white, and her manner of talking, and even of feeling, would have made her at home in any middle-class white household. Eliza was better bred and educated than her fellow slaves, more middle class than the uncouth white trader who purchased her son. And her decision to escape from the trader's clutches did not even stem from self-interest, but only from the desire to protect her child. Her single act of defiance was nothing more than an act of maternal love. It would have been difficult for even the most conservative readers of *Uncle Tom's Cabin* to withhold their sympathy from Eliza.

Stowe tried to evoke guilt as well as sympathy in her white readers by suggesting that the brutality of the slave system was caused not just by evil, brutal white men but by decent, good-hearted slaveowners as well. It would have been easy—too easy—for Stowe to portray the man who owned Eliza Harris as mean and unfeeling. But if she had done so, her readers would have found it equally easy to dismiss the scene from their own conscience. It is always possible to find excesses in any social system. To make Eliza's owner a decent, civilized, caring person, a man who would sell any of his slaves only reluctantly, and who did so for a reason that most northern whites could understand—in order to pay off a business debt—was a shrewd literary and political stroke.

Stowe drove the point home in a passage that directly addressed her humane readers:

> It is you considerate, humane men, that are responsible for all the brutality and outrage committed by these wretches; because, if it were not for your sanction and influence, the whole system could not keep foothold for an hour. If there were no planters except such as that one [a particularly brutal slaveowner], the whole thing would go down like a millstone. It is your respectability and humanity that licenses and protects his brutality.
>
> Are you educated and he ignorant? You high and he low? You refined and he coarse? You talented and he simple? In the day of a future Judgement, these very considerations may make it more tolerable for him than for you.

It was the slave system itself that was evil, not just its excesses. Nobody was free of moral responsibility for it, and the more personally "humane" an individual might be, the deeper his or her responsibility lay.

Many people in the North were prepared for such a message. The year before Harriet Beecher Stowe wrote *Uncle Tom's Cabin,* northerners had for the first time become clearly implicated in the overt protection of the slave system. In 1850 Congress had passed, and the president had signed, a highly controversial bill known as the Fugitive Slave Law, which made it a federal crime punishable by six months' imprisonment and a fine of $1,000 for anyone, even in a free state, to aid in the concealment or rescue of a slave who had escaped from bondage.

What the Fugitive Slave Law meant was that if a nonfictional Eliza Harris had managed to cross the river from Kentucky into the free state of Ohio, and had managed there to encounter a family that was sympathetic to her plight, it would have been a criminal offense if that family had failed to turn her over to the authorities for deportation back into slavery. In Chapter 9 of *Uncle Tom's Cabin,* Stowe dramatized just such a situation.

The house in which Eliza was about to take refuge proved to be the residence of a fictional member of the Ohio state legislature, a senator named John Bird. And as Stowe would have it, the state of Ohio had just that week passed a law that was the exact fictional equivalent of the federal Fugitive Slave Law. Senator Bird arrived home that very day and acknowledged to his horrified wife that he himself had actively supported passing the law. The senator patiently reminded his wife that he personally opposed the slave system, but it was necessary to put aside mere "private feeling" when there were "great public interests involved."

But Mrs. Bird refused to let her husband forget his private feelings. She asked him what he would do if a runaway slave were suddenly to appear at their doorstep. And she answered the question for him: "Oh, nonsense, John! You can talk all night, but you wouldn't do it. I put it to you, John—would you, now, turn away a poor, shivering, hungry creature from your door?"

At just this moment Eliza Harris appeared at the doorway. And, of course, Mrs. Bird was correct. Her politician-husband quickly melted, and within a few minutes he had put on his boots and was making plans to escort the two runaways to the house of a notorious local abolitionist, where they would be helped on their way to Canada. For all his theoretical intentions and hard-hearted political logic, the senator became a criminal—a criminal who broke the very law he had just helped to pass.

Stowe did not let the point go unnoticed. Just before Senator Bird left with the two fugitives, his wife put her hand on his and said, with tears in her eyes, "Your heart is better than your head, John. Could I have ever loved you, had I not known you better than you know yourself." Mrs. Bird's lesson to her husband was also the lesson that

HARRIET BEECHER STOWE. Harriet Beecher Stowe began *Uncle Tom's Cabin* in 1850, when she was thirty-eight. She had written little before this novel, only some stories based on her girlhood in Connecticut, but the passage of the Fugitive Slave Law in 1850 drove her into action.

Harriet Beecher Stowe was trying to teach her male readers: to trust their hearts—and their wives.

Stowe had carefully manipulated the situation to make it easy for Senator Bird (and for the readers of the novel) to sympathize with the two runaways. Eliza and her child looked and behaved exactly like "well-bred" white people. Stowe knew exactly what she was doing—what she had to do in order to force her readers to feel sympathies that many of them had never experienced toward any black person.

Eliza Harris had managed to escape to freedom. But it was not just her story, dramatic as it was, that gave the book its extraordinary impact. Stowe aroused that response by telling a very different story, about a very different slave. It was the story of Uncle Tom and the people around him that provided the novel with its title and with the material for all but three of its last thirty-five chapters. The character Uncle Tom did not resemble any actual African American enslaved in the United States. He was a literary fantasy, the fictional invention of a New England woman, a minister's daughter. Stowe wished to evoke the figure of a gentle, powerless black man who managed to retain his moral strength and integrity in the face of infinite provocation and pain, and whose terrible suffering and death brought redeeming solace, even love, to those around him. The story of his suffering and death was nothing less than a conscious retelling, set in the political context of the United States in 1850, of the biblical passion of Jesus of Nazareth.

Steaming down the Mississippi under the watchful eye of the slave trader who owned him, Tom one day glimpsed a beautiful little white girl. With her golden hair, her deep blue eyes, and her gentle expression, she seemed to him almost like one of the angels out of the New Testament that the young son of his former owner had often read to him. And she acted like an angel, too, giving away fruit and candy to the slaves in Haley's gang. Tom engaged the child in conversation, and she quickly took a liking to him. "Where are you going?" she asked, and he answered, "I am going to be sold to somebody. I don't know who." Then the child spoke eagerly: "My papa can buy you; and if he buys you, you will have good times. I mean to ask him this very day." And she did. When her father asked why she wanted Tom, the girl replied simply, "I want to make him happy."

And so Tom acquired a new home. For the next five years, he found himself living not on a brutal cotton plantation—not yet—but in a beautiful villa in New Orleans. His official job was to care for the family's riding horses. But the dirty work was performed by a lower servant under Tom's direction, and Tom himself wore a collared suit and shiny boots. Tom's actual function was simply to provide Eva St. Clare with friendly companionship. And he did have "good times."

Augustine St. Clare, the little girl's father, turned out to be an extraordinary man—a true aristocrat, wealthy, intelligent, and generous, and a complicated, tortured soul who detested slavery but felt powerless to change it. At the time St. Clare purchased Tom for his daughter, they were being accompanied on their trip down the Mississippi by a cousin from Vermont, a middle-aged spinster who was coming to New Orleans for an extended visit. Ophelia St. Clare—Miss Ophelia, as she was generally addressed—was a prim, smug woman who disdained slavery, and the South itself. She was quick to display her faith in Yankee superiority. For that reason, during Tom's first weeks in his new home, Augustine St. Clare found himself engaging in long arguments with his New England cousin.

To begin with, Augustine St. Clare detested slavery with a passion equal to that of any northern abolitionist:

> "Strip it of all its ornament, and what is it? Why, because my brother Quashy [any black person] is ignorant and weak, and I am intelligent and strong, therefore I may steal all he has, keep it, and give him only such and so many as suits my fancy. Whatever is too hard, too dirty, too disagreeable, for me, I may set Quashy to doing. Because I don't like work, Quashy shall work. Because the sun burns me, Quashy shall stay in the sun. Quashy shall earn the money, and I will spend it. Quashy shall lie down in every puddle, that I may walk over dry-shod. Quashy shall do my will, and not his, all the days of his mortal life, and have such chance of getting to heaven as I find convenient. This I take to be about what slavery is. I defy anybody on earth to make anything else of it. Talk of the abuses of slavery! Humbug! The thing itself is the essence of all abuses."

But St. Clare insisted, at the same time, that the condition of black people was not likely to improve even if they were emancipated. Such improvement would require ongoing time and effort, and the white people of the North—for all their theoretical disapproval of slavery—were just as racist in their feelings as the slaveowners themselves:

> "Suppose we should rise up tomorrow and emancipate, who would educate these millions, and teach them how to use their freedom? The fact is, we are much too lazy and impractical, ourselves, ever to give them much of an idea of that industry and energy which is nec-

essary to form them into men. They will have to go north, where labor is the fashion. And tell me, now, is there enough Christian philanthropy, among your Northern states, to bear with the process of their education and elevation? You send thousands of dollars to foreign missions; but could you endure to have the heathen sent into your towns, and villages, and give your time, and thoughts, and money, to raise them to a Christian standard? If we emancipate, are you willing to educate? How many families, in your town, would take in a Negro man and woman, teach them, bear with them, and seek to make them Christians?"

For that matter, St. Clare believed that free society, with its capitalist factories, treated its powerless people not much differently from the way southern society treated its slaves:

"We are in pretty good company, for all that. Look at the high and the low, all the world over, and it's the same story—the lower class used up, body, soul, and spirit, for the good of the upper. The planter is only doing, in another form, what the aristocracy and capitalists are doing by the lower classes: that is, appropriating them to their use and convenience."

In his bleaker moments, St. Clare even sounded like Karl Marx. He could hear "a muttering among the masses, the world over," and he predicted that, before too long, they would make an international revolution:

"I tell you, if there is anything that is revealed with the strength of a divine law in our times, it is that the masses are to rise, and the under class become the upper one."

One day St. Clare arrived home with an unexpected present for his Yankee cousin—an eight-year-old slave girl. The girl had previously been owned by a pair of drunken men who whipped her so often that both her back and her spirit had become hard and calloused. Her skin was black, her woolly hair formed into braids that stuck out in all directions, and her expression was shrewd and cunning. Her name was Topsy.

Ophelia did not like black people very much to begin with, and she reacted to Topsy with undisguised discomfort. "Augustine," she exclaimed, "what in the world have you brought that thing here for?" And St. Clare responded, with a whimsy that his cousin was not yet able to fathom:

"For you to educate. You're always preaching about educating, so I thought I would make you a present of a fresh-caught specimen, and let you try your hand on her. Try now, and give her a good orthodox New England bringing-up, and see what it'll make of her."

"I don't want her, I am sure. I have more to do with 'em now than I want to."

Finally, Ophelia agreed that it might be a good idea to convert this young heathen to civilized ways. First, she gave Topsy a bath and some new clothes. Then she began to interview the grinning child:

"How old are you, Topsy?"
"Dunno, Missis." [A grin]
"Who was your mother?"
"Never had one." [Another grin]

"Never had any mother? What do you mean? Where were you born?"

"Never was born. [Her face serious now] Never had no father nor mother, nor nothin'. I was raised by a speculator, with lots of others."

"Have you ever heard anything about God, Topsy?" [No response—just another broad grin]

"Do you know who made you?"

"Nobody, as I knows on. [A short, sharp laugh] I 'spect I grow'd. Don't think nobody never made me."

Undaunted, Ophelia began Topsy's "education" by instructing her in sewing and in reading, and the girl proved an adept student. But her behavior was another story. Topsy seemed unable to distinguish right from wrong, and truthfulness from lying. She stole things, and once, when Miss Ophelia caught her red-handed, Topsy simply denied her guilt. Then, when Miss Ophelia scolded her for denying the theft, Topsy promptly "confessed" a whole series of offenses—offenses that Miss Ophelia knew she could not possibly have committed. Nothing Topsy said could be believed. Miss Ophelia was flabbergasted:

"What in the world did you tell me you took those things for, Topsy?"

"Why, Missis said I must 'fess, and I couldn't think of nothin' else to 'fess."

Ophelia's rules for bringing up children simply had no effect. In desperation, she began to whip the little slave girl. But even the whippings had no effect. Topsy would scream and groan and beg for mercy. But half an hour later, she would be laughing about it to the other slave children.

Finally, Ophelia was ready to admit defeat. "I never saw such a child as this," she told St. Clare. "What is to be done with her?" And he replied, "You have stated a serious question; I wish you'd answer it. . . . You have talked a great deal about our responsibilities in educating, cousin. I really wanted you to try with one child, who is a specimen of thousands among us."

"It is your system makes such children," Ophelia protested. And St. Clare responded: "I know it; but they are made—they exist—and what is to be done with them?"

But there was reason for hope—and it was St. Clare's own daughter, Eva, who instinctively knew what was to be done. St. Clare may have treated his slaves with paternal benevolence, but Eva treated them as her equals, and with unselfconscious affection. Once, her father asked her whether she would prefer living in a place without slaves or "to have a houseful of servants, as we do." The child's answer was earnest and unhesitating—and it was surprising:

"Why, of course, our way is the pleasantest."

"Why so?"

"Why, it makes so many more round you to love, you know."

As it happened, it was with Topsy herself that Eva first demonstrated the extraordinary power of her unbounded love. Two years had passed, by now, and little had changed in the St. Clare household. Topsy was about eleven, and Miss Ophelia had still failed to make any real contact with her. One day St. Clare heard his Yankee cousin screaming at the girl for some petty offense. Then Miss Ophelia came in and lamented her inadequacy:

> "Augustine, I don't know what to do. I've taught and taught. I've talked till I'm tired. I've whipped her. I've punished her in every way I can think of. And she's still just what she was at first. I shall have to give her up."

Eva was in the room, listening. At just this point, she silently motioned for Topsy to follow her out of the room. The two children walked together into a secluded area nearby. Both Augustine and Ophelia followed, curious. The scene that unfolded was a revelation. Eva was speaking to Topsy with fervent intensity, and there were tears in her eyes as she spoke:

> "What does make you so bad, Topsy? Why don't you try and be good? Don't you love anybody, Topsy?"
>
> "Dunno nothing 'bout love. I loves candy and sich, that's all."
>
> "But, Topsy, if you'd only try to be good, you might—"
>
> "Couldn't never be nothin' but a nigger, if I was ever so good. If I could be skinned, and come out white, I'd try then."
>
> "But people can love you, if you are black, Topsy. Miss Ophelia would love you, if you were good."
>
> "No—she can't bear me, 'cause I'm a nigger! She'd soon have a toad touch her. There can't nobody love niggers, and niggers can't do nothin! I don't care!" [Beginning to whistle]

Here, Eva impulsively put her hand on Topsy's shoulder.

> "Oh, Topsy, poor child, I love you! I love you, because you haven't had any father, or mother, or friends—because you've been a poor, abused child! I love you, and I want you to be good. I wish you would try to be good, for my sake."

Suddenly, Topsy too began to weep; the tears rolled down her cheeks and fell, one by one, on Eva's hand. Then, overcome, she started to sob out loud. Finally, Topsy managed to speak, and her words were as new to her as her tears:

> "Oh, dear Miss Eva, dear Miss Eva! I will try, I will try—I never did care nothin' about it before."

As Ophelia observed this scene, she was honest enough with herself to recognize why Eva had managed to reach Topsy so easily while she herself had failed to do so in two years.

Eva had taught Ophelia a lesson—that love itself, sincerely felt and openly expressed, could accomplish in a moment what neither lectures nor punishments could achieve in years. And Eva's lesson about the power of love might be even more important than her father's earlier lesson about the uselessness of education. For it promised to yield an answer to the deeply disturbing question that St. Clare had posed to her (and to himself) two years earlier: "What is to be done?"

The answer went beyond love, to death—and redemption. The first to die was Eva. Her long, Christ-like death was the culmination and fulfillment of her love, and also a sacrificial testimony against the slave system and every other form of social organization that was based on power.

In the two years that had passed since Eva had defended slavery on the grounds that "it makes so many more round you to love," she had come to learn something about the dark reality of slavery. Protected though she was, she could not help overhearing stories about the brutalization of slaves in other households. These stories caused her to feel an emotional anguish that she experienced as real physical pain.

The illness that now stole upon Eva would probably have been diagnosed by a physician as consumption (tuberculosis). But Eva herself was convinced that it was caused by the pain of suffering slaves, pain that had sunk into her heart. She knew the Bible well, and she soon came to identify her own approaching death with the crucifixion of Jesus.

One day, Eva spoke seriously about her thoughts to the slave Tom, who remained her constant companion:

> "Uncle Tom, I can understand why Jesus wanted to die for us. . . . I've felt that I would be glad to die, if my dying could stop all this misery. I would die for them, Tom, if I could."

As her death approached, Eva's sense of its meaning became even clearer. A few weeks before she died, Eva completed her transformation from little girl to Christian evangelist. She had her long hair cut short. ("Come, shear the sheep!" she said.) She sent for all the slaves in the household to gather round her bedside. First, she told these "dear friends" how much she loved them all, and how much she wanted them to be happy. Then she presented each one in turn with a lock of her hair as a final token of her love. In a torrent of grief, the slaves fell to their knees, and wept, and kissed the little girl. The last to approach Eva for her gift was Topsy:

> "Oh, Miss Eva, I've been a bad girl—but won't you give me one, too?"
> "Yes, poor Topsy! To be sure, I will. There—every time you look at that, think that I love you, and wanted you to be a good girl!"

Eva's death, a few weeks later, completed Topsy's conversion. As the child's corpse lay in her bed on the day after her peaceful death, the black girl approached the lifeless body, then flung herself to the floor with a wild and doleful cry:

> "Oh, Miss Eva! Miss Eva! I wish I'se dead, too—I do! She said she loved me—she did! Oh, dear! Oh, dear! There ain't nobody left now—there ain't!"

But now it was Miss Ophelia who came forward to comfort Topsy. She helped the grieving child to her feet and led her gently out of the room. At last she was able to touch the black girl, and her eyes, too, were moist as she spoke.

"Topsy, you poor child, don't give up! I can love you, though I am not like that little dear child. I hope I've learnt something of the love of Christ from her. I can love you. I do. And I'll try to help you grow up a good Christian girl!"

It was Eva herself—the "little Evangelist"—who had saved Topsy, and, in death, she was now saving Ophelia as well. Eva had been infused first with the spirit of Jesus, and then with his power. There was a message that she conveyed to everyone who came in contact with her. Uncle Tom had spoken of it to Ophelia just a few hours before Eva's death:

"Miss Eva, she talks to me. The Lord, he sends his messenger in the soul. When that ar blessed child goes into the kingdom, they'll open the door so wide, we'll all get a look in at the glory."

Eva's mantle now passed to Tom, who closely resembled her in his piety, his patience, and his selfless, boundless love. It was to Tom that Augustine St. Clare turned in his sorrow, in part because Tom reminded him so much of his daughter. Once, he confided to his slave, "It seems to be given to children, and poor, honest fellows, like you, to see what we can't. How comes it? How do you know there's any Christ, Tom? You never saw the Lord."

Tom's response was quick and sure: "Felt him in my soul, Mas'r—feel him now!" And Tom went on to associate his faith with his own experience as a helpless slave, at the mercy of a social system that had separated him, perhaps permanently, from his own family:

"Oh, Mas'r, when I was sold away from my old woman and the children, I was jest a'most broke up. I felt as if there weren't nothin' left; and then the good Lord, he stood by me, and he says, 'Fear not, Tom'; and he brings light and joy into a poor feller's soul—makes all peace."

St. Clare was powerfully moved by Tom's words, and by the sincerity in his voice. And his response, so reminiscent of Topsy's earlier response to Eva, marked the beginning of his own redemption. St. Clare put his head on his slave's shoulder, grasped his hand, and said, "Tom, you love me."

It was true—Tom did love his master. But that did not mean he liked being a slave. So when St. Clare told Tom that he had promised the dying Eva that he would set him free, Tom reacted with such great joy that St. Clare was disturbed:

"You haven't had such bad times here, that you need to be in such raptures, Tom."

"No, no, Mas'r! 't ain't that—it's bein' a free man! That's what I'm joyin' for."

But it was not to be. One evening, while trying to break up a fight between two drunken men, St. Clare was accidentally stabbed, and he died soon after being carried back to his house. Two weeks later, Tom was taken to a slave warehouse in New Orleans and held there with other slaves for sale at auction. In the days before the auction took place, potential buyers were free to walk in and examine the available merchandise. It was now that Tom first saw the awful man who would be his next—his last—owner. The man was shabbily dressed, short but brutally muscular. His expression was coarse, his neck was thick, and his head was shaped almost like a bullet. His hands were heavy and dirty. As he elbowed his way through the warehouse, the man briefly paused in front of an attractive teenage mulatto girl who was standing next to her mother. He put out his dirty hand toward her, and passed it roughly over her arm, her neck, and her bosom. Then, as the girl began to cry, he pushed her away and moved on. The next slave to catch his eye was Tom himself. The man grabbed Tom by the jaw and pulled open his mouth in order to inspect his teeth, rolled up Tom's sleeve to examine his muscles, and finally made him jump up and down to demonstrate his physical condition. A little later, when the auction began, both Tom and the mulatto girl were purchased by the bullet-headed man—the one for labor, the other for sex.

Tom's new master was Simon Legree, the owner of a cotton plantation along the Red River in Texas, just west of the Louisiana border, and it was there that Legree now headed with his new property. As the steamboat made its way up the muddy river, Simon Legree engaged in a systematic effort to break Tom's spirit. He put his new slave in handcuffs. He took away all the possessions Tom had acquired over the years, including his hymn book and his extra clothing. ("One suit has to do for one year on my place," he announced.) Then he told Tom to look him in the eye and proceeded to deliver a well-planned speech of introduction:

> "Now, d'ye see this fist? Heft it! [bringing his fist down on Tom's hand] Look at these yer bones! Well, I tell ye, this yer fist has got as hard as iron knocking down niggers! I never see the nigger, yet, I couldn't bring down with one crack. . . . I don't show no mercy!"

For the first time in his life, Tom found himself working in the cotton fields. The Legree plantation had once been an elegant estate, but it had become run-down and shabby under Legree's ownership. The slave quarters were crowded, dirty, and devoid of furnishings. Dogs and horses roamed the grounds at will; the lawn had grown up in weeds, and several of the windows in the main house had been shattered or boarded up. Legree even used the wallpaper in his living room to record his financial records with chalk. It was characteristic of the man to do this—for Simon Legree regarded his plantation only as an instrument to make money. He acted more like the common stereotype of a Yankee capitalist than a southern gentleman. In fact, Legree actually was a Yankee—he had been born and raised in New England. And he regarded his slaves as temporary investments, who were to be worked to death and then replaced with new ones. Legree was quick to acknowledge that his plantation, Tom's new home, was literally a death camp: "I don't go for savin' niggers. Use up, and buy more, 's my way—gives you less trouble, and I'm quite sure it comes cheaper in the end."

Tom worked hard and without complaint, and at the end of a day his basket was always filled with the required amount of cotton. Legree never had cause to criticize Tom's productivity or his obedience. But Legree wanted something else, too. He wanted to control Tom's soul as well as his body—to destroy his spirit and turn him into a selfish brute like the other slaves on the plantation, and like Legree himself. But Tom was not willing to surrender his humanity, for he knew it was his only remaining source of freedom. The real struggle between Tom and Simon Legree was therefore a spiritual one. In this struggle Tom fought long and hard—and, at the end, with success.

One day, working in the fields, Tom came to the aid of a woman whose strength had failed her. He silently removed all the cotton from his sack and transferred it to the woman's so that she would be able to return from the fields with her daily quota. Legree learned that Tom had given away his cotton to help a fellow slave. He could have confronted Tom with his act of generosity and punished him for it. But Legree's plan was more diabolical than that. Instead, he angrily pretended that the woman Tom had assisted was still short of her quota, and he promised to have her whipped for her laziness. Then he called Tom over and, offering to "promote" him to a higher position on the plantation, demanded that he be the one to administer the whipping. Tom refused—politely but firmly: "I beg Mas'r's pardon; hopes Mas'r won't set me at that. It's what I ain't used to—never did—and can't do, no way possible."

In a real rage this time, Legree struck Tom across the face with a strap, and went on to pummel him with his massive fists:

"There! Now will ye tell me ye can't do it?"

"Yes, mas'r. I'm willin' to work night and day, and work while there's life and breath in me. But this yer thing I can't feel it right to do; and, Mas'r, I never shall do it—never! Mas'r, if you mean to kill me, kill me. But as to raising my hand agin anyone here, I never shall—I'll die first!"

Legree now realized for the first time that he was faced with a powerful adversary. He began to ridicule Tom:

"Well, here's a pious dog, at last, set down among us sinners!—a saint, a gentleman, and no less, to talk to us sinners about our sins! Powerful holy crittur he must be!"

And then he started to debate with Tom about a slave's moral obligations to his master:

"Here, you rascal—didn't you never hear, out of yer Bible, 'Servants, obey your masters?' Ain't I yer master? Didn't I pay down twelve hundred dollars, cash, for all there is inside yer old cussed black shell? Ain't yer mine, now, body and soul? Tell me!"

But this question only filled Tom's heart with a sudden gleam of triumphant joy. And as the tears and the blood flowed together down his face, Tom raised his eyes and defiantly proclaimed his independence:

"No! No! No! My soul ain't yours, Mas'r! You haven't bought it—ye can't buy it! It's been bought and paid for, by one that is able to keep it."

For the time being, Legree had failed. With a sneer, he now ordered his two black slave overseers to take Tom to the junk room of the building that housed the plantation's cotton gin. There, in the depths of Legree's earthly hell, amid damaged cotton and broken machinery, the two overseers gave Tom the first flogging of his life.

STOWE'S BEST-SELLER. Nobody expected *Uncle Tom's Cabin* to be very widely read or sold. As Harriet Beecher Stowe wrote the year after its publication, "Having been poor all my life and expecting to be poor the rest of it, the idea of making money by a book which I wrote just because I could not help it, never occurred to me. It was therefore an agreeable surprise to receive $10,000 as the first fruits of three months' sale." The advertisement shown here refers to an edition published for German-speaking immigrants to the United States.

But Tom's crisis was just beginning. In the coming days, as he recovered from his whipping and returned to work in the fields, Tom began to give way to despair. For the first time, even the Bible seemed to lose its power to restore his spirit. One evening, as Tom sat alone and dejected by a small fire, Simon Legree approached him and made one final effort to conquer the soul of his slave:

> "Well, old boy, you find your religion don't work, it seems! I thought I should get that through your wool at last. You were a fool, for I meant to do well with you, when I bought you. You might have had easy times; and instead of getting cut up and thrashed every day or two, ye might have had liberty to lord it round, and cut up the other niggers; and ye might have had, now and then, a good warming of whiskey punch. Come, Tom, don't you think you'd better be reasonable? Heave that 'ar old pack of trash in the fire [pointing to Tom's Bible], and join my church!"

Tom continued to sit in silence. It was the heaviest moment in his life. After Legree had left, Tom sat for endless moments, gazing vacantly into the fire, like a man in shock. Then, suddenly, he saw a vision of the face of Jesus, crowned with thorns, buffeted and bleeding. Gradually, the vision changed: The sharp thorns became rays of glory, shining out from the head, and Tom heard a calm voice assuring him that he, too, would finally overcome. When Tom came to his senses, the fire had gone out, and he was painfully cold—but his spirit had been restored.

From that moment on, Tom knew only peace. The sorrows of his life seemed to be over, and his misfortunes were no longer able to hurt him. Even Legree realized that his power over his slave was totally gone, and that Tom was a free man. ("I hate him! I hate him!" Legree began to mutter to himself.) Tom now devoted all his energy to assisting his fellow slaves in their work, and comforting them in their distress. At first, most of them were incapable of responding to Tom's benevolence—it was so unfamiliar in their experience. But after months of persistence, Tom's efforts began to take hold. Gradually, this silent, patient man—a man who was ready to bear everyone's burden but who sought help from nobody—began to exercise a strange power. Like Eva St. Clare before him, Tom began to awaken the long-suppressed humanity in the brutalized people around him.

And like Eva, Tom began to look forward to death—not at the hands of disease, but at those of Simon Legree.

His opportunity soon arrived. One day, two of Legree's female slaves escaped from the hellish plantation. They had invited Tom to join them, but he refused—just as he had refused years earlier to escape with Eliza Harris from his old owner in Kentucky. As badly as Legree wanted to recapture the pair, he wanted even more to take his revenge against Tom, who was known to be a confidant of the two fugitives. It was with both these purposes in mind that Legree ordered his overseers to bring Tom to the main house:

"Well, Tom, do you know I've made up my mind to KILL YOU?"

"It's very likely, Mas'r."

I have done—just—that—thing, Tom, unless you'll tell me what you know about these yer gals! . . . D'ye hear? Speak!"

"I han't got nothing to tell, Mas'r."

"Do you dare to tell me ye don't know?"

"I know, Mas'r; but I can't tell anything. I can die!"

Tom was a strong man, and it took him two full days to die from the savage whipping he now received. On the second day, he received an extraordinary visit from a young white man whom Tom had known and loved years earlier, the son of his old owner in Kentucky—the gentleman farmer who had reluctantly sold him away to pay his debts. The farmer's son had remembered Tom with affection and loyalty, and over the intervening years he had managed to raise the money to buy Tom back and return him to the old farm in Kentucky—where, even now, Tom's wife and children continued to live. After a long search, the young man had succeeded in finding Tom. He arrived at the Legree plantation to arrange the purchase in the final minutes of Tom's life, just in time to allow him to die in the company of a friend.

Tom's death thus became an occasion of reunion—a symbolic return to his earthly home as well as his heavenly one. His last words were a message of farewell to his wife and family, and then to everyone he had known in earlier, happier times:

"Tell 'em all to follow me—follow me! Give my love to Mas'r, and everybody in the place! Ye don't know! 'Pears like I loves 'em all! I loves every creatur' everywhar! It's nothing but love! Oh, Mas'r George, what a thing 'tis to be a Christian!"

Simon Legree was standing nearby as Tom died. The young visitor from Kentucky asked Legree to sell him Tom's body so that it might be returned to Kentucky for burial. "I don't sell dead niggers," Legree snapped back. He had lost Tom's soul, and now he let his body go for free.

Slavery, the West, and the Fate of the Republic

When Harriet Stowe wrote *Uncle Tom's Cabin*, the issue of slavery had already been plaguing her family for many years. In 1832, the family had joined countless other people in the migration to the West. Her father Lyman Beecher was one of New England's most famous ministers. At the invitation of the wealthy abolitionist who had bailed William Lloyd Garrison out of jail in 1831, Beecher had decided to move from Boston to Cincinnati, Ohio, to become the head of a new college, Lane Theological Seminary. He took along his large clan and his future son-in-law Calvin Stowe, who was to become a teacher at Lane. Beecher planned to use his new position to spearhead a vast campaign to "evangelize the nation."

What Beecher did not anticipate was the way the slavery question was going to impose itself on him, his family, and many other evangelical Protestants. Almost as soon as he took over the theological seminary, one of the students, thirty-four-year-old Theodore Weld, began to preach against slavery. He recruited some of his fellow students to spend time in the African-American community of Cincinnati, teaching and preaching to the free blacks who lived in the city's impoverished neighborhoods. Distressed at this development, Lane Theological Seminary's governing board voted to expel Weld and his group. Lyman Beecher and Calvin Stowe supported the decision.

The problem, from Beecher's point of view, was that Arthur Tappan, one of Lane's wealthiest benefactors, supported Weld in the controversy and withdrew his support from the seminary. This meant hard times for the Beecher family. And when Harriet Beecher married Calvin Stowe in 1836, it meant hard times for them too. The next fourteen years were difficult, for Harriet Beecher Stowe wanted to write stories—not about slavery yet, but sentimental tales with a religious message. But she had seven children during the next fourteen years, and began to think of herself as "a mere drudge with few ideas beyond babies and housekeeping." She was able to publish a collection of short stories in 1841 about life in traditional New England. Then, from 1841 to 1850, she published nothing.

Lyman Beecher's initial theory was that the task of evangelicalism was to save the nation's soul. Perhaps after that task was completed, he thought, slavery would go away. In the meantime, he thought, abolitionism was a distraction from God's work. But slavery would not leave the Beechers and the Stowes alone. Harriet's sister Catherine Beecher got involved in a public quarrel about whether women should speak in public about slavery (she thought not). The 1837

THE BEECHER FAMILY. Lyman Beecher is surrounded by his extensive family. On his right is Catherine Beecher, the author of the *Treatise on Domestic Economy*. Harriet Beecher Stowe is at the right end of the row of women. Henry Ward Beecher, who became an outspoken critic of slavery, is standing at the far right. He is the only man in the picture who has not given in to the new craze for beards that began just before the Civil War. Everyone in the picture follows the prevailing fashion of the day, which was not to smile for the camera.

murder of an abolitionist editor, Elijah Lovejoy, by a mob in Alton, Illinois, moved one of Harriet's brothers, Edward, to condemn slavery publicly. By the mid-1840s, both her father and husband had begun to attack slavery from the pulpit.

Harriet Beecher Stowe was being pulled in contradictory directions. She dreamed of being a writer and thought that as a woman she had special moral insights that could find legitimate expression in literature. But there was her family to care for and a sense that the condemnation of slavery was the proper business of men, anyway. Then came an event that seemed so monstrous

that it appeared to *demand* that she find the time to write. As part of the Compromise of 1850, a federal law was enacted making it a crime for any citizen of a free state to assist runaway slaves, and requiring federal marshals to help catch them and return them to slavery. Writing against a law like this was not just a diversion from family life. It became, suddenly, as solemn and significant as motherhood itself.

The ways slavery altered the lives of the Beechers and the Stowes were a microversion of the national history. For most whites in the North and the South, slavery as a political question was something to be avoided if possible. But the question kept threatening not only to break to the surface of politics, but to become the central question of American political life. It had surfaced in 1819–1820 in the controversy over the admission of Missouri to the Union. During the 1820s and 1830s, most politicians had done everything they could to keep slavery out of public debates. But as more and more people moved west and new states had to be admitted to the Union, the question whether they were to be slave or free became more and more urgent. The astonishing public success of *Uncle Tom's Cabin* was further proof of how salient the problem of slavery had become in the minds of Stowe's overwhelmingly white, middle-class audience. Westward expansion and slavery became so inextricably linked that the nation was hastening to disunion and civil war.

"MANIFEST DESTINY"

As Whigs and Democrats squared off for the elections of 1844, expansion was on most people's minds. From every section of the country the clamor rose for the United States to push its boundaries westward to the Pacific Ocean.

Ever since the Louisiana Purchase, Americans had looked longingly at the northern territories of Mexico. Americans also turned their sights to Oregon, the far northwest territory that Britain and the United States both claimed and jointly controlled. Missionaries and promoters who had gone there sent back enticing descriptions of the richness of the soil and the wonders of the climate. Their reports were reprinted in newspapers all over the country, and Americans suddenly found themselves in the grip of "Oregon fever"—thousands set out for that territory. Similarly, many began to succumb to "California fever."

Many Americans had long dreamed of an American republic stretching from the Atlantic to the Pacific. But as the election of 1844 approached, the call to expand American dominion intensified, propelled by a powerful ideology of expansion that was captured in the phrase "Manifest Destiny." Ever since the Revolution, orators and writers had proclaimed that America was providentially chosen to spread the light of liberty over a despotic globe. But it was no longer enough to be an example. As John L. O'Sullivan, a leading Democratic editor, put it when he coined the phrase:

> [It is] the right of our manifest destiny to overspread and to possess the whole of the continent which Providence has given us for the development of the great experiment of liberty and federative self government entrusted to us.

It has been argued—rightly—that Manifest Destiny was a rationale for imperialism. It certainly was not the first time European Americans had used an idea of their own moral superiority to justify taking other people's lands. But expansion also kept open the promise of an inexhaustible fund of available new land. This was as much a psychological as an economic asset. America, as the Whig publicist Calvin Colton put it, was "a country of self-made men," constantly striving for "self-improvement" and "success." The "race of life," as Abraham Lincoln referred to it, carried a heavy burden of anxiety. People had to strive constantly, never knowing when they had arrived, in constant fear—especially after the depression of 1837—that they would fail and have to start all over again.

Americans were a peculiarly pastless people. Their sense of a special national history and heritage did not look back but pointed ever onward. Mired in the anxieties and hardships of day-to-day life in the present, many people constructed dreams of how much better things would be in the future. Physically, the West represented land; psychologically, it provided the geography of the imagination. So long as there was "virgin land" open to the hardy and the enterprising—in American values, the morally deserving—the future remained bright, and fulfillment possible.

THE MEXICAN WAR

What Americans call the Mexican War was actually the final armed struggle in a sequence of conflicts lasting more than a decade. The first phase was the war of Texas independence, which took place in 1835–1836. Then, in 1841, a second, brief war was fought between the Republic of Texas and Mexico as a result of Texan efforts to occupy even more Mexican territory. The third and final phase was a declared war between the United States (now including Texas as a state) and Mexico in 1846–1847. This long sequence of wars would be a dominant issue in American political life during the 1840s. The wars' outcomes would pose the fateful issue of the politics of the 1850s. The final act in the drama would be the American Civil War, but some of its origins lay in another, older struggle—the revolution that brought Mexico independence from Spain.

MEXICAN INDEPENDENCE

In August of 1821, a twenty-five-year-old Virginian named Stephen Austin was making his way toward San Antonio, the capital of the Mexican province of Tejas. He was going to try to persuade the Spanish governor of the province to allow him to inherit a Spanish land grant made to his father. At dawn on a Sunday morning, a group of Tejanos rode into Austin's camp, shouting "Viva Independencia!" Austin and the little group of Americans who were with him took up the shout. Mexico had gained independence from Spain and had become a republic. After Austin reached San Antonio, the governor confirmed the land grant. A process had begun that would bring thousands of American immigrants into Mexico and make it one of the main focuses of the expansive ambitions of Manifest Destiny.

The Mexican struggle for independence had been a very difficult and bloody ten-year revolution against Spain. During the revolution, the people of the northern province of Tejas had suffered even more than most Mexican people. At the time of independence, the Hispanic population of Tejas was only about one-third of what it had been a decade earlier.

Tejas was a problem for the government in Mexico City. The loyalty of the Tejanos was uncertain; the government even tried to forbid them to carry weapons. The government was having difficulty pacifying the Native American tribes in the area. And, to make matters worse, there were already about 3,000 Anglo-Americans living in Tejas, most of them illegal aliens, "wetbacks" who had crossed the Sabine or the Red River without permission. Many of them were outlaws or frontier ruffians, far outnumbering the tiny force of 200 men the Mexican government had in Tejas.

To try to deal with this impossible situation, the Mexican government decided to legalize what it could not prevent. The result was the Colonization Law of 1825. It permitted unrestricted immigration from the United States or Europe into both Tejas and the province just south of the Rio Grande, Coahuila. The law guaranteed immigrants' land titles and constitutional rights and even exempted them from taxes for four years. It worked all too well. By 1830, there were 7,000 Anglo-Americans in Tejas, and still only about 3,000 Mexicanos. In 1830, an anxious Mexican government repealed the Colonization Law, not only outlawing immigration from the United States but expressly forbidding anyone to bring slaves into Tejas. But the government could not enforce the law, and in 1834 immigration was made legal again. By this time, there were about 20,000 *norteamericanos* in Tejas, and they were coming across the border at the rate of a thousand a month.

There were also certain compatibilities between Mexico and the United States that encouraged Anglo-American migration into both Tejas and Alta California. Mexico was not only a republic, but, like the United States, it had adopted a federal system. Its constitution contained many of the same guarantees of liberty that were in the United States Constitution. Perhaps more important, most members of the governing Mexican elite had the same brutally racist and genocidal attitudes toward Native Americans as had many white people in the United States. In fact, the initial victims of Mexican independence were the Native American peoples of California, for a situation soon developed that bore considerable resemblance to the fate of the Civilized Tribes of the American Southeast during the period of Cherokee removal.

Many Native Americans in California had adapted to a mission system created by members of the Franciscan order with the backing of the Spanish government. In 1834, Mexican citizens anxious for land persuaded their government to shut down the missions and expel the Franciscans. A small fraction of the mission lands that the Native Americans had farmed were granted to the mission Indians. But most of their lands were soon lost to confidence men. The remainder of the mission lands and large cattle herds were granted to Hispanic *rancheros*. Soon about 800 families owned much of the best land in California.

Many of the mission Indians remained behind to labor for the *rancheros* as they had labored for the friars. But their conditions of life worsened drastically. Their death rate was twice that of slaves in the southern part of the United States—so high that California's Native American population would drop by 20 percent in less than fifteen years. The story was as old as the story of the European conquest of North America. The hunger for land overrode the ancient injunctions against killing and coveting. And Anglo-Americans were as land-hungry as any Spanish Americans, as events in Tejas were about to prove.

TEXAN INDEPENDENCE

After Mexico's revolution, the administrations of both John Quincy Adams and Andrew Jackson tried to buy Tejas from Mexico. But the sums they offered were pitifully small. Henry Clay even argued that Mexico ought to give away all its vast northern territory, from the Rio Grande to the Pacific, so that the capital city of Mexico would be more centrally located!

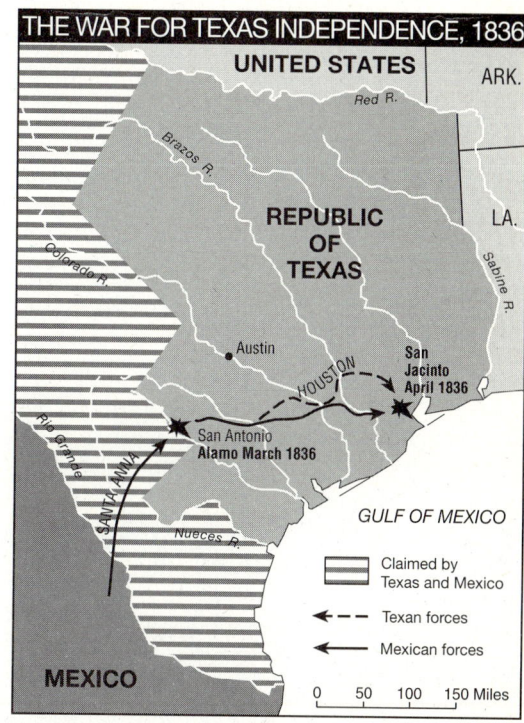

Meanwhile, the immigrants from the United States were becoming increasingly problematic for Mexican authorities. The Colonization Law required them to accept Catholicism, but they spurned the law. They smuggled goods from the United States, evading Mexican tariffs. In 1829, Mexico formally abolished slavery, but the *norteamericanos* kept the slaves they had brought with them to work their cotton plantations. In 1832, when the commander of the garrison at Galveston arrested a group of Anglo-Americans for a petty crime, a major riot resulted.

In such tense situations, the most trivial incident—even a practical joke—can set off a major historical event. In 1835, an Anglo-American in Galveston packed a container with sawdust, marked it "for export," and presented it to a Mexican customs official for inspection. The customs inspector's pride was challenged, and he tried to arrest the man. An angry mob gathered and troops were summoned. Soon Anglo-Americans all over what they named Texas had risen in open rebellion, declaring themselves an independent nation. They were joined by substantial numbers of Hispanic Tejanos.

The Texas revolution was the result of a number of things. One was racism, a deep conviction on the part of most Anglo-Americans that the Mexicans of Spanish and Spanish–Native American descent were inferior people not fit to govern. Another was a different kind of racism, which made the Texas rebels defend slavery against Mexican attempts to abolish it. A third was a demand for "liberty" from the rule of the man who in 1834 had made himself practically the dictator of Mexico, General Antonio López de Santa Anna. Santa Anna had abolished the federal system, threatening the states' rights convictions of many Mexicans and all the Anglo-American immigrants.

By fall, Texan revolutionary forces had taken San Antonio, in the process capturing most of the Mexican troops in Texas. The next spring, a revolutionary convention issued a declaration of independence and a constitution for the Republic of Texas. A few days later, Santa Anna reached San Antonio at the head of an army of somewhere between 4,000 and 7,000 men, determined to put down the rebels and restore Mexican control. The rebel commander, Sam Houston, took his little army out of the city. But a group of about 150 men decided to mount a suicidal defense. They were led by William Travis, a passionate, proslavery southerner. The force included a number of Mexicanos and two legendary frontier figures, Davy Crockett and Jim Bowie. The rebels took up positions in an old mission, the Alamo, and held Santa Anna at bay for twelve days. Toward the end, Travis asked the most prominent of the Mexican Tejanos, Juan Sequin, to ride out of the Alamo in a rainstorm carrying a desperate plea for help to Sam Houston. Sequin made it, but by the time he found Houston's force, it was too late. On the morning of the thirteenth day, Mexican troops finally scaled the walls of the Alamo, and when the fighting stopped, almost all the defenders were dead. Seven armed defenders, six other men, one woman, and one child surrendered. Santa Anna ordered his troops to pour oil on the dead bodies and burn them.

Less than a month later, a larger force of 330 Texans surrendered to Santa Anna in the town of Goliad. They were marched out of town as prisoners, then executed. But Santa Anna was moving slowly, and time was on the side of the Anglo-Americans and their Tejano allies. As the weeks passed, hundreds of Americans crossed over from Louisiana to join Houston's army. Finally, at the end of April 1836, the rebels surprised Santa Anna's army in east Texas on the banks of the San Jacinto River, where the city of Houston was eventually built. After two days of fighting, Santa Anna himself was taken prisoner and forced to sign a treaty recognizing the Republic of Texas. Mexico repudiated the treaty, and Santa Anna was exiled to Cuba. But for the moment, at least, Texas was "free."

THE TEXAS QUESTION

The Anglo-Americans in Texas hoped that their republic would immediately be annexed by the United States and become a state. But the professional politicians in Washington were wary. They knew full well that the admission of another slave state might bring a repetition of the Missouri crisis of 1819–1820. Both Whigs and Democrats understood that if either party split along sectional lines, it could not win a presidential election. Andrew Jackson privately favored annexation, but decided not to propose it because he feared it would divide the Democratic party. Martin Van Buren felt the same.

Texas political leaders, reasoning that if they were going to be kept waiting at the threshold they might as well take advantage of their independence, went to war again with Mexico in 1841. They laid claim to a vast stretch of territory reaching far to the west and north of the present borders of the state. The president of the republic, Mirabeau Buonaparte Lamar, led a Texan army to Santa Fe to try to establish by force a claim to an enormous empire in the Southwest. But this war was mercifully short. The Texans were soundly beaten, and Lamar withdrew his force—though not Texas's territorial claims.

William Henry Harrison's death in 1841 put a proslavery, proannexation southerner, John Tyler, in the White House. In 1843, he negotiated a treaty of annexation with the Republic of Texas. But he could not muster the two-thirds vote in the Senate that was constitutionally required for ratification. In fact, the treaty was decisively defeated, 35 to 16. So the "Texas question" became the hot potato of the 1844 election, and for a while it looked as though no presidential candidate was willing to hold it. The two men who expected to be the Democratic and Whig candidates for president, Martin Van Buren and Henry Clay, decided to try to keep the issue out of the election. Like the good party men they were, they struck a deal: neither of them would endorse the immediate annexation of Texas, so that the issue of slavery could be kept out of the election. By the party standards of the day, this decision appeared to be shrewd politics. But the arrangement was going to backfire on both Clay and Van Buren.

When Van Buren refused to endorse annexation (or to flatly oppose it), he antagonized southern Democrats. At their nominating convention, they blocked Van Buren, and the party nominated a Tennessean, James K. Polk. He was an ardent expansionist and a protégé of Andrew Jackson—"Young Hickory," his partisans called him. Clay, on the other hand, won the Whig

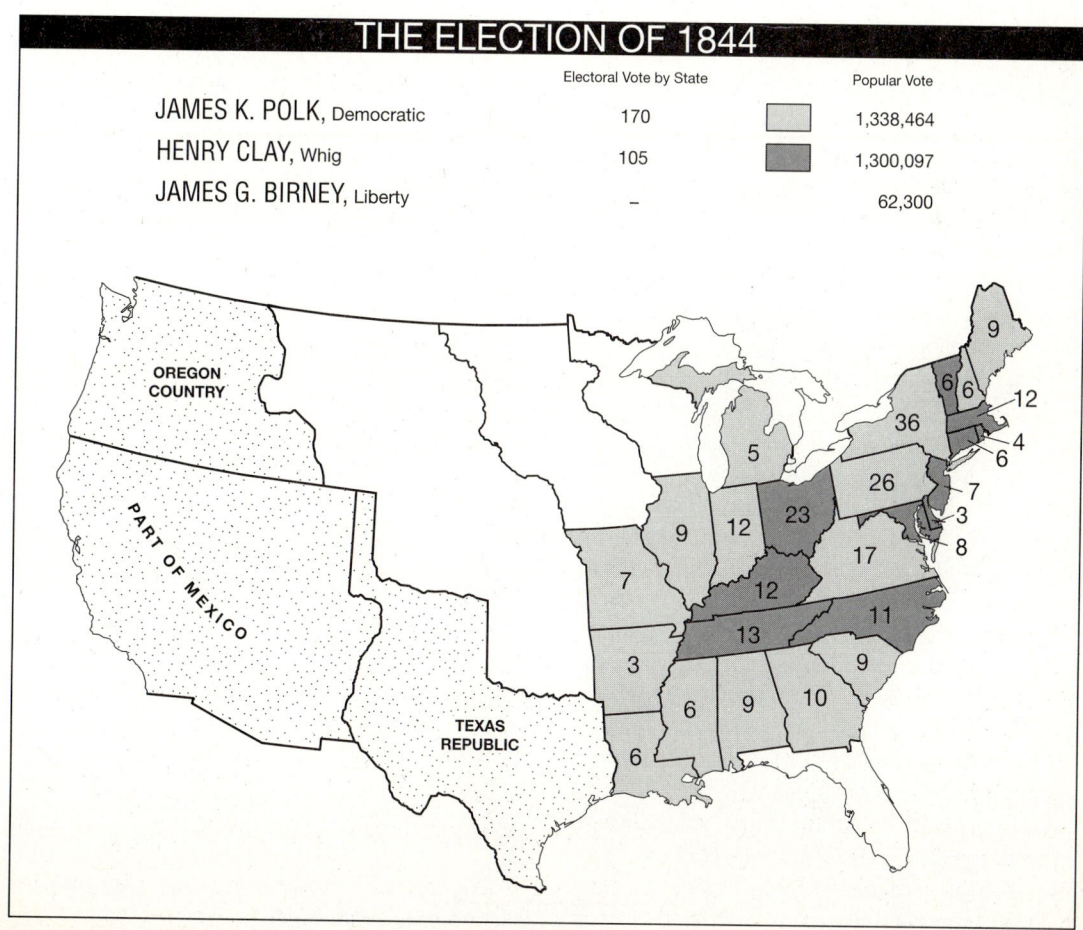

nomination easily (he had been campaigning for it full-time for two years). But he failed to anticipate a shrewd gamble on Polk's part. Polk's strategy was to come out strongly for the annexation of Texas but to balance it with something that would tempt Northerners to support him. So he proposed the annexation of both Texas and Oregon, all the way up to the latitude of 54°/40′— far above the present boundary with Canada—even if it meant another war with the British.

The Democrats' slogan "Fifty-four Forty or Fight" narrowly carried the day in a close election. But the campaign had brought the question of slavery nearer to the center of American politics than it had been for a generation. In fact, the slavery issue probably cost Henry Clay the prize for which he had been working so long. A change in the vote of one state, New York, would have given the presidency to Clay. He lost in New York by only about 5,000 votes out of almost half a million cast. And it was painfully obvious where those votes could have come from. James G. Birney, the candidate of a small, antislavery third party, the Liberty party, had received almost 16,000 votes. None of these voters would have been likely to vote for a slaveholder like Polk. If Birney had not been in the race, most of them would probably have gone to Clay, and the Whigs would have carried New York and won the presidency. As it was, the fate of Texas, of Mexico, and of the United States itself was in James K. Polk's hands.

Polk was a shrewd man, and he had a political vision—to restore the dominion of the Democratic party. His political hero was Andrew Jackson. Like Jackson, he thought that the president embodied the people's will. What the people willed was expansion, and he would give it to them. And if he could fuse expansion with the Jacksonian idea that government should deny special privileges to any interest or group, he believed the Democrats could lead a unified nation to even greater heights of prosperity and power.

Even before Polk was inaugurated, his Texas goals were met. Congress annexed Texas, by joint resolution of both houses (which required only majority votes) rather than by treaty (which needed a two-thirds vote in the Senate). After a lot of blustering talk on both sides, the United States and Britain came to an agreement on Oregon's border with Canada. "Fifty-four Forty or Fight" was a campaign slogan for Polk: his real interest was in California, so he settled for setting the border at the forty-ninth parallel, much farther south than Polk had proposed in the campaign.

WAR

But Polk's ambitions reached much further than Texas and Oregon. He was determined to have about half of Mexico, too—Alta California and New Mexico (which included present-day Nevada, Utah, Arizona, and New Mexico).

When the United States annexed Texas, Mexico broke diplomatic relations with the United States. Polk then tried a combination of military pressure and diplomacy. He ordered the navy to be ready to seize the California city of Monterey in case war came. And he sent General Zachary Taylor to Texas with a sizable army to take up a position on the Nueces River, which Mexico had always regarded as the southern border of Tejas. Then he ordered John Slidell to Mexico to try to negotiate a Texas border settlement and to offer to purchase California and New Mexico.

Mexico's governing elite was outraged by the combination of military threat and the offer of money for land. The government refused to talk to Slidell. An important newspaper in Mexico City later described the American offer as a form of banditry:

> Es esencia do contrato do compra-venta, que el consentimiento sea mutuo y espontáneo. No se puede comprar cuando el dueño de una cosa no quiere venderla. "Me vendes o te asesino," es el lenguaje del salteador.[1]

In January 1846, Polk ordered Taylor to move his army across the Nueces to the Rio

---

[1] *It is the essence of an agreement to buy and sell that the consent be mutual and spontaneous. You cannot buy when the owner of a thing does not want to sell it. "Sell to me or I'll murder you" is the language of the assailant.*

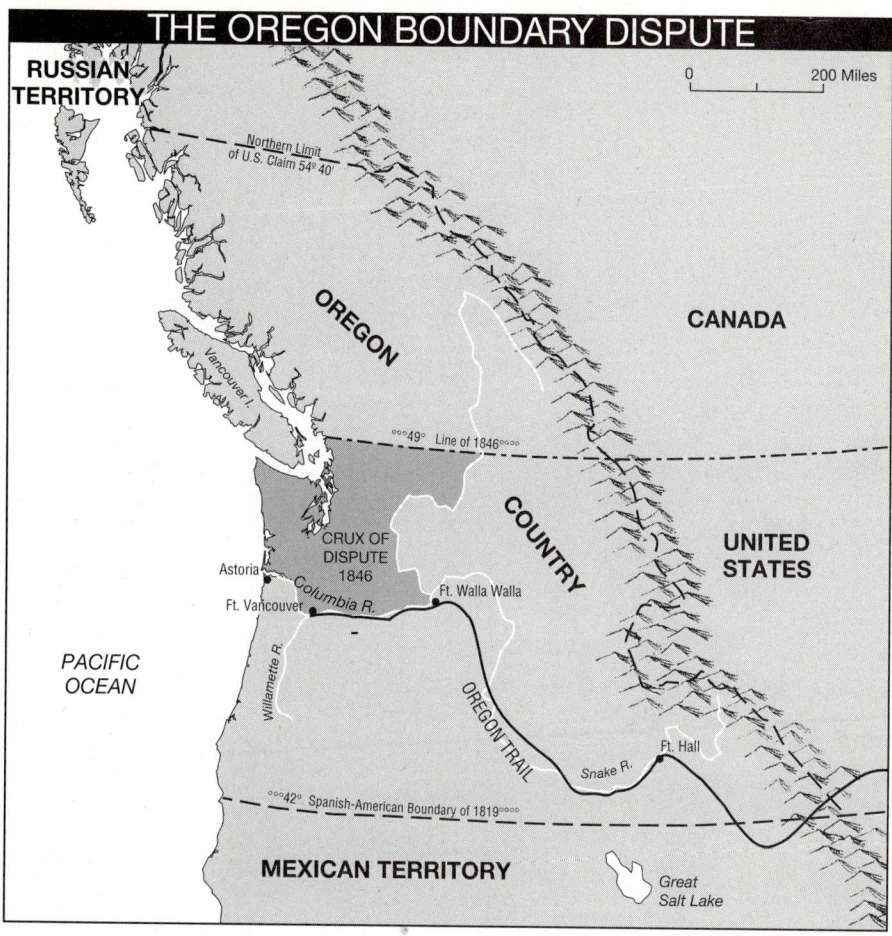

Grande—knowing full well that the Mexican government could only interpret this as an invasion and an act of war. On April 24, a detachment of United States soldiers was attacked on the north bank of the Rio Grande by a much larger body of Mexican troops. General Taylor sent a curiously worded message to Polk. "Hostilities," he said, "may now be considered as commenced." When he got the message, Polk was already busy writing a message asking Congress for a declaration of war. Congress was ready and waiting. On May 13, the Senate voted for war 40 to 2, and the House 174 to 14.

Polk's initial strategy was to fight a brief border war in Texas, occupy California with a small force, then make peace. He apparently had no wish for a war to the finish and no idea how fierce the Mexican resistance would be. Now came a secret offer from Santa Anna, who was still living in forced exile in Cuba. If the United States would allow him to "escape" and return to Mexico, he would see to it that Polk's strategy worked. The Americans decided to trust him. What they got was not the deal they had bargained for, but a Santa Anna who rallied his people to a heroic resistance.

For their part, the Mexicans were both proud and confident—at least the well-off and educated Mexicans who had access to government and the press. The year before the war began, a writer in *La Voz del Pueblo* in Mexico City boasted that Mexico's soldiers were hardened

GENERAL WINFIELD SCOTT'S ENTRY INTO MEXICO CITY. In March 1847 the American army captured Mexico City. This print appeared in a history of the war by George W. Kendell, who was one of the first reporters to go into battle with an army.

professionals who would easily turn back the American armies:

> Nuestros soldados han nacido bajo las cureas de los caones, se han mecido al estallido de la artillería; su educación, su alimento, su vivir ha sido la guerra. ¿Cómo podrán resistirlos los que han pasado su vida en el ocio de la paz? Mexico debía armarse y hacer una grande expedición terrestre y marítima para forzar los Estados Unidos a adoptar unánimemente la religión católica apostólica y romana, a sangre y fuego.[2]

[2] *Our soldiers were born under the stocks of the cannons, they have been rocked to the crack of artillery. Their education, their nourishment, their life has been war. How can those who have spent their lives in the idleness of peace resist them? Mexico should arm herself and conduct a great expedition, by land and sea, to force the United States, in blood and fire, to unanimously adopt the apostolic Roman Catholic religion.*

The strident tones of American Manifest Destiny had found their echoes among some Mexican leaders.

⋆⇌⋆

Once war began, the United States' opening move was to march an army of about 2,000 from Kansas to Santa Fe. This army, led by General Stephen W. Kearney, took Santa Fe easily and set out for its second objective, San Diego and Los Angeles. But even before Kearney could arrive, the American settlers of California, led by Captain John C. Frémont, had organized a rebellion of their own and proclaimed the "Bear Flag Republic."

Zachary Taylor, who sported the nickname Old Rough and Ready, crossed the Rio Grande into Mexico and finally met and defeated an army that Santa Anna was rushing northward, at the town of Buena Vista in February 1847. Santa Anna gave up any further effort to dislodge Taylor in order to meet a new and more serious

American threat. An American army was moving by sea toward Vera Cruz, with the obvious intention of mounting an overland attack on the capital of Mexico. The Americans were commanded by General Winfield Scott—he was called Old Fuss and Feathers because he wore ornate uniforms and insisted on a strict discipline.

After a siege, Scott forced Vera Cruz to surrender. Then he began a long and difficult campaign, moving across rough terrain toward Mexico City and meeting stiff and skilled resistance in battle after battle. Finally, in September 1847, he was at the fortress of Chapultepec, just south and west of the capital. The garrison consisted largely of the teenage cadets of the Mexican military academy. But the boys fought with desperate heroism—easily matching that of the hardened American frontiersmen at the Alamo—and died to a man. Scott's artillery now had a clear command of the capital. Santa Anna, after some complicated negotiations, agreed to the Treaty of Guadalupe Hidalgo. In the treaty, Mexico accepted the Rio Grande border, and ceded California and New Mexico to the United States. In return, the United States agreed to pay Mexico the modest sum of $15 million and to take care of any claims American citizens might have against Mexico as a result of the war.

The war was a mild one for the Americans. It cost them 3,000 casualties, but they increased their territory by more than one-third. Like the War of 1812, this one had its heroes, its myths, and its slogans. It gave the Marines the first line of their hymn, "From the halls of Montezuma." It thrust new presidential contenders into the national spotlight: Scott, Taylor, and Frémont. It yielded the slogan "Remember the Alamo." And it gave a pair of young officers, Ulysses S. Grant and Robert E. Lee, their first real experience of war—an experience they would take into battle again fifteen years later.

Polk had fulfilled America's Manifest Destiny with skill and determination. When he left office in 1849, the United States had spread its dominion over all the territory between the oceans, north of Mexico and south of Canada. But his expansionism had once again injected slavery into politics and unleashed forces of division far more powerful than anyone had imagined. The contrast between Polk's aggressive southwestern expansion and his willingness to settle for less than all of Oregon angered many northerners, who already viewed Polk with suspicion. When, during the Mexican War, Polk asked Congress for money for "adjustment of a boundary" between Mexico and the United States, David Wilmot, a Democratic representative from Pennsylvania, introduced an amendment that would make it "an express and fundamental condition" that slavery be forever excluded from any territory gained from Mexico. (Wilmot also wanted to exclude all blacks from the newly acquired territories.) A rider attached to an insignificant bill by an obscure first-term congressman, the Wilmot Proviso—though never enacted—had an enormous political impact and pushed the slavery controversy to a much higher plane.

SLAVERY AND EXPANSION

It is ironic that when the antislavery movement concentrated on the states where slavery existed, it made little headway, but when the focus shifted to the territories where slavery did not yet exist, the issue became so explosive it eventually split the nation apart. There are several reasons for this. The Constitution clearly denied Congress the authority to abolish slavery in the states. But the territories were a different matter: they belonged to the whole nation. The precedents of the Northwest Ordinance and the Missouri Compromise seemed to give Congress the authority to prohibit slavery in the territories.

It was primarily racism that kept most northerners from embracing abolitionism. Like Miss Ophelia, most northerners had a deep, almost visceral antipathy to African Americans. They were no more eager than southerners to have blacks as free and equal members of their society. To them, abolitionism threatened to turn millions of blacks loose on white society, a prospect that during the 1830s provoked dozens of northern mobs to attack abolitionists and free blacks, killing one white abolitionist and dozens of blacks. When Wilmot introduced his proviso, most northerners were still perfectly content to let slavery remain in the states where it already existed. They still denounced abolitionists as fanatical "amalgamationists" hell-bent on destroying the Union. Nonetheless, many had become convinced that slavery was the direct antithesis of all that they associated with freedom. In its essence, slavery robbed people of their labor, the very instrument by which free men and women determined their own destinies.

The question of slavery in the territories divorced race from the issue of slavery and made the "slavery question" a matter of fundamental principle, far removed from the reality of America's black slaves. For northerners and southerners alike, the territories represented the future. The conflict over slavery in the territories thus became a struggle for control of the future. Most slaveholders believed their way of life could endure and thrive only if they had full freedom to take their slave property into the open territories. To deny them that right, they believed, was to deprive them of the foundation of their present prosperity and their dreams for the future. To the citizens of the free states, the open territories also symbolized an open future, full of opportunity. But many now considered the expansion of slavery to be incompatible with their own freedom to make the best life their talent and labor would allow. They feared that slavery would jeopardize their future if it was permitted to enter the territories they themselves might want to go into. Slavery seemed to them to give slaveholders an unfair advantage in "the race of life." With only their own labor, how could they possibly compete with the labor and capital the planter could extract from his slaves?

SLAVERY AND POLITICS: THE ELECTION OF 1848

The encroachment of slavery on ordinary politics was unmistakable in the elections of 1848. Expansion had led the Democrats to victory in 1844, but in 1848 it left them in disarray. The sectional fissures were deep, and in many northern states, feuding between antislavery and conservative Democrats wracked the party. In spite of his success in carrying out his program, Polk stepped aside (when he won the nomination in 1844 he stated that he would serve only one term.) The Democrats nominated Lewis Cass of Michigan. Cass, firmly opposed to the Wilmot Proviso, argued that the people in the territories should decide the issue. This "popular sovereignty," he insisted, was in accord with the American tradition of local autonomy. Besides, it would remove the whole problem from national politics.

The Whigs were split between "conscience" Whigs, who were increasingly antislavery and anti-South, and "cotton" Whigs, who did not want to disrupt the alliance between southern planters and northern merchants and textile manufacturers. But with the Democrats even more bitterly divided, the Whigs had a good chance to regain the presidency. Again they turned to a military hero and nominated General Zachary Taylor, who had spent most of his adult life on the frontier fighting Native Americans. The Whigs did not even adopt a party platform. Any position they might take was sure to antagonize voters, so they decided to stand for nothing. The tactic worked, and Taylor won the election.

If the major parties' desperate avoidance of the territorial issue was testimony to the power of that issue, the most ominous sign of how the question was beginning to disrupt ordinary politics was the emergence of a new political party. In August several thousand reformers, Democrats, and conscience Whigs gathered in Buffalo, New York, and established the antislavery Free-Soil party. The party nominated Martin Van Buren for the presidency and called for an end to the expansion of slavery, a homestead act, internal improvements, and a new tariff. The new party's significance lay less in its electoral success or failure than in the range of people and ideas it brought together. It drew humanitarian reformers who until now had condemned politics as unprincipled and sordid and had worked outside the political arena, and it drew young politicians who were willing to stake their careers on antislavery. Perhaps most revealing of all, the new party attracted some established Whig and Democratic politicians who had always thought of themselves as loyal party men; now they had decided to cast their lot with a political party that was as much an instrument of a moral crusade as it was an electoral machine.

THE CRISIS AND COMPROMISE OF 1850

The politics of avoidance could not work forever. It had elected Taylor, and for three years Congress simply left the new territories unorganized.

But avoidance was no longer possible when, in 1849, nearly 80,000 "Forty-niners" flocked to California after the discovery of gold at Sutter's Mill. California had to have some kind of civil organization. President Taylor, though a southern slaveholder, was a staunch Unionist. A military man, he believed in firm action and decided that it was time to put the territorial issue to rest. He devised a straightforward plan to skip the territorial stage and have the people of the territories won from Mexico adopt constitutions and apply directly for statehood.

Southern leaders were shocked. By September, Californians had already ratified a Free-Soil constitution and New Mexico was about to follow suit. If the antislavery forces were permitted to keep slavery out of California and New Mexico, how could they be stopped from keeping it out of all future territories? If California and New Mexico came into the Union as free states, power might shift so decisively to the North that slavery in the South itself would be endangered. All over the South, alarmed southerners held rallies denouncing the attack on their institutions and rights. Amid threats of secession, southern leaders called for a convention in Nashville to plan a concerted response to the threat they faced.

The vehemence of the southern response alarmed Unionists everywhere. Henry Clay, "the Great Pacificator," the border-state senator who had worked out the Missouri Compromise, began work on a new compromise, designed to settle the full range of issues by giving each side some of what it wanted. He proposed that California be admitted as a free state but that New Mexico and Utah be organized as territories without any restrictions on slavery. He proposed that the interstate slave trade be prohibited from operating in the nation's capital, but that slavery there be abolished only if the people of the District of Columbia and Maryland agreed and if slaveholders were compensated for their slaves. Finally, he called for a stringent federal law requiring the return of fugitive slaves to their masters.

For months, debate over the compromise raged, drawing forth the best rhetorical efforts of two generations of political leaders. Clay urged northerners to drop their insistence on the abstract Wilmot Proviso and be content with California and the probability that New Mexico would eventually become a free state. To the dying Calhoun, so sick he had to have his speech read for him, the compromise would solve nothing. He insisted that the Union could be preserved only if the political balance between North and South was made permanent and the South's rights to take its slaves into the territories and have its runaway property returned were guaranteed. If the North could not agree, he warned, "tell us so and let the states we both represent agree to separate and part in peace. If you are unwilling we should part in peace, tell us so, and we shall know what to do when you reduce the question to submission or resistance."

Daniel Webster rose to answer Calhoun. He spoke, he began, "not as a Massachusetts man, not as a Northern man, but as an American. I speak today for the preservation of the Union. Hear me for my cause." He too pleaded for the North to give up its adherence to the Wilmot Proviso, and he pleaded with the South to surrender its talk of secession. Now it was time for the other flank to speak. William Seward, an antislavery Whig from New York, condemned the compromise as "morally wrong and essentially vicious." The Constitution, he argued, did not protect slavery in the territories because there was "a higher law than the Constitution" that had preserved the land for liberty and justice.

Brilliant and moving oratory was not enough to pass Clay's "omnibus bill." On July 31, Free-Soilers, antislavery Whigs, and southern "fire-eaters" (proslavery extremists) combined in a parliamentary ploy that ripped the compromise to shreds, piece by piece. A dejected Clay surrendered leadership of the compromise forces to Senator Stephen Douglas of Illinois. Douglas broke the bill into separate measures and secured a different majority for each item of the compromise. The sudden death of President Taylor, who had opposed the compromise, removed the threat of veto, and by September the major mea-

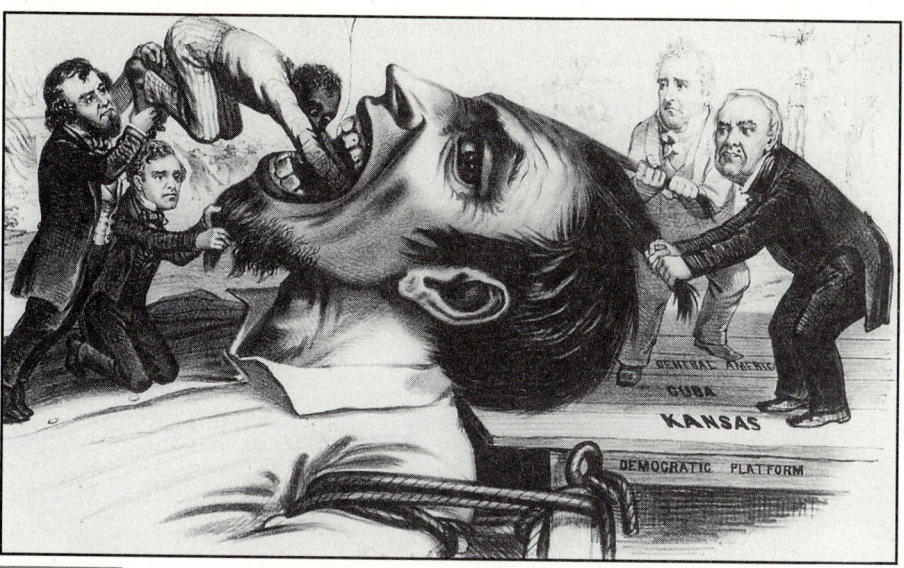

FORCING SLAVERY DOWN THE THROAT OF A FREE-SOILER. In this Free-Soil cartoon, the Democrats—Stephen Douglas and Franklin Pierce on the left, James Buchanan and Lewis Cass on the right—are shoving both slavery and black people down the throat of a white Free-Soiler. Neither Free-Soilers nor their opponents were above trying to exploit white racial prejudices for their own political advantage.

sures had been signed into law by President Millard Fillmore.

All over the country people celebrated. The crisis had been resolved, the Union saved. In New Orleans a huge rally applauded the compromise and honored its architects; in New York a hundred leading merchants set up a Union Safety Committee to strengthen support for the measure; in the Middle West, Whigs and Democrats swore to stand by the compromise. Stephen Douglas "vowed never to make another speech on the slavery question. Let us cease agitating, stop the debate, drop the subject. If we do this, the Compromise will be recognized as a final settlement."

The election of 1852 indicated how deeply most longed for a "final settlement." The Democratic platform pledged the party to full support of the compromise and promised to resist "agitation" of the slavery issue "under whatever shape or color the attempt may be made." The convention nominated Franklin Pierce of New Hampshire, a lackluster politician whom all factions of the party could accept. Though the Whigs were more deeply divided, their platform also endorsed the compromise. Again they turned to a military man, General Winfield Scott, to bridge their divisions. When Scott did not back the compromise strongly enough, many southern Whigs deserted to Pierce, who carried all but four states and all the states of the lower South. It looked as if the compromise might in fact hold as the final settlement of the crisis that had brought the Union to the brink of division.

It was a thin thread for keeping the fabric of the Union together. A highly vocal minority of southern leaders utterly rejected the compromise and tried to undermine it. Even moderate southerners were suspicious of the compromise. In the North an equally vehement minority condemned the compromise as a moral outrage because it included a fugitive slave law. Ralph Waldo Emerson vilified Daniel Webster for moral treachery, and Harriet Beecher Stowe sat down to write the novel that did so much to transform northern thinking about slaves and slavery. As a result, the compromise helped undermine its own chances for success. Still it might have worked, largely because so many Americans wanted it to work and had already begun to sanctify it as a sacred, inviolable act. But the Compromise of 1850 could hold together only if the problem that had brought about the crisis in the first place—slavery in the territories—could be avoided.

THE RESUMPTION OF EXPANSION

The Democratic party was a party of expansion. Men like Douglas and Pierce hoped that with the issue of slavery out of the way, the United States could resume its destined march of expansion and progress. Pierce insisted that his administration "would not be controlled by any forebodings of evil from expansion" and turned his attention toward Cuba. Proslavery forces had long eyed Cuba with its slave and plantation economy. They had aided one abortive expedition designed to provoke a Texas-style revolution in Cuba and were busy organizing another. Although Pierce repudiated this adventure, he authorized his minister to Spain, Pierre Soulé of Louisiana, to try to buy Cuba, and he ordered the American ministers to France and England to meet with Soulé to discuss how the United States should handle the Cuban question. The ministers sent a memorandum to the State Department saying that if Spain refused to sell or did anything that might hamper American interests, the United States would be fully justified in taking Cuba by force. When the memo leaked to the press as the notorious Ostend Manifesto, the uproar forced Pierce to repudiate the mission. But the damage had been done. Pierce was condemned as a tool of the proslavery forces, and northern fears of an aggressive slave power intensified.

THE KANSAS-NEBRASKA ACT

But it was expansionism of a more ordinary sort that brought the issue of slavery in the territories back into politics. A continental railroad was needed to connect the West Coast—especially gold-rich California—to the rest of the country. Where to put canals, turnpikes, county seats, and railroads had always provoked intense political maneuvering. The transcontinental railroad was no exception. All the major cities along the Mississippi scrambled to be selected as the eastern terminal. Jefferson Davis, the Mississippi senator and proslavery expansionist whom Pierce had selected as secretary of war, was especially eager to secure a southern route. He sent teams to survey five possible routes and arranged the appointment of a southern railroad promoter, James Gadsden, to negotiate the purchase of land needed for the best southern route.

Senator Stephen Douglas of Illinois was equally intent on securing a northern route. He believed that America's destiny lay in the "Great West," the vast expanse that stretched from the Mississippi to the Rocky Mountains. Unlocking that destiny demanded development, and development demanded railroads. However, it made the most sense to put the Pacific railroad through lands that were already settled, organized, and surveyed. The preferred southern route lay fully within existing states and organized territories, whereas the northern route went through a huge expanse of unorganized territory. As chairman of the Senate committee on the territories, Douglas introduced a bill to organize the Nebraska Territory (the huge tract that lay between Iowa and Missouri and the Utah Territory) without reference to the issue of slavery. But under the Missouri Compromise of 1820 (see Chapter 7), slavery was excluded from the territory Douglas wanted to organize, and southern senators blocked the bill. Douglas agreed to amend the bill in a way that would repeal the Missouri Compromise and divide the territory in two. The issue, Douglas argued, should be decided by "popular sovereignty" by the votes of the inhabitants of the territories. But at the same time, Douglas and many others expected that under popular sovereignty the southern portion, Kansas, would likely become a slave state and the northern portion, Nebraska, a free state. Douglas's maneuver worked:

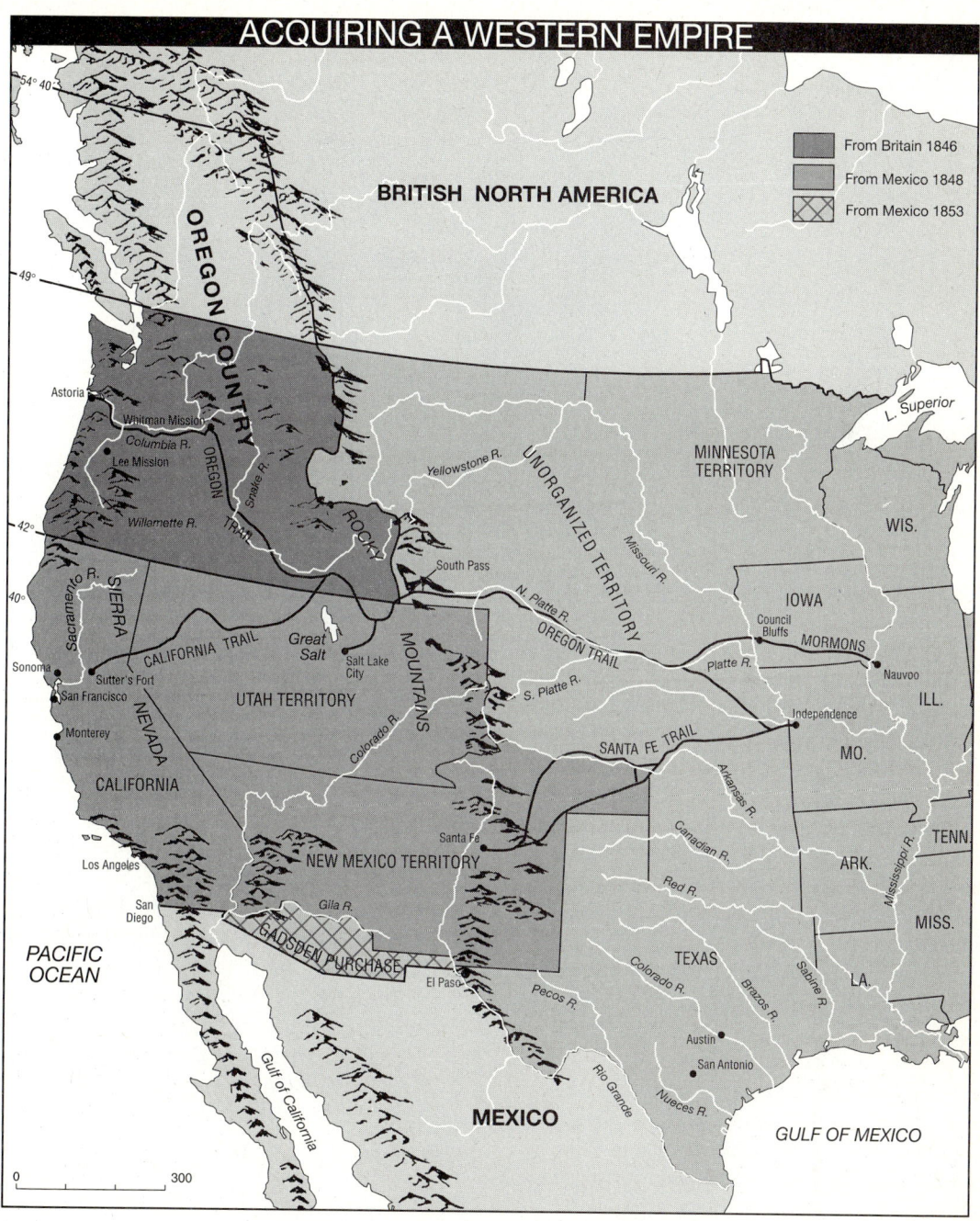

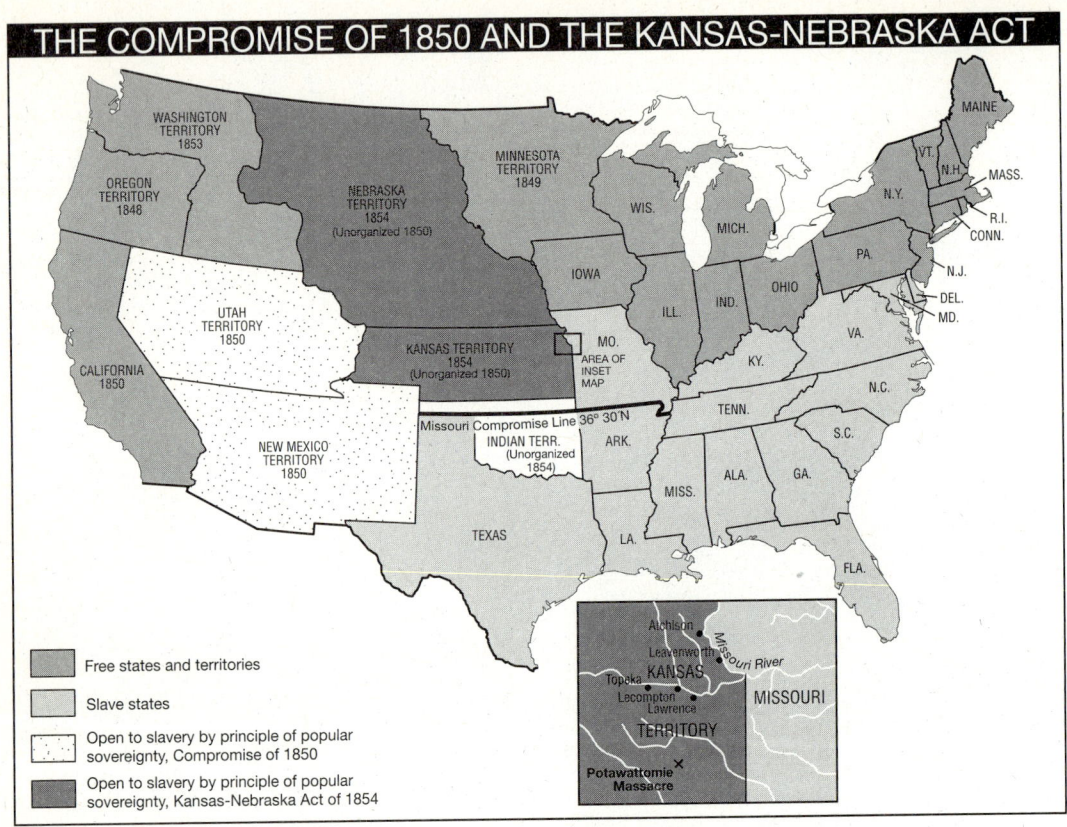

the Kansas-Nebraska Bill passed both houses and Pierce signed it into law.

The reaction in the North was vehement. Antislavery leaders condemned the act as a monstrous plot by slaveholders to spread slavery into all the territories of the Union, while moderates condemned the repeal of the Missouri Compromise as the "violation of a sacred pledge." Douglas had known that tampering with the Missouri Compromise would "raise a hell of a storm." But he was confident that he could ride it out and that the controversy would quiet down once people began to reap the benefits of the bill and see the wisdom of the formula of popular sovereignty. He was dead wrong. Because Douglas himself considered slavery in the territories a bogus issue, he failed to realize how deeply many northerners and southerners had come to feel about it.

"BLEEDING KANSAS"

The rush to control Kansas began. New England emigrant aid societies sent more than a thousand settlers into Kansas, while southern promoters sponsored a large proslavery migration. Initially, there were probably more pro- than antislavery voters in Kansas. But the proslavery forces were not going to leave anything to chance. On the eve of the territorial election, nearly 5,000 proslavery voters crossed from Missouri into Kansas and used intimidation, force, and fraud to steal the election. When this fraudulently elected legislature—which Pierce, under intense proslavery pressure, let stand—convened, it expelled the few antislavery legislators who had been elected and made it a felony to challenge the existence of slavery in Kansas. The outraged Free-Soilers countered with their own "free state convention," drew up a constitution, and proceeded to elect their own territorial legislature. Popular sovereignty had not solved the issue; it had established two implacably hostile governments in Kansas, neither of which had a clear claim to legitimacy.

Pierce did nothing to solve the problem. Extremists on both sides began to arm themselves. Many of the "border ruffians" who crossed into Kansas carried guns, and antislavery groups all over the North sent rifles to the antislavery settlers. In a territory near anarchy, with people on both sides living in terror of what the other might do, it was only a question of time before real violence occurred. In May 1856, a proslavery marshal led a posse into the antislavery stronghold of Lawrence to arrest two local officials for "treason." The posse destroyed the press of the antislavery newspaper and burned many of the buildings in the town. Later, abolitionist John Brown retaliated with a raid on the proslavery town on Pottawatomie Creek. Brown and his seven men dragged five unarmed men from their cabins, killed them with axes, and mutilated their bodies.

The violence even spilled over into Congress. Senator Charles Sumner of Massachusetts delivered a fiery speech on "the crime against Kansas," singling out Senator Andrew Butler of South Carolina for special abuse. Sumner's attack outraged Butler's nephew, Preston Brooks, a congressman from South Carolina, who came up behind Sumner one day when the Senate was not in session and caned him into insensibility. Fistfights broke out between individual congressmen, and some men even began to come to sessions armed. Pierce sent a new governor to Kansas, who was able to put a lid on the violence there. But "Bleeding Kansas" had already had a profound effect on American politics.

THE RISE OF THE REPUBLICAN PARTY

For nearly twenty years the contest between two national parties had structured American politics. In 1856 that system fell apart. The Whig party had barely survived the election of 1852. In the North, the Whigs were badly damaged by the rise of the "Know Nothings," an assortment of secretive, "nativist" groups that capitalized on widespread anti-immigrant and especially anti-Catholic feeling. Called Know Nothings because their members vowed to answer "I know nothing" when asked questions about their organizations, the Know Nothings combined calls for temperance legislation with calls for restrictive anti-immigrant measures, including tighter naturalization laws and prohibitions against Catholics holding public office. By 1854, the Know Nothings had drained away a large portion of the Whig constitutency, showing great electoral strength in the East and even gaining control of the Massachusetts legislature. Moreover, the Kansas-Nebraska Act effectively destroyed the Whig party as a national party. Almost all the southern Whigs had joined their Democratic counterparts to support the bill, and almost all the northern Whigs had opposed it. They could no longer stay in the same party. Most of the southern Whigs became Democrats, making the South increasingly a one-party region. The situation in the North was more chaotic. Anti-Nebraska Whigs were cut loose from their own party but could hardly join the southern-dominated Democratic party. Kansas had also driven many antislavery Democrats from their party. By the fall of 1854, the old political groupings were disintegrating, and people were coming together in new ways under a bewildering range of labels. The most important of these was the Republican party, which sprang up in a number of different places, drawing together Free-Soilers, anti-Nebraska Democrats, and conscience Whigs, and, in a number of places in the East, allying with the Know Nothings.

The campaign for the 1856 election began amid the violence in Kansas and in the Capitol. When the Republicans gathered in Philadelphia for their first convention, there was an exuberant, almost festive air about the proceedings. They were on a crusade, and they were confident. They adopted a platform denouncing the Ostend Manifesto and calling for the exclusion of slavery from the territories and the immediate admission of Kansas as a free state. They nominated General John C. Frémont, the hero of California and a staunch Free-Soil man. The Democrats for their part endorsed the Kansas-Nebraska Act and extolled popular sovereignty as the only way to deal with slavery in the territories. Rejecting Douglas as too controversial, they turned to James Buchanan, a loyal party man who was untainted by Kansas and whose participation in the Ostend Manifesto made him acceptable to the South.

Buchanan won the election, carrying all the slave states except Maryland, and six free states; Frémont carried the other eleven northern states. In 1854, the Know Nothings had been as strong and in some places stronger than the newly forged Republican party. But by 1856, a large portion of the Know Nothing adherents, increasingly inspired by antislavery and antisouthern sentiments, shifted their allegience to the Republican party. The Democrats won partly because they were still able to hang on as a national party, but their grip was weak. Without its solid hold on all the southern states, the party would have lost the election. Frémont had run well even in the states Buchanan had won—a small shift in Pennsylvania and Illinois would have given him the election. Republicans also controlled most of the state governments in the North, giving them the local base from which to take control of northern politics. In only two years, the Republican party had risen from the chaos of Kansas to become the most powerful force in northern, if not national, politics.

REPUBLICAN IDEOLOGY

The Republican party was far more than a loose coalition drawn together around the single issue of slavery in the territories. It offered northerners a view of the world that expressed their goals, addressed their fears, and contained an increasingly compelling explanation of what was happening to the country. The Republican slogan, "Free soil, free labor, free men," embodied the values most northerners held. "Free soil," of course, was a code for the insistence that the territories be kept open as an area in which free white men could build a better future. The notion of "free labor" embodied the ideal of the self-made man: the right to the fruits of his own work. By providing them with the means to rise beyond any dependency that might keep one person under the dominion of another, free labor enabled free men to fulfill the destiny manifest in their own talents and work.

Republican ideology contained an equally powerful indictment of slavery and southern society, portraying them as the antithesis of "free soil, free labor, free men." Again and again, Republicans pointed to the South's seeming lack of industriousness and progress, its lack of cities, factories, railroads, schools. Even southern agriculture seemed retarded, especially among poor whites, who could not compete with slave labor. The South had "no middle class of intelligent farmers, artisans, and mechanics who constitute the real strength, who make the real wealth and are justly the pride and glory of the free states." Many northerners clearly believed that slavery undermined the work ethic that characterized free society, creating pampered, wasteful, and self-indulgent masters, degraded slaves, and ignorant and lazy poor whites. And this was the system the slavocracy wanted to impose on all the territory to which free men might want to go.

Republican ideology thus fused two powerful emotions: firm dedication to an ideal of freedom and an equally intense dislike of slavery. The antislavery movement converted few northerners to abolition, but it did have a powerful effect on their feelings about slavery. The abolitionist Theodore Weld's *American Slavery As It Is: The Testimony of a Thousand Witnesses* (1839) bombarded hundreds of thousands of readers with example after example of the cruelty of slavery. Countless tracts portrayed the slave South as a depraved society that undermined all the discipline and self-restraint that a generation of northern ministers and reformers had extolled. But it was probably *Uncle Tom's Cabin,* more than any other single thing, that inspired in northerners such intense feelings about slavery. The novel offered no new arguments about slavery; its ideas had been around for at least a decade. What it did do was transform how people felt about slavery. By forcing her white readers to respond to at least some black slaves as human beings with many of the same feelings, values, and aspirations as themselves, Stowe forged a bond of sympathy between reader and slave that led many readers to an intense loathing of the institution. To most northern readers of *Uncle Tom's Cabin,* slavery was no longer an abstraction but something they had an almost tangible sense of, something they had come to hate.

The Republican party tapped the growing hatred of slavery and gave it political direction. It offered a crusade to rid the nation of slavery, a program that promised to place slavery on "a course to ultimate extinction." Along with their proslavery counterparts, Republicans believed that slavery—like so much else in American life—had to expand or die. They argued that if it could be contained within the states where it already existed, it would eventually wither and die from lack of nourishment. To many Republicans this was what the politics of the last decade had been about: a struggle not just for "free soil" but to redeem the United States as a genuinely free society. As William Seward put it, Americans were locked in an "irrepressible conflict," one that sooner or later would determine whether the nation would become "entirely a slaveholding or entirely a free labor nation."

THE RUSH TO DISUNION

THE DRED SCOTT CASE

When politics cannot seem to deal with an issue, Americans often turn to the Supreme Court for a resolution. On March 6, 1857, two days after Buchanan's inauguration, the Court handed down its decision in *Dred Scott* v. *Sanford.* Scott was a slave who belonged to an army doctor in Missouri. The doctor took Scott to Illinois and the Minnesota Territory before returning to Missouri. Scott sued for his freedom on the ground that the Missouri Compromise prohibited slavery in Minnesota. In the Court's six-to-three decision, Roger B. Taney, a Maryland slaveholder whom Jackson had appointed as chief justice, declared that blacks were not citizens, and hence Scott could not bring suit. He denied Scott's claim that his residence in Minnesota had made him free, arguing that the Missouri Compromise itself had been unconstitutional because slaves were property and the Fifth Amendment flatly forbade Congress from taking property without "due process of law."

It was a stunning decision. Buchanan expected it to be "the final settlement," but the decision only polarized the issue even further. Proslavery forces were exuberant: their most radical argument now had the sanction of the highest court in the land. Consternation and fury greeted the decision in the North. Democrats like Stephen Douglas were in a tough position: if they went along with the insistence of the southern majority in their party that the party endorse the decision, they would have to repudiate popular sovereignty, the basis of their appeal to northern voters. Republicans condemned the decision totally. They argued that Taney's argument was merely an "obiter dictum," a piece of incidental reasoning that was not binding as constitutional law, and they denounced the Court for usurping legislative powers. Worst of all, the decision threatened to spread slavery even into the free states of the North. To Republican leaders, the logical extension of Taney's argument was that nothing could prevent slaveholders from moving into the free states with their slave property.

In the meantime, the turmoil in Kansas had not subsided. Buchanan appointed a new territorial governor and instructed him to see to it that Kansas, "by fair and regular vote, unaffected by fraud and violence," adopt a constitution and apply for statehood. The vast majority of Kansans were now Free-Soilers, but the proslavery legislature disqualified most of them from voting and rigged the districts so that the proslavery minority would control the constitutional convention. Most of the Free-Soilers boycotted the convention, which met in the temporary capital of Lecompton and drew up a constitution that guaranteed the rights of all existing slaveholders to keep their slave property. They gave the voters a choice between a constitution with slavery and one that banned the future importation of slaves. Free-Soilers in Kansas and Republicans elsewhere denounced Lecompton as a "great swindle," while proslavery forces in Kansas and elsewhere endorsed it as a formula that was fully consistent with the *Dred Scott* decision.

The Lecompton constitution solved nothing, and it provoked an irreparable split in the Democratic party. Buchanan claimed that the Lecompton referendum gave Kansas a "fair" choice and urged Congress to accept the constitution in the interests of national peace. But Douglas considered it a betrayal of popular sovereignty and led the attack in the Senate on Buchanan and the Lecompton constitution, infuriating the southern members of the party.

JOHN BROWN'S RAID

Ostend, Bleeding Kansas, the *Dred Scott* case, Lecompton—they all seemed to many northerners to be frightening proof of the power of the slavocracy. When John Brown left Kansas, his obsession with slavery only deepened. Now he was determined to strike out against it. Like Nat Turner, Brown considered himself God's instrument for the destruction of slavery. He devised a plan to take a small band of men into the Virginia mountains and sally forth to liberate slaves. These he would organize into a black state, which would in turn provoke a general slave insurrection. In October 1859 Brown led his band of eighteen men, including two of his sons and five blacks, in an assault on the federal arsenal at Harper's Ferry, Virginia. He captured the armory easily, but there was no slave uprising—only a few slaves lived in the area, and none of them had been told about the raid. State and federal troops quickly forced Brown to retreat to an engine house near the arsenal. The next day, troops stormed the engine house, killing ten of Brown's men and capturing Brown and most of the others. Brown was quickly tried by a Virginia court, condemned for treason, and executed.

John Brown's raid had as powerful an effect on southerners as *Uncle Tom's Cabin* had had on northerners. The novel had seemed to expose the awful reality of slavery; the raid seemed to expose the terrifying reality of the northern threat to the South and its peculiar institution. The specter of slave insurrection had long haunted southerners. But just as ominous was that supposedly respectable northerners had supported Brown and that men like Ralph Waldo Emerson and Henry Ward Beecher now embraced him as a martyr. Brown's raid seemed all too clearly to be the result of ideas like Seward's "higher law" doctrine. If to many northerners the spread of slavery to the free states flowed logically from the *Dred Scott* decision, to many southerners "the crimes of

JOHN BROWN. Before his trial and execution, most Americans looked upon John Brown as a dangerous fanatic. But the dignity and calmness with which he met his end helped transform him into a martyr. After he was sentenced to death, he declared, "If it is deemed necessary that I should forfeit my life for the furtherance of the ends of justice and mingle my blood with the blood of millions in this slave country, I say let it be done."

John Brown" were simply "the practical illustrations of the doctrines of the Republican party." As Americans entered the new year and prepared themselves for the presidential election, Seward's "irrepressible conflict" seemed frighteningly near.

THE ELECTION OF 1860

The Democratic party was the only national political institution left. But it was bitterly divided when it met late in April 1860 in Charleston, South Carolina, to select its nominee. A majority of the delegates came from the North and favored Douglas. But his stand on Lecompton and positions he had taken in his 1858 campaign for the Senate had made him anathema to the South. At Freeport, Illinois, Douglas's challenger for the Senate seat, Abraham Lincoln, had pointedly asked Douglas whether the people of a territory could exclude slavery before a state constitution was established. If Douglas answered no, he would repudiate popular sovereignty and alienate the North; if he said yes, he would repudiate the *Dred Scott* decision and alienate the South. Instead, Douglas had suggested that people could evade *Dred Scott* if they used local police regulations to keep slaveholders from coming into a territory. For southerners, *Dred Scott* was the test of a northern candidate's acceptability; with his "Freeport heresy," as they dubbed it, Douglas had failed the test.

The southerners demanded a platform that denied Congress and territorial legislatures the authority to exclude slavery from a territory, and they called for federal protection of slavery in the territories. When the convention refused to give it to them, the delegates from seven states of the lower South walked out. After a second attempt to bring the party back together had the same result as the first convention, the northerners nominated Douglas. Southern Democrats then called a convention of their own and nominated John Breckinridge of Kentucky as their candidate. The last of the national parties had foundered on the issue of slavery in the territories.

The prospects for a Republican victory were very good, even though it was purely a sectional party. When they gathered in Chicago, party leaders were determined not to squander the advantage the Democrats' split gave them. They adopted a broad, carefully worded platform, hoping to counter the notion that they were a bunch of one-idea fanatics. They called for a homestead act, a transcontinental railroad, internal improvements, and a protective tariff. They indicated that they would not interfere with slavery where it existed but remained adamantly opposed to the extension of slavery. The convention rejected William Seward of New York, the best known of the Republican leaders, because he was too controversial and had made too many enemies in the party. On the third ballot, the convention turned to Abraham Lincoln, the ex-Whig from Illinois who had fought Douglas so well in 1858. Lincoln had few enemies, was firm on slavery and other issues, and had achieved national prominence with his eloquent exposition of Republican antislavery doctrine. It was also thought he would be a stronger candidate in Illinois, Pennsylvania, and Indiana—states the Republicans had to carry to win the election.

The two sections had become so deeply alienated from each other that the election was less a national contest than two regional elections. In the South, it was between Breckinridge and John Bell (the candidate of the Constitutional Union party, which a group of elder statesmen had put together in a desperate attempt to head off disunion), who together won more than 80 percent of the southern vote. In the North, the contest pitted Douglas against Lincoln, who between them received more than 80 percent of the vote in that region. Though Lincoln received only 40 percent of the popular vote, he won a clear majority of the electoral vote, carrying every northern state but New Jersey, which split its vote between Douglas and Lincoln. (Though nearly a million more people voted for Lincoln's opponents than voted for him, he would have won the election even if all the other votes had been cast for a single opponent.) The returns did not give a very clear picture of what people wanted. A *national* majority had certainly not endorsed the Republican party; it had voted for one extreme or the other—for either Lincoln or Breckinridge—rather than for the candidates in the middle. Read another way, the returns had little comfort for the South: nearly 70 percent of the voters in the nation had taken positions that seemed clearly in opposition to the extension of slavery.

SOUTHERN RESPONSE TO LINCOLN'S ELECTION

All during the spring and summer of 1860, southern leaders had tried to figure out what to do if and when the "Black Republicans" won the White House. Talk of secession and even war was rife, and the election returns were scarcely in before the secessionist tide began to flow. Within a week of the election, the South Carolina legislature called for a convention to consider secession, and by the end of November five more states had followed suit. In all the other slave states of the upper and lower South, secessionists grabbed the initiative and began the rush to division.

The speed with which the secessionists took command surprised almost everyone but the secessionists themselves. Secession was far more than a panicked reaction to the election of Lincoln. That event was merely a catalyst that propelled a well-prepared and eager secessionist party to the fore. In many ways, the secessionists were the direct political counterpart of the Republicans. Essentially, they too were rev-

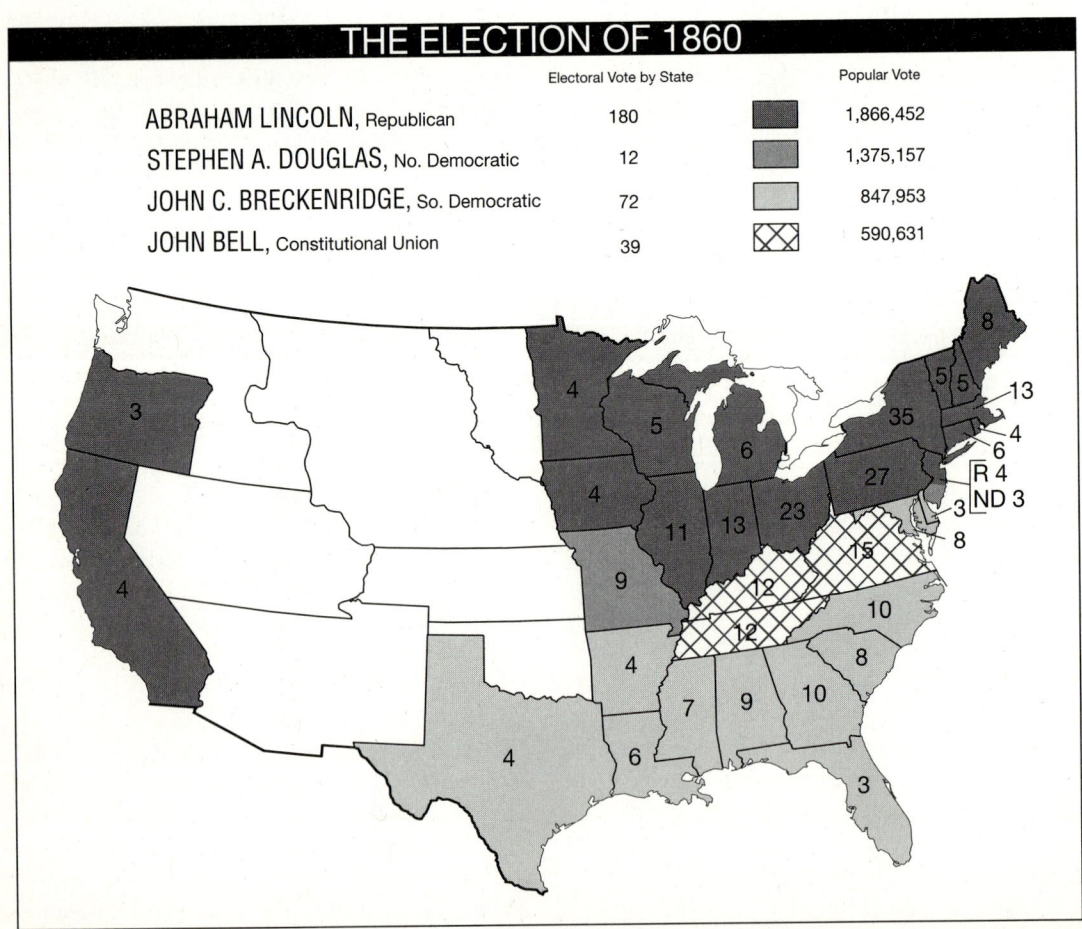

olutionaries, motivated by an ideology as far-reaching as antislavery Republicanism. And now many southerners found their interpretation of the events to be as compelling as the Republicans' interpretation had come to be to so many northerners.

As early as 1850, southern fire-eaters also had glimpsed an "irrepressible conflict." Calhoun and Davis both had warned the North that the South might be forced to break the Union if northerners did not stop attacking southern institutions and guarantee the right of slavery to expand and prosper. But the secessionist ideology promoted by the southern radicals was not purely defensive; it incorporated all the ideas by which southern leaders and intellectuals had convinced themselves that slavery was a positive good and the South a superior civilization. The secessionists were fighting not only to ward off Yankee aggression but to expand and enhance a civilization that in their eyes appeared far finer and nobler than the money-grubbing materialism of the so-called free society of the Yankee North. They saw themselves as true southern patriots cast in the American revolutionary tradition of Patrick Henry. By the early 1850s they had begun to dream of an independent slaveholding republic and to work as hard as they could to bring it about. In 1860 they had been working for nearly a decade to alert the southern people to the true nature of Yankee tyranny and to lead them out of the Union and into a republic that would let southern civilization expand and flourish as it was destined to do.

So long as the Democrats held national power and so long as the South controlled the Democratic party, the radicals failed to gain broad support for secession. But after 1856 the logic of events—the rise of a Republican party that spoke of an "irrepressible conflict" and talked of the day when the whole society would be free of the sin of slavery; a Democratic party

AN ANTI-LINCOLN CARTOON. This cartoon tries to discredit Lincoln by associating him with all the isms that most Americans condemned as madness and depravity. Here Horace Greeley, whose *New York Tribune* advocated many of the reforms of the period, leads Lincoln to the insane asylum, followed by a motley collection of Mormons, free-love advocates, feminists, and other supposedly unsavory types.

CHRONOLOGY

1820	Missouri Compromise agreed to	1846 (cont'd)	
1821	Mexico wins independence from Spain		Mexican War ended by Treaty of Guadelupe Hidalgo;
1824	Mexican government passes Colonization Law allowing immigration from the United States to Mexico		Wilmot Proviso introduced in House of Representatives
1834	Mexico closes California's Franciscan missions, grants land and herds to *rancheros*;	1848	Zachary Taylor (Whig) defeats Lewis Cass (Democrat) and Martin Van Buren (Free-Soil) in presidential election
	General Antonio López de Santa Anna suspends Mexico's federal constitution	1849	California gold rush begins, and the territory applies for statehood
1835	Texas revolution begins	1850	Zachary Taylor dies, and Millard Fillmore becomes president;
1836	Texas wins independence from Mexico		
1837	Abolitionist editor Elijah Lovejoy killed by mob in Illinois		Compromise of 1850 completed
1841	William Henry Harrison dies;	1852	Franklin Pierce (Democrat) defeats Winfield Scott (Whig) in presidential election
	John Tyler becomes president;		
	Texas president Mirabeau Buonaparte Lamar leads military expedition against Santa Fe, and is defeated	1854	Kansas-Nebraska Act becomes law
		1856	Republican party founded;
1844	Tyler's treaty to annex Texas defeated in Senate;		James Buchanan (Democrat) defeats John C. Frémont (Republican) in presidential election
	Martin Van Buren defeated in try for Democratic nomination;	1857	Supreme Cour decides *Dred Scott* v. *Sanford;*
	James K. Polk (Democrat) defeats Henry Clay (Whig) in presidential election;		Kansas adopts Lecompton Constitution, which Congress rejects
	Oregon boundary dispute with Britain settled.	1859	John Brown raids federal armory in Harper's Ferry, Virginia, and is hanged
1845	Texas annexed by joint resolution of Congress;	1860	Abraham Lincoln (Republican) defeats John Breckinridge (Southern Democrat), John Bell (Constitutional Union), and Stephen Douglas (Democrat) in presidential election
	Polk orders General Zachary Taylor to move his army to the Nueces River		
1846	Mexico rejects American offer to purchase territory;	1861	By mid-February, seven southern states secede and set up Confederate States of America
	Polk orders Taylor across the Nueces, war declared;		

that had essentially repudiated the *Dred Scott* decision; and a northern population that made a martyr of a madman who had tried to provoke a slave insurrection—such events made the radicals' arguments more and more compelling. With the triumph of the Black Republicans, it seemed clear that the time for the South to rise against the tyranny that was determined to deprive it of its rights and liberty had come. The secessionists were well prepared to seize the moment, and they did. By February 1861, more than a month before the inauguration of Lincoln, seven states of the lower South—South Carolina, Mississippi, Florida, Alabama, Georgia, Louisiana, and Texas—had seceded. They adopted a provisional constitution for the Confederate States of America and selected Jefferson Davis as provisional president. The day of wrath and judgment that Augustine St. Clare had warned of and that Abraham Lincoln later referred to as "this mighty scourge of war" was close at hand.

SUGGESTIONS FOR FURTHER READING

UNCLE TOM'S CABIN

Uncle Tom's Cabin is readily available in several paperback and hardcover editions. The best discussion of this novel is the opening chapter of Edmund Wilson, *Patriotic Gore: Studies in the Literature of the American Civil War* (1961). Stowe's novel is criticized for its racist assumptions in James Baldwin, *Notes of a Native Son* (1971). Edward Wagenknecht, *Harriet Beecher Stowe* (1965), is a good short biography. Charles H. Foster, *The Rungless Ladder: Harriet Beecher Stowe and American Puritanism* (1954), discusses the theological sources of the novel. Milton Rugoff, *The Beechers* (1981), tells the story of that extraordinary family. Jeanne Boydston et al., *The Limits of Sisterhood: The Beecher Sisters on Women's Rights and Woman's Sphere* (1988), contains an excellent set of documents. Robert H. Abzug, *Passionate Liberator: Theodore Dwight Weld and the Dilemma of Reform* (1980), is a biography of the abolitionist who managed to embroil the Beecher family in the antislavery issue.

EXPANSION IN THE 1840s

Albert K. Weinberg, *Manifest Destiny* (1935), is the classic account of American expansionism. Charles G. Sellers, Jr., *James K. Polk: Continentalist, 1843–1846* (1966), is a relatively sympathetic account. Otis Singletary, *The Mexican War* (1960), and K. Jack Bauer, *The Mexican-American War* (1974), provide good one-volume treatments of the Mexican War. William R. Brock, *Parties and Political Conscience* (1979), establishes the political context of sectional conflict during the 1840s. The story of Mexico's attempt to govern and retain its northern territories is admirably treated in Donald J. Weber, *The Mexican Frontier, 1821–1846: The American Southwest Under Mexico* (1982). The southern understanding of the politics of slavery and expansion is well covered in William Cooper, *The South and the Politics of Slavery, 1828–1856* (1978).

THE 1850s

David Potter, *The Impending Crisis, 1848–1861* (1976), is the best introduction to the events of this decade. Michael F. Holt, *The Political Crisis of the 1850s* (1978), is a recent analysis of changing party alignments. For the Compromise of 1850, see Holman Hamilton, *Prologue to Conflict* (1964). Eric Foner, *Free Soil, Free Labor, Free Men* (1970), is an important book about the political ideology of the early Republican party. The enforcement of the Fugitive Slave Law is the subject of Stanley Campbell, *The Slave Catchers* (1968). Biographies of two contrasting figures also illuminate some of the key events of the period: Robert W. Johannsen, *Stephen A. Douglas* (1973), and Stephen P. Oates, *To Purge This Land with Blood: A Biography of John Brown* (1970). Don E. Fehrenbacher, *Prelude to Greatness* (1962), deals with Abraham Lincoln during the 1850s. Dwight Dumond, ed., *Southern Editorials on Secession* (1931), and Harold C. Perkins, ed., *Northern Editorials on Secession*, 2 vols. (1942), provide a good sampling of newspaper opinion on the crisis of the Union.

Chapter 13

His Terrible, Swift Sword

Episode: Abraham Lincoln—From Politics to Martyrdom

The Mighty Scourge of War

- Building and Equipping Armies
- Strategy—Theory and Practice
- The Struggle Begins
- Leadership and Opposition in Wartime
- War and Slavery
- The Struggle Climaxes
- The Election of 1864
- The Struggle Ends
- The Toll of Total War

THE EPISODE: *If the importance of historical figures can be measured by the amount of attention that historians and biographers pay to them, then Abraham Lincoln was surely the most important American. In this chapter, we look in some detail at several crucial moments and themes in his career as president.*

The first is the secession crisis, which the new president confronted when he took office in March of 1861. The second is Lincoln's attempt to define the Civil War as the ultimate test of the principles of republican government, an attempt he began soon after the war started and that climaxed at Gettysburg, Pennsylvania, in 1863, when he said that the cause of the Union was the cause of "government of the people, by the people, for the people." The third is his halting, tentative effort to confront the question of slavery and the relationship between the preservation of the Union and freedom for African Americans. The fourth is his assassination and the public mourning that followed, which made it clear that he had become the symbol, in the North at least, of both union and liberty.

We chose these moments and themes not only because they are intrinsically interesting and important, but because they also reveal much about a transformation in the man. When he ran for president in 1860, Abraham Lincoln was a folksy, practical, politically shrewd Illinois politician with a flair for words. If he had died then, nothing he had done would have made him more than a footnote to history. When he did die less than five years later, most Americans would agree that he was the nation's savior, the Great Emancipator, the embodiment of their highest national aspirations.

THE HISTORICAL SETTING: *Abraham Lincoln did not cause the Civil War. In a sense, the war caused him—made him into the leader and the monumental memory he became. Understanding what happened to Abraham Lincoln after 1861 means understanding what happened to the nation during a war of a duration, nature, and destruction that no one did anticipate—or could have anticipated—in April 1861.*

The momentous questions he confronted during every day of his two terms as president were the same questions that were also confronted by American men and women, North and South, white and African American. Would there be war? If the war came, who would fight and what would be the strategies of battle? Who would prevail, and how? And what would be the political, economic, and social fate of millions of African Americans held in slavery, not only in the states that formed the Confederacy but in several states that remained loyal to the Union?

Abraham Lincoln—From Politics to Martyrdom

As the winter of 1860–1861 ended, the new president came quietly, even somewhat secretly, into Washington to take his oath of office. He was about to face a reality no other American president had to face: a divided union. And no one, not even men who had agreed to serve in his cabinet, not even the political friends who had helped engineer his nomination and win his election, knew what his strategies and policies would be. Most people who thought about Abraham Lincoln at all thought of him as a western lawyer, as a pretty good stump speaker, and—above all—as a shrewd politician. And they were, in the main, right. Lincoln had shown a remarkable ability to find moderate positions about slavery, positions he knew were not far from the opinions of the Northern voters who had elected him.

No one could have predicted that four years later, a murdered Abraham Lincoln would leave the capital as the greatest national hero since George Washington. When his body returned westward, back to Illinois, it was no longer the political figure, or even the political leader, that people mourned. It was a dedicated, heroic martyr to what Lincoln had managed to define as a national crusade. He had managed to transform an ugly civil war into a spiritual struggle for principles much higher than the political unity of a nation. His death put the seal on that transformation.

He began his presidency by playing a complicated political "game," as he sometimes called it. The game became war. And war changed Abraham Lincoln. The change was not complete: the shrewd politician remained always a part of him. But he began to see the war as something more than politics, more even than battle and suffering. Part of him began to think of it as a religious experience, in which a nation that seemed to have been chosen by God for special blessings was now being put through a special trial and punishment. He began to insist more and more that the war was a kind of blood sacrifice demanded by God as a payment for the long sin of slavery. And when, at the war's end, he paid with his own blood, dramatic proof seemed to be given that his redefinition of the war was correct.

As Lincoln prepared to take office, the political situation was so delicate and so dangerous that even his practical skills had only a slender chance. Seven states in the lower South had already seceded and had established a new federal government for themselves, the Confederate States of America. Several states in the upper South, particularly Virginia, Maryland, and Kentucky, were poised to join the new Confederacy.

ABRAHAM LINCOLN, 1860 AND 1865. The first portrait shows Lincoln in June 1860, at the opening of his presidential campaign. The second, taken just four days before his assassination, reveals the psychological and physical toll the Civil War had extracted from Lincoln.

All the federal officials in the seceded states had either given allegiance to the Confederacy or had been replaced by secessionists. The Confederacy had taken over almost all the federal property within its borders—the post offices, the customs and land offices, even the forts and arsenals. All that remained of visible federal authority were two forts. One was Fort Pickens, far off in Pensacola, Florida; the other was Fort Sumter in Charleston Harbor, in the heart of secession country.

Then, as inauguration day approached, there was a strange lull. Everyone waited to see what Lincoln would do. He made no public statements. The only prediction anyone could hazard was that his actions would be—characteristically—cautious, secretive, and essentially political. In Lincoln's mind, the best direction things could go was clear: secession would somehow be stopped without violence; the Union would be restored. And this would be done without compromising the basic Republican position on slavery in the western territories. The problem was, did he have the means and the power to work out such a political solution?

The answer would surely lie with Virginia. If he could manipulate events carefully enough so that Virginia stayed in the Union, then surely Maryland and Kentucky, probably Tennessee and Missouri, would follow Virginia's lead. Time would take its toll on the weak and isolated Confederacy. Good sense might win out, and one by one the seceding states could come back into the Union.

At this point, Lincoln saw the problem in terms that were legal, political, and constitutional. It was illegal for any state to secede. He had no doubt of that. But it was equally unconstitutional for the federal government to interfere at all with slavery in any of the states. The political bargain he wanted was for the upper South to accept this political settlement, remain in the Union, and keep their slave system as long as they could make it last.

But it was a tricky situation. If Lincoln did anything that even seemed hostile, he might provoke the border states and the upper South, especially Virginia, into joining the Confederacy, leaving the Union in a much more vulnerable position if and when war came. But he could not simply ignore secession: The people who had elected him expected Lincoln to stand up to the slave power, not give in to it. Should he try to get national institutions going again and send Republican postmasters, judges, and customs officials into the Confederacy? Should he try to reclaim federal property? What about Fort Pickens and Fort Sumter? There had already been one crisis over Fort Sumter. On December 26 Major Robert Anderson had moved his Union garrison out of Fort Moultrie, far out in the harbor, into Sumter. But outraged South Carolinians had demanded the total evacuation of federal troops. After three days of vacillation, President Buchanan had rejected the Confederate demand and the first Sumter crisis had died down. But Fort Sumter had become an important symbol: to the North it was an emblem of the endurance of the Union; to the South it was a galling sign of Yankee aggression.

Lincoln announced his policy in his first act as president, his inaugural address. He began by reassuring the South. His administration would not "directly or indirectly interfere with the institution of slavery where it exists." Lincoln then flatly declared that the Union remained unbroken. "No state," he insisted, "can lawfully get out of the Union; and acts of violence within any state or states against the authority of the United States are insurrectionary." He warned that he would use "the power confided to me to hold, occupy, and possess the property and places belonging to the government." But then, his resolve to defend the Union unmistakable, he assured the South that there would be "no bloodshed or violence unless it be forced upon the national authority." He would deliver the mails only if the South wanted them delivered, and he would not "force obnoxious strangers into the South to carry out Federal business." Even though he had "the strict legal right" to do so, he would "forgo, for the time, the use of such offices" because any attempt to do otherwise "would be so irritating and so nearly impracticable."

Finally, Lincoln insisted again on his peaceful intentions. "In your hands, my dissatisfied fellow countrymen, and not mine, is the momentous issue of Civil War—the government will not assail you. You can have no conflict, without being yourself the aggressors."

Lincoln was carefully walking a political tightrope, trying to avoid as long as possible any action that would set events on an irreversible course to war. His policy was designed to buy some political time to get his administration set up and to let Unionist sentiment in the South regroup. But the policy was also aimed toward making sure that if war did come, the responsibility for starting it would lie not with Lincoln but with his "dissatisfied fellow countrymen." It would be easier to rally the political support needed to wage war if the Confederacy rather than Lincoln was seen as the aggressor. Also, if Lincoln started the war, all the remaining slave states would probably join the Confederacy, and then Britain and France, leaping at the chance to split the American empire, might formally recognize the Confederacy as a separate nation.

Lincoln's policy of "masterly inactivity," as *The New York Times* dubbed it, rested on the assurance of his military advisers that Fort Sumter could hold out indefinitely and stand as a continuing symbol of the unbroken Union. But the day after Lincoln delivered his inaugural address, Major Anderson sent the surprising word that his provisions would last only four to six weeks. He would have to surrender Fort Sumter unless 70,000 troops were sent to relieve him.

So Sumter would have to be reinforced or evacuated. Neither alternative was very desirable in political terms. Sending military relief would certainly bring civil war. It would surely drive the upper South and quite possibly the border states as well into the Confederacy. But evacuation also had political risks. It would probably avoid war for a time and might help Southern Unionists. But it might push reunion ever further away by confirming the secessionists' claim that the North lacked the will to fight, thus strengthening their political grip on the Confederate states. The impact of evacuation on Northern opinion could be even more disastrous. Most Northerners, and especially the Republican majority that had elected Lincoln, would surely consider evacuation a betrayal of his pledge to "hold and possess" federal property. This might so discredit him as a political leader that his capacity to govern would collapse. And that, Lincoln feared, would lead to the collapse of the Republican party, the political force that had finally succeeded in wresting the federal government away from the slave power. Everything the Republicans had fought for during six long years would be lost forever.

Lincoln proceeded cautiously. He asked each of the members of his cabinet for a written response to the suggestion that provisions only, not fresh troops, be sent to Fort Sumter. Only one man, Postmaster General Montgomery Blair, urged that course. The others feared that even this would lead to war. Secretary of State William Seward argued most vehemently against sending provisions, insisting that the evacuation of Sumter was the only possible way, short of war, to end the crisis and restore the Union. Lincoln listened to the debate but did not express a firm position of his own. Those around him certainly thought he had accepted the overwhelming opinion of his cabinet that the fort would have to be surrendered. In fact (unknown to Lincoln), Seward privately assured some Confederate commissioners who had come to Washington to demand recognition of the Confederacy that Sumter would be evacuated. The commissioners knew that Lincoln could not possibly accept their demand for recognition, but they hoped to use his formal refusal to prove their contention that his real intent was hostile. Arguing that Sumter was about to be evacuated, Seward persuaded the commissioners to delay asking for an immediate answer to their demand. He himself favored evacuation and was dead certain that the inexperienced Lincoln would follow his seasoned advice.

But Lincoln had not decided to pull out of Fort Sumter. Seward and the others had misread his silence as an endorsement of evacuation. (Lincoln usually listened to advice, but he rarely revealed his own intentions until he was ready to act.) Though it seemed likely that Sumter would have to be abandoned, Lincoln was reluctant to take the step and played for more time. He had ordered the troops waiting aboard ship in Pensacola Harbor to move into Fort Pickens. This quiet, relatively unprovocative act might let him turn Pickens into the symbol of an unbroken Union. He sent Stephen Hurlbut, a Charleston-born friend, to South Carolina to find out how strong the Union sentiment there really was.

But the clamor for action was mounting. The rumors of an impending evacuation of Sumter were eroding Lincoln's support, and disillusionment over his "weakness" and "inaction" began to set in. "The country feels no more assurance as to the future than it did on the day Mr. Buchanan left Washington," *The New York Times* editorialized. "The people want something to be decided on—some standard raised—some policy put forward which shall serve as a rallying point for the abundant but discouraged loyalty of the American heart." Lincoln's old friend Senator Lyman Trumbull of Illinois introduced a resolution in the Senate declaring that it was "the duty of the President to use all the means in his power to hold and protect the property of the United States."

Hurlbut reported back that Unionism was utterly dead in South Carolina and all but extinct in other seceding states. He was sure that the Confederacy would accept nothing but "unqualified recognition of absolute independence," and he believed that nothing done "by the government will prevent the possibility of armed collision." Major Anderson in the meantime sent back word that he could hold out no longer than April 15. So on March 29 Lincoln ordered that an expedition to provision Sumter be prepared, "to be used, according to circumstance."

Still, the president hesitated. For weeks he had waited for word from Pensacola, but when it finally came, on April 6, it was not what Lincoln had hoped to hear. The order to garrison Fort Pickens, sent by sea rather than land, had taken a long time to get there. When it finally had arrived, it had not been obeyed! The captain of the troopship, acting on orders issued under Buchanan, would not take orders from the army and refused to act until a navy superior told him to. Now lack of supplies would force the surrender of Sumter before Pickens could be established as the symbol of the Union. And so, finally, Lincoln sent a message to Governor Pickens of South Carolina, informing him that "an attempt will be made to supply Fort Sumter with provisions only, and that if such attempt be not resisted, no effort to throw in men, arms, or ammunition will be made without further notice, or in case of an attack upon the fort." On April 9 the expedition, carrying provisions for a year, set forth with an armed escort.

Lincoln's message to Governor Pickens surprised and angered Southern leaders, who thought that Seward had spoken for Lincoln when he had promised the evacuation of Sumter. But secessionists were also becoming impatient with the inactivity of their leaders. The United States flag fluttering above the fort, in full view of Charlestonians, was a continuing affront to the idea of Southern independence. The Confederates acted. At 4:30 A.M. on April 12, 1861, before the relief expedition had time to arrive, shore batteries opened fire on Fort Sumter. The next day Major Anderson surrendered the fort and withdrew his forces, and on the following day, April 14, Lincoln, declaring that the South had fired the first shot, issued a call for 75,000 volunteers to put down the insurrection.

Lincoln's efforts to avoid the war had been political—naturally enough, for the situation was political until one side or the other began to shoot. And the political task had suited his personality and his talents. Now, confronted with a war that quickly became more deadly and more enduring than anyone on either side expected, what would Lincoln do? What was there in his character that would emerge under the intense pressure of armed conflict?

Initially, some of his work was still mainly political. He had to organize the government for war. He had to take full control of his party, which was as yet merely a loose electoral coalition. Few Republicans felt much loyalty to the "little Illinois lawyer," as Secretary of State William Seward had once called Lincoln. He had become president through a combination of adroit maneuvering and accident. Now he had to spend enormous amounts of time handing out the favors and the offices that would create political loyalties.

But in the midst of the politics, a new Lincoln began to find his voice. He developed a special way of talking about the war—no longer as a war for the Union, or just as a combat forced on the government by a few hotheads in the South. In his language, the war gradually became a test of the principles of freedom and democracy—for white people, at least. On July 4, in a message calling Congress into special session, Lincoln stated the argument he was to use for the next four years: that the struggle was not between North and South, or between union and secession, but a struggle for the rights of the people. The real issue, he declared,

> embraces more than the fate of these United States. It presents to the whole family of man the question whether a constitutional republic, or a democracy—a government of the people, by the same people—can or cannot maintain its territorial integrity against its domestic foes. It presents the question whether discontented individuals, few in number, can arbitrarily break up their government and thus practically put an end to free government upon the face of the earth.

These brief words summarized a brilliant rhetorical strategy. There were three interlocking steps. First, identify the Union cause as the cause of "the people," the cause of democracy. Second, make the outcome a test case of the cause of democracy not just in the United States but for the whole world, "the family of man." Third, make the outcome the ultimate test case: if democracy cannot survive here and now, then it can never survive anywhere.

From that July 4 address to the end of the Civil War in 1865, Abraham Lincoln continued to insist on these principles. They were somewhat illogical: there was no sound reason why democracy might not fail in the United States and still succeed in other places. And they were somewhat unrealistic: there was in fact little or no democracy for the "family of man" in the world. But neither logic nor realism was at stake for Lincoln. He understood the necessity of enabling his countrymen to believe they were embarked on an ennobling crusade. And he plainly came to believe it himself.

Lincoln's definition of the war got its most famous statement two years later, in November 1863. He traveled to Gettysburg, Pennsylvania, where the Union armies had turned back a Confederate advance in one of the bloodiest battles of the war just three months earlier. Lincoln's speech came at the end of a long ceremony dedicating a military cemetery. This short address came to represent his greatest performance as a writer, speaker, and ideological leader of his people. His strategy had not changed. He still defined the war as a war for democracy, for all the world, and for all time. But the tactics had become even more skillful.

First, Lincoln sanctified democracy by making it into an inheritance. "Four score and seven years ago," he began, "our fathers brought forth on this continent a new nation, conceived in Liberty, and dedicated to the proposition that all men are created equal." No more skillful sentence was ever written by an American president. "Four score and seven years" sounded much more ancient and more holy than "eighty-seven." And "our fathers brought forth . . . conceived . . . " was the language of procreation and birth. It stood in superb dramatic contrast to the place of death he had come to dedicate. Again, the logic and the accuracy were questionable. The United States was already heavily populated by immigrants whose "fathers" had not "brought forth" the nation at all. And it was equally true that the fathers who had "conceived" the nation included a great many slaveholding Virginians and South Carolinians. But once again, logic and realism were not what counted. Lincoln was making the war into an act of faith.

In his next paragraph—and the Gettysburg Address consisted of only two paragraphs—he began to make this religious message clear. The first sentence used the words *dedicate, consecrate,* and *hallow:* "But in a larger sense, we cannot dedicate, we cannot consecrate, we cannot hallow, this ground. The brave men, living and dead, who struggled here, have consecrated it . . . " (Those brave men, of course, were all Union soldiers, for nothing in Lincoln's way of defining the struggle could admit Confederate dead to a share in "the unfinished work . . . so nobly advanced.") The issue was, in the end, dedication—not the dedication of a cemetery but the need for dedication of those who lived on to complete the work. And so Lincoln ended with a ringing plea that "we here highly resolve that these dead shall not have died in vain—that this nation, under God, shall have a new birth of freedom—and that government of the people, by the people, for the people, shall not perish from the earth."

Lincoln had, by the force of his words more than by any other means, made the war into a crusade. But while he worked out the definition of the crusade as a struggle to defend democracy for all time, a nagging, often private dilemma would not go away. Lincoln's fine speech at Gettysburg did not mention the problem of slavery. Was that part of the crusade? Did "our" fathers include African-American fathers? Did "a new birth of freedom" include freedom and some measure of equality for slaves? This part of Lincoln's drama was never settled with anything like the clarity and coherence of his mighty assertion of liberty and democracy as the real stakes of war. But his halting, indecisive attempts to confront the issue of slavery are still a central thread in the story of his movement toward heroic martyrdom.

While Lincoln was defining the war as democracy's struggle for survival, other men around him wanted a different, more radical definition. For them, slavery was the issue. Charles Sumner, a Massachusetts senator and the leader of the abolitionist wing of the Republican party, insisted that Lincoln strike immediately at slavery—both as an act of justice and as a military measure to weaken the Confederacy. Frederick Douglass, the leading black abolitionist, declared that "the innermost logic of events will force it upon them in the end: that the war is a war for and against slavery." A leading white abolitionist, Wendell Phillips, spoke in even more demanding terms to the North: "Seize the thunderbolt God has forged for you, and annihilate the system that has troubled your peace for seventy years."

But Lincoln hung back. He knew that somehow slavery was "the root of the rebellion." And he knew he did not like it. He could not remember a time when he did not believe that "if slavery is not wrong, nothing is wrong." At the same time, he shared the view of most Northern white voters that black people were racially inferior to whites. Even if he considered fighting the war *against* slavery, he could not conceive of it as a war *for* black freedom and equality. He was also deeply convinced that the Constitution did not give him any power to interfere with slavery within the states.

Most of all, the idea of emancipating slaves by executive order went against Lincoln's political instincts. He knew that a leader who defied public opinion might lose his capacity to lead at all. He had not been elected on an abolitionist platform (and no Republican could have been elected that way). The support he enjoyed early in the war came to him as the friend of the Union, perhaps as the friend of democracy and liberty for whites, but not as the friend of black slaves. Most of all, Lincoln feared that the political outcome of any attempt to emancipate the slaves would be to drive the border states, especially Kentucky, into the Confederacy. "To lose Kentucky," he said, "is nearly the same as to lose the whole game. Kentucky gone, we could not hold Missouri, nor, as I think, Maryland. These all against us, the job on our hands is too large for us. We would as well consent to the separation at once, including the surrender of this capital."

But Frederick Douglass was right: the "innermost logic of events" did keep forcing the question of slavery to the surface. In the most practical way, military commanders operating in places like Missouri and Maryland had to deal with the status of slaves. Twice, in August 1861 and then again in May 1862, Union generals in the field issued orders declaring the slaves of rebels or slaves who had come within Union battle lines free. Lincoln quickly and unambiguously canceled both orders, to the dismay of abolitionists in the North.

Lincoln was in trouble. And he groped for a solution. He proposed the old idea of colonization—sending freed slaves out of the country. He even had agents scouting out suitable land in Central America. He promoted the idea of encouraging slaveholders to give up their slaves voluntarily, in return for federal government compensation.

But he was beginning a private journey toward a new policy. During the spring of 1862, he slipped down into the telegraph room of the White House. It was the only

LINCOLN AND HIS CABINET. Lincoln selected his cabinet carefully, making sure that the many factions of his party were represented. From left to right: Edwin M. Stanton, secretary of war; Salmon P. Chase, secretary of the treasury; Lincoln; Gideon Welles, secretary of the navy; Caleb Smith, secretary of the interior; William H. Seward, secretary of state; Montgomery Blair, postmaster general; Edward Bates, attorney general.

place he could hide from the nagging politicians and office seekers who dogged his tracks all day. There he wrote out a draft proclamation of emancipation, which he put away to use in case he needed it.

It waited for two months, until July 1862. He continued to try to rally support for his plan for voluntary, gradual, and compensated emancipation followed by colonization. But the support did not come quickly enough nor in great enough strength. On July 13 Lincoln hinted to two members of his cabinet that emancipation might become a "military necessity." A week later, on July 21, he called the rest of the cabinet together to read them his draft of an emancipation proclamation. The cabinet was stunned by the policy change. They argued the question back and forth while the president listened. Finally, he was persuaded to wait again. The Union was still losing battle after battle. At home and in Europe, a proclamation might seem to be only a clumsy attempt to draw public attention away from the military blundering and defeats. Back into Lincoln's desk drawer went the draft, to wait for at least a Union victory.

While he waited, the president suffered, publicly and privately. In public, he was accused of being "an Ass for the Slave Power to ride." Horace Greeley, editor of the *New York Tribune,* an influential Republican paper, printed an open letter to the president: "On the whole face of this wide earth, Mr. President, there is not one determined, intelligent champion of the Union cause who does not feel that all attempts to put down the Rebellion and at the same time uphold its inciting cause are preposterous and futile."

The *Tribune* letter gave Lincoln a chance to restate, in the clearest possible way, his continued analysis of the relationship between the war and slavery. He did wish, he wrote in reply, that "all men everywhere be free." But—and the but was the same one that had dogged him since his election—"My paramount object is to save the Union and is not either to save or to destroy Slavery. If I could save the Union without freeing any slave I would do it, and if I could save it by freeing all the slaves, I would do it, and if I could do it by freeing some and leaving others alone, I would also do that."

That answer might satisfy some, even most, Northerners. But the private suffering was harder to deal with. Lincoln had begun to brood over the meaning of the war—especially of the Union defeats—in a way that went far beyond politics and public opinion. After one particularly disastrous military failure, he sat in his study at night and thought about God. "We are whipped again." That much was clear. If God was all powerful, as Lincoln devoutly believed He was, then why did the slaveholders keep winning? Maybe God had something in mind that neither Union nor Confederacy could know. "God wills this contest, and wills that it should not end yet," he thought. "By His mere quiet power, He could have either saved or destroyed the Union without human contest." Alone, at night, Lincoln began to wonder whether he "might be an instrument in God's hands for accomplishing a great work." He even began to look for some kind of sign from God.

The sign—or something like it—came on the battlefield. The Confederates invaded Maryland at summer's end, in 1862. This time they were stopped cold. The Union commander wired that he had won a great victory, a statement Lincoln soon learned was somewhat exaggerated. But he proclaimed the victory anyway. Lincoln went to his cabinet and told them he had made a covenant with God that when victory came in Maryland, he would consider it an indication of the Divine Will that he should move forward in the cause of emancipation.

The next day, September 22, 1862, Lincoln issued his Emancipation Proclamation. He had come only a little distance. The proclamation did not free a single slave until New Year's Day 1863, and then it declared only that the slaves in Confederate territory were to be freed. Since most of that territory was still very firmly in the hands of the Southerners, the proclamation could hardly be enforced. In fact, the proclamation suggested a very odd paradox: that slavery was illegal in rebel states but still perfectly all right in Union states like Kentucky or Missouri—in the city of Washington itself, if it came to that.

But Lincoln had done one decisive thing. He had settled one question firmly that no one had considered settled before. If the Union won the war, then slavery in the American South would effectively come to an end. Now the war was not just a war for the Union but against slavery. It was not yet a war for African-American rights—and it never would become quite that. But it was a very different thing from the intricate political game it had been when the president took office.

Abraham Lincoln's sense that the Civil War had some sort of deep, religious meaning deepened over the next year and a half. The casualty lists grew to appalling proportions on both sides. But the months and the battles favored the Union, whose armies now advanced in the unanticipated role of liberating armies for black slaves. No one, including Lincoln, had any clear idea what liberation might mean in fact and in practice. But Frederick Douglass's "logic of events" had done its work. When on March 4, 1865, Lincoln again climbed the steps of the Capitol to deliver his second inaugural address, the end was in sight. He knew everything he said would be studied with care by men and women, blacks and whites, in the North and in the South. And so he tried once more to say what the war signified, to give some explanation of the reasons he thought the nation had to endure what it was going through.

When the war had begun almost four years earlier, he began, no one on either side had guessed that it would last so long, or that it would be transformed into a war against slavery. But that had been God's will. He had given the Americans this long and "terrible war," perhaps as a punishment for the offense of slavery. "Fondly do we hope, fervently do we pray," Lincoln went on, "that this mighty scourge of war may speedily pass away." His language had the accents of the Old Testament prophets. And he did not hold back: "Yet if God wills that it continue until all the wealth piled by the bondsman's two hundred and fifty years of unrequited toil shall be sunk, and until every drop of blood drawn with the lash shall be paid by another drawn with the sword, as was said three thousand years ago, so still must be said, the judgements of the Lord are true and righteous altogether."

But in the religious world of Abraham Lincoln and of most of his countrymen, North and South, the Lord did not only judge, he forgave. So Lincoln ended with a plea that echoed more the New Testament than the Old. "With malice toward none; with charity for all; with firmness in the right as God gives us to see the right, let us strive to finish the work we are in; to bind up the nation's wounds, to care for him who shall have borne the battle, and for his widow, and his orphan—to do all which may achieve a just and lasting peace, among ourselves and with all nations." Here were the words so central to the New Testament: *charity, light, care, peace.* When he lay dead a few weeks later, the vocabularies of both testaments would echo back over him, and he would be compared to Moses, then to Jesus.

At Appomattox Courthouse in Virginia on April 9, 1865, Robert E. Lee surrendered his Army of Northern Virginia to Ulysses S. Grant. By April 14—which was Good Friday—it had all begun to sink in: armed resistance in the South was practically over. The sadness that had seemed to weigh so heavily on Lincoln lifted a bit. That night, he and his wife would go to the theater. A new English comedy, *Our American Cousin,* had just opened at Ford's Theater, and the Lincolns were in just the right mood for such a play. During the third act, John Wilkes Booth, a member of the famous Booth family of actors, slipped into the president's box, pointed a derringer at Lincoln's head, and pulled the trigger. Lincoln slumped forward, with the bullet that had passed through his brain now lodged just behind his right eye. He probably never knew what had happened. He was carried, deeply unconscious, to a house across the street. All through the night, the hopeless vigil of the doctors, of high government officials, and of Lincoln's son, Robert, continued. Then, at 7:22 in the morning, Lincoln died. The secretary of war, Edwin Stanton, was heard to mutter, "Now he belongs to the ages."

Stanton was right. What now began was a drama of grief that seemed almost boundless. War and victory had made Lincoln a hero. Now death transformed him into a near-saint. "The heart grows sick and faint," wrote the *Washington National Republican* on this day before Easter. "The pen almost refuses to trace the details of the tragedy." Crowds had gathered in the rain outside the house where Lincoln lay dying. "At 7:30 the tolling of bells announced to the lamenting people that he had ceased to breathe. His great and loving heart was still." Immediately, the streets were crowded with "people, men, women, and children, thronging the thoroughfares. It seemed as if everyone was in tears." As the bells tolled, offices, government buildings, and stores all closed. The black crepe of mourning replaced the red, white, and blue bunting that only a few days earlier had been put up to celebrate Lee's surrender. It was the same everywhere. As the telegraph hurried the news over the land, people gathered in the streets to express and share their horror, bewilderment, and grief.

To many, the loss was personal—something that had happened directly to them, not just to the nation. Some could barely contain their rage and struck out at anyone who uttered anything against the fallen president. Black freedmen were numbed by the word that the president was dead. One young girl remarked that she thought she could "never love God anymore." Walt Whitman expressed his sense of loss in a poem. News of the assassination had come to him just as the lilacs, portent of spring, rebirth, and renewal, had come into blossom:

> When lilacs last in the dooryard bloom'd
> And the great star early droop'd in the western sky in the night,
> I mourn'd, and yet shall mourn with ever-returning spring.

> *Ever-returning spring, trinity sure to me you bring,*
> *Lilac blooming perennial and drooping star in the west,*
> *And thought of him I love.*

The press and public orators struggled to find ways to comprehend and interpret the tragedy. What dumbfounded the people, wrote the *New York Herald,* was that such a thing could have happened to the American Republic. The real "horror of the deed," the *Boston Transcript* insisted, was "the fact that the victim was the kindliest and most magnanimous of great magistrates and seemed to fall martyr to his own goodness." In Lincoln's hometown, a newspaper that had not always supported the president described the event this way:

> Just in the hour when the crowning triumph of his life awaited him; . . . when he could begin clearly to see the promised land of his longings—the restored Union—the assassin's hand at once put a rude period to his life and to his hopes. As Moses of old, who had led God's people through the gloom and danger of the wilderness, dies when on the eve of realizing all that his hopes had pictured, so Lincoln is cut off just as the white wing of peace begins to reflect its silvery radiance over the red billows of war.

As the first shocked grief poured forth, plans for the funeral and burial were made. Several groups laid claim to the body. The City Council in Springfield, Illinois, insisted that Springfield "should be the final resting place for all of him that remains mortal." New York papers urged construction of a monument that would contain his remains. The Commission of Public Monuments in Washington declared that the body ought to be deposited in the vault that had been prepared for George Washington under the rotunda of the Capitol. But the distraught widow insisted (as had Washington's family) that his dust shall lie among his own neighbors and kin. Lincoln would be returned to Springfield for burial, but not directly and immediately as Mary Lincoln wanted. Her husband also belonged to the public. Secretary of War Stanton, in charge of the official arrangements, thought it was important that as many people as possible have a chance to take part in the farewell to Lincoln.

At noon on Wednesday, April 19, the official funeral service took place in the East Room of the White House. At the same hour, people all over the country gathered in their churches for simultaneous services. Lincoln's pastor eulogized the president and pointed to the belief in the "justness and goodness of God" that had been "an anchor to his soul" and had "emboldened him in his path of duty." Then a procession, led by an African-American regiment, followed by half a dozen other military units, thirty bands, and then another African-American regiment, carried the body past a vast crowd of blacks and whites, soldiers and wounded veterans, to the Capitol, where the open casket lay in state for two days. "The procession of saddened faces came pressing forward at the rate of three thousand persons per hour. The Rotunda, which was lighted only by a sort of twilight hue, was filled with solemn stillness, unbroken save by the rustling of the dresses of female mourners, and occasionally a deep sigh from some of those passing the coffin."

Then, on April 21, a nine-car funeral train left Washington for the long journey back to Springfield. The train retraced the route that just four years earlier had carried Lincoln to his inauguration. It stopped in ten cities along the way. Everywhere it was

LINCOLN'S FUNERAL TRAIN. This nine-car train carried Lincoln across the land to his grave in Springfield, Illinois.

the same: a procession through the city, ceremonies in a hall where the body lay in state, throngs of people filing past the coffin to get a last glimpse of the "face of our great friend." In Philadelphia 100,000 people joined the procession; 300,000 more looked on, as the hearse bearing the casket made its way to Independence Hall, "the Temple of American Liberty," to lie in state. When the body arrived at the hall, three women placed a cross of pure white flowers on the casket. It was, according to the silk streamer attached to it, "A Tribute to our Great and Good President Fallen a Martyr to the Cause of Human Freedom—'in my Hand No Price I Bring, Simply My Cross to Cling.'"

In every city, banners along the route that the procession took proclaimed their messages: "His Memory, like the Union he Preserved, is not for a day, but for all time"; "God's noblest work, an honest man"; "Weep, generous nation, weep; the sad, swift removal of him whom Heaven indulgent sent to man. Too good for earth, to Heaven art thou fled, and left the Nation in tears." At numerous ceremonies, Lincoln's second inaugural address was read again and again. Orators and clergymen tried to capture the meaning of the man and the tragedy. Lincoln's "death, which was meant to sever the Union beyond repair, binds it more firmly than ever," George Bancroft declared. "The country may need this imperishable grief, to touch its inmost feelings. The grave that receives the remains of President Lincoln, receives a martyr to the Union, and the monument which arises over his body will bear witness to the Union."

Not only the cities mourned. As the train passed through hamlet, countryside, and town, it went through arches with banners and emblems, past bands playing re-

THE EXECUTION OF THE CONSPIRATORS. John Wilkes Booth, killed trying to resist capture, escaped trial for the assassination of Lincoln. But four others were tried and, on July 7, 1865, publicly executed. One of them, Mary E. Surratt, in whose boardinghouse some of the plotting had taken place, was probably innocent of any involvement in the crime, a victim of the hysteria and desire for revenge that Lincoln's assassination provoked.

quiems, and regiments of militiamen and Union soldiers. Everywhere, at every hour and in every kind of weather, people thronged to see the train. At midnight, in Syracuse, New York, 35,000 people stood in a drenching rain as the train passed by. During the nights, all along the way, "a pillar of fire" guided the cortege as "at every crossroads the glare of innumerable torches illuminated the whole population from age to infancy, kneeling on the ground, their clergymen leading them in prayers and hymns."

After twelve days and more than 1,600 miles, the funeral train reached Springfield, Illinois. At ten in the morning on May 3, the casket was closed, carried to the waiting hearse, and taken by one last procession to Oak Ridge Cemetery.

The long journey was over. Stanton had said that Lincoln belonged to the ages. As the funeral train had made its way across the nation, the people themselves had poured out on him the accumulated grief of four years of war and taken possession of him. "Give him place, oh, ye prairie," the Reverend Henry Ward Beecher had said as the cortege passed through New York. "Ye winds that move over the mighty prairies of the west, chant his requiem. Ye people, behold the martyr, whose blood pleads for fidelity, for law, for liberty." From Lincoln's words and acts, out of their own needs, from historical myth and their religious traditions, they had transmuted the Lincoln many of them had once ridiculed and condemned into Lincoln the martyr—the good and pure Lincoln, who had befriended the lowly slave, and sacrificed himself for liberty and the Union. "Washington the Father, Lincoln the Savior of his Country" countless banners along the way proclaimed.

The Mighty Scourge of War

When Lincoln summoned the North to combat, few people were really surprised. War talk had been going on for a long time. But neither side was at all ready for war. The United States scarcely had a military establishment: its army existed mainly to fight Native Americans and consisted of about 20,000 soldiers scattered in remote frontier forts. Its navy was made up of about ninety ships, most of which were obsolete, out of commission, or in foreign ports. In addition, Americans were largely an agricultural people, living in a huge, sparsely populated, decentralized society.

BUILDING AND EQUIPPING ARMIES

The first task was to create armies. There was no shortage of men willing to fight. Northerners and Southerners both greeted the call to arms with naive enthusiasm. After witnessing the huge Union rallies in the city, one New Yorker declared, "It seems as if we never were alive till now; never a country till now." All over the nation, men, many scarcely more than boys, rushed to volunteer. The big question was "not who shall go to the wars, but who shall stay at home." Local communities themselves organized companies, platoons, and regiments. With a motley assortment of uniforms and weapons, with fiery speeches, and with knapsacks crammed with cakes and mementoes from wives, mothers, and sweethearts, the volunteers went off to war, flushed with idealism, eager to serve the sacred cause of Union or Southern independence. Death did not frighten the eager volunteers. If it did come, it would be heroic: "And for life, wrote one young man in words many on both sides would have echoed, if the Nation will take me, I do not see that I can put myself—experience and character—to any more useful use."

Each side expected its valor in a righteous cause to bring quick victory. *The New York Times* predicted it would take only thirty days to put down the "local commotion." The seventy-four-year-old general-in-chief, General Winfield Scott, thought it might take up to a year to bring the Confederacy to terms. On the other side, one Southerner predicted quick victory because "the Yankee army is filled with the scum of creation and ours with the best blood of the grand old Southland." There was one dissenting and, as it turned out, prescient voice, that of William T. Sherman. Shortly after the firing on Fort Sumter, he stated: "I think it is going to be a long war—very long—much longer than any politician thinks."

In July Lincoln asked Congress to authorize the enlistment of 400,000 volunteers for three years. Congress actually authorized 100,000 more than Lincoln requested and even more,

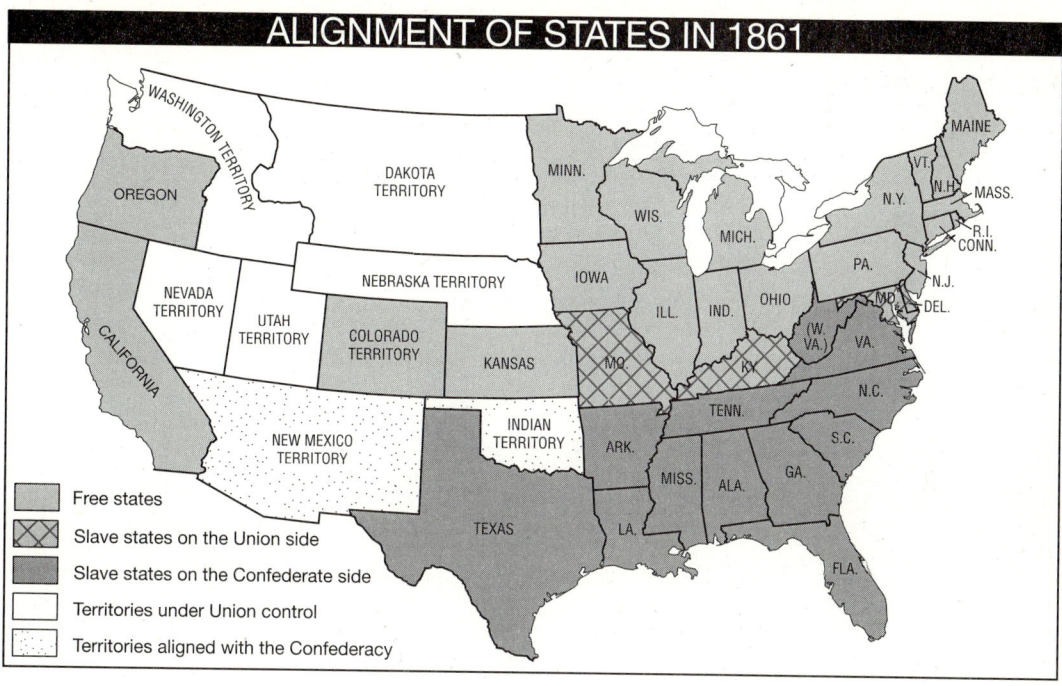

700,000 all told, met the call for volunteers. Even more quickly, the South mobilized for war. More than a month before the firing on Fort Sumter, the Confederate Congress issued a call for 100,000 men. In May, it authorized recruiting an additional 400,000 troops. The flood of volunteers had to be turned into disciplined armies. There was not much to build on. Their only military experience was the musters of local militia, to which most able-bodied white men had gone each month for a little haphazard drill, a lot of speechmaking, and even more drinking. Discipline was also a problem: Southerners and Northerners alike were an independent lot, with scant experience or liking for regimentation. In addition, at the company level, the volunteers elected their own officers, who in turn elected the regimental officers (up through the rank of major.) One Northern soldier complained that his regiment could "only justly be called a mob and one not fit to face the enemy." A more serious problem was the lack of an adequate and experienced officer corps. Of the 1,000 officers with any formal military training (about three-quarters of whom joined the Confederacy), none had ever commanded more than a few battalions. At the higher levels, command was often conferred because of political connections or local prominence rather than military competence. Throughout the war, but especially in the first two years, the war efforts of both sides and particularly the North were plagued by the incompetence of "political generals."

Creating and fielding armies also demanded kinds of economic and governmental organization that neither side had. Both sides, and particularly the North, possessed considerable resources, but in 1861 neither economy (especially the South's) was designed for feeding, equipping, and transporting large armies. The North's textile mills, for example, produced hundreds of thousands of yards of cloth each year, but this cloth was still turned into finished clothing (like uniforms) in small workshops. And the nearly 10,000 miles of Southern railroad (as much railway, in proportion to population, as the North had) did not constitute a genuine transportation

CONFEDERATE VOLUNTEERS. With the outbreak of hostilities both sides had to scramble to build armies from new volunteers and from any existing prewar militia companies. Both sides greeted the outbreak of war with confidence and enthusiasm. Here the Sumter Light Guards, which became part of the 4th Georgia Infantry Regiment, stand at review in April of 1861.

system, since few of the railroads were hooked up to each other.

There was a similar lack of administrative machinery. Except for the postal service, the federal government played only a small role in people's lives. With a minuscule military establishment, no federal taxes or national banking system, and no educational or welfare agencies, the experienced officials or bureaucratic mechanisms needed to prepare for and conduct war did not exist. Near-chaos reigned for much of the first year. Leroy P. Walker, the Confederacy's first secretary of war (whose filing system consisted of piling papers on a chair), turned away tens of thousands of volunteers because he did not know what to do with them. The Union's first secretary of war, Simon Cameron, like Walker a political appointee with no relevant experience, was equally unable to cope with the flood of recruits and military contracts. As a result, corrupt profiteers had a heyday, getting exorbitant prices for often worthless equipment. One large lot of Northern uniforms, for example, was made of shoddy, a pressed woolen fabric that disintegrated in a hard rain.

Not until well into the second year of the war did many of these problems begin to get worked out. Lincoln shipped Cameron off to a relatively innocuous ambassadorship in Russia and replaced him with Edwin Stanton, who ran the War Department from then on with incorruptible efficiency. Confederate president Jefferson Davis, too, found more competent personnel, and by 1862 the Confederacy had an ordinance chief who was able to procure 20 million cartridges for a 400,000-man army. (When the Confederacy declared war, it had only 20 cartridges per soldier.)

STRATEGY—THEORY AND PRACTICE

Economic strength, population, and military power go hand in hand, and when war began, the North seemed to have an overwhelming advantage in men and economic resources. Its population of 22 million was more than double that of the South, and it had more than three times as many white men of military age. This later advantage was partly offset by slavery. Slaves did much of the work at the home front that free men had to do in the North. This enabled the Confederacy to draw nearly 80 percent of eligible white men into the army. (Only about half of the eligible Northerners served in the war.) The North's industrial output and its overall wealth were more than ten times that of the South. In materials necessary for war, the North's advantage was even greater: it possessed eleven times as many ships, and produced fifteen times as much iron, seventeen times as much textiles, and thirty-two times as many arms. Its transportation—by river, canal, and especially rail—was much superior. It produced more than twenty times the number of locomotives, possessed four times the amount of rolling stock and more than twice the density of rail mileage.

JEFFERSON DAVIS. Though a reluctant secessionist, Davis was a firm and unrelenting champion of the Confederacy. Like Lincoln, he was often vilified by opponents who objected to his handling of the war. Imprisoned for two years after the war, he remained a believer in the righteousness of the Southern cause to the end of his life. He refused to request official amnesty and never regained United States citizenship.

The South did have some things working in its favor. The most important was that it could pursue a defensive strategy. Jefferson Davis (a West Point graduate who would have preferred to lead the Confederate armies rather than head the government) knew that the Confederacy did not have to conquer the North to achieve its war aims. It would cost far less in men and resources to force the Union to fight in the South than it would to invade the North. Davis's strategy was to have the Confederate army fight close to its economic base and use the military advantages of defense, familiar territory, and short supply lines to win a few major battles. In addition, the South would be fighting at home, against a hated, invading army. Eventually, Davis believed, the North would find the price of victory too high and would grant the Confederate States of America independence, just as a war-weary and frustrated Britain had granted the American colonies their independence. Indeed, historical precedent, not only that of the American Revolution, but Napoleon's fate in Russia as well, seemed to work in the South's favor. The Confederacy was simply too vast, its people too determined, to be conquered.

Northern strategy, not surprisingly, was almost the mirror opposite. By the nature of its paramount goal—to save the Union—the North had to go on the offensive. Only if the South was thoroughly defeated, Lincoln and his military advisers believed, could it be forced to give up its claim to independence. Lincoln knew that even with its economic superiority the North faced a task that would strain its will and resources to the utmost. And he recognized, too, the link between economic and military strength. To strangle the South economically, he declared a naval blockade, hoping to keep the Confederacy from importing the war materials it needed. A blockade was difficult—the vast Southern coastline had nearly 200 harbors and coves where cargo could be landed—and, especially in the early years of the war, was easily penetrable. Still, over the long haul, the blockade would be a valuable weapon. And, in fact, with a naval force that reached nearly 500 ships by 1864, the Northern blockade reduced Southern cotton exports to one-tenth of their prewar volume and Southern trade to one-third. On land, Lincoln planned a two-pronged attack. In the West, Northern armies would invade and try to cut the Confederacy in two, while in the East, they would strike at the Southern capital of Richmond.

These were the grand designs. But geography and the conventions of military doctrine shaped how they were put into practice. Until the last year of the war, almost all the fighting in the East took place in the narrow area between the Blue Ridge Mountains and the Atlantic Ocean and between the James and Potomac rivers, the narrow corridor between Richmond and Washington. In the thinking of the day, capital cities had great military, political, and symbolic significance. According to strategic doctrine, capturing the enemy's capital could itself bring victory, and loss of one's own might well bring defeat.

The war in the West was very different. There, the changing border between Union and Confederacy stretched for over a thousand miles. In this vast theater, warfare took many forms. The long border exposed both sides to quick strikes and raids. Along the Missouri and Kansas border, a marauding guerrilla warfare of the most brutal sort took place. (Indeed, Jesse and Frank James, the most notorious bandits in American history, got their start as members of William C. Quantrill's Confederate guerrilla band.) In the West, too, the Mississippi, Tennessee, and Cumberland rivers opened up avenues into the heart of the Confederacy.

THE STRUGGLE BEGINS

If the war could be won (or lost) quickly, as a lot of people on both sides expected it would be, then the decisive action would surely come in the East. If the war had to be fought in the heartland beyond the Appalachian Mountains—in Kentucky, Tennessee, or Mississippi—then it would be long and bitter.

During the first spring and early summer of war, 1861, not much happened on the battlefields. Both sides were getting ready. Then Lincoln decided to try for the quick victory that would end the war. He ordered General Irvin McDowell, who commanded about 30,000 inexperienced troops, to march south from Washington toward the Virginia town of Manassas, to do battle with a smaller Confederate army commanded by General P. G. T. Beauregard. In mid-July McDowell moved. Beauregard waited just south of a muddy little creek (or "run" as country people called it) named Bull Run. The two armies met on July 21. Several times the federal soldiers charged Beauregard's lines. Each time, they were driven back. Then Beauregard ordered a counterattack. The heat, the clamor, and the unexpectedly heavy casualties all took their toll on the young and green federal soldiers. The Union forward units panicked and ran back across Bull Run. The panic spread, and before it was over, McDowell had to retreat all the way to Washington.

The retreating soldiers brought only a few of their dead and wounded. But they also brought a blunt, wordless message. The war would not be won and lost in a few weeks in northern Virginia. It would be long and bloody. The first force of Union volunteers had enlisted for three months. Now Lincoln set out to raise a force of hundreds of thousands, recruited not for a few weeks but for three years. The Confederate leaders began the same grim task.

The winter of 1861–1862 was another season of regrouping, supply, and training on both sides. And when the war heated up again, it was in the West, and it was savage. The Confederate armies in Kentucky were grouped around Bowling Green in the east and Columbus in the west. A Union commander, Ulysses S. Grant, received permission to move south from Illinois to drive a wedge between the armies and try to gain control of the Tennessee River. He succeeded in capturing two Confederate forts just inside Tennessee before the Confederate commanders could get their armies in position to challenge his advance. Then he quickly headed southward up the river. By early April he had reached Pittsburg Landing,

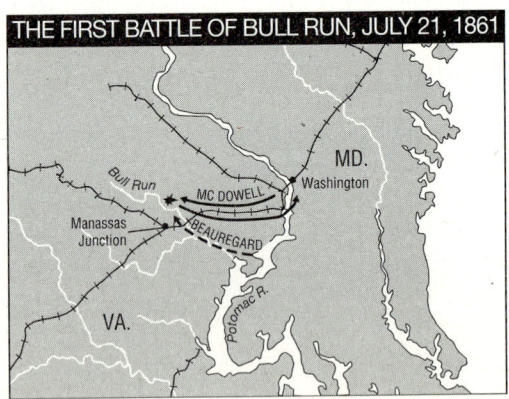
THE FIRST BATTLE OF BULL RUN, JULY 21, 1861

near the Mississippi border and a crucial rail junction at Corinth, Mississippi.

Meanwhile the two Confederate forces in the West, split by Grant's maneuver, had fallen back, abandoning the western half of Tennessee. The two armies, one commanded by Beauregard, the other by Albert Sidney Johnston, came together in northern Mississippi. Sooner or later they and Grant's force would have to meet. The Southern commanders decided to strike at Grant before Union reinforcements, racing down from Louisville, could reach him. They attacked near a Tennessee country church called Shiloh on April 6.

The struggle was ferocious. The Confederate generals had 40,000 troops to throw at Grant, who had about 33,000 men. The first day ended in stalemate, but the corpses piled up. Then Grant's reinforcements arrived, and after the second day, the Southerners had to break off their attack.

Neither army had been broken or destroyed at Shiloh. But two things were now clear. First, the Confederate forces had not been able to drive Grant's threatening army out of the Deep South. Second, the war was going to be more savage than even Bull Run had hinted it would be. On the fields and in the woods at Shiloh, nearly 2,000 Union soldiers and 2,000 of the Confederacy's best troops lay dead. Another 16,000 were wounded, of which another 2,000 would soon die. Victory was now a question of which side could stand the carnage longer, could continue to pour men and guns into one titanic battle after another, and could go on hauling away the wagonloads of the dead and wounded.

Strategically, the Union was very close to accomplishing a major goal: controlling the Mississippi. In April 1862, the same month as Shiloh, Flag Officer—soon to be Admiral—David Farragut captured Mobile and New Orleans for the Union. A little later, he had moved up the Mississippi to Baton Rouge. Grant took Corinth, Union forces occupied Memphis, and now most of the river was theirs, except for the strong Confederate fortress at Vicksburg. Things looked

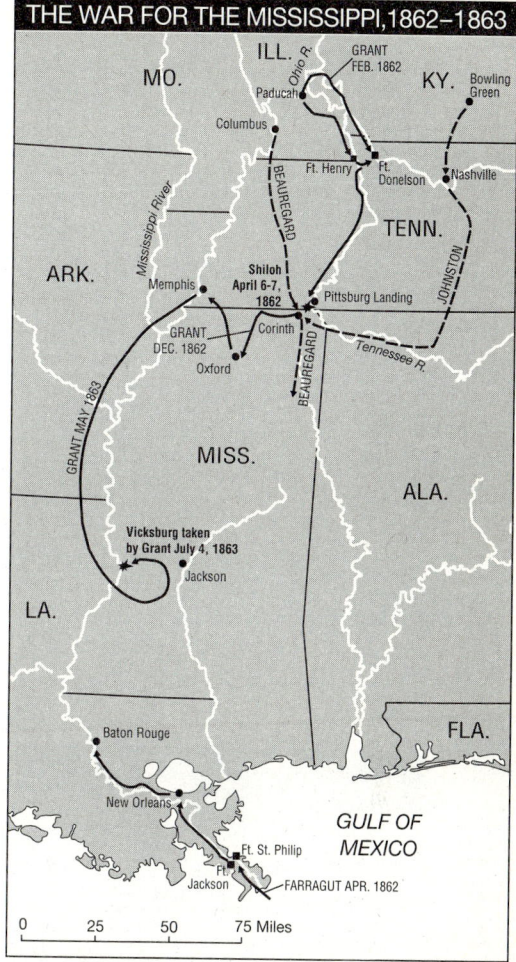

bleak for the Confederacy as the Union forces in the West pushed relentlessly forward. Even in the East, the prospects were dark: young General George McClellan, who now commanded the Army of the Potomac, had moved 100,000 men to within five miles of Richmond. The *New York Tribune* confidently proclaimed in late May, 1862, that it took "no very far reaching prophet to predict the end of this struggle."

The *Tribune* was mistaken. While the Union attack in the West went forward, the war in the East became a bloody standoff. Neither the Union's failures nor the Confederacy's successes were decisive enough to bring either side within sight of final victory or defeat.

McClellan had convinced Lincoln to let him try to take Richmond, not by land this time but by sea and up the peninsula between the York and James rivers—that same peninsula where Charles, Lord Cornwallis, had surrendered to George Washington in 1781. Confederate armies led by a new commander, Robert E. Lee, and his ablest lieutenant, General Thomas J. "Stonewall" Jackson, met the threat and turned McClellan back. The major battles of the campaign lasted seven days and took 20,000 Confederate and 15,000 Union casualties. But Lee had won. The Army of the Potomac was driven back down the peninsula.

Lincoln ordered McClellan's army home to Washington, determined to attack Richmond overland. But Lee and Jackson now moved north, hoping to defeat other Union forces near Washington before McClellan's army could complete its withdrawal and regroup. And they succeeded. A second battle near Manassas, the Second Battle of Bull Run, August 29–30, 1862, was the most decisive Confederate victory yet.

Now Lee took the offensive. His army was exhausted and low on provisions. Still, he decided on a daring stroke. A decisive conquest in the North might lead the European powers to recognize the Confederacy and even induce the North to ask for peace. So instead of pausing to rest and regroup, Lee moved his army into Maryland, knowing that the federal army would have to place itself between him and the capital, leaving Virginia's farmers free to take in the fall harvest without the presence of massive Union armies. McClellan moved out to meet the threat and threw an army of almost 90,000 at Lee's 50,000 near Sharpsburg, Maryland, at a stream called Antietam Creek.

On September 17 Lee's men and McClellan's fought three pitched battles on the same field. The Confederate lines bent under overwhelming pressure. Then, when it was clear that one more Union assault would bring a massive defeat, Jackson rushed to Lee with reinforcements. Still, McClellan might have won with one more charge. But he held back and even gave Lee another day to withdraw.

Antietam was the bloodiest single day of the war. At its end, 2,100 men in Union blue and 2,700 in Confederate gray lay dead. Over 18,000, of whom 3,000 would soon die, had been wounded. Lincoln called it a victory and used it as the occasion for the Emancipation Proclamation. But he mourned McClellan's failure to follow up on his apparent advantage, and he relieved McClellan as commander. In the East, as in the West, some things had become clear, at least for the time being. Neither side had an overwhelming advantage in the field. The Union was not able to manage a successful offensive against Richmond. But neither was Lee able to operate successfully outside Virginia. Any Union commander who wanted to defeat Lee had to be prepared to accept appalling casualties and keep attacking, again and again.

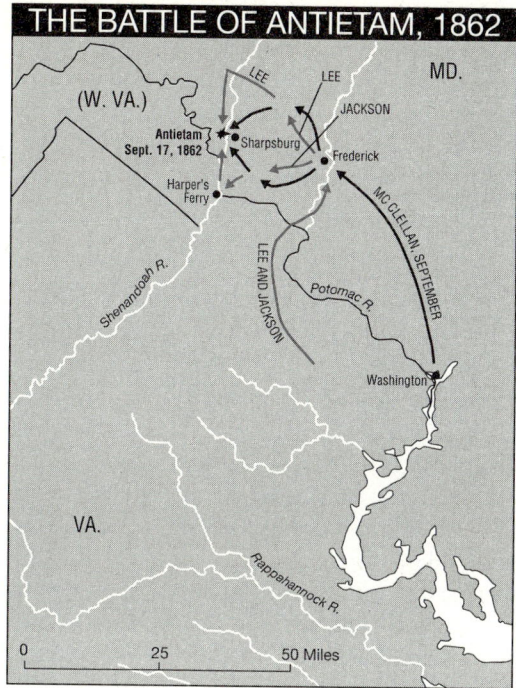

Such an officer was the man Lincoln chose to replace McClellan, General Ambrose E. Burnside. Burnside shocked Lee and Jackson by driving his Army of the Potomac across the Rappahannock River, near Fredericksburg, Virginia, and attacking strong Confederate positions on the high ground near the town. The Confederates held. Burnside sent his men again up the heights. Again they failed. The bewildered general commanded another attack. Another failure. And by the end of the battle, Burnside had lost 12,000 men in his disastrous effort. The two exhausted armies dug in for a winter of waiting on the opposite shores of the Rappahannock.

The next spring, another new general, "Fighting Joe" Hooker, took charge of the Army of the Potomac. But his luck against Lee was no better than McClellan's or Burnside's had been. Hooker tried moving upriver, then across the Rappahannock, to outflank Fredericksburg. Lee and Jackson met him at Chancellorsville, in early May 1863, and defeated him decisively. But by now the Confederacy was so weakened that no Southern general could assemble the supplies and fresh troops necessary to take decisive advantage of any victory. Once more, Lee had won, but he had won only time and stalemate. And time and stalemate were now clearly the allies of the Union.

⸺⚍⚏⸺

The fortunes of war are not made only on the battlefield. From the perspective of long-range strategy, the Union's successes in the West put it in a fairly strong position. But it did not seem that way to the Northern people. The Civil War was the first American war to get vivid daily newspaper coverage, and it was in the eastern theater that the most dramatic, closely watched, and highly publicized fighting took place. There in the early years of the war the North took a pounding, and this was far more important than Union victories in the West at Shiloh and Corinth in shaping the politics and diplomacy that could determine the outcome of the war.

Diplomacy played an important part in the Confederacy's overall strategy. From the outset, Davis hoped to secure recognition and support from the European powers, especially England and France. The South's confidence that Britain would come to its aid lay in the importance of its cotton to the English economy. Nearly 20 percent of Britain's population was dependent on textiles for its livelihood; cotton goods made up over 40 percent of its exports, and it got more than 80 percent of its raw cotton (700 million pounds per year) from the South. This situation, and the fact that Britain's own imperial designs in the Western Hemisphere would be well served if the American Union fell apart, brought that country very close to recognizing the Confederacy. As it was, in thinly disguised fashion Britain supplied the South with blockade-running ships and, at the risk of provoking war with the North, had even taken orders for two ironclad rams that could easily have broken the Northern blockade. Still, prudence and certain hard economic facts—the fact that Britain, having stockpiled a great deal of cotton before hostilities, had not yet felt much of an economic pinch; the fact that its merchants were profiting handsomely from trade with both sides; the fact that it imported a great deal of Northern wheat—dictated caution. Though leaning heavily toward the Confederacy, the British government chose to look carefully before it leaped; it waited to see how the war was going before it did anything that might provoke the North's open hostility. Lincoln knew that the British had their eyes trained on the battlefield. That was one of the reasons he so hastily proclaimed Antietam a major victory and issued the Emancipation Proclamation. He hoped to swing British public opinion behind the Northern cause.

Those at home also watched the eastern theater with concern. Northern morale—the willingness of the people of the North to endure the suffering of war—was almost as important for Northern victory as what happened on the battlefield. Lincoln knew that one of his greatest tasks was to keep up support for the war, and he tried at every point to strengthen commitment to the Union as a cause worthy of any sacrifice. Moreover, Confederate strategy was aimed directly at Northern morale. Davis expected Southern independence to come from the Confederacy's ability to hold off defeat until a weary Northern public turned against the war. The strategic importance Lee attached to the destruction of a Northern army lay in the impact he hoped it would have on Northern and foreign opinion.

Lincoln was acutely aware of how precarious Northern morale was in the summer and fall of 1862. Enthusiasm for the war had waned with the end of any hope for a quick victory, and many people were beginning to wonder if there would be *any* victory. Discontent with the administration's conduct of the war was mounting, and the war weariness threatened to slip into opposition to the war itself. Already there were those who argued that the North should stop fighting and negotiate with the Confederacy about rejoining the Union. Lincoln issued his Emancipation Proclamation partly to line up antislavery fervor solidly behind the administration and to draw more blacks into the Union's war effort. If things in the East kept going as they were, the North's will to fight might well give out.

LEADERSHIP AND OPPOSITION IN WARTIME

As the war ground on inexorably, opposition to Lincoln and Davis mounted. Northerners and Southerners increasingly blamed the seeming weakness and incompetence of their respective leaders for the hardship, suffering, and frustration they had to endure. Throughout the war, opponents portrayed Lincoln as a well-meaning but hapless bungler. To many Southerners, Davis seemed petty, aloof, bogged down in detail, and incapable of strong leadership. But oddly enough, Lincoln and Davis were also accused of being too forceful and were vilified as dictators and tyrants.

In large measure, the charge of tyranny reflected the fact that the war had led to an unprecedented centralization of government power on both sides. In 1863 the North reinstituted a national banking system. The Confederate and Union governments both levied new forms of taxation. The North imposed duties on most goods and adopted an income tax, while the South introduced a tax that required each planter and farmer to contribute 10 percent of his produce to the government. By early 1863 both sides had turned to conscription to help fill their armies. The opposition to the draft was intense, especially because the conscription acts contained exemption clauses that let the rich avoid the draft by hiring substitutes.

Finally, both presidents used executive authority in unprecedented ways. Lincoln used his authority as commander in chief to initiate limited emancipation, and Davis used executive authority to impress slaves for work on military projects and to confiscate agricultural produce for the Confederate army. Lincoln also used his war powers to control and stifle opposition to the war effort. After the firing on Fort Sumter, the administration arrested a number of Maryland citizens for pro-Confederate actions, including a judge and several members of the legislature. Chief Justice Roger Taney (who had delivered the infamous Dred Scott decision) ruled against Lincoln's suspension of the right of habeas corpus, but Lincoln ignored Taney's ruling, arguing that Article I, Section 9, of the Constitution gave the president the power to suspend the right "when in Cases of Rebellion or Invasion the Public Safety may require it." Just after issuing the Emancipation Proclamation, Lincoln issued an executive order formally suspending the writ of habeas corpus and empowering the military to arrest and detain without trial "all Rebels and Insurgents, their aiders and abettors within the United States, and all persons discouraging volunteer enlistments, resisting militia drafts, or guilty of any disloyal practice." More than 13,000 editors, public officials, and others who spoke out against such war policies as the draft or advocated making peace with the Confederacy were arrested and detained often without formal charges or trial. Jefferson Davis and Confederate military authorities took similar actions, though to a lesser extent. From an administrative point of view, these were all pragmatic measures dictated by military necessity, but to the Northerners and Southerners who experienced them, they were forms of centralization and regimentation—tyranny—that went against long-standing traditions of local autonomy.

Lincoln and Davis also found it increasingly difficult to muster the unified support needed to carry out the policies necessary for victory. The Republican party itself was divided between the moderates, for whom union was the overriding issue and who opposed actions directed against slavery, and the radicals, who insisted that the war become a crusade to end slavery. Lincoln constantly had to try to balance the conflicting demands of these two wings of his own party. Most Northern Democrats initially lined up behind the war effort, a few like Secretary of War Stanton even became Republicans of a decidedly radical stamp. But partisan politics quickly reasserted itself. The Democrats, too, were divided between "War Democrats," who supported the war effort and "Peace Democrats," dubbed Copperheads (after a particularly venomous and well-camouflaged snake) who advocated "the Constitution as it is, the Union as it was." The Peace Democrats, led by Ohio congressman Clement Vallandingham (a descendant of Southerners married to the daughter of a prominent Maryland planter) drew most of their support from the border states and the lower portions of Ohio, Indiana, and Illinois, which were heavily populated by migrants from Southern states.

From early 1862 on, even the War Democrats subjected administration policies—and especially Lincoln's leadership—to unrelenting attack. They attacked the seeming incompetence, especially when the Union armies seemed to falter, and strategic idiocies of the administration as well as the corruption. And, especially after suspension of habeas corpus and the institution of a draft, they denounced Lincoln as a tyrant. But War and Peace Democrats alike leveled their most vociferous and unrelenting attacks against the administration's new policy on slavery embodied in the Emancipation Proclamation. For more than a decade before the Civil War, the Democratic party had loudly proclaimed itself "the white man's party." Once again they made race their principal cause. "The United States," one Democratic senator thundered, "shall be the white man's home . . . and the nigger shall never be his equal." Party newspapers proclaimed the key questions in such terms as "White Supremacy or Negro Amalgamation," "Can Niggers Conquer Americans," and "Shall the Working Classes Be Equalized With Negroes." In the fall 1862 elections, such appeals made some inroads. Democratic governors were elected in New York and New Jersey, and the Democrats secured majorities in the Ohio and Indiana legislatures. But in national terms, the administration won important reendorsement of its leadership and policies, including emancipation, as the Republicans retained firm control of Congress.

There was far less opposition to the war effort in the Confederacy than in the Union. But Jefferson Davis had even greater problems than Lincoln did in getting the support he needed. Many planters, though steadfastly loyal to the Confederacy, opposed Davis's policies and did all they could to evade or subvert them. Davis's efforts also ran afoul of the doctrine of states' rights. His own vice president, Alexander Stephens, led the opposition to Davis's alleged usurpations of state sovereignty, and the governors of Georgia and North Carolina continually obstructed Davis's efforts to develop and carry out a unified policy. This dissension and disaffection proved insurmountable, even for one as singlemindedly dedicated to Southern independence as Jefferson Davis.

WAR AND SLAVERY

The Emancipation Proclamation transformed the war into an official crusade against slavery. It made it clear that victory by the North would

DRAFT RIOT IN NEW YORK CITY, 1863. Violent riots broke out in New York and other Northern cities in reaction against Abraham Lincoln's conscription policies. Most of the rioters were workers who were especially angered because men with enough money could buy their way out of being drafted. The riots were only one manifestation of widespread dissatisfaction with Lincoln's administration. In the South, Jefferson Davis also met with major resistance to his policies.

mean not only the restoration of the Union but the end of the institution of slavery. Lincoln justified his executive act legally and as a matter of policy as a "military necessity." This was partly pretense—a way for Lincoln to sell a controversial shift in policy to a reluctant Northern public—but only partly. The assault on slavery had very real significance for the outcome of the war. In the first place, of course, slavery was a vital resource for the South. As Frederick Douglass put it, slavery was "the very stomach of this rebellion." Slaves provided the bulk of the labor force at home and provided much of the labor that directly supported the Confederate war effort. They constituted two-thirds of the workforce of the South's two largest ordnance works as well as providing cooks, servants, construction laborers, and teamsters for the Confederate armies. With its slave labor force, the Confederacy was able to enlist a far larger portion of its white male population into its armies. Moreover, as the war dragged relentlessly on and especially as the Northern armies moved into the Confederacy, the African Americans became a direct and necessary asset for the Northern forces. Emancipation paved the way for recruiting the ex-slaves of the Confederacy as the servants, teamsters, and construction laborers the Union armies needed as they invaded the South.

Well before the Emancipation Proclamation made the end of slavery official Northern policy, the institution of slavery had begun to fall apart, due to the "friction and abrasion" of war. By the end of 1861, runaways to Union armies were increasingly treated as "contraband" of war, rather than returned to their masters under the terms of the Fugitive Slave Act of 1850s, which still remained in force. In August Congress passed the first of two Confiscation Acts, which authorized military commanders to seize all property used in aid of rebellion. In July of 1862, it expanded the authority even more and declared that the slaves of planters supporting the rebellion would be "deemed captives of war and shall be forever free" once they fell behind Union lines.

Almost from the outset of the war the Union armies became de facto armies of liberation. Early in 1862 Northern armies captured the Sea Islands off the coast of Georgia and South Carolina. The fleeing planters tried to take their slaves with them, but an overwhelming majority resisted these efforts and came under the (sometimes dubious) protection of the Union forces. By the end of the summer of 1862, tens of thousands more erstwhile slaves had come within the reach of Northern forces as they captured the lower Mississippi and penetrated into Tennessee and northern Alabama. Masters everywhere tried to keep news of the approach of the Northern armies and the progress of the war away from their slaves, but slaves devised ways of finding out anyway. In Forsythe, Georgia, a slave who was responsible for bringing the newspaper to his mistress always showed it to the local black preacher before he delivered it. House servants often overheard their masters talking and returned to the quarters with information about the whereabouts of the Union armies. More than once, a master awoke to find that many if not all of his slaves had slipped away in the night to become contraband.

The war altered the lives of almost everyone, subjecting them to wholly unforseen circumstances. As men went off to war, women in both North and South found themselves taking on roles and responsibilities from which they usually had been excluded, forced to manage farms, shops, and stores. In the North, women came to make up nearly one-third of the manufacturing labor force. (In 1860, they constituted less than one-quarter of the labor force.) The war also brought thousands of women into paid and volunteer positions as nurses and medical aides and, under the leadership of such women as Clara Barton, paved the way for the establishment of nursing as a profession open to women.

But no group was as severely buffeted about by the war as were the slaves. The war directly affected nearly a million and a half and brought another half a million slaves under

Union control. Many slaveholders in areas most vulnerable to Union attack—especially the Georgia and South Carolina low country and the Mississippi valley—abruptly moved their slaves to the interior and to Texas. Tens of thousands became refugees subject to the vagaries of warfare; others became roaming fugitives, seeking safety in the backwoods. Many slaves found themselves "liberated" by Union armies, only to be subjected to recapture by Confederate forces once the Union Army had retreated or moved on.

There was no settled policy about what to do with the tens of thousands of contraband as they came under Union control. It wasn't even very clear who had authority over them. As confiscated property they technically fell under the jurisdiction of the Treasury Department, but they were under the immediate jurisdiction of the occupying Northern army. Contraband camps and freedmen's villages were hastily improvised, rations and clothing issued. Calls went out to various Northern benevolent associations for help. From the outset, efforts were made to convert the contraband population into a nonslave labor force. Here, too, variety ruled the day. A number of the former slaves, whether in contraband camps or not, were quickly mobilized to provide the Union armies with the labor needed to build roads and bridges, transport supplies, etc. They theoretically worked for wages, but, after deductions for food, clothing, medicine, and supplies for their families, this often amounted to little. A large number were set to work on plantations, run either by Northerners who leased confiscated and abandoned plantations, by Southerners who had taken an oath of allegiance to the Union, or, through superintendents, by the government itself. All together, at least 475,000 former slaves (and some free blacks) participated in one form or another of these government-organized free-labor systems during the war years.

In the Sea Islands, which early fell to the Union, there was a self-conscious attempt to provide a model for the transition from slavery to free labor. The plantations there were conducted by superintendents recruited from Northern antislavery missionaries. They set up schools to give the freedmen the education deemed essential to the transition to freedom and set out to turn the former slaves into genuine "free-laborers" and thereby prove the viability of the free-labor system for the plantation South. In the Mississippi Valley (which contained nearly two-thirds of the former slaves under Union control), a system closer to the old plantation system prevailed. General Nathaniel Banks, a far cry from the antislavery superintendents in the Sea Islands, issued regulations that required all contraband to contract for labor under terms that in effect traded labor for food and shelter and established procedures for enforcing "continuous and faithful service, respectful deportment, correct discipline and perfect subordination."

There was another vision held by some antislavery radicals and by a number of former slaves of how the transition from slavery to freedom might take place. Confiscated lands could be leased or sold in small plots of forty acres to the freedmen themselves. Several small steps in this direction were taken during the war. Under the Direct Tax Act of 1861, 5,000 acres of land confiscated in the Sea Islands for failure to pay taxes was sold to former slaves. In January of 1865, General William Tecumseh Sherman issued Special Field Order No. 15, which set aside the Sea Islands and abandoned land reaching thirty miles inland along the coast from South Carolina to northern Florida for the settlement of freedmen on their own homesteads. By war's end, 40,000 freedmen occupied these lands and approximately 20 percent of the lands in government hands were being farmed under one arrangement or another by former slaves.

The recruitment of former slaves (and free blacks from North and South alike) into the Northern armies delivered another telling wartime blow against slavery. African-American soldiers, recruited from the free black population of southern Louisiana, were first used in 1862. From the spring of 1863 on, the government strove to maximize the recruitment of African Americans into the Northern army. All together, nearly

AFRICAN-AMERICAN SOLDIERS.

180,000 African Americans served in the Union forces (about 10 percent of the Union total). Of these, 33,000 (71 percent of the military-age African-American male population) came from the free states, 42,000 from the border states, and 94,000 from the Confederacy. Initially, African-American military units were used largely as a labor force, and as guard forces they were kept out of combat. (Many Union soldiers, especially Democrats from southern Ohio, Indiana, and Illinois, were virulently antiblack.) But by the last two years of the war, African-American regiments were regularly engaging in some of the most deadly battles.

The recruitment of African Americans increased Union manpower at a time of particularly pressing need. But African-American units, relishing the role of liberator, also attacked slavery more directly. They were heavily used to protect contraband camps and as they moved up the rivers of the Atlantic coast and through southern Louisiana they often aided slaves in their escape from their masters. Their presence in Northern armies had another, less tangible but nonetheless important, impact on slavery. It helped combat antiblack prejudice and strengthen support for the idea of emancipation. "The bravery of blacks in battle" helped skeptical, if not hostile soldiers (as well as the public back home) move from opposition to anything that smacked of "a fight for the abolition of slavery" to the ability to "take to emancipation readily."

Ironically, the use of African-American soldiers in the Union armies had its greatest *direct* impact on slavery in the border states. In Delaware, Maryland, Kentucky, and Missouri, which were exempted from the terms of the Emancipation Proclamation, slavery remained legal. In these states, the Union army furnished a major route out of slavery. Against the opposition of slaveholders, the War Department issued orders in 1863 and 1864 that offered freedom to slaves (and compensation to owners) in the border states who would enlist. Although the owners protested the orders and often forcibly tried to keep their slaves from enlisting, and even visited reprisals on their families, thousands flocked to the recruiting offices. In Delaware and Maryland, more than 25 percent of the African-American men of military age enlisted; in Missouri, 39 percent percent; and in Kentucky, a staggering 57 percent did so.

THE STRUGGLE CLIMAXES

At the end of April 1863, Grant had put the Mississippi River town of Vicksburg under heavy siege. The situation was critical. If Vicksburg fell, as it must if not given massive support from the East, then Confederate communications with the states west of the river would be cut. Lee had to decide whether to send an army west to raise the siege. He decided on another, daring strategy, designed to try for a victory that might force the Union to move part of Grant's forces east. So once more Lee invaded, this time not just into Maryland, but into Pennsylvania.

As Lee moved north, Hooker moved too, keeping his army between the enemy and Washington. 'But Hooker did not attack. Chancellorsville had been a painful lesson. He finally asked Lincoln to remove him from command, and the hapless Army of the Potomac now received yet another new commander, George G. Meade. With Lee about ten miles inside Pennsylvania, Meade moved in on the rear of the advancing Confederates.

On July 1, 1863, Lee sent a brigade of infantry into the town of Gettysburg, hoping to seize shoes for his army. The infantry stumbled onto some Union cavalry units, and there was a brief skirmish. Messengers on both sides rode away toward their main armies, asking for quick reinforcements. Neither commander had chosen Gettysburg as a battlefield. But Lee could not keep moving northward once the Army of the Potomac had found him and was at his rear, able to cut him off from Virginia. The Union commander, Meade, could not give Gettysburg to Lee. The town was just too important. It was a junction for a dozen different roads, one of them leading straight into Baltimore.

All day long on July 1, both armies rushed men toward Gettysburg. Lee was a bit closer, so he managed to get 25,000 soldiers into action on that first day. Meade managed to move up about 20,000. The Union's forward units fought and fell back, then fought again. (One Northern unit, after ferocious fighting, retreated in a panic through the town of Gettysburg, to take up new positions on Cemetery Hill. As they rushed sweating and frightened past the gates of the town's cemetery there, some of them may have noticed a small sign, a memory of more peaceful days. It read, "All persons found using firearms in these grounds will be prosecuted with the utmost rigor of the law." The good citizens of Gettysburg wanted their dead to sleep in peace.)

ULYSSES S. GRANT.

The Struggle Climaxes

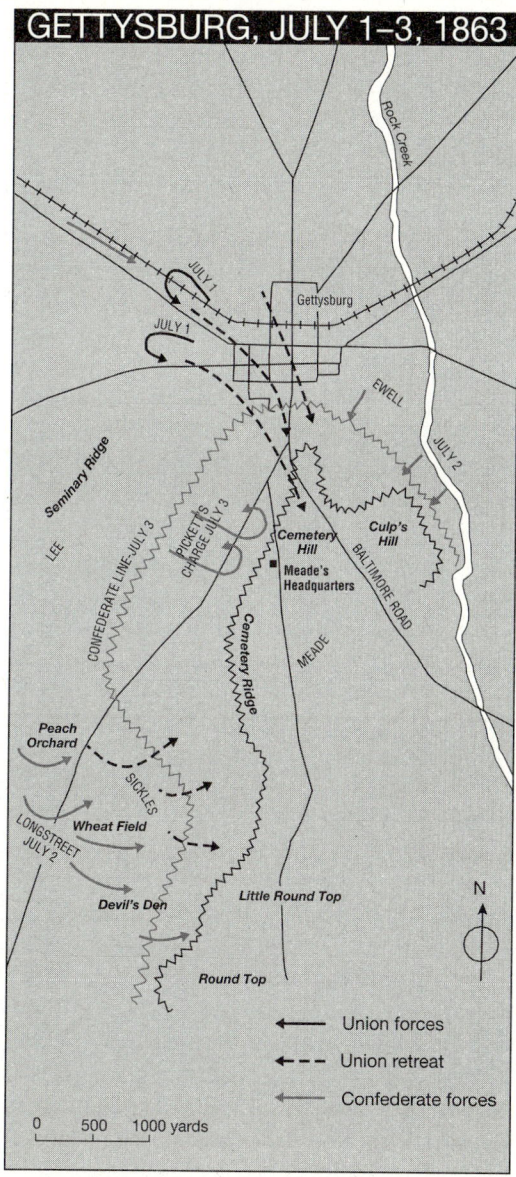

or how long it would take it to fall upon him. But he was encouraged by the success of his men on that first day, when they had seemed able to drive the Union troops back toward the ridgetop with ease. In fact, Lee was fighting a war of morale, hoping he could break the spirit of the Union soldiers at Gettysburg and that a victory here would damage the Union's will to continue the war.

So Lee decided to try to turn both Union flanks on July 1. He ordered General Richard Ewell to take Cemetery Hill, on the Union right, "if practicable." But Ewell, who commanded the corps that Stonewall Jackson had once led, was not willing to risk his men. He was certain that the enemy was securely dug in on the hill and had a lot of artillery ready to fire into his advancing troops. So he held back.

Lee also ordered a larger force, commanded by General James P. Longstreet, to attack the Union left and to try to take the hills, known as

ROBERT E. LEE.

At the end of the first day's fighting, Meade's soldiers had fallen back into tight and powerful defensive positions on the long hook-shaped ridge south and west of Gettysburg. Time was on Meade's side. Every hour, he could expect fresh men and supplies. Lee was reluctant to attack because he did not know where the rest of the great Army of the Potomac was,

Little Round Top and Round Top, at the southern end of Cemetery Ridge. Longstreet's charge fell short and only succeeded in driving some Union cavalry units off the forward slopes of the ridge.

Lee's hope had been that attacks by Ewell and Longstreet would tempt Meade to move forces out of the center of his line to defend its open flanks. Meantime, he was massing almost the entire Confederate artillery in the center, ready for an assault on the third day. Despite Ewell's decision not to attack Cemetery Hill, and despite Longstreet's bloody and costly failure, Lee decided to go ahead with his plan. In fact, given the state of battle and the state of the war, he probably had no choice but to launch an all-out attack.

By noon on July 3 the Confederates had everything ready. About 143 cannon were massed near the center of the field. At 1:00, Lee ordered them to fire. They were answered by a barrage of equal ferocity from the heights. It was the single heaviest exchange of artillery of the entire war. But as the exchange wore on, two things happened. The Confederate guns dug themselves more deeply into the earth on each recoil, pointing their barrels higher. Their shots began to fly above the Union positions, where the infantry crouched behind defenses they had dug for themselves the day before. Second, Union commanders, understanding that a massive infantry assault would soon be coming, ordered their artillery gradually to fall silent and wait. In fact, Meade had anticipated Lee's strategy, and was ready for the assault on his center. He had placed a lot of artillery there and had some of his best and toughest troops defending that part of the line.

Lee and his generals may have been convinced they had a good chance to break the Union's lines. Or Lee may have felt he had no choice but to continue his attack, no matter what. He could hardly take up a defensive position this deep into enemy territory. And he could not retreat without dooming Vicksburg to surrendering to Grant. Whatever the reason, Lee ordered 13,000 men, commanded by General George Pickett, to charge Cemetery Ridge. Pickett formed his men in parade-ground order and sent them forward. The Union artillery opened up, followed by a withering fire from a strong center held by some of the most seasoned troops in the Army of the Potomac. And still the Confederates came. A few of them actually reached Union breastworks along the ridgeline. But only a few. The rest were dead or wounded on the field, and the few who did make it to Union lines had no choice but to die, surrender, or run back down the slope under the same deadly fire.

As the charge began, Pickett had three brigade commanders. Two were now dead and the third badly wounded. The thirteen colonels in his division were all dead. And three-fourths of his men were dead, wounded, or captured.

All in all, the Confederate armies had lost between 25,000 and 30,000 men at Gettysburg. (Lee had lost seventeen generals in the three days of battle.) Meade had lost about 23,000 men. But he had held. News came quickly that on July 4, just one day after the failure of Pickett's charge, Vicksburg had fallen to Grant.

THE ELECTION OF 1864

By early 1864, as both sides regrouped for the upcoming spring campaigns, it was clear that the Union was headed toward victory. But, ironically, Lincoln's political future did not seem nearly so clear-cut. In the first place, one-term presidencies seemed to have become the tradition: no one since Andrew Jackson in 1832 had been elected to a second term in office. Lincoln was a master at maneuvering through the complex and shifting factional warfare within the Republican party. But in the summer of 1864 he stirred up a hornet's nest of opposition in Congress with his veto of the Wade-Davis Bill, which set stringent conditions for the return of Confederate states to the Union after the increasingly inevitable Union victory. The bill passed by a large enough margin to sustain an ordinary veto. But Lincoln blocked it with a "pocket veto." The bill had been passed at the very end of the legislative session, so Lincoln simply killed it by refusing to sign it. Lincoln's opponents worked to replace him, first, with his secretary of the treasury, Salmon P. Chase, a wildly ambitious but inept politician, and then with General John C. Frémont. But Lincoln had firm control of party machinery and, in the end, easily won renomination to the renamed "National Union party." To broaden its base, the party turned for its vice presidential candidate to a Tennessee Democrat, Andrew Johnson, who had been unstinting in his support of the administration's war effort.

War weariness also diminished Lincoln's prospects. As spring passed into summer and summer headed toward fall, the quick, final victory that the Northern press had predicted so confidently in May seemed remote indeed. Sherman seemed stalled outside Atlanta, Grant stalemated outside Petersburg, Virginia. Instead of victory, the summer had given the Northern people 100,000 more casualties. Wasn't everyone "tired of this damnable tragedy," one Democratic newspaper asked. In late August, the Democrats gathered in Chicago. As expected they nominated General George C. McClellan, a staunch opponent of emancipation but also a supporter of the restoration of the Union by force. By late August even Lincoln feared defeat. He even went so far as to ask his cabinet to endorse a memorandum pledging that if he were defeated, they would back him as he carried out his "duty" to work with the new president-elect to "save the Union between the election and the inauguration" because the very terms of his successor's election would have rendered it impossible to "save it afterwards."

THE DESTRUCTION OF CHARLESTON, SOUTH CAROLINA. As the Union armies pressed into the South they left much in ruins, visiting a destruction upon the civilian population that few other Americans have ever experienced. Note the former slaves sitting against the column at the center of this photograph by Matthew Brady, the noted photographic chronicler of the Civil War.

Lincoln was unduly pessimistic. He was rescued by the fall of Atlanta, his own political skills, and his ability to provide the Northern public with a sense of the higher, sacred meaning of the war. He won a solid victory that amounted to a clear endorsement of his definition and conduct of the war. His margin of victory in the electoral college was 212 to 21, and his popular vote a healthy 55 percent (as opposed to 48 percent in the same states in 1860.) The Republicans won huge majorities in both houses of Congress. Lincoln emerged from the election with the support he needed to see the cause through to victory.

THE STRUGGLE ENDS

The end was all but inevitable, but still the fighting and dying continued. Union troops occupied Chattanooga, Tennessee, in August. Then a Union force moved down into Georgia. They were beaten there in the fierce battle of Chickamauga in 1863, one of the few fights in which the Confederates outnumbered the Union troops.

But the victory counted for little. A month later, in the battle of Chattanooga, Grant's army drove the South off its positions on the ridges and mountains around the city.

Once the Union armies had taken unchallenged control of Chattanooga, Atlanta lay before them, and then the sea. The South, already divided along the Mississippi, could now be split a second time by a line of soldiers stretching from Kentucky across Tennessee and Georgia to the Atlantic. This mission was not to be Grant's. Lincoln called him east to take command of the Army of the Potomac. The West was left under the command of William Tecumseh Sherman.

In the spring of 1864, the end drew nearer—though still it would not come. Grant embarked on the most vicious offensive of the war, attacking Lee day after day in May in a terrible struggle known as the Wilderness Campaign. The Southerners fell back, but they continued to kill with deadly skill. They cost Grant 55,000 casualties in a little less than a month. But they suffered 30,000 of their own, losses they could no longer afford.

Meanwhile, in May, Sherman had begun his move southeastward from Chattanooga. It took him three months to reach Atlanta, but reach it he did. Then he set off on one of the most remarkable military marches in history. He ordered his men to advance along a front fully sixty miles wide, feeding off the countryside and destroying civilian property as they went. By December he was in Savannah.

For nine months the armies of Grant and Lee had been entrenched around Richmond, Grant waiting, Lee unable to attack. Defeat for the Confederacy was becoming more and more obvious with every dispatch from Georgia. Then Grant finally moved to surround Lee's force. The Confederate army, now numbering only about 25,000, made a desperate lunge westward, trying to escape encirclement, but it failed. Lee surrendered his army at Appomattox Courthouse, Virginia, on April 9, 1865. There were a few days more of scattered fighting in the Carolinas. But the war had finally ended. So had the lives of 600,000 soldiers.

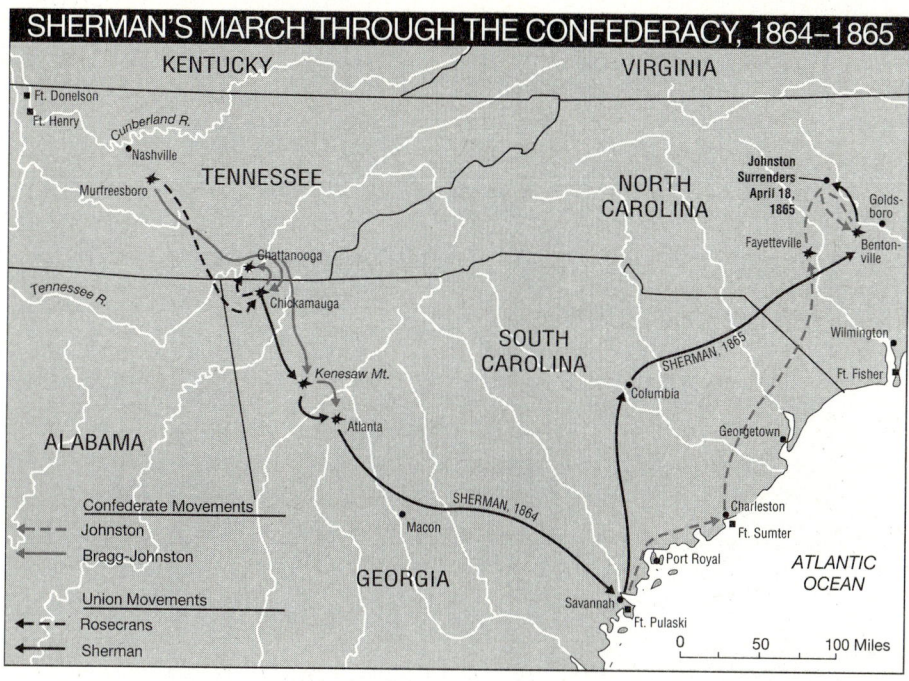

THE TOLL OF TOTAL WAR

In the North, there was an outpouring of jubilation, then a sense of completion and deliverance that was sealed in the ritual of mourning and transfiguration that carried Lincoln to his martyr's grave. To the ex-slaves, it was also time for jubilation—the day of deliverance longed for and promised in so many spirituals. Among the defeated whites of the South, especially those of the planter class, there was shock and disbelief, fear and uncertainty; their ordeal, it seemed, was far from over. All around them was chaos and destruction—no money, little food, a society and economy in shambles. Many wondered how or if they would survive and what might become of them. Would their lands be seized? Would they be tried and hanged as traitors, especially now that some Southern fanatic had killed the seemingly magnanimous Lincoln? Some also experienced an overpowering sense of loss. Not only had the Confederate armies been defeated, Southern civilization seemed also to have been destroyed. It was more than some could bear. On June 17 Edmund Ruffin, an early and vehement secessionist, who had been chosen to pull the lanyard that opened fire on Fort Sumter, made a final entry in his diary: "I here proclaim my unmitigated hatred to Yankee rule and the perfidious, malignant, and vile Yankee Race." Then he placed the muzzle of his gun in his mouth and pulled the trigger with a forked stick.

The final push to the bloody end had made clear what the decisive year of 1863 had already suggested. This was a war unlike any previous war. The Civil War has been called the first modern war, for good reasons. It was the first railroad war, with unprecedented quantities of troops and supplies transported over unprecedented distances. While Sherman conducted his siege of Atlanta, sixteen trains rushed him 1,600 tons of supplies each day. In addition, the huge armies—ten times the size of any previous units—using new technologies of destruction—trench warfare, repeat-firing rifles—had brought about an unprecedented mass slaughter. As Walt Whitman wrote in 1863, "The heart grows sick of war after

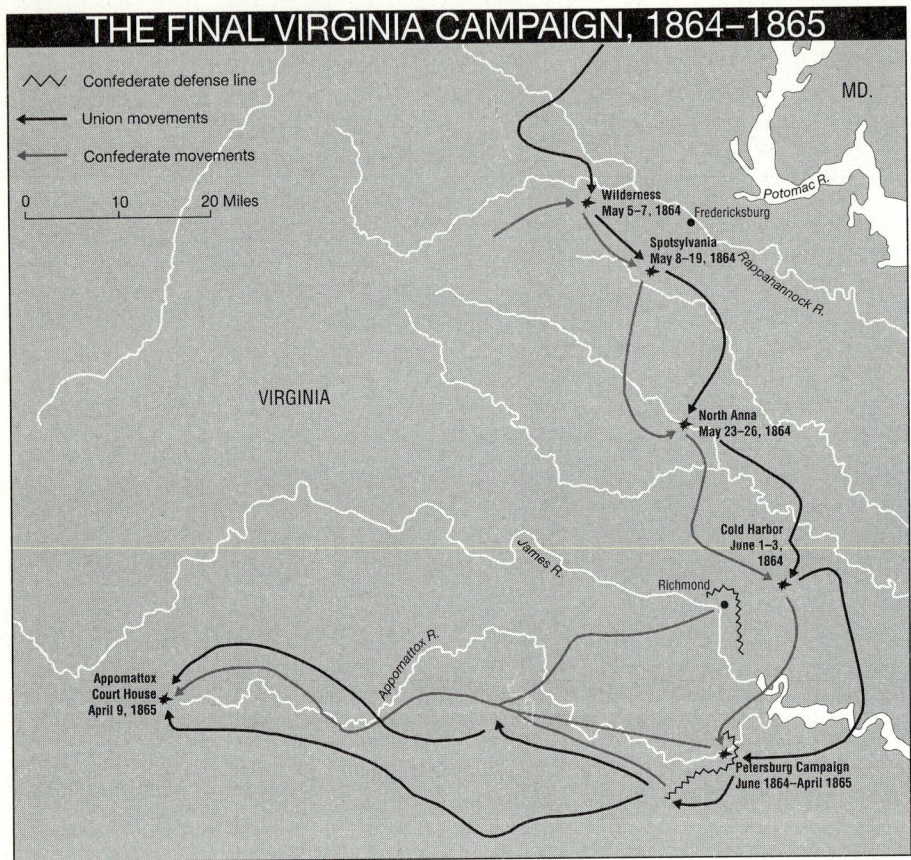

Confederate dead at Antietam. Most of the photographs of Civil War battle scenes were taken several days after the battles and had a more ordered and composed aspect to them. This photograph was taken shortly after the battle and shows the casualties as they fell.

all, when you see what it really is—every once in a while I feel so horrified and disgusted—it seems to me like a great slaughterhouse and the men mutually butchering each other."

But what more than anything else set the Civil War apart from earlier wars was its character as a total war. Wars traditionally had been fought by professional armies, which jockeyed for territory until some kind of negotiated settlement was reached. Partly because of the new technologies of war and partly because each side was fighting for a principle it would not compromise, the Civil War became the first total war in modern times. It pitted not just two armies, but two societies—each by the end fully mobilized for the effort—against each other. Victory came not with the taking of territory but with the destruction of the other society's capacity to fight. Sherman grasped the brutal logic of total war. As he put it, as he embarked on his march to the sea, "We are not only fighting hostile armies, but a hostile people. We must make old and young, rich and poor, feel the hand of war." And victory and defeat were themselves total: a destroyed South held on until it was forced into unconditional surrender. At the end, the Confederacy was in no position to negotiate a peace—it surrendered because it could no longer carry on.

UNION DEAD AT GETTYSBURG.

CHRONOLOGY

1860	Abraham Lincoln (Republican) elected president;	1863 (cont'd)	
	South Carolina secedes		Battle of Chancellorsville;
1861	Mississippi, Alabama, Georgia, Florida, Louisiana, Texas secede;		Battle of Gettysburg;
			Grant captures Vicksburg;
	Firing on Fort Sumter;		Draft riots in Northern cities;
	Border states, Arkansas, Virginia, Tennessee, North Carolina secede;		Lincoln begins a reconstruction program
		1864	Grant named Union general in chief;
	First battle of Bull Run (Manassas)		Siege of Petersburg;
1862	Battle of Shiloh;		Sherman captures Atlanta;
	Robert E. Lee named commander of the Army of Northern Virginia;		Lincoln reelected president;
			Sherman's march to the sea and capture of Charleston
	Second battle of Bull Run;	1865	Confederate government flees Richmond;
	Battle of Antietam;		Lee surrenders to Grant at Appomattox Courthouse;
	Lincoln drafts preliminary Emancipation Proclamation;		
			Lincoln assassinated, Andrew Johnson becomes president;
	Battle of Fredericksburg		
1863	Lincoln issues Emancipation Proclamation;		Thirteenth Amendment abolishing and outlawing slavery ratified

SUGGESTIONS FOR FURTHER READING

ABRAHAM LINCOLN

The literature on Abraham Lincoln is voluminous. Four important new books have been published in the past three years: Merrill D. Peterson, *Lincoln in American Memory* (1994); Mark E. Neely, *The Last Best Hope of Earth* (1993); Philip S. Paludan, *The Presidency of Abraham Lincoln* (1994); and Garry Wills, *Lincoln at Gettysburg* (1992). Benjamin Thomas, *Abraham Lincoln* (1952), is a good single-volume biography; it is somewhat surpassed by Stephen B. Oates, *With Malice Toward None: The Life of Abraham Lincoln* (1977) and *Abraham Lincoln: The Man Behind the Myths* (1988). Lawanda Cox, *Lincoln and Black Freedom* (1981), is a very useful study of the decision for emancipation. David Donald, *Lincoln Reconsidered* (1958), and Richard Current, *The Lincoln Nobody Knows* (1951), provide refreshing perspectives on Lincoln as a politician. Edmund Wilson, *Patriotic Gore* (1962), treats Lincoln's mystical attachment to the Union and his deepening religious sentiments during the war. David Potter, *Lincoln and His Party in the Secession Crisis* (1942), remains the best study of the subject. John Hope Franklin, *The Emancipation Proclamation* (1963), is a succinct history of how the document came about; Allan Nevins, *Lincoln and the Gettysburg Address* (1954), is a solid account of that famous oration. Ralph Borreson, *When Lincoln Died* (1965), is a detailed account of Lincoln's assassination and funeral. T. Harry Williams, *Lincoln: Selected Speeches and Letters* (1960), is an excellent sampling of the president's own writings.

CIVIL WAR

An excellent overview of the period is James McPherson, *Ordeal by Fire* (1982). The same author's *Battle Cry of Freedom* (1988) covers much the same ground, but in a somewhat more readable fashion. James G. Randall and David Donald, *The Civil War and Reconstruction*, 2d ed. (1961), is an older work but is still a useful survey. An excellent study of secession in one state is Michael P. Johnson, *Toward a Patriarchal Republic: The Secession of Georgia* (1977).

Two fine recent studies of the armies and battles of

the war are Michael Barton, *Good Men: The Character of Civil War Soldiers* (1981), and Gerald F. Linderman, *Embattled Courage: Combat in the Civil War* (1977). William S. McFeely, *Grant: A Biography* (1981), is essential reading. Sherman's Georgia campaign is discussed in rich detail in *March to the Sea and Beyond* (1985). The causes of Northern victory and Confederate defeat are discussed in David Donald, ed., *Why the North Won the Civil War* (1960); Richard E. Beringer, Herman Hattaway, Archer Jones, and William N. Still, Jr., *Why the South Lost the Civil War* (1986); Herman Hattaway and Archer Jones, *How the North Won* (1983); and Gabor S. Borritt, *Why the Confederacy Lost* (1992). The life of the common soldier is the subject of Bell Irvin Wiley's pioneering works, *The Life of Johnny Reb* (1943) and *The Life of Billy Yank* (1952). Allan Nevins, *The War for the Union,* 4 vols. (1959–1971), Bruce Catton, *This Hallowed Ground* (1956) and *Centennial History of the Civil War* (1961–1965), and Douglass Southall Freeman, *R. E. Lee,* 4 vols. (1934–1935), provide full, readable accounts of the military history of the Civil War. T. Harry Williams, *Lincoln and the Radicals* (1942), argues that Lincoln and the radicals were in continuing opposition; whereas Hans L. Trefousse, *The Radical Republicans* (1968), stresses their cooperation. Emory L. Thomas, *The Confederate Nation* (1979), is a good single-volume treatment. Charles Ramsdell, *Behind the Lines in the Southern Confederacy* (1944), discusses the internal political conflicts within the Confederacy. The lives of African-American women are treated in Jacqueline Jones, *Labor of Love, Labor of Sorrow* (1985). Other valuable works on African Americans and the war include Benjamin Quarles, *The Negro in the Civil War* (1953); James McPherson, ed., *The Negro's Civil War* (1965); and Dudley Cornish, *The Sable Arm: Negro Troops in the Union Army,* 2d ed. (1987). James L. Roark, *Masters Without Slaves* (1977), describes the breakdown of the plantation system during the war and Reconstruction. Ira Berlin, et al., *Slaves No More: Three Essays on Emancipation and the Civil War* (1992) is an enormously valuable discussion of the impact of the war on slavery.

Politics and ideology in the North are the subjects of Earl J. Hess, *Liberty, Virtue, and Progress: Northerners and Their War for the Union* (1988); Eric Foner, *Politics and Ideology in the Age of the Civil War* (1980); and Dale Baum, *The Civil War Party System* (1984).

George Fredrickson, *The Inner Civil War* (1965), and Edmund Wilson, *Patriotic Gore* (1962), provide superb discussions of the intellectual impact of the war. Ralph Andreano, ed., *The Economic Impact of the American Civil War* (1962), contains a number of important articles assessing the economic dimensions of the war. James L. Roark, *Masters Without Slaves* (1977), analyzes the plight of Southern planters during the Civil War and Reconstruction.

Collections of documents include Frank Moore, ed., *Rebellion Record,* a twelve-volume compilation put together in the 1860s and reprinted in a modern edition in 1977; Francis T. Miller, *The Photographic History of the Civil War,* 10 vols. (1957), is the most extensive of the many collections of Civil War photographs. Frank Freidel, ed., *Union Pamphlets of the Civil War* (1967), provides a valuable collection of Northern writings. See also Harold Hyman, ed., *The Radical Republicans and Reconstruction* (1967). C. Vann Woodward, ed., *Mary Chesnut's Civil War* (1981), and Robert Myers, *The Children of Pride* (1972), provide invaluable insight into Southern life during the war. An especially rich collection of documents concerning the experiences of African Americans in the South during the war is Ira Berlin, et al., eds., *Freedom: A Documentary History of Emancipation* (1982–1993). Particularly valuable is Ira Berlin, et al., *Free at Last: A Documentary History of Slavery, Freedom, and the Civil War* (1993), a one-volume paperback containing documents from all four volumes in the Freedom series.

Chapter 14

Reconstruction

Episode: Edisto Island—Land and Freedom

REUNION AND RECONSTRUCTION

- Lincoln's Plan for Reconstruction
- Presidential Reconstruction Under Johnson
- Radical Reconstruction
- Redeeming the States

THE EPISODE: After four long years, the Civil War had once and for all determined that the American Republic could not be divided. But the society that had to be reunited was very different from the one that had split apart in 1861. The war had destroyed the institution of slavery. But the question of the place of the former slaves in American society, of the degree of "freedom" white America would grant them, remained very much an open question.

There was no absence of possible and deeply conflicting answers to the question. The victorious Northerners were deeply divided over the matter. Most of them did not want to see blacks elevated to a position of civil and social equality—especially in the North. Even most abolitionists doubted that the former "bondsmen" were fully ready for freedom and envisioned a period of tutelage in the ways of freedom.

The defeated white Southerners—especially the former slaveowners—were much clearer in their answer. Whatever "system" was devised for the former slaves, they wanted it to be one that provided former masters with a dependent labor force and relegated blacks to a position of clear social subordination.

The newly freed blacks were no less clear in their answer than their former masters. They wanted "independence," freedom from anything that resembled the domination that ownership had entailed. And they wanted land.

Historians traditionally portrayed the newly freed blacks as relatively passive—bystanders or pawns—in a battle over Reconstruction fought out by ex-Confederates and northern Republicans. More recently, historians have pointed out that, on the contrary, the newly liberated blacks moved quickly—though by no means always successfully—to claim their newfound freedom and turn it to their own ends.

One place they did so was Edisto Island, off the coast of South Carolina. There in 1865 and early 1866, the issue of the place of the freedman in Southern society was immediately and fully joined, as all the parties—the freedmen, the former masters, and divided Northerners—fought to create their particular vision of a "reconstructed" South.

THE HISTORICAL SETTING: Lincoln once said that the issue that the Civil War was fought over was union but that the cause was slavery. Similarly, the formal issue that dominated what historians have called Reconstruction (the period from 1865 to 1877) was "reunion." But what "caused" the process of reunification to take so long—it took more than twice as long as the war itself—and made it such a bitter and violent process was the question of the place the former slaves would occupy in the new and different South.

The battle over the freedman was fought on two fronts. In Washington, between president and Congress, between moderate and Radical Republicans, and between Democrats and Republicans. But it was fought with greatest intensity in the South. The nature of the question itself—and, quite literally, the deadly seriousness with which it was taken—is sufficient to account for much of the intensity and violence of the battle. But it also took place under conditions that no Americans other than the southerners have ever faced—military occupation. "Reconstruction" took place, not simply within the context of a military defeat, but within a framework of conquest and an occupation that endured longer and with greater bitterness than the Allied occupation of Japan and Germany after World War II.

Edisto Island—Land and Freedom

Early on the morning of October 19, 1865, a small steamer carried General Oliver O. Howard from Savannah, Georgia, up the South Carolina coast to Edisto Island just twenty miles below Charleston. Veteran of the battles of Gettysburg and Atlanta and of Sherman's march to the sea, Howard was the Commissioner of the Bureau of Refugees, Freedmen, and Abandoned Lands (popularly known as the Freedmen's Bureau), the agency established in March of 1865 to aid the former slaves in their transition from slavery to freedom. He was on his way to Edisto, a settlement of nearly 4,500 blacks, almost all of whom were recently liberated former slaves, to explain recent changes in federal policy regarding "abandoned and confiscated lands."

In less than ten months, the freedmen on Edisto Island had transformed it from a war-torn, abandoned waste into a burgeoning community of independent farmers. Before the war one of the largest and most populous of the sea islands, Edisto early succumbed to the vicissitudes of war. In late 1861 most of the white owners fled the island to get away from the approaching Union forces. They and Confederate troops tried to take their slaves with them to the mainland, but the slaves resisted and fled to the periphery of the island, where they built huts and eked out a livelihood fishing and hunting. In early 1862 federal troops occupied the island and many of the slaves returned to their home plantations as squatters and as paid laborers on the plantations now run by Northern "supervisors." But in July 1862, the federal army abandoned Edisto, leaving more than 2000 acres of planted crops in the soil and evacuating the more than 2,000 former slave inhabitants. Then at the end of 1864, the war once again transformed Edisto Island.

As General William Tecumseh Sherman's army cut its sixty-mile swath across Georgia from Atlanta to Savannah, it produced another army, a refugee army made up of the tens of thousands of homeless, landless, impoverished former slaves who flocked to the Union forces as the army of their liberation. Something had to be done about the immediate problem of the refugees. A little more than three weeks after Sherman captured it, Secretary of War Edwin Stanton went to Savannah to survey the situation. At the suggestion of the Reverend James Lynch, a 26-year-old black minister from Baltimore who had gone to Savannah to work with the ex-slaves there, Stanton organized a meeting with Sherman, himself and his aides, and twenty black churchmen from the area. Sherman saw little point to the meeting, called to deal with what he referred to in a letter to his wife as "that Negro nonsense." To him, the meeting smacked of the poison politics of Washington. Besides, he resented sitting down almost as an equal with members of a race that he believed should never be "put on any equality with Whites"

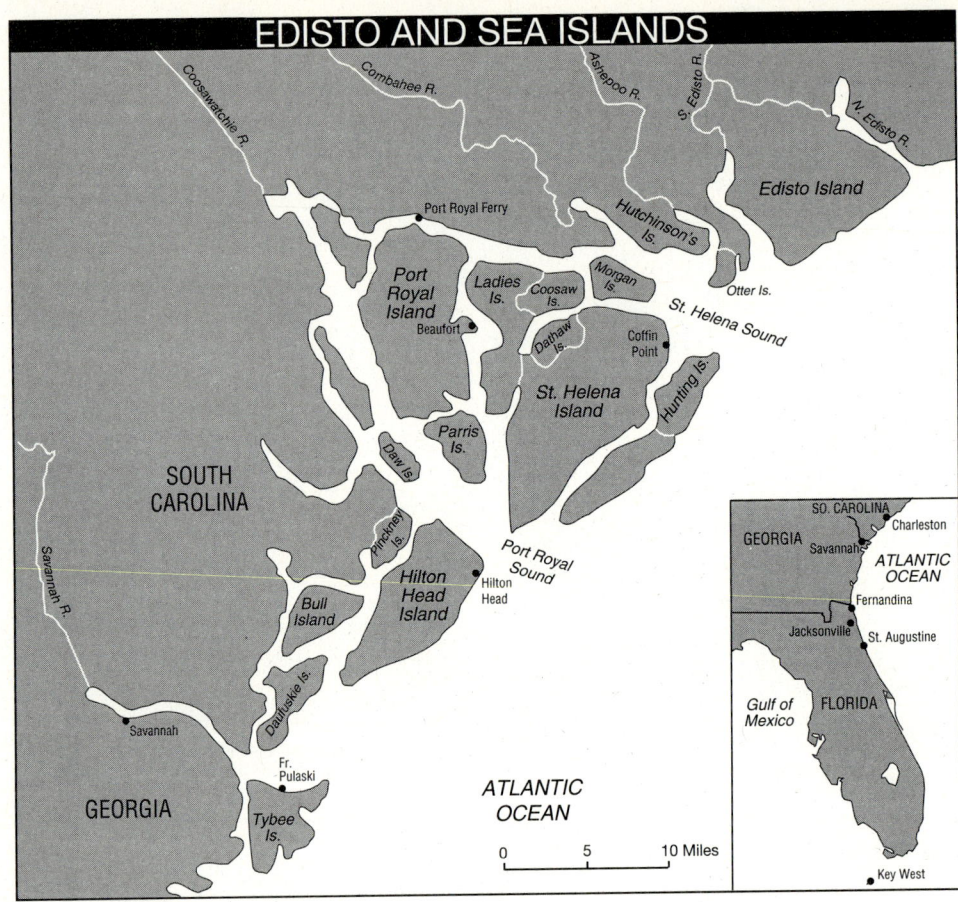

at a meeting called to solicit *their* views about what they wanted from their new freedom.

Stanton conducted the meeting as a species of military or judicial board of inquiry. The churchmen were asked to select a spokesman and to answer a set of carefully selected, written questions. All but one of the twenty black leaders, ranging in age from 26 to 72, were from the Savannah area: five had been "free born," three were former slaves who had been freed at the death of their masters, three had purchased their own freedom before the war, and the remaining eight had remained slaves until "the army freed" them. They selected as their spokesman Garrison Frazier, aged 67, who had served as a minister for thirty-five years and in 1856 had "bought himself and his wife, paying $1,000 in gold and silver," as their spokesman. Stanton composed his questions as a catechism designed to determine the extent of the former slaves' understanding of the principles of American freedom. The churchmen prepared their answers with subtlety and care. They knew it was a test. They and Stanton knew full well that even strongly antislavery whites doubted whether "the poor, debased" former slaves were ready or even capable of freedom. They were determined to prove that there was enough "understanding and intelligence" among the former slaves to sustain freedom and prosper under it. After first eliciting a clear and subtle exposition of the acts of Congress and "President Lincoln's proclamation, touching the condition of the colored people in the Rebel States," Stanton moved directly to the key question. "State," he asked, "what you understand by Slavery and the freedom that was to be given by the President's proclamation." The answer came back clear and succinct. "Slavery is," Frazier asserted, "receiving by *irresistible power* the work of another man, and not by his *consent*," whereas "the freedom, promised by the proclamation, is taking us from under the yoke of bondage and placing us where we can reap the fruit of our own labor, take care of ourselves and assist the Government in maintaining our freedom." Stanton then posed the obvious follow-up: How, he asked, do "you think you can take care of yourselves, and how can you best assist the government in maintaining your freedom?"

The question was not quite so simple and innocent as it seemed. A good deal was riding on the answer. Few ideas were more deeply embedded in the white consciousness than the notion that the former slaves were "lazy," either, in the racist version, because of inborn racial characteristics, or, in the antislavery version, because slavery itself had made enslaved blacks that way. Unless carefully and gradually nurtured in the ways and responsibilities of freedom, such thinking went, the ex-slaves were destined to remain a "degraded" and "dependent" people. Moreover, most whites (North and South alike) envisioned the ex-slaves becoming a free, largely agricultural wage-labor force. The churchmen could have answered, "give us steady work and good wages and we will take care of ourselves." But they didn't. They knew what they wanted and Frazier stated it clearly and unmistakably: "The way we can best take care of ourselves is to have land, and turn it and till it by our own labor."

There was a good deal of meaning packed into this simple sentence. Freedom meant to the former slaves just what it meant to whites in North and South alike—independence, freedom from dependence upon and control by others. And just as did most free whites, especially in the South, the freedmen associated independence with the ownership of land, with possession of what was aptly called a "homestead." With a homestead, a man as the "head of household" who held title to the land could secure, protect, and provide for his family. With their own land to turn and till with their own hand, the former slaves hoped, black wives and children would no longer be forced to labor in the fields of whites. Wives might even be able to forswear fieldwork altogether to attend more fully to the tasks of nurture, child rearing, and the domestic production their families required. So that the key point shouldn't be lost, Frazier concluded simply, "We want to be placed on the land until we are able to buy it and make it our own."

After the meeting Stanton asked Sherman for his suggestions about what to do with the newly freed fugitives that had flocked to his army. Sherman came up with a surprising proposal: he suggested turning the confiscated and abandoned land in the Sea Islands off the coast of South Carolina and Georgia over to the refugees. Four days later, on January 16th, 1865, after much discussion and careful reworking of several drafts, Sherman issued Special Field Order No. 15. It was a revolutionary document. It set aside the Sea Islands and "the abandoned rice fields along the rivers for thirty miles back from the sea" from Charleston south to the St. Johns River in Florida, for the "settlement of the negroes now made free by the acts of war." According to the provisions of the Order, whenever "three respectable negroes, heads of families" selected a "locality clearly defined," a settlement would be established in which "themselves and such others as may choose to settle near them" would be given "a plot of not more than forty acres of tillable land."

As soon as Sherman issued Field Order No. 15, former inhabitants who had evacuated Edisto, landless inhabitants from nearby islands, and refugees who had followed Sherman's army into Savannah flocked to the island and its rich lands. By the fall of 1865, the island held more than 4,500 people, and nearly 550 households had managed to "establish a home on their own lands." Just as rapidly they put in their crops. "The crops on these lands," the Freedmen's Bureau agent on the Island reported, "look remarkably well considering the lateness of the season when they were planted. The cotton and the corn crop looks much better than those seen on either of the other sea islands. There are one thousand and three acres of excellent cotton planted, and nearly two thousand acres of corn, also nearly two hundred acres of rice besides many acres of vegetables." The freedmen of Edisto not only laid claim to land and put in their crops. They also, the Bureau agent reported, "feel it their duty as well as a privilege of establishing a simple form of Gov–among themselves." The inhabitants established a system of "selectmen and constables elected by the people." In addition, they had a "Constitution & laws of this Civil Gov . . . about ready" for submission to the deputy commissioner for his approval. The inhabitants also established the practice of holding a "general meeting" each Saturday in which they discussed "general issues" and read reports on local and national doings from a black newspaper, *The South Carolina Leader,* and other Republican newspapers.

Howard was not eager to meet with the freedmen of Edisto but considered it his "duty" to do so. Dubbed the "Christian General" because of his piety and dedication to "good works," Howard considered himself an "ardent friend of the Negro," one of their truest "champions" in the federal government. As did the freedmen themselves, he believed that the best policy for the former slaves was to settle them on homesteads of their own. The legislation that established the Freedmen's Bureau, in fact, contained a clause that extended to "the several insurrectionary states" the Sherman formula for settling freedmen on forty-acre homesteads carved out of lands "abandoned" by or "confiscated" from those who had supported the Insurrection. Howard had worked quickly to implement the land policy. On July 28, 1865, he issued a Circular (# 13) firmly enunciating the policy and ordered his assistant commissioners to survey the lands, settle freedmen and their families on specified plots, and provide them with formal, written "certificates" of possession. (By October 1865, freedmen occupied 16,000 acres on Edisto Island, and Howard's assistant commissioner for South Carolina and Georgia, General Rufus Saxton, had issued Circular 13 grants to 367 Edisto families.)

But now "the Christian General," friend and protector of the freedmen, was on his way to Edisto Island to inform the people there of a dramatic reversal of federal land policy. President Andrew Johnson had established a new policy to "restore" the once "abandoned" land to former owners who had been pardoned under the terms of an

WILLIAM TECUMSEH SHERMAN. More than any other general, Sherman understood that defeating the Confederacy demanded a "total" war, directed at the civilian population and the Confederate armies alike, that would destroy the enemy's capacity and will to fight. He conducted this "modern" form of warfare with devastating effectiveness in his march through Georgia and the Carolinas in late 1864.

amnesty proclamation Johnson had issued the previous May. Johnson, further, ordered Howard to withdraw Circular 13. The new policy even challenged the validity of land grants bestowed under Special Order No. 15. Howard's "hard task" was to tell the Edisto inhabitants that they would have to give up their farms and surrender their land to the very men who had fought the Union armies that had liberated the slaves.

General Howard and his entourage—consisting of his brother; Colonel John Alvord, an old abolitionist and head of the Freedmen's Savings Bank; and Colonel William Whaley, a lawyer and representative of the former owners who himself had owned one of the largest plantations on the island—did not know what awaited them on the island. Howard certainly expected to find anger and disappointment. But he also thought he could persuade the Edisto inhabitants to accept his proposal for working out a "just" solution to which freedmen and former owners could both agree. Howard had met with the former owners the night before. They all, but especially Whaley, impressed him as "gentlemen" of moderation who fully accepted the reality of slavery's demise and had genuine concern for the freedmen's welfare. Armed with this belief in the planters' good faith, he was sure that in the end he could convince the freedmen to adopt his formula by which the freedmen would "contract" with the owners for their labor. Under these "contracts," the Edisto farmers would agree to exchange a set amount of labor either for wages, a lease for land, or the opportunity to buy a parcel of land. A Board of Supervisors—made up of a representative of the planters, a representative for the freedmen, and an agent of the Freedmen's Bureau—would work out specific contracts, which were then subject to approval by the assistant commissioner of the Bureau or his designated agent.

Rumor had preceded him that Howard was coming to the Island to take away the freedmen's land. The more than 2,000 men, women, and children gathered in a large church in the center of the island to hear what the General had to say could not contain their anger and sense of betrayal. The hall was filled with "noise and confusion" and to Howard the eyes of his audience "flashed unpleasantly." The Edisto islanders called on their most powerful medium of expression as the crowd turned to "the Lord's Songs." The church rang out with the sorrowful sounds of the spirituals, "Wandering in the Wilderness of Sorrow and Gloom" and "Nobody Knows the Trouble I Seen." When Howard "endeavored as clearly and gently as [he] could to explain the wishes of the President as they were made known to me in an interview I had just before leaving Washington," he was met with anguished cries of "No! No!" One man, described by Howard as "very black, thick set and strong" cried out from the balcony, "Why, General Howard, why do you take away our lands? You take them from us who are true, always true to the government! You give them to our all-time enemies! That is not right!"

Finally, in desperation, Howard asked the assembly to select a committee to prepare a more formal response. He beseeched the group to be charitable toward their former owners. And he specified the condition of their tenure on the land under "our President's actions," explaining that they had "no absolute title but simply occup[ied] the homesteads." He urged the committee to come up with a way to "make the best possible terms with the holders of the titles." The next day the committee gave Howard its written response. "With painful Hearts" the committee informed Howard that the people of Edisto could not sign the kinds of contracts "you wished us to Sign." Instead, they went on

> General we want Homesteads; we were promised Homesteads by the government; If It does not carry out the promises Its agents made to us, If the government Having concluded to befriend Its late enemies and to neglect to observe the principles of common faith between Its self and us Its allies In the war you said was over, now takes away from them all right to the soil they stand upon save such as they can get by again working for *your* late and their *all time enemies*. If the government does so we are left In a more unpleasant condition than our former . . .
>
> We can only do one of three things   Step Into the public *road or the sea* or remain on [the land] working as In former time and subject to their will as then. We can not resist It In any way without being driven out homeless upon the road.
>
> You will see this Is not the condition of really freemen
>
> You ask us to forgive the land owners of our Island. *You* only lost your right arm In war and might forgive them. The man who tied me to a tree & gave me 39 lashes & who stripped and flogged my mother and sister & who will not let me stay In His empty Hut except I will do his planting and be satisfied with His price & who combines with others to keep away land from me well knowing I would not Have any thing to do with Him If I had land of my own—that man, I can not well forgive.

The former owners were confident. They sensed that momentum was on their side. They had the president squarely in their corner and understood Howard to have committed himself to the restoration of their lands. But they also knew they had pow-

BLACK REFUGEES CROSSING THE RAPPAHONNOCK RIVER, VIRGINIA, 1862. From early in the war, the incursion of Northern forces into the Confederacy produced a growing army of black refugees, as tens of thousands of slaves availed themselves of the opportunity warfare opened up to place themselves beyond slavery's grasp. Sherman issued Special Field Order No. 15 to resolve the "refugee problem" that surrounded his conquering army.

erful enemies in the North and realized that conditions remained volatile and unsettled. At the very moment, the Senate Judiciary Committee in Washington was considering a bill to extend the life and powers of the Freedmen's Bureau that contained a provision to validate the Sherman grants in the Sea Islands for the lifetime of the head of household currently on the land. The owners were determined to regain possession of the land and get a labor force bound to them by contract as quickly as possible. They believed that Howard had agreed that their "lands would be restored *first,* and the agreements with the freedmen "arranged *afterwards.*" They wanted the freedmen under contract to them or off the land by the beginning of the new year, and insisted that Captain A. P. Ketchum, the Freedmen's Bureau agent for Edisto, go with them to Edisto and tell the farmers that if they did not sign contracts by Jan. 1, 1866, they would be removed from the land.

    The freedmen were no less determined. The Edisto farmers realized the severity of the blow to their hopes for land and feared they might in the end have to leave the land they now occupied. But they were not about to give up without a fight. They also knew they had two things going for them. They were *on* the land: they might not have clear titles but, some 4,500 strong, they in fact *occupied* Edisto Island. They wouldn't be easily dislodged. In fact, when one of the planters went to the island to try to claim his land, the inhabitants forced him to turn back. Panic-stricken, he told his fellow planters that "the Negros on that Island are armed and have announced their purpose to allow no white man on it." Second, the Edisto farmers possessed a new and very important kind of freedom: their labor was now theirs to give or withhold. As the churchmen had told Stanton and Sherman, they were free "to reap the fruit of our own labor." Above all else the planters wanted their land back, but they also wanted and needed the freedmen's labor. Cotton prices were very good and the planters were desperate to recoup from the personal economic devastation the war had visited upon them. Plantations with no one to work them would do the owners little good.

The Edisto freedmen had some important allies of their own. Their anguished plea for land and justice had clearly moved Howard. As he reported to his superior, Secretary of War Stanton, "They will submit with evident sorrow to the breaking of the promise of General Sherman's order. The greatest aversion is exhibited to making contracts, and they beg and plead for the privilege of renting or buying land on the island . . . I am convinced that something must be done to give these people and others the prospect of homesteads." And he replied to the Edisto committee that "You are right *in wanting homesteads* and will *surely be defended in the possession of every one* which you shall purchase or have already purchased." He made it clear that he would work to secure them lands *somewhere,* pointing out that "Congress must meet before any public lands can be had and before I can buy any for you." In the meantime, he urged them to "enter into contracts, leasing or for wages or purchase when possible for next year."

The Edisto committee knew that, in the end, men in Washington would determine their fate. They told Howard that they intended to petition Congress. Howard assured them that he "would see to it that [their petition] is not passed by without proper attention." They even appealed directly to President Johnson himself to prove himself "a true friend of the poor and Neglected race" by granting them the "protection and Equal Rights [and] with the privilege of purchasing A Homestead—A Homestead right here in the Heart of South Carolina." In their petitions to both, they based their claims on their loyalty, their standing as freemen, and the actions of the government itself:

> Here is where secession was born and Nurtured. Here is where we have toiled nearly all Our lives as slaves and were treated like dumb Driven cattle. This is our home, we have made These lands what they are. We were the only true and Loyal people that were found in posession of these Lands. We have been always ready to strike for Liberty and humanity yea to fight if needs be To preserve this glorious union. Shall we who Are freedmen and have been always true to this Union have the same rights as are enjoyed by Others? Have we broken any Laws of these United States? Have we forfieted our rights of property In Land? If not then are our rights as A free people and good citizens of these United States To be considered before the rights of those who were Found in rebellion against this good and just Government (and now being conquered) come (as they Seem) with penitent hearts and beg forgiveness for past offences and also ask if thier lands Cannot be restored to them. Are these rebellious Spirits to be reinstated in their *possessions* and we who have been abused and oppressed For many long years not to be allowed the Privilege of purchasing land But be subject To the will of these large Land owners? God Forbid.
>
> We have been encouraged by Government to take Up these lands in small tracts, receiving Certificates of the Same . . . We are ready to pay for this land When Government calls for it. And now after What has been done will the good and just government take from us all this right and make us Subject to the will of those who have cheated and oppressed us for many years. God Forbid!

Howard's subordinates in South Carolina were sympathetic to the Edisto farmers' plea for their homesteads. The assistant commissioner of the Bureau, General Saxton, in fact, was determined to resist restoration as long as possible in the hope that Congress would at least partially honor the Sherman grants on the island. Even though he considered it his "solemn duty" to secure "just" contracts between the former owners and the people of Edisto, Captain H. P. Ketchum, the Bureau agent responsible for Edisto, refused to issue any orders of restoration until a contract was secured and approved. And he refused to approve of any contract to which the freedmen did not freely and mutually agree. Saxton and Ketchum were not about to force the freedmen to sign contracts for "hire," nor would they try to force them off the island if they did refuse to sign. The road to "restoration" was proving a bit more rocky than the owners had reckoned.

A "somewhat discomposed" William Whaley confronted Ketchum directly over his failure to carry out his duties as the owners saw them. He threatened to "write the President immediately" and report that the agents of the Bureau were deliberately subverting Johnson's formally declared policy to restore abandoned land to its rightful owners. But Ketchum cleverly turned the tables on Whaley. Had the pardoned owners, he asked pointedly, in fact selected a person to represent them on the Board of Supervisors called for in Howard's Field Order laying out the procedures for the restoration of the lands? They had not. Whaley claimed that he understood Howard to have said that the lands would first be restored to the owners who would then work out an agreement with the freedmen. Ketchum warned Whaley that if he did "write the President" as he threatened, it would be clear to all that he would be making demonstrably false statements that "could not be substantiated." Whaley, seeming "better contented," backed down. (But, to cover himself and the Bureau in the event Whaley did go to the president, Ketchum sent Howard a detailed account of the meeting.)

GENERAL OLIVER OTIS HOWARD. A native of Maine and a graduate of West Point, Howard underwent religious conversion during a Methodist revival in 1853 at the age of 23. The experience shaped his sense of himself as a soldier in the Union cause and the antislavery cause and as commissioner of the Freedmen's Bureau. A wounded veteran of the battles of Fredericksburg and Gettysburg, he commanded one of Sherman's armies in the March to the Sea.

The owners moved quickly to recoup their position as reasonable men perfectly willing to work out a "just" arrangement with the inhabitants of Edisto Island. The next day, they informed Ketchum that they had selected Whaley as their representative on the Board of Supervisors. Shortly thereafter "the planters of Edisto Island" sent to Howard and Ketchum a formal resolution that declared their entire "willingness to comply with General Howard's order for the restoration of lands on Edisto Island." They avowed that it was their "intention to deal justly and generously with the freedmen with whom we may contract and to do all in our power to promote their physical welfare and moral improvement and to labor to give the greatest success to the system of free labor which has been inaugurated." The planters were in for another surprise. The Edisto freedmen selected a black man as their representative, Charles Branwell, a 40-year old minister "of intelligence and influence, one of those with whom the Secretary of War had a conference at Savannah." Whaley immediately sent Howard a telegram objecting to Branwell. He wanted to know if Howard had in mind only white men when he specified that "citizens" should be selected as the representatives on the supervisory boards. Howard agreed that such had been his intent. When it became clear that Ketchum considered Branwell a citizen and was unwilling to exclude him from the board without an explicit order from Howard, the "Edisto planters" were furious. Whaley "became quite violent," according to Ketchum's report to Howard, and "declared the Dred Scott decision the law of the land, and said he would rather have his plantation 'sunk' than submit to having a black man on the board." Ketchum urged Howard not to remove Branwell, a "fair and generous man" who would "do as much as any man can to bring about an understanding between the freedmen and former owners." In addition, removal would only deepen the "distrust of the people, which is almost universal on the island," making agreement between owners and freedmen almost impossible to achieve.

Howard agreed to let Branwell remain on the Edisto board. Branwell told the board that he did not think the Edisto farmers would agree to contract for *wages*, though he promised to try to get the farmers to consider the planters' proposals fairly. In early December Ketchum went with several of the planters to visit their respective plantations. Once again the farmers were adamant: they absolutely refused to make "simple contracts for service *with their former owners*," even though Branwell had succeeded in wresting more favorable terms from the former owners. This intransigence baffled some of the Bureau and other federal officials. It seemed to indicate an inability of "the colored people to appreciate this style of agreements." Formal, written contracts for wages were a standard feature of free Northern society. But the freedmen saw the matter very differently. They feared that such contractual arrangements, especially ones that bound them to the owners for a full year, would amount to a surrender of the very hard-won independence that to them was the essential difference between slavery and freedom. They were unwilling to agree to anything that threatened to resubject them to the control of their former masters. As one observer put it, the freedmen "consider the effect of this class of contracts as a practical return to slavery."

Once again the owners went over the head of the Freedmen's Bureau officials in South Carolina. The planters' Washington agent, Henry Trescot, complained to President Johnson that Saxton and Ketchum were deliberately thwarting government policy. He alleged that they had ordered Branwell to ask "the freedmen in Edisto" if they would be willing to purchase land from the owners if the government would help them "buy the land of the former owners." The very question, the owners argued, simply exacerbated the freedmen's stubbornness: so long as Bureau agents "encouraged" them to believe that there was a chance to hold on to the land, the Edisto inhabitants would continue to refuse to sign contracts with the owners. Moreover, Saxton's actions, Trescot told Johnson, had fostered such a "spirit of resistance among the freedmen" that General Daniel Sickles, the federal commander of the South Carolina military district, had been forced to send in troops to ensure "order." So long as Saxton "controls [the South Carolina] department of the Bureau," Trescot insisted, solving the impasse between the freedmen and the former owners would remain an "utter impossibility." The only solution was the immediate "removal of General Saxton."

The planters also tried to enlist General Sickles on their side. The owners sent him a long petition claiming that the agents of the Freedmen's Bureau were motivated by a "factious spirit of opposition to accommodation" and used their "pernicious influence" to prevent the freedmen from making contracts. The petition was a clever move. The planters knew of the rivalry between the army and the Freedmen's Bureau and knew that Sickles, who thought that Bureau agents in his military district should be under his command, resented Bureau disregard of his authority and interference with things he considered military affairs.

"Slave" quarters on an Edisto Island plantation after the white owners had fled but before the Union forces evacuated the island. The man in the foreground is clothed in a Union uniform.

The planters' petition, complete with five attached "documents," made two key points: (1) the planters had acted in full good faith; and (2) the Bureau agents, especially Captain Ketchum, had ignored the express orders of Johnson and Howard and were subverting clearly established and declared policy. Ketchum, the planters alleged, claimed that if the freedmen refused to contract at all, "the entire plan of settlement was thereby defeated" and "the whole matter must be referred back to General Howard for a decision." To the owners, this interpretation of Howard's order "gives the freedmen in possession a veto upon all proceedings for adjustment whatsoever." Clearly, the petitioners insisted, this was "not contemplated by General Howard . . . and would not be tolerated by him." They concluded that the "just and equitable settlement of General Howard" had been dangerously delayed by his agents in the field and was "in danger of being defeated altogether," and they invited Sickles to investigate the facts and take "such action" as he deemed proper. They knew full well what action they wanted Sickles to take. They conceded that Howard's order "contemplated the restoration of the lands in question as soon as contracts approved by the board should be made," but insisted that "the Freedmen were required to enter into such contracts before January 1, 1866 or else to leave the island." The petition was designed to lay the groundwork for Sickles to "forcibly remove" the freedmen if they persisted in their refusal to contract with the landowners. As they reminded him in their petition, Sickles had already acted "in regard to Edisto" when he sent a detachment there to counter the "hostile attitude of the Freedmen" that had denied "access to the island to the landowners."

General Sickles dispatched one of his key aides, Colonel Edwin Tremain, to "investigate and report on the petition of certain pardoned owners of land on Edisto Island." Tremain's findings were not exactly what the owners wanted nor, probably, what Sickles expected. He found wholly unsubstantiated the allegations "against the faithfulness and integrity of Ketchum" (who, Tremain assured Sickles, "voluntarily invited my inspection of all the documents on file in his office, . . . and desired me to express to General Sickles his gratification at being able to lay the whole matter fully and frankly before him.") In fact, Tremain found that Ketchum followed the letter and spirit of Howard's instructions scrupulously. The planters based their case against Ketchum on a document Ketchum had submitted to the Board of Supervisors asking it to consider the "subject of the freedmen's leasing and buying of lands, and if so upon what terms." They claimed that this action was calculated to foster the inhabitants' intransigence and thereby render accommodation "utterly impossible." Tremain found that this was not the case. Ketchum presented the proposition only to the board. Barnwell, instead of using it to prevent the "negroes from contracting," in fact agreed not to take the proposition to the freedmen and had "not yet done so." Even more to the point, Tremain reported that Howard's written orders expressly directed Ketchum to "ascertain if leases could be made and, if contracts for service could not be arranged, to execute, if possible, *leases* for the freedmen." Moreover, he pointed out that the purchase of land was expressly one of "the modes of settlement" Howard himself had proposed. Finally, Tremain found no basis for the claim that the freedmen had to contract by Jan. 1, 1866 or leave the island. On the contrary, Tremain cited Secretary of War Stanton's telegraph to Howard after his Edisto meeting stating that Stanton "did not understand your orders [from President Johnson] require you to disturb the freedmen in their possession at present, but only to ascertain whether a just and mutual agreement can be made between the pardoned owners and the freedmen, and, if it can, to carry it into effect." Tremain concluded from this that since no agreements had been reached and no new orders issued, there was no ground for imposing the Jan. 1, 1866 deadline on the freedmen.

Oddly enough, despite its full exoneration of Ketchum, Tremain's report to Sickles actually acknowledged the accuracy of the owners' assessment of the situation they faced. All Howard's instructions, "assumed that an agreement could be made with the freedmen by their former owners." But, "the real trouble," Tremain concluded, "is the freedmen will not make agreements with these gentlemen." The reason was really very simple. "Believing," as they did, "that assistance may possibly be afforded by the United States securing them in some manner the continued possession of the lands in question, it is not unnatural," Tremain pointed out, "that they should for present refuse to contract with parties, who—as the negroes believe—have no claim against them." After all, he went on, under the existing orders, "if the freedmen and pardoned owners agree, restoration follows; if they do not agree, restoration is in abeyance." In effect, the freedmen of Edisto were conducting a kind of strike. In the end, it came down to one question: "can an agreement be effected?"

Once again a delegation made its way across the sound to Edisto Island. Colonel Tremain, accompanied by Captain Ketchum, a few aides, and a "deputation of planters" headed by William Whaley set out to make one more effort to see if "some *agreement* might not be determined upon by which the pardoned owners would receive the services of the resident negroes, and the latter a just and remunerative compensation." The prospects for agreement were not entirely favorable. The pardoned owners had not been idle. "Time," as they pointed out to Sickles, "was all important." "If they did not effect their arrangements for labor at once, the crop for the ensuing year must be lost." Whaley "repaired" to Washington, where he secured a meeting with the president attended by General Howard. Whaley came away from the meeting, he told Tremain, with the "expressed intention of the President to restore immediately in case the freedmen were unwilling to contract or lease." Tremain sensed, he later reported, that the owners, armed with Johnson's assurances, didn't really want an agreement but would be "quite satisfied" if they came away from Edisto able to "show the unwillingness of the freedmen to do either."

The pardoned owners urged Tremain to summon the Edisto inhabitants to a general meeting and inform them straight out that the government "required them to contract" by a set time or "leave the island." Tremain bluntly told the planters that in fact he had no authority to tell the freedmen that they were *required* to contract or leave the island. He pointed out that a meeting such as they proposed could only serve to inflame matters. He advised, instead, that the owners go to their estates and "*converse* with the freedmen" and "attempt an agreement of some kind with the resident negros there."

The party learned that on the next day the Edisto farmers were to hold their weekly public meeting. It might be "advisable" for them to attend. When the delegation of white men arrived the meeting had been in progress for over an hour. It continued, "orderly and attentive" for two additional hours. Ketchum asked permission to address the meeting and explained that the "planters present wished to confer with them on matters of great interest to both." Ketchum knew how angry the freedmen were and that their distrust of the former owners ran deep. He was apprehensive about how the assemblage would react to the planters' attempt to persuade them to contract or lease.

Adopting the pose of a stern but kindly father, he pointed out that while the government "demanded that the colored people should be treated like men," it was equally "their duty to be considerate and respectful." He advised them to be "business-like and patient" with their former owners, to resist being "carried away by personal prejudice" and warned them to follow "individual judgement" and not let themselves be "led astray" by some who "would claim to be leaders."

Ketchum then introduced Tremain. He spoke very briefly, stressing that the government "desired" them to make agreements with the owners. It could be in their best interest to do so, he said, if some "mutual understanding" could be achieved. He then told them that "their enemies" claimed that the freedmen were lazy and did not want to "earn their bread by the sweat of their brow" and asked them who "proposed to work and who did not." The count, he reported to Sickles, was unanimous: "all expected to work for a living." He then introduced Whaley, who, according to Tremain, spoke "in excellent and considerate terms." The freedmen listened closely without interrupting. Whaley assured them that the planters were willing to do whatever was "fair and reasonable" in arranging contracts or leases, all of which would be for a year. He closed by offering the freedmen a bit of advice. He stated unequivocally that the former owners had "unquestionable titles" to the land and would soon return to them. The people of Edisto would be well advised to come to terms with Whaley and his colleagues.

Tremain then asked the chairman of the meeting if some of their "own leading speakers" would give their views. The speakers were clear about what they did and

This photograph, taken after the "liberation" of the slaves but probably before 1864 when the freedmen set up individual farmsteads, depicts a "domestic" scene—"wash day—" on Edisto Island. It appears carefully composed but nonetheless reflects the division of work roles of men and women among the freedmen. The women are shown at work at the household tasks that were their province, but the men are bystanders. (The boy with the man at the left of the picture reflects the status of the father as "head" of household.)

did not want. They wanted to "secure for themselves a *home*, . . . somewhere." Above all else, they wished to "*own lands* and to have some security for this result before working again under their former masters." All were opposed to the year contract system. Before the meeting closed, Tremain asked the assembly to select a committee to meet with him, Ketchum, and the owners later that evening. The committee that had written Howard and petitioned the Congress and the president reassembled. But before it met with the visitors to the island, the committee conducted a session with its constituents.

Tremain asked the chair of the committee, Henry Bram, to reply for the committee to the proposals that the owners had presented to the general meeting earlier in the day. Again Bram repeated the simple plea that the churchmen had made to Stanton and Sherman and that the committee had sent to Howard, the president, and to Congress. Their desire was to "acquire land" because only land could "secure their liberty." They of course would prefer land near their old homes, but, if necessary they would go elsewhere. They did not expect "large possessions," but simply a "little plot of ground" upon which as a freedman one could establish a "home for his family from which no one would have a right to eject him, and in the possession of which he would be secured by the laws of the land." The committee pointed out that most of the families on the island had "a little money and wished to buy."

Then the committee made a surprise move that for the moment at least caught the "deputation of planters" off guard. They proposed that the planters "*sell to the freedmen, or to each head of a family, a plot of ground from one to five acres in size,* as might be determined by direct agreement or by decree of the Supervisory Board." The freedmen were perfectly willing to "pay a reasonable price." What was a reasonable price? the owners wanted to know. The committee could not give a specific number but suggested that "tax evaluation" might be taken as a suitable basis. The owners immediately objected,

The freedmen, as well as their northern supporters, put great stock in education. As soon as the Sea Islands fell under Union control, northern freedmen's aid societies sent northern "missionaries"—the majority of whom were unmarried young women from New England—south to set up and conduct schools. The Penn School, shown in this photo, was sent in prefabricated sections to St. Helena Island by the Pennsylvania Freedmen's Relief Association.

suggesting that such a figure was for tax purposes and did not represent a fair sale price. At this point, Captain Ketchum suggested that tax evaluation "might not always be inappropriate" since the planters themselves had used tax evaluations when they claimed estates worth less than $20,000 and thereby made themselves eligible for the general pardons that gave them the claim to have their lands restored. At this point, Tremain asked the committee if the people would be willing to contract "for service" with "their former masters" if the owners would agree to sell them a plot of ground from one-half to five acres. The response was immediate. If "the planters would sell them *even one acre*, they would then make agreements for service." Tremain turned to Whaley, the planters' representative, for his response. "I am not authorized to consider them," Whaley replied. His instructions "contemplated only *contracts or leases*" and he had "nothing to say on the subject of sales." When Tremain asked the other planters for their response, they repeated Whaley's answer. There was little more to say so, the meeting adjourned.

Whaley's silence spoke volumes. The pardoned owners feared that even selling small parcels of land to just a few freedmen would make the others even more reluctant to engage as hired laborers. Besides, it was increasingly clear that there was little chance that they would have to concede on the land question. Time now seemed clearly on their side. And it was. On Jan. 9, General Saxton, the freedmen's strongest advocate, was removed from office. Less than two weeks later the Senate Judiciary Committee eliminated from the Freedmen's Bureau Bill the provision that would have given the holders of Sherman grants lifetime title to the land. General James Beecher (brother of Harriet Beecher Stowe, commander of a black regiment in the war, and military officer under Sickles in charge of the Sea Islands) moved quickly to settle the confused matter of "so called land titles." A large number of the Edisto farmers held "certificates" from Saxton but many did not and many of those who did held certificates to lands other than those they had cultivated. Beecher ordered that "such parties and such parties alone" who held duly authenticated certificates to accurately surveyed lands that they had actually occupied and cultivated "should not be disturbed in possession" of the land. He ordered all others "removed from the plantations" if they persisted in their "refusal to contract."

With great bitterness and reluctance a large number of Edisto farmers signed a contract for lease or hire. In the winter months of 1866 there weren't many places they could go where conditions would be any better. By mid-summer of 1866, a Bureau official reported, Edisto Island was settled and orderly and the freedmen "will make enough during the present year to comfortably clothe them and support them until they have time to make contracts for the ensuing years." But the freedmen of Edisto Island had not surrendered their hope for land. Many still refused to contract, even if it meant expulsion from Edisto. They had learned that under a new act of Congress some land for homesteading had been opened up in Florida. "The freedmen are much exercised about the Homestead Act," Saxton's successor, General R. K. Scott, reported to Howard, "and are holding meetings in each District to devise ways and means of migration." In January of 1867 a large party of Edisto inhabitants led by Henry Bram left Edisto for St. Johns River in Florida to establish homesteads on the "abundance of Government land" that had been set aside for "freedmen and refugees." "Persons," Bram wrote General Scott, "are anxious to take up this opportunity as they are pressed daily to leave their present quarters or make a contract which they are opposed to do." The freedmen suffered defeat at Edisto Island, but the dream "to have land and turn and till it" endured.

Reunion and Reconstruction

When the Confederate armies lay down their arms in unconditional surrender in April of 1865, the nation faced two distinct but intertwined tasks. One task was reunion, or "restoration" as Andrew Johnson preferred to call it, "binding the nation's wounds" and returning the seceded states to full and equal participation in all the political processes of the nation. Normal political and governmental operations had to be restored on the local and state levels. With the collapse and surrender of the Confederacy, civilian authority in many areas simply evaporated as occupying northern forces became the major source of law and order. Procedures had to be established for electing members from the "insurrectionary" states to the national Congress in Washington. But what should be the terms of these "restorations," and who would determine them? The terms of surrender had ensured that ordinary Confederate soldiers would not be held as prisoners or treated as traitors. But what about officers, Confederate officials, and the planters who had supported secession and rebellion—what should be their role in restored governments and in the national polity?

The nation also faced another, even more troublesome task—namely, the task of "reconstructing" the defeated South, of determining what kind of society would replace the slave-based society that the war had irrevocably destroyed. As a Memphis, Tennessee newspaper put it in 1865, "the events of the past five years have produced an entire revolution in the social system of the entire Southern country." There were no clear or settled answers to the question, "What shall we do with the Negro," which General Oliver Howard asked when he took over command of the Freedmen's Bureau. And no question was more controversial or more bitterly contested. But one thing was clear—as General Howard and the Edisto planters such as William Whaley quickly learned. The freedmen and their former owners had very different and essentially incompatible ideas about what they wanted to replace the old master-slave relationship.

By the summer of 1865 most slaveholders had relinquished their slave property. But they still held on to the attitudes that had justified holding blacks in bondage. Even though many masters had trusted *individual* slaves with important tasks and responsibilities, they nonetheless considered blacks as a whole to be childlike people, whom they had fed, clothed, housed, and cared for. And most had convinced themselves that their own slaves were loyal and happy, content with the lot to which their race had consigned them. The former masters thus had great difficulty even imagining blacks as anything but a dependent and subservient people. Masters were perplexed, angered, and even hurt when their slaves (often led by personal or house servants, who had been considered most loyal) left them, refused to work, or stole tools and food.

As the reality of the death of slavery sunk in, the former masters were determined that whatever replaced it would come as close as possible to the control and subordination of blacks that had characterized slavery. Slavery had been, first and foremost, a labor system. The former owners, above all else, wanted whatever "free labor" system replaced it to provide them with a labor force that they could depend on and control. But slavery was also a social system and a system of race relations and control. In early 1865, one black soldier saw his former master among a group of Confederate prisoners. "Hello massa," he shouted, "bottom rail on top dis time." The former masters were determined to do all in their power to see that this reversal did not become a permanent state of affairs. After all, even William Whaley, whom whites and blacks alike had accounted a "good master," went into a rage when told that a black man would serve as his equal on the Edisto Island Board of Supervisors. The former owners were no less determined to exclude the freedmen from civil equality and participation in the polity and thereby maintain white supremacy and return the freedmen to a position of social inferiority and subordination.

The response of the ex-slaves to their new status varied. In some places—particularly in the rice country of South Carolina—accumulated anger and bitterness burst forth in open defiance and occasional violence. Former slaves on the Middleton plantation near Charleston burned the main house and broke open the grave vaults in the family cemetery and scattered the bones. The cook on a plantation in Florida on which "never before" had there been "a word of impudence from any of our black folk," bluntly told her mistress that "if she want dinner she kin cook it herself." In Charleston and Richmond, emancipation brought outpourings of jubilation. In Charleston thousands of blacks turned out for a huge parade, complete with soldiers, bands, tradesmen with their tools, and a contingent of children bearing a banner that declared "We Know No Master but Ourselves." At the center of the celebration was a mock funeral with a coffin blazoned with the motto, "Slavery Is Dead."

In more remote, rural areas the initial response was more confused. Word of emancipation penetrated many places slowly and often in a garbled way. A few slaves wondered if emancipation meant that they now belonged to Lincoln. When slavery ended, there was nothing definite to take its place. The freedmen possessed a number of agricultural and other skills, but they were a people suddenly released from bondage, with few personal possessions and no money, property, or housing. It was not at all clear what they should do, where they should go, or how they could feed, clothe, and shelter themselves. Some set off for places from which they had been sold, hoping to reunite with their families. Others stayed where they were, working for their former masters or for nearby planters. Others, essentially refugees of war, roamed about and flocked to Union encampments in search of food, shelter, and protection.

In spite of all the confusion and uncertainty, as the Edisto people made clear, the ex-slaves possessed a clear and definite idea of the difference between slavery and freedom. One former slave put it to his former master this way: "If I cannot do like a white man I am not free. I see how the poor white people do. I ought to do so too, or else I am a slave." But, above all else, it was "independence"—the condition that from the American Revolution on white Americans had most associated with liberty—that the former slaves saw as the essential hallmark of their newfound freedom. They often asserted their desire for independence—for freedom from the control and dependence on masters that had defined their lives under slavery—in subtle ways. A rural and agricultural population tied to land and place, most were reluctant to leave areas they regarded as home. But, refusing to stay in quarters that reminded them of their previous situation, they often moved to huts scattered around their

FREED AFRICAN AMERICANS IN RICHMOND, VIRGINIA. A major problem after the war was the future of the former slaves. Slavery ended without a clear sense of what was to take its place. All over the South, freed men and women drifted to the cities in search of work or simply to test their newfound freedom.

former master's lands. Some moved to a neighboring planter's land to demonstrate that the tie to their former master had indeed been broken. For many, simply the act of moving, whatever the distance, was a gesture of liberation, a deliberate exercise of the choice and freedom that had been denied them under slavery.

Many blacks, as the Edisto planters learned to their frustration, firmly resisted contracting for their labor, a refusal many whites condemned as a sign of laziness and irresponsibility. But many freedmen were suspicious of anything that seemed to bind them and their labor to any white man. Possession of their labor had been one of the essential marks of their enslavement. Indeed, many thought themselves justified in taking food, tools, and mules from their former masters as payment morally due them for their previous labor. But land was probably the most important token of freedom—a parcel of land that was their own. Again and again, blacks during Reconstruction pleaded for land, "forty acres and a mule," that would enable them to establish their independence and set up households where husbands and wives could work for themselves and rear and protect their children. Even when they suffered a defeat as on Edisto Island, they continued to seek out ways to get a parcel of land—by moving on, saving bit by bit until they could purchase some when and if economic and political conditions changed, banding together to buy a large enough tract to set up a small black community.

LINCOLN'S PLAN FOR RECONSTRUCTION

Lincoln had begun to plan for the aftermath of war well before the end of the fighting. He hoped to restore political relations as quickly and with as little animosity as possible. On December 8, 1863, he issued the Proclamation of Amnesty and Reconstruction as a kind of companion piece to his earlier Emancipation Proclamation. Drawing on his constitutional authority to grant pardons for federal offenses, he offered "full pardon" and the restoration of all property "except slaves" that might have been abandoned or confiscated during the war to anyone who had engaged in rebel-

"The Freedmen's Bureau." The Freedmen's Bureau was controversial in the North as well as the South. Democrats condemned it as a tool of "radicals" designed to promote "Negro equality," and some conservative Republicans attacked it as the cause of much of the racial strife in the South. Here, *Harper's Weekly,* a highly influential northern publication, counters these attacks, showing the Bureau "agent," here depicted as a black man, as an agent of peace.

lion but was now willing to swear an oath of loyalty to the United States, the Constitution, and to all acts freeing the slaves. (High civil and military officials of the Confederacy were excluded). Once 10 percent of the number voting in the 1860 election had taken the oath of allegiance, a state government could be established, which the "national Executive" would recognize. (Lincoln took care to point out that only the houses of Congress could authorize seating members from such reconstructed states.) Once a state government was established, it was required to call a constitutional convention or amend its prewar constitution to formally abolish slavery. No provision was made for the enfranchisement of former slaves. Since blacks had not been eligible to vote in 1860, under the terms of Lincoln's proclamation they were excluded from the suffrage.

The Republican leaders in Congress wanted a much tougher procedure than that contained in Lincoln's proclamation. They wanted to guarantee what they considered true loyalty to the Union. In July 1864, Congress passed the Wade-Davis Bill, which Lincoln "pocket-vetoed." (An outright veto likely would have been overridden, so Lincoln, who ten days before the bill would become law without his signature, had simply ignored the bill thereby killing it since Congress had adjourned before the ten days were up.) The bill required action by 50 percent of the eligible electorate. More important, it contained provisions for an ironclad oath—a pledge of past as well as future loyalty—which was designed to bar all former secessionists and Confederate officeholders from political participation. The Wade-Davis Bill did not provide for black suffrage, though some Republicans had tried to have such a provision included in the bill.

Lincoln was not unmindful of the troubling question of the freedmen, nor was he unaware of the tricky relationship between race and the politics of reunion. But just as he had initially subordinated slavery to the task of preserving the Union, he now placed highest priority on reestablishing normal political relations. In some ways, in fact, just as was the Emancipation Proclamation, his Proclamation of Amnesty and Reconstruction was a wartime measure. It was issued in late 1863, after the victories of Gettysburg and Vicksburg and the capture of Memphis. With large parts of five Confederate states under Union control, some form of "loyal" civil government was highly desirable. In addition, such generous and nonpunitive terms might induce lukewarm supporters of the Confederacy to abandon the cause. Moreover, Lincoln thought reconstruction could be best achieved if the question of the freedmen was separated from the process of political reunion: if the ordinary political machinery was reestablished, the nation would be better able to work out what the freedman's place in American society should be.

Although Lincoln worked hard for the passage of the Thirteenth Amendment abolishing slavery, he had always been reluctant to push for civil and social equality for blacks, partly because of his awareness of the depth of American racism and partly because he shared some of that prejudice. Still, at the time of his death, he had begun to work on the problem of the freedmen and on the politics of that problem. When Louisiana in 1864 drew up its constitution under the provisions of Lincoln's proclamation, he wrote the governor "a private letter" urging Louisiana to consider giving the vote to "some of the colored people," especially "the very intelligent and those who have fought gallantly in our ranks." On March 3, 1865, he signed a bill creating the Freedmen's Bureau. The bill gave federal protection and aid to ex-slaves and contained a limited provision for giving them land, a provision that looked forward to the possible establishment of a landholding black yeomanry. In his "last speech," delivered on April 11, 1865, just three days before his assassination, Lincoln declared that he would "prefer that [the vote] were conferred on the very intelligent and those who serve our cause as soldiers" and promised to deliver "some new announcement" on Reconstruction very soon. John Wilkes Booth made certain that no such announcement was ever made.

PRESIDENTIAL RECONSTRUCTION UNDER JOHNSON

Lincoln's successor, Andrew Johnson, fully intended to carry out the policy Lincoln had begun. He, too, hoped to restore normal political institutions and relations as quickly as possible. There was considerable support, especially in the country at large, for such an approach. Declaring that "we want true Union and concord in the quickest possible time," the *Springfield Republican*, an important Massachusetts newspaper, called for an end to the "reproaches and invectives" that prolonged "the spirit and the evils of the war after the war itself has terminated." But at the same time, there was equally strong sentiment in the North, and especially among both moderate and Radical Republicans in Congress, that the terms of "restoration" not deprive the Union of its hard-won victory. They wanted the "errant states" returned to the Union, but only if they absolutely repudiated secession and if the freedom and basic civil rights of the freedmen were guaranteed. Furthermore, they wanted arrangements that would grant those southerners who had opposed secession dominant power and for the time, at least, exclude ex-Confederate leaders from the political process. Andrew Johnson came to the presidency with some important credentials. Like Lincoln he was a self-taught man of humble origins and great ambition, who used politics as a road to power and standing. He had held office almost continuously for more than thirty years, including two terms as governor of Tennessee, and a term as U.S. Senator. From 1862 until his election as vice president, he served as military governor of Tennessee. His Unionist credentials

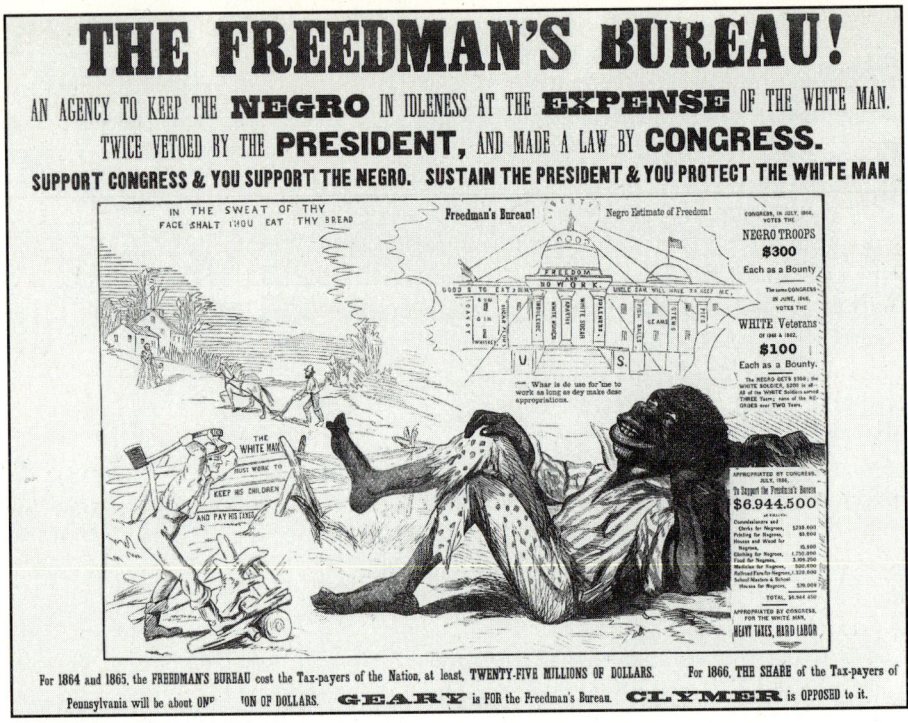

From well before the Civil War, the Democratic party had based much of its electoral appeal on race, presenting itself as the champion of "the white man." As this broadside from 1866 demonstrates, the Democrats continued during Reconstruction to play "the race card" at every opportunity.

were impeccable. In political terms, he seemed to have the support of two important, but not always compatible, constituencies. A former Democrat and strong southern Unionist, he could draw support from Union Democrats and southern Whigs. But, initially, he also had the support even of some Radical Republicans, some of whom thought he was preferable to the seemingly more moderate Lincoln. He loathed the old planter gentry as "a cheap, purse-proud set" nowhere near the moral equal of "the man who earns his bread by the sweat of his brow," and declared again and again during the war that "treason is a crime and must be made odious."

But Johnson also took office with some severe disadvantages. Some Republicans regarded him with suspicion as a former Democrat and a southerner who had once held slaves. In addition, many Republicans in Congress considered reconstruction a legislative rather than an executive responsibility. Johnson also lacked the political power Lincoln had amassed through his adroit dispensing of favors and patronage. Even more important, Johnson lacked the stature—the legitimacy—Lincoln had acquired as the head of state who had seen the Union through to victory and the first president since Andrew Jackson to win reelection. Even with all these assets, Lincoln had run into stiff opposition to his approach to Reconstruction. But Johnson's greatest weakness was more personal. He lacked Lincoln's understanding of the politics of governing—when to follow and when to lead "popular opinion," when to consult and when to keep his own counsel, the need for flexibility and compromise, the crucial importance of timing. Johnson was a loner, proud and suspicious, who rarely consulted others. His most loyal supporter in the cabinet, Secretary of the Navy Gideon Welles, even conceded that Johnson "has no confidants and seeks none."

ANDREW JOHNSON. When Tennessee seceded in June 1861, Johnson—alone among Southern senators—refused to resign and join the Confederacy. Lincoln quickly appointed him military governor of Tennessee. His staunch Unionism and effectiveness in restoring civilian rule there made him a logical choice as Lincoln's running mate in 1864.

Rigid and intolerant of opposing views, he was quick to equate disagreement with enmity and treachery.

So Johnson charged ahead. Congress was not in session when he took office, and he proceeded to carry out his own plan for Reconstruction by executive action, without consulting the Republican leaders of Congress. Here, too, he partly followed Lincoln's example. Lincoln had jailed opponents to the war, ended slavery in the Confederate states, and instituted a draft—all by executive action. He had launched Reconstruction by proclamation and vetoed the Wade-Davis Bill because he opposed its more stringent conditions and thought Reconstruction was properly an executive function. Johnson issued his own Amnesty Proclamation. He renewed the promise of amnesty to most ex-Confederates, but did make one major modification in Lincoln's policy. He expanded the number of categories of persons to be exempted from general amnesty and required people with more than $20,000 in taxable property to seek individual presidential pardons. In addition, he set three conditions for a rebel state's reentry into the political system: the state had to nullify its ordinance of secession, accept the Thirteenth Amendment, and repudiate all Confederate debts.

Johnson moved quickly to restore the Confederate states to the Union. He granted recognition to the governments in Arkansas, Tennessee and Louisiana sponsored by Lincoln under his 1863 proclamation, named the loyal government established in western Virginia as the legitimate government of the whole state, and named a provisional governor of North Carolina and directed the calling of a convention to draw up a new constitution. By July of 1865, he had appointed provisional governors for the remaining six states of the old Confederacy with similar injunctions to hold conventions to establish constitutions that would meet the conditions of his Amnesty Proclamation of May 29. Johnson, arguing like Lincoln that there had been no legal basis for secession, insisted that the states had never legally been out of the Union and hence retained the power to set their own rules on who could vote. He also assured southern leaders that Congress was constitutionally bound to accept these governments. Under the leadership of many ex-Confederates, the South moved quickly. When Congress came back into session in December, it was presented with a fait accompli: all but Texas had set up state governments filled with many former slaveholders and Confederate leaders and had sent senators and representatives to Washington to claim their seats in the new Congress.

Johnson and most white southerners thought political reconstruction was substantially complete. Johnson's major goal was political reunion. He also had a more personal, political agenda. His amnesty procedures were designed to restore the southern states to local control. (Though he used executive authority to achieve this, Johnson remained loyal to his lifelong democratic commitment—his middle name was Jackson—to states' rights and local autonomy.) But he wanted that control in the hands of southerners who had been if not always antisecession Unionists, at least reluctant Confederates. Even more importantly, he wanted the new political alignment to once and for all break the old "slavocracy's" domination of southern politics. He expected these new leaders—and leaders from the old elite who could regain political standing only through Johnson's individual pardon—to provide crucial political support for his own ambition to win the presidency on his own in 1868.

Johnson's decision to rescind General Sherman's Special Field Order No. 15 was part of this political strategy. But it also reflected his vision of what a reconstructed South should look like. Johnson had been antislavery, less out of regard for the black slaves than out of hatred of the planters' power. As he once put it, "Damn the Negroes! I'm fighting these traitorous aristocrats, their masters." He even once declared that he wished "to God that every head of family in the United States had one slave to take the drudgery and menial service off his family." The "new south" he envisioned remained a "white man's" society. Under his proclamations for instituting new governments only white men who had taken oaths of allegiance could participate in the political process. Moreover, he believed that only the states themselves, not Congress and certainly not the executive branch, had the power to define the franchise. He insisted that "white men alone must manage the South" and in his State of the Union address in 1867 went so far as to declare that blacks possessed "less capacity for government than any other race."

BLACK CODES

As soon as the ex-slaveholders found themselves regaining local power, they moved rapidly to reestablish their economic and social dominion, to return the freedmen to a position of social subordination and keep them as a cheap source of plantation labor. In fact, even before regaining formal power, some whites had resorted to violence to try to keep the newly freed blacks in a subordinate position. In May of 1866 in Memphis and in July in New Orleans white mobs aided by some police killed dozens of blacks. Mississippi, South Carolina, and Alabama enacted Black Codes (the other states followed in early 1866), designed to erect state controls that would clearly and carefully define the place of the former slaves in post–Civil War southern society. The codes were multifaceted. Some permitted freedmen to hold property, enter into contracts, contract legal marriages, and sue in the courts. But they also restricted rights. No codes, of course, permitted black voting, and all prohibited freedmen from serving on juries and prohibited intermarriage. (Most northern states also prohibited these things as well.) Other codes restricted blacks to agricultural labor or positions as "servants," forbade carrying firearms, and imposed curfews on them. But it was in the area of labor that the codes were most restrictive. As William Trescot, the agent who pleaded the Edisto planters' cause in Washington, put it, "This question of the control of labor underlies every other question of state interest." The most severe labor codes were passed in Mississippi and South Carolina. Such codes required freedmen to sign annual contracts. In Louisiana and Florida, the contracts extended to "all the members of the family able to work." (As freedmen moved off large estates and onto homesteads, black women had withdrawn from the kinds of field labor they had done under slavery.) If freedmen broke their contracts, they lost all back wages and were subject to arrest by any white man. Vagrancy laws were passed, under which unemployed blacks who could not pay their fines for vagrancy could be bound out to work for anyone who paid their fine.

To many in the North, the new South that Johnson's Reconstruction had ushered in seemed frighteningly similar to the old South. Most of the ex-Confederates seemed right back in power. They filled the state legislatures. And the former vice president of the Confederacy, Alexander Stephens, six former cabinet members, nine generals, and more than fifty members of the Confederate legislature had been elected to the national

Congress by the reconstructed states. Moreover, the Black Codes seemed to have reestablished slavery under another name. As the *Chicago Tribune* thundered, "We tell the white men of Mississippi that the men of the North will convert the state of Mississippi into a frog pond before they will allow any such laws to disgrace one foot of soil over which the flag of freedom waves."

Northerners were divided over what they wanted out of Reconstruction, and few were eager to grant equality to blacks. (Twelve northern states still refused to give the franchise to blacks.) Still, they had opposed slavery, fought and won a war that had come about partly because of slavery, and they did not want to see it restored under some new guise. But most upsetting of all, those who had led the rebellion—those responsible for the terrible war—refused to acknowledge defeat. Mississippi and Texas rejected the Thirteenth Amendment, South Carolina refused to nullify its ordinance of secession, and members of the old slavocracy demanded seats in Congress. In Louisiana a government filled with conservative Unionists, Democrats, and former secessionists was elected on a platform that proclaimed the state government to be a structure "for the exclusive benefit of the white race." It seemed as if Reconstruction was about to deprive the North of the victory for which so many of its men had died.

When the new Congress returned to Washington, it refused to seat the senators and representatives from the former Confederate states. Even moderate Republicans were deeply disturbed at the apparent turn of events. They opposed the Radicals' call for the enfranchisement of the freedmen, fearing that if the party embraced the measure it would lose crucial support in the North. They were alarmed by the repressiveness of many of the newly installed regimes. As Senator Lyman Trumbull of Illinois, a leading moderate, put it, unless there was "some legislation by the nation for his protection," the ex-slave stood in danger of being "abused and virtually reenslaved." The Republicans set up a Joint Committee on Reconstruction, headed by a moderate and dominated by moderates even though it contained the strong-willed Radical Republican, Representative Thaddeus Stevens of Pennsylvania. (The most vociferous Radical in the Senate, Charles Sumner of Massachusetts, who desperately wanted to be on the committee, was excluded as too "ultra.") Army officers, officials from the Freedmen's Bureau, some freedmen and southern Unionists testified before the committee about a rising tide of antiblack hostility and neo-Confederate, anti-North sentiment.

CONGRESSIONAL RECONSTRUCTION

Moderates like Lyman Trumbull and Senator John Sherman of Ohio did not want to throw out the governments organized under Johnson. But they did want to give some protection to the freedmen. Lyman Trumbull, perhaps the most influential man in Congress, introduced two bills early in 1866. The first was a measure to extend the life and expand the scope of the Freedmen's Bureau by giving it funding of its own and extending jurisdiction of its agents to cases involving actions against blacks. It authorized Bureau agents to punish officials who denied blacks the "civil rights belonging to white persons." But to the bitter disappointment of the Edisto farmers the final version of the bill dropped an earlier provision that would have extended at least temporarily their possession of land granted to them under Sherman's special order. Trumbull's second measure was a civil rights Bill. The bill was designed to give legislative substance to the Thirteenth Amendment. It declared all people born in the United States (except Native Americans) citizens and specified that without regard to race they all possessed equal rights to make contracts, to sue in the courts, and to "full and equal benefit of all laws . . . for the security of persons and property." In potentially its most radical feature, it made civil rights a federal responsibility by giving federal officials the authority to bring suits in federal courts against violations. Trumbull (as were most other moderates) was certain he had Johnson's support. He had met with Johnson in late December and believed that "the President wishes no issue with Congress and if our friends would be reasonable we would all get along harmoniously." The moderates considered both bills the height of "reasonableness."

Johnson—to the horror of Congress and the glee of Democrats and southern leaders "restored" to power under Johnson's procedures—vetoed both bills. (Both were later resubmitted and passed over his veto.) In his veto messages, Johnson not only condemned the specific measures, he also challenged the bills' constitutional legitimacy. The Freedmen's Bureau bill, he declared in a statement that challenged the authority of the then-sitting Congress to pass *any* Reconstruction legislation, was unconstitutional because it was passed by a Congress that contained no members from the "eleven states which are to be mainly affected by its provisions." He condemned the Civil Rights Bill as an unconstitutional violation of states' rights and an unconstitutional "stride towards centralization and the concentration of all legislative powers in the national government."

The moderates countered with the Fourteenth Amendment, a complex measure designed to give some basic protection to the ex-slaves in a form that the moderates hoped the South would accept. The amendment contained the basic features of the Civil Rights Act. By constitutional amendment it declared all "persons born or naturalized in the United States" to be citizens (and thereby nullified the Dred Scott decision) and prohibited any state from depriving "any person of life, liberty, or property, without due process of law." But it also reduced the political power of the old southern elite by barring from public office anyone who had ever sworn fidelity to the Constitution and then participated in rebellion. The Radicals tried to get a black suffrage clause included in the amendment. The rights of the freedmen was not the Republicans' only concern. Johnson's Reconstruction plan threatened them with the loss of their political power, and many Republicans were more concerned with holding on to political power than with the rights of blacks. With the end of slavery, southern representation in the House of Representatives would be increased by about twenty seats, since for purposes of apportionment a slave had been counted as only three-fifths of a person. Republicans, especially the Radicals, feared that the exclusion of southern blacks from the vote would ensure the election of unreconstructed rebels, who would join with pro-southern Democrats to drive the Republicans from power. But the moderates resisted the radical demand for a suffrage clause. Instead, the amendment only threatened to reduce southern representation if blacks were not permitted to vote. Nor did it contain any provision for the confiscation or redistribution of lands—the measure to which Stevens was most committed. It was clear, however, that the Republican Congress would not accept any state

THADDEUS STEVENS. Like Lincoln, a former Whig who played an important role in founding the Republican party, Stevens was a Republican congressman from Pennsylvania. During the war he served as chairman of the powerful House Ways and Means Committee, and after the war he became the leader of the radical Republicans in the House and one of the leading advocates of the distribution of confiscated lands to the freedmen.

back into the Union that did not ratify the amendment.

President and Congress were now at complete loggerheads. Johnson denounced the amendment and even urged southerners to reject it. He decided to take the issue of Reconstruction directly to the voters in the upcoming congressional elections. Contrary to custom, Johnson went on the political hustings, denouncing the Republican Congress and further polarizing the issue. Johnson was confident that popular opinion would rally to him. "The right of each state to control its own affairs," was an idea cherished in all parts of the country. Johnson was also certain that few northern whites really supported the expansion of black civil rights. When he asked an election rally, "What does the veto mean?" a supporter shouted back, "It is keeping the nigger down." These were the issues, moreover, by which he hoped to build his own electoral base of a coalition of Democrats, conservative and moderate Republicans, and southern Unionists. But he miscalculated. He underestimated the impact of southern actions—especially the violence against the former slaves and the defiant rhetoric of many restored southern officeholders—on northern opinion. Northern willingness to "forgive" only went so far. Not far below the surface was deep and residual northern anger over the terrible war that they thought the South had visited on the country. Johnson's campaign was a disaster, and the voters overwhelmingly repudiated his policies. The Republicans, now increasingly under the influence of Sumner and Stevens, won more than two-thirds of the seats in both houses, enough to override any presidential veto.

Most of the members of the newly constituted southern legislatures were firmly opposed to the Fourteenth Amendment, which would remove many of their members from office. But white southerners were also angry and felt a deep sense of betrayal. Many had complied with Lincoln's and Johnson's requirements in good faith—a number had condemned the outbreak of violence against blacks and the harshest measures of the restored legislatures—only to have new and harsher conditions imposed on them in what seemed like an all-too-familiar resurgence of Yankee tyranny. Amid fiery denunciations of the fanatical South-hating Republicans, all the southern states except Tennessee, which was eager to have its congressional delegation seated, rejected the Fourteenth Amendment, further infuriating the Republicans in Congress. "The last one of the sinful ten has flung back into our teeth the magnanimous offer of a generous nation" was how Representative James Garfield of Ohio saw it. It was now two years after the end of the fighting, and North and South were further from reconciliation than ever. In his last major speech, Lincoln had pleaded for Americans "to bind up the nation's wounds"; two years of Reconstruction politics had only poured salt on them.

RADICAL RECONSTRUCTION

An aroused Republican Congress came to Washington in December 1866 determined to impose a new style of Reconstruction on a dismayed and angered South. The Republicans moved quickly to consolidate their power and to ensure that neither the courts nor the president thwarted their will. When the Supreme Court issued a ruling that seemed to challenge the validity of the military courts of the Freedmen's Bureau, they reduced the size of the Court, depriving Johnson of the chance to make any appointments to it. When in 1868 the Court seemed about to challenge the Reconstruction Acts the Radicals had passed, they took jurisdiction over such matters away from the Court. But it was Johnson's power that the Republicans were most determined to check. The election had given them the votes to nullify his veto power. The Republicans were equally determined to nullify his use of executive authority, especially his powers as commander in chief (the powers Lincoln had used so effectively during the war to bypass Congress). They enacted legislation that required all military orders, including those of Johnson, to go through General-in-Chief Ulysses S. Grant. The Republicans were also worried that Johnson would try to use federal patronage to create a political machine that would be loyal to him. To thwart this possibility, they passed the Tenure of Office Act, which was designed to prevent Johnson from firing people opposed to his policies.

Radicals, convinced that Johnson would use all means at his disposal to thwart Reconstruction policies passed even over his veto, opened up a campaign to impeach him and remove him from office. They argued that a public official could be removed for "grave misuse of his powers, or any mischievous nonuse of them—for any conduct which harms the public or perils its welfare." Moderates, believing that a president could be removed from office only if he did something that would be indictable as a crime if he were a private citizen, succeeded in blocking two initial attempts to launch impeachment proceedings against Johnson.

In early 1867, the Radicals succeeded in passing a resolution calling for an impeachment investigation, but the House Judiciary Committee, dominated by moderates, declined to act. For a time, Johnson seemed to relent in his efforts to subvert congressional Reconstruction policy and let it be known that his administration would implement the laws Congress had passed. But after Congress adjourned in August, Johnson suspended Secretary of War Stanton (who actively supported the Radicals) and enlisted Ulysses S. Grant as interim secretary. Then, against Grant's wishes, Johnson removed from their commands Generals Philip Sheridan and Daniel Sickles, effective administrators and clear supporters of congressional policy, leading some moderates to change their minds and endorse impeachment. By a 5 to 4 margin, the House Judiciary Committee recommended to the full House that Johnson be impeached for "usurpation of power." The fall elections brought more conservative members into the House, which failed to vote on the measure.

But the impeachment issue was by no means dead. Under the provisions of the Tenure of Office Act, the Senate had to agree before Stanton could be removed from office. Technically, he was only suspended until the Senate acted. When the Senate refused to concur, Grant stepped aside and Stanton returned to his office. Johnson retaliated on February 21, 1868, and ordered Stanton removed, whereupon Stanton barricaded himself in his office. This apparently blatant violation of the Tenure of Office Act pushed many moderates to support impeachment and on February 24 the House voted by 126 to 47 to impeach Johnson. Under the Constitution, the House votes articles of impeachment—the equivalent of an indictment in criminal law—and the Senate acts as the court that conducts the trial on the charges. For eleven weeks an enthralled public watched the Senate proceedings. In the end, despite the complex legal issues as to what constituted legitimate grounds for removing a president from office, what was on trial was Johnson's unrelenting attempt to thwart Republican Reconstruction. But some moderates who deplored

Charles Sumner. A senator from Massachusetts, Sumner was the best known advocate of Radical Reconstruction in the Senate. A powerful orator, he was less effective as a legislative leader than Stevens and was often outmaneuvered by moderates.

Johnson's actions were equally fearful of setting a precedent under which a two-thirds majority of Congress could remove a president who opposed congressional policies, thereby perhaps permanently undermining the balance of powers that lay at the heart of the American constitutional system. Johnson, finally realizing the precariousness of his position, moderated his own behavior. He stopped publically denouncing Congress and promised moderates that he would enforce all the Reconstruction Acts. On May 16, 1868, the Senate finally voted. Seven Republicans and twelve Democrats voted against impeachment. By one vote impeachment failed to secure the two-thirds majority needed for conviction.

In the spring and early summer of 1867, the Republican Congress passed a series of Reconstruction Acts that envisioned a political structure and society very different from that being "restored" under Johnson's mode of reconstruction. Lincoln and Johnson had argued that since secession itself was illegal, the Confederate states had never really been out of the Union. But the Radicals insisted that by rebelling, the states had forfeited their statehood, committing "state-suicide," as Sumner called it. Radicals pushed for a far-reaching plan that would disenfranchise ex-Confederates for a long time, confiscate land for homesteads for the freedmen, and establish a system of federally supported schools. But they settled for a considerably less radical plan that declared the Johnson governments illegal and divided the conquered South into five military districts. The commander of each district, with the aid of the army, was required to prepare the states for readmission by registering all adult black males and all adult white males not disenfranchised by the Fourteenth Amendment. This new electorate would then elect delegates to conventions that were required to draw up state constitutions that guaranteed the vote to blacks and ratified the Fourteenth Amendment. Once the constitution was ratified by popular vote, elections could be held and the state's representatives would be readmitted to Congress. Ironically, by putting the word *male* into the Constitution for the first time, the Fourteenth Amendment erected a constitutional barrier to opening the franchise to women. It is doubly ironic—though not surprising—that while requiring the black vote in a reconstructed South, the Republicans still resisted extending the requirement to the North. Fearing an adverse reaction in the 1868 elections, moderate Republicans resisted the Radicals' call for a constitutional amendment prohibiting the denial of the right to vote "on account of race, color, or previous condition of servitude." In fact, it was not until the Republicans began to lose power in the North in 1870 that they passed the Fifteenth Amendment, granting suffrage to black males in the North and South.

"Radical," or Republican, Reconstruction might not have taken such radical steps as barring the old political elite from power for a generation or laying the economic foundations for the development of an independent black yeomanry. From one perspective, in fact, the term "radical" is something of a misnomer. Those denominated "Radicals" from whom the label derived never gained clear control of Congress and never succeeded in passing their most radical social measures. Nonetheless, Republican Reconstruction did amount to a very real *political* revolution. It brought black voters into the center of the political process and, for a time, gave them very real political power in a way and to a degree that would have been simply unimaginable to most northern or southern whites even two years earlier. By September of 1867, the military supervisors had registered approximately 725,000 black and 650,000 white voters. (Between 100,000 and 175,000 white voters were probably disenfranchised. Over 25 percent of the eligible white voters failed to register either out of apathy or as a protest against the whole new system.) Moreover, blacks constituted a majority of the voters in five states.

The freedmen greeted the franchise with almost as much enthusiasm as they had emancipation itself. All over the South black voters mobilized almost as rapidly as freedmen had flocked to Edisto Island when Sherman's Special Field Order No. 15 was issued. Every institution—but especially the black churches—lent itself to polit-

"And Not This Man?" This woodcut by Thomas Nast was designed to enlist northern support for the franchise for blacks. It evokes the idea that blacks used to claim equal rights from the Revolution through World War II, the idea that as defenders willing to die for the nation, they deserved the freedom for which they had fought.

ical organization. Political notices were read at "churches, societies, leagues, clubs, picnics and all other gatherings." Branches of the Union League (founded in the North as a club to rally support to the Union cause) sprung up everywhere as a major instrument for political education and voter mobilization. One startled observer declared, "You never saw a people more excited on the subject of politics than are the negroes of the south. They are perfectly wild." In areas free of violence and intimidation (see below) voter turnout often reached nearly 90 percent.

THE REPUBLICAN COALITION IN THE SOUTH

The first step in the making of Radical Reconstruction in the South was the mobilization of a Republican coalition that could dominate the writing of the new constitutions and secure control of state and local government. The coalition was composed of three key groups. Certainly the largest group consisted of the newly enfranchised blacks. Throughout the whole period, they were the electoral backbone of the Republican party in the South, constituting from 60 to 85 percent of the Republican vote. But blacks were a majority of the population in only three states—South Carolina, Mississippi, and Louisiana. They were one-quarter of the population in three states, and between 40 and 47 percent in the remaining four states of the old Confederacy. Thus, even with some (short-lived) disenfranchisement of whites, Republican power required varying degrees of white electoral support. This support came from two groups. The smallest component of the Republican coalition—in no place did it make up more than 2 percent of the electorate—consisted of northerners, dubbed "carpetbaggers" by resentful southerners who portrayed them as lowly, grasping, and greedy men, little better than "maggots feeding on Southern misfortune." In fact, the "carpetbaggers," the majority of whom were veterans of the Union army, were a well-educated, middle-class group of ambitious men in their twenties and thirties that included teachers, agents of the Freedmen's bureau, and investors in many cotton plantations. Although they constituted a minuscule portion of the electorate, they held a widely disproportionate number of the key public offices in the Reconstruction governments: they made up nearly 18 percent of the delegates to the constitutional conventions, and sixty of them served in Congress during Reconstruction.

The second group of whites in the Republican coalition consisted of southern whites, dubbed "scalawags" and condemned as "lepers" by many of their countrymen. There were, in general, two quite different groups of scalawags. A number came from the ranks of the former southern Whigs and Unionists who had opposed secession and were often of considerable local prominence and political experience. The largest group of southern white supporters of Republicans were those from the up-country regions, where there had been few slaves and where resentment of the planter aristocracy that had largely controlled antebellum politics was deepest. These up-country Republicans had been Union loyalists during the war and were often the most vehement in demands that the "rebels" be barred from office and their lands confiscated. To them, Republican Reconstruction, initially at least, represented the opportunity to once and for all bring "the reign of the would be aristocracy" to a "close."

The Republican coalition was a fragile and vulnerable one, made up of not always compatible groups with different interests, ideas, and priorities. For the more prominent and wealthy former Whigs and southern Unionists in the coalition, adherence to the Republican party was often perceived as an avenue to political power. Such men hoped to become the leaders of a new South built by securing the support of the freed blacks and the whites who resented the old planter and Confederate leadership as the agents who had brought war and destruction on the South. But the interests and wishes of such leaders were often at odds with those of the whites from the hill country, where slavery had been less of a presence. But most unstable of all was the biracial character of the Republican coalition. The newly freed slaves and poorer whites had a number of interests in common—the need for education and basic welfare, access to land and credit, limitations on the power of economic elites. But race cut deep, especially when economic conditions seemed to put whites and blacks in competition for scarce and dwindling resources. In the prolonged and deepening "hard times" that plagued much of the rural South in the decades following the Civil War, racial antagonism only intensified. At the same time as blacks struggled to gain access to land, an increasing number of poor whites found themselves *losing* land, a loss that made the Democrats' call for restoring the South as a "white man's country" all the more powerful.

As soon as registration was complete, the states elected delegates to the constitutional conventions. Less than half the registered whites but more than 80 percent of registered blacks cast ballots for delegates. Nearly 18 percent of the delegates were carpetbaggers. These delegates, typically in their thirties, were well-educated professionals who often chaired the key committees and drafted the key provisions of the new constitutions. Southern whites made up the largest group of delegates, the majority of whom were farmers, artisans, and merchants from the up-country who had little previous political experience. Blacks constituted a large block of 265 delegates overall, about half of whom had been born in slavery. At least 80, thirty of whom had spent most of their lives in the North, had been born free. At least 40 of the black delegates had served in the Union armies. In most states, the black delegates were relegated to minor roles, but in South Carolina and Louisiana experienced free-born delegates played a major role in shaping the final document.

As soon as the new constitutions were drafted, the battles for ratification were joined. In

"**The First Vote.**" To the former slaves the vote was as much a measure of freedom as the possession of land. This idealized depiction of "the first vote" by Nast is careful to represent the new black voters not as poor, uneducated farmers and agricultural laborers but as solid citizens no different from white voters, as artisans, as veterans, and as well-appointed gentleman. But by 1874, Nast and *Harpers* had retreated from their support of blacks and depicted black legislators in the southern states as corrupt, illiterate buffoons.

many places, conservatives worked strenuously to defeat ratification. They were sure that in the presidential election coming up in 1868 northern whites would turn against the Republican attempt to force "Negro rule" on the South. If the Democrats prevailed, perhaps things could be reversed and self-rule without black suffrage restored. In many places, the antiratification forces resorted to intimidation and violence, using a new terrorist organization, the Ku Klux Klan, to keep blacks away from the polls. But their major tactic was a voter boycott. Ratification required a majority of *registered* voters. There was little chance of getting more votes against ratification than for it, but if enough whites stayed away from the polls ratification would not win the majority it needed. The tactic succeeded in defeating ratification in Alabama: the vote was 70,812 to 1,005 in favor of ratification, but only 43 percent of the registered voters cast ballots. The Republicans in Congress retaliated by passing an additional Reconstruction Act that changed the requirements for ratification: henceforth it would only require a majority of those actually voting. By July of 1867, six states had ratified their constitutions by majorities ranging from 51 percent to 72 percent in South Carolina and had elected Republican governors and legislatures. It took until 1869 for Texas, Mississippi, and Virginia to complete the process that established—for a time at least—Republican rule in each of the states of the old Confederacy.

The North finally had reconstructed states it could accept as legitimate, full-fledged members of the Union. But to many white southerners these governments were never legitimate, and they were determined to do whatever it took to undermine them. To them, Republican Reconstruction was an unmitigated nightmare, and it left a century-long legacy of bitterness. There was, first, the tyranny—the imposition by military force of governments and rulers that they themselves would never have chosen. Moreover, it was an imposition by *outsiders*, by conquerors. Not only was Republican Reconstruction the act of a national government from which southerners had been excluded, it also turned local government *in* the South over to "invaders" from the North. It was a long-standing American axiom that government rested on the consent of the governed, and the majority of white southerners had certainly never consented to the kinds of governments that military Reconstruction forced on them. In fact, of course, in several of the states a majority of *all* Southerners—that is, of blacks and whites—had consented to them. But to most white southerners, the greatest of the horrors of Republican Reconstruction was that it subjected them to "Negro rule," a rule they condemned as wholly incompetent and corrupt.

The charge of "Negro rule" had a kind of truth to it. The Reconstruction governments did bring blacks into the political process and give them real political power: nearly 80 percent of Republican voters were blacks, freedmen were elected and appointed to local and national office—fourteen were elected to the House of Representatives and two were elected to the U.S. Senate—and the governments passed legislation to meet the demands and needs of the newly empowered black constituency. Indeed, it was precisely this *fact* of black political power that rendered these governments so illegitimate in the eyes of most southern whites. White supremacy was not an idea they were about to surrender. But at the same time, the conservative portrait of "Negro rule" was also largely a mythic creation, designed to delegitimize these governments not only in the eyes of white southerners but in northern eyes as well. Although black suffrage was essential for keeping these regimes in power, their electoral base, especially in the beginning, extended beyond the ex-slaves. Many former Whigs, southern Union men, and antisecessionists initially allied themselves with the new Republican governments. Many whites in nonslaveholding regions who had always resented the rule of the planter elite, voted for and participated in the Reconstruction governments. Moreover, only 6 percent of the congressmen elected during Reconstruction were blacks, who never held more than 20 percent of the local offices. In no state did blacks dominate or control the government. There was not a single elected black governor, and only in South Carolina was there ever a black legislative majority. Moreover, the range of ability, education, and competence among black officeholders was not wildly different from the range among most white officeholders in the North or South. Opponents of the Reconstruction governments castigated the carpetbaggers as "too depraved, dissolute, dishonest, and degraded to get" even "the lowest places" in their home states. But, in fact, they were more highly educated, competent, and probably more idealistic than the officeholders in most states in the Union. The Reconstruction governments certainly contained corruption, but they were no more corrupt than their lily-white counterparts before or after the war.

The Reconstruction governments were in many ways reform governments. Their constitutions were more advanced than many in the North. They not only established universal manhood suffrage, but also mandated public school systems for both races. Many of the constitutions called for the expansion of governmental responsibility for social warfare. The South Carolina constitution—the most far-reaching—for example, called for an integrated school system, abolished imprisonment for debt, provided for public support for "the aged, infirm, and helpless poor" (persons whom under slavery, masters had been responsible for), and called for "the division and sale of unoccupied lands among the power classes." The Reconstruction governments spent comparatively little time trying to achieve social equality between whites and blacks. Instead, they concentrated on such things as public education and eliminating the undemocratic features of the antebellum political system, by which the planter elite had maintained its dominion—things that benefited poor whites as well as the freedmen.

REDEEMING THE STATES

In standard political terms, there was much about the Reconstruction governments for the former slaveholders and old planter elite to oppose. They redistributed power and advocated programs that were often against the old elites' perceived interests. Moreover, the burden for paying for schools and welfare fell most heavily on them. But such considerations were not the ultimate source of opposition. Their opponents considered these governments to be wholly illegitimate—an outrage. Illiterate black field hands who could vote while former planters could not, blacks who held office, uppity ex-slaves who mocked their former masters, black soldiers who now patrolled whites—all these things in the eyes of the former slaveholders turned Republican Reconstruction into "Black Reconstruction." "Negro rule" became the galling symbol of all the horrors of Radical Reconstruction, of all they had lost, of the defeat they had suffered and the degradation they now felt.

The opposition struck back against the hated Reconstruction governments with all the means at their disposal. They were determined to regain control of politics and government and "redeem" the South by purging it once and for all of the twin specter of Yankee dominion and "Negro rule." They appealed to white supremacy to draw support of the poorer whites away from the Republicans. For the most part they relied on the ballot box for victory, but in many areas they used intimidation and violence against blacks and their allies to so reduce the black vote as to grant them electoral victory.

At the center of the resort to violence and intimidation were secret organizations like the Ku Klux Klan, which served as a kind of guerrilla force to restore white supremacy. In the words of Eric Foner, a leading historian of Reconstruction, the Klan and similar organizations, such as the Knights of the White Camellia and the White Legions, sought "to destroy the Republican Party's infrastructure, undermine the Reconstruction state, reestablish control over the black labor force, and restore racial subordination in every aspect of Southern life." Democrats—and many subsequent scholars—asserted that Klan violence and terrorism stemmed largely from the racial hatreds of poor whites, that violence was not something the "better sort" condoned. To be sure, a number of southern whites were appalled by the violence (though very few condemned it in public). But in areas of its greatest strength, the Klan drew members from across the social spectrum. Moreover, its leadership (which did not always participate directly in the overt violence itself) came from "respectable gentlemen." And many other "leading men" lent tacit support to the institution so long as it served their political and social purposes.

The Klan directed some of its terror against black schools and churches. In some areas, the Klan "enforced" labor contracts by whipping blacks who challenged or "disobeyed" their employers. Often "prosperous" blacks and those in positions considered too "elevated" for blacks were assaulted. But black officeholders and leaders were the major target of Klan violence. (Scalawags were also frequent targets.) More than thirty of the blacks who served in the constitutional conventions in 1867 were attacked and seven were murdered. In Arkansas, more than 200 political murders, including the assassination of a Republican congressman, took place in 1868 alone.

"TWO MEMBERS OF THE KU KLUX KLAN IN THEIR DISGUISES." The Ku Klux Klan began as a secret, relatively harmless fraternal order, but by early 1868 it had become a terrorist organization, filled with Confederate veterans and led by more than two dozen generals and colonels. Its hoods and robes, ostensibly intended to keep their identities secret, were thought to play on the alleged "superstition" of blacks and to add to the terror of the Klan.

The Klan's greatest strength was in areas of the Piedmont, where blacks were a minority or only a bare majority and where the population was evenly divided between Democrats and Republicans. (In the early and mid 1870s paramilitary "White Legions" operated extensively in Louisiana, Texas, Arkansas, and Alabama.) The Klan was largely absent from low-country South Carolina and Georgia, but was very active in a number of counties around Atlanta and in western Alabama and was deeply entrenched in the central Piedmont regions of North and South Carolina. In Jackson County, Florida, more than 150 people were killed; in Spartanburg County, South Carolina, the Klan whipped hundreds of Republicans and destroyed their livestock and farm property; and in Union County, where almost the entire white population belonged to the Klan, eleven blacks were killed and several hundred whipped.

By itself the campaign of violence did not bring about the "redemption" of the South. But its importance should not be underestimated. It seriously crippled the Republican infrastructure by decimating its leadership and intimidating others out of taking their places. It kept large numbers of black voters from the polls—in districts with the greatest Klan presence, the black vote was often reduced to almost nothing. (In the Klan-dominated counties of Georgia in 1868, for example, only a little over 100 out of more than 9,000 registered black voters cast ballots; in a group of 21 parishes in Louisiana, a Republican vote that had reached more than 26,000 was reduced to 500.) The violence undermined the Republicans in yet another way. Even in power (both locally and nationally) it seemed unable to protect its supporters. Only in Arkansas and Tennessee did Republican governors successfully use state force to combat the Klan. The campaign of terror alarmed northern Republicans. Two "force bills" and a Ku Klux Klan Act were passed by Congress, and in 1871 President Ulysses S. Grant initiated federal prosecutions in Mississippi. In South Carolina, Grant placed a few counties under martial law. These measures succeeded for a time in cutting down on violence and reducing the power of the Klan, which had lost much of its force by 1872. But after that the laws were unevenly enforced and when the White Legions resorted again to violence in Louisiana, Mississippi, and Alabama the Republican administration in Washington only intervened in a few, particularly dramatic—and well-publicized—cases.

It did not take long for "redemption" to begin reclaiming southern states. In states like Tennessee, Virginia, and North Carolina, where white voters had a clear majority, the "redeemers" gained control by 1870. In fact, in Virginia and Tennessee, opposition Democrats had controlled the state legislature from the beginning. It did not take long to regain the governorships. After only one year of Republican rule, Georgia followed suit in 1871, through the combination of the Democrats' success in drawing white voters away from the Republicans and a significant reduction of black votes in Klan areas. (In Alabama, the Democrats won control in 1870, lost it in 1872, and regained it permanently in 1874.) The battles for redemption in the deep South where there were black majorities were prolonged, intense, and violent. The Democrats successfully used white supremacy, and the reduction of taxes (the social measures of the Republican governments fell most heavily on property owners, who were especially hard hit by a continuing agricultural depression) to pry whites away from the Republicans. In Texas, which they captured in 1873, the Democrats were aided by a massive migration of southern whites, which reduced the Republican coalition to a minority.

In Louisiana and Mississippi, the contest was especially intense and violent. In Louisiana, extensive violence—and considerable fraud on both sides—plagued every election from 1868 to 1876. The Democratic and Republican candidates in 1872 both claimed victory. The Democratic claimant, John McEnery, organized a militia and tried to take control of New Orleans police stations. In April of 1873, a clash between the largely black state militia (few whites were willing to serve under Republican administrations) and armed whites in upstate Louisiana left two white men and more than seventy blacks dead. In the fall of 1874, the White Legion tried to take over New Orleans and set McEnery up as governor. Some 3,500 Legionnaires overran the militia and police forces and captured city hall, the state house, and the arsenal. Only after the arrival of federal troops did they withdraw. In Mississippi conditions were not much different. As the 1875 Mississippi election approached, whites were determined to keep blacks and Republicans away from the polls, and the governor feared a bloodbath if he used black militia to oversee the elections. When he asked for federal help, the Grant administration refused, declaring that "the whole public are tired of these annual autumnal outbreaks in the South." The Democrats swept to power, aided by the White Legions, and Mississippi too joined the ranks of the redeemed.

In the end, redemption amounted to a stunningly successful counterrevolution. The "redeemer" governments didn't repeal everything the Reconstruction governments had tried to accomplish. The public school systems—perhaps the most lasting achievement of Republican Reconstruction—remained intact but with severely reduced funds. Fiscal, social welfare, and land policies that had been directed toward blacks and poorer whites were scaled back if not largely abandoned. But what redemption did overturn was the revolution in political power that had given blacks a very real—though by no means dominant—place in the political community and thus, for a time, established the framework within which they might achieve equal standing as "free men."

Blacks were not immediately excluded from the political process. And the pace and process of restoring "white rule" and white supremacy varied from place to place. Some black officeholding continued after redemption: a few remained in several legislatures and even in Congress, they retained seats on some city councils, and some enclaves of black power like the second

MEMBERS OF THE MISSISSIPPI STATE LEGISLATURE, 1874–1875. This official roster of the Mississippi Senate shows the membership of the last legislature before Mississippi was "redeemed" in 1876. Note the arrangement of the profiles and the relegation of the blacks to the bottom two rows. Note also the presence of one woman, Miss Adies Ball, a black woman who was the Senate postmistress.

congressional district in North Carolina and areas in the South Carolina backcountry persisted until near the end of the century. Similarly, black suffrage was not completely rolled back with redemption. But what was broken with remarkable haste was the *effectiveness* of black political participation as state after state moved to make the Fourteenth and Fifteenth amendments "dead letters on the statute book." Black officeholders found themselves increasingly isolated and their powers curtailed. Local offices in areas with large black electoral majorities were stripped of much of their authority, which was transferred to county commissioners or appointed officials. Districts were redrawn to dilute the black vote and city-wide rather than ward elections were instituted. Along with the border and former slave states of Delaware, Kentucky, and Maryland, the "redeemed" states instituted a series of measures—poll taxes, residency requirements, and, in some places, property qualifications—that reduced the black electorate. And finally, especially in the Deep South, the threat—and fact—of antiblack violence was used to return blacks to subordination.

The former slaves and their free black allies fought hard, even after "redemption," to preserve their schools and hold on to whatever land they had. Despite the turmoil, the fickleness and reversals of policy, and the violence and intimidation, they persisted in their quest for land and independence. Availing themselves of the small window of opportunity the Reconstruction governments—and the Fourteenth and Fifteenth Amendments—provided them, by the end of Reconstruction nearly 20 percent of the blacks in the South succeeded in securing at least a parcel of "land [to] turn and till by [their] own labor." But white unity, continuing intimidation, and the ever deepening indifference of the North isolated the ex-slaves politically and made their rights—and even, oftentimes, their hard-won land—ever more vulnerable.

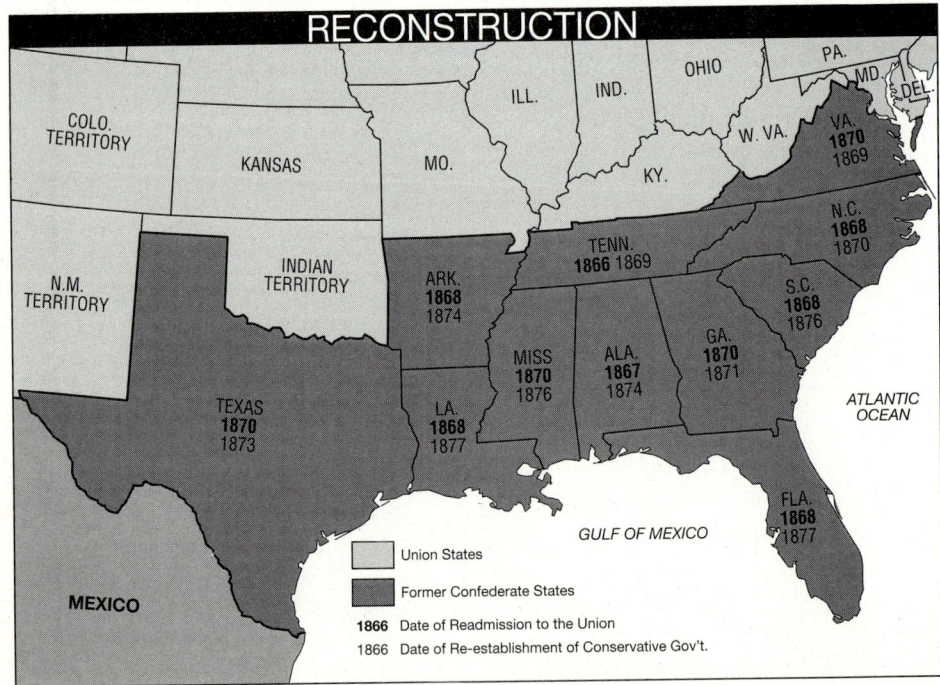

THE END OF RECONSTRUCTION

By 1876 only Louisiana, South Carolina, and Florida remained unredeemed. Even there the hold of Reconstruction was precarious, dependent on the continuing presence of federal troops. The election of 1876 removed this prop, largely because most northerners (at best minimally interested in the welfare of the ex-slaves) no longer cared very much about what was happening in the South. The Republican retreat from the politics of reconstruction really began with the passage of the Reconstruction Acts of 1867 and the election of General Ulysses S. Grant as president in 1868. In many ways, Grant's strong victory—he won 55 percent of the northern vote and carried every northern state but Oregon, New Jersey, and New York—represented an endorsement of Republican Reconstruction. But it also was believed to have finally "settled" the issue of Reconstruction—to have set the policies and procedures by which it would at long last be carried out—and opened the way for the nation and especially the North to return to the ordinary concerns of politics. (In fact, except for "force bills" and the Ku Klux Klan Act, no additional reconstruction measures were passed.) In his inaugural address of 1869, Ulysses S. Grant called for "peace," which most northerners took to mean relief from the turmoil of Reconstruction politics.

The election of 1872 indicated how rapidly northern concerns had shifted. It was not only the South that came out of the Civil War a changed society. A number of important changes—the development of a modern transportation system and mechanized agriculture, a series of technological innovations that underlay industrialization and the emergence of a wide-scale factory system—were well under way by the outbreak of war. (In fact, they were central in enabling the North to win the war.) But the war dramatically accelerated these changes. Moreover, it radically shifted the regional distribution of wealth, both by increasing the wealth in the North and because of the impoverishment that the war brought to the South. In 1860, southern whites had 95 percent *more* per capita wealth than northern whites: in 1870, northern whites had 44 percent more than southern whites. Production (both industrial and agricultural) had been about even on a per-capita basis at the outbreak of war: by 1870, it was nearly 60 percent greater in the North. And in 1870, the South contained only 12 percent of the overall national wealth. The North wanted to get back to business, and business didn't require paying any real attention to the South and what might be happening there.

In 1872, many liberal Republicans who had been staunch in their concern for black rights, including Charles Sumner, turned against the Republican party and supported the Democratic nominee, Horace Greeley, himself an old Whig-Republican, who focused his campaign largely on the corruption of the Grant administration. By the mid-1870s, northerners were more preoccupied with the politics of corruption and agrarian discontent, and with the problems of inflation, tariffs, and railroads, than with Reconstruction or, certainly, the fate of the former slaves.

The election of 1876 resulted in a bizarre deadlock between Rutherford B. Hayes, the Republican nominee, and his Democratic opponent, Samuel J. Tilden. In exchange for the disputed electoral votes of South Carolina, Florida, and Louisiana, Hayes, who had narrowly lost the popular vote to Tilden, promised to remove all remaining federal troops from the South, thus putting a symbolic end to the Reconstruction that in all essential respects had already come to an end. In his second inaugural address, Lincoln had linked the survival of the Union to the fate of the slaves. Slavery had ended and the mighty scourge of war was lifted, but twelve years of Reconstruction had made it clear that white Americans were far from ready to make good on the promise of emancipation.

CHRONOLOGY

1861	Planters flee Edisto Island; blacks remain and plant crops under Union supervision
1862	Union forces evacuate Edisto
1863	Lincoln issues the Emancipation Proclamation;
	Lincoln issues the "Proclamation of Amnesty and Reconstruction"
1864	Congress passes Wade-Davis Bill; Lincoln vetoes it;
	Sherman captures Atlanta and Charleston, South Carolina
1865	Sherman and Stanton meet with twenty black leaders in Charleston, South Carolina;
	Sherman issues Field Order No. 15;
	Blacks return to Edisto Island and establish family farms;
	Freedmen's Bureau established; General O. O. Howard appointed commissioner;
	Lincoln assassinated, Johnson becomes president;
	Johnson issues his Amnesty Proclamation;
	Thirteenth Amendment ratified;
	Johnson rescinds special Field Order No. 15;
	General Howard visits Edisto Island to explain Johnson's policy
1866	Johnson recognizes southern state governments established under his reconstruction plans;
	Southern legislatures adopt "Black Codes";
	Republican Congress refuses to seat members elected from the former Confederate states;
	Johnson vetoes Freedmen's Bureau Bill and Civil Rights Act;
	Congress passes Fourteenth Amendment;
	Republicans win large majorities in both houses;
	Republicans pass Civil Rights Bill and Freedmen's Bureau Bill (without provision protecting black land titles) over Johnson's veto;
	Ku Klux Klan established
1867	In continuing search for land, Henry Bram leads migration of Edisto inhabitants to Florida;
	Congress passes set of Reconstruction Acts, establishing Military Reconstruction;
	Congress passes Tenure of Office Act
1868	Arkansas, Alabama, Florida, Louisiana, North Carolina, South Carolina are readmitted to Union and elect representatives to Congress under provisions of Military Reconstruction;
	Fourteenth Amendment ratified;
	Violence against blacks in the South escalates;
	Johnson impeached, not convicted;
	Ulysses S. Grant (Republican) elected president
1869	Congress passes Fifteenth Amendment granting vote to adult black males
1869–1871	Tennessee, North Carolina, Virginia "redeemed"
1870	Congress passes two "force bills" and the Ku Klux Klan Bill in response to antiblack violence
1872	Grant reelected president
1872–1874	Texas, Alabama, Arkansas, Georgia "redeemed";
	White Legions established in Louisiana, Texas, Arkansas, and Alabama
1875	Grant refuses to send federal troops to oversee Mississippi election
1876	Rutherford B. Hayes (Republican) elected president;
	Federal troops withdrawn from the South, Reconstruction officially ends
1877	Louisiana and Florida "redeemed"

SUGGESTIONS FOR FURTHER READING

EDISTO ISLAND: LAND AND FREEDOM

Willie Lee Rose, *Rehearsal for Reconstruction* (1964), is the classic study of Reconstruction during the Civil War in the Sea Islands and contains important material concerning Edisto Island. William S. McFeely, *Yankee Stepfather: General O. O. Howard and the Freedmen* (1994), devotes a chapter to Edisto. Vincent Harding, *There Is a River: The Black Struggle for Freedom in America* (1981), Edward Magdol, *A Right to the Land: Essays on the Freedmen's Community* (1977), and Eric Foner, *Reconstruction: America's Unfinished Revolution* (1988), also contain discussion of the struggle over Edisto Island. Ira Berlin, et al., "The Terrain of Freedom: The Struggle over the Meaning of Free Labor in the U. S. South," *History Workshop,* 22 (Autumn 1986), reprints the Edisto farmer's petitions to Howard and Johnson.

REUNION AND RECONSTRUCTION

The best, most comprehensive treatment of Reconstruction is Foner, *Reconstruction: America's Unfinished Revolution* (1988.) James McPherson, *Ordeal by Fire: The Civil War and Reconstruction* (1982), has a short but very useful discussion. John Hope Franklin, *Reconstruction After the Civil War* (1961), and Kenneth M. Stampp, *The Era of Reconstruction* (1965), are useful short, general accounts. W. E. B. du Bois, *Black Reconstruction* (1935), remains a classic, pathbreaking study. W. McKee Evans, *Ballots and Fence Rails* (1966), is a superb study of the politics of Reconstruction on the local level in North Carolina. Lawanda Cox and John Cox, *Politics, Principle, and Prejudice* (1965), and William Gillette, *The Right to Vote* (1969), treat race and politics in this period. Eric McKitrick, *Andrew Johnson and Reconstruction* (1966), is a thorough study of early presidential Reconstruction. Hans Trefousse, *Andrew Johnson* (1991), is a useful recent biography. Dan T. Carter, *When the War Was Over: the Failure of Self-Reconstruction in the South, 1865–1867* (1985), is a provocative and highly suggestive study of the early years of Reconstruction. William S. McFeely, *Grant* (1981), is the best study of Grant's presidency. The same author's *Yankee Stepfather: General O. O. Howard and the Freedmen* (1968), is a useful study of the Freedmen's Bureau. James L. Roark, *Masters Without Slaves: Southern Planters in the Civil War and Reconstruction*, is a superb study of a complex subject. Michael Perman, *The Road to Redemption* (1984), is a solid study of the overall subject of redemption. Allen Trelease, *White Terror* (1967), remains the best treatment of the role of the Ku Klux Klan and white terrorism in defeating Reconstruction. C. Vann Woodward, *Reunion and Reaction* (1951), and William Gillette, *Retreat from Reconstruction* (1980), describe the end of Reconstruction.

The story of blacks in Reconstruction is explored in a number of works. Especially valuable for setting the Civil War context for postwar developments is Ira Berlin, et al., *Slaves No More: Three Essays on Emancipation and the Civil War* (1992). Among the most notable studies of the freedmen during Reconstruction are Joel Williamson, *After Slavery* (1966), and Leon Litwack, *Been in the Storm So Long* (l979), and Thomas Holt, *Black Over White* (l977). Ronald E. Butchart, *Northern Schools, Southern Blacks, and Reconstruction: Freedmen's Education, 1862–1875* (1980), is a solid study of the important topic of the freedmen's quest for education. Other important books on Reconstruction and its impact on white and black southerners alike are Paul D. Escott, *Many Excellent People* (1985), and Stephen Hahn, *The Roots of Southern Populism* (1983). Morgan Kousser and James McPherson, eds., *Region, Race, and Reconstruction* (1982), is a valuable collection of essays.

Rupert S. Holland, ed., *The Letters and Diary of Laura M. Towne* (1970), is a superb collection of letters from a young woman who went to the South Carolina Sea Islands to teach the ex-slaves. Though they deal with the period of the Civil War, the four volumes in *Freedom: A Documentary History of Emancipation*, edited by Ira Berlin, et al., *The Destruction of Slavery* (1986), *The Black Military Experience* (1983), *The Wartime Genesis of Free Labor: the Lower South* (1991), and *The Wartime Genesis of Free Labor: the Upper South* (1993), are invaluable.

The Declaration of Independence

The Constitution of the United States of America

Amendments to the Constitution

The Declaration of Independence

In Congress, July 4, 1776. The unanimous Declaration of the thirteen United States of America.

When in the Course of human events, it becomes necessary for one people to dissolve the political bands which have connected them with another, and to assume among the powers of the earth, the separate and equal station to which the Laws of Nature and of Nature's God entitle them, a decent respect to the opinions of mankind requires that they should declare the causes which impel them to the separation.

We hold these truths to be self-evident, that all men are created equal, that they are endowed by their Creator with certain unalienable Rights, that among these are Life, Liberty and the pursuit of Happiness.

That to secure these rights, Governments are instituted among Men, deriving their just powers from the consent of the governed,

That whenever any Form of Government becomes destructive of these ends, it is the Right of the People to alter or to abolish it, and to institute new Government, laying its foundation on such principles and organizing its powers in such form, as to them shall seem most likely to effect their Safety and Happiness. Prudence, indeed, will dictate that Governments long established should not be changed for light and transient causes; and accordingly all experience hath shown, that mankind are more disposed to suffer, while evils are sufferable, than to right themselves by abolishing the forms to which they are accustomed. But when a long train of abuses and usurpations, pursuing invariably the same Object evinces a design to reduce them under absolute Despotism, it is their right, it is their duty, to throw off such Government, and to provide new Guards for their future security.

Such has been the patient sufferance of these Colonies; and such is now the necessity which constrains them to alter their former Systems of Government. The history of the present King of Great Britain is a history of repeated injuries and usurpations, all having in direct object the establishment of an absolute Tyranny over these States. To prove this, let Facts be submitted to a candid world.

He has refused his Assent to Laws, the most wholesome and necessary for the public good.

He has forbidden his Governors to pass Laws of immediate and pressing importance, unless suspended in their operation till his Assent should be obtained; and when so suspended, he has utterly neglected to attend to them.

He has refused to pass other Laws for the accommodation of large districts of people, unless those people would relinquish the right of Representation in the Legislature, a right inestimable to them and formidable to tyrants only.

He has called together legislative bodies at places unusual, uncomfortable, and distant from the depository of their public Records, for the sole purpose of fatiguing them into compliance with his measures.

He has dissolved Representative Houses repeatedly, for opposing with manly firmness his invasions on the rights of the people.

He has refused for a long time, after such dissolutions, to cause others to be elected; whereby the Legislative powers, incapable of Annihilation, have returned to the People at large for their exercise; the State remaining in the mean time exposed to all the dangers of invasion from without, and convulsions within.

He has endeavored to prevent the population of these States; for that purpose obstructing the Laws for Naturalization of Foreigners; refusing to pass others to encourage their migrations hither, and raising the conditions of new Appropriations of Lands.

He has obstructed the Administration of Justice, by refusing his Assent to Laws for establishing Judiciary powers.

He has made Judges dependent on his Will alone, for the tenure of their offices, and the amount and payment of their salaries.

He has erected a multitude of New Offices, and sent hither swarms of Officers to harrass our people, and eat out their substance.

He has kept among us, in times of peace, Standing Armies without the Consent of our legislatures.

He has affected to render the Military independent of and superior to the Civil power.

He has combined with others to subject us to a jurisdiction foreign to our constitution, and unacknowledged by our laws; giving his Assent to their Acts of pretended Legislation:

For quartering large bodies of armed troops among us:

For protecting them, by a mock Trial, from punishment for any Murders which they should commit on the Inhabitants of these States:

For cutting off our Trade with all parts of the world:

For imposing Taxes on us without our Consent:

For depriving us in many cases, of the benefits of Trial by Jury:

For transporting us beyond Seas to be tried for pretended offences:

For abolishing the free System of English Laws in a neighbouring Province, establishing therein an Arbitrary government, and enlarging its Boundaries so as to render it at once an example and fit instrument for introducing the same absolute rule into these Colonies:

For taking away our Charters, abolishing our most valuable Laws, and altering fundamentally the Forms of our Government:

For suspending our own Legislatures, and declaring themselves invested with power to legislate for us in all cases whatsoever.

He has abdicated Government here, by declaring us out of his Protection and waging War against us.

He has plundered our seas, ravaged our Coasts, burnt our towns, and destroyed the lives of our people.

He is at this time transporting large Armies of foreign Mercenaries to compleat the works of death, desolation and tyranny, already begun with circumstances of Cruelty & perfidy scarcely paralleled in the most barbarous ages, and totally unworthy the Head of a civilized nation.

He has constrained our fellow Citizens taken Captive on the high Seas to bear Arms against their Country, to become the executioners of their friends and Brethren, or to fall themselves by their Hands.

He has excited domestic insurrections amongst us, and has endeavoured to bring on the inhabitants of our frontiers, the merciless Indian Savages, whose known rule of warfare, is an undistinguished destruction of all ages, sexes and conditions.

In every stage of these Oppressions We have Petitioned for Redress in the most humble terms: Our repeated Petitions have been answered only by repeated injury. A Prince, whose character is thus marked by every act which may define a Tyrant, is unfit to be the ruler of a free people.

Nor have We been wanting in our attentions to our British brethren. We have warned them from time to time of attempts by their legislature to extend an unwarrantable jurisdiction over us. We have reminded them of the circumstances of our emigration and settlement here. We have appealed to their native justice and magnanimity, and we have conjured them by the ties of our common kindred to disavow these usurpations, which, would inevitably interrupt our connections and correspondence. They too have been deaf to the voice of justice and of consanguinity. We must, therefore, acquiesce in the necessity, which denounces our Separation, and hold them, as we hold the rest of mankind, Enemies in War, in Peace Friends.

We, Therefore, the Representatives of the United States of America, in General Congress, Assembled, appealing to the Supreme Judge of the world for the rectitude of our intentions, do, in the Name, and by the Authority of the good People of these Colonies, solemnly publish and declare, That these United Colonies are, and of Right ought to be, Free and Independent States; that they are Absolved from all Allegiance to the British Crown, and that all political connection between them and the State of Great Britain, is and ought to be totally dissolved; and that as Free and Independent States, they have full Power to levy War, conclude Peace, contract Alliances, establish Commerce, and to do all other Acts and Things which Independent States may of right do.

And for the support of this Declaration, with a firm reliance on the protection of divine Providence, we mutually pledge to each other our Lives, our Fortunes, and our sacred Honor.

John Hancock
(MASSACHUSETTS)

New Hampshire
Josiah Barlett
William Whipple
Matthew Thornton

Massachusetts
Samuel Adams
John Adams
Robert Treat Paine
Elbridge Gerry

Delaware
Caeser Rodney
George Read
Thomas McKean

New York
William Floyd
Philip Livingston
Francis Lewis
Lewis Morris

New Jersey
Richard Stockton
John Witherspoon
Francis Hopkinson
John Hart
Abraham Clark

North Carolina
William Hooper
Joseph Hewes
John Penn

Maryland
Samuel Chase
William Paca
Thomas Stone
Charles Carroll of
   Carrollton

South Carolina
Edward Rutledge
Thomas Heywood, Jr.
Thomas Lynch, Jr.
Arthur Middleton

Rhode Island
Stephen Hopkins
William Ellery

Connecticut
Roger Sherman
Samuel Huntington
William Williams
Oliver Wolcott

Pennsylvania
Robert Morris
Benjamin Rush
Benjamin Franklin
John Morton
George Clymer
James Smith
George Taylor
James Wilson
George Ross

Virginia
George Wythe
Richard Henry Lee
Thomas Jefferson
Benjamin Harrison
Thomas Nelson, Jr.
Francis Lightfoot Lee
Carter Braxton

Georgia
Bulton Gwinnett
Lyman Hall
George Walton

The Constitution of the United States of America

The preamble establishes the principle of government by the people and lists the six basic purposes of the Constitution.

We the People of the United States, in Order to form a more perfect Union, establish Justice, insure domestic Tranquility, provide for the common defence, promote the general Welfare, and secure the Blessings of Liberty to ourselves and our Posterity, do ordain and establish this Constitution for the United States of America.

ARTICLE I LEGISLATIVE DEPARTMENT

Section 1. All legislative Powers herein granted shall be vested in a Congress of the United States, which shall consist of a Senate and House of Representatives.

Section 2. The House of Representatives shall be composed of Members chosen every second Year by the People of the several States, and the Electors in each State shall have the Qualifications requisite for Electors of the most numerous Branch of the State Legislature.

Representatives serve two-year terms. They are chosen by those electors (that is, voters) who are qualified to vote for members of the lower house of their own state legislature.

The number of representatives allotted to a state is determined by the size of its population. The 14th Amendment has made obsolete the reference to "all other persons"—that is, slaves.

A census must be taken every ten years to determine the number of representatives to which each state is entitled. There is now one representative for about every 470,000 persons.

No Person shall be a Representative who shall not have attained to the Age of twenty-five Years, and have been seven Years a Citizen of the United States, and who shall not, when elected, be an Inhabitant of that State in which he shall be chosen.

Representatives and direct Taxes shall be apportioned among the several States which may be included within this Union, according to their respective Numbers, which shall be determined by adding to the whole Number of free Persons, including those bound to Service for a Term of Years, and excluding Indians not taxed, three-fifths of all other Persons. The actual Enumeration shall be made within three Years after the first Meeting of the Congress of the United States, and within every subsequent Term of ten Years, in such Manner as they shall by Law direct. The Number of Representatives shall not exceed one for every thirty Thousand, but each State shall have at Least one Representative; <u>and until such enumeration shall be made, the State of New Hampshire shall be entitled to chuse three, Massachusetts eight, Rhode Island and Providence Plantations one, Connecticut five, New York six, New Jersey four,</u>

Source: House Document #529. U.S. Government Printing Office, 1967.
Note: The Constitution and the amendments are reprinted here in their original form. Portions that have been amended or superseded are underlined. The words printed in the margins explain some of the more difficult passages.

Pennsylvania eight, Delaware one, Maryland six, Virginia ten, North Carolina five, South Carolina five, and Georgia three.

When vacancies happen in the Representation from any State, the Executive Authority thereof shall issue Writs of Election to fill such Vacancies.

The House of Representatives shall chuse their Speaker and other Officers; and shall have the sole Power of Impeachment.

Section 3. The Senate of the United States shall be composed of two Senators from each State, chosen by the Legislature thereof, for six Years; and each Senator shall have one Vote.

Immediately after they shall be assembled in Consequence of the first Election, they shall be divided as equally as may be into three Classes. The Seats of the Senators of the first Class shall be vacated at the Expiration of the second Year, of the second Class at the expiration of the fourth Year, and of the third Class at the Expiration of the sixth Year, so that one third may be chosen every second Year; and if Vacancies happen by Resignation, or otherwise, during the Recess of the Legislature of any State, the Executive thereof may make temporary Appointments until the next Meeting of the Legislature, which shall then fill such Vacancies.

No Person shall be a Senator who shall not have attained to the Age of thirty Years, and been nine Years a Citizen of the United States, and who shall not, when elected, be an Inhabitant of that State for which he shall be chosen.

The Vice President of the United States shall be President of the Senate, but shall have no Vote, unless they be equally divided.

The Senate shall chuse their other Officers, and also a President pro tempore, in the absence of the Vice President, or when he shall exercise the Office of President of the United States.

The Senate shall have the sole Power to try all Impeachments. When sitting for that Purpose, they shall be on Oath or Affirmation. When the President of the United States is tried, the Chief Justice shall preside: And no Person shall be convicted without the Concurrence of two thirds of the Members present.

Judgment in Cases of Impeachment shall not extend further than to removal from Office, and disqualification to hold and enjoy any Office of Honor, Trust or Profit under the United States: but the Party convicted shall nevertheless be liable and subject to Indictment, Trial, Judgment and Punishment, according to Law.

Section 4. The Times, Places and Manner of holding Elections for Senators and Representatives, shall be prescribed in each State by the Legislature thereof; but the Congress may at any time by Law make or alter such Regulations, except as to the Place of chusing Senators.

The Congress shall assemble at least once in every Year, and such Meeting shall be on the first Monday in December, unless they shall by Law appoint a different Day.

Executive authority refers to the governor of a state. The Speaker, chosen by and from the majority party, presides over the House. Impeachment is the act of bringing formal charges against an official. (See also Section 3.)

The 17th Amendment changed this method to direct election.

The 17th Amendment also provides that a state governor shall appoint a successor to fill a vacant Senate seat until a direct election is held.

The Vice President may cast a vote in the Senate only to break a tie.

The president *pro tempore* of the Senate is a temporary officer; the Latin words mean "for the time being."

No President has ever been convicted on charges of impeachment. In 1868 the Senate fell one vote short of the two-thirds majority needed to convict Andrew Johnson. Thirteen other officials—eleven federal judges, one senator, and one secretary of war—have been impeached; five of the judges were convicted.

Elections for Congress are held on the first Tuesday after the First Monday in November in even-numbered years.

The 20th Amendment designates January 3 as the opening of the congressional session.

Each house of Congress decides whether a member has been elected properly and is qualified to be seated. (A quorum is the minimum number of persons required to be present in order to conduct business.) The House once refused admittance to an elected representative who had been guilty of a crime. The Senate did likewise in the case of a candidate whose election campaign lent itself to "fraud and corruption."	**Section 5.** Each House shall be the Judge of the Elections, Returns and Qualifications of its own Members, and a Majority of each shall constitute a Quorum to do Business; but a smaller number may adjourn from day to day, and may be authorized to compel the Attendance of absent Members, in such Manner, and under such Penalties as each House may provide.

Each House may determine the Rules of its Proceedings, punish its Members for disorderly Behavior, and with the Concurrence of two thirds, expel a Member.

Each House shall keep a Journal of its Proceedings, and from time to time publish the same, excepting such Parts as may in their Judgment require Secrecy; and the Yeas and Nays of the Members of either House on any question shall, at the Desire of one fifth of those Present, be entered on the Journal.

Neither House, during the Session of Congress, shall, without the Consent of the other, adjourn for more than three days, nor to any other Place than that in which the two Houses shall be sitting. |
| Congressmen have the power to fix their own salaries. Under the principle of *congressional immunity*, they cannot be sued or arrested for anything they say in a congressional debate. This provision enables them to speak freely.

This clause reinforces the principle of separation of powers by stating that, during his term of office, a member of Congress may not be appointed to a position in another branch of government. Nor may he resign and accept a position created during his term. | **Section 6.** The Senators and Representatives shall receive a Compensation for their Services, to be ascertained by Law, and paid out of the Treasury of the United States. They shall in all Cases, except Treason, Felony and Breach of the Peace, be privileged from Arrest during their Attendance at the Session of their respective Houses, and in going to and returning from the same; and for any Speech or Debate in either House, they shall not be questioned in any other Place.

No Senator or Representative shall, during the Time for which he was elected, be appointed to any civil Office under the Authority of the United States, which shall have been created, or the Emoluments whereof shall have been encreased during such time; and no Person holding any Office under the United States, shall be a Member of either House during his Continuance in Office. |
| The House initiates tax bills but the Senate may propose changes in them.

By returning a bill unsigned to the house in which it originated, the President exercises a *veto*. A two-thirds majority in both houses can override the veto. If the President receives a bill within the last ten days of a session and does not sign it, the measure dies by *pocket veto*. Merely by keeping the bill in his pocket, so to speak, the President effects a veto. | **Section 7.** All Bills for raising Revenue shall originate in the House of Representatives; but the Senate may propose or concur with Amendments as on other Bills.

Every Bill which shall have passed the House of Representatives and the Senate, shall, before it become a Law, be presented to the President of the United States; If he approve he shall sign it, but if not he shall return it, with his Objections to that House in which it shall have originated, who shall enter the Objections at large on their Journal, and proceed to reconsider it. If after such Reconsideration two thirds of that House shall agree to pass the Bill, it shall be sent, together with the Objections, to the other House, by which it shall likewise be reconsidered, and if approved by two thirds of that House, it shall become a Law. But in all such Cases the Votes of both Houses shall be determined by Yeas and Nays, and the Names of the Persons voting for and against the Bill shall be entered on the Journal of each House respectively. If any Bill shall not be returned by the President within ten Days (Sundays excepted) after it shall have been presented to him, the Same shall be a Law, in like Manner as if he had signed it, unless the Congress by their Adjournment prevent its Return, in which Case it shall not be a Law. |
| The same process of approval or disapproval by the President is applied to resolutions and other matters passed by both houses (except adjournment). | Every Order, Resolution, or Vote to which the Concurrence of the Senate and House of Representatives may be necessary (except on a question of Adjournment) shall be presented to the President of the United States; and before the Same shall take Effect, shall be approved by him, or being disapproved by him, shall be repassed by two thirds of the Senate and House of Representatives, according to the Rules and Limitations prescribed in the Case of a Bill. |

Section 8.   The Congress shall have Power to lay and collect Taxes, Duties, Imposts and Excises, to pay the Debts and provide for the common Defence and general Welfare of the United States; but all Duties, Imposts and Excises shall be uniform throughout the United States;

To borrow money on the credit of the United States;

To regulate Commerce with foreign Nations, and among the several States, and with the Indian Tribes;

To establish an uniform Rule of Naturalization, and uniform Laws on the subject of Bankruptcies throughout the United States;

To coin Money, regulate the Value thereof, and of foreign Coin, and fix the Standard of Weights and Measures;

To provide for the Punishment of counterfeiting the Securities and current Coin of the United States;

To establish Post Offices and post Roads;

To promote the Progress of Science and useful Arts, by securing for limited Times to Authors and Inventors the exclusive Right to their respective Writings and Discoveries;

To constitute Tribunals inferior to the superior Court;

To define and punish Piracies and Felonies committed on the high Seas, and Offenses against the Law of Nations;

To declare War, grant Letters of Marque and Reprisal, and make Rules concerning Captures on Land and Water;

To raise and support Armies, but no Appropriation of Money to that Use shall be for a longer Term than two years;

To provide and maintain a Navy;

To make Rules for the Government and Regulation of the land and naval Forces;

To provide for calling forth the Militia to execute the Laws of the Union, suppress Insurrections and repel Invasions;

To provide for organizing, arming, and disciplining the Militia, and for governing such Part of them as may be employed in the Service of the United States, reserving to the States respectively, the Appointment of the Officers, and the Authority of training the Militia according to the discipline prescribed by Congress;

To exercise the exclusive Legislation in all Cases whatsoever, over such District (not exceeding ten Miles square) as may, by Cession of particular States, and the acceptance of Congress, become the Seat of the Government of the United States, and to exercise like Authority over all Places purchased by the Consent of the Legislature of the State in which the Same shall be, for the Erection of Forts, Magazines, Arsenals, dock-Yards, and other needful Buildings; And

To make all Laws which shall be necessary and proper for carrying into Execution the foregoing Powers, and all other Powers vested by this Constitution in the Government of the United States, or in any Department or Officer thereof.

Section 9.   The Migration or Importation of such Persons as any of the States now existing shall think proper to admit, shall not be prohibited by the Congress prior to the Year one thousand eight hundred and eight, but a tax or duty may be imposed on such Importation, not exceeding ten dollars for each Person.

The privilege of the Writ of Habeas Corpus shall not be suspended unless when in Cases of Rebellion or Invasion the public Safety may require it.

These are the *delegated,* or *enumerated,* powers of Congress.

Duties are taxes on imported goods; *excises* are taxes on goods manufactured, sold, or consumed within the country. *Imposts* is a general term including both duties and excise taxes.

Naturalization is the process by which an alien becomes a citizen.

Government *securities* include savings bonds and other notes.

Authors' and inventors' rights are protected by copyright and patent laws.

Congress may establish lower federal courts.

Only Congress may declare war. *Letters of marque and reprisal* grant merchant ships permission to attack enemy vessels.

Militia refers to national guard units, which may become part of the United States Army during an emergency. Congress aids the states in maintaining their national guard units.

This clause gives Congress the power to govern what became the District of Columbia, as well as other federal sites.

Known as the *elastic clause,* this provision enables Congress to exercise many powers not specifically granted to it by the Constitution.

This clause concerns the slave trade, which Congress did ban in 1808.

The writ of *habeas corpus* permits a prisoner to appear before a judge to inquire into the legality of his or her detention.

> *A **bill of attainder** is an act of legislation that declares a person guilty of a crime and punishes him or her without a trial. An ex post facto law punishes a person for an act that was legal when performed but later declared illegal.*
>
> *The object of Clause 4 was to bar direct (per person) taxation of slaves for the purpose of abolishing slavery. The 16th Amendment modified this provision by giving Congress the power to tax personal income.*

No Bill of Attainder or ex post facto Law shall be passed.

No capitation, or other direct, Tax shall be laid, unless in Proportion to the Census or Enumeration herein before directed to be taken.

No Tax or Duty shall be laid on Articles exported from any State.

No Preference shall be given by any Regulation of Commerce or Revenue to the Ports of one State over those of another; nor shall Vessels bound to, or from, one State, be obliged to enter, clear, or pay Duties in another.

No Money shall be drawn from the Treasury, but in Consequence of Appropriations made by Law; and a regular Statement and Account of the Receipts and Expenditures of all public Money shall be published from time to time.

No Title of Nobility shall be granted by the United States: And no Person holding any Office of Profit or Trust under them, shall, without the Consent of the Congress, accept of any present, Emolument, Office, or Title, of any kind whatever, from any King, Prince, or foreign State.

> *States are hereby forbidden to exercise certain powers. Some of these powers belong to Congress alone; others are considered undemocratic.*
>
> *States cannot, without congressional authority, tax goods that enter or leave, except for a small inspection fee.*

Section 10.   No State shall enter into any Treaty, Alliance, or Confederation; grant Letters of Marque and Reprisal; coin Money; emit Bills of Credit; make any Thing but gold and silver Coin a Tender in Payment of Debts; pass any Bill of Attainder, ex post facto Law, or Law impairing the Obligation of Contracts, or grant any Title of Nobility.

No State shall, without the Consent of the Congress, lay any Imposts or Duties on Imports or Exports, except what may be absolutely necessary for executing its inspection Laws: and the net Produce of all Duties and Imposts, laid by any State on Imports or Exports, shall be for the Use of the Treasury of the United States; and all such Laws shall be subject to the Revision and Controul of the Congress.

No State shall, without the Consent of Congress, lay any duty of Tonnage, keep Troops, or Ships of War in time of Peace, enter into any Agreement or Compact with another State, or with a foreign Power, or engage in War, unless actually invaded, or in such imminent Danger as will not admit of delay.

ARTICLE II   EXECUTIVE DEPARTMENT

Section 1.   The executive Power shall be vested in a President of the United States of America. He shall hold his Office during the Term of four Years, and, together with the Vice President, chosen for the same Term, be elected, as follows.

> *Federal officials are ineligible to serve as presidential electors.*

Each State shall appoint, in such Manner as the Legislature thereof may direct, a Number of Electors, equal to the whole Number of Senators and Representatives to which the State may be entitled in the Congress: but no Senator or Representative, or Person holding an office of Trust or Profit under the United States, shall be appointed an Elector.

The Electors shall meet in their respective States, and vote by Ballot for two persons, of whom one at least shall not be an Inhabitant of the same State with themselves. And they shall make a List of all the Persons voted for, and of the Number of Votes for each; which List they shall sign and certify, and transmit sealed to the Seat of the Government of the United States, directed to the President of the Senate. The President of the Senate shall, in the Presence of the Senate and House of Representatives, open all the Certificates, and the Votes shall then be counted. The Person having the greatest

Number of Votes shall be the President, if such Number be a Majority of the whole Number of Electors appointed; and if there be more than one who have such Majority, and have an equal Number of Votes, then the House of Representatives shall immediately chuse by Ballot one of them for President; and if no Person have a Majority, then from the five highest on the List the said House shall in like Manner chuse the President. But in chusing the President, the Votes shall be taken by States, the Representation from each State having one Vote; a quorum for this Purpose shall consist of a Member or Members from two thirds of the States, and a Majority of all the States shall be necessary to a Choice. In every Case, after the Choice of the President, the Person having the Greatest Number of Votes of the Electors shall be the Vice President. But if there should remain two or more who have equal Votes, the Senate shall chuse from them by Ballot the Vice President.

The 12th Amendment superseded this clause. The weakness of the original constitutional provision became apparent in the election of 1800, when Thomas Jefferson and Aaron Burr received the same number of electoral votes. The 12th Amendment avoids this possibility by requiring electors to cast separate ballots for President and Vice President.

The Congress may determine the Time of chusing the Electors, and the Day on which they shall give their Votes; which Day shall be the same throughout the United States.

No person except a natural born Citizen, or a Citizen of the United States, at the time of the Adoption of this Constitution, shall be eligible to the Office of President; neither shall any Person be eligible to that Office who shall not have attained to the Age of Thirty-five Years, and been fourteen Years a Resident within the United States.

A naturalized citizen may not become President.

In a Case of the Removal of the President from Office, or of his Death, Resignation, or Inability to discharge the Powers and Duties of the said Office, the same shall devolve on the Vice-President, and the Congress may by Law provide for the Case of Removal, Death, Resignation or Inability, both of the President and the Vice President, declaring what Officer shall then act as President, and such Officer shall act accordingly, until the Disability be removed, or a President shall be elected.

The Vice President is next in line for the presidency. A federal law passed in 1947 determined the order of presidential succession as follows: (1) Speaker of the House; (2) president pro tempore of the Senate; and (3) Cabinet officers in the order in which their departments were created. This clause has been amplified by the 25th Amendment.

The President shall, at stated Times, receive for his Services, a Compensation, which shall neither be encreased nor diminished during the Period for which he shall have been elected, and he shall not receive within that Period any other Emolument from the United States, or any of them.

Before he enter on the Execution of his Office, he shall take the following Oath or Affirmation:—I do solemnly swear (or affirm) that I will faithfully execute the Office of the President of the United States, and will to the best of my Ability, preserve, protect and defend the Constitution of the United States.

Section 2. The President shall be Commander in Chief of the Army and Navy of the United States, and of the Militia of the several States, when called into the actual Service of the United States; he may require the Opinion in writing, of the principal Officer in each of the executive Departments, upon any subject relating to the Duties of their respective Offices, and he shall have Power to Grant Reprieves and Pardons for Offenses against the United States, except in Cases of Impeachment.

This clause suggests written communication between the President and the principal officer in each of the executive departments. As it developed, these officials comprise the Cabinet—whose members are chosen, and may be replaced, by the President.

He shall have Power, by and with the Advice and Consent of the Senate, to make Treaties, provided two thirds of the Senators present concur; and he shall nominate, and by and with the Advice and Consent of the Senate, shall appoint Ambassadors, other public Ministers and Consuls, Judges of the supreme Court, and all other Officers of the United States, whose Appointments are not herein otherwise provided for, and which shall be established by Law: but the Congress may by Law vest the Appointment of such inferior Officers, as they think proper, in the President alone, in the Courts of Law, or in the Heads of Departments.

Senate approval is required for treaties and presidential appointments.

> Without the consent of the Senate, the President may appoint officials only on a temporary basis.

> The President delivers a State of the Union message at the opening of each session of Congress. Woodrow Wilson was the first President since John Adams to read his messages in person. Franklin D. Roosevelt and his successors followed Wilson's example.

The President shall have Power to fill up all Vacancies that may happen during the Recess of the Senate, by granting commissions which shall expire at the End of their next Session.

Section 3. He shall from time to time give to the Congress Information of the State of the Union, and recommend to their Consideration such Measures as he shall judge necessary and expedient; he may, on extraordinary Occasions, convene both Houses, or either of them, and in Case of Disagreement between them, with Respect to the Time of Adjournment, he may adjourn them to such Time as he shall think proper; he shall receive Ambassadors and other public Ministers; he shall take Care that the Laws be faithfully executed, and shall Commission all the Officers of the United States.

Section 4. The President, Vice-President and all civil Officers of the United States, shall be removed from Office on Impeachment for, and Conviction of, Treason, Bribery, or other high Crimes and Misdemeanors.

ARTICLE III   JUDICIAL DEPARTMENT

> Federal judges hold office for life and may not have their salaries lowered while in office. These provisions are intended to keep the federal bench independent of political pressure.

Section 1. The judicial Power of the United States, shall be vested in one supreme Court, and in such inferior Courts as the Congress may from time to time ordain and establish. The Judges, both of the supreme and inferior Courts, shall hold their Offices during good Behaviour, and shall, at stated Times, receive for their services, a Compensation, which shall not be diminished during their Continuance in Office.

> This clause describes the types of cases that may be heard in federal courts.
> The 11th Amendment prevents a citizen from suing a state in a federal court.

Section 2. The judicial Power shall extend to all Cases, in Law and Equity, arising under this Constitution, the Laws of the United States, and Treaties made, or which shall be made, under their Authority;—to all Cases affecting Ambassadors, other public Ministers and Consuls;—to all Cases of admiralty and maritime Jurisdiction;—to Controversies to which the United States shall be a Party; to Controversies between two or more States;—between a State and Citizens of another state;—between Citizens of different states;—between Citizens of the same State claiming Lands under Grants of different States, and between a State, or the Citizens thereof, and foreign States, Citizens or Subjects.

> The Supreme Court handles certain cases directly. It may also review cases handled by lower courts, but Congress in some cases may withhold the right to appeal to the highest court or limit appeal by setting various conditions.

In all Cases affecting Ambassadors, other public Ministers and Consuls, and those in which a State shall be Party, the supreme Court shall have original Jurisdiction. In all the other Cases before mentioned, the supreme Court shall have appellate Jurisdiction, both as to Law and Fact, with such Exceptions, and under such Regulations as the Congress shall make.

> The 6th Amendment strengthens this clause on trial procedure.

The trial of all Crimes, except in Cases of Impeachment, shall be by Jury; and such Trial shall be held in the State where the said Crimes shall have been committed; but when not committed within any State, the Trial shall be at such Place or Places as the Congress may by Law have directed.

> Treason is rigorously defined. A person can be convicted only if two witnesses testify to the same obvious act or if he or she confesses in court.

Section 3. Treason against the United States, shall consist only in levying War against them, or in adhering to their Enemies, giving them Aid and Comfort. No Person shall be convicted of Treason unless on the Testimony of two Witnesses to the same overt Act, or on Confession in open Court.

The Congress shall have Power to declare the Punishment of Treason, but no Attainder of Treason shall work Corruption of Blood, or Forfeiture except during the Life of the Person attained.

ARTICLE IV RELATIONS AMONG THE STATES

Section 1. Full Faith and Credit shall be given in each State to the public Acts, Records, and judicial Proceedings of every other State. And the Congress may by general Laws prescribe the Manner in which such Acts, Records and Proceedings shall be proved, and the Effect thereof.

Section 2. The Citizens of each State shall be entitled to all Privileges and Immunities of Citizens in the several States.

A Person charged in any State with Treason, Felony, or other Crime, who shall flee from Justice, and be found in another State, shall on demand of the executive Authority of the State from which he fled, be delivered up, to be removed to the State having Jurisdiction of the Crime.

<u>No Person held in Service or Labour in one State, under the laws thereof, escaping into another, shall, in Consequence of any Law or Regulation therein, be discharged from such Service or Labour, but shall be delivered up on Claim of the Party to whom such Service or Labour may be due.</u>

Section 3. New States may be admitted by the Congress into this Union; but no new State shall be formed or erected within the Jurisdiction of any other State; nor any State be formed by the Junction of two or more States, or parts of States, without the Consent of the Legislatures of the States concerned as well as of the Congress.

The Congress shall have Power to dispose of and make all needful Rules and Regulations respecting the Territory or other Property belonging to the United States; and nothing in this Constitution shall be so construed as to Prejudice any Claims of the United States, or of any particular State.

Section 4. The United States shall guarantee to every State in this Union a Republican Form of Government, and shall protect each of them against Invasion; and on Application of the Legislature, or of the Executive (when the Legislature cannot be convened) against domestic Violence.

ARTICLE V AMENDING THE CONSTITUTION

The Congress, whenever two thirds of both Houses shall deem it necessary, shall propose Amendments to this Constitution, or, on the Application of the Legislatures of two thirds of the several States, shall call a Convention for proposing Amendments, which, in either Case, shall be valid to all Intents and Purposes, as part of this Constitution, when ratified by the Legislatures of three fourths of the several States, or by Conventions in three fourths thereof, as the one or the other Mode of Ratification may be proposed by the Congress: Provided that no Amendment which may be made prior to the Year One thousand eight hundred and eight shall in any Manner affect the first and fourth Clauses in the Ninth Section of the first Article; and that no State, without its Consent, shall be deprived of its equal Suffrage in the Senate.

ARTICLE VI GENERAL PROVISIONS

All Debts contracted and Engagements entered into, before the Adoption of this Constitution, shall be as valid against the United States under this Constitution, as under the Confederation.

Punishment for treason extends only to the person convicted, not to his or her descendants. (Corruption of blood means that the heirs of a convicted person are deprived of certain rights.)

States must honor each other's laws, court decisions, and records (for example, birth, marriage, and death certificates).

Each state must respect the rights of citizens of other states.

The process of returning a person accused of a crime to the governmental authority (in this case a state) from which he or she has fled is called *extradition*.

The 13th Amendment, which abolished slavery, makes this clause obsolete.

A new state may not be created by dividing or joining existing states unless approved by the legislatures of the states affected and by Congress. An exception to the provision forbidding the division of a state occurred during the Civil War. In 1863 West Virginia was formed out of the western region of Virginia.

A *republican* form of government is one in which citizens choose representatives to govern them. The federal government must protect a state against invasion and, if state authorities request it, against violence within a state.

An amendment to the Constitution can be proposed (a) by Congress, with a two-thirds vote of both houses, or (b) by a convention called by Congress when two-thirds of the state legislatures request it. An amendment is ratified (a) by three-fourths of the state legislatures or (b) by conventions in three-fourths of the states. The twofold procedure of proposal and ratification reflects the seriousness with which the framers of the Constitution regarded amendments. Over 7,000 amendments have been proposed; only 26 have been ratified.

> The *supremacy clause* means that if a federal and a state law conflict, the federal law prevails.

This Constitution, and the Laws of the United States which shall be made in Pursuance thereof; and all Treaties made, or which shall be made, under the Authority of the United States, shall be the supreme Law of the Land; and the Judges in every State shall be bound thereby, any Thing in the Constitution or Laws of any State to the Contrary notwithstanding.

> Religion may not be a condition for holding public office.

The Senators and Representatives before mentioned, and the Members of the several State Legislatures, and all executive and judicial Officers, both of the United States and of the several States, shall be bound by Oath or Affirmation, to support this Constitution; but no religious Test shall ever be required as a Qualification to any Office or public Trust under the United States.

ARTICLE VII RATIFICATION

> The Constitution would become the law of the land upon the approval of nine states.

The Ratification of the Conventions of nine States shall be sufficient for the Establishment of this Constitution between the States so ratifying the Same.

DONE in Convention by the Unanimous Consent of the States present the Seventeenth Day of September in the Year of our Lord one thousand seven hundred and eighty-seven and of the Independence of the United States of America the Twelfth. In Witness whereof We have hereunto subscribed our Names.

G° WASHINGTON
Presid^t and deputy from
VIRGINIA

Attest: William Jackson, Secretary

Delaware
Geo: Read
Gunning Bedford, jun
John Dickinson
Richard Bassett
Jaco: Broom

Maryland
James McHenry
Dan: of St Thos Jenifer
Danl Carroll

Virginia
John Blair
James Madison Jr.

North Carolina
Wm Blount
Richd Dobbs Spaight
Hu Williamson

South Carolina
J. Rutledge
Charles Cotesworth
  Pinckney
Charles Pinckney
Pierce Butler

Georgia
William Few
Abr Baldwin

New Hampshire
John Langdon
Nicholas Gilman

Massachusetts
Nathaniel Gorham
Rufus King

Connecticut
Wm Saml Johnson
Roger Sherman

New York
Alexander Hamilton

New Jersey
Wil: Livingston
David Brearley
Wm Paterson
Jona: Dayton

Pennsylvania
B Franklin
Thomas Mifflin
Robt. Morris
Geo. Clymer
Thos. FitzSimons
Jared Ingersoll
James Wilson
Gouv Morris

Amendments to the Constitution

[The date following each amendment number is the year of ratification.]

AMENDMENT I (1791)

Congress shall make no law respecting an establishment of religion, or prohibiting the free exercise thereof: or abridging the freedom of speech, or of the press; or the right of the people peaceably to assemble, and to petition the Government for a redress of grievances.

Establishes freedom of religion, speech, and the press; gives citizens the rights of assembly and petition.

AMENDMENT II (1791)

A well regulated Militia, being necessary to the security of a free State, the right of the people to keep and bear Arms, shall not be infringed.

States have the right to maintain a militia.

AMENDMENT III (1791)

No Soldier shall, in time of peace, be quartered in any house, without the consent of the Owner, nor in time of war, but in a manner to be prescribed by law.

Limits the army's right to quarter soldiers in private homes.

AMENDMENT IV (1791)

The right of the people to be secure in their persons, houses, papers, and effects, against unreasonable searches and seizures, shall not be violated, and no Warrants shall issue, but upon probable cause, supported by Oath or affirmation, and particularly describing the place to be searched, and the persons or things to be seized.

Search warrants are required as a guarantee of a citizen's right to privacy.

AMENDMENT V (1791)

No person shall be held to answer for a capital, or otherwise infamous crime, unless on a presentment or indictment of a Grand Jury, except in cases arising in the land or naval forces, or in the Militia, when in actual service in time of War or public danger; nor shall any person be subject for the same offence to be twice put in jeopardy of life or limb; nor shall be compelled in any criminal case to be a witness against himself, nor be deprived of life, liberty, or property, without due process of law; nor shall private property be taken for public use, without just compensation.

To be prosecuted for a serious crime, a person must first be accused (indicted) by a grand jury. No one can be tried twice for the same crime (double jeopardy). Nor can a person be forced into self-incrimination by testifying against him- or herself.

AMENDMENT VI (1791)

In all criminal prosecutions, the accused shall enjoy the right to a speedy and public trial, by an impartial jury of the State and district wherein the crime shall have been committed, which district shall have been previously ascertained by law, and to be informed of the nature and cause of the accusation; to be confronted with the witnesses against him; to have compulsory process for obtaining witnesses in his favor, and to have the Assistance of Counsel for his defense.

Guarantees a defendant's right to be tried without delay and to face witnesses testifying for the other side.

AMENDMENT VII (1791)

In suits at common law, where the value in controversy shall exceed twenty dollars, the right of trial by jury shall be preserved, and no fact tried by a jury, shall be otherwise reexamined in any court of the United States, than according to rules of the common law.

A jury trial is guaranteed in federal civil suits involving more than twenty dollars.

AMENDMENT VIII (1791)

Excessive bail shall not be required, nor excessive fines imposed, nor cruel and unusual punishments inflicted.

AMENDMENT IX (1791)

The enumeration in the Constitution, of certain rights, shall not be construed to deny or disparage others retained by the people.

The listing of specific rights in the Constitution does not mean that others are not protected.

AMENDMENT X (1791)

The powers not delegated to the United States by the Constitution, nor prohibited by it to the States, are reserved to the States respectively, or to the people.

Limits the federal government to its specific powers. Powers not prohibited the states by the Constitution may be exercised by them.

AMENDMENT XI (1798)

The Judicial power of the United States shall not be construed to extend to any suit in law or equity, commenced or prosecuted against one of the United States by Citizens of another State, or by Citizens or Subjects of any Foreign State.

A state cannot be sued by a citizen or another state in a federal court. Such a case can be tried only in the courts of the state being sued.

AMENDMENT XII (1804)

The Electors shall meet in their respective states and vote by ballot for President and Vice-President, one of whom, at least, shall not be an inhabitant of the same state with themselves; they shall name in their ballots the person voted for as President, and in distinct ballots the person voted for as Vice-President, and they shall make distinct lists of all persons voted for as President, and of all persons voted for as Vice-President, and of the number of votes for each, which lists they shall sign and certify, and transmit sealed to the seat of the government of the United States, directed to the President of the Senate;—The President of the Senate shall, in presence of the Senate and House of Representatives, open all the certificates and the votes shall then be counted;—The person having the greatest number of votes for President, shall be the President, if such number be a majority of the whole number of Electors appointed; and if no person have such majority, then from the persons having the highest numbers not exceeding three on the list of those voted for as President, the House of Representatives shall choose immediately, by ballot, the President. But in choosing the President, the votes shall be taken by states, the representation from each state having one vote; a quorum for this purpose shall consist of a member or members from two-thirds of the states, and a majority of all the states shall be necessary to a choice. <u>And if the House of Representatives shall not choose a President whenever the right of choice shall devolve upon them, before the fourth day of March next following, then the Vice-President shall act as President, as in the case of the death or other constitutional disability of the President:</u>—The person having the greatest number of votes as Vice-President, shall be the Vice-President, if such number be a majority of the whole number of Electors appointed, and if no person have a majority, then from the two highest numbers on the list, the Senate shall choose the Vice-President; a quorum for the purpose shall consist of two-thirds of the whole number of Senators, and a majority of the whole number shall be necessary to a choice. But no person constitutionally ineligible to the office of President shall be eligible to that of Vice-President of the United States.

Revises the process by which the President and Vice President were elected (see Article II, Section 1, Clause 3). The major change requires electors to cast separate ballots for President and Vice President. If none of the presidential candidates obtains a majority vote, the House of Representatives—with each state having one vote—chooses a President from the three candidates having the highest number of votes. If no vice presidential candidate wins a majority, the Senate chooses from the two candidates having the highest number of votes. The underlined portion was superseded by Section 3 of the 20th Amendment.

AMENDMENT XIII (1865)

Section 1. Neither slavery nor involuntary servitude, except as a punishment for crime whereof the party shall have been duly convicted, shall exist within the United States, or any place subject to their jurisdiction.

Abolishes slavery.

Section 2. Congress shall have power to enforce this article by appropriate legislation.

AMENDMENT XIV (1868)

Section 1. All persons born or naturalized in the United States, and subject to the jurisdiction thereof, are citizens of the United States and of the State wherein they reside. No state shall make or enforce any law which shall abridge the privileges or immunities of citizens of the United States; nor shall any State deprive any person of life, liberty, or property, without due process of law; nor deny any person within its jurisdiction the equal protection of the laws.

This section confers full civil rights on former slaves. Supreme Court decisions have interpreted the language of Section 1 to mean that the states, as well as the federal government, are bound by the Bill of Rights.

A penalty of a reduction in congressional representation shall be applied to any state that refuses to give all adult male citizens the right to vote in federal elections. This section has never been applied. The underlined portion was superseded by Section 1 of the 26th Amendment. (This section has also been amplified by the 19th Amendment.)

Section 2. Representatives shall be apportioned among the several States according to their respective numbers, counting the whole number of persons in each State, excluding Indians not taxed. But when the right to vote at any election for the choice of electors for President and Vice-President of the United States, Representatives in Congress, the Executive and Judicial officers of a State, or the members of the Legislature thereof, is denied to any of the male inhabitants of such State, being <u>twenty-one</u> years of age, and citizens of the United States, or in any way abridged, except for participation in rebellion, or other crime, the basis of representation therein shall be reduced in the proportion which the number of such male citizens shall bear to the whole number of male citizens twenty-one years of age in such state.

Any former federal or state official who served the Confederacy during the Civil War could not become a federal official again unless Congress voted otherwise.

Section 3. No person shall be a Senator or Representative in Congress, or elector of President and Vice-President, or hold any office, civil or military, under the United States, or under any State, who, having previously taken an oath, as a member of Congress, or as an officer of the United States, or as a member of any State legislature, or as an executive or judicial officer of any State, to support the Constitution of the United States, shall have engaged in insurrection or rebellion against the same, or given aid or comfort to the enemies thereof. But Congress may by a vote of two-thirds of each House, remove such disability.

Makes legal the federal Civil War debt, but at the same time voids all Confederate debts incurred in the war.

Section 4. The validity of the public debt of the United States, authorized by law, including debts incurred for payment of pensions and bounties for services in suppressing insurrection or rebellion, shall not be questioned. But neither the United States nor any State shall assume or pay any debt or obligation incurred in aid of insurrection or rebellion against the United States, or any claim for the loss or emancipation of any slave; but all such debts, obligations and claims shall be held illegal and void.

Section 5. The Congress shall have power to enforce, by appropriate legislation, the provisions of this article.

AMENDMENT XV (1870)

Gives ex-slaves the right to vote.

Section 1. The right of citizens of the United States to vote shall not be denied or abridged by the United States or by any State on account of race, color, or previous condition of servitude.

Section 2. The Congress shall have power to enforce this article by appropriate legislation.

AMENDMENT XVI (1913)

Allows Congress to levy direct taxes on incomes.

The Congress shall have power to lay and collect taxes on incomes, from whatever source derived, without apportionment among the several States, and without regard to any census or enumeration.

AMENDMENT XVII (1913)

Provides for election of senators by the people of a state, rather than the state legislature.

The Senate of the United States shall be composed of two Senators from each State, elected by the people thereof, for six years; and each Senator shall have one vote. The electors in each State shall have the qualifications requisite for electors of the most numerous branch of the State legislature.

When vacancies happen in the representation of any State in the Senate, the Executive authority of such State shall issue writs of election to fill such vacancies: Provided, That the legislature of any State may empower the executive thereof to make temporary appointments until the people fill the vacancies by election as the legislature may direct.

This amendment shall not be so construed as to affect the election or term of any Senator chosen before it becomes valid as part of the Constitution.

AMENDMENT XVIII (1919)

Section 1. After one year from the ratification of this article, the manufacture, sale, or transportation of intoxicating liquors within, the importation thereof into, or the exportation thereof from the United States and all territory subject to the jurisdiction thereof for beverage purposes is hereby prohibited.

Legalizes prohibition—*that is, forbidding the making, selling, or transporting of intoxicating beverages. Superseded by the 21st Amendment.*

Section 2. The Congress and the several States shall have concurrent power to enforce this article by appropriate legislation.

Section 3. This article shall be inoperative unless it shall have been ratified as an amendment to the Constitution by the legislatures of the several States, as provided in the Constitution, within seven years from the date of the submission hereof to the States by the Congress.

AMENDMENT XIX (1920)

The right of citizens of the United States to vote shall not be denied or abridged by the United States or by any State on account of sex.

Congress shall have power to enforce this article by appropriate legislation.

Gives women the right to vote.

AMENDMENT XX (1933)

Section 1. The terms of the President and Vice-President shall end at noon on the 20th day of January, and the terms of Senators and Representatives at noon on the 3d day of January, of the years in which such terms would have ended if this article had not been ratified; and the terms of their successors shall then begin.

The "lame duck" amendment allows the President to take office on January 20, and members of Congress on January 3. The purpose of the amendment is to reduce the term in office of defeated incumbents known as "lame ducks."

Section 2. The Congress shall assemble at least once in every year, and such meeting shall begin at noon on the 3d day of January, unless they shall by law appoint a different day.

Section 3. If, at the time fixed for the beginning of the term of the President, the President elect shall have died, the Vice-President elect shall become President. If a President shall not have been chosen before the time fixed for the beginning of his term, or if the President elect shall have failed to qualify, then the Vice-President elect shall act as President until a President shall have qualified; and the Congress may by law provide for the case wherein neither a President elect nor a Vice-President elect shall have qualified, declaring who shall then act as President, or the manner in which one who is to act shall be selected, and such person shall act accordingly until a President or Vice-President shall have qualified.

Section 4. The Congress may by law provide for the case of the death of any of the persons from whom the House of Representatives may choose a President whenever the right of choice shall have devolved upon them, and for the case of the death of any of the persons from whom the Senate may choose a Vice-President whenever the right of choice shall have devolved upon them.

Section 5. Sections 1 and 2 shall take effect on the 15th day of October following the ratification of this article.

Section 6. This article shall be inoperative unless it shall have been ratified as an amendment to the Constitution by the legislatures of three-fourths of the several States within seven years from the date of its submission.

AMENDMENT XXI (1933)

Repeals the 18th Amendment.

Section 1. The eighteenth article of amendment to the Constitution of the United States is hereby repealed.

States may pass prohibition laws.

Section 2. The transportation or importation into any State, Territory, or possession of the United States for delivery or use therein of intoxicating liquors, in violation of the laws thereof, is hereby prohibited.

Section 3. This article shall be inoperative unless it shall have been ratified as an amendment to the Constitution by conventions in the several States, as provided in the Constitution, within seven years from the date of the submission hereof to the States by the Congress.

AMENDMENT XXII (1951)

Limits a President to two full terms or one term plus two years of a previous President's term.

Section 1. No person shall be elected to the office of the President more than twice, and no person who has held the office of President, or acted as President, for more than two years of a term to which some other person was elected President shall be elected to the office of the President more than once. But this Article shall not apply to any person holding the office of President when this Article was proposed by the Congress, and shall not prevent any person who may be holding the office of President, or acting as President, during the term within which this Article becomes operative from holding the office of President or acting as President during the remainder of such term.

Section 2. This article shall be inoperative unless it shall have been ratified as an amendment to the Constitution by the legislature of three-fourths of the several States within seven years from the date of its submission to the States by the Congress.

AMENDMENT XXIII (1961)

By giving the District of Columbia three electoral votes, Congress enabled its residents to vote for President and Vice President.

Section 1. The District constituting the seat of Government of the United States shall appoint in such manner as the Congress may direct:

A number of electors of President and Vice-President equal to the whole number of Senators and Representatives in Congress to which the District would be entitled if it were a State, but in no event more than the least populous State; they shall be in addition to those appointed by the State, but they shall be considered, for the purposes of the election of President and Vice-President, to be electors appointed by a State; and they shall meet in the District and perform such duties as provided by the twelfth article of amendment.

Section 2. The Congress shall have power to enforce this article by appropriate legislation.

AMENDMENT XXIV   (1964)

Section 1. The right of citizens of the United States to vote in any primary or other election for President or Vice-President, for electors for President or Vice-President, or for Senator or Representative in Congress, shall not be denied or abridged by the United States or any State by reason of failure to pay any poll tax or other tax.

Forbids the use of a poll tax as a requirement for voting in federal elections.

Section 2. The Congress shall have power to enforce this article by appropriate legislation.

AMENDMENT XXV   (1967)

Section 1. In case of the removal of the President from office or of his death or resignation, the Vice-President shall become President.

Outlines the procedure to be followed in case of presidential disability.

Section 2. Whenever there is a vacancy in the office of the Vice-President, the President shall nominate a Vice-President who shall take office upon confirmation by a majority vote of both Houses of Congress.

Section 3. Whenever the President transmits to the President pro tempore of the Senate and the Speaker of the House of Representatives his written declaration that he is unable to discharge the powers and duties of his office, and until he transmits to them a written declaration to the contrary, such powers and duties shall be discharged by the Vice-President as Acting President.

Section 4. Whenever the Vice-President and a majority of either the principal officers of the executive departments or of such other body as Congress may by law provide, transmit to the President pro tempore of the Senate and the Speaker of the House of Representatives their written declaration that the President is unable to discharge the powers and duties of his office, the Vice-President shall immediately assume the powers and duties of the office as Acting President.

Thereafter, when the President transmits to the President pro tempore of the Senate and the Speaker of the House of Representatives his written declaration that no inability exists, he shall resume the powers and duties of his office unless the Vice-President and a majority of either the principal officers of the executive department or of such other body as Congress may by law provide, transmit within four days to the President pro tempore of the Senate and the Speaker of the House of Representatives their written declaration that the President is unable to discharge the powers and duties of his office. Thereupon Congress shall decide the issue, assembling within forty-eight hours for that purpose if not in session. If the Congress, within twenty-one days after receipt of the latter written declaration, or, if Congress is not in session, within twenty-one days after

Congress is required to assemble, determines by two-thirds vote of both Houses that the President is unable to discharge the powers and duties of his office, the Vice-President shall continue to discharge the same as Acting President; otherwise, the President shall resume the powers and duties of his office.

AMENDMENT XXVI (1971)

Lowers the voting age to eighteen.

Section 1. The right of citizens of the United States, who are eighteen years of age or older, to vote shall not be denied or abridged by the United States or any state on account of age.

Section 2. The Congress shall have the power to enforce this article by appropriate legislation.

Credits

Unless otherwise acknowledged, all photographs are the property of Scott, Foresman and Company. Page abbreviations are as follow: (T) top, (C) center, (B) bottom, (R) right.

1: John Carter Brown Library, Brown University; **5:** John R. Freeman and Co., London; **12:** Copyright the British Museum; **14:** John Carter Brown Library, Brown University; **16:** Private Collection; **22:** National Portrait Gallery, Smithsonian Institution; **25:** Photograph Courtesy of the Museum of The American-Indian Heye Foundation; **27:** Arizona Historical Society; **28:** Copyright the British Museum; **30:** Ernest Haas; **33:** Bibliteca Medices Laurenziana; **35:** Library of Congress; **36:** Stokes Collection, New York Public Library, Astor, Lenox and Tilden Foundations; **37:** Public Archives of Canada; **41:** From *The American Pilgrim's Way New England*, Marcus B. Hirish, 1907; **43:** Smithsonian Institution; **47:** Detail, Map of Virginia. Courtesy of The Edward E. Ayer Collection, Courtesy of The Newberry Library, Chicago; **50:** Rare Book Division/New York Public Library, Astor, Lenox and Tilden Foundations; **52:** Copyright the British Museum; **53:** National Portrait Gallery, Smithsonian Institution; **55:** Courtesy Ingham Fosler Collection, Imperial Tobacco Limited; **57:** Society of Antiquaries, London; **60:** From *The New World,* Stefan Lorant Collection 1946; **62:** Copyright the British Museum; **65:** Detail, Map of Virginia Courtesy of the Edward E. Ayer Collection, Courtesy of The Newberry Library, Chicago; **72:** Courtesy of the John Carter Brown Library, Brown University; **79T:** Courtesy American Antiquarian Society; **79B:** From *New England's Prospect,* William Wood, 1634; **81:** From *News From America,* John Underhill, 1638; **83T:** Stokes Collection/New York Public Library, Aston, Lenox and Tilden Foundations; **83B:** Courtesy of the New York State Museum; **89:** Detail, *Penn's Treaty With The Indians*, 1771-1772, Benjamin West. Courtesy of Pennsylvania Academy of the Fine Arts; **92:** Copyright the British Museum; **95:** Courtesy Peabody Essex Museum, Salem, MA; **104:** Courtesy of Harvard University Art Museums; **107:** From Ralph Gardiner, *England Grievance Discovered In Relation To The Coal Traders* London, 1655; **111:** The Colonial Williamsburg Foundation; **112:** Library of Congress; **113:** *Penn's Treaty With The Indians* 1771-1772, Benjamin West. Courtesy Pennsylvania Academy of the Fine Arts; **117:** The Edward E. Ayer Collection, Courtesy of The Newberry Library, Chicago; **120:** Courtesy American Antiquarian Society; **122:** Library of Congress; **125:** British Gallery of Historical Portraits; **126:** Courtesy of the John Carter Brown Library, Brown University; **127:** Courtesy American Antiquarian Society; **133:** Library of Congress; **137:** Library of Congress; **140:** New York Public Library, Aston, Lenox and Tilden Foundations; **141:** National Anthropological Archives/Smithsonian Institution; **144:** St. Augustine Historical Society; **146:** Library of Congress; **150:** Rare Book Division, New York Public Library, Astor, Lenox and Tilden Foundations; **152:** Stokes Collection, New York Public Library, Astor, Lenox and Tilden

Foundations; **154:** From Victor Collot, *Voyage Dans L'amerique Septentrionale,* 1826, plate 16/ Courtesy of The Newberry Library, Chicago; **155:** National Anthropological Archives/ Smithsonian Institution; **156:** Courtesy of the John Carter Brown Library, Brown University; **157:** The Institute of Texan Cultures, San Antonio, Texas; **159L:** Musco de America, Madrid; **159R:** Musco de American, Madrid; **162:** National Portrait Gallery, London; **166:** Maryland Historical Society, Baltimore; **167:** Courtesy of the John Carter Brown Library, Brown University; **169:** National Army Museum, London; **170:** From the Collection of the Louisiana State Museum; **175:** Detail, *Surrender of Lord Cornwallis,* 1787-1794, John Trumbull. Copyright Yale University Art Gallery; **179:** Courtesy Museum of Fine Arts, Boston; **181:** Antiquarian Society, Concord, Mass. All rights reserved; **182:** Courtesy of the Bostonian Society, Old State House; **183:** Library of Congress; **186:** I. N. Phelps, Stokes Collection Miriam & Ira D. Wallach Division of Art, Prints and Photographs/New York Public Library, Astor, Lenox and Tilden Foundations; **189:** Massachusetts Historical Society; **212:** *Surrender of Lord Cornwallis,* 1787-1794, John Trumbull. Copyright Yale University Art Gallery; **215:** Detail, Washington's Farewell to his officers, 1865, Alonzo Chappel. Courtesy Chicago Historical Society; **218:** Washington's Farewell to his officers, 1865, Alonzo Chappel. Courtesy Chicago Historical Society; **221:** National Gallery of Art, Washington, D.C. Andrew W. Mellon Collection; **223:** Virginia State Library and Archives; **227:** National Portrait Gallery, Smithsonian Institution; **230:** The Museum of the City of New York; **240:** New York Public Library, Astor, Lenox and Tilden Foundations; **245:** Library of Congress; **247:** Courtesy American Antiquarian Society; **251:** Library of Congress; **255:** Courtesy Independence National Historical Park. Eastern National Parks and Monuments Association Park; **260:** In the Collection of the Corcoran Gallery of Art, Gift of William Corcoran; **262:** Courtesy of The Newberry Library, Chicago; **267:** The New-York Historical Society, New York City; **276:** The New-York Historical Society, New York City; **277:** Library of Congress; **279:** Thomas Jefferson Memorial Library; **283:** Montana Historical Society, Helena; **286:** Library of Congress; **293:** Detail, The Trail of Tears, 1942. Robert Lindneux. Woolarac Museum, Bartlesville, Oklahoma; **296:** Western History Collections, University of Oklahoma Library; **300:** Courtesy American Antiquarian Society; **301:** National Anthropological Archives, Smithsonian Institution; **302:** Western History Collections, University of Oklahoma; **303:** National Anthropological Archives, Smithsonian Institution; **307:** George Lowrey, Attributed to George Catlin. Accession no. 0126.2180. Thomas from the Collection of Gilcrease Institute of American History & Art, Tulsa; **313:** Detail, The Trail of Tears, 1942. Robert Lindneux. Woolarac Museum, Bartlesville, Oklahoma; **318:** American Museum of Natural History; **321:** From *Harper's New Monthly Magazine*, March 1854; **325:** Field Museum of Natural History, Chicago Neg. A93851c; **329:** The New-York Historical Society, New York City; **333:** Cincinnati Historical Society; **336:** The Museum of American Political Life, University of Hartford, Photograph by Sally Anderson-Bruce; **342T:** Cincinnati Historical Society; **342B:** Cincinnati Historical Society; **344:** Cincinnati Historical Society; **346:** Cincinnati Historical Society; **348:** The Boston Athenaeum; **353:** Print Collection, Miriam & Ira D. Wallach Division of Art, Prints & Photographs. New York Public Library, Astor, Lenox and Tilden Foundations; **356:** The Historic New Orleans Collection. Accession no. 1974.25.14.167; **361:** In the Collection of the Corcoran Gallery of Art, Museum Purchase, Gallery Fund; **363:** National Portrait Gallery, Smithsonian Institution/Art Resource, New York; **365:** Museum of Political Life, University of Hartford. Photograph by Steven Laschever; **366:** St. Louis Art Museum; **372:** The New-York Historical Society, New York City; **379:** The Metropolitan Museum of Art, Gift of I. N. Phelps Stokes, Edward S. Hawes, Alice Mary Hawes, Marion Augusta Hawes, 1937; **387:** Peabody Essex Museum, Salem, MA; **389:** Bettmann Archive; **393:** Collection of The New-York Historical Society, New York City; **395:** Massachusetts Historical Society; **400:** Library of Congress; **401:** The Museum of the City of New York; **402:** Collection of The New-York Historical Society, New York City; **403:** Courtesy of the Fairbanks Museum and Planetarium, St. Johnsburg, VT; **408:** Courtesy The Brooklyn Museum, Dick S. Ramsay Fund 57.68/; **410:** The Metropolitan Museum of Art, Gift of I. N. Phelps Stokes, Edward S. Hawes, Alice Mary Hawes, Marion Augusta Hawes, 1937; **414:** Culver Pictures; **416:** Peabody Essex Museum, Salem, MA; **417:** New York Public Library, Astor, Lenox and Tilden Foundations; **418:** The Metropolitan Museum of Art, The Chester Dale Collection, Bequest of Chester Dale, 1962. (64.97.4); **419:** Robert Frost Library, Amherst College Library; **426:** Library of Congress; **438:** Library of Congress; **444:** Missouri Historical Society; **450(both):** Library of Congress; **451:** Library of Congress; **459:** Collection of the Louisianna State Museum; **463:** Library of Congress; **468:** Stowe-Day Foundation, Hartford, CT; **471:** Stowe-Day Foundation, Hartford, CT; **480:** The Granger Collection, New York; **484:** Stowe-Day Foundation, Hartford, CT; **492:** Library of Congress; **497:** The New-York Historical Society, New York City; **504:** Library of Congress; **507:** Library of Congress; **511:** The National Archives; **514L:** Chicago Historical Society; **514R:** Library of Congress; **520:** Library of Congress; **525:** Courtesy of The Illinois State Historical Library; **526:** The National Archives; **530:** Library of Congress; **531:** Courtesy The Museum of the Confederacy, Richmond, Va.; **538:** The New-York Historical Society, New York City; **541:** Library of Congress; **542:** Library of Congress; **543:** Library of Congress; **545:** The National Archives; **548:** Library of Congress; **549:** Library of Congress; **553:** The New-York Historical Society, New York City; **559:** Library of Congress; **561:** Library of Congress; **563:** Library of Congress; **565:** The New-York Historical Society, New York City; **568:** The New-York Historical Society, New York City; **569:** From the Penn School Collection. Permission granted by Penn Center, Inc., St. Helena Island, SC; **573:** Library of Congress; **574:** "The Freedmen's Bureau" drawing by A. H. Ward July 25, *Harper's Weekly* 1868; **576:** Library of Congress; **577:** Library of Congress; **580:** Library of Congress; **582:** Courtesy of The Bostonian Society, Old State House; **584:** from *Harper's Weekly*; **586:** *Harper's Weekly* 1867; **589:** Rutherford B. Hayes Presidential Center, Fremont, Ohio; **591:** Library of Congress

Index

Page numbers in italics refer to art.

Abolitionists, 456, 494
Acoma, pueblo destruction, 69–70
Adams, John, 178, 183, 186, *189*, 190, 239, 351
   in election of 1800, 277
   negotiations with France, 282
   nomination for President, 275
   as president, 232
Adams, John Quincy, 279, 335, 352
   in 1824 presidential campaign, 355–56
   Garrison's reaction to, 391
   inaugural address, 363
   opinion on Cherokees, 305
   presidency of, 357–58
   views on party politics, 357
Adams, Samuel, 178–80, *179*, 188, 190
Adams-Onis Treaty of 1819, 354
Adena (Ohio), Great Serpent Mound, *25*
African Americans. *See* Africans, Blacks, Slavery
African culture, 136
Africans. *See also* Blacks, Slaves
   forced immigration of, 109, 149, 150
Agriculture. *See also* Farming
   of Cherokees, 299, 302
   in colonies in the 18th century, 164
   commercialization of, 330
   Erie Canal to move crops, 328
   expansion in North, 323–30
   expansion in South, 319–23
   market expansion, 330–31

Alabama, 297, 320
   cotton cultivation, 445
   statehood, 320, 367
Alamo, 488
Alaska, 159, 160
Albany, 82, 328
   council meeting with Iroquois League (1754), 168–69
Albany Argus, 362
Albemarle County, 111
Alden, John, accused as wizard, 103–4
Alexandria, 225
Algonquians, 12, *12*, 26
Alien and Sedition Acts, 275
Alta, California, 486, 490
Alvord, John, 559
American Home Missionary Society, 407
American merchant vessels, British warships seizure of, 282
American Revolution, 176–213
   war-debts from, 228–29, 272
American Slavery As It Is (Weld), 502
"American System," 356
American Tract Society, 407
"Americanized" Indians, 324
Amherst, General Jeffrey, 170
Amnesty proclamation
   by Johnson, 559, 577
   by Lincoln, 573, 575
Anastasia Island, 144
Anderson, Robert, 515
Andover Theological Seminary, 301
Andros, Sir Edmund, 128

Anglo-Dutch War (1652–1654), 119
Angola, 150
Annapolis Convention (1786), 226, 227
Antietam Creek, 534, *548*
"Antifederalist" political faction, 245
Antislavery advocates, 502
   Garrison as, 393, 394
   views of blacks, 412, 556–57
Antislavery tracts, 469
Apaches, 26, 34
Appomattox Courthouse, 523, 546
Arizona, 490
   pueblo in, 27
Arkansas, 577
Arkansas River, 31
Army of the Potomac, 534
Arondelle, Peter, 65
Arroyo Hondo, 259, 264
Articles of Confederation, 216, 226, 233
   achievements under, 235–37
   amendments to, 235
   convention to strengthen, 227
   major problems of, 237–39
Assumption, in Hamilton plan, 273
Athapascans, 26
Athapaskan, 26
Atlanta, 545, 546
Atlantic (locomotive), *400*
Attucks, Crispus, 185
Auburn, New York, 412
Austin, Stephen, 486
"Awakening," evangelical, 118, 405–7
Azores, 29

I–1

Aztecs, 19
    Spanish discovery of, 29

Backcountry. *See* Frontier; Westward expansion
Bacon, Nathaniel, 125, *125*
Bacon's rebellion (Virginia, 1676), 123–25
Balboa, Vasco Núñez de, 29
Baltimore, Maryland, 400
    national nominating convention (1839), 338
Bancroft, George, 350
Bank, national, 273–74. *See also* Bank of the United States
Bank of the Commonwealth (Kentucky), 353
Bank of England, 373
Bank notes, 353
    as currency, 352
Bank of the United States, 274, 353
    Jackson's opposition to, 371
    recharter bill (1830), 369–72
    state taxes on, 354
Bankruptcy, 353
    fear during Confederation Period, 237
Banks, General Nathaniel, 540
Banks, state, 352
Baptists, 80, 163–64, 405
Barbados, 90, 110
Barlowe, Arthur, 11
Barnard, G. N., *446*
Basset, Lieutenant James, 187
Bates, Edward, *520*
Battle. *See* location names
Bear, John W., 347
"Bear Flag Republic," 492
Beauregard, General P. G. T., 532, 533
Beecher, Catherine, 412, 483
    A Treatise on Domestic Economy, 409, 419
Beecher, General James, 570
Beecher, Henry Ward, 504
Beecher, Lyman, 483
Beecher family, *484*
Bell, John, 505
Benavides, Antonio de, 136
Bennett, Edward, 56
    plantation attack, 63
Benton, Thomas Hart, 354
Bering, Vitus, 158–59
Bering Strait, passage across, 24
Berkeley, Sir John, 56, 63
Berkeley, Sir William (Virginia governor), 125
Berkeley Hundred, 58
Bernard, Francis, governor of Massachusetts, 187, 188
Beverley, Robert, 51

Bible, New Testament translation into Cherokee, 301
Biddle, Nicholas, 369
Bight of Biafra, 150
Bill of Rights, 248–49
"Bills" of rights, in state constitutions, 236
Biloxi Bay, 116
Bingham, George Caleb, "The County Election," *366*
Birney, James G., 490
Birth control, 409
Birthrate, decline in the 19th century, 407–9
Bishop, Bridget, 105
Black codes, 578–79
Black Reconstruction, 588
"Black Republicans," 506
"Black Seminoles," 317, 318
Blackbeard, 111, *112*
Blacks. *See also* Edisto Island, Freed People, Runaway slaves, Slaves
    antislavery advocate views of, 412, 556–57
    population in South, 584
    randomly murdered after Nat Turner's rebellion, 437
    in Republican coalition, 584
    southern white views of, 571–72
    status after Civil War, 554
    voting rights, 574, 583
    after redemption, 592
Blair, Montgomery, 516, *520*
"Bleeding Kansas," 500–1
Blennerhassett, Harman, 263
Blunt, Dr. Thomas, 436
Bonner, John, *186*
Book of Mormon, 413
Booth, John Wilkes, 523, 526
Boston, 74, 400
    in 1769, *186*
    British army in, 177, 180–81, *181*
    Garrison in, 391
    population in 1770s, 25
    poverty in, 165
    riots, 187–88
    suspected witches in, 105
    Whitefield in, 163
Boston Associates, 403
Boston Gazette, 178, 184
Boston Massacre, 171, 177–93, *184*
    publicity campaign after, 189
    ropewalk fight, 180
    sentencing of soldiers, 191
    trial, 190–92
Boston Post, 148
Boston Tea Party and Coercive Acts, 199–201
Boston Transcript, 524
Boudinot, Elias, *300*, 301, *302*, 305, 308, 309, 311, 312, 314

Bowen, Nathan, 164
Bowie, Jim, 488
Bowlegs, Billy, 319
Braddock, Major General Edward, 168
Braddock's Road, 222
Bradford, William, 76
Bradshaw, Giles, 63
Bram, Henry, 569, 570
Brantley, Ethelred T., 427
Branwell, Charles, 564
Breckinridge, John, 505
Br'er Rabbit, 452
Brief Relation of the Destruction of the Indies, A (Las Casas), 9
Brief Sketch of the Trial of William Lloyd Garrison, A, 394
Britian. *See* England
British army
    in Boston, 177, *181*
    in colonies in 1760s, 170, 171
    desertions in, 182
    officers, 180
    relations with Boston residents, 180–81
    removal from Boston, 188
British colonies, American ships barred from, 237
British goods, colonial nonimportation agreement, 177
Brook Farm, 413, 418
Brooks, Preston, 501
Brown, John, 501, 504–5, *504*
Brownists, 75
Bryan, Jonathan, 143, 144, 146, 148
Bubonic plague, 78
Buchanan, James, 502, 515
"Buckeye Blacksmith," 347
Buffalo, 328, 330
Bull, Lt. Governor William, 135, 138
Bull Run, Battles of, 532, 534
Bureau of Refugees, Freedmen & Abandoned Lands, 555. *See also* Freedmen's Bureau
Burk, Sergeant Mark, 182
Burnside, General Ambrose E., 535
Burr, Aaron, 252, 253–69, *267*, 270
    arrest for Mexico invasion plans, 263
    arrest order issued, 265
    debt of, 253, 254
    defeat in election for governor, 254
    duel, 253, 270
    in election of 1800, 277
    Hamilton criticism of, 254
    land grant of, 260
    marriage and divorce, 269
    Ohio seizure of ships, 265
    as politician, 270
    preparation for West control, 263
    trial for treason, 266–69
    westward travel, 257–58

INDEX   I–3

Burroughs, George, 102
Butler, Andrew, 501
Byrd, William, 112
Byrd, William II, 165

Cabot, John, 9, 29
Cabot, Sebastian, 9
Caboto, Giovanni (John Cabot), 29
Cabrillo, Juan Rodríguez, 31
Cadillac, Sieur de, 154
Cádiz expedition, 20
Cahokia, 25
Caldwell, Samuel, 185
Calhoun, John, 337, 355, 369, 371, 456, 507
    as Jackson running mate, 358
California, 31
    application for statehood, 496
    ceded to U.S., 494
    Drake's claim of, 37
    gold discovery, 496
    mission system in, 487
    Native American population in, 158
    Spanish settlements in, 157
"California fever," 485
Calvert, Cecilius (Lord Baltimore), 74
Cambridge University, 10
Cameron, Simon, 530
Canada, 282
    agreement on border with Oregon, 490
    demilitarization of border, 354
    as trade route, 328
    War of 1812, 287
Canary Islands, 29
Cannibals All: Or Slaves Without Masters, 457
Cape Fear, North Carolina, 31
Capital cities, capture as Civil War goal, 532
Capps, William, 60–61
Caribbean, Columbus in, 28
Carolina Outer Banks, as settlement site, 11
Carolinas, 90, 130. *See also* North Carolina, South Carolina
    loss of slaves to Florida, 135
    separation of, 111
    settlement of, 110–12
    slavery introduction to, 110
    western settlement, 151–52
Carpetbaggers, 584–85, 585
Carr, Patrick, 185, 189
Carroll, John, 185
Cartier, Jacques, 32
Casa de Contratación, 8
Cass, Lewis, 495
Castillo de San Marcos, 142
Cayugas, 26, 119, 120, 155

Census of 1790, 283
Central America, 29
Ceremonial mounds of Native Americans, 25, 25
Champlain, Samuel de, 36
    drawing of Quebec, 38
Chancellorsville, 535
Chapultepec, 493
Charles I, King of England, 23, 78
    execution, 74
Charles II, King of England, 109
    Carolina grants from, 110
Charlesfort, 35
Charleston, South Carolina, 110
    Civil War destruction, 545
    epidemic in, 138
Charter of Freedoms and Exemptions, 83–84
Chase, Salmon P., *520,* 545
Chase, Samuel, 280
Chattanooga, Tennessee, 546
Cheat River, 224
Cherokee Nation v. *State of Georgia,* 308
Cherokee National Academy, 299
Cherokee Phoenix, 299, *300,* 301, 305, 309
Cherokees, 155
    1817 treaty with, 298
    adoption of constitution, 305
    agriculture of, 299, 302
    "blood law" of, 310, 315
    chief, *307*
    fur trade decline by, 299
    intermarriage, 116–17
    Jackson's efforts to gain treaty, 309–10
    meeting with Tecumseh, 326–27
    names for, 295
    Oglethorpe contact with, 141, 143
    pressure to cede territory, 304
    regimental support at battle of Horseshoe Bend, 297, 304
    removal policy, 469
    territory surrender, 295, 297
    trade with, 296
    tribal government of, 298
    vote on treaty, 311
Cherokees' forced migration to Oklahoma, 294, 295–315, 319
    appeal to Supreme Court, 308
    arrival in Oklahoma, 314
    colonial land needs and, 304–5, 306–7
    conditions of, 314
    Georgia land distribution, 308
    Indian Removal Law, 306
    political opposition to, 306
    roundup of, 313
Chesapeake, 286, 287
Chesapeake Bay, *14,* 15, 35, 40, 50, 130

colonization, 70–74
    in late 17th century, 120–21
    religious revival, 163
    slavery established, 90
Chickamauga, battle of, 546
Chickasaws, 145, 316, 327
Chisholm v. *Georgia* (1793), 280
Choctaws, 316, 327
Christianity, 58. *See also* Missionaries, Religion
    Pueblo rejection of, 123
    of slaves, 453
Church of England, 163
    Puritan opposition to, 75
Church of Jesus Christ of Latter-Day Saints, 413–14
Churchill, Sarah, 100, 102
Cibola, 31
Cincinnati, 330, 335, 401
Cincinnati Court of Common Pleas, 336
Cincinnatus, 341
City of Raleigh corporation, 20
Ciudad Juárez, 117
"Civil Body Politic," 76
Civil Rights bill, 580
Civil War. *See also* Confederate States of America, Union army
    administrative system for, 530
    beginnings of, 532–36
    building and equipping armies, 528–30
    casualties, 533, 534, 544, 546
    climax, 542–44
    consequences, 547–49
    diplomacy in, 535
    end, 546
    Fort Sumter, 515–16
    leadership and opposition, 536–38
    Lee's surrender, 523, 546
    religious meaning to Lincoln, 521, 522
    and slavery, 538–42
    strategy, 530–32
    surrender terms, 571
    in West, 532
Clark, William, 283
Clay, Henry, 306, 309, 337, 347, 355, 360–67, *361,* 487, 489–90, 496
    efforts to gain Presidential nomination, 338–39
    loss of presidential election, 490
    Missouri Compromise, 367
    role in presidential election of 1824, 357
Clerke, Charles, 160
Clinton, DeWitt, 328
Cobb, Thomas W., 367
Cole, Joseph, *182*
Cole, Nathan, 162

Colonies, English attempt to consolidate, 128
Colonists
   attitudes toward Britain, 171–72
   Raleigh's first contingent, 11–12
   views on Revolution, 176
   women as, 56–57, 71, 74
Colonization, 2, 68–87
   Chesapeake Bay, 70–74
   deaths during, 73
   early goals, 68
   early settlements, 2, 23
   English approach, 37–40
   financing, 2, 10–11, 16, 37–38
   historical setting, 2
   in late 17th century, 109
   middle colonies, 82–85
   Native American lifestyle before, 50–51
   Native American role in, 2
   Native Americans' reaction to Virginians, 61–63
   New England, 74–82
   patterns, 85–86
   privateering vs., 18
   Raleigh as advocate, 8–9
   reasons for European interest, 68–69
   in Southwest, 34–35, 69–70
Colonization Law of 1825, 486, 487
Colton, Calvin, 485
Columbia, 273
Columbus, Christopher, 28
Comanches, 156
Commerce regulation, as Congressional power, 241
Communal societies, 413
Compromise of 1850, 484, 495–98
Confederate army, 530
Confederate Congress, call for army volunteers, 529
Confederate states, restoration to Union, 577
Confederate States of America, 508, 513
   attack on Fort Sumter, 517
   efforts toward diplomatic recognition, 535
   former officials in Congress, 578–79
   Maryland invasion, 521
   surrender, 549
   takeover of federal property, 514
Confederation, 233–39. *See also* Articles of Confederation
   debts of, 272
   government, 234–35
   Washington complains about, 226–27
Confederate soldiers, surrender terms for, 571

Confessions of Nat Turner, The, 425
Confiscation Acts, 539
Congregationalists, 405
   missionaries to Cherokees, 299
Connecticut, 80
   abolition of slavery in, 248
   constitution for, 235–36
Connecticut River, 160, 323
Conquistadors, 30
"Conscience" Whigs, 495
Conscription, 536
Constitution of the United States of America (text), A–6—A–14. *See also* Philadelphia Convention
   Amendments (text), A–15—A–22
      Thirteenth, 575, 579
      Fourteenth, 580, 581, 592
      Fifteenth, 592
   Bill of Rights, 248–49
   ratification, 230–31, 244–45
   strict construction of, 278, 284
   treason definition in, 266
Constitution ("Old Ironsides"), 287
Constitutional issues, political parties and, 366
Constitutionality, of laws, 279, 280
Constitutions
   for Carolina, 110
   conventions for post-War south, 585
   of post-war Southern states, 583
Continental army, Washington farewell to, 217
Continental Congress, 216, 233
contraband, slaves as, 539, 540
Contracts, 280
   freed Blacks' views on, 564
   required from freed people, 578
Convention of 1818, 354–55
Cook, Captain James, 160
Cooper, James Fenimore, 416, 417, 418, 419
Cooper, Thomas, 456
Copley, John Singleton, *179*
Copperheads, 537
Cornwall, Connecticut, 300–1
Cornwallis, surrender at Yorktown, 216
Coronado, Francisco Vasquez de, 31
Corporations, rise of, 398–99
"Corrupt Bargain," 357
Cortes, Hernando, 29
Corwin, Jonathan, 93, 105
Cory, Giles, 106
Cory, Martha, accused as witch, 97–98
Cosío, Antonio Valverde y, 156–57
Cotton, 321–22
   slavery and, 443–45
Cotton gin, *321*, 444
Cotton mills, in New England, 403–4

"Cotton" Whigs, 495
Council of the Indies, 8
Court of Oyer and Terminer (Massachusetts), 105–6
Courts. *See also* Judiciary, Supreme Court
   federal, 242, 279
   in Massachusetts in 1690s, 93
   under Articles, 234
Covenant Chain, 155
Crawford, William, 355–56
Creeks, 145, 155, 288, 297, 316
   council house, *155*
   forced cession of land, 316–17
   meeting with Tecumseh, 326–27
   Oglethorpe negotiations with, 141
   territory ceded by, 297
Creoles, 121, 166
   Mexican-born Spaniards as, 158
Criminals, treatment of, 412
Croatoan, 18
Crockett, Davy, 306, 343–44, 488
Cromwell, Oliver, 74
Cuba, 498
Cumberland Island, 140
Currency, in early 1800s, 352. *See also* Debt, Paper money, Panic of 1819, Panic of 1837

Dale, Sir Thomas, 42, 51
Danbury, Connecticut, hat manufacturers, 398
Dare, Ananias, 15
Dare, Eleanor, 15
Dare, Virginia, 17
Daucks, Marie, 57
Davis, Captain Caleb, 135
Davis, Jefferson, 498, 507, 508, 531, *531*
   authority of, 536–37
   opposition to, 536
   problems of, 538
Dayton, Jonathan, 258, 260–61, *260*, 262
de Soto, Hernando, 25, 31
Debt
   of Burr, 253, 254
   of Indians, 296
   national in 1800, 278
   in Panic of 1819, 352
   of Revolution and Confederation, 236–37, 272
Debt repayment, Madison opposition, 273
Debtors, laws to protect, 238
Decentralized power, 278
Declaration of Independence, 205–6 (text), A–3—A–5
"Declension," 118
Deerskins, 135
   trade in, 111

Delaware
  Constitution ratification, 245
  slavery during Civil War, 541
Delaware Bay, 84
Delaware Indians, 168, 324, 326
  germ warfare against, 170–71
Delaware River, 82
Democratic party, 334, 336, 359, 375–76
  in 1840 political campaign, 350
  depression blamed on, 374
  split in 1860, 505
Democratic-Republican societies, 274
Democratization
  political parties and, 375–76
  of politics, 360
Depression of 1837, 485
Deseret, 413
Desertions, by British soldiers, 182
Detroit, 154, 170, 224–25, 287
Devil, colonists' belief in, 91
Dew, Thomas, 456
D'Ewes, Simonds, 64
Dickinson, Emily, 416, 418, 419, *419*
Dickinson, Jane, 66
Diplomacy. *See also* Louisiana purchase, War of 1812, Mexican war, Foreign nations, *Treaties by name*
  in Civil War, 535
  with Indians, 155
Direct Tax Act of 1861, 540
Discourse of Winter Planting (Hakluyt), 10
Disease
  bubonic plague, 78
  in Chesapeake, 73
  in early Virginia settlements, 59
  European impact on Native Americans, 2, 29, 30, 33–34, *33*, 154
"Disease filter," 24, 33
District of Columbia, 273
  slavery in, 496
Dix, Dorothea, 412
Dominion of New England, 128
Dongan, Thomas, 120, 128
Doublehead, 295
Douglas, Stephen, 496, 497, 498, 500, 503, 505
Douglass, Frederick, *450*, 519, 520, 522, 539
Drake, Sir Francis, 14, 37
Dred Scott v. Sanford, 503–4, 580
"Due process of law," 503
Duke's Laws (New York, 1665), 119
duPont, E. I., 329
Durham House, 10
Dutch, rebellion in New York, 128–29

East Florida, 255
East India Company, 38

Eaton, John, 309, 370
Eaton, Peggy O'Neale, 371, *372*
Economic growth
  in the 18th century, 164–65
  in the 19th century, 397–404
Edisto Island, 554–70
  black on supervisory board, 564
  government on, 558
  plans for forcible removal of blacks, 566
  planters' meeting with blacks, 567–70
  planters' petition, 566
Education
  public schools, 400
  for women, *410*
Edwards, Jonathan, 161–62
  Faithful Narrative of the Surprising Work of God, 162
"Eirik the Red's Saga," 28
El Dorado, 19
El Paso, 123
El Paso del Norte, 117
Elections
  of 1800, 275, 276–77
  of 1824, 355–57
  of 1828, 334, 358–59, 368–69
  of 1836, 338
    voting statistics, 373
  of 1840, 334, 335–50, *351*
    voting statistics, 350
    Whig almanac cartoon, *348*
    Whig political rally, *346*
  of 1844, 485
    Texas question, 489–90
  of 1848, slavery in, 495
  of 1852, 497
  of 1856, 501
  of 1860, 505–6
  of 1862, 537
  of 1864, 544–46
  of 1866, 581
  of 1868, 593
  of 1876, 593
Electoral college, 242, 243, 246–47, 271, 351
  and political campaign strategy in 1840, 340
  selection by voters, 356–57
Elite
  in Chesapeake Bay, 121
  deference to, 166–67
  in political office, 360
  power in post-war South, 580
  southern white resentment of, 587
Elizabeth I, Queen of England, 5–6, *16*, 17
  and Raleigh's right to colonize, 10–11
  relationship with Raleigh, 6, 18–19, 20

Ellyott, Mary, 56
Emancipation, 424, 442
  by executive order, 519
  draft of proclamation, 521
  gradual, 441
  proclamation issued, 522
  slave reaction to, 572
Emancipation Proclamation, 536, 537
Emathla, Charley, 317
Embargo, by Jefferson, 384
Embargo Act, 286
Emerson, George Barrell, *410*
Emerson, Ralph Waldo, 416, *418*, 497, 504
Encomienda, 123
England. *See also* British army, Great Britain
  Burr request for aid from, 256–57
  colonial attitudes toward, 171–72
  colonial involvement in conflict with France, 134
  colonization by, 37–40, 48
  early settlements, 2
  government financial problems in 1760s, 169
  immigration from, 150
  labor system, 71
  naval superiority in War of 1812, 287
  in Northwest Territory, 281
  South need for help from, 535
  textile manufacture in, 40
  textile mills, 322
  trouble in early 1800s, 284–87
  war with Spain (1739), 139
English, Philip, 102
English Civil War, 23
English Navigation Acts, 116, 119
Enumerated imports, 273
Epidemic, in Charleston, South Carolina, 138
"Era of Good Feeling," 352
Erie Canal, 328–30, 399, 401
Eriksson, Leif, 28
Essex, Earl of, 19
Europe
  in Civil War strategy, 534
  impact on U.S., 281
  social problems in 1600s, 68–69
  U.S. opposition to Western Hemisphere intervention, 355
European diseases, impact on Native Americans, 2, 29, 30, 33–34, *33*, 154
Europeans
  first contacts with Native Americans, 28–32
  first impressions of America, 2
Evangelical "awakening," 118
  in middle-class, 405–7
Evangelical Family Library, 407

Evangelism, tracts for, 406–7
Everglades, Seminole in, 319
Ewell, General Richard, 543
Ex-slaves
    enfranchisement, 574
    as refugees, 555
    in South Carolina, 572
    testing of understanding of freedom, 556–57
    Union army recruitment of, 539, 540–41, *541*
Executive branch
    creation, 242
    defining, 271–72
    presidential control of, 272

Factors (trade agents), 116
Faithful Narrative of the Surprising Work of God (Edwards), 162
Fallen Timbers, battle of, 323
Family
    in the 18th century, 167
    in the 19th century, *408*, 487–910
    of slaves, 449–52
Famine, in Europe, 69
Faneuil Hall, 188
Farming
    family, 114, 330
    on frontier, 153, *153*
    specialization, 330
Farragut, David, 533
Federal property, Confederate takeover of, 514
Federal system of government, 243
    test of, 270
Federalist, The, 245
Federalist party, 245, 351
    amendments to Constitution, 248
    destruction of, 279, 351
    vs. Republicans, 274–76
Feminist movement, 410–11
Fernandes, Simão, 16–17
Ferriter, Nicholas, 185
"Fifty-four Forty or Fight," 490
Fillmore, Millard, 372, 497
Finney, Charles Grandison, 406
"Fire-eaters," 496
First Continental Congress, 216, 233
First Seminole War, 317
Fishing, near Newfoundland, 10, 29, 37
Fishing trade, in New England, 114
Fitzhugh, George, 457
Five Nations, 119
Florida, 69, 593
    as British possession, 169
    changes in control of, 148
    French landing, 36
    in late 17th century, 121–22

    Spanish control, 255, 316
    Spanish settlements, 35
    Spanish surrender of, 354
    terrain as Seminole advantage, 318
Floyd, John, 440–41, 456, 459
Foner, Eric, 588
Force Bill, 369, 589
Ford's Theater, 523
Foreclosures, 353
Foreign Affairs Department, 272
Foreign policy. *See also* Diplomacy
    in early U.S., 280–83
    of Monroe, 354–55
    under Constitution, 243
Fort McHenry, 288
Fort Orange, 82
Fort Pickens, 514, 516, 517
Fort Pitt, 152, 170
Fort San Luís, 122
Fort Sumter, 514, 515–16
    attack on, 517
Fort Ticonderoga, 287
Fort Washington, 335
Fourth of July, 349
France
    colonial involvement in conflict with England, 134
    colonization by, 48
    control of American interior, 116–17
    early settlements, 2
    exploration in North America, 31–32
    in far north, 36
    landing in Florida, 36
    negotiations in late 1700s, 282–83
    South need for help from, 535
    U.S. pledge of aid to, 282
    weaknesses in interior control, 168
Francis, Salathiel, 432
Franciscans
    conflict with Pueblos, 123
    in Florida, 121–22
    in Texas, 117
Franklin, Benjamin, 164, 183, 233, 284
    autobiography, 404
    plan for union at Albany, 168–69
    on Whitefield, 163
Franklin Clubs, 404–5
    Garrison as member, 386
Frazier, Garrison, 556
Free blacks, 454
    in early 1800s, 424
Free Press (Newburyport), 390–91
Free society, 457
"Free soil, free labor, free men," 502
Free-Soil party, 495, *497*
    in Kansas, 500
Freedman's Bureau Bill, 570
    Johnson's veto, 580

Freed people. *See also* Edisto Island, Ex-slaves, Emancipation
    conflict over status, 554
    contracts required from, 578
    education, 569
    in political affairs, 587
    reaction to vote, 583–84
    restrictions on, 578
    social subordination of, 578
Freedmen's Bureau, 555, 558, 561, 565, 579
    creation, 575
Freedom, ex-slave views of, 556–57, 572
Frémont, General John C., 492, 502, 545
French explorers, in Southeast, 26
French Huguenots, 35
French and Indian War, 168–69, 176
    effects of, 169–72
    Shawnees in, 323
French Protestant Huguenots, in Carolinas, 110
French Revolution, 281
Frethorne, Richard, 65–66, 67
Frontier. *See also* Westward expansion
    colonists' move to, 170
    during Confederation Period, 238
    eastern views and control of, 152–53, 222–23
    farming in, 153
    proclamation to restrict access to, 171
    settlement of, 151–54
Frontier wars, 122–29
Fugitive Slave Act of 1850, 470, 496, 539
Fulton, Robert, 402
Fur trade, 36, 68, 119, 134
    by French, 168
    by Russians, 159
    decline by Cherokees, 299
    in New Netherland, 82–83

Gadsden, James, 498
Gage, General Thomas, 182–83
Galveston, 487
Gálvez, José de, 157–58
Gamboa, Sarmiento de, 19
Gárces, Francisco, 158
Garfield, James, 581
Garrick, Edward, 184
Garrison, Abijah, 383
Garrison, Fanny, 384–85, 388–89
Garrison, Helen Eliza Benson, *389*
Garrison, James, 381–82, 383, 384
Garrison, Joseph, 383
Garrison, William Lloyd, 380–96, *387*, 412, 419–20

early writings, 388
education, 386
financial problems, 394
imprisonment, 394–96
The Liberator, 380, *395*, 456, 469
lifestyle, 382
mob action against, *393*, 413
mother's impact on, 390
as printer, 390
reaction to J. Q. Adams, 391
realization of freedom, 395–96
as social reformer, 391–92
Garrison family, 380–96
desertion by father, 384
social change affecting, 397
Garzía, Francisco, 136
Gates, Sir Thomas, 42
General Court (Massachusetts colonial legislature), 105
General Court (Plymouth), 76
General Land Office, 235
Genèt, Edmond, 282
Genius of Universal Emancipation, 394
George III, King of England, 169–70
Georgia, 135. *See also* Cherokees' forced migration to Oklahoma
as buffer between Florida and South Carolina, 134, 151
cotton cultivation, 445
creation, 151
"redemption," 590
slavery in, 148, 151
slavery prohibition in, 151
Spanish attack to remove English, 147
western settlement, 151–52
Germany, immigration from, 149, *150*
Gettysburg
battle, 542–44, *549*, 575
Lincoln's address, 375, 518–19
Gilbert, Adrian, 6
Gilbert, Humphrey, 6, 7
Gilbert, John, 6
Glorious Revolution (England, 1688), 128
Glover, Witch, 91
Gold
discovery in California, 496
English search for, 39
Spanish search for, 30
Goldfinch, Captain-Lieutenant John, 184
Goliad, 488
Good, Sarah, 92–93, 96
execution, 106
questioning of, 93–95
Governor's Island, 82
Gracia Real de Santa Teresa de Mose, 136
Graffenried, Count Christophe von, 111

Grand Settlement of 1701 (Montreal), 120
Grant, Ulysses S., 494, 532–33, *542*, 581, 589
in cabinet, 582
election, 593
Lee surrender to, 523, 546
Vicksburg seige, 542
Gray, Samuel, 185
Great Awakening, 160–64
Great Britain. *See* England, British army
Great Compromise, 241
Great Lakes, 154
discovery, 32
Greeley, Horace, 343, 347, 593
criticism of Lincoln, 521
Green, William, 180
Green Corn ceremony, 50–51
Greenland, 28, 29
"Greenlanders' Saga," 28
Greenville, Ohio community, 324, 325
Greenville treaty (1795), 323–24
Grenville, Sir Richard, 13
Grey, Lord of Wilton, 7
Guadalupe Hidalgo, treaty of, 494
Guale, 121
Guerrilla tactics
by Nat Turner, 435
by Seminoles, 319
in West during Civil War, 532
Guiana, 19, 21, 29
Raleigh expedition to, 21–23
Guilds, 71
Gullageenah, 301

Habeas corpus, 241, 243
Lincoln suspension of, 537
Halfway Covenant, 118
Hamilton, Alexander, 229, 235, 239, 244–45, *245*, 270, 272, 275, 351
criticism of Burr, 254
death of, 253
program for debt repayment, 272–74
Hammond, James, 456
Harper's Ferry, Virginia, 504
Harriot
Thomas, 14–15, 21
Principal Navigations, Voyages, Traffics, & Discoveries of the English Nation, 10
Harrison, William Henry, 287, 326, 334, 373, 489
1840 campaign engraving, *342*
age at election, 340
attack on Prophetstown, 327

death, 375
election campaign, 335–50
as Indiana Territory first governor, 336
political image of, 341
positions on campaign issues, 340
Hartford Convention, 289–91
Hathorne, John, 93–97, 99–106
records as witchcraft trial evidence, 105
Hawaiian Islands, 160
Hawthorne, Nathaniel, 416, *416*
Hayes, Rutherford B., 593
Headrights, 71–72, 121
in Massachusetts Bay, 78–79
Henrico, 56, 58
Henry, Prince of Portugal (the Navigator), 28
Henry, Prince of Wales, 21
Hermitage, 360
"Hero of New Orleans," 356
Hewes, George Robert Twelves, 180–81, 182, *182*, 185, 186, 191
"Hickory Clubs," 337
Hicks, Elijah, 302
Hilyer, Joseph, 185
The History of the World (Raleigh), 21
Holland, 75, 82
Homestead, for freed blacks, 557
Homestead Act, 570
Hooker, "Fighting Joe," 535, 542
Hooker, Thomas, 80
Hopewell, 18
Hopewell Indian culture, 25
Hopis, 31, 34
Horseshoe Bend, battle of, 297, 304
House of Representatives, 241, 271
election of 1824, 357
presidential election determined by, 277
southern representation increase after Civil War, 580
voting for, 243
House of Seven Gables, The (Hawthorne), 416
Houston, Sam, 488
Houston, Texas, 488
Howard, Charles, 19–20
Howard, General Oliver O., 555, 558, 562, *563*, 571
Hudson River, 31, 82
Huguenots, 6
Hundley, D. R., 457
Hurlbut, Stephen, 516, 517
Hurons, 36
Hutchinson, Anne, 80, 187
Hutchinson, Lieutenant Governor Thomas, 186–88, 191
Hylton v. United States, 280

Iceland, 29
Illinois, 235
  statehood, 367
Illinois Central Railroad, 399
Immigration, *401. See also* Colonization
  in 1840s, 399
  in 18th century, 149–51
  in late 17th century, 109
  Mexican control for Texas, 486
  to Carolinas, 110
  and working conditions, 415
Impeachment, 242, 280
  against Johnson, 582–83
Implied powers, 284
Imported goods
  amendment giving Congress power to tax, 235
  colonial refusal to use, 179
  tariff on, 272
Impost, 272
Impressment, 281, 285–86
Incas, 19, 30
  Spanish discovery of, 29
Income tax, during Civil War, 536
Indentured servants, 71, 85, 110
  in Chesapeake Bay area, 120
  shift to slavery, 150
Independence, ex-slave views of, 572
Independent Treasuries system, 373
Independent Treasury Bill, 374
Indian, John, 92, 95, 96
Indian removal, need for land and, 322–23. *See also* Cherokees' forced migration to Oklahoma
Indian Removal Act, 306, 308, 317
Indian Territory (Oklahoma), 294, 310
  Cherokee arrival, 314
Indian trade, in Southeast, 135
Indian village, 12
Indian wars, in Carolinas, 112
Indiana, 235
  statehood, 367
Indiana Territory, Harrison as first governor, 336
Indians of North America. *See* Native Americans
Indigo, 111, 167
  as cash crop, 443–44
Industrial revolution, 398
Information revolution and political parties, 364
Inns of Court in London, 6
Internal improvements, Adams as advocate, 357
Interstate commerce, 280
Interstate slave trade, 496
Inventions, 402
  and cotton production, 322
Ireland, immigration from, 150
Irish war (1580), Raleigh's role in, 7–8

Ironworks, 56
Iroquois League, 112, 119–20, 155
  Albany council meeting (1754), 168–69
Iroquois tribes, 26
Irrigation projects, by Southwest Native Americans, 34
Irving, Washington, 266, 267, 415, 417

Jackson, Andrew, 288–89, 304, 404
  in 1824 presidential campaign, 356
  in 1828 election, 358
  background, 360
  battle against Seminoles, 317
  Burr's visit with, 258
  efforts to gain treaty with Cherokees, 309–10
  inaugural address, 363
  involvement in Burr's plans, 265
  political party development, 370–72
  pressure on Cherokees, 307
  relations with Indians, 297–98
  support for Indian removal, 305–6
  on Texas annexation, 488
  Van Buren as choice for successor, 373
  veto of Bank charter bill, 369
Jackson, Anne, 56, 66, 67
Jackson, John, 56, 67
Jackson, John (gunsmith), 66
Jackson, Colonel Richard, 336–37
Jackson, Thomas J. ("Stonewall"), 534
Jackson, William, 56
Jacobs, George, 100–2
Jacobs, Margaret, 102
Jacobs, Mrs., as suspected witch, 102
James, 65
James, Duke of York, 119
James, Frank, 532
James I, King of England, 20, 21, 39–40
James II, King of England, 105, 127–28
James, Jesse, 532
James River, 15, 39
Jamestown, 2, 18, 21, 39, 40–42, 48, 68
  early deaths in, 41
  first colonists to, 40–41
  Native American political groupings near, 26
  warning of Indian attack, 63
Japazaws, 53
Jay, John, 244–45, 282
Jay Treaty, 282
Jefferson, Thomas, 221, 239, 246, 272, 351. *See also* Republican party

  appointment of Louisiana governor, 257
  and Burr, 265, 266
  cartoon (1795), 276
  debt of, 320
  in election of 1800, 277
  Monticello, 279
  negotiations over Louisiana border, 259
  news of Burr's western plans, 263
  nomination for President, 275
  and political party formation, 274
  political philosophy, 278
  re-election, 278–79
  Republicanism of, 277–79
Jenkins, Thomas, 139
Jesuits, 35, 157
Jesup, General Thomas, 318
Johnsbury, Vermont, 403
Johnson, Andrew, 545, 577
  amnesty proclamation, 559
  characteristics, 575–76
  Congressional reaction to, 581–82
  impeachment process, 582–83
  policy of land restoration, 558–60
  Reconstruction under, 575–81
Johnston, Albert Sidney, 533
Joint Committee on Reconstruction, 579
Joint-stock companies, 15, 37–38, 85, 109
  for Jamestown, 40
  for river transportation to West, 226
Jones, Alice, 57
Jonson, Ben, 4
Journal of the Times, 393
Judiciary, 242, 279–80
  in Virginia and New Jersey plans, 240
Judiciary Act of 1789, 279
Judiciary Act of 1801, 280

Kahnungdclageh, 295
Kansas
  Lecompton constitution, 504
  statehood application, 503–4
Kansas-Nebraska Act, 498, 500
Karlsefm, Thorfinn, 28
Kearney, Stephen W., 492
Kennebec River, 40
Kentucky, 255, 263, 320, 520
  secession plans, 513, 514
  slavery during Civil War, 541
Ketchum, A. P., 561, 563, 566, 567, 570
Key, Francis Scott, 288
Keymis, Lawrence, 23
Kieft, Willem, 83
Killpatrick, James, 145

Killpatrick, John, 138
Kilroy, Matthew, 185
Kimber, Edward, 140, 146, 151
King Caucus, 358
"King Cotton," 320–23, 445
King George's War (1744–1748), 168
King Philip's War (New England, 1675–1676), 125–26
King William's War (1689–1697), 168
Kino, Eusebio Francisco, 157
Knickerbocker History of New York (Irving), 415
Knights of the White Camellia, 588
Know Nothings, 501, 502
Knox, Henry, 184, 185, 272
Ku Klux Klan, 586, 588–89
Ku Klux Klan Act, 589, 593

La Caroline (Florida), 35
La Salle, René Robert Cavelier, Sieur de, 116
Labrador, 28
Labrobe, Benjamin Henry, *166*
Lacour, Peter, 230
Lafayette, Marquis de, 281
Lake Champlain, 288
Lake Okechobee, Seminole battle near, 319
Lake of the Woods, 225
Lalawethika, 324
Lamar, Mirabeau Buonaparte, 488–89
Land
    as blacks' goal, 569–70, 573
    ceded by Creeks, 297
    colonial threat to Indian, 62
    for colonists, 68, 71
    for freed blacks, 557
    grants to railroads, 399
    as Indian common property, 325
    loss of fertility in East, 320
    loss of Native American, 487
    need in North, 327–28
    policy after Civil War, 558–60
    promise to Virginia colonists, 55
    as settlers' goal, 124
    speculation in, 322
Land grants, 85
    for Austin, 486
    in New York, 119
Land holdings, of Washington, 220
Land titles, 128
Lane, Ralph, 11, 13
Lane Theological Seminary, 483
Last of the Mohicans, The (Cooper), 416
Law, connection to politics, 362
Lawes Divine, Morall and Martiall, 42
Lawrence, James, 287
Lawson, Deodat, 97, 98
Leatherstocking, 416, 417, 419
Leaves of Grass (Whitman), 416, 418

Lecompton constitution, for Kansas, 504
Lee, Robert E., 494, 534, *543*
    surrender to Grant, 523, 546
Legal profession, changes in 19th century, 361–62
Leisler's Rebellion, 128–29
Leopard, 286
Leoyne, Pierre, Sieur d'Iberville, 116
Levant Company, 38
"Levying war," 266, 268
Lewis, Meriwether, 283
Liberator, The, 380, 395, 456, 469
Liberty Tree, in Boston, 178
Lillie, Theophilus, 177
Lincoln, Abraham, 347, 361, 375, 505, 512–27, *514*
    assassination and funeral, 523–25
    authority of, 536–537
    cabinet, 516, *520*
    campaign debates in 1840, 350
    cartoon to discredit, 507
    democratic principles of, 518
    on equality for blacks, 575
    execution of conspirators in assassination, 526
    Gettysburg address, 375, 518–19
    government organization for war, 517–18
    opposition to, 536
    Reconstruction plan, 573–75
    southern response to election, 506–8
    on Stowe's impact, 464, 467
    veto of Wade-Davis bill, 544
    views on secession, 514–15
Literature
    by and for women, 410
    captivity narrative, 126
    growth in 19th century, 415–20
Little Ice Age, 69
Lloyd, Frances Maria, 383
"Lobsterbacks," 177
Lockport, New York, 328, *329*
Locomotive (*Atlantic*), 400
Log Cabin (Whig campaign paper), 343, 347
Log Cabin Campaign, 334, 335–50
London
    in the 16th century, 4
    Tower of, 19
London Bridge, 5
Long Island, 80
    settlement of, 119
Longstreet, General James P., 543
Los Angeles, 158
Lost Colony, 16, 18
    planning by Raleigh, 15
Louisiana, 154, 255, 256, 577, 579, 593
    border of, 259, 354

post-Civil War constitution, 575
statehood, 367
Louisiana Purchase, 284, 289
Louisville, 401
Lovejoy, Elijah, 484
Lowell, Massachusetts, 403, 414–15
Lowrey, George, *307*
Loyalists, 178
Lucas, Eliza, 111
Lundy, Benjamin, 394
Luther, Martin, 4
Lynch, James, 555

McClellan, George, 533–45
McClernand, John, 350
McCormick, Cyrus, 330
    automatic reaper, 330
McCulloch v. Maryland (1819), 280, 354
McDonough, Thomas, 288
McDowell, General Irvin, 532
McEnery, John, 590
MacIntosh, Ebenezer, 178–79
Madison, James, 226, 229, 235, 244–45, 272, 273, 279, 286–87, 351
    creation of Virginia Plan, 240
    debt of, 320
    and political party formation, 274
    as writer of Bill of Rights, 248
Magellan, Ferdinand, 29
Maine, 40, 367
Malaria, 73
Manassas (Second Battle of Bull Run), 534
Manhattan Island, 82
Manifest Destiny, 485, 486, 494
Mann, Horace, 412
Manteo, 15
Manumission, 424
Marbury v. Madison (1803), 280
Marcy, William Learned, 363
Market capitalism, 322
    and slavery, 442–45
Market economy
    agriculture and, 330–31
    expansion of, 352
    expansion and removal of Cherokees, 294
"Marmaduke," 56
Marshall, John, 266, 279–80, 308, 354
    and treason definition, 268
Martin's Hundred, 63, 66, 72
Mary I, Queen of England, 5
Maryland, 69, 226. *See also* Chesapeake colonies
    colonization, 74
    ratification of Articles of Confederation, 234
    rebellion in 1689, 129

Maryland (continued)
  secession plans, 513, 514
  slavery during Civil War, 541
  slavery in, 496
  Susquehannock Fort, 124
Massachusetts
  abolition of slavery in, 248
  Constitutional ratification, 245
  courts in 1690s, 93
  negotiation of new charter with William and Mary, 128
Massachusetts Bay, 74, 77–82, 91
  company charter, 78
  company seal, 77
  compared to Pennsylvania, 113–14
  first royal governor, 104
  headright system modification, 78–79
  in late 17th century, 117
  new colonization approaches in, 78
  witchcraft panic, 99
Massasoit, 76
Matagorda Bay, 116
Mather, Cotton, 91, 92, 106
Mather, Increase, 128
Maverick, Samuel, 185
Mayas, 29
Mayflower, 76
Mayflower Compact, 76
Meade, George G., 542
Measles, 33
Mechanics' Union of Trade Associations, 415
Melville, Herman, 416, 419
Memominees, 324
Memphis, 575
Menéndez, Francisco, 136, 137, 147
Menéndez de Avilés, Pedro, 35
Mercantilism, 115–16
Merchants. *See also* Commerce, Trade
  British and French warship interception, 285–86
  in New England, 118
Merry, Anthony, 256, 261
Metacom, 125, 126
Methodists, 151, 405
  missionaries to Cherokees, 299
Mexican War, 486–94
Mexico, 256
  independence, 486–87
  northern territories, 485
  Spanish acceptance of northern limit, 354
  Spanish control, 255
  Texas war in 1841, 488
Mexico City (Tenochtitlán), 29, 30
Miamis, 324, 326
Miccusukee, 316
Michigan, 235
Middle class, 380, 405

religious revival, 405–7
Middle Colonies, 90, 130
  colonization, 82–85
  growth of, 116
  religious revivals, 161
  trade development, 114
"Midnight judges," 280
Minuit, Peter, 82, 84
Mission system, in California, 157–58, 487
Missionaries
  Franciscans in Florida, 121–22
  in Southwest, 34, 69–70
  to Cherokees, 299
Mississippi River, 116, 284
  Coronado discovery, 31
  French control, 156–60, 168
  steamboats on, 322
  Union control of, 533
Mississippi (state), 320, 579, 587
  black code in, 578
  cotton cultivation, 445
  members of state legislature, 1874–1875, 591
Mississippian culture, 25–26
Missouri
  admission to union, 367, 485
  secession plans, 514
  slavery during Civil War, 541
Missouri Compromise, 367–68, 494, 500
Mobile, Union capture, 533
Mobile Bay, 116
Moby Dick (Melville), 416, 419
Mohawks, 26, 119, 155
  chief, 156
Mohegans, 80–81
Monongahela River, 224
Monroe, James, 279, 284, 352
  debt of, 320
  foreign policy, 354–55
Monroe Doctrine (1823), 355
Monterey, 158, 490
  soldier and wife, 159
Montezuma, 30
Montiano, Manuel de, 136, 144, 147–48
Monticello, 279
Montigny, Dumont de, 117
Montreal, 287
Moore, James, 142
Moore, Thomas, 427, 429
"Moors," 28
Moravians, 151–52
Mormons, 413
Morris, Robert, 235
Morse, Samuel, 402
Mose, 136–37
  capture of, 143–44
  recapture by Spanish, 145
Mott, Lucretia, 411

Mount Vernon, 217, 220
"Mr. Madison's War," 290
Muscovy Company, 38
Muskogee, 316
Mutual Benefit Society of Journeymen Cordwainers, 415
Mystic, Connecticut, 81

Napoleon, 283, 284–85
  negotiations for New Orleans, 283
  Waterloo defeat, 289
Narragansetts, 26, 80
Narrative of the Life of Frederick Douglass, 450
Narrative of the Troubles with the Indians in New England (Hubbard), 126
Nast, Thomas, 584
Nat Turner's rebellion, 424, 424–39, 456
  attack on plantations, 436
  failure of, 433
  need for secrecy, 430–31
  planning, 429–31
  random murdering of blacks after, 437
  tensions in Virginia after, 440
  white response to, 435–37
Natchez, 261, 265
Natchez Indians, 26
Natchitoches, 261
National bank, 273–274. *See also* Bank of the United States
National capital, creation, 273
National Committee (Cherokees), 298–99, 302–3
National government
  division of powers with states, 243
  limits on powers, 243
  need for, 216
"National party" (Cherokees), 310
National Philanthropist, 391
National Trades Union, 415
National Union party, 545
"Nationalist" political faction, 245
Native Americans, 24
  alliance by, 296–97
  ancestors of, 24
  in California as Mexico independence victims, 487
  children as intermediaries with colonists, 51–54
  and clash of empires, 154–56
  colonization and, 2, 48
  cultures of, 24–27
  enslavement of, 111
  European disease impact on, 2, 29, 30, 33–34, 33, 154
  first contacts with Europeans, 28–32

French trade with, 36
germ warfare against, 170–71
Great Serpent Mound in Ohio, *25*
individual English persons in communities, 66–67
life before colonization, 50–51
Oglethorpe relations with, 141
in Ohio Valley, 155–56, 168, 323
Pilgrim relations with, 76
population decline, 154
   in California, 158
and Raleigh, 23
reactions to Virginia colonization, 61–63
rebellions in 1670s and 1680s, 122–27
relations with early Virginia settlers, 42–44
religion of, 34
resistance to cultural change, 70
Spanish relations in California, 158
tensions in Ohio Valley, 223
treaties ceding land, 324
violence against New Netherland, 84
Virginia's goal to convert, 58–61
weapons for, 135
woman and child by J. White, *28*
women from lower Mississippi Valley, *117*
work roles, 26
Native Americans' attack on Virginia plantations, 49–50, 62–63, 72–73
   aftermath, 64–66
   captives taken, 66–67
Nauvoo, 413
Navahos, 34
   Spanish arrival in Southwest, *30*
Navajos, 26
Navigation Acts of England, 116, 119
Negro rule, 588
Nemattanew, Jack of the Feathers, 51, 55, 61
Neolin (Delaware Prophet), 156
Netherlands, as English enemy, 119
Neutrality, 282
   1790s to early 1800s, 281–82
Nevada, 490
"New Albion," 37. *See also* California
New Bern, 112
New California, 158
New Echota, 299, 308
   treaty of, 311–12
New England, 90, *126,* 130
   colonization, 74–82
   Dominion of, 128
   French exploration, 36
   growth of, 116
   in late 17th century, 117–18, 127

Native Americans in, 26
   opposition to English control in late 17th century, 127
   opposition to western expansion, 289
   trade by, 114
New Hampshire
   abolition of slavery in, 248
   Constitutional ratification, 245
New Harmony, 413
New Jersey, 119
New Jersey Plan for Constitution, 240–41
New Lights, 163
New Mexico, 34, 69, 156, 490
   application for statehood, 496
   ceded to U.S., 494
New Netherland, 82–84, 90, 109. *See also* New York
   English seizure, 119
New Orleans, 154, *170,* 282, 288, 401
   battle, 287
   French control of, 283
   Jackson defense of, 288
   Jackson politics in, 358
   Spanish control, 169
   Union capture, 533
New Sweden, 84–85
New York, 90
   colony seal, *120*
   Constitutional ratification, 245
   in election of 1800, 276–77
   in election of 1828, 358
   expansion, 327
   importance of Erie Canal to, 328
   in late 17th century, 119–20
   poverty in, 165
   reaction to Glorious Revolution, 128
New York City, 400–1
   draft riots (1863), *538*
   as first capital, 231
New York Daily Whig, 343
Newburgh, New York, 217
Newburyport, 384
Newfoundland, 21, 31
   fishing near, 10, 29, 37
   Norse in, 28
Newport, Christopher, 52
Newspapers, 365
   in 1840 presidential campaign, 347–48
   coverage of Civil War, 535
   growth of, 364
Niagara River, 287
Nicholls, Richard, 119
Nigeria, 150
Niles, Hezekiah, 337
Nile's Weekly Register, 337
Non-Intercourse Act of 1809, 287

Nonimportation agreement, 177, 180
Norse voyagers, 28
North
   advantage at Civil War beginning, 530
   agricultural expansion in North, 323–30
   land needs in, 327
   morale in Civil War, 536
North Africans, 28
North America
   French explorations, 31–32
   interior trade and settlement, 116–17
   Spanish in, 30
North Carolina, 320, 577. *See also* Carolinas
   backcountry, 153
   Constitutional ratification, 245
   early economy, 112
   early settlers in, 111
   "redemption," 590
Northerners, in post-Civil War south, 584–85
Northumberland, Earl of, 21
Northwest Ordinance, 235, 494
Northwest passage, 39
   search for, 159–60
Northwest Territory
   British in, 281
   slavery prohibition in, 235
Nueces River, 490
Nuestra Señora de Guadalupe, 117
Nullification crisis, 368–69
   Jackson response to, 371
Nurse, Rebecca, 106

Ogle, Charles, 344
Oglethorpe, James, *140,* 151
   attack on St. Augustine, 139
   relations with Indians, 141, 143
   sickness, 146
Ohio, 235, 255, 327
Ohio Valley, 154
   English interest in, 168
   Native Americans in, 25, 155–56, 168, 223, 323
   Washington land holdings in, 220, 221
   Washington's plan to connect to Atlantic, 224–25
Ojibways, 324
Oklahoma, 294
Oñate, Juan de, 34, 69–70
Oneida, New York, 413
Oneidas, 26, 119, 155
Onondagas, 26, 119, 120, 155
Ontario, 327
Opechancanough, 49, 54, 55, 59–60, 61, 72–73

"Open Door" (The Prophet), 324, 327
Ordinance of 1787, 235
Oregon, 31, 485
   border with Canada, 490
Oregon Country, 354–55
Orinoco, 19, 21, 23
Orleans Territory, 258
Osburne, Sarah, 93, 94, 96
   questioning of, 95
Osceola, 317, *318*
   capture, 318–19
Ostend Manifesto, 498, 501–2
O'Sullivan, John L., 485
Ottawas, 324
Ouachita land grant, 263
Ouachita River, Burr land grant on, 260
Oxford University, 6, 10

Pacifist movement, 393
Packenham, General Sir Edward, 288
Palmes, Richard, 185, 191
Pan-Indian alliance, Tecumseh plan, 325
Panama, 29
Panic of 1819, 352–54
Panic of 1837, 373, 415
Paper money, 238
   from state banks, 353
Parahunt, 53
Parker, James, 435
Parris, Betty, 91, 107
Parris, Samuel, 91–92, 105, 107, 109, 118
   views on trade dangers, 114–15
Patawomekes, 53
paternalism, in slave relations, 457
Paterson, William, 240
Patriarchy, 167
Patronage, 363–64, 371
Patroonship system, 82
Patuxets, 77
Pawnees, 156
"Pays d'en haut," 119
"Peace Democrats," 537
Peacetime army, 182
Pelham, Henry, 189
Penn, William, 112, 113, *113*
   negotiation with Delawares, *113*
Pennsylvania, 90
   abolition of slavery in, 248
   Constitutional ratification, 245
   population mix, 114
   settlement of, 112–14
   trade in, 114
   western settlement, 151–52
Pensacola, 116
   Jackson capture, 288
"People," political parties and, 364, 366

"People's choice," Harrison image as, 349
Pequot War of 1636–1637, 80–81
Pequots, 26
Peralta, Pedro de, 34
Percy, George, 51
Perea, Fray Estevan de, 69
Perry, Oliver Hazard, 287
Petersburg, Virginia, 545
Philadelphia, *167*, 400
   in 1787, 229
   Penn's planning for, 113
   poverty in, 165
   trade unions in, 415
Philadelphia Convention, 239–44, *240*
   attitudes toward democracy, 243–44
   call for, 227
   checks and balances, 242–43
   federal government powers, 241–42
   Great Compromise, 241
   Virginia and New Jersey plans, 240–41
   Washington as president, 229–30
Philip II, King of Spain, 17
Philip III, King of Spain, 23
Phillips, Wendell, 519
Phips, Sir William, 104–5, 106
Pickering, John, 280
Pickett, General George, 544
Pierce, Franklin, 497, 498, 500
Pilgrims, 75–77
Pinckney, Charles, 147
Pinckney, Eliza Lucas, 165–66
Piracy, 11. *See also* Privateering
Pitt, William, 169
Pittman, Philip, *170*
Pittsburgh, 401
Pizarro, Francisco, 30
Plaine Man's Pathway to Heaven, The (Dent), 58
Plantations
   in Carolinas, 111
   mistress of, 458
Plattsburgh, battle of, 288
Plymouth, 40, 74, 75–77
   Indian fighting in, 125–26
Pocahontas, 26, 44, 51–52, 53, *53*, 54, 70
   in England, 58
Pocket veto, 544–45
Poem on the Late Massacre in Virginia (Brooke), 61
Political parties, 271–80, 334, 351–55
   Constitution silence on, 246–47
   and constitutional issues, 366
   creation, 360
   development of, 270
   in election of 1840, 334
   fundamental purpose, 374

   Jackson's creation of, 358
   Jackson's role in developing, 370–72
   Republicans vs. Federalists, 274–76
   and "the people," 364, 366
   theory of, 362–66
   Washington on, 275
Political rallies, by Whigs, 345–47, *346*
Political spoils, 363–64
Political stability, under Articles of Confederation, 238
Political system, development for 1840 election, 351
Political theory, development after Revolution, 233
Politics
   connection to law, 362
   democratization of, 360
   European events and, 281
Polk, James, 489–90, 495
   and Mexican War, 490
Polygamy, by Mormons, 413
Pontiac's War, 170
Popé, 123
Popular sovereignty, 495, 498, 501
Popular vote for president, in 1824, 357
Population
   in 19th century, 399–400
   increase 1789–1820s, 270
   increase 1810 to 1840, 320
   increase in early 1800s, 283
   proportion of white and black in slave states, *455*
Populus, 178
Port Royal Sound, South Carolina, 35
Portolá, Captain Gaspar de, 158
Portugal, 10
   early explorations, 28
Pory, John, 59
Potawatomis, 324, 326
Potomac project, 226
Potomac River, 222, 273
   Washington search for connections to, 224
Potomac River Company, 226
Pott, Ralph, 66
Pottery, 164
Powhatan, 18, 26, 34, 42, *43*, 48, 50, 51, 54, 72
Practice of Piety, The (Bayly), 58
Pratt, Orson, 414
Presbyterians, 405
President of U.S., 242. *See also* Election, *individual presidents*
   election of, 243, 246–47, 277
   powers of office, 230
   proper address of, 271–72
   veto by, 242, 273

INDEX

Presidios, 156
Preston, Captain Thomas, 182, 183, 185, 187, 190
Privateering, 11, 14, 16–17, 38
    Blackbeard, 111, *112*
    James I opposition to, 21
    vs. colonization, 18
Privy Council, 17
Proclamation of 1763, 171
Proclamation of Amnesty and Reconstruction, 573, 575
Proctor, Alice, 63–64
Proctor, Elizabeth, 99
Proctor, John, 99
Property
    concentration of ownership in 19th century, 398
    as voting qualification, 236, 238
    abolition of, 364
Property-owning classes, in South, 454
The Prophet, 324
"Prophetstown" (Tippecanoe), 287, 325–26
    attack on, 327, 336
Proprietary colony, Pennsylvania as, 113
Proprietors, colonies as property of, 109
Proslavery argument, 455–60
Protestantism, 4–5, 405
    in Maryland, 74
Providence, 78
Prynne, Hester, 419
Public lands, specie payment required for purchase, 373
Public schools, 400, 588, 590
Publishing industry, 416
Pueblo Indians, 26, 34–35
    rebellion against Spanish, 90
Pueblo revolt (New Mexico 1680), 123
pueblos, 27, 31
Puritan settlements, 57
Puritans, 75, 117–18
    English persecution of, 78
    opposition in England, 23
    view on trade dangers, 114
Putnam, Anne, 108

Quakers, 112–13, 164
    success in trade, 116
Quantrill, William C., 532
Quasi-War, 283
Quebec, 2, 32, 36, *38*, 44, 168
    English capture of, 169, *169*
Queen Anne's War (1702–1713), 168

Racism, 455, 457. *See also* Blacks, Native Americans, Slavery

of northerners, 469, 494
    in Texas revolution, 488
Radical Reconstruction, 581–88
Radical Republicans, 576, 580
Radicalism, 380
Railroad(s), 399
    in Civil War, 529–30, 547
    transcontinental, 498
Raleigh, Sir Walter, 2, 3–23, 22
    as advocate for colonization, 8–9
    at Oxford University, 6
    enemies, 20
    execution, 3–4, 23
    History of the World, The, 21
    "Lost Colony" planning, 15
    marriage, 18–19
    and Native Americans, 23
    plan to attack Spanish ships, 11
    relationship with Queen Elizabeth, 6, 18–19, 20
    Roanoke planning, 10
    role in Irish war, 7–8
    search for South American wealth, 19
    treason charges, 3, 20
Raleigh, Wat, 22, 23
Rancheros, 487
Rappahonnock River, 535
Reagan, Ronald, 340
Reck, Captain Philipp von, 138
Reconstruction, 554, 571
    black codes, 578–79
    Congressional, 579–81
    end of, 593
    Johnson's plans, 575–81
    Lincoln's plans, 573–75
    North reaction to, 579
    opposition to government, 588
    Southern reaction to government, 587
Reconstruction Acts of 1867, 581, 583, 593
Red Clay, 308
Red Sticks, 297, 317, 327
"Redeemer" governments, 590
Reese, Piety, 432
Reformers, 392, 411–14
    women as, 410–11
Refugees, ex-slaves as, 555
Regulators, 153
Religion
    in 16th century Europe, 4
    behavior in New England meetinghouse, 97–98
    conversion experiences, 161
    conversion of runaway slaves, 136
    diversity in New York, 128
    in East in 1700s, 160–64
    Lloyd family split by, 383
    of Native Americans, 34

    New England in late 17th century, 117–118
    as reason for colonization, 39
    of slaves, 453
Religious beliefs
    colonists' belief in Devil, 91
    of Nat Turner, 427–29
Religious conflict, Pueblos vs. Franciscans, 123
Religious conversions, 405
Religious freedom, 160
    as French colonial goal, 35
    for Quakers in Pennsylvania, 112
Religious leaders, of pre-colonial Native Americans, 50–51
Religious persecution, in Europe, 69
Religious revivals, 134, 397
    in 18th century, 156
Religious teaching, The Prophet to Native Americans, 324
Religious toleration, 128
    in Holland, 75, 82
    in Maryland, 74
    in Rhode Island, 80
Repartimiento, 123
"Republican" government, 238
Republican party, 351, 362, 501–3
    in 1860 election, 505
    division during Civil War, 537
    Philadelphia convention in 1856, 501
Republican Reconstruction, 583
Republicanism, of Jefferson, 277–79
Republicans, vs. Federalists, 274–76
Revenge, 147
Revenue Act of 1764 (The Sugar Act), 194–95
Revere, Paul, 189
    engraving of Boston Massacre, *183*
Review of the Debate of the Virginia Legislature in 1831 and 1832, 456
Revolution of 1800, 277–78
Revolution, paying off debts from, 236–37
Rex v. *Preston,* 190
Rhode Island, 80, 235
    abolition of slavery in, 248
    constitution for, 235–36
    Constitutional ratification, 245
Rice, 165
    in Carolinas, 111
    as cash crop, 443–44
Richardson, Ebenezer, 177–78
Richmond, Union attempts to control, 534
Ridge, The, 295–96, *296,* 297, 299
    death, 315
    property of, 300
    resistance to forced migration, 307
    in Washington, 305

Ridge, John, 300–1, *301*, 309, 310–11
   death, 314
Rio de Espíritu Santo, 31. *See also* Mississippi River
River transportation
   joint-stock company to develop, 226
   Washington analysis in northern Virginia, 224
Rivers, navigable in South, 322
Roanoke colony, 3, 11–15, *14*, 37
   Native Americans in, 26
   Raleigh's planning for, 10
Rochester, New York, 330, 401
Rolfe, John, 44, 52, 64, 70, 72
Roman Catholics, 4, 74
Ross, Betsy, 167
Ross, John, 303–4, *303*, 305, 309, 310, 312
   death, 315
   involvement in Cherokee migration, 313
   loss of home, 308
Rowlandson, Mary, *Narrative,* 126, *127*
Ruffin, Edmund, 547
Ruffin, Thomas, 449
Runaway slaves, 248, 449
   adoption of Seminole culture by, 317
   laws against hiding, 470
   recapture after Revolution, 316
Runaway slaves to Spanish Florida, 135–48
   Mose, 136–37
   St. Augustine attack, 139–46
   South Carolina insecurity in, 137–39
Rush-Bagot agreement, 354
Russian, exploration and traders, 158–59

Sabine River, 259, 264
Sacajawea, 283
Sacs, 324
Sagadahoc, 40
St. Augustine, 2, 35, *37*, 44, 122, 135, *144*
   attack on, 139–46
   role in slave uprising, 134
   siege, 144–45
   South Carolina delay in support for attack of, 142
St. John's River, 35, 140
St. Lawrence River, 32
St. Louis, 258, 401
St. Simons Island, 140, 147
Salem, settlement, 78
Salem witchcraft accusations, 90–108, 115, 161
   children's first accusations, 92–93
   compensation of victims, 107
   confessions, 105
   end of panic, 106–8
   executions, 102, 105, 106, *107*
   expansion of panic, 99
   questioning of accused, 93–99
   restrictions on court proceedings, 128
   as struggle with Devil, 118
Salzburgers, *150*, 151
San Agustin, 35. *See also* St. Augustine
San Antonio, 156, *157*, 486, 488
San Diego, 158
San Francisco Bay, 158
San Gabriel, 158
San Jose, 158
San Juan, 35
Sandys, George, 64
Santa Anna, 491
Santa Anna, General Antonio Lopez de, 488
Santa Barbara, 158
Santa Elena, 35
Santa Fe, 2, 34, 44, 69, 70, 123
Savage, Thomas, 52–53, 54
Savannah, Georgia, *152*, 546
Saxton, General, 563, 565, 570
Scarlet Letter, The (Hawthorne), 416, 419
Schermerhorn, John, 311
Scotland, immigrants to Carolina from, 110
Scots-Irish, in Carolina, 110
Scott, General R. K., 570
Scott, General Winfield, 312, *492*, 493, 497, 528
Sea Islands, 540. *See also* Edisto Island
   Union capture, 539
Secession, 506–8, 513
   legal status of states after, 577
   Lincoln's views on, 514–15
   proposed by Hartford Convention, 291
   Southern threat of, 496
   threatened by South Carolina in 1828, 369
Secession of Western states
   Burr plans for, 255
   funding for, 259
Second Bank of the United States, 353–54. *See also* Bank of the United States
Second Great Awakening, 405
Second Seminole War, 318
Second War for Independence, 289
Sedition Act of 1798, 275–76
Seider, Christopher, 178, 180
Self-made man, 360–61, 404–5, 485, 502
Seminole culture, adoption by runaway African-American slaves, 317
Seminoles
   removal treaty with, 317
   violence to keep lands, 316–19
Senate, 241, 271
   Burr as president, 253
   election of, 246
Seneca Falls, New York, 411
Seneca Falls Declaration, 411
Senecas, 26, 119, 155
Separation of powers, 242
   absence under Articles, 234
   political parties and, 364
Separatists, 75
Sequin, Juan, 488
Sequoya, *300*
Serra, fray Junípero, 158
Seven Years' War, 168
Seward, William, 496, 503, 505, 516, 520
Shakers, 413
Shakespeare, William, 4
   The Tempest, 41
Shamans, 51, 52
Shannon, 287
Sharpsburg, Maryland, 534
Shawnees, 323
   Tecumseh, 287, 296, 320, 324–27
Shays, Daniel, 227–28, *227*
Shays's Rebellion (Massachusetts), 227, 238
   Washington reaction to, 228
Sheridan, Philip, 582
Sherman, John, 579
Sherman, William Tecumseh, 528, 546, *559*
   march through Georgia, 545, 549, 555
   Special Field Order No. 15, 540, 557–58, 559
   rescinding by Johnson, 578
Shiloh, battle of, 533
Shoemakers, 415
Shute, Samuel, 166
Shuttuck, Job, 227
Sickles, Daniel, 582
Sickles, General Daniel, 565
Sioux, 26
Six Nations, 119
Sketch Book (Irving), 415
Slave auction, *444*
Slave codes, 445
   in Virginia, 441, 442
Slave culture, 452
Slave rebellion. *See also* Nat Turner's rebellion
   South Carolina, 1739, 134
   South fear of, 504

Slave states, proportion of white and black population, 455
Slave trade, 114, 150–51
 interstate, 496
 profit from, 443
 restrictions on Congress to regulate, 242
 in *Uncle Tom's Cabin,* 465
Slavery, 233
 in 18th century, 165–66
 in Chesapeake Bay, 90, 120–21
 Civil War and, 538–42
 as Civil War issue, 519–21
 in civilization, 456
 Constitution silence on, 246, 247–48
 and cotton, 443–45
 economic viability of investment in, 442–43
 in election of 1848, 495
 and expansion, 494–98
 in Georgia, 148, 151
 introduction in Carolinas, 110
 master's power, 448–49
 Mexico abolition of, 487
 as national institution during Revolution, 442
 as political issue, 367
 prohibition in Georgia, 151
 prohibition in Northwest Territory, 235
 proslavery argument, 455–60
 slave responses to, 449–53
 as social system, 446–49
 as Southern feature, 442
 in territories, 494–95
 Texas rebels defense of, 488
 Virginia legislature debate on, 441
 Virginian attitudes on, 440–41
Slaves, *111, 122.* See also Ex-slaves, Runaway slaves to Spanish Florida
 at work, *446*
 in Baptist church, 164
 as contraband, 539, 540
 counting for congressional representation, 241
 family of, 449–452
 importation from Africa, 109
 kin structure of, 165, 452
 legal status, 447
 names of, 425–26
 native-born, 165
 religion of, 453
 in South Carolina, 137–38
 speculation in, 322
 varieties of experience, 447–48
Slidell, John, 490
Smallpox, 30, 33
 in germ warfare, 170–71

Smerwick (Irish fortress), 7
Smith, Caleb, 520
Smith, Hyrum, *414*
Smith, John, 34, 40–42, *41,* 44, 50, 52, 61, 64
Smith, Joseph, 413, *414*
Smith, Senator John, 262
Society of the Cincinnati, 228
Sociology for the South: Or the Failure of Free Society, 457
Sons of Liberty, 177, 178
Soulé, Pierre, 498
South. *See also* Confederate States of America, *specific states*
 agriculture expansion in, 319–23
 at Civil War beginning, 531
 economic changes from Civil War, 593
 ideal of womanhood, 458–60
 naval blockade of, 531
 opinion of North as threat to society, 507
 railroad during Civil War, 529–30
 reaction to Reconstruction government, 587
 removal of federal troops, 593
 Republican coalition in, 584–88
 response to Lincoln's election, 506–8
 social structure of, 453–55
 social system after Civil War, 571
South America, Spanish explorations, 29–31
South Carolina, 69, 579, 587, 593. *See also* Carolinas
 backcountry, 153
 black code in, 578
 commitment to slavery, 110
 delay in support for St. Augustine attack, 142
 ex-slaves in, 572
 Jackson's response to nullification movement, 371
 racial tensions in, 137–39
 secession plans, 506
 threatened secession, 369
 wealth of, 134
Southwest
 colonies in, 34–35, 69–70
 cultural mix within, 35
 Navaho wall painting of Spanish arrival, *30*
Spain
 Burr request for funding from, 258
 colonization by, 48
 control of American interior, 116–17
 early explorations, 28
 early settlements, 2
 importation of Africans to Americas, 9

 land controlled in beginning of the 19th century, 255
 presence in Texas, 156
 settlements in California, 157
 settlements in Florida, 35
 South American explorations, 29–31
 as superpower, 8
 threat of war with, 262
 war with England (1739), 139
Spanish, in North America, 30
Spanish Armada, 17
Spanish espionage rolls, Wilkinson on, 254
Spanish explorers, in Southeast, 26
Spanish ships, Raleigh's plan to attack, 11
Special Field Order No. 15
 by Sherman, 540, 557–58, 559
 rescinding by Johnson, 578
Specie, 352
"Specie Circular," 370, 373
Spectral evidence, 106, 107
Spelman, Henry, 53, 54, 65
Springfield Republican, 575
Squanto, 76–77
Squatter farmers, Washington encounter with, 222
Squirrel (Chickasaw chief), 145
Stamp Act of 1765, 187, 195
Stamp Act Congress, 196–97
Stamp Act riots, 178
Standard of living
 in the 18th century, 134, 149, 164–65
 in the 19th century, 404
Stanton, Edwin, 520, 523, 530, 555, 556–58, 562, 582
Stanton, Elizabeth Cady, 411
State banks, 352
State courts, constitutional restrictions on, 243
State law, constitutionality of, 280, 354
States
 constitutional restrictions on, 243
 creation of constitutions, 235
 declaration of federal law unconstitutional, 369
 division of powers with national government, 243
 powers under Articles, 234
 quarrels among, 238
 suits against, 290
States' rights, 278, 538
Steamboats, 322, 402
Stephens, Alexander, 538, 578–79
Stevens, Thaddeus, 339, 579, *580*
Stone, William, 74
Stono Rebellion, 138

Stoughton, William, 103, *104*, 105, 106
Stowe, Calvin, 483
Stowe, Harriet Beecher, 467–69, *471*, 497
    desire to write, 484
    Lincoln on impact of, 464, 467
    Uncle Tom's Cabin, 464–82. See also *Uncle Tom's Cabin* (Stowe)
Stuyvesant, Peter, 84, *84*
Sugar, 445
    trade in, 114
Sumner, Charles, 501, 519, 579, *582*, 593
Supreme Court, 242, 279, 280, 503–4, 581
    Cherokee appeal to, 308
"Supreme law of the land," 280
Surratt, Mary E., 526
Susquehannock Fort (Maryland), *124*
Susquehannocks, *65*, 84
Sweden, 84

Talleyrand, Charles, 282
Tallmadge, James, 367
Taney, Roger, 537
Taney, Roger B., 503
Tappan, Arthur, 483
Tariff of Abominations, 358, 368–69
Tariff on imported goods, 272
Taxation
    on alcoholic beverages, 273
    British and colonial, 170
    as Congressional power, 241
    creation of system, 272
    on distilled liquor, 274
    during Civil War, 536
    under Articles, 237
Taylor, Zachary, 319, *365*, 450, 490, 495, 496
Teach, Edward (Blackbeard), 112
Tears of the Indians, The (Las Casas), 9
Technology
    in 19th century, 402–4
    in Civil War, 547, 548
Tecumseh, 287, 296, 320, 324–27, *325*
    alliance with British, 327
    as leader, 326
    meeting with Creeks and Cherokees, 326–27
Telegraph, 402
Ten Lost Tribes of Israel, 24
Tennent, Gilbert, 161
Tennent, William, 161
Tennessee, 255, 320, 577
    "Redemption," 590
    secession plans, 514
Tenochtitlán, 29, 30

Tenskwatawa (The Prophet), 324, 327
Tenton, Parnell, 57
Tenure of Office Act, 582
Territories
    presidential power to acquire, 284
    slavery in, 494–95
Texas, 117, 579, 587
    annexation of, 488–90
    border with Louisiana, 354
    independence, 487–88
    Spanish claim on, 259
    Spanish presence in, 156
    treaty of annexation with, 489
    U.S. attempts to purchase, 487
    war with Mexico in 1841, 488
Textile industry
    in Britain, 322
    in England, 40, 322
    in New England, 414–15
    techological changes, 403
Thames, battle of, 287
Thirty Years' War, 69
Thoreau, Henry David, 416, 417–18, 419
Thorpe, George, 49–50, 58–61, 67
    friendship with Indians, 59
    Indian attack on, 62–63
Thorpe, Georgius, 58
Throckmorton, Bess, 18
Tiger (ship), 12
Tilden, Samuel J., 593
Timucua, 121
Tippecanoe, 287, 325–26
    battle of, 327, 336
"Tippecanoe Clubs," 337
"Tippecanoe and Tyler Too," 345
Tituba, 92, 103, 109, 115
    questioning of, 95–97
Tobacco, 21, *122*, 320
    advertisement, *55*
    as cash crop, 443–44
    production increases, 73
    in Virginia, 49, 55, 70
Tocanahowi, 141
Tomochichi, 141, *141*
Tories, 246
Tower of London, Raleigh in, 19, 20–21
Townshend Acts, 197–99
Tracts, on antislavery, 469
Trade
    with Cherokees, 296
    dishonesty with Indians, 141
    in late 17th century, 114–17
    mercantilism, 115–16
    to connect country, 225
Trade routes, *115*
    Americas as barrier, 31–32
    Canada as for Northwest, 328

    search for, 39
    to west, need for, 221–22
Trade unions, in Philadelphia, 415
Trail of Tears, 294, 295–315, *313*
Transcendentalism, 418
Transcontinental railroad, 498
Transportation
    for cotton, 322
    railroad beginnings, 399
    and western expansion, 498
Travis, Joseph, 429, 431
    death, 431–32
Travis, William, 488
Treason
    Burr's plans as, 256
    definition by Chief Justice Marshall, 268
    definition in Constitution, 266
    Raleigh charged with, 3, 20
Treasury Department, 272
Treaties, to cede Indian land, 324, 326
Treaty of 1778, 282
Treaty of 1817 with Cherokees, 298
Treaty, Jackson's efforts with Cherokee, 309–10
Treaty of annexation with Texas, 489
Treaty of Fort Gibson, 317
Treaty of Fort Wayne, 326
Treaty of Ghent, 289
Treaty of Greenville (1795), 325
Treaty of Guadalupe Hildalgo, 494
Treaty of Moultrie Creek, 317
Treaty of New Echota, 311–12
Treaty of Paris (1763), 169
    ratification by Congress, 217
Tremain, Colonel Edwin, 566–67, 568, 570
Trescot, Henry, 564–65
Trescot, William, 578
Trumbull, Lyman, 516, 579
Tsenacommacoh, 50
Tubman, Harriet, *450*
Turner, Benjamin, 426
Turner, Nat. *See also* Nat Turner's rebellion
    capture of, 438–39, *438*
    expectations of, 426
    religious beliefs, 427–29
Turner, Samuel, 427, 432
Turner's Nat, *426*
Tuscarora Indians, 111–12, 119, 137, 155
Tyler, John, 375, 489
    as vice-presidential candidate, 339–40
Tyler, Royall, 188
Tyranny, 170
    criticism against Lincoln, 536
    peacetime army as risk of, 182

Uncle Tom's Cabin (Stowe), 464–82,
    502–3, 504
  advertisement for, *480*
  excerpts, 465–67, 471–82
  political impact, 467
  public demand for, 467
Underground Railroad, *450*
Underhill, John, 81
Unemployment, 165, 415
Union
  restoration of Confederate states to, 577
  secession threat to, 496
Union army
  creation, 528
  declaring freedom of slaves within battle lines, 520
  Lincoln's reaction to defeats, 521
  recruitment of ex-slaves, 539, 540–41, *541*
Union League, 584
Unionism, in South, 517
"Unit rule," 339
Universal manhood suffrage, 334, 364
Urbanization, 400–2
Utah, 490, 496
Utopian communities, 413

Vaca, Cabeza de, 30–31
Vagrancy laws, 578
Vallendingham, Clement, 537
Van Buren, Martin, 334, 335, 336, 363, 369, 495
  background, 360
  brooch, *336*
  as Jackson's choice for successor, 373
  loss of presidential nomination, 489
  presidential victory, 338
  reaction to 1840 loss, 350
  on Texas annexation, 488
  Whig campaign against, 341, 343
Van Ness, John, 358
Van Rensselaer, Kiliaen, 82
Vanderdussen, Alexander, 145
Vanderlyn, John, 267
Vann, Joseph, 302
Vargas, Diego de, 123
Vera Cruz, American army move toward, 493
Vermont, abolition of slavery in, 248
Verrazzano, Giovanni, 31
Vesey, Denmark, 424
Vespucci, Amerigo, 29
Vice-president
  election of, 246–47
  Tyler as candidate, 339–40
Vicksburg, 533, 542, 575
Virginia, 40, 44, 226, 577, 587
  Bacon's rebellion (1676), 123–25
  colonization, 70–73
  Constitutional ratification, 245
  early deaths in, 59
  early plantations, 49–67
    aftermath of attack, 64–66
    captives taken, 66–67
    Native American attack, 49–50, 62–63, 72–73
  food shortage in early colonies, 66
  House of Burgesses, 72
  legislative debate on slavery, 441
  lottery, 57
  Native Americans' conversion, 58–61
  Native Americans' reaction to colonization, 61–63
  Native Americans' relations, 42–44
  "redemption," 590
  secession plans, 513, 514
  tensions after Nat Turner's rebellion, 440
  western settlement, 151–52
Virginia Company, 40, 70–71
  charter loss, 73
  colonial risks from poor planning, 73
  financing of colonization, 72
  new policy, 54–56
  planned violence against Native Americans, 64
Virginia General Assembly, 59
  first meeting, 56
Virginia and Kentucky Resolutions, 276
Virginia plan, 240–41
Virginia Slave Code, 441, 442
Visscher, John, 5
Von Reck, Captain Philipp, 138
Voting. *See also* Elections, Political parties
  for House Representatives, 243
  qualifications for, 236, 238
Voting rights, of ex-slaves, 574, 583
Voz del Pueblo, La, 491

Wade-Davis Bill, 574
  Lincoln's veto, 544
Walden, or Life in the Woods (Thoreau), 416, 417–18, *417*
Walker, David, 424
Walker, John, Jr., 310
Walker, Leroy, 530
Walker, Patrick, 180
Waller, Levi, 434
Wampanoags, 76, 125
Wampum, 82–83, *83*, 84–85
Wanchese, 15
War of 1812, 287–89, 319–20
  Harrison in, 336
"War Democrats," 537
War Department, 272, 541
War Hawks, 289
War of Jenkins' EAr, 139
Ware v. *Hylton,* 280
Warren, Mary, 99–100
Warren, William, 185
Wars. *See also* American Revolution, War of 1812, Mexican War, Civil War
  colonial (1670s and 1680s), 122–29
  in Europe, 69
  in Native-American culture, 27
Washington, D.C., 273
  British capture, 288
  burning (1814), *286*, 287
Washington, George, 168, 216, 217–31, *221*
  as aristocrat, 219
  cartoon (1795), *276*
  death, 232
  farewell to army, 217, *218*
  finances, 220
  first inauguration, *230*, 231
  as Philadelphia convention.president, 229–30
  in public affairs, 219
  re-election, 275
  reaction to Whiskey Rebellion, 274
  reputation, 229
  resignation of power, 218
  travel west, 222–24
  as president, 271
Washington National Republican, 523
Waterhouse, Edward, 49, 62
Waterloo, Napoleon's defeat, 289
Wayne, General Anthony, 323
Webster, Daniel, 306, 337, 338, 347, 350, 361, 373, 375, 496, 497
Weed, Thurlow, 339
Weld, Theodore, 483
  American Slavery As It Is, 502
Welles, Gideon, *520*, 576
Werowance, 50
Wesley, John, 151
West. *See also* Western expansion
  in 18th century, 156–60
  Evangelism in, 407
West Florida, 255
Western lands, during Confederation Period, 238
Western states, Burr plans for secession, 255

Westward expansion, 224, 294, 498–501
  1789–1820s, 270
  boundary agreements, 355–56
  British trouble in early 1800s, 284–87
  by new nation, 283–89
  and commercial agriculture, 331
  in late 17th century, 125
  Louisiana Purchase, 284
  Manifest Destiny, 485
  New England opposition to, 289
  proclamation to restrict, 171
  slavery and, 367, 494–98
Whaley, William, 559, 563, 567, 568, 570, 572
Wheat cultivation, 328
Whig party, 246, 334, 337, 359–60, 375–76, 501
  call for national convention, 338
  campaign songs, *344*
  split in, 375, 495
  strategy in 1840 election campaign, 340–50
Whiskey Rebellion, 274
White, Hugh Lawson, 184, 338, 373
White, John, 14–18
  painting of Carolina Algonquian village, *12*
  painting of Indian woman and child, *28*
  painting of The Flyer, *52*
White House, appropriations as campaign issue, 344–45
White Legions, 588, 589, 590
Whitefield, George, 148, 151, 162–63, *162*

Whitehead, Catherine, 432
Whitman, Walt, 416, 418, 523–24, 547
Whitney, Eli, 321, 444
Wilderness Campaign, 546
Wilkinson, James, 254–56, *255*, 260–61
  appointment as Louisiana governor, 257
  at Burr's trial, 267
  betrayal of Burr, 264
  conflict of interest, 259–60
  warning to Jefferson, 264
William and Mary, negotiation of new Massachusetts charter, 128
William of Orange, 128
Williams, Abigail, 91, 97, 98, 107
Williams, Robert, 63
Williams, Roger, 80
Wilmot, David, 494
Wilmot Proviso, 494, 496
Wingina (Roanoke chief), 13
Winnebagos, 324
Winslow, Edward, 76
Winthrop, John, 77, *79*
Wirt, William, 308
Wisconsin, 235
Witches, death penalty for, 105, 107
Women
  in the 18th century, 167
  as colonists, 56–57, 71, 74
  during Civil War, 539
  education for, *410*
  in evangelist movement, 407
  Hispanic in California, 158
  landholdings in South Carolina, 110

  literature by and for, 410
  Native American, 26–27
  as Quakers, 113
  Raleigh's recognition of skills, 15
  as reformers, 410–11
  revivals' impact on, 164
  right to vote, 364
  role changes in the 19th century, 409–10
  Southern ideal, 458–60
  under Dutch law, 119
  voting barrier from 14th Amendment, 583
Women's rights, 411
Woodmason, Charles, 153
Workers' movements, in the 19th century, 414–15
Working Men's Party, 415
World Anti-Slavery Convention, 411
Wragg, Joseph, 146
Wyandots, 324
Wyatt, Sir Francis, 54, 59

X, Y, Z affair, 282

Yamacraws, 141
Yamasee Indians, 112, 136
Yeardley, Sir George, 54, 59
"Yeoman" farmers, Jefferson's views on, 278
Young, Brigham, 413
"Young Hickory," 489

Zunis, 31, 34